BUS

7/30 61

FROM EMPIRE TO EUROPE

FROM EMPIRE TO EUROPE

The Decline and Revival of British Industry
Since the Second World War

GEOFFREY OWEN

HarperCollins*Publishers*

HarperCollins*Publishers*
77–85 Fulham Palace Road,
Hammersmith, London w6 8jb

www.**fire**and**water**.com

Published by HarperCollins*Publishers* 1999
3 5 7 9 8 6 4 2

A catalogue record for this book is
available from the British Library

ISBN 0 00 255682 0

Set in PostScript Linotype Minion by
Rowland Phototypesetting Ltd,
Bury St Edmunds, Suffolk

Printed and bound in Great Britain by
Clays Ltd, St Ives plc

Contents

PART III

Institutions and Policies

Acknowledgements

Most of this book was written while I was on the staff of the Centre for Economic Performance at the London School of Economics. The CEP is an inter-disciplinary research centre funded by the Economic and Social Research Council.

I am grateful to Richard Layard, Director of the CEP, for inviting me to join the Centre and for his advice and encouragement while the book was in preparation. I received a considerable amount of help from other LSE colleagues, especially Peter Abell, Charles Bean, Stefan Behringer, Nick Crafts, Susanne Espenlaub, Leslie Hannah, Alexander Lehmann, David Marsden, David Metcalf, Andrew Oswald, Ray Richardson, Ansgar Richter, Razeen Sally and Ralph Turvey.

Many other people in business and academia, and former colleagues on the *Financial Times*, gave generously of their time to provide me with information and suggestions. I would particularly like to thank the following: Martin Adeney, David Andrews, Sir Robert Atkinson, John Barber, Sir William Barlow, Howard Barrett, Sir Malcolm Bates, Christopher Beauman, Sir Jonathan Benn, Dennis Bexson, Robert Bischof, David Buck, David Edgerton, Michael Evans, Richard Freeman, Michael Goddard, John Grieve-Smith, Edward Hadas, John Harper, Trevor Harrison, David Henderson, Angus Irvine, Edgar Jones, Matthias Kipping, Sir Arthur Knight, David Kynaston, Richard Lambert, Ian Mackintosh, Peter Marshall, Colin Mayer, Andrew Nahum, Nicholas Owen, John Plender, Garel Rhys, John Roberts, Geoffrey Rose, Mary Rose, David Sawers, Janet Sidaway, Anthony Slaven, John Wilson, Basil Woods, Chris Woodwark, Ivan Yates and Sir Richard Young.

I am grateful for the skilful and constructive editing by Charles Drazin and Lucinda McNeile at HarperCollins.

I owe a special debt of thanks to my wife, Miriam. The book could not have been completed without her constant support and active involvement in the project.

Falling Behind and Catching Up

In the summer of 1995, a ceremony was held at the Aylesford paper mill in Kent, one of Britain's largest paper-making sites, to mark the successful commissioning of a newsprint machine. In forest-rich countries such as Canada or Finland, this would have been an unremarkable event. But for Britain the Aylesford project had a special significance. It was the first new machine to be built at the mill for more than thirty years. Based on recycled paper, it produced newsprint which was competitive in cost and quality with imports. The project was financed by two non-British companies, one from Sweden and the other from South Africa. By investing £250m at Aylesford, they were contributing to the revival of an industry which twenty years earlier had seemed in the grip of irreversible decline.

What happened in paper-making during the 1980s and 1990s illustrates the central theme of this book – the delayed modernisation of British industry. For the first decade after the war British paper-makers led a comfortable existence. Domestic demand was strong, and import competition was restrained by tariffs and quotas. These easy conditions came to an abrupt end in 1959 when the Conservative government under Harold Macmillan decided to participate in the European Free Trade Association (EFTA). This was a grouping of countries outside the six-nation Common Market, and it included Sweden and Finland, both of which had large, efficient paper industries based on cheap electricity and ample supplies of wood.[1]

As tariffs among the EFTA countries came down, the Nordic paper producers used their cost advantage to increase their exports to Britain. British firms strove to come to terms with a difficult trading environment. Mills and machines were closed down, and some of the leading British companies lost faith in the industry's future. But the economics of paper-making in Britain were not as unfavourable as the pessimists supposed. For some grades of paper, being near to the market turned out to be more important than being near to the forests. In addition, Britain had a man-made 'forest' of its own: improvements in recycling technology created new opportunities for using waste paper instead of imported woodpulp as the feedstock for paper production. The gloom began to lift in the early 1980s, and over the next fifteen years a remarkable transformation of the industry took place, involving new investment and changes of ownership. Some of the new projects, like the Aylesford newsprint machine, were undertaken by foreign companies. But there was also a new spirit of confidence among the surviving British-owned firms, targeting sectors of the market where a UK-based producer could compete successfully against imports.

A similar chain of events took place in other industries: profitable growth in the first few years after the war, a struggle to cope with increasing international competition in the 1960s and 1970s, and, finally, integration into the world market. The form which integration took varied according to the circumstances of each industry and the amount of ground that had been lost in earlier years. The revival of the British motor industry, for example, which had almost been given up for dead at the end of the 1970s, owed a great deal to the decision by three Japanese companies – Toyota, Honda and Nissan – to choose Britain as the site of their first European assembly plants. By the end of the 1990s, after Jaguar had been bought by Ford, Rover by BMW and Rolls-Royce Motors by Volkswagen, virtually the whole of the British motor industry had passed into foreign control. While this was a blow to national pride, the willingness of these companies to invest on a large scale in British car factories was an indication of how much had changed since the dark days of the 1970s.

With or without the involvement of foreign companies, the 1980s saw a vigorous effort throughout British industry to correct past mistakes and to build defensible positions in the world market. Guest Keen and Nettlefolds (GKN) was an old-established company which had diversified in the interwar years from its original base in steel-making into a wide range of steel-using businesses, and it continued to do so in the 1950s and 1960s. Most of its sales were to customers in Britain and the Commonwealth. In the second half of the 1970s, when competition increased and profits came under pressure, a new approach was necessary. As Trevor Holdsworth, chairman of the company from 1979 to 1986, put it later: 'We were drifting uncertainly into the future without a clear strategy. A new generation of senior executives was emerging and we set about trying to make sense of our inheritance. We had to find new products, new technology and we had to spread internationally.'[2] The chosen path for expansion was in vehicle components, and over the next decade GKN converted itself into a leading supplier to the world motor industry, with a strong market position in Continental Europe and the US. Other companies went through similar upheavals. The common elements were specialisation and internationalisation, and a drive to raise manufacturing efficiency closer to the best world standards.

What precipitated these changes? Why did they occur in the 1980s, and not thirty years earlier?

During the 1970s a series of shocks – Britain's entry into the Common Market, the rise of Japan and the newly industrialising countries, the slow-down in the world economy after the first oil crisis – exposed weaknesses in British industry which had been partially obscured and more easily toler-ated in the earlier post-war years. By the end of the decade companies such as GKN were forced to take a more critical look at themselves, and decide which of their businesses, if any, could compete on the world stage.

These external pressures coincided with a change in the political climate within Britain. The election of a Conservative government under Margaret Thatcher in May 1979 heralded a break with the past in the management of the economy. A fierce determination to defeat inflation through strict monet-ary and fiscal policies was combined with a greater emphasis on competition and deregulation. Virtually all the industries which had been nationalised since 1945 – and some, like the telephone network, which had been in government hands since the 1920s – were transferred to the private sector. The labour relations system, which had been partly responsible for Britain's reputation as the sick man of Europe, was drastically reformed.

A third ingredient was the phenomenon which came to be known as globalisation. During the 1980s increasing cross-border investment altered the structure of several major industries, paper and cars being two notable examples. Many of the world's leading companies built or acquired factories in their major markets, and organised their manufacturing and distribution on an international basis. Britain benefited from this process because, thanks to Margaret Thatcher, it had become a more attractive location for invest-ment. The Conservative government was also more relaxed than its prede-cessors about allowing former 'national champions' to be acquired by foreign companies; no objection was raised when BMW bought Rover, or when ICL, the computer manufacturer, was sold to Fujitsu of Japan.

The combined effect of international competition, domestic policy reform and foreign investment brought to an end a long period in which productivity in British manufacturing had grown more slowly than in other European countries (TABLE 1.1). After years of falling behind, Britain was catching up.

This book describes how the transition came about. It focuses on firms and the people who ran them, and on the domestic and international environment in which they were operating. The aim is to identify the reasons for Britain's poor industrial performance, compared to other European countries, in the first thirty years after the war, and to assess the significance of the changes that occurred in the 1980s and 1990s.

TABLE 1.1 *Labour productivity in manufacturing 1960–95*

(annual average per centage increase in output per hour worked)

	1960–73	1973–9	1979–95
Britain	4.1	1.0	4.3
France	6.6	4.4	3.1
Germany	5.7	4.2	2.2

Source: US Department of Labor, Bureau of Labor Statistics.

What firms can do in international competition is constrained by the economics of the industry they are competing in and by the conditions which they face in their home base: countries provide a better 'global platform' for some industries than for others.[3] In some cases companies may derive a competitive advantage from the size and character of domestic demand for their products. In others the crucial factor may be ease of access to essential raw materials. But the most important influence on the international competitiveness of companies, especially in manufacturing, is the extent to which they are helped or hindered by national institutions and policies. To take one example, the US has developed since the Second World War a large and sophisticated community of venture capitalists, who have supported the growth of start-up firms in high-technology industries such as electronics and biotechnology. While access to venture capital is not the only reason for the success of American companies in these industries, it is an institutional asset which other countries do not possess.

Institutions and policies have been central to the long-running controversy about British industrial decline. Three culprits which have figured prominently in the debate – the financial system, the training and education system and the labour relations system – are given special attention in this book. The financial system is accused of failing to provide manufacturing companies with the constructive, long-term support which is available in other countries. The education system has been criticised for being too detached from the world of industry, leading to an inadequate supply of technical and managerial skills. The labour relations system is held responsible for the collapse of strike-prone industries such as shipbuilding and cars, and more generally for the slow growth of productivity in British industry as a whole between the 1950s and the 1970s. These institutional weaknesses have been aggravated, some commentators believe, by policy errors on the part of post-war governments. The management of the economy has been erratic, while micro-economic or 'supply-side' policies, ranging from nationalisation to the promotion of mergers, have often been ill-considered and counter-productive.

Opinions differ about the relative importance of these factors, and about the extent to which some of the alleged weaknesses – for example, the 'short-termism' of British financial markets – continue to put British firms at a disadvantage today. This book seeks to shed light on these issues by making comparisons across countries and across industries. It examines how British firms in a number of major industries responded to international competition after the Second World War, and compares their response with that of their counterparts in other European countries, principally Germany and France; the list of industries covered is set out in TABLE 1.2.

Some British industries did better than others, and the same was true in the two Continental countries. At the end of the 1990s British-owned firms ranked among the world leaders in chemicals and pharmaceuticals, but not in cars. German companies were outstandingly successful in mechanical engineering, but not in computers or television sets. French manufacturers out-performed their British counterparts in cars, but not in machine tools. The purpose of the industry case studies contained in later chapters is to explore the reasons for these national strengths and weaknesses, and thus to illuminate the larger question of how institutions and policies have affected industrial performance.

In studying the interaction between firms, industries and nations, history matters at all three levels. Although the book is primarily concerned with events after 1945, each of the case studies begins by examining the earlier history of the firms and industries concerned. Did British industry enter the post-war period with managerial and technical weaknesses inherited from the past, or was its poor performance after 1945 due to the things that were done or not done in the post-war period itself?

This is a book about British manufacturing, not about the British economy. The focus on manufacturing is not meant to imply that making things is a more important activity than providing services. The proportion of the workforce employed in manufacturing has been declining for many years in Britain, as it has in other industrial countries, and the trend is certain to continue. A nation's economic strength cannot be considered in terms of manufacturing alone, and some might argue that, by excluding non-manufacturing sectors such as the media and financial services, this book is underplaying the things which British firms are good at. Nevertheless, the post-war history of British manufacturing is a large and complex subject in its own right, and the focus on this part of the economy seems justified in view of the many unresolved controversies which surround it.

TABLE 1.2 *The case study industries in 1988*

Industry	No of employees (000s)	Exports (£m)	Imports (£m)
Engineering (non-electrical and electrical machinery)	789.3	12,502	12,966
Chemicals (incl. pharmaceuticals)	554.9	15,930	14,380
Electronics	306.6	9,834	12,624
Motor vehicles	264.7	5,136	11,262
Textiles	254.1	2,250	4,340
Aircraft	170.5	5,430	3,955
Iron and steel	154.2	2,573	2,237
Shipbuilding	72.0	259	183
Pulp, paper and board	32.6	735	3,740

Source: *Industrial Structure Statistics*, OECD, Paris, 1992.

PART I

---•◦•---

Historical Background

PART I

Historical Background

TWO

————————•○•————————

The Consequences of Coming First

There is a widely held view that British industrial decline began in the closing decades of the nineteenth century and has continued remorselessly ever since. According to this account, British entrepreneurs, having led the world in the first industrial revolution, failed to adapt to competition from the two late-industrialising countries, Germany and the US. British industry was locked into a set of institutions and management practices which had become obsolete. The financial system was not well organised to supply risk capital for the new industries of the second industrial revolution; the education system did not produce enough scientists and engineers; and the labour relations system slowed down the introduction of new manufacturing methods.

It is certainly true that Britain was caught up by the US and Germany between 1870 and 1914. It is also true that the institutions and capabilities which the two late-comers developed were different from those on which the British industrial revolution had been based. One well-known example is the emergence in Germany of the big universal banks, led by Deutsche Bank, which made long-term loans to their industrial clients and organised stock market flotations for them, while British banks concentrated almost entirely on short-term lending. Another is the creation in the US towards the end of the nineteenth century of large, professionally managed corporations, while British businessmen still clung to what Alfred Chandler, the American business historian, has called personal capitalism – a structure of small, family-controlled firms, lacking the economies of scale enjoyed by their US counterparts.[1]

A much-debated issue is whether Britain's inability to match these and other innovations constitutes an entrepreneurial failure, and, if so, whether the failure was sufficiently serious and long-lasting to be relevant to what happened after 1945. Was it a disadvantage to have come first?

The Growth of British Industry from 1750 to 1870

Britain's industrial revolution, which began in the second half of the eigh-teenth century, was driven by technological change in three sectors. The pace-setter was cotton textiles. The substitution of machines for human effort in the spinning and weaving of cotton generated a huge domestic and international demand for a fabric which had previously been too expensive to capture a mass market. Second, new iron-making techniques – the replace-ment of charcoal by coke in the smelting of iron ore and the 'puddling' process for refining pig iron – increased the supply and lowered the price of wrought iron, which became the building block of the industrial revolu-tion.[2] The third breakthrough was the steam engine, first used for pumping water out of coal-mines and later replacing water power in driving machinery of all kinds.

Why did this burst of technological progress occur in Britain and not elsewhere? France was arguably a richer economy at the start of the eighteenth century and more advanced in science. But Britain had several advantages which, taken together, made the industrial revolution possible.[3] One was an ample supply of cheap and accessible coal. Another was an endowment of mechanical skills which had been built up in old-established trades such as clock-making and the manufacture of ship's instruments. The great inventors and engineers of the industrial revolution were predominantly craftsmen, trained in the workshop, and their skills were practical rather than theoretical. Some of them worked closely with scientists, and their lack of formal edu-cation did not preclude 'a rational faith in the orderliness and predictability of natural phenomena, even if the actual laws underlying physics and chemis-try were not fully understood.'[4] To describe them as tinkerers hardly does justice to their achievements, but they relied on experience and intuition, not on scientific knowledge.

The initial stimulus for exploiting these innovations came from domestic demand. Although society was organised hierarchically with the aristocrats at the top and the labouring poor at the bottom, differences in spending patterns were less extreme than in other parts of Europe. Britain was also a more unified economy than its European neighbours, with an efficient trans-port system, so that regions could specialise in particular industries, as Lanca-shire did in cotton textiles, and serve a national market.

The provision of education for the mass of the population was poor, but the technologies which were being introduced did not depend on a highly educated labour force. Most of the necessary skills could be learned on the job. Where craftsmanship was called for, as in the metal-working industries, apprenticeship was the principal means of acquiring and transmitting skills. This system, adapted from the medieval guilds, suited employers because it was a cheap and efficient form of training which could be administered largely by the craftsmen themselves. It suited the craftsmen because it preserved their status as a highly paid group set apart from the growing mass of semi-skilled and unskilled workers. A distinctive feature of factory organisation in the first phase of the industrial revolution was the use of skilled workers as 'internal contractors', responsible for organising the work of less skilled employees.[5]

The political and economic environment was highly conducive to entrepreneurship and the pursuit of wealth. Since the Glorious Revolution of 1688 Britain had been a peaceful, orderly society. The old conflicts between King and Parliament been resolved without the upheaval which engulfed France at the end of the eighteenth century. The King could not borrow or tax without the consent of the country's wealth-holders, and, unlike France, Britain developed financial institutions which provided a secure basis for private commercial activity.[6] The ruling élite was a landowning aristocracy which, far from resisting industrialisation, saw it as an opportunity for making themselves richer. Although the landowners were rarely entrepreneurs in their own right, they supported new businesses with patronage and money, and were eager to exploit the coal and iron ore that lay under their estates. Success in business was seen as a way in which 'middling' people from non-aristocratic backgrounds could lift themselves into a higher social category. A business career was particularly attractive for religious dissenters who were barred from politics and public service. But while this group supplied a large number of well-known industrialists, there was no special merit in being an outsider. Entrepreneurial talent came from a variety of sources, including foreign immigrants as well as the younger sons of the aristocracy.

Industrialisation took place without direction or control from the state. The role of the government was to ensure that no obstacles were put in its way. The authorities maintained public order, guaranteed the security of property, and upheld a legal system which was helpful to entrepreneurs. *Laissez-faire* was the guiding principle in most areas of public policy well before Adam Smith published his *Inquiry into the Nature and Causes of the Wealth of Nations* in 1776. The major exception was in overseas trade, where Britain, like other European countries, had been committed since the seventeenth century to mercantilism. Under this doctrine domestic industry was protected by tariffs; trade with the colonies was reserved for British manufacturers and merchants; and the colonies produced only those commodities which the mother country wanted. These arrangements, providing secure markets for British-made goods, were helpful for British manufacturers in the seventeenth and early eighteenth centuries,[7] but overseas trade was not the principal driver of the industrial revolution. It was not until the early decades of the nineteenth century that Britain's leading industries came to depend on exports to maintain their rate of growth.

By this time there was a range of commodities – textiles, coal, iron, machinery – of which Britain was the world's largest and lowest-cost producer. In these circumstances mercantilist policies were not only unnecessary, but positively harmful to the continuing prosperity of exporters. They needed access to a wider range of markets than the colonies could provide, but this was only possible if the importing countries were free to export their food and raw materials to Britain. As long as British agriculture was protected against import competition, exports of British manufactures were held back. This conflict of interests formed part of the battle between manufacturers and landowners over free trade, culminating in the repeal of the Corn Laws in 1846.

The free trade controversy marked the emergence of the urban middle class as a powerful force which had to be integrated into the political system. Henceforth the aristocrats, if they were to hold on to the reins of power, had to govern with the consent of the industrial bourgeoisie. Protection was abandoned because the ruling class accepted, or at least acquiesced in, 'the middle-class view that one species of wealth, namely passive property in land, had no right to abuse its political power to exact a toll from another, namely active capital in industry and commerce'.[8] Of the two main political parties, the Liberals were the vehicle through which manufacturers and merchants pursued their campaigns for free trade and parliamentary reform. But, once the argument over the Corn Laws issue had been settled, it was not long before the Conservatives, under Disraeli, came to terms with free trade.[9] The principles on which the economy should be run were broadly accepted by both parties.

A more serious threat to political stability came from the working class. As the shift of labour to the factory gathered pace, there was sporadic resistance from handloom weavers and other workers whose skills were being made obsolete. After the end of the Napoleonic wars working-class resentment over working conditions and the lack of political representation took a more violent form. The Chartists, whose influence was at its peak in the 1830s and 1840s, contained a faction which believed in physical force as a means of changing society. But Britain never came close to revolution. Timely concessions to labour interests (including legislation to improve working conditions in factories), together with the prosperity of the mid-Victorian age, helped to bring about what Harold Perkin has called a 'viable class society'.[10] The radicalism of the Chartists gave way to 'New Model' trade unions, formed by craftsmen and other skilled workers who constituted the so-called aristocracy of labour. In the industries where these unions gained a firm hold, such as textiles, iron-making and engineering, most employers came to accept that well-organised trade unions could contribute to the stability of the workplace. While disputes over wages and working conditions continued, union leaders and employers shared many of the same assumptions, including a belief in free trade. Both of them saw the Liberals as their natural allies.

Thus, despite the social strains resulting from industrialisation, there was no political upheaval which might have halted the growth of British industry. Overseas, the long period of peace which followed the Battle of Waterloo allowed British manufacturers to consolidate their position in international trade. A rising proportion of British exports during this period went to the primary producing countries which supplied the food and raw materials that Britain needed. These links were strengthened by the financial, commercial and shipping services which Britain, through the merchants and traders of the City of London, was well equipped to provide. Britain was the world's banker and clearing house as well as its workshop, and supplied most of the capital with which the primary producing countries built up their mines, their ports and their railways. Earnings from overseas investments and commercial services were essential to Britain's prosperity, since they offset a growing deficit in goods.

As a free-trading country Britain was the natural outlet for exports from other European countries, and to a lesser extent the US, as they built up their industries. For Richard Cobden, chief architect of the repeal of the Corn Laws, free trade was in everyone's interests, not just those of Britain, and he tried to persuade other governments that the abolition of tariffs would create the conditions for an era of peace and prosperity in Europe.[11] But protectionist pressures, aggravated by the economic depression which began to affect most parts of Europe in the 1870s, proved too strong. Germany's decision to raise its tariffs in 1879 was part of a general retreat into protectionism throughout Western Europe, which continued up to and beyond the First World War.

In the 1870s Britain was still by far the largest exporter of industrial goods, accounting for about 40 per cent of world trade in manufactures, but competition was beginning to cause concern. The old rival, France, with its limited natural resources, slow-growing population, and predominantly agricultural economy, had slipped back, but a serious threat to British supremacy was coming from Germany and the US. A second industrial revolution was under way, and in some of the new fields – electricity, the internal combustion engine, organic chemistry – the newcomers, not Britain, were taking the lead.

The Rise of American Industry

In the US, as in Britain, the first factory-based industry was cotton textiles, based on water power and located mainly in New England. The use of steam power increased after the Pennsylvania coal fields were opened up in the 1830s, but it was not until the construction of the railway and telegraph networks in the 1840s and 1850s that America's two great advantages as a manufacturing country, the wealth of its raw materials and its huge home market, could be exploited on a larger scale. The railway boom gave a boost to the growth of the iron industry, and encouraged the exploitation of more distant natural resources, notably the Mesabi iron ore mines of Minnesota. The US was richly endowed with other minerals, including oil; the first oil strike was made at Titusville, Pennsylvania, in 1859.

To make full use of these assets the US needed a combination of rising demand, entrepreneurial skill, and supportive policies and institutions.[12] The population, swollen by immigration, rose much more rapidly than Britain's between 1870 and 1913 (TABLE 2.1). But the difference with Britain was not just a matter of size. Incomes in the US were more equal and consumer tastes more similar. These conditions favoured the manufacture of standard-ised goods for a mass market, and entrepreneurs had an incentive to design machinery which would permit low-cost, high-volume production. A well-known example was the Bonsack cigarette-making machine, introduced in 1884, which could turn out 125,000 cigarettes a day; the best that a skilled worker could do was 3,000 cigarettes a day.[13] Manufacturers of branded consumer goods like tobacco and soap were among the first to build sales networks throughout the US. Some of the metal-working industries adopted what became known as the American system of manufactures, a way of making standard machinery from interchangeable components. Pioneered in government armouries for the production of small arms, it was taken up by manufacturers of sewing machines, typewriters and other products for which there was a large, homogeneous demand. The greatest triumph of the American system, achieved by Henry Ford shortly before the First World War, was the mass-produced automobile.[14]

TABLE 2.1 *Population growth 1870–1913*

(in millions)

	1870	1913
US	39.9	97.2
Britain	31.4	45.6
Germany	39.2	67.0
France	38.4	39.8

Source: Angus Maddison, *Dynamic forces in Capitalist Development*, Oxford, 1991, pp. 228–31.

Another distinctive feature of industrialisation in the US was the scarcity of skilled labour. The British apprenticeship system was transplanted to North America in colonial times, but it never established deep roots.[15] The US was a dynamic, settler society in which labour was more mobile than in Britain. Opportunities for self-employment were greater, and the restrictions on personal freedom which apprenticeship entailed were less acceptable. Hence employers had difficulty in retaining the apprentices they had trained. Attempts to impose sanctions on runaway apprentices were unsuccessful and, except in a few trades such as printing, the system had virtually died out by the end of the nineteenth century. Since American manufacturers did not have access to the pool of skilled workers which was available in Britain, they looked for manufacturing methods which economised on the use of craft skills.

In the early stages of industrialisation American employers used the British internal contracting system, but as the volume of production rose and expensive investments were made in high-output machinery, these informal arrangements were no longer adequate. Tighter discipline and closer supervision were needed. In the 1890s Frederick W. Taylor, a production engineer at a leading steel company, worked out new ways of organising and motivating shop floor employees in order to ensure that machinery was used productively. Taylor's approach, which was set out in his *Principles of Scientific Management*, published in 1911, was to establish scientifically how much time and effort a particular task required, and to reward workers who consistently achieved those standards. The 'Taylorist' style of management, giving workers less control over the pace and organisation of work, was resisted by the American trade unions, which, like their British counterparts, were organised on craft lines. But American employers were not prepared to compromise on the principle of managerial control. 'British employers generally chose to accommodate the craft workers; US employers, to confront them.'[16]

The increasing scale of manufacturing operations brought with it the need for well-trained, technically competent managers. The Morrill Land Grant Act of 1862, providing federal support for the creation of new universities, led to an expansion of engineering education. One of the new institutions was the Massachusetts Institute of Technology, which formed close links with the electrical engineering industry. The first business school – the Wharton School of Finance and Commerce at the University of Pennsylvania – was opened in 1881. The expansion of commercial education put pressure on the older, classical universities to make their teaching more relevant to the needs of industry.[17] Harvard's Graduate School of Business Administration, modelled on the Harvard Law School, was founded in 1908.

The professionalisation of management was accelerated by the wave of mergers which took place around the turn of the century. Entrepreneurs in industries making high-volume, standardised goods invested heavily in machinery and equipment, and profitability depended on keeping this expensive plant fully employed, and on avoiding destructive price wars. When cartels were prohibited by the Sherman Antitrust Act of 1890, mergers were seen as a more secure means of keeping competition under control. Several industries acquired an oligopolistic structure, which was to persist with little fundamental change until after the Second World War. An extreme case was United States Steel Corporation, which at the time of its creation in 1901 accounted for 65 per cent of America's steel-making capacity. Most of the big mergers which took place around the turn of the century involved the transfer of ownership from the original founders or their descendants to outside investors, and the appointment of salaried executives to senior posts.

Industrialisation in the US was characterised by scale, organisation and raw-material intensity. The US did not have any great reputation at this stage for scientific originality. As in Britain, American technology was oriented to the shop floor and built on practical experience.[18] American entrepreneurs were good at taking inventions made elsewhere, like the internal combustion engine, and adapting them to local conditions. Even in electrical engineering, which was an outstanding American success, Thomas Edison was a brilliant experimenter, not a trained scientist, although he recognised the need for scientifically trained colleagues to translate his ideas into practice. The growth of the US electrical industry rested on organisational skills – the construction of an integrated system for generating, transmitting and distributing electricity – and on the recognition that, once the system was in place, a mass market was waiting to be tapped.

The Rise of German Industry

At the start of the nineteenth century the German states lagged behind France and Britain in economic development, but the pace quickened in the 1840s. A powerful boost came from railway construction, and heavy industry played a more central role in German industrialisation than it did in Britain. One of Europe's largest concentrations of coking coal was in the Ruhr valley in Westphalia, and within the space of thirty years this previously agricultural region was transformed into the powerhouse of German industry. Alfred Krupp built his first iron-works in Essen in 1836; by 1873 this firm's labour force had increased to 16,000.[19] The engineering industry also benefited from the railway boom. In the 1840s most of Germany's locomotives were imported from Britain, but Borsig in Berlin and other German manufacturers gradually reduced their dependence on British technology and developed their own designs. By the 1860s import substitution was complete and Borsig was competing with British manufacturers in export markets.

The rapid growth of the iron and steel industry paralleled what had happened in the US, but in other respects Germany followed a different path. The division of the country into separate states meant that a unified market was slow to emerge. Even after the formation of the customs union in 1834 and the unification of the country under Prussian leadership in 1871, the domestic market was more fragmented than that of the US, and there was little scope for mass production. Since Germany was also poor in natural resources, apart from coal, entrepreneurs had to find other ways of catching up. They did so through skill rather than scale. Instead of tackling their British and American competitors head-on, they looked for market niches and sought to tailor their products to the needs of specific customers. In cotton textiles, for example, while the British were supplying large quantities of yarn and cloth to India and other distant countries, German mills concentrated on higher-income European customers who were willing to pay a premium for quality and variety.[20] In engineering the focus was on custom-designed machinery produced in small batches.[21]

This strategy was crucially dependent on the skills of the workforce. Like Britain, Germany relied on apprenticeship as the principal means of skill formation, but, in contrast to Britain, it was supplemented by government-financed vocational schools at which apprentices received part of their training. In addition, most states established technical high schools, later upgraded to universities, for the training of engineers. The classical universities were reformed, and, although their mission was strictly non-vocational, the systematic pursuit of knowledge for its own sake contributed to the scientific advances – notably in chemistry – which underpinned the success of German entrepreneurs in the second industrial revolution.

Scientific and technical education was one of the means by which German industry made up for its late start. Another was a financial innovation, the universal bank, which had no counterpart in Britain or the US. Local financial networks were less highly developed than in Britain, and heavy industry needed large amounts of initial capital.[22] From the middle of the nineteenth century, and more extensively after 1870, the gap was filled by the universal banks, which combined commercial and investment banking under the same roof. The three leading *Grossbanken* – Deutsche Bank, Dresdner Bank and Commerzbank – formed a continuing relationship with their industrial clients, often becoming shareholders and taking seats on their boards of directors.

The influence of the *Grossbanken* was largely confined to heavy industry. In states such as Baden and Württemberg, which had a long pre-industrial tradition of skilled craftsmanship, the typical manufacturing enterprise was the family-owned firm, specialising in a narrow range of products.[23] Operating in such industries as textiles and mechanical engineering, they formed networks in which firms sub-contracted to each other the responsibility for particular components or manufacturing processes. The cutlery industry in Solingen, in the lower Rhineland, was a well-known example. These firms did not need large amounts of capital, and their financial requirements were met by local savings and cooperative banks.[24] Despite the rise of a few large companies, such as Krupp and Siemens, industry in Germany was much less concentrated than in the US at the time of the First World War.

Another difference from the US was that German manufacturers depended to a greater extent on exports. Trade policy was a contentious issue in German politics, as it was in Britain. But whereas British manufacturers favoured free trade and the landowners protection, in Germany the opposite was the case. Manufacturers wanted to keep imports out so that they could build up their industries. The landowners were large exporters of grain and feared that the imposition of a tariff would provoke retaliation, putting their overseas business at risk. The fall in grain prices in the 1870s, together with growing competition from American grain exporters, brought a change of heart, and tariffs were introduced in 1879. This represented a shift away from British-style liberalism towards the more nationalistic economic policy advocated by such thinkers as Friedrich List. List's *National System of Political Economy*, published in the 1840s, was intended as a riposte to Adam Smith, and called for a national effort to resist Britain's industrial expansion.[25]

The lack of enthusiasm for free markets was also reflected in a tolerant attitude on the part of the German authorities towards cartels. Price-fixing and market-sharing agreements spread widely in German industry in the closing decades of the nineteenth century. In 1897, seven years after the Sherman Act was passed in the US, the German supreme court confirmed the legality of cartels.[26]

The abandonment of free trade was the product of a pragmatic alliance between two previously hostile interest groups, the landowners and the industrialists. Their common enemy was an increasingly assertive working class. Trade unions began to organise themselves in the 1870s and the political arm of the labour movement, the Social Democratic Party, won nearly 500,000 votes in the Reichstag elections of 1877. The reaction of the ruling oligarchy was repression, balanced by attempts to de-politicise the working class through social insurance and other welfare measures. In contrast to Britain, no 'viable class society' emerged in Germany before the First World War, and there was no scope for the compromise between unions and employers which took place in Britain between 1850 and 1870. This had important consequences for the character of the German trade union movement. Although union membership was at first largely confined to skilled workers, the driving force was not, as in Britain, the desire to protect craft jobs against incursions from semi-skilled and unskilled workers, but the need for a common front against employers and the state. The German trade union movement was more class-based than craft-based.

The constitution of the German Reich, as devised by Bismarck at the time of unification, has been described as 'an autocratic monarchy with a few parliamentary trimmings'.[27] This archaic political system perpetuated social strains which were to have catastrophic consequences in the inter-war years, but it did not prevent the rapid build-up of manufacturing industry. The distinctive features of German industrialisation were the commitment to technical education and workforce skills, the close links between heavy industry and the big banks, the special importance of small, craft-based firms, and the reliance on cartels and protection.

The British Response to Competition

American and German competition affected different British industries in different ways. As far as the older industries are concerned, there was no obvious sign of entrepreneurial failure before 1914. The cotton textile industry, for example, continued to dominate the world market. Although export growth slowed down after 1870, this was due, not to a loss of competitiveness, but to the build-up of production behind tariff walls in countries which had previously imported from Britain. Similarly the shipbuilders faced no serious challenge from the US or Germany. Even in steel, where production in Britain fell behind that of Germany and the US soon after the turn of the century, this was largely for reasons outside the control of British steel-makers. Germany and the US were still in their catch-up phase, and steel consumption was rising more rapidly than in Britain. Both countries also protected their steel industries with tariffs. Thus British steel-makers were restricted from selling to the two most dynamic overseas markets, while their own home market was fully exposed to imports. In these circumstances a fall in Britain's share of world steel production and exports was unavoidable.[28]

The situation in the newer industries was more worrying. In electrical engineering, for example, none of the British entrepreneurs who came into the industry in the 1880s, following the invention of the incandescent lamp, built companies to match the size and technical strength of General Electric in the US, or Siemens and AEG in Germany. This has been blamed by historians on a variety of factors, including lack of support from the capital markets[29] and a distinctively British inability to create and manage large companies.[30] But a more important factor was a domestic environment which slowed down the growth of demand for electricity. In Britain, unlike the US and Germany, urbanisation was well advanced by the time electricity became available, and an extensive network of gas lighting was in place. The existence of this network was a disincentive to the rapid introduction of electricity, and it was reinforced by regulations designed to protect the interests of the gas-lighting suppliers.[31]

The other celebrated British failure was in the chemical industry, above all in dyestuffs, where German firms pioneered the new technique of synthetic organic chemistry and established a virtual world monopoly. But it was not a uniquely British failure. The American chemical industry was as far behind in this field as its British counterpart; up to the First World War the US market for synthetic dyestuffs was supplied mainly from Germany and Switzerland. There were, moreover, other branches of the industry where British entrepreneurs did well. One was soap-making, where William Lever built up what was to become one of Britain's leading multinational companies. Another was rayon or artificial silk. The viscose process for making rayon yarn was patented by two British scientists, C. F. Cross and E. J. Bevan, in 1892, and brilliantly exploited by Courtaulds, the textile company. Courtaulds became the world's largest rayon manufacturer, with a profitable subsidiary in the US.[32]

At the level of individual industries, old and new, the British response to American and German competition between 1870 and 1914 was patchy but by no means disastrous.[33] World trade in manufactures had become a three-horse race, and the early leader could hardly have been expected to remain dominant on all fronts. Were there, nevertheless, institutional weaknesses, inherited from the first industrial revolution, which were holding industry in Britain back?

One obvious gap, especially compared with Germany, was in the field of technical education. In 1870 British universities were not well equipped to serve the new, science-based industries. Oxford and Cambridge had played no part in the industrial revolution, and had no interest in the world of industry. Nevertheless, although Britain started late in this field, it recovered well. New universities with a strongly technical bent were established in several provincial cities during the last years of the nineteenth century, and the Imperial College of Science and Technology was founded in London in 1908. There was also an expansion of part-time technical education below the university level. The British approach was more decentralised, less system-atic and more market-led than in Germany, but by 1914 the gap between the two countries was narrowing. Sidney Pollard, the economic historian, has suggested that Germany's investment in technical education and the role of the state in it 'may not imply German superiority, simply a different tradition and a different place in the sequence of world industrialisation'.[34]

Some historians believe that the creation of the universal bank gave German entrepreneurs a competitive advantage because it provided access to long-term capital on terms which were not available in Britain.[35] British commercial banks, even after the mergers that took place towards the end of the century, generally steered clear of long-term lending to industry, while the merchant banks in the City – Barings, Rothschilds and the rest – were preoccupied with raising capital for foreign borrowers. There were flaws in the financial system during this period, but financial markets were sufficiently well-developed to ensure that few creditworthy entrepreneurs were starved of finance. There is no clear evidence that the outflow of capital to support railway construction and other infrastructure projects overseas diverted funds from investment in domestic industry.[36] The German universal bank was a response to a particular set of circumstances – a late-developing country undergoing a very rapid process of industrialisation – that did not exist in Britain.

As for the impact of trade unions on industrial performance, labour relations in Britain went through a stormy period around the turn of the century, and again in the years immediately preceding the First World War. This was due partly to a change in the character of trade-unionism, arising from the emergence of more militant 'general' unions which represented semi-skilled and unskilled workers. Labour relations became more adversar-ial, and in industries such as engineering, where craft unions were strong, the number of disputes over working practices and demarcation increased. But the employers generally came out on the winning side in these disputes, and the labour relations system was probably not a significant brake on efficiency and technical progress in manufacturing before 1914.

The late Victorian and Edwardian entrepreneur has been criticised by some historians for his reluctance to break away from craft control – the practice of delegating to skilled workers part of the responsibility for the organisation of work. The argument is that this practice delayed the introduc-tion of 'Taylorist' techniques, which called for tighter supervision of shop floor labour.[37] But for most British employers craft control was not a com-petitive disadvantage in the conditions which they faced before the First

World War. In shipbuilding, for example, where craft control was solidly entrenched, productivity in Britain was higher than in the US and Germany, and there was no reason to abandon a well-tried production system which was working satisfactorily. This point is also relevant to Alfred Chandler's strictures about personal capitalism. The main reason for the creation of giant companies in the US towards the end of the nineteenth century was the nature of the domestic market. Firms which were manufacturing on a large scale needed to take direct control over the procurement of raw materials and the distribution of finished products. In Britain, with a smaller home market and more highly developed networks of merchants and other intermediaries, there was less need for manufacturers to integrate backward into raw material purchasing or forward into marketing and distribution.[38] Lancashire cotton was the classic case of a successful industry which was both horizontally and vertically disintegrated, with most firms specialising in one part of the production chain.

The comparison with Germany is less clear-cut. In industries where German companies were bigger than their British counterparts, this, too, was mainly due to the character and timing of German industrialisation. The iron-masters of the Ruhr were building a new industry from scratch in an undeveloped region. They needed to do more things for themselves than was necessary in Britain, and to integrate more operations on the same site. Some German companies, of which Thyssen and Siemens are examples, did adopt organisation methods similar to those of the big American corporations.[39] But many of Germany's industries, such as mechanical engineering, were as fragmented, and as dominated by family-owned concerns, as in Britain.

Britain, Germany and the US in the Inter-war Years

One of the consequences of the First World War was to consolidate the position of the US as the world's leading industrial power. American manufacturers were well placed to profit from the booming domestic demand of the 1920s and to exploit internationally the managerial advances which they had made before the war. Their most spectacular success was in the mass-production industries; US manufacturers accounted for three-quarters of the world's car exports in the inter-war years. But there was also a push forward in science-based industries as large American firms began to adopt the German approach to company-financed research. The discovery of nylon by Du Pont in 1930 was the direct result of this company's decision to build up a team of first-class scientists and engineers and give them the same facilities which they would have enjoyed in an academic environment.[40] American Telephone and Telegraph created in Bell Laboratories what was to become America's foremost industrial research institution.[41]

The broadening of American industrial capabilities was reinforced by new managerial techniques. Alfred Sloan at General Motors, which overtook Ford as America's largest car manufacturer during the 1920s, showed how economies of scale in large, multi-product companies could be combined with efficient central coordination. The General Motors multi-divisional structure, which separated the day-to-day management of the car businesses – Chevrolet, Pontiac, Cadillac and so on – from the supervisory role of the head office, was widely imitated in the US and later in Europe. Sloan was an example of the kind of professional manager who filled many of the top executive posts in American industry. The separation of ownership and control, which had been a distinctive feature of American capitalism before the war, was taken further as companies increased in size through mergers and acquisitions.

The rise of American industry provoked a mixture of admiration and fear in Europe. Businessmen made pilgrimages to Detroit and tried to learn how the Americans were able to combine high productivity, high wages and high standards of living.[42] Of the leading European countries, Germany was the most influenced by American ideas, but its ability to maintain its pre-war momentum of growth, let alone catch up with the US, was constrained by the legacy of the war. The establishment of the Weimar Republic in 1919, and the integration of the working class into the political and economic system, left unresolved many of the political tensions which had existed under the Kaiser. Employers, especially the coal and steel magnates of the Ruhr, resented the new-found power of organised labour, and sought to roll back the concessions they had been forced to make at the end of the war.

The economy was damaged by the onerous terms of the Versailles peace settlement, compounded by the sluggish growth of world trade. Between 1919 and 1924 industrial production was running at between a half and three-quarters of the 1913 level.[43] The situation improved in the second half of the 1920s after inflation had been brought under control and capital began to flow in from the US. But most of these funds were withdrawn when the world depression began to bite. With the banking system in crisis and the political parties unable to reconcile their differences, Germany was plunged into a period of political turbulence which culminated in the appointment of Hitler as Chancellor in 1933. Within the confines of a command economy a partial recovery took place in the second half of the decade, but economic efficiency took second place to the two overriding national objectives: military supremacy and industrial autarky.

The response of German industry to these events was defensive. The first priority after the war was to rebuild the industrial base. In heavy industries rationalisation through merger was seen as a means of cutting costs and reducing competition. Thyssen was the prime mover in the formation, in 1926, of a giant steel-making group, Vereinigte Stahlwerke (Vestag), which accounted for about half the industry's output. This merger, partly financed by US capital, facilitated plant closures and led to some improvement in productivity, but Vestag was an unwieldy creature and difficult to manage effectively.[44] In the chemical industry a process of consolidation, which had started before the war, led in 1925 to the creation of IG Farben, embracing all the leading dyestuffs companies. But rationalisation did little to improve the efficiency of German industry; one historian has described it as 'simply a vogue-word used to describe the mistaken investments made in the 1920s'.[45] It was accompanied by a further proliferation of cartels, some of which, as in steel, were extended internationally.

The stagnation of the inter-war years did not erase what had been achieved in Germany before 1914. Investment in skills through technical schools and universities was maintained, and the apprenticeship system was strengthened by the Nazis, albeit for political rather than economic reasons; factory-based training, part of a programme for building 'works communities', was a way of detaching workers from their loyalty to trade unions. While German engineering firms lost ground to the Americans in mass-produced lines – the Solingen cutlery-makers, for example, had nothing with which to counter the Gillette safety razor – they continued to be highly competitive in skill-intensive capital goods such as machine tools. IG Farben was the undisputed leader in the world chemical industry, spending more on research than its American and British competitors. But German manufacturers tended to continue along lines which had been set before the war, rather than develop new activities. There was a particular weakness, partly due to the instability of the economy, in consumer products.[46] The electrical industry was slow to invest in the large-scale production of domestic appliances, and the motor industry, most of which was still attached to craft-production methods, performed poorly until the second half of the 1930s.

For Britain the inter-war period was not as politically traumatic as in

Germany, and the social strains arising from high unemployment were handled more successfully. But the war and its aftermath undermined many of the assumptions which had guided governments and entrepreneurs since the middle of the nineteenth century. The 1920s saw the collapse of the liberal world economic order on which British hegemony had been based. The attempt to restore the old order was responsible for what is often seen as a serious error – the return to the gold standard in 1925 at sterling's pre-war exchange rate. Although this decision could be defended as a contribution to the revival of international trade, it weakened the competitiveness of British exporters at a time when overseas markets were contracting. Yet, whatever the merits of the return to gold, the British government on its own could have done little to halt the spread of protectionism. The one country which might have done so, the US, maintained its high tariff policy; the Hawley–Smoot Tariff of 1930 has been widely blamed for exacerbating the world depression. Britain's own attachment to free trade finally gave way with the abandonment of the gold standard in 1931 and the introduction of a general tariff in the following year.

The collapse of world trade had a disastrous effect on Britain's staple industries which had traditionally exported a large proportion of their production. After the brief post-war boom had faded, the cotton textile industry was faced with a huge surplus of capacity which persisted throughout the inter-war period. Some of its important Asian markets were invaded by Japanese textile exporters, and India was building up its own textile production. Cost reduction was the order of the day, but the one major attempt at reorganisation – the concentration of more than a hundred spinning mills in the Lancashire Cotton Corporation – did little to improve the industry's competitiveness. The situation in shipbuilding was much the same. A surge in orders after the war, as owners replaced tonnage that had been damaged or destroyed, was followed by a prolonged slump. Some yards were closed in the 1930s as part of a capacity reduction programme co-ordinated by the Bank of England, but the adjustment was far from complete by the time of the Second World War.

The positive feature of the inter-war period was the progress made in newer industries. The four-way merger which created Imperial Chemical Industries (ICI) in 1926 was in part a defensive response to the formation of IG Farben in the previous year, but the new company was strongly committed to research. ICI's invention of polythene in 1933 was the counterpart to Du Pont's nylon, showing that in the new technology of polymer chemistry German firms no longer had the field to themselves. There was a partial recovery in electrical engineering and a promising start in the new field of electronics; television and radar were two innovations for which British engineers could claim most of the credit. In the motor industry British manufacturers were no match for Ford and General Motors in exports, but by European standards the two leading firms, Morris and Austin, did well, skilfully adapting Fordist techniques to the conditions of a much smaller home market.

There were improvements, too, in management and organisation. The formation of ICI was one of several large-scale mergers which took place in the inter-war period, and although not all of them were successful, these structural changes had a positive effect on managerial efficiency.[47] The merger movement, and the increasing trend for large companies to raise capital on the London Stock Exchange, created opportunities for the merchant banks in the City of London (which were facing a dearth of overseas business) to strengthen their links with domestic industry. As companies got bigger and family control was diluted, more professional managers were appointed to senior executive posts. Some of them came into industry via the accountancy profession; the accountancy firms, in their role as auditors, provided their staff with a training in management which was a partial substitute for a business school education of the American type.[48]

Given the difficult international environment, British industrial performance in the inter-war years was creditable, at least in comparison with other European countries.[49] As TABLE 2.2 shows, Germany and Britain were roughly on a par in terms of manufacturing productivity at the end of the

TABLE 2.2 *Manufacturing output per person employed 1899–1935*

(Britain = 100)

	US/Britain	Germany/Britain
1899	195.4	94.7
1913	212.9	119.0
1925	234.2	95.2
1935	207.8	102.0

Source: S. N. Broadberry, *The Productivity Race*, Cambridge, 1997, p. 36.

1930s, as they had been just before the First World War, and not far apart in their share of world manufacturing production (TABLE 2.3). The failure, if there was one, was in relation to the US, where productivity was more than double the European level. The American lead was based on a large, tariff-free home market, an abundance of raw materials, and institutions and policies which encouraged entrepreneurship and innovation.

TABLE 2.3 *Shares of world manufacturing output, 1913 and 1938*

(per centage of total)

	1913	1938
US	32.0	31.4
Germany	14.8	12.7
Britain	13.6	10.7
Japan	2.7	5.2
France	6.1	4.4
Italy	2.4	2.8
Others	28.4	32.8

Source: Paul Bairoch, 'International Industrialisation Levels from 1750 to 1980', *Journal of European Economic History*, vol. 11, no. 2, Fall 1982.

Britain's early start in the industrial revolution had left some lasting legacies, some of which would prove troublesome after the Second World War. One was a large commitment to older industries, such as cotton textiles and shipbuilding, which had been built up during the nineteenth century. Another was a pattern of trade originating from the days when Britain exchanged the products of the first industrial revolution – textiles, coal, iron – for food and raw materials from the primary producing countries. The bias towards non-European markets was reinforced by the protectionism of the inter-war years. The newer industries, in particular, became increasingly dependent on the dominions and colonies; in 1938 three-quarters of Britain's electrical machinery and car exports went to imperial markets. This was to a large extent the inevitable result of high tariffs in other European countries, but it encouraged the view that overseas trade should be based on complementarity rather than competition. Trade with developing countries, inside and outside the Empire, seemed more natural than trade between industrial countries which had similar industrial structures and produced similar goods.

Britain's distinctive industrial history had left its mark on the three institutions which were referred to in the first chapter – the financial system, the education system and the labour relations system. But in all three fields a process of evolution had taken place before and after the First World War, and none of them can be seen as a fatal disability which condemned British industry to decline after 1945. The labour relations system, for example, had stabilised after the drama of the 1926 General Strike. If attitudes on the part of unions and employers were adversarial, there was a pragmatic recognition that a *modus vivendi* had to be worked out, and that orderly procedures for dealing with disputes were in everyone's interests. It can hardly be said that this was a worse preparation for the post-war period than the bitterness which characterised German labour relations during the 1920s and early 1930s, leading to the extinction of the trade union movement under the Nazis.

A damaging consequence of the inter-war depression was the retreat from liberalism in British economic and industrial policy. The abandonment of free trade in 1932 was accompanied by the spread of price-fixing and market-sharing arrangements, condoned and even encouraged by the government in the hope that they would encourage rationalisation. The lack of internal competition, together with protection against imports, created an environment which was not conducive to industrial efficiency. But these policies were not confined to Britain; the cartel habit was even more deeply entrenched in Germany.

Britain was not the only country with awkward legacies from the past, and British industry was not obviously less well equipped than its European competitors to benefit from the more favourable international environment that prevailed after the Second World War. Explanations for what went wrong after 1945 have to be found in the post-war period itself.

THREE

Britain, Germany and France after the Second World War

W here did Britain go wrong after 1945? This question began to exercise the minds of politicians and economists at the end of the 1950s as they compared Britain's relatively sluggish rate of growth with the spectacular performance of Germany, France and Italy. Many people felt that British industry, whether through its own mistakes or those of governments, had thrown away its opportunities at the end of the war. With their manufacturing capacity largely intact, British firms seemed to be in a strong position to make permanent gains in world markets at the expense of their pre-war competitors. Yet it was Germany, not Britain, which had an 'economic miracle', based on an extraordinarily rapid increase in exports. At the same time France and Italy, which had been laggards before the war, made a greap leap forward. By 1960 these three countries were threatening to overtake Britain and in some industries had already done so.

By historic standards the British economy performed well during this period. In common with the rest of Western Europe, Britain benefited from a world economic climate which was far more benign than in the 1920s and 1930s. Thanks to the leadership of the US, now converted to the virtues of free trade, the pre-war system of cartels and protection was dismantled, paving the way for a golden age of economic growth which helped all the European nations raise their productivity and their living standards closer to the US level. The British people, as the Prime Minister, Harold Macmillan, remarked in 1957, had 'never had it so good'.[1] Yet the Continental countries did even better, and it was this disparity which gave rise to a growing sense of national failure, reflected in books such as Michael Shanks' *The Stagnant Society*. The backwardness of much of British industry, Shanks wrote in 1961, 'is becoming almost a music-hall joke'.[2]

A large part of the divergence with the Continental countries – and this was often overlooked in the general gloom about Britain's deficiencies – was due to two factors over which neither British governments nor British companies had any control.[3] First, the Continental countries had suffered more extensive damage during the war, and so were starting from a lower base. It was inevitable that once the damage had been repaired and rational economic policies introduced, they would enjoy some years of exceptionally rapid recovery. Most of the destruction had been to transport and communications rather than to factories. This was particularly true of West Germany, where new investment in plant and machinery during the war had exceeded losses from bombing and demolition.[4]

Second, Germany and France had larger agricultural sectors than Britain. As economic growth gathered pace in the 1950s, they could transfer labour from low-productivity farming into high-productivity industry, a transition which Britain had gone through many years before.[5] In 1950 only 6 per cent of the British labour force was engaged in agriculture, compared with 28 per cent in France and 24 per cent in Germany. Whereas Britain was faced with labour shortages in the first decade after the war, the two Continental countries had a pool of surplus labour on which to draw. In Germany the pool was enlarged by refugees from Soviet-controlled East Germany, many of whom had useful skills and were strongly motivated to contribute to the revival of the country.

TABLE 3.1 *Shares of world exports of manufactures 1929–73*

per cent

	Britain	Germany*	Italy	France	US	Japan
1929	23.8	15.5	3.9	11.6	21.7	4.1
1937	22.3	16.5	3.7	6.2	20.5	7.4
1950	24.6	7.0	3.6	9.6	26.6	3.4
1964	14.0	19.5	6.2	8.5	20.1	8.3
1973	9.1	22.3	6.7	9.3	15.1	13.1

*The German figures for 1929 and 1937 are 71 per cent of contemporary Germany; the figures for 1950–73 are for the Federal Republic.

Source: R. C. O. Matthews, C. H. Feinstein and J. C. Odling-Smee, *British Economic Growth, 1856–1973*, Oxford, 1982, p. 435.

Yet these two factors on their own are not enough to explain how the Continental countries converted post-war reconstruction into a period of sustained economic growth which lasted until the early 1970s. By 1973, as TABLE 3.1 shows (previous page), Germany's share of world exports of manufactures was more than twice as large as Britain's. This was not a continuation of pre-war trends. Something had changed to give the Continental countries a lift which was missing in Britain. As a first step towards exploring what had changed, this chapter considers the differences between Britain, Germany and France in the aftermath of the war, and the policy choices which were made in the three countries at that time.

The Social Market Economy in Germany

For the first three years after the war, the German economy was in a chaotic state, and living conditions were worse than they had been at any time during the war. The Nazi system of economic management, including price controls and food rationing, was still in place, but there was no central authority to administer it. The country was divided into four occupied zones, and, until the merger of the British and American zones in 1947, there was little co-ordination between them. Normal market incentives were not functioning, and the currency, the Reichsmark, had lost most of its value; firms and households relied extensively on barter and the black market. The slow pace of recovery was due as much to the policies of the occupying powers as to the effects of the war. The victors insisted that Germany must be made to pay for the destruction it had caused. This was to involve reparations, in the form of plant and equipment which would be dismantled and exported to the victorious nations, and restrictions on German industrial production. The main target was heavy industry, especially coal and steel, which was to be cut back in favour of light industry and agriculture. Although extreme ideas about the 'pastoralisation' of the German economy were quickly dropped, these measures contributed to a general state of demoralisation in the country.

The turning-point came in 1947, when the Truman administration in the US recognised that punitive policies towards Germany were damaging the interests of the West; a prosperous and united Europe could not be achieved with a permanently weakened Germany. With the announcement of the Marshall Plan and the subsequent merger of the three Western zones, the stage was set for the creation of the Federal Republic of Germany as an independent state, firmly tied to the Western alliance.

How this state should be organised, and how relations between West Germany and its neighbours should be regulated, were far from clear at the time of the Marshall Plan. The French government was determined to prevent the resurgence of a powerful neighbour that might again threaten France's security as it had done three times in the previous eighty years. A particular concern was the coal and steel complex in the Ruhr, which, the French argued, should be either drastically reduced in size or placed under international control. These fears were not easily reconciled with the American view that the revival of German industry was vital for the rest of Europe; unless Germany resumed its former role as the main supplier of capital goods to its Continental neighbours, Europe would be dependent for an indefinite period on American equipment and American money.

The Americans wanted to mould West Germany, and Western Europe as a whole, in their own image – an efficient, competitive, capitalist economy tempered by the reforms of Franklin Roosevelt's New Deal.[6] But they did not try to impose a detailed blueprint on a cowed West German population. It was for the Germans themselves, subject to Allied approval on key points, to design their own institutions. The outcome was a blend of Americanisation and home-grown ideas.

The Social Democratic Party (SPD), whose prestige was high because of its opposition to the Nazis, believed that capitalism had failed and that it should be replaced by planning, public ownership and 'economic democracy'; the last had been a long-standing party objective since the 1920s – an equal share for employees and trade unions in the running of the economy and in the management of companies. The Christian Democrats, a new party which united several of the centre-right parties of the Weimar period, were opposed to socialism, but a strong faction within the party had doubts about the free market as the principal regulator of economic activity. The party's 1947 programme, known as the Ahlen programme, declared that 'the capitalist economic system has failed to do justice to the vital political and social interests of the German people', and called for the public ownership of major enterprises.[7] Even the Free Democrats, a union of pre-war liberal parties, took a cautious line on the restoration of free markets.

The most coherent analysis of Germany's past history and current situation came, not from the political parties, but from a group of academics who had been pondering the flaws in the country's political and economic system since the 1920s. One of the leading figures was Walter Eucken, who was appointed Professor of Economics at the University of Freiburg in 1927 and continued in that post throughout the war. Others such as Wilhelm Ropke and Alexander Rustow went into exile after Hitler's rise to power, but they remained in contact with one another during the war.

The principal lesson which this group drew from the collapse of the Weimar Republic and the disasters that followed was that a third way had to be found between unbridled *laissez-faire* and the collectivism that had failed so abysmally under the Nazis. At the heart of their philosophy, sometimes called Ordo-liberalism, was the need for strict safeguards against the concentration of power, whether in the hands of government or of organised interest groups. The government's influence over the economy must be limited in scope and governed by clear rules, so that the temptation to intervene for short-term political reasons would be eliminated. An independent central bank, with a remit to resist inflation and maintain the value of the currency, was part of this rules-based framework. The conduct of fiscal and monetary policy must be consistent and predictable, with anti-cyclical measures kept to a minimum. The highest priority must be given to the promotion of competition; the prevalence of cartels and tariffs was seen as one of the principal causes of the malfunctioning of the German economy under the Weimar Republic. But the Ordo-liberals did not envisage a passive, nightwatchman state. The government had to be strong enough to ensure that the rules of the market economy were enforced. It also had responsibilities in the social field, at least to the extent of providing a safety net for the disadvantaged. The approach was nearer to classical liberalism than to the Keynesianism which became fashionable in Britain and in the US after the war. It was an attempt to redefine liberalism in a form suitable for a modern society.[8]

These ideas were actively promoted by Eucken and others after the war, but at that time the tide of opinion was running in favour of a planned economy in which the price mechanism would play only a limited role. When the American and British authorities set up a Bizonal Economic Administration in 1947, most of the senior posts were held by Social Democrats and trade-unionists. A mild form of socialism, as favoured by the British, seemed a likely outcome when the Germans resumed control of their affairs. But an advisory committee was established on which pro-market economists, including Eucken, were represented, and they had an important influence on the debate which preceded the currency reform in June 1948.

The reform itself, which involved the introduction of a new currency, the Deutschmark, to replace the Reichsmark, was the responsibility of the occupation authorities, but the other changes which were made at the same time – above all, the removal of almost all controls over prices and wages – reflected the victory of the liberals over the *dirigistes* within the Economic Administration. The man who was responsible for implementing the reforms, and had a large part in shaping them, was Ludwig Erhard.

The son of a shopkeeper in Fürth, northern Bavaria, Erhard was trained as an economist at the Nuremberg School of Commerce and worked for a market research organisation from 1928 until 1942. He then set up his own research institute and from this base he developed ideas about the post-war economy which, though not directly influenced by Eucken and his colleagues, placed the same emphasis on competition and sound money.[9] In 1944 he circulated a memorandum to bankers and industrialists which included proposals for a currency reform and the phased removal of government controls. Erhard was not an active opponent of the Nazis, but he had kept his distance from them, and when Fürth was liberated by the Americans in April 1945, he was asked to take charge of economic administration in the area. Later in 1945 he was appointed to the post of economics minister in the new Bavarian government. Although Erhard fell out with other members of the administration and resigned in January 1947, he continued to propagate his views, and in September of that year he was invited to head a committee on currency reform within the Bizonal Economic Administration. A few months later the director of the Administration, Johannes Semler, was removed from office after making critical remarks about the policies of the occupying powers, and Erhard was appointed to take his place.

The 1948 reforms were spectacularly successful. 'On the morning after the introduction of the Deutschmark, people accepted money in exchange for goods and labour services, the shop windows were full of goods which had previously been unavailable – at least legally – and black and grey markets were reduced to an almost negligible role.'[10] This was the first step towards the revival of the German economy, but several crises had to be overcome before Erhard's policies were firmly in place. A wave of price increases in the autumn of 1948 prompted demands for the reimposition of price controls. Despite a one-day general strike Erhard stood firm, the new central bank[11] tightened monetary policy and the threatened upsurge in inflation was brought under control.

Erhard's growing reputation as the architect of economic recovery made him a valuable asset to whichever political party secured his support; he himself had no political ties, although his sympathies were with the Free Democrats. Konrad Adenauer, leader of the Christian Democrats, saw in Erhard a powerful weapon with which to defeat the Social Democrats in the first Federal elections, to be held in August 1949. The Ahlen programme was dropped and the Christian Democrats adopted a pragmatic version of the Ordo-liberal doctrine. The conversion of the principal conservative party to liberalism was an important event in post-war Germany; before the war the parties of the right, influenced by vested interests in industry and agriculture, had put more weight on nationalism and autarky than on the virtues of competition.[12]

Although the Christian Democrat share of the vote in the elections was not much higher than that of the Social Democrats – 31 per cent to 29 per cent – the support of smaller parties, including the Free Democrats, was sufficient to give the non-socialist parties a clear majority, and Erhard was installed as economics minister in the new Federal government. Less than a year later another crisis threatened to derail his policies. The outbreak of the Korean War led to a worldwide shortage of raw materials and semi-finished goods as the Americans and their allies scrambled to re-equip their armed forces. A combination of higher prices and rising imports put the German balance of payments into deficit, and Erhard came under pressure to reimpose controls on the allocation of raw materials. Adenauer's confidence in his economics minister was shaken, and there was a risk that Erhard would resign or be dismissed. But although import liberalisation was briefly suspended, the market economy proved to be more flexible than Erhard's critics had expected, and by the spring of 1951 the 'economic miracle' was back on course.

The impressive performance of the German economy under Erhard's stewardship made the alternative prescriptions offered by the Social Democrats increasingly irrelevant. Heavy defeats in the 1953 and 1958 elections prompted a reformist group within the SPD to rethink the party's commitment to planning and nationalisation. The anti-capitalist element was out of touch with events, and the party's conversion to the principles of the market economy was formalised at the Bad Godesberg conference in 1959; the rhetoric of the class struggle was abandoned. The slogan on which the Social Democrats united – 'as much competition as possible, as much planning as necessary' – did not eliminate differences with the Christian Democrats on aspects of economic policy, but there was a broad consensus in both parties about the priority that should be given to competition and free markets.

The opposition to Erhard's insistence on competition came more from cartel-minded businessmen than politicians. The anti-cartel law which he introduced in 1952 met strong resistance, and when it was finally passed in 1957 it was weaker than Erhard would have preferred. The rules on monopolies were mild, and there were too many loopholes and escape clauses. But the law established the principle that cartels and other restrictive practices were unacceptable, and helped to wean German industry away from the anti-competitive practices which had been widespread before the war.

In pressing for action against cartels Erhard could count on support from the Americans, who regarded the introduction of US-style antitrust policies as a way of injecting dynamism into the German economy. The other aspect of competition policy to which the US attached great importance – the break-up of dominant firms – was more contentious. Two of the principal targets for the American trust-busters were IG Farben and Vestag; other large companies, including Siemens and Bosch, were briefly considered as candidates for break-up, but no action was taken against them. Erhard agreed with the Americans on the need to prevent monopoly, but had no objection to bigness if it could be justified on economic grounds. He was concerned that an over-drastic approach to deconcentration would weaken the ability of German companies to compete in world markets. IG Farben was broken up, but the three main successor companies – Bayer, Hoechst and Badische Anilin und Soda Fabrik (BASF) – were large enough to hold their own against the world leaders in the chemical industry, such as Du Pont in the US and ICI in Britain. In steel, the ties between steel-making and coal-mining were partially broken, but deconcentration was milder than the more enthusiastic American trust-busters had hoped for. The outcome was an industrial structure nearer to the American model of competitive oligopoly than to German practice in the 1920s and 1930s.[13]

The strongest safeguard against a return to cartels was not domestic competition policy, but the openness of the German economy to imports.[14] Erhard was an enthusiastic proponent of free trade, and Germany was the pace-setter in European trade liberalisation; the average level of tariff protection was reduced from 19.6 per cent to 10.6 per cent during the 1950s. Imports of manufactured goods, principally from neighbouring European countries, increased rapidly, adding to the competitive pressure on German industry.[15] Erhard favoured the widest possible free trade area and the minimum amount of government intervention in regulating exports and imports. When the French foreign minister, Robert Schuman, put forward the idea of a European Coal and Steel Community (ECSC) in 1950, Erhard was not enthusiastic.

He disliked the idea of a supranational authority to control European trade in steel, suspecting that it might be a vehicle through which the German and French steel-makers could recreate their pre-war cartels. But there were great political attractions in the scheme for West Germany. It offered the prospect of defusing French anxieties over the future of the Ruhr, bringing to an end Allied controls over German steel production, and confirming the status of the Federal Republic as an acceptable partner in European affairs. These were the issues which mattered most to Adenauer, and the Coal and Steel Community proved to be a decisive step towards European political integration.[16]

On this larger issue, too, Erhard did not see eye to eye with his Chancellor. He was concerned that the proposed European Economic Community – first put forward by the Dutch foreign minister, Johan Willem Beyen, in 1953 – would be pushed by France in an illiberal direction. A better alternative, in Erhard's view, was a free trade area covering Western Europe as a whole, including Britain. But Adenauer was more interested in the political than the economic aspects of the Common Market, seeing it as a means of binding West Germany into the Western alliance and strengthening the Federal Republic's ties with France. The row between the two men simmered on after the Common Market had come into operation in 1958, and Erhard was disappointed, as were other liberals within the German government, when General de Gaulle vetoed Britain's application to join the EEC in 1963. However, although the creation of the Common Market had a distorting effect on the pattern of trade – most notoriously in the field of agriculture – it had the offsetting advantage for West Germany of opening up the two most protected European markets, France and Italy. The process of tariff reduction within the EEC was almost certainly faster than it would have been in a looser free trade area, and in that sense the creation of 'Little Europe' had a positive effect on the growth of West German exports.[17]

Membership of the Common Market did not alter the fundamentally liberal thrust of German economic policy. But there were other reforms which had to be made if the social market economy was to function effec-tively. Conflict-prone labour relations had contributed to the instability of the Weimar Republic, and the collusion of many employers with the Nazis made the trade union movement even more determined to reassert itself after 1945. The unions were in a strong political position because of their opposition to fascism, and their demands for public ownership and 'econ-omic democracy' were regarded sympathetically by the Labour government in Britain. But nationalisation faded from the political agenda after the defeat of the Social Democrats in the 1949 election, and the unions concentrated their efforts on the issue of codetermination – the sharing of power between employee representatives and shareholders in the management of companies.

The unions had made a significant advance on this front in 1947, when the British authorities in the Ruhr agreed that the reconstituted steel companies should assign half the seats on their supervisory boards to employee representatives.[18] But this was only an interim arrangement. Final decisions had to await the establishment of the Federal Republic, and by that time the employers, some of whom regarded codetermination as socialism by the back door, had recovered their self-confidence. It was only through the patient diplomacy of Konrad Adenauer that a compromise was reached in 1951, confirming the arrangements that had been made in the Ruhr in 1947, but imposing a more limited form of codetermination in other industries. This was at best a partial victory for the unions, and it was followed by the Works Constitution Act of 1952, which was widely regarded as a defeat. All companies with more than fifty employees were obliged to have a works council, but council members were appointed by the workforce as a whole, not by the trade unions, and there were strict limitations on what the councils could do. They could not, for example, initiate a strike; their role was to act as mediators between management and workforce.

The strengths of the new system were that it entrenched the rights of employees in a legal framework which was designed to encourage co-operation between the two sides, without seriously impeding managerial freedom. Day-to-day issues in the factory, which were the domain of the works council, were separated from bargaining over wages, which took place at a regional or industry level. The two-tier arrangement was facilitated by the reorganisation of the trade union movement into a small number of industrial unions, each of which bargained on behalf of all blue-collar employees in its industry. Although relations between unions and employers remained uneasy for several years after the new laws had been passed, the bitterness of the Weimar years gradually faded. Even hard-line employers who had barely reconciled themselves to the existence of trade unions recognised that a fresh start had to be made.

The labour relations reforms, like other parts of the new order which took shape in West Germany in the late 1940s and early 1950s, combined a determination to learn from past mistakes with elements of continuity. Most of the interest groups which helped to build the new order – political parties, trade unions and employers' organisations – had existed in much the same form under Weimar.[19] But the reforms corrected weaknesses that had prevented the Weimar Republic from functioning effectively. The other crucial difference from the Weimar days was an exceptionally favourable economic environment, for which the US was largely responsible. The importance of the Marshall Plan lay not so much in its financial contribution to the modernisation of German industry as in opening the way towards free trade in Europe and creating the conditions for West Germany's reintegration into the world economy.[20]

Modernisation in France

The fall of France in 1940 has been described as 'a psychological avalanche that buried pre-war certainties and created a new landscape on which reformers could build anew'.[21] From it sprang a collective sense of national failure, and a conviction that fundamental reforms were needed to reverse the country's economic decline. France appeared to be trapped in a state of permanent inferiority *vis-à-vis* its neighbour on the other side of the Rhine. Breaking out of this trap was the over-riding objective for post-war French governments. It was to be achieved by industrial modernisation and by preventing Germany from dominating Europe as it had done before the war. The hope was that, if this twin-track policy could be implemented quickly, France would displace Germany as the strongest industrial power on the Continent.

France's backwardness could be traced partly to the slow pace of industrialisation in the nineteenth century, partly to the crippling effects of the 1930s depression. France had kept pace with the German states in the early phase of the industrial revolution, but the governments of the Third Republic, established in 1870, did not regard the promotion of industry as an important policy objective. Prosperity and social harmony were thought to depend on preserving a balance between agriculture and industry; Germany and the US, with their pell-mell rush for industrialisation, were not seen as models which France should imitate. This did not prevent an impressive French performance in some of the industries of the second industrial revolution. The French motor industry, for example, was the largest in Europe before the First World War, and France was also the leader in aircraft production. In the 1920s modernising elements in French business sought to propagate scientific management, mass production and other American techniques. But with the onset of the Depression, which came later in France than in other European countries and bit more deeply, French industry reverted to a defensive and inward-looking posture, with an increase in cartelisation and greater reliance on colonial markets.

This was the legacy which faced General de Gaulle's provisional government when it was installed in Paris in September 1944. The government was a coalition in which the three main parties were the Communists, the Socialists and the Christian Democrats or MRP (Mouvement Républicain Populaire). The Communist Party, then at the peak of its influence, did not seek to promote a revolution, but rather to retain its hold on power, to preserve the unity of the left and to ensure that France did not align itself with the US-dominated Western alliance. It was also eager to participate in the task of national recovery, pressing its trade union allies to increase production and to refrain from strikes.

The economic programme was a compromise between the disparate elements in the coalition. Most of the basic industries, including electricity, gas and coal, were taken into public ownership, as were the leading banks and insurance companies (the nationalisation of Renault was a special case, prompted by the owner's collaboration with the Pétain régime during the war). While these measures gave the government control over some key industrial sectors, they were not part of a comprehensive plan to direct the economy from the centre. Pierre Mendès-France, minister of national economy in the provisional government, tried to formulate such a plan, which would be administered by a strong planning office attached to his department. But he was opposed by other ministers, notably René Pleven at the Ministry of Finance, a former businessman and close ally of de Gaulle. Mendès-France resigned in the summer of 1945 and the Ministry of Finance established a dominant influence over economic policy.

The shift away from socialism became more pronounced when the Communists left the coalition in 1947. In April of that year an unofficial strike broke out at Renault in protest against the government's wages policy. The strikers were at first denounced by the Communist Party. But as support for the strike spread, the Communists came under intense pressure to reverse their stance. When they did so, the government insisted that the maintenance of its wages policy was a matter of confidence, and that if the Communists were not prepared to support it they should resign. What emerged after 1947, under governments of a predominantly centrist or centre-right composition, was a distinctively French form of managed capitalism. Its inspiration was not a coherent body of doctrine akin to Ordo-liberalism in Germany, but the conviction on the part of an influential group of politicians, economists and government officials that the archaic structures of the French economy could be reformed only through purposive intervention by the state.

A central figure was Jean Monnet, appointed by General de Gaulle in January 1946 to head a small planning body, the Commissariat Général au Plan. Monnet was a businessman who had close ties with the US and he greatly admired the dynamism of American industry. He was also well aware, given France's dependence on US aid, that any modernisation plan had to be framed in a way which was credible to American policy-makers. Monnet was convinced that French industry had to be made fit enough to face up to international competition. The first step was to rebuild and expand the basic industries which had been damaged in the war. The first Monnet Plan, published at the end of 1946, gave priority treatment to six sectors – coal, steel, electricity, railways, agricultural machinery and cement – which were given privileged access to public funds. In other industries modernisation commissions were established, consisting of government officials, businessmen and trade union leaders. The Planning Commission had no powers of compulsion, but the planners were able to put pressure on firms by using the government's control over the allocation of credit, foreign exchange and essential raw materials.

Many of the targets set in the first plan were missed, and there may have been over-investment in basic industries to the detriment of the rest of the economy.[22] But the existence of the plan, and the skill of Monnet and his colleagues in persuading businessmen to co-operate with it, helped to change attitudes.[23] The choice, Monnet insisted, was between modernisation and decadence, and this was a slogan which struck a chord in the country at large. The drive for modernisation affected civil servants as well as businessmen. The old administrative élite – products of the Ecole Polytechnique and the other grandes écoles – had played little part in the reforms that followed liberation; many of these officials had served in the Vichy administration, and they were widely blamed for contributing to the stagnation of the inter-war years. But de Gaulle believed that his plans for restoring the grandeur of France depended on a cadre of highly trained administrators dedicated to the service of the state. To combat the narrow-minded conservatism of the older schools, a new graduate school of public administration, the Ecole Nationale d'Administration (ENA), was set up in 1945. All senior civil servants were recruited through ENA; its curriculum was broader and less technical than that of the older schools. Although ENA did not democratise civil service recruitment in the way that some of its architects had hoped – its students continued to come mainly from the Parisian middle and upper classes – it helped to propagate a technocratic view of the state as a promoter of modernisation.[24] The technocrats were in command, too, in the newly nationalised enterprises. The spirit of the times was personified by the flamboyant head of Renault, Pierre Lefaucheux, a businessman who had played an active part in the resistance. Although he had socialist sympathies, he saw the company as *une entreprise-pilote*, setting an example of dynamism and innovativeness for the rest of the motor industry.[25]

The first Monnet Plan had an important international dimension.[26] What was at stake was France's place in Europe and, above all, its relationship with Germany. If France could take advantage of Germany's defeat to build up its industrial strength, the balance of power on the Continent might be permanently altered in France's favour. In this context the steel industry had a special significance. The French steel mills, concentrated mainly in Lorraine, had always obtained most of their coking coal from the Ruhr. The expansion of steel-making capacity envisaged in the Monnet Plan was based on the assumption that German steel production would be held well below its pre-war level. This would ensure that adequate supplies of coal would be available to France and that the enlarged French steel industry would take over from Germany as the principal supplier to Continental markets. In the aftermath of the war, when Allied policy towards Germany was in its punitive phase, these ambitions seemed realistic. But after the announcement of the Marshall Plan France had to accept that West Germany would soon be created as a sovereign state and reintegrated into the European economy. While the Americans recognised French sensitivities over the Ruhr, they were not willing to contemplate permanent curbs on German steel pro-duction. France had to find alternative means of fulfilling its industrial ambitions while protecting itself against German domination.

The outcome of this reappraisal came in 1950 with the proposal for a European Coal and Steel Community (ECSC), presented to the world by Robert Schuman, the foreign minister, but largely devised by Jean Monnet. The primary motive was political. It was a way of dealing with one of the most contentious issues in Franco-German relations and establishing a new partnership between the two countries. It was also an imaginative approach to European integration, and for that reason attracted the immediate support of the Americans. John Foster Dulles, Secretary of State, saw the Schuman Plan as 'brilliantly creative', while President Truman described it as 'an act of constructive statesmanship'.[27] But Monnet also saw the plan as a way of shaking up a conservative and cartel-minded steel industry; he regarded the Treaty of Paris, which established the Community, as Europe's first antitrust law. In the event, the impact of the Community on competition was more limited than Monnet had hoped. Although intra-European trade in steel increased, national governments continued to intervene in the industry for political and social reasons. Yet the treaty marked a shift away from the privately regulated cartels of the past and established a concept of European interdependence which could be applied to other sectors.

For the shift to go further, a transformation would have to take place in the attitudes of French businessmen. France was a highly protected country, and in the early 1950s some 40 per cent of its overseas trade was with the colonies. Monnet and his colleagues knew that intra-European trade offered far greater possibilities for industrial modernisation than trade with the Empire. A possible way forward was to continue the sectoral approach, extending to other industries the same principle which had been applied to coal and steel. But the Beyen Plan, which proposed the elimination of tariffs on all industrial goods among the six member countries of the ECSC, involved a much bigger leap in the direction of free trade.[28] The initial French reaction was hesitant, partly because of the weakness of the balance of payments, but by 1955, when the foreign ministers of the six ECSC countries met in Messina to consider the Beyen Plan, France's trade position had improved and the advocates of free trade were in a stronger position to argue their case. As they saw it, sectoral arrangements along the lines of the Coal and Steel Community had serious limitations. 'The French renaissance had to be completed by pushing the whole of French manufacturing into a competitive common market ... Either France renounced liberalisation, modernisation and its hopes for the future, or it took the economic risk.'[29] That risk was taken when France signed the Treaty of Rome in 1957, and the next decade saw a rapid reorientation of French exports towards its Common Market partners (TABLE 3.2).

For France, as for Germany, intra-European trade was crucial to the high rate of economic growth which was achieved in the 1960s. But France's approach to economic policy was more erratic than that of the Federal Republic. The most glaring failure was persistent inflation; successive governments were unable either to control public spending or to impose a German-style monetary policy. Consistency in economic management was not helped by the fragmentation of the political parties, leading to a series of short-lived coalitions. While the withdrawal of the Communists in 1947 had removed

TABLE 3.2 *Destination of French exports 1952–73 (per centage of total)*

	Former French colonies	Six EEC countries	Other OECD countries
1952	42.2	15.9	27.3
1958	37.5	22.2	24.4
1962	20.8	36.8	27.9
1968	13.5	43.0	27.0
1973	9.2	48.6	27.5

Source: W. J. Adams, *Restructuring the French Economy*, Brookings, 1989, p. 178.

the risk of a swing to the left, none of the conservative parties commanded the same solid national support as the Christian Democrats in West Germany. General de Gaulle formed his own party, the Rassemblement du Peuple Français (RPF), rather than accept the leadership of the MRP. Political and social divisions were exacerbated by the colonial wars in Indo-China and Algeria, culminating in 1958 in a political crisis, the return of General de Gaulle to power and the inauguration of the Fifth Republic. The new constitution provided for a stronger presidency, and economic policy became more coherent.

The reform process in France differed from Germany in two other respects. First, the French government did little to promote internal competition. Although a law against price-fixing was passed in 1952, enforcement was lax, and cartels continued much as they had done in the 1930s. Second, there was no overhaul of labour relations. Like their German counterparts, most French employers before the war had been hostile to trade unions, and resented the concessions which had been forced on them at the time of the Popular Front government in 1936. After liberation in 1944 there were hopes that relations between capital and labour could be put on a new footing. One of the first acts of the provisional government was to require all firms with more than 100 employees to establish *comités d'entreprises*, or plant committees, through which managers and employees could work together to increase production. These committees were helpful in coping with the short-term problems of reconstruction, but there was no fundamental change in the labour relations system. The *comités d'entreprises* left behind 'a residue of mundane achievement and a sense of unfulfilment'.[30]

Thus the impetus for reform in France after the war was more limited than in Germany, and left some old institutions and attitudes intact. The biggest changes were the national consensus in favour of industrial modernisation and the recognition that a new relationship with Germany had to be forged. One of Monnet's most valuable contributions, according to his biographer, was to promote a shift in attitudes among France's ruling élite 'from the pretensions of a moth-eaten great power to the realism of a medium-sized but ambitious economic one'.[31] It was the weakness of France's position after the war which encouraged bold and imaginative solutions to its problems, and in this context the Schuman Plan was crucial.[32] The European Coal and Steel Community allowed France to assume a position of leadership in building post-war Europe, and pointed the way to the fuller exposure of French industry to German competition.

Britain's post-war Consensus

In Britain the outcome of the war was an occasion for relief and self-congratulation. While it was recognised that the war could not have been won without American help, there was a justifiable pride in the courage and unity of the British people, and in the resilience of Britain's institutions. The concentration of effort and resources on winning the war had been achieved, as one participant wrote later, with 'a spirit of social cohesion and a perception of fairness which could hardly have been bettered'.[33] When Winston Churchill displaced Neville Chamberlain as Prime Minister in 1940, he invited senior Labour politicians to join the war cabinet, including Clement Attlee as Deputy Prime Minister and Ernest Bevin, head of the Transport and General Workers Union, as Minister of Labour. There was close co-operation between government, employers and trade unions throughout the war, and in planning for post-war reconstruction. The Beveridge report on social insurance, published in 1942, and the 1944 White Paper on employment policy reflected a broad agreement across the political spectrum on the priorities which should guide post-war governments: to maintain full employment and to prevent a repetition of the social hardships of the inter-war years.

Much of this consensus survived Labour's victory in the 1945 general election. Although the election campaign was acrimonious – Churchill claimed that the socialist state which Labour wanted to introduce could not be run without a Gestapo, while Aneurin Bevan, a Labour left-winger, insisted that the election represented 'a struggle for power between Big Business and the people'[34] – the gap between the parties was less wide than the rhetoric suggested. Labour's landslide victory did not mark the conversion of Britain to socialism.[35] By presenting a manifesto which combined social reform with an extension of government control over the economy, the Labour Party convinced the voters that it was more likely than the Conservatives to ensure that the unemployment and stagnation of the 1930s did not return. Labour, under the cautious leadership of Clement Attlee, was offering a set of measures that built on the wartime consensus and added to it a number of social programmes, including the creation of a National Health Service, that were widely agreed to be necessary. Attlee and most of his closest colleagues favoured a mixed economy in which the role of government would be powerful but not overwhelming. There was also an assumption that the partnership between government, employers and unions which had been established during the war would continue.

The most pressing economic problem was the financial legacy of the war. The war had been paid for by borrowing, mainly from sterling area countries, and by the sale of overseas investments, supplemented by aid from the US under the Lend–Lease programme. With the abrupt termination of this programme at the end of the war, Britain was faced with an alarming gap between its foreign exchange outgoings, including debt repayments and overseas military expenditure, and its income from exports.[36] A new American loan was negotiated at the end of 1945, but strict conditions were attached to it, including a requirement that the pound should be made freely convertible into dollars in 1947; there was also pressure from the Americans to dismantle the imperial preference system and open up the British market to imports.

Britain's balance of payments remained fragile throughout Labour's period in office, necessitating a strenuous effort to hold back domestic consumption in favour of exports. Because of this financial weakness, Britain's economic situation after the war was not as favourable as it seemed compared to Germany and France. Although Britain had sustained less physical damage, the two Continental countries did not have a large foreign debt to service, nor did they have the international obligations which stemmed from Britain's shared responsibility with the US and the Soviet Union for supervising the transition from war to peace. The Labour government had the difficult task of correcting the balance of payments while at the same time pursuing its social objectives and fulfilling its overseas commitments. Despite severe setbacks, including the abandonment of sterling convertibility in 1947 and the devaluation of the pound in 1949, the balancing act was successful. By the time Labour left office in 1951, Britain's overseas finances had been strengthened, full employment had been maintained, and a substantial social programme had been carried through.

Some historians have argued that the Attlee government devoted too much attention and resources to social welfare at the expense of what should have been a much higher priority – the modernisation of industry.[37] But Attlee and his colleagues were well aware of the need for higher productivity. The problem was not that their priorities were wrong or that too much money was spent in other areas, but that their industrial policies were not well conceived. In its election manifesto Labour had committed itself to planning and an extension of the public sector through nationalisation. How the plan was to be formulated, and what machinery would be set up to implement it, was left vague. Most of the wartime controls – over imports, over access to foreign exchange, over the allocation of raw materials – were still in place, and they were used by the government to support the export drive. But no new planning instruments were introduced. The proposed National Investment Board, which was to 'determine social priorities and promote better timing in private investment', was not set up, perhaps because the government thought that, by nationalising some of the most capital-intensive industries, it would have sufficient control over investment.[38] In principle the extension of public ownership enabled the government to plan at least part of the economy. But there was no link between nationalisation and planning. The impetus behind nationalisation was partly ideological. For left-wingers like Aneurin Bevan it was a way of ensuring that 'effective social and economic power passes from one order of society to another'.[39] But most ministers saw public ownership as a way of solving particular problems in particular sectors, not as a step towards a socialist economy. Three of the industries which were taken over, gas, electricity and the railways, had been subject to government regulation before the war. The regulatory arrangements had not worked well, and public ownership could be defended as a more effective means of ensuring that these 'natural monopolies' were managed effectively in the public interest.[40] The most ideologically motivated nationalisation was that of steel, but even this could be presented as a way of dealing with the structural weaknesses in the industry which had not been tackled in the 1930s.

No serious consideration was given to extending public ownership beyond steel to other manufacturing industries, and the drive for higher productivity in the private sector took the form of exhortation and persuasion. The most active propagandist was Stafford Cripps, who served first as President of the Board of Trade and later as Chancellor of the Exchequer. He created a production efficiency service within the Board of Trade, supported the establishment of the British Institute of Management, and with Marshall Plan funds helped to set up the Anglo-American Council on Productivity, which sent teams of managers and workers to the US to study American manufacturing methods. Cripps also established working parties in a number of industries soon after the war, through which employers and unions could identify obstacles to higher productivity and work out plans for removing them. The government intended to convert these bodies into development councils with statutory powers, and legislation for this purpose was passed in 1947. But employers were unenthusiastic, fearing that the councils would cut across the work of existing trade associations. Only a few were were set up, and, apart from the Cotton Board (an existing organisation which was reconstituted as a development council), they were in minor industries.[41]

An important strand in the productivity drive was the promotion of greater co-operation between trade unions and employers. But the government did not contemplate any major change in the institutions of collective bargaining, still less a wholesale reform of the labour relations system. The only initiative which might have altered relationships at the shop floor level was an attempt in 1947 to relaunch the factory-based joint production committees, which had had some success during the war. However, many employers saw the committees as a step towards workers' control, while the unions were anxious to ensure that they did not trespass into the field of wages and conditions, which should be left to the established channels of collective bargaining.[42] Some union leaders were also concerned that joint production committees might be used as a vehicle for Communist shop stewards to increase their influence. Although the TUC and the major unions were fully supportive of the productivity drive, they were wary of any moves which might restrict their bargaining freedom. The employers, for their part, were determined to maintain their managerial prerogatives and to resist any encroachment either from the state or from the unions.[43] For the government to have banged heads together, or to have imposed labour relations reform by legislation, was politically out of the question. Ministers needed the co-operation of the trade unions in holding wages down (and in preventing strikes), and that of the employers in increasing production and exports. Thus the status quo was preserved.

An alternative approach for promoting industrial efficiency would have been to inject more competition into the economy, by taking action against price-fixing agreements and by opening up the home market to imports. But the Labour Party's attitude to competition was ambivalent. Many of its members were suspicious of the profit motive and preferred public ownership or public regulation to unfettered competition. Others argued that in industries where nationalisation was not feasible, private enterprise should be forced to become more enterprising, and this called for a vigorous competition policy. The 1945 manifesto contained a promise that 'anti-social' restrictive practices in industry would be prohibited. But it was not until 1948 that a Monopolies and Restrictive Practices Commission was set up, with limited powers. There was no automatic assumption that cartels were against the public interest; each case had to be looked at on its merits. By 1951 the Commission had published only two reports, and its impact on the behaviour of companies was negligible. Cartelisation was probably even more pervasive in the early 1950s than it had been in the 1930s.[44]

As for competition from imports, the weakness of the balance of payments ruled out any immediate removal of the tariff and quota restrictions which had been in force since 1932. The government was also determined to retain imperial preference, despite strong criticism from the US. Friction with the Americans over trade policy increased after the announcement of the Marshall Plan. The US government was pressing for Britain to take the lead in European economic integration, but Ernest Bevin, the Foreign Secretary, insisted that Britain was 'not just another European country'.[45] As leader of the Commonwealth and America's most important ally, Britain wanted to co-operate with the US in managing a one-world system which would include the Continental countries, but not as a separate trading bloc. In 1950, in a decision which had profound implications for future relations with Continental Europe, the Attlee government decided against membership of the European Coal and Steel Community.[46] Britain was not prepared to cede sovereignty over two of its most important industries to a supranational authority. The Labour Party was also hostile to the idea of Britain throwing in its lot with countries which did not share its commitment to full employment and a planned economy. Many people in the Party deplored the electoral swing to the right in France and Germany. Aneurin Bevan saw the defeat of the German Social Democrats in 1949 as 'one of the blackest days in the history of post-war Europe',[47] and there was a widespread feeling that economic liberalism as practised on the Continent was a prescription for social injustice.[48]

Some economists in the Board of Trade favoured membership of the Coal and Steel Community on the grounds that the steel industry would benefit from being exposed to European competition, but this was a minority view. The negative reaction to the Schuman Plan was indicative not only of the government's lack of enthusiasm for competition, but also of the low priority which it attached to trade with Europe. In the immediate aftermath of the war Germany's absence from world markets created an opportunity for British manufacturers to increase their exports, and some of the restrictions imposed on Germany – for example, the ban on aircraft production – were designed to help British industry. But the idea of Britain replacing Germany as the main supplier of manufactured goods to European markets was not seriously entertained, even less so after the US change of policy in 1947. The general assumption was that in due course Germany would resume its pre-war trade position in Europe, and that British industry would have little to gain from entering into head-on competition with German manufacturers in their natural market. As an internal government memorandum put it as early as 1946, 'where German essential goods compete with the United Kingdom, it will be better for Germany to supply Europe and ourselves to concentrate on non-European markets'.[49]

In relation to Europe, as in most other areas of domestic and foreign policy, the Conservative government which took office in 1951 continued along broadly the same lines as its predecessor. In 1952 another opportunity to join the European Coal and Steel Community was rejected, and the British government played no part in the negotiations which led to the creation of the Common Market. Its position was that since the bulk of the country's trade was outside Europe, it would gain nothing from membership of a narrow European trade bloc which might discriminate against the rest of the world. The movement towards European integration seemed 'at best irrelevant to Britain's economic self-interest and at worst a political nuisance which had to be tolerated, if only in public, because of the Americans'.[50]

In contrast to France and Germany, the challenge which Britain faced in the first decade after the war did not call for a radical break with pre-war institutions and policies. The biggest change was the enlargement of the government's role in managing the economy and the focus on full employment as the prime economic objective. This was the consensus which emerged from the war, and Labour was remarkably successful in fulfilling the goals laid down in the 1944 White Paper. Keith Middlemas has suggested that the Attlee government may have been almost too successful in setting the pattern of post-war Britain. 'It may, in the long run, have been unfortunate that so much was achieved in an extraordinarily fluid period at the war's end which then set quickly in a particular mould before the 1950s began. Subsequently, the system could not easily be altered, even if it appeared no longer suitable to changing circumstances.'[51]

In the first half of the 1950s the system did not appear to need changing. Living standards were rising, unemployment and inflation were kept low, and the mixed economy which had been forged during and after the war seemed capable of meeting the aspirations of the people. In the second half of the decade this comfortable state of affairs came under threat on two fronts. First, the British economy was clearly under-performing in comparison with West Germany and other Continental countries. Second, social consensus was breaking down. With full employment taken for granted, self-restraint on the part of trade unions and their members in pressing for higher wages was fading fast. In the 1960s the search began, first under the Conservatives and then under Harold Wilson's Labour government from 1964 to 1970, for ways of remedying the flaws in the post-war settlement.

Continuity and Change

The policy choices made in Germany, France and Britain in the 1940s and early 1950s flowed from the lessons which each country drew from its experience before and during the war. The shock to the political and economic system was far greater in France and Germany than in Britain, and the break with the past more complete. There was a strong desire in both countries to correct the errors which were responsible for earlier disasters. In France this meant state-sponsored industrial modernisation; in Germany, the decentralisation of economic power, with strict rules for the conduct of fiscal and monetary policy and a strong emphasis on competition. In both countries, too, European political and economic integration was given a high priority, as a means of preventing further wars and as a competitive stimulus for industry.

There were many differences between the two countries. France nationalised the leading banks and financial institutions, Germany did not. France adopted a system of indicative planning, Germany did not. Germany reformed its labour relations system, France did not. While Germany was cutting its tariffs unilaterally, France remained one of the most highly protected countries in Europe until the formation of the Common Market. The fact that both countries grew very fast despite these differences cautions against putting too much weight on particular reforms as a source of economic success. But the continuity with pre-war institutions and policies was greater in Britain than in either France or Germany, and this had an important impact on industrial performance, as the next ten chapters will show.

PART II

Industries and Firms

—•○•—

FOUR

Textiles: Misdirected Modernisation

As the first factory-based industry and one of the principal drivers of the industrial revolution, the textile industry has a special place in British economic history. The extraordinary growth of the cotton textile sector, in particular, was a triumph for the mill owners and merchants of Lancashire. In the 1880s more than 80 per cent of world cotton-cloth exports came from Britain. The subsequent decline of this part of the industry, beginning in the inter-war period and accelerating after 1945, was to a large extent the inevitable result of the spread of industrialisation. The production of cotton textiles, with its relatively simple technology, low capital requirements and easily transportable raw material, was a natural starting-point for developing countries as they began to build up their industries. Many of them moved on from cotton to make a wider range of textiles and clothing, and their low labour costs gave them a competitive advantage in overseas markets. From the 1950s onwards, despite the protective barriers which were raised against them, manufacturers in the developing countries steadily increased their share of world textile production and exports, and the shift is continuing.

Low-cost imports posed particular problems for the British textile industry, especially the cotton textile sector, because of its exceptional size at the start of the post-war period. The response was to restructure the industry through mergers and take-overs. This turned out to be a mistake. Many of the mergers which took place in the 1960s were unwound in the 1980s and 1990s. By contrast, the two most successful European textile industries, those of Italy and Germany, relied mainly on small and medium-sized firms, targeting sectors of the market which were less vulnerable to competition from imports. They also benefited to a far greater extent than the British industry from the expansion of intra-European trade in the 1950s and 1960s. This is a case where the long-standing British bias towards non-European export markets proved to be a serious disadvantage.

1750–1914: Lancashire's Triumph

Before the industrial revolution the production of wool textiles was Britain's largest manufacturing industry, and cotton was an expensive luxury. But cotton was a more versatile material – washable, easily dyed and printed, comfortable to wear in hot weather – and a huge market was waiting to be tapped if the price could be brought within reach of the mass of the population. This became possible in the second half of the eighteenth century when hand spinning and later weaving were replaced by machines. The invention of the spinning mule and the powerloom led to a shift of production from the home to the factory, and a sharp fall in manufacturing costs.[1] As prices came down, domestic demand expanded rapidly, but from the early decades of the nineteenth century the main impetus to the growth of the industry came from exports. In 1850 more than 80 per cent of Britain's cotton textile production was shipped overseas, representing nearly half the country's total exports. Wool textile manufacturers also adopted the factory system during this period, but their growth was less spectacular, mainly because export opportunities, largely confined to countries with a warm climate, were more limited.

Two distinctive features of the cotton textile industry were its geographical concentration and its fragmented structure. Lancashire had been an important centre of linen production since the seventeenth century, and the pre-industrial putting-out system, whereby spinning and weaving were carried out in the worker's home, had created a pool of skill and experience on which factory owners could draw. There was also an array of middlemen who bought the raw materials, co-ordinated the various stages of the production process and handled the marketing of the finished cloth.[2] Lancashire had other advantages – a damp climate, easy access through the port of Liverpool to supplies of raw cotton (mainly from the US), and nearby reserves of cheap coal. Once the momentum of growth had been established, new entrants gravitated to the area where suppliers and sub-contractors were already in place. For example, Hibbert & Platt, which as Platt Brothers was to become the world's largest textile machinery manufacturer, was founded in Oldham in 1822, and its presence helped to make that town a leading cotton spinning centre.[3]

Establishing a spinning mill or a weaving shed needed only a modest amount of capital, and from the start the industry was made up of small enterprises. Although combined spinning and weaving firms were not uncommon in the early years, the trend as the industry grew in size was towards specialisation by function, and each firm, whether engaged in spinning, weaving or finishing, generally concentrated on a narrow range of products. Administrative costs were kept low by delegating to middlemen much of the responsibility for buying and selling. A central role was that of the merchant-converter, who, having secured an order, bought grey cloth from the weaving mill and arranged for it to be bleached, printed or dyed. Foreign trade was in the hands of export merchants, many of whom – like Nathan Mayer Rothschild, who moved from Frankfurt to Manchester in 1799 – came from overseas. Manufacturers rarely had direct contact with the final customer for their products. This dense network of inter-connected businesses generated what economists have called external economies of scale. Firms did not need to 'internalise' functions which could be handled more efficiently by other members of the network.

The management of production within the mill depended on a compromise, sometimes an uneasy one, between employers and their most experienced workers. Before the advent of the factory the spinner or weaver, working from home, was given a contract for a piece of work, and he was expected to hire other workers, usually including members of his family, to get the job done. The factory owners adopted a modified version of this arrangement – internal contracting – whereby the senior spinner or weaver hired and supervised other workers in return for a fixed payment based on output.[4] These senior workers organised themselves into trade unions, seeking to negotiate a fair price for each piece to be produced, and to prevent employers from cutting wages when trade was depressed. Despite initial resistance, employers gradually came to terms with trade unions, and by the end of the nineteenth century the cotton industry unions were among the strongest in the country.[5]

Thanks to its early technical lead and efficient organisation, the Lancashire industry established a competitive advantage which was not seriously challenged before the First World War. Germany was the second largest exporter of cotton textiles, but in 1913 its share of world exports, measured by value, was only 10 per cent, compared with Britain's 55 per cent.[6] The US was not a significant exporter, even though its industry was in some respects more technically advanced than its British counterpart. The scarcity of skilled labour in the US encouraged entrepreneurs to develop new machines – the ring spindle and the automatic loom – which could be operated by inexperienced workers. There were also differences in the structure of the industry. To produce long runs of standard cloth, which was what the US market wanted, the automatic loom had to be fed with yarn of consistent quality, and spinning and weaving operations had to be closely linked. Large, integrated mills were built to accommodate spinning and weaving under the same roof. American employers also dispensed with the system of internal contracting, so that the organisation of work was in the hands of managers rather than workers; trade unions were never as strong in the US cotton textile industry as in Lancashire.

The markets which Lancashire served were too varied to permit high-volume, standardised production on the US model, and, since skilled workers were in ample supply, only a few firms installed ring spindles and automatic looms. There were some large textile amalgamations in Britain around the turn of the century, principally in the finishing trades and in fine spinning; among the largest companies formed at that time were Calico Printers Association, Bleachers Association and Fine Spinners and Doublers Association. But these were horizontal mergers of competing firms, and they were designed more to reduce price competition than to achieve economies of scale. The same was true of English Sewing Cotton, a group of Lancashire sewing-thread manufacturers who came together in 1897 to counter the aggressive tactics of the dominant Scottish thread producer, J and P Coats. The bulk of the industry consisted of small, specialised firms.

If Lancashire was no longer at the forefront in technology at the end of the century, the old machinery still had plenty of life left in it, and there is no sign that entrepreneurial dynamism was fading. The mule and the Lancashire loom, in the hands of experienced workers, provided the flexibility which was needed to supply the world market with a vast range of yarns and fabrics. Although the growth of exports slowed down after 1870, this was mainly due to the build-up of textile production behind tariff walls in countries which had previously imported from Britain. Continental Europe and the US had been major customers for British cloth in the early part of the century, and, as these countries became more self-sufficient, the direction of British exports shifted to less developed countries. The two biggest markets just before the First World War were China and India, with India alone taking 45 per cent of Britain's cloth exports.

With hindsight, the industry can be criticised for allowing itself to become too dependent on India, especially as Indian entrepreneurs were beginning to develop a factory-based industry of their own. But it was not unrealistic to suppose that if the Indian market declined, others would be found to take its place.[7] In the decade leading up to the war the cotton textile industry was successful and expanding. With 620,000 employees, it was Britain's largest manufacturing industry, and, despite the growth of newer industries, it still accounted for a quarter of the country's exports. But Lancashire's prosperity, like that of the British economy as a whole, depended on a set of conditions which came to an end after the First World War.

The Inter-war Years: Lancashire in Crisis

The cotton industry came through the war in good condition, despite some reduction in output as a result of restricted imports of raw cotton. The expectation that profits would continue at a high level prompted a wave of financial speculation in the industry. Some mills took on large bank over-drafts, while others were bought by financial syndicates in the belief that they could be refloated on the stock exchange at a higher price. Hence the industry was poorly prepared for the downturn in trade which began in 1920. Purchasing power in the primary producing countries that absorbed the bulk of the industry's exports was affected by the low level of commodity prices, and there was a continuing trend towards import substitution. In India, for example, indigenous production had increased during the war, and Indian mill owners were clamouring for more protection. The 11 per cent tariff imposed in 1921, up from 3.5 per cent before the war, was nominally a revenue-raising measure, but it was greatly resented in Lancashire, and the Manchester Chamber of Commerce lobbied hard to get it reduced.[8] But there was another, more ominous development which affected Lancashire's share of Asian markets in the inter-war years – competition from Japan.

Japanese entrepreneurs had bought their first spinning machines from Platt Brothers in the 1860s, and the cotton textile industry played a similar role in Japan's industrial development as it had in Britain a hundred years earlier. Exports, principally to China and other neighbouring countries, rose strongly after the turn of the century. As production increased, the larger firms installed ring spindles and automatic looms, some of which were designed and built in Japan. The industry was less fragmented than in Lancashire, and there was a greater degree of co-operation across its various sectors. Overseas marketing was handled not by a proliferation of export merchants as in Britain, but by a handful of powerful trading companies.[9] By the mid-1930s Japan had overtaken Britain as the leading exporter of cotton textiles.

The response in Lancashire to falling demand and increasing competition had two main strands. One was to reduce capacity through rationalisation. The biggest merger of the inter-war years was the formation of Lancashire Cotton Corporation in 1929; it absorbed 96 firms and 109 mills, accounting for about a fifth of the industry's spinning capacity. The Bank of England took the initiative in getting this venture off the ground. The Governor, Montagu Norman, was concerned about the stability of the banks which had lent heavily to the Lancashire mills in the early post-war years.[10] The new company had a shaky start, but when Frank Platt, an exceptionally able manager, was installed as managing director in 1932, rationalisation proceeded more swiftly, and about half the spindles which had been brought under its control were scrapped.[11] Platt was an enthusiastic proponent of reorganisation, and he helped to promote the Cotton Spinning Industry Act of 1936, which gave statutory backing to an industry-wide scrapping scheme, financed by a levy on the manufacturers.

The other strand was to seek government help in preserving the industry's export markets. Lancashire's attachment to free trade was discarded with remarkable speed in the inter-war years.[12] The cotton industry welcomed the imposition of the tariff in 1932, not only because it protected the home market, but also because it provided a bargaining weapon in negotiations with overseas governments. Japan was the principal target, and the Manchester Chamber of Commerce used its influence in Whitehall to limit Japanese exports. Because of the industry's importance as employer and exporter – and the presence of sixty Lancashire MPs in the House of Commons – 'King Cotton' carried considerable political weight, and the government agreed in 1934 to impose quotas on Japanese exports to the colonies.[13]

These were defensive reactions to the crisis. Were there other steps which Lancashire could have taken to improve its competitive position? Some historians believe that modernisation was held back by the inability of employers and trade unions to break away from a labour-intensive production system which had become entrenched in the years of prosperity.[14] What was needed, according to this view, was a shift to high-throughput technologies, based on ring spindles and automatic looms. This would have required changes in the structure of the industry – a move from small, specialised firms to large, vertically integrated companies – and changes in the way labour was managed. Instead, employers adopted the simpler strategy of lowering the costs of operating their existing machines, by using inferior grades of cotton and by intensifying the pace of work. There were several serious strikes in Lancashire between 1929 and 1932 over these issues.

Whether the industry would have done better in the inter-war years if it had reorganised itself on American lines is far from clear.[15] There was a great deal of debate inside and outside Lancashire at the time about what structural changes were needed to meet Japanese competition. A report published in 1934 by Political and Economic Planning (PEP), an independent research organisation, called for greater co-operation between the different sections of the industry and for the creation of new industry-wide associations to co-ordinate the activities of member firms.[16] The separation of manufacturing from marketing was regarded as particularly harmful; the interests of the manufacturer, according to the PEP report, had too often been sacrificed to those of the merchant. The authors argued that more horizontal amalgamations were desirable in order to reduce destructive price competition, but they rejected US-style vertical integration, on the grounds that such a structure would limit the industry's ability to produce the variety of yarns and fabrics which its customers needed. The way forward, they suggested, was a greater emphasis on high-quality products which would be less vulnerable to Japanese competition.

The industry's reaction to the PEP report, and to prescriptions offered by other bodies, was lukewarm. Most firms preferred to muddle their way through the crisis in the hope of better times. There was, indeed, no easy solution to Lancashire's problems. The industry's extreme dependence on exports made it exceptionally vulnerable to the collapse of world trade and to the rise of new competitors. The two other principal sectors of the British textile industry – wool textiles, based in Yorkshire, and hosiery and knitwear, based mainly in the East Midlands and Scotland – were in a more favourable situation. The wool textile manufacturers had never expanded to the same extent as the cotton mills, and although they were badly affected by the depression in world trade, employment fell by only 11 per cent between 1912 and 1937, compared to 42 per cent in cotton. The growth of hosiery and knitwear in the inter-war years was mainly geared to the home market. A useful boost to trade came from the wider use of rayon in women's stockings, and some manufacturers began to develop their own brands. Another development which was to have important consequences for the textile industry as a whole was the emergence of multiple retailers, led by Marks & Spencer, as major customers for the hosiery and knitwear firms.

Lancashire cotton was the unsolved problem, and it was one which, because of the industry's size and economic importance, governments could not ignore. The first step towards intervention was the Cotton Spinning Industry Act of 1936, followed by the Cotton Industry (Reorganisation) Act of 1939, which provided for a statutory Cotton Board to fix minimum prices and to set production quotas for individual firms. Although this second Act was suspended after the outbreak of war, a Cotton Board made up of employer and employee representatives was established in 1940 to act as a co-ordinating body on export policy and other matters, and to assist the government in dealing with wartime emergency measures.[17] As a result of the transfer of labour to the armed forces, some 40 per cent of the industry's capacity was temporarily closed, and the mills which remained in operation concentrated on military contracts and the production of yarns and fabrics under the 'utility clothing' scheme.

The Cotton Board was also involved in planning for post-war reconstruction. In 1943 it produced a report for the Board of Trade which suggested, among other things, that the necessary re-equipment of the industry would depend on stable prices, and this would require a price maintenance scheme of the sort envisaged in the 1939 Act. Another view, pressed by Frank Platt following a mission which he led to the US in 1944, was that the industry should be reorganised along American lines, with more standardisation, more vertical integration and more investment in new equipment.[18] No consensus on these issues had been reached by the end of the war.

1945–1960: A Short-Lived Boom

As the country's largest exporter, the cotton textile industry had a central role to play in the post-war export drive. 'Britain's bread', as the slogan put it, 'hangs by Lancashire's thread.' With Japanese and German textile manufacturers temporarily out of action, there was no problem in finding customers. The constraint was the shortage of labour, and, although production increased strongly in the first five years after the war, exports in 1950 were only half the 1937 level (TABLE 4.1). These were years of full order books and high profits, a welcome relief from the inter-war depression. But the industry was well aware that it had to prepare for the return of its pre-war competitors to the world market. In September 1945, Stafford Cripps, President of the Board of Trade in the new Labour government, set up a working party, consisting of employers, trade union representatives and outside experts, to examine the industry's future.

All the members of the working party agreed that 'the one thing that must be avoided is the enjoyment of this period as a fool's paradise of easy profits at the end of which the industry, and all those who rely on it for

TABLE 4.1 *Output and exports of cotton and allied textiles 1937–65*

(in million square yards)

	Output	Exports
1937	4,532	2,002
1945	1,928	531
1950	2,937	1,017
1955	2,568	689
1965	1,900	300

Source: Marguerite Dupree, 'Struggling with Destiny: The Cotton
Industry, Overseas Trade Policy and the Cotton Board, 1940–1959'.
Reprinted by permission from *Business History*, vol. 32, no. 4, published
by Frank Cass & Company, 900 Eastern Avenue, Ilford, Essex, England.
Copyright Frank Cass & Co Ltd.

employment, may find themselves in worse difficulties even than those of
the inter-war years'.[19] But when it came to proposals for action, opinions
were divided. Some favoured a drastic programme of rationalisation. Others
argued against larger groupings on the grounds that, unlike their American
counterparts, British mills needed the flexibility to meet the needs of widely
varying markets. 'To compare the American industry, with its vast and highly
protected home market and its minor interest in exports, with the British
industry, which exports half its products to markets all over the world, is to
compare organisations which are geared up for entirely different functions.'[20]

The lack of unanimity disappointed Cripps, but he had no blueprint of
his own to offer. Although nationalisation was favoured by the trade unions,
it would have been a disruptive and controversial measure at a time when
the urgent priority was to maximise production for export, and it was not
seriously considered by the government. One of the few concrete results from
the working party's deliberations was the Cotton Industry (Re-equipment
Subsidy) Act of 1948, which made funds available for re-equipment to firms
which agreed to form larger groups. But the take-up was small. Most manufacturers, scarred by their pre-war experience, took a cautious view of the
industry's prospects, and were content to run their existing equipment with
as much labour as they could obtain, without much investment in new
machinery.[21] Their biggest fear was that when the post-war boom came to

an end, the industry would be plunged into another crisis of over-capacity, as had happened in the 1920s.

The boom did indeed come to an end in 1952, partly because of a shift of consumer spending away from clothing towards domestic appliances, partly because of increasing competition in export markets. The stabilisation of Lancashire's export trade in the 1930s had depended on imperial preference and on discrimination against Japanese exports to the colonies. Both these props were weakened after the war by the US-led drive for freer trade, starting with the signature of the General Agreement on Tariffs and Trade (GATT) in 1947. Quotas on Japanese exports to the colonies were removed, and it was no longer possible to manipulate tariffs in Lancashire's favour. By the mid-1950s Japanese textile manufacturers had returned to the world market in full force.

At the same time an unexpected threat materialised in the domestic market. Under the agreement reached between Britain and the Commonwealth countries at the Ottawa conference in 1932, most imports from the Commonwealth were allowed to enter Britain free of duty. This gave an opportunity for the textile industries of India, Pakistan and Hong Kong to build up their sales in Britain. Imports from these three countries increased rapidly during the 1950s, and by the end of the decade Britain had become a net importer of cotton cloth for the first time since before the industrial revolution.[22] Another factor working to Lancashire's disadvantage was the growing popularity of knitted fabrics in applications previously served by cotton cloth. Two of the biggest growth areas were warp knitted fabric for shirts and sheets, and double jersey knitting for dresses and suits. The expansion of the knitting industry during the 1950s was linked to the wider use of the new synthetic fibres, principally nylon and polyester.

The reaction to these events, once again, was defensive: an attempt to keep prices up through a price-fixing agreement, and an appeal to the government for help on imports. After 1951 the industry was dealing with a Conservative government which was inclined to leave Lancashire to its fate. Peter Thorneycroft, President of the Board of Trade in the 1951–5 Churchill government, insisted that the industry's future lay in its own hands. 'The government', he told the Cotton Board in 1952, 'has no featherbed to offer you and very little shelter in the harsh winds of competition which are blowing through the world today.'[23] In the second half of the decade, however, the political tide began to turn in Lancashire's favour. With a general election in prospect, the Prime Minister, Harold Macmillan, was fearful of loss of support in an area which supplied a large number of Conservative

MPs, and he agreed to support the industry's efforts to secure a voluntary restriction on imports from the three main Commonwealth suppliers. The ceilings negotiated in 1958 were higher than Lancashire had hoped for, but ministers were at least taking an interest in the industry's problems.

In the following year the government went further, acceding to the industry's request for a state-supported scrapping scheme. The Cotton Industry Act of 1959 was designed to eliminate 50 per cent of the industry's spinning capacity and 40 per cent of its weaving capacity. Two-thirds of the costs of scrapping surplus machinery were funded by the government, with a levy on the industry providing the rest. In addition, a re-equipment subsidy was made available to firms which installed new machinery. This was a new departure in government–industry relations, a foretaste of the interventionism which was to characterise British industrial policy in the 1960s and 1970s, but it did little to improve the industry's competitiveness. The Act accelerated the rate of scrapping of surplus equipment, but expenditure on modernisation was much lower than the government had anticipated.[24] The main reason for the disappointing response was the continuing uncertainty over imports.

This was a uniquely British problem, arising from Britain's obligations to the Commonwealth. Although the increase in textile exports from Japan and other low-cost producers was causing concern among other industrial countries, they were more highly protected than Britain. In 1960 cotton textile imports accounted for 35 per cent of domestic consumption in Britain, compared with 5 per cent in the six Common Market countries and only 1 per cent in the US.[25] The Lancashire mill owners have been criticised for failing to modernise in the first decade after the Second World War, but it is far from certain that large-scale investment in ring spindles and automatic looms would have put them in a better position to resist the import invasion.[26] Such investment would only have made sense if they had been able to use the new equipment intensively, and that would have required an expanding demand for long runs of standard fabrics, which did not exist.

These issues were anxiously debated as the flow of cheap imports increased, and the 1959 Act did nothing to resolve them.[27] It was clear that new initiatives were needed, from the industry or the government or both, to save the industry from continuing decline.

The 1960s: Merger Mania

By the early 1960s advocates of rationalisation on the US model were gaining ground. They argued that the industry's weakness stemmed in large part from the lack of co-ordination between its different sections, and that this could only be remedied by consolidation into larger groups. Control over all phases of the production chain, from spinning and weaving through to finishing and distribution, would also make the manufacturers less vulnerable to the stock fluctuations which were a notorious feature of the textile business. Another argument was that the growing use of synthetic fibres was eroding the traditional boundaries between processes.[28] The successful textile company would need to be a multi-fibre, multi-process operation, enjoying economies of scale in production and carrying sufficient weight in the market to bargain effectively with customers. This last point was particularly important because of the increasing dominance of the multiple retailers, especially Marks & Spencer, in the clothing trade.

An articulate exponent of this view was Cyril Harrison, chairman of English Sewing Cotton. This company, originally a sewing-thread producer, had diversified into spinning and weaving. Harrison made several further acquisitions in the 1950s and early 1960s, but his resources were limited, and if the industry was to be restructured in a substantial way an outside catalyst was needed. That catalyst then appeared in the form of Courtaulds, a larger and wealthier company than English Sewing Cotton, and one which had particular reasons for intervening in Lancashire's affairs.

Courtaulds had built its reputation in the nineteenth century as a weaver of silk mourning crêpe; the original family company, Samuel Courtauld, was founded in 1849. In 1904, in a classic entrepreneurial coup, it secured the rights to the manufacturing process for viscose rayon. Once the process had been fully commercialised, rayon proved to be a huge money-spinner. Courtaulds was one of Britain's most profitable manufacturing companies between the wars. But it failed to capitalise on its success. Regarding itself as a textile rather than a chemical company, it did not invest in research and missed out on the development of synthetic fibres, the first of which was Du Pont's nylon.[29] Courtaulds' involvement in nylon came about through a partnership with Imperial Chemical Industries (ICI), which under the terms of its technical agreement with Du Pont was licensed to manufacture nylon in Britain. The two British companies formed a joint venture, British Nylon

Spinners, which began producing nylon commercially in 1949.[30] The next breakthrough in synthetic fibres was polyester, invented by scientists at Calico Printers Association (CPA) in 1942. The rights to this process were secured by ICI and, much to the irritation of Courtaulds, it chose to exploit the new fibre independently, under the brand name Terylene, rather than through British Nylon Spinners. The first Terylene plant came on stream in 1954.

Courtaulds was in a difficult position. Its largest business was rayon, but this was the oldest and slowest-growing of the man-made fibres. It was shut out of polyester by the CPA patents, and had only a half share in British Nylon Spinners. One way forward was to step up its own research. Work began in the early 1950s on an acrylic fibre, launched in 1957 as Courtelle, but by that time a rival product from Du Pont, Orlon, was already well established in the market. Another was to expand in textiles. Courtaulds had retained an interest in weaving through Samuel Courtauld, and this side of the business was enlarged in 1957 by the purchase of British Celanese, a company which had extensive textile and garment-making operations as well as being Courtaulds' last remaining competitor in rayon; it also had a pilot plant for the production of nylon, using a different process from that used in British Nylon Spinners. A third strand in Courtaulds' strategy was to diversify outside fibres and textiles, principally in paints and packaging. The architect of the diversification programme was Frank Kearton, a scientist who had joined Courtaulds in 1946 as head of the chemical engineering department; he had previously worked for ICI, and had been involved in the atomic weapons project during the war. Kearton quickly established a reputation within the company as a forceful and determined manager, and was appointed to the board in 1952.

The partnership with ICI in British Nylon Spinners did not go smoothly. There were arguments over the prices which ICI charged for intermediate chemicals, and as both companies built up their separate fibres activities there was increasing scope for conflicts of interest. In the summer of 1960 Paul Chambers, newly appointed chairman of ICI, suggested to his opposite number at Courtaulds, John Hanbury-Williams, that the two companies should merge. Although Hanbury-Williams favoured this idea, his colleagues did not, and the matter was dropped. A year later Chambers revived the proposal, arguing that a merger would not only tidy up the situation in British Nylon Spinners, but would also create a powerful British fibre group which would compete more effectively against Du Pont and the other world leaders. Chambers pointed out that, whereas in Britain British Nylon Spinners made nylon, Courtaulds made acrylic fibre and ICI made polyester, Du Pont had all three fibres under its own control.

After several months of inconclusive talks, Chambers decided in December 1961 that the only way of breaking the log-jam was to appeal directly to the shareholders of Courtaulds, offering to buy their shares in exchange for shares in ICI. This would have been the biggest merger in British corporate history, and in resorting to a hostile take-over Chambers was using a technique which was still highly controversial. Some of the Courtaulds directors, including Kearton, accepted the logic of ICI's arguments, but objected to the terms being offered. Others, especially the two members of the Courtauld family who sat on the Board, were determined to keep the company independent.

If there was a possibility of a compromise, it was removed by clumsy tactics on the part of ICI, and an acrimonious battle began. Although Kearton was a relatively junior member of the board, he played a prominent part in the defence campaign. At a memorable press conference in the middle of the contest, he lashed into ICI's record, complaining about the high prices ICI charged for its chemicals, contrasting the slow development of Terylene with the success of Courtelle, and predicting a sharp fall in ICI's profits. As the company's historian records, Kearton 'threw figures about with cheerful abandon and some inaccuracy . . . raised laughs, bubbled with ideas and was the total antithesis of the old, stuffy Courtaulds'.[31] By conveying the impression that Courtaulds was about to enter a new era of profitable growth, Kearton helped to shift opinion in the City of London away from ICI. The outcome was an embarrassing defeat for Paul Chambers, leaving ICI with an unwanted 38 per cent shareholding in Courtaulds.

The effect of the bid on Courtaulds was to sharpen the need for a clear strategic direction, and to enhance the reputation of Frank Kearton, inside and outside the company. Although some of his colleagues were uncomfortable with his egocentric personality and erratic temper, Kearton brought a new dynamism to a company which had become a rather sleepy member of the British establishment. He was appointed deputy chairman in 1961 and chairman three years later.

Kearton had reached the conclusion before the ICI bid that diversification did not provide a long-term future for Courtaulds and that there were limits, because of competition from ICI, Du Pont and others, to what the company could do as a fibre producer. The alternative was to move further into textiles, both as a captive outlet for fibres and as a growth business in its own right.[32] Kearton and his colleagues convinced themselves that the decline of the Lancashire cotton industry could be halted by an injection of capital, technology and modern management, and that, once modernisation was complete, it would be able to compete with low-cost imports from developing countries.[33] Both Kearton and his finance director, Arthur Knight, were influenced by the example of the integrated textile companies in the US, which, despite high wages, produced fabrics as cheap as or cheaper than European mills. The key to their success lay in scale and standardisation, producing long runs of standard fabrics in large, well-equipped factories, and this was the model which Courtaulds planned to replicate in Britain. As one of Kearton's fellow directors put it, 'it is a concept of genius, worthy of England's best days, that the brains of the new fibres should assume the responsibility of putting fresh life into the traditional textiles'.[34]

The initial plan, formulated in 1962, was the 'Northern project', whereby Courtaulds would take over five of the largest spinning companies in Lancashire – Lancashire Cotton, English Sewing Cotton, Tootal, Combined English Mills, and Fine Spinners and Doublers. ICI, as a major shareholder in Courtaulds, was consulted about the proposal and agreed to participate; Courtaulds was to take a 55 per cent stake in the new group, ICI the remaining 45 per cent. Negotiations on this five-way deal broke down because one of the companies thought that its shares were undervalued, but the appetite for mergers had been whetted. In 1963 two of the five, English Sewing Cotton and Tootal, got together, with ICI and Courtaulds each taking a minority stake, and in the following year Courtaulds bought Lancashire Cotton and Fine Spinners and Doublers. This was the start of an extraordinary wave of take-over activity which transformed the structure of the textile industry over the subsequent decade.

Unlike the 1959 Act, this was a private-sector solution to Lancashire's problems, but Kearton looked to the government for support on the issue of imports. He argued that temporary protection was justified while the industry was being reorganised. The Conservatives were still in office, and they were anxious not to offend the Commonwealth. However, ministers applauded what Courtaulds was doing in Lancashire and were willing to consider granting some relief, perhaps replacing the voluntary quotas on Commonwealth imports with tariffs. By this time the first steps had been taken on an international level to regulate the flow of textile imports from developing countries. In 1961 the US government took the lead in promoting an agreement between the principal exporting and importing countries which limited the growth of imports from developing countries to 5 per cent a year; the importing countries were also allowed to take restraining measures if imports threatened to disrupt their domestic market. This agreement was initially limited to cotton textiles and clothing, but was converted in 1973 into the Multi Fibre Arrangement (MFA), covering all fibres.[35]

Courtaulds welcomed these moves, but they did not directly affect Britain's duty-free imports from the Commonwealth, which remained the industry's greatest anxiety. In October 1964, thirteen years of Conservative rule came to an end with the election of a Labour government under Harold Wilson, and the change seemed likely to be helpful for Courtaulds. Wilson had made industrial modernisation a central plank of his election campaign. He believed that many British firms were too small to compete effectively against larger international competitors, and that a major programme of rationalisation was needed. What Courtaulds had started to do in textiles was in line with this philosophy, and Kearton was much admired by Labour ministers. In 1966 the government set up a new agency, the Industrial Reorganisation Corporation (IRC), to promote mergers, and Kearton was appointed chairman. In this role he had a hand in some of the biggest mergers of the 1960s, including the creation of British Leyland Motor Corporation and the amalgamation of the three big electrical companies, GEC, AEI and English Electric. The IRC did not involve itself in the restructuring of the textile industry, not because Kearton was chairman, but because the merger movement was rolling along at a spanking pace and needed no prodding from Whitehall.

The awkward matter of ICI's shareholding in Courtaulds was resolved in 1964 with an agreement which swapped these shares for Courtaulds' stake in British Nylon Spinners. Courtaulds was now free to go ahead with an independent nylon venture and to compete against ICI in polyester. But it was a late-comer in both markets, and this reinforced the case for acquiring textile and garment companies which would provide guaranteed outlets for the company's fibres. Kearton's aim was to secure a share of about 30 per cent in the various markets in which its fibres were sold. In cotton spinning this was to be achieved through acquisitions. In weaving, since most of the existing mills were regarded as too small, the company built new factories on greenfield sites, making full use of the government grants which were available in areas of high unemployment.[36] Outside Lancashire, Kearton bought hosiery and knitwear companies in the East Midlands; they were important customers for Courtelle and nylon. He also acquired wholesalers, some with well-known brand names, in the hope of establishing a counterweight to the multiple retailers. Kearton resented the power which Marks & Spencer exerted over the garment and textile trade.

As a large manufacturer of synthetic fibres, ICI had as much interest as Courtaulds in an efficient textile industry, but it had no wish to own textile companies. Its policy was to take minority stakes in selected firms and encourage them to make further acquisitions. Of the six companies supported by ICI during the 1960s, the strongest was Viyella. This was the creation of an ambitious entrepreneur, Joe Hyman, who, unlike Kearton, had spent his entire career in the textile business. He had started as a merchant-converter and his instincts were those of a merchandiser. In 1957 he bought control of a knitwear company, Gainsborough Cornard, which supplied nylon lingerie to Marks & Spencer and other retailers. Four years later he engineered a merger with a larger East Midlands firm, William Hollins, which owned the well-known Viyella brand.[37] The merged group was renamed Viyella International, with Hyman as chief executive. He was determined to push into Lancashire, which he believed would be transformed by polyester/cotton blends, just as nylon had revolutionised the knitting industry.[38]

In 1963 Hyman persuaded ICI to take a minority stake in Viyella as part of a £13m injection of equity and loan capital, and he promptly embarked on a flurry of acquisitions. Like Kearton, Hyman believed in the virtues of size, but his approach was more market-driven than that of Courtaulds; one of his greatest successes was to establish the Dorma brand as the market leader in polyester/cotton sheets.

Although ICI's investments were not directed against Courtaulds, there was an obvious risk of conflict as the two companies pursued their separate strategies. With Courtaulds now moving into nylon and polyester, they were competing for the same customers. Kearton himself appears to have had doubts about the wisdom of a head-on fight. In 1966 he suggested a deal whereby the two companies would merge their fibre interests in a single, jointly owned company, and Courtaulds would combine its textile interests with those of Viyella. But ICI was now making handsome profits from nylon and Terylene, and the idea of an all-British fibres merger was no longer as attractive as it had seemed to Chambers five years before.[39]

The next move came from Hyman, who had become disenchanted with ICI's textile policy. He thought that ICI was 'Balkanising' the industry by taking minority stakes in a number of textile companies and encouraging them to undertake expansion programmes which they were incapable of managing. He pointed to the example of Carrington & Dewhurst, one of ICI's clients, which was building up its knitting and finishing interests in direct competition with Viyella. In 1967 Hyman broke his links with ICI and a few months later launched a take-over bid for English Sewing Cotton, in which both ICI and Courtaulds still held minority interests. English Sewing Cotton rejected Hyman's offer and arranged a friendly merger with Calico Printers Association; the merged company was renamed English Calico.

Up to this point the Labour government, though not directly involved in the restructuring process, had taken a benevolent stance. In 1966 it had responded to the industry's pleas for protection by introducing a system of global quotas on textile imports from developing countries, including the Commonwealth. The manufacturers regarded the quotas as far too high, and continued to press for tighter controls. The government then invited the Textile Council (the old Cotton Board reconstituted to embrace other fibres) to conduct a thorough study of the issue as part of a wide-ranging investigation of the industry's prospects.

In the meantime a small time bomb was ticking away in another part of the Whitehall machine. In 1965 the Board of Trade had asked the Monopolies Commission to examine the rayon market. This was in line with the established policy, dating back to the Monopolies and Restrictive Practices Act of 1948, whereby industries in which a single company accounted for more than half the market could be subjected to review by the Commission. Courtaulds was virtually the sole supplier of rayon, and the Commission had to decide whether its dominance adversely affected the public interest. Kearton and his colleagues were upset that the Board of Trade had referred them to the Commission, pointing out that any monopoly power which Courtaulds might enjoy in rayon was constrained by competition from other fibres. They were even more upset when the Commission found, in its report of 1968, that the company's monopoly in rayon was against the public interest, and recommended that Courtaulds should be barred from making further acquisitions in textiles if such acquisitions gave it more than 25 per cent of the relevant market.[40]

This left the government in a dilemma, committed to two apparently contradictory policies – promoting mergers with one hand, attacking monopoly with the other. While the government delayed its response to the Commission's report, Courtaulds announced, in January 1969, yet another large take-over bid, for English Calico. This was the last straw for the ICI directors. They feared that, if the bid went through, Courtaulds would have such a tight grip on the textile industry that their own fibre business would be at risk. They hatched an alternative scheme whereby English Calico, Carrington & Dewhurst and several other firms would come together in a consortium, with ICI holding a 40 per cent stake. At the same time they pressed the Board of Trade to block the Courtaulds bid. Faced with this 'confrontation between two great powers',[41] the government set up a committee. Edmund Dell, Minister of State at the Board of Trade, conducted an inquiry into the structure of the industry, which concluded by recommending a temporary standstill on mergers among the five major textile groups – Courtaulds, Viyella, Carrington & Dewhurst, English Calico and Coats Patons.[42]

The weakest of these five was Carrington & Dewhurst, which with ICI's money behind it had embarked on a series of ill-judged acquisitions, culminating in a disastrous attempt to establish Crimplene, ICI's brand name for textured polyester filament yarn, in West Germany. As the largest shareholder and a major fibre supplier, ICI could not afford to let the company collapse. The solution was to merge it with Viyella, which, though no longer financially linked to ICI, was an important customer for its fibres. In December 1969, Joe Hyman, who had fallen out with his fellow directors, was dismissed from his post as chairman. ICI promptly announced its intention to bid for Viyella and then to sell it to Carrington & Dewhurst. This would give ICI 64 per cent of the combined company and contravene the government's merger standstill. Another government committee was set up, this time under Harold Lever, the Paymaster General, who recommended that ICI should be allowed to go ahead with the Carrington/Viyella merger, on condition that it reduced its voting power to not more than 35 per cent. The merger provided a short-term solution for Carrington's problems, but had the unfortunate consequence of weakening Viyella, which had been one of the most progressive firms in the industry. Viyella's senior managers opposed the merger, and several of them left shortly after it was completed. The new company, known as Carrington Viyella, never achieved the sense of mission which Hyman had briefly inspired in the 1960s.

The purpose of all this take-over activity, confused though it was by inter-company rivalries, was to strengthen the competitiveness of the industry. How well it had done so was one of the questions addressed in the Textile Council's report, commissioned by the government in 1967 and finally published in March 1969.[43] Not surprisingly, given the role played by Courtaulds in drawing up the report, the Council concluded that the restructuring process had been wholly beneficial. Pointing to the modernisation and re-equipment which was then under way, the report predicted that costs in cotton spinning and weaving would be reduced by 25 per cent and that by the mid-1970s the leading firms would be at least as efficient as their Continental counterparts. The shift towards scale and vertical integration would make possible longer production runs, better quality control and more effective monitoring of stocks at each stage in the production chain. The one proviso was that the government must take a firmer line on imports. The government welcomed the report, agreed with its conclusions, and – in a decision which was seen in the industry as marking a fundamental change of policy – announced that tariffs on Commonwealth imports would be imposed from the start of 1972.[44] Lancashire seemed set for a fresh start.

The 1970s: The Grand Design Unravels

The 1960s were a decade in which managers, politicians and financiers had an exaggerated belief in mergers as a means of improving industrial performance. A few industries benefited from greater concentration, notably the electrical industry which is discussed in Chapter 8, but most of the others did not, the extreme case being the failure of British Leyland Motor Corporation (Chapter 9). Kearton's grand design, applauded by the government and praised by most outside commentators, was flawed in two major respects.

First, it was based on a misreading of the market. The expectation was that a modernised industry, producing long runs of yarns and fabrics, would compete profitably against low-cost imports and become a major exporter to other European countries. But the commodity products which were the main focus of Courtaulds' investment programme continued to be subject to fierce price competition, and the shift to a capital-intensive mode of production could not prevent a further loss of market share to imports from developing countries, even with the higher levels of protection which came into force in 1972. Moreover, the European market was very different from that of the US, being less homogeneous and more geared towards design and quality. Instead of a growing demand for standard, mass-produced fabrics, European consumers wanted more differentiated, more colourful and more stylish fabrics. This called for flexibility on the part of textile manufacturers and quick response to changing fashions. The structure which Kearton had put in place was not well suited for these conditions.

The second mistake was to under-estimate the disadvantages of vertical integration. The use of textile and garment companies as captive outlets for fibres was to tackle the problem from the wrong end: the fibre supplier, not the customer, called the tune. It was a technocratic approach which perhaps suited Kearton's background and experience, but the management skills required for the mass production of fibres were different from those needed in textiles and clothing. The synergies which were supposed to flow from putting the various stages in the production process under single ownership were largely illusory.

The cracks in the grand design first became evident during the recession which followed the first oil shock at the end of 1973. This coincided with Britain's entry into the Common Market, and the home market came under attack from Continental fabric suppliers, which over the preceding decade had pursued a very different strategy from Courtaulds. Instead of scale and standardisation, they had put more emphasis on design and technical innovation. Imports from the Continent rose sharply in the second half of the 1970s, and the British textile industry, having neglected European markets in the 1950s and 1960s, was not well equipped to respond. With some exceptions at the top end of the market, British manufacturers lacked products suitable for European consumers, and had little experience of marketing and distribution on the Continent.

Kearton retired from the chairmanship of Courtaulds in 1975. His successor, Arthur Knight, brought more order into an organisation which had been built up in a highly personal way by his predecessor; a new divisional structure was introduced, with clearer lines of accountability. Knight also began to reverse the policy of vertical integration, giving managers of each business greater freedom to buy or sell in the best market, instead of being tied to in-house suppliers and customers. But the fundamental problem was an excess of spinning and weaving capacity, planned for a market which had not materialised. One of the large new weaving plants, at Skelmersdale, was closed down in 1977, and there were cutbacks in other parts of the business. By the time of Knight's retirement in 1979, the errors made by Kearton had been partially corrected, but profits in the textile business remained poor, and Courtaulds was losing money on its two newest fibres, nylon and polyester. Contrary to the predictions of the 1969 Textile Council report, the creation of large textile groups had not halted Lancashire's decline, nor had mergers brought much benefit to other parts of the industry. Courtaulds and Coats Patons had bought up several of the leading hosiery and knitwear manufacturers in the East Midlands, but the subsequent performance of these firms was worse than that of the ones which stayed independent. The largest and most profitable of the independents was Nottingham Manufacturing, owned and run by the Djanogly brothers, which was a major supplier of knitwear to Marks & Spencer. According to one account, 'Courtaulds and Coats

Patons were large, highly centralised companies with little experience or understanding of the hosiery and knitwear industries, and their problems occupied little time at board meetings.'[45] Here, as in Lancashire, vertical integration had been a mistake.

The 1980s and 1990s: Adjustment to International Competition

The redirection of Courtaulds which had begun under Arthur Knight was taken further by his successor, Christopher Hogg. Appointed chairman in 1979 at the age of forty-three, Hogg belonged to a new generation of managers who came to the fore in British industry during the 1980s. Educated at Oxford, Hogg had taken a master's degree at the Harvard Business School, worked as a merchant banker in the City, then joined the staff of the Industrial Reorganisation Corporation. Recruited by Kearton in 1970, he made an outstanding success of running the paints subsidiary, the most profitable of the company's non-textile activities.

Within a few months of becoming chairman Hogg was faced with a drastic fall in profits resulting from the so-called Thatcher recession. The new Conservative government under Margaret Thatcher imposed tight monetary policies in an effort to stamp out inflation, and the consequent rise in interest rates led to an unintended overvaluation of sterling, putting extreme pressure on exporting and import-competing industries. The immediate task was to cut costs, and the programme of plant closures which had started under Knight was accelerated. Hogg's long-term strategy was to focus only on those businesses which had a realistic chance of becoming internationally competitive. As he said in 1981, 'you've got to be reasonably certain that you can make money against the worst that imports can challenge you with'.[46]

An early decision was to discontinue the production of nylon and polyester, businesses in which Courtaulds was too small to compete against ICI and the other major suppliers. This left the long-established rayon business and Courtelle, where the company's market position was stronger. In textiles, Hogg saw that Courtaulds had no future as a producer of commodity yarn and fabric, which would always be under attack from low-cost suppliers; most of the weaving plants which Kearton had built on greenfield sites were closed down, as were several of the Lancashire spinning mills. Another change from the Kearton era was Hogg's determination to rebuild friendly relations with Marks & Spencer, the principal customer for Courtaulds' hosiery and knitwear. Unlike most of the other multiple retailers, Marks & Spencer bought almost all its clothing in Britain, and it was willing to enter into a long-term relationship with suppliers. This was how the Djanogly brothers at Nottingham Manufacturing had built their success, and Hogg aimed to win a larger share of Marks & Spencer's business, while also promoting Courtaulds' own brands – Kayser Bondor, Wolsey, Gossard and others – to other retailers.

The old policy of vertical integration had been largely abandoned by Knight, and Hogg established Courtaulds Textile Group as a separate subsidiary in 1985. The management skills required in textiles and clothing – design flair, fashion consciousness, quick response – had little application for the rest of Courtaulds, which consisted mainly of capital-intensive chemical and industrial businesses. To run the Textiles Group Hogg appointed Martin Taylor, a former financial journalist, who set in train a radical overhaul of the business. 'We found that in too many products we were number 4 or 5 in Britain, and number 29 in Europe. We had to make ourselves more international, and we had to simplify, do fewer things.'[47] Lancashire spinning and weaving were cut back even further, and the Samuel Courtauld weaving business, the oldest part of the company, was sold to a Japanese company. At the same time Courtaulds continued to invest in products such as stretch fabric where it had a technical edge over its rivals.

The assumption on which these plans were based was that protection against low-cost imports was likely to diminish and eventually disappear. Although the Multi Fibre Arrangement was renewed for a further five years in 1981, the developing countries were increasingly hostile to a system which had been envisaged as a short-term measure to give the older textile industries time to reorganise. The Uruguay Round of GATT trade negotiations, which began in 1986, ended five years later with an agreement that the MFA would be phased out by 2005. This was in line with the forecasts made by Martin Taylor and his colleagues. The only businesses worth having were those which could survive in an open world market: Courtaulds had to turn itself into an international company. In the mid-1980s 90 per cent of the products which Courtaulds Textiles sold were made in Britain, and 90 per cent of its sales were in Britain. The objective, over a period of a decade, was to reduce the first of these two figures to 40 per cent, by sourcing more goods in cheaper overseas locations, and the second to 50 per cent, by exporting more British-made products and by overseas acquisitions.

In 1989 Hogg took the separation between fibres and textiles to its logical conclusion, floating Courtaulds Textiles on the stock exchange as an independent company; this was an early example of 'demerging', a practice which was to become fashionable during the 1990s. Although Taylor left the company in 1993 to be chief executive of Barclays Bank, the strategy of specialisation and internationalisation which he and Hogg had set in place was maintained. The final step in the unwinding of Kearton's grand design came in 1996, when the remaining Lancashire spinning mills were sold to Shiloh, an old-established firm run by Edmund Gartside, the third generation of a family which had controlled the business since 1874. Shiloh's survival was based on flexibility, service and the ability to respond quickly to a wide variety of customer demands – not the characteristics of the giant vertical enterprise which Kearton had constructed in the 1960s.[48]

During the 1990s the British textile industry continued to contract as more firms shifted part of their production overseas, but at the end of the decade Courtaulds Textiles appeared to be securely placed with a much narrower portfolio of businesses, principally lace and stretch fabrics, lingerie and hosiery, casualwear and underwear. Marks & Spencer was by far its largest customer, accounting for more than 40 per cent of sales, but substantial progress had also been made in internationalising the company along the lines mapped out in the mid-1980s.[49] Indeed Courtaulds Textiles performed rather better during this period than its former parent. Courtaulds, having shed the textile operation, spent most of the decade trying to build a coherent business out of three disparate activities – fibres, paints and packaging materials. In 1998 it was taken over by the Dutch chemical group, Akzo Nobel, and the name 'Courtaulds' became the exclusive property of the textile company – a reversal of history, since Samuel Courtauld had been founded as a textile business 150 years earlier.

While Hogg and Taylor were setting Courtaulds on a new course, the other textile groups which had been formed during the merger wave of the 1960s were going through upheavals of their own. Carrington Viyella, like Courtaulds, was hard hit by the recession of the early 1980s, and it was no longer of much interest to ICI, its principal shareholder. The huge profits which ICI had made in nylon and Terylene in the 1960s had evaporated in the 1970s as a result of worldwide over-capacity, and fibres were no longer regarded as a core business. But Carrington Viyella had an array of strong or potentially strong brands – Viyella, Dorma, Van Heusen and others. These assets attracted the attention of David Alliance, an entrepreneur somewhat in the Hyman mould. Alliance, scion of an Iranian textile merchanting family, had come to Britain in 1959. Starting in Manchester as a merchant-converter, he began buying up near-bankrupt textile manufacturers, and he used Spirella, one of the acquired firms, as the vehicle to build a substantial household textile business. The biggest purchase was that of Vantona in 1975, making Alliance one of the largest household textile manufacturers in Europe. The decline of Carrington Viyella – and ICI's obvious eagerness to sell out – presented Alliance with an opportunity to expand his empire at a favourable price; he bought the company in 1982. This marked the end of a highly unprofitable diversion for ICI in the textile business.[50]

Alliance was a shrewd buyer of companies, and his acquisitions were guided more by opportunism than by strategic planning. A remarkable coup was the purchase of Nottingham Manufacturing in 1985, giving Alliance a big stake in the East Midlands knitwear industry. This was followed by the acquisition of Coats Patons in 1986 and Tootal in 1991. Alliance's group, now called Coats Viyella, had become the largest textile company in Britain, even bigger than Courtaulds Textiles. However, as the industry's experience since 1960 had shown, size was no guarantee of success, and Coats Viyella's performance during the 1990s was poor. The most consistently profitable operation was sewing thread, the original Coats business, which had few links with other parts of the group. The spinning and weaving operations were sold in a management buy-out in 1995, and two years later the company announced plans for a demerger. The thread business was to be separated from the garment, household textiles and retailing activities, which would be grouped together under the Viyella name and floated as an independent company. A few months later the demerger was deferred because of un-favourable stock market conditions.

The decline of Coats Viyella was confirmation, if any was needed, that the future of the industry did not lie in big, diversified groups. As Martin Taylor remarked in 1989, 'experience has shown time and time again in the last twenty-five years that it is easier to assemble large groups with apparently formidable strengths than it is to manage them'.[51] To survive in the 1990s companies had to find defensible market positions, based on a well-established brand name, or close relations with a major customer like Marks & Spencer, or a technical advantage which rivals could not easily imitate. Another essential skill was the ability to manage an international supply chain, whether through wholly owned overseas subsidiaries or through contractual arrangements. This was particularly important as Marks & Spencer moved away from its previous reliance on British suppliers, and bought more of its clothing from overseas; by 1999 the proportion of its goods sourced within Britain had dropped to 65 per cent, and the figure was expected to fall further to about 50 per cent within a few years.[52]

As with most of the industries described in this book, the 1980s and 1990s saw an internationalisation of the British textile industry. In conditions of free or nearly free trade the only manufacturing activities likely to remain in Britain were those which, for technical or commercial reasons, had a competitive edge over low-cost producers in the developing countries. At the end of the 1990s, after three decades of restructuring, the British textile industry was drastically reduced in size, and the mistakes made during the merger mania of the 1960s had been largely reversed. Although the contraction in employment was certain to continue as more production was shifted overseas, what was left of the industry was better equipped to compete in the world market.

Missing Out on Europe

How did British performance in textiles compare with that of other European countries? In the 1950s and 1960s the British textile industry faced two problems which its European counterparts did not share – the unfinished task of adapting Lancashire cotton to its changed position in the world, and the early exposure to low-cost imports from developing countries. Lancashire was in the direct line of fire from imports, and, because of its size at the start of the post-war period, the contraction was bound to be more severe than in the two other main sectors of the industry (TABLE 4.2). On the

TABLE 4.2 *Employment in British textiles, 1914–84*

	Cotton and silk	Wool and worsted	Hosiery and knitwear
1924	572,000	262,000	97,500
1954	538,100	197,200	122,800
1984	32,500	41,900	90,100

Source: Based on Stanley Chapman, 'Mergers and Take-overs in the Post-war Textile Industry'. Reprinted by permission from *Business History*, vol. 30, no. 2, published by Frank Cass & Company, 900 Eastern Avenue, Ilford, Essex, England. Copyright Frank Cass & Co Ltd.

other hand, it was not inevitable that, by the mid-1990s, the cotton textile sector in Britain would be smaller than in Italy, Germany or France (FIGURE 4.1).

FIGURE 4.1 *Cotton textile sector spinning production, selected European countries, 1957–95*

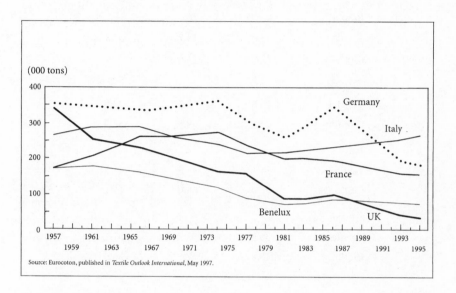

Source: Eurocoton, published in *Textile Outlook International*, May 1997.

Part of the explanation relates to intra-European trade. TABLE 4.3 shows the extent to which Continental manufacturers depended on exports to neighbouring Common Market countries in the 1960s; for British firms, the shift to Europe did not get under way until later. As tariffs within the EEC came down, the Continental manufacturers were operating in a fast-growing, homogeneous market which was more effectively protected against low-cost imports than Britain. The industries which made the best use of this opportunity were those of Italy and Germany.

The Italians had the initial advantage of low labour costs, but this factor became less important as wages and living standards rose, and the success of the industry was based on design flair, flexibility and speed of response to changing customer demands. A unique feature of the Italian industry was

TABLE 4.3 *Exports of textiles and clothing from Britain, Germany, France and Italy to the six original Common Market countries as a per centage of total exports of textiles and clothing*

	1960	1970	1980
Britain			
Textiles	13.0	14.7	33.4
Clothing	17.0	17.6	34.6
Germany			
Textiles	20.8	42.3	43.0
Clothing	23.0	59.8	54.0
Italy			
Textiles	31.1	44.5	48.7
Clothing	36.0	68.0	65.1
France			
Textiles	30.9	53.7	57.2
Clothing	15.2	57.6	56.6

Source: Michael Breitenacher, Sergio Paba and Gianpaolo Rossini, 'The Cost of "non-Europe" in the Textile-Clothing Industry', IFO-Institut, December 1987.

its dependence on small, family-owned firms clustered together in districts which concentrated on particular segments of the market, such as Prato which specialised in wool textiles and Carpi in knitwear.[53] This cottage industry structure, which bore some resemblance to nineteenth-century Lancashire, involved a high degree of co-operation among members of each network, while trade associations and other industry-wide organisations provided common services in such areas as overseas marketing, research and training. A few large firms such as Benetton did emerge, but they relied on small sub-contractors for much of their manufacturing. Of the larger European countries, only Italy has maintained a substantial trade surplus both in textiles and in clothing (TABLE 4.4).

The other European success story was the West German textile industry.

TABLE 4.4 *Exports and imports of textiles and clothing in 1995*

(figures in $bn)

	Germany	Britain	Italy	France
Textiles				
Exports	14.20	5.16	12.67	7.47
Imports	12.16	7.70	6.32	7.49
Balance	+2.04	−2.54	+6.35	−0.02
Clothing				
Exports	7.38	4.65	14.04	5.62
Imports	24.23	8.34	4.60	10.29
Balance	−16.85	−3.69	+9.44	−4.67

Source: *Textile Outlook International*, July 1997.

When low-cost imports first posed a threat in the early 1960s, the response among German manufacturers was to go for a capital-intensive, mass-production strategy similar to that of Courtaulds in Britain. But it soon became clear that the savings in labour costs would not be enough to withstand import competition in the simpler types of yarn and fabric, and that the future for the industry lay in doing things which manufacturers in the developing countries could not match – differentiated, technically demanding, fashion-sensitive products, generally made in small batches.[54] Most firms looked for niches where they could combine the use of modern technology with a strong emphasis on marketing.[55] This strategy suited the small and medium-sized companies which constituted a large part of the German textile industry. Between the mid-1960s and the mid-1970s, when the British textile industry was going through a wave of mergers, the concentration ratio in Germany hardly changed (TABLE 4.5).

The adjustment process in Germany was market-led, with the Federal government playing almost no role.[56] Requests for protection were met with the argument that the German economy as a whole depended on free trade and that the textile industry must adjust as best it could to the changing international division of labour. The government was more interested in

TABLE 4.5 *Concentration in European textiles 1966–75*

(the figures refer to the per centage share of textile employment accounted for by the top 3, 5 and 10 firms in each country)

	Britain	Germany	France	Italy
1966				
Top 3 firms	16	4	10	6
Top 5 firms	21	6	12	9
Top 10 firms	28	11	14	na
1975				
Top 3 firms	40	5	17	8
Top 5 firms	53	7	19	12
Top 10 firms	70	16	21	16

Source: Brian Toyne et al., *The Global Textile Industry*, Allen & Unwin, 1984, p. 86.

keeping markets open for the country's capital goods industry (including the textile machinery makers) than in preserving jobs in textiles; Germany was more liberal than other Common Market countries in its application of the Multi Fibre Arrangement.[57] The fact that, in contrast to Britain, there were no large concentrations of textile employment in particular regions reduced the textile industry's lobbying power. Nor was it necessary for the synthetic fibre manufacturers to involve themselves directly in the reorganisation of the industry as they did in Britain. While they provided technical advice and support, they did not acquire textile firms.[58]

High German wages made it difficult for the labour-intensive clothing industry to remain competitive, and during the 1960s many apparel manufacturers began to transfer production to countries with low labour costs. This was often done in co-operation with their fabric suppliers. Under the outward processing system authorised by the European Commission, German-made fabric was made up into garments outside Germany and then re-imported free of duty. International sub-contracting allowed German clothing manufacturers to reduce their production costs while concentrating more of their attention on marketing and distribution.[59]

The least successful of the three largest Continental textile industries was that of France.[60] In common with much of the rest of French industry, the textile manufacturers were highly protected during the 1950s, and much of their export trade was with the colonies. The opening-up of the domestic market following the creation of the EEC put the industry under greater pressure, and the government, which had taken little interest in textiles in the early post-war years, sought to encourage modernisation. In line with the prevailing belief in 'national champions', attempts were made to restructure the industry into larger groups, somewhat along the lines of what was happening in Britain during the same period.[61] Although concentration did not go as far as in Britain, some large textile conglomerates were formed, including Prouvost, DMC, Agache-Willot, and Boussac, and they were not much more successful than their British counterparts.

What prevented the British textile industry from following a strategy similar to that pursued in Germany or Italy? There had been a long tradition, especially in Lancashire, of supplying yarns and fabrics in large quantity to non-European countries, and the industry was organised in a way which suited this trading pattern. Post-war developments in world textile trade made these arrangements obsolete. With hindsight, the right response to developing-country competition in the 1950s and 1960s would have been a shift to high-value-added fabrics, which were less vulnerable to competition from low-cost imports, and a reorientation of overseas marketing to Continental Europe. But this would have required a change of mindset in a long-established industry which had been struggling for years with continuous decline and chronic over-capacity. As it was, the attempt by Courtaulds to breathe new life into the industry led in the wrong direction.[62] It is conceivable that if Courtaulds had not intervened in the way that it did more firms might have pursued a specialisation strategy along German or Italian lines, although whether this would have led to a spontaneous revival of the industry must be open to question.

Britain's delayed entry into the Common Market was a disadvantage, and it was not the only factor which slowed down the Europeanisation of the industry. The concentrated structure of the retail trade, and the domination by Marks & Spencer in particular, made it difficult for manufacturers to establish their own brands in competition with retailers' brands, except at the top end of the trade. Manufacturing under contract for Marks & Spencer was a profitable business, guaranteeing steady orders for firms which could meet the retailer's specifications.[63] This tended to reinforce the industry's attachment to long runs of relatively undifferentiated products. If the retail market had been as fragmented as in Italy or Germany, there would have been greater opportunity for manufacturers to develop independent design and marketing skills, and to promote their own brands. The distinctive character of the British clothing market helped to isolate the textile industry from Continental Europe. Many of the East Midlands knitwear producers, for example, preferred to concentrate on the British retail trade, offering medium-quality, low-fashion products at low prices, rather than build up their export business.[64]

Because of history and because of the Commonwealth connection, the British textile industry faced a very difficult adjustment after the Second World War. The attempt to solve the problem through scale, standardisation and vertical integration was a mistake. As for the three institutional weaknesses mentioned in Chapter 1 – labour relations, training and education, and the financial system – none of them seem central to the textile story. Labour relations were generally stable throughout the post-war period. The trade unions did not resist the modernisation efforts of the 1960s, and they were largely passive during the contraction which took place in the 1980s and 1990s. On the issue of skills, the German industry's emphasis on up-market, technically demanding fabrics may have been facilitated by the well-organised apprenticeship system, but deficiencies in British training arrangements played no more than a marginal role in the textile industry's decline. There were, after all, some successful firms, like the Scottish knitwear producers, operating at the high-fashion end of the trade. That there were not more of them cannot be blamed on a shortage of workforce skills. Equally, the textile industry was not held back by lack of support from banks and financial institutions; it may even have been too easy for Courtaulds to finance its ambitious investment and acquisition programme. If there was a weakness in the financial system, it lay in the failure of shareholders and their advisers to scrutinise more rigorously the claims made by Courtaulds and others about the benefits of large-scale mergers.

The impact of public policy was unhelpful. Successive governments cannot be criticised for the failure of Kearton's grand design since they were not responsible for initiating or implementing it. They were, however, sympathetic to the plan and, by partially conceding the industry's demands for protection, they may have encouraged unrealistic ideas of what could be achieved through scale and standardisation. The government would have done better to have left the industry alone, as the German government did, instead of intervening in an erratic and inconsistent way. According to a study carried out by the Organisation of European Co-operation and

Development, 'Government policies for the textile and clothing industries have primarily affected the rate at which change has occurred, rather than the direction or broad thrust of change'.[65] Britain's experience confirms this judgement. Government intervention had the effect of delaying the textile industry's integration into the world market; this is a theme which will recur in later chapters.

FIVE

Shipbuilding: Imprisoned by History

I f there is one industry which symbolises Britain's transition from imperial power to 'just another European country', it is shipbuilding. At the end of the nineteenth century Britain had the largest shipbuilding industry in the world, the largest merchant fleet and the largest navy. The combination of circumstances which underpinned that supremacy began to fall apart in the inter-war years, and at a faster rate after 1945. One by one the great shipyards on the Clyde, the Tyne and the Wear wilted in the face of foreign competition, and no amount of support from the government could stop the rot. By the end of the 1990s only fragments were left of an industry which had once ruled the world.

This is often seen as an egregious British failure, attributable to specifically British weaknesses. Incompetent managers and bloody-minded trade-unionists figure prominently in popular explanations of what went wrong. Yet other European shipbuilders fared almost as badly. Even the Swedish shipbuilding industry, much admired in the 1950s and 1960s for its technical progressiveness and its stable labour relations, was overwhelmed by competition from low-cost yards in Japan and South Korea, the two countries which have come to dominate the world shipbuilding scene. The near-demise of merchant shipbuilding in Britain is as much a European as a British phenomenon. What was distinctive about the British case was the size of the industry at the start of the post-war period, and the extent to which its response to competition was conditioned by its earlier history.

The Sources of British Supremacy before 1914

In the second half of the nineteenth century the shipbuilding industry went through a technological transformation, from wooden sailing ships to steam-powered vessels with hulls made of iron and later steel. By exploiting this opportunity better than their counterparts in other countries, Britain's shipbuilders established a commanding position in the world market which was not seriously challenged until after the First World War. The US and Germany, despite their rapid progress in other sectors, lagged behind Britain in shipbuilding. The failure of the Americans was particularly striking, since they had been the leaders in the sailing ship era. No British yard could match the speed and efficiency of the American clippers, which were at the height of their success between 1830 and 1850.[1]

Britain had two advantages which the US and Germany lacked. One was the depth of experience in iron-making and steam power which had been accumulated since the start of the industrial revolution. The potential superiority of iron over wood, in reducing the weight of the vessel and the thickness of its hull, was recognised towards the end of the eighteenth century, but it took several decades of experimentation before corrosion and other technical problems were fully overcome.[2] By the 1860s the seaworthiness of iron vessels was no longer in doubt, and the substitution of steel for iron in the following decade marked a further advance. The shipbuilders benefited from the invention in 1867 of the open hearth furnace, which produced steel of a more consistent quality than the older Bessemer process. Similarly, the development of steam engines for marine application involved a long period of incremental improvement before sail was finally displaced. The introduction of more efficient compound engines and the replacement of the paddle by the screw propeller – both developments starting in the 1850s – reduced coal consumption to the point where steam was more economical than sail even on the longest voyages. The next breakthrough was the steam turbine – invented in 1884 by Charles Parsons, a British engineer – which was well suited for high-speed naval ships and passenger liners. The first turbine-powered ship was launched on the Tyne in 1894, and a few years later the Cunard Company installed steam turbines in its two transatlantic liners, the *Lusitania* and the *Mauretania*.

Technical progress depended on close co-operation between shipbuilders, steel-makers and engine manufacturers. Whereas the production of wooden ships had been scattered across a large number of locations, the second half of the nineteenth century saw a concentration of shipbuilding in regions which combined suitable port facilities with access to coal, iron and a well-established engineering industry. By 1900 more than two-thirds of the industry's production came from the Clyde in Scotland and the Tyne, Tees and Wear in the north-east. Other important centres were Birkenhead on the Mersey, where the Laird brothers were among the first to take up iron shipbuilding, and Barrow-in-Furness, where the shipyard was built by the owners of the local ironworks; in 1897 it was acquired by Vickers, the armaments manufacturer. Belfast, where Edward Harland and Gustav Wolff opened their shipyard in 1861, was a less obviously attractive location, since most of its coal and iron had to be imported. But labour was cheap, the port was the main outlet for the Irish linen trade, and there were close links with the Liverpool shipowners across the Irish Sea.

The other British advantage was the size of the merchant fleet. Like other maritime nations, Britain had traditionally protected its shipping industries by restricting trade with the colonies to British-owned and British-built vessels. The shift towards free trade in the 1840s and 1850s was resisted by the shipowners, who feared that without the protection provided by the Navigation Acts they would lose ground to foreign competition.[3] But the repeal of these laws in 1850, far from heralding the decline of Britain's maritime industries, marked the start of a period of spectacular growth. Steamship services were introduced which enabled the British fleet not only to retain the bulk of the colonial trade, but also to win the lion's share of trade between foreign countries. By 1890 the steam tonnage on the British register amounted to 5m tons, compared with just under 3m tons for all the other maritime countries put together, and all these ships were built in British yards. Another source of domestic demand was the Royal Navy, especially in the period between 1890 and 1914 when the race for naval superiority with Germany was in full swing. While some of these ships were built in government-owned dockyards, an increasing proportion of the Navy's requirements was contracted out to private shipbuilders. Some firms such as Vickers and John Brown (which owned one of the largest yards on the Upper Clyde) specialised almost entirely in naval ships. The specifications for battleships and other naval vessels were more demanding than for merchant ships, and helped to raise the technical competence of the industry.[4]

The size of the home market allowed yards to specialise in serving the needs of individual customers and thus to gain experience in designing and building particular types of ship. The leading firms in Glasgow and Belfast won fame for their large, luxurious passenger liners, while yards in the north-east tended to concentrate on general-purpose cargo ships. The coal trade was important for Wearside yards, which built simple, low-cost vessels for tramp operators. Specialisation rarely involved the construction of identical ships; each vessel was purpose-built to suit the owner's requirements. The flow of orders fluctuated, and shipbuilders needed the flexibility to move from one sector of the market to another in line with the state of demand.

As in cotton textiles, the home market was the base from which the shipbuilders could build up their export sales. But the shipbuilders, even at the height of their international success, remained more dependent on domestic business than the Lancashire cotton mills. While 80 per cent of Lancashire's textile production was for the overseas market, only 20 per cent of new launchings in Britain between 1900 and 1914 were for foreign buyers. This was partly due to protectionism in overseas countries. Several foreign governments treated their maritime industries as an instrument of national security, and obliged their shipowners to buy only from national yards.

Employment in shipbuilding rose from 75,000 in 1870 to nearly 200,000 in 1914. The way in which this workforce was organised and managed reflected the traditions of the industry, dating back to the days of wood and sail, and the state of shipbuilding technology.[5] As a complex, assembly industry, shipbuilding was dependent on craft skills. In the sailing ship era the most important skills were those of the shipwrights, responsible for building up the carcass of the ship. The transition from wood to metal called for skills which the shipwrights did not possess, and the yards recruited craftsmen from other industries, principally construction and engineering. The industry's skilled workforce was made up of a large number of distinct crafts, each of which had a clearly defined set of skills.

Apprenticeship was the means by which the craftsman acquired his skills. It was also the qualification for membership of one of the craft-based trade unions which established themselves in the industry after 1850. One of the main functions of the union was to preserve the integrity of the apprenticeship system; this meant, among other things, constant vigilance to ensure that jobs which had traditionally been performed by its members were not assigned to unskilled workers or to members of other unions. The strongest union was the Boilermakers Society, which represented the majority of skilled workers in the steel trades.

Although the scope for mechanisation increased as technology advanced, fluctuations in the flow of new orders, and variations in the type of ship required, made firms reluctant to invest in machinery which might be idle for a substantial part of the time. It was also difficult, for the same reasons, to provide continuity of employment. Workers were hired and fired as the demand for particular skills rose and fell. These employment practices were made possible by the existence in each of the main shipbuilding regions of a pool of mobile labour on which employers could draw, and by the ability of strong trade unions to give their members a degree of protection against insecurity of employment.[6] Workers could expect to be dismissed, and to move to another yard, when the part of the ship on which they were working was completed. If no work was available in neighbouring yards, they looked to the union for financial support.

These arrangements suited the employers because labour costs were kept low, but the division of the workforce into separate crafts, each represented by a different union, meant that, when new machines or new methods were introduced which altered the distribution of skills or created the need for new ones, demarcation disputes were likely to arise. Each union was determined to protect the rights of its members to their existing jobs, and, if possible, to win a share of any new work that might be available. Strikes over demarcation increased in the closing decades of the century, prompting efforts by employers and unions to devise new conciliation procedures. The establishment of national organisations – the Shipbuilding Employers Federation and, on the union side, the Federation of Shipbuilding and Engineering Trades – helped to bring some order into the industry's collective bargaining arrangements. But the individual unions were not willing to surrender power to a central body; the Boilermakers, in particular, were frequently in conflict with other unions.

There were moments when employers, irritated by persistent demarcation disputes and by union-imposed restrictions on how workers could be deployed, favoured a more aggressive labour relations strategy.[7] In 1898 the engineering employers won a decisive victory over the principal craft union in engineering, the Amalgamated Society of Engineers, over the issue of managerial prerogatives, and some shipyard owners wanted to apply the same rules in shipbuilding.[8] In 1902 employers on the Clyde proposed to their colleagues in the north-east a concerted attack on union-imposed restrictions. This would involve the freedom to deploy unskilled labour on new machinery, the detachment of foremen from union influence, and discretionary power to sub-divide the work process where this was felt to be desirable. But it proved impossible to maintain a united front among a notoriously individualistic group of employers. Some companies, especially in the north-east, had no stomach for an all-out fight. As G. B. Hunter of

Swan Hunter, the largest shipyard on the Tyne, put it, 'we in the north of England want to work by agreement with the trade unions. We think we can manage the men better by so doing'.[9]

Although labour relations in shipbuilding were adversarial, workers and their unions recognised that changes in technology and organisation were essential if the industry was to retain its dominant position in the world market. Disputes over demarcation and other issues were seen as part of the give-and-take between the two sides which allowed the necessary adjustments to take place. The unions, moreover, performed a number of useful services; they administered the apprenticeship system and, through their welfare payments, helped to maintain the attachment of skilled workers to the industry during recessions.[10]

There was another reason why employers needed the co-operation of their skilled workers. In the days of wooden shipbuilding the yard owner customarily sub-contracted part of the work to the shipwright, who hired, supervised and paid other, less skilled workers. Although sub-contracting began to die out after the transition to steam and iron, the industry continued to rely on self-supervising gangs or teams of workers, who were 'given only the vaguest of instructions and then left to organise the work among themselves'.[11] The head of the team, a senior member of the relevant union, was given considerable responsibility. The foreman to whom he was nominally responsible belonged to the same union, and was no less concerned to protect the interests of the craft. There was no strong incentive to change these arrangements as long as the industry was doing well.

Productivity in shipbuilding was higher in Britain than in any other country before the First World War.[12] In Germany, Britain's strongest competitor in other industries, shipbuilding had developed slowly up to the 1890s, partly because of inadequate supplies of high-quality steel. Support from the government, in the form of protection and subsidies, gave the industry the confidence to expand and modernise, and after the turn of the century German yards were turning out ships which matched the British in quality. But despite lower wages production costs were higher than in Britain. This was partly a matter of scale; German merchant ship launchings were about one-sixth of the British level before the First World War. But a more important reason was the scarcity of skilled labour, which forced German firms to spend more on machinery. This was an expensive overhead, which, because of fluctuations in demand, could not be kept in continuous operation.[13]

Like cotton textiles, shipbuilding was an industry in which there was no sign of entrepreneurial failure in Britain before the First World War. The production methods which had been developed since the middle of the nineteenth century, together with the skills and experience of managers and men, suited the conditions in which the industry was operating at that time. These conditions changed radically in the inter-war years, and, like the textile manufacturers described in the last chapter, the shipbuilders had great difficulty in adjusting to the new environment.

The Inter-war Years

For the first two years after the First World War new orders flowed into British shipyards at a high level as tonnage which had been lost in the war was replaced. Most of these orders came from British owners, who assumed that the growth of international trade would quickly return to its pre-war path and that Britain would resume the dominant role in world shipping which it had had before the war. Both these assumptions turned out to be wrong. The volume of sea-borne trade remained below the pre-war level until 1924, and, after a brief upturn in the second half of the 1920s, fell back again under the impact of the world depression. Within this declining market British shipowners faced growing competition from foreign fleets, some of which were protected and subsidised by their governments. There were also changes in the composition of world trade which worked to Britain's disadvantage. Coal exports, which had been the staple business for many British tramp operators, declined in importance as the volume of oil shipments increased.

Several firms had enlarged their yards after the war on the expectation of continuing growth in demand, and in 1920 the industry had the capacity to produce about 4m tons of merchant shipping a year. Output reached a peak of 2.1m tons in 1921, but for the rest of the decade it averaged little more than 1m tons a year, falling to below 700,000 tons between 1930 and 1939. To make matters worse, naval orders, which had accounted for about a quarter of the industry's workload before the war, virtually dried up in the 1920s, and remained at a low level until the onset of rearmament in the mid-1930s. The warship specialists were forced to compete for merchant ship orders, adding to the problem of over-capacity and low prices.

What had been a source of strength for the shipbuilders – their close ties to British shipowners – now became a weakness, since all the growth in sea-borne trade in the inter-war years was secured by non-British owners. Between 1913 and 1939 British-registered merchant tonnage remained virtually unchanged at about 18m tons, while the world fleet expanded from 43m tons to 69m tons. Part of the decline in Britain's share was due to subsidised competition, but there were also some missed opportunities. Before 1914 the few oil tankers in service were owned either by oil companies or by governments as part of their naval fleets. After the war the oil companies supplemented their own tonnage with vessels chartered from independent tanker owners. This business did not appeal to British tramp operators, partly because they had invested heavily in traditional cargo vessels after the war and lacked the resources to tackle a new market. One historian has suggested that British shipowners had a contemptuous attitude to oil tankers, 'which they seem to have regarded as being hardly ships at all, much as the American sailing shipowners in the nineteenth century turned their backs on steamships, which they regarded as floating kettles not worthy of their consideration'.[14] British shipowners allowed a gap in the market to open up, which others were quick to fill. By the end of the 1930s Norwegian entrepreneurs had built up the largest independently owned tanker fleet.

British shipowners were also slow to take up the diesel engine. This form of propulsion, invented in Germany in the 1880s and adapted for marine purposes after the turn of the century, gained wider acceptance in the inter-war years. It was particularly attractive in countries which did not have an indigenous source of coal. By 1939 more than 60 per cent of the Norwegian fleet was equipped with diesel engines, compared with 26 per cent in Britain. Some of this lag reflected the composition of the British fleet. In passenger liners, for example, which were more important for British owners than for the Scandinavians, the steam turbine was more economic than the diesel. But the long attachment to coal and steam bred a cautious attitude towards the diesel engine which was not shared overseas.[15]

The shipbuilders did not find it easy to break away from an approach to designing, building and selling ships which was geared to the needs of British owners. Most of them had a close relationship with a small number of British owners from whom they derived the bulk of their orders; the export trade was regarded as marginal and unpredictable. But even if British shipbuilders had been more aggressive in pursuing export business, there would still have been a need to reduce the industry's capacity. The idea of an industry-wide rationalisation scheme was first broached by the warship builders in 1925, and the discussions were broadened to include the rest of the industry. The Bank of England helped to promote rationalisation through the creation in 1930 of National Shipbuilders Security (NSS), a financial holding company. Financed by a levy on each firm which participated in the scheme, the NSS was given the power to buy up and close down shipyards which were surplus to requirements. Between 1930 and 1935 38 yards were permanently shut, sterilising some 1.4m tons of building capacity.[16]

The capacity reduction scheme was an unusual exercise in collective self-help in an industry which in the past had found great difficulty in maintaining a common front on any issue. Previous inhibitions about government intervention were laid aside as the industry's plight worsened. Both shipowners and shipbuilders pressed for action to counter subsidised foreign competition. In 1934 the government agreed to provide a temporary subsidy for tramp operators, and in the following year a scrap-and-build scheme was introduced; loans were made available to British shipowners to scrap old ships and order new ones in British yards.

If the response of the employers to the inter-war crisis was defensive, the same was true of the unions. High unemployment made the unions even more determined to preserve traditional demarcations between trades, and less co-operative in their response to technological change. The replacement of riveting by welding provoked a lengthy dispute. The employers proposed the creation of a new class of skilled worker, the ship-welder, to be organised and trained outside the existing union structure. Inconclusive negotiations took place, but no national agreement was reached. The allocation of welding work within individual yards was determined in the time-honoured way, 'through a process of competitive struggle between groups of skilled workers and their unions for control of the new process'.[17]

Delays in the introduction of welding in the 1930s did not put British yards at a serious competitive disadvantage. The technology was not yet fully developed, and the shipbuilders were understandably concerned that a premature rush into welding might damage their reputation for building high-quality vessels.[18] But the reaction of the unions was symptomatic of the lack of trust between managers and workers, which was exacerbated by high unemployment.

The inter-war depression made it more difficult for employers and unions to shake off attitudes and habits which had taken root before the war. The employers were more interested in cutting costs than in a radical reform of the industry's labour relations system or in altering the traditional approach to the organisation of work. Other shipbuilding nations were putting more emphasis on the pre-planning of production and on organising the flow of materials so as to economise on the use of skilled labour. This was the start of a transformation in shipbuilding techniques which was to be taken much further after the Second World War.[19]

The Post-war Boom in World Shipping

The Second World War, like the first, was followed by a worldwide surge in orders, and this time the boom did not quickly evaporate as it had done in the 1920s. From the early 1950s the world economy entered a golden age of growth, which continued for the following twenty years, and sea-borne trade increased at a rate which had no historical precedent. World shipbuilding output, which had fluctuated between 2m and 7m tons a year between the wars, rose to 36m tons in 1975. Yet Britain's shipbuilders signally failed to profit from this favourable environment. Annual output from British yards was virtually static in the 1950s and 1960s (TABLE 5.1).

TABLE 5.1 *Britain's share of world merchant ship launchings 1950–95*

	British launchings (000 gross tons)	World launchings (000 gross tons)	British share of world total (per cent)
1950	1,324	3,492	37.9
1960	1,332	8,356	15.9
1975	1,304	35,897	3.6
1985	172	18,156	0.9
1995	126	22,467	0.6

Source: Lloyd's Register of Shipping.

In the early post-war years production in Britain was held back by the scarcity of labour and materials, but these shortages had eased by the early 1950s, and cannot account for the stagnation of output for the rest of the decade. Part of the explanation was the cautious view which British shipbuilders took about the future course of demand. Always anxious lest another depression was round the corner, they were determined to avoid the mistake that had been made after the First World War, when over-investment was followed by a prolonged slump. But two new forces were at work, neither of which sat easily with the skills and experience of British shipbuilders.

The first was a change in the market for ships, leading to a loosening of the ties between national owners and builders. The most striking development was the rapid growth of the so-called flags of convenience. This was a post-war device whereby owners registered their ships outside their home country, principally in Panama, Liberia and Honduras, partly for tax reasons, partly to avoid restrictions imposed by their home governments on manning levels and wage rates.

The second force was a change in the way ships were designed and built. In oil tankers and bulk carriers there was a trend towards scale and standardisation. There was also a growing demand for technically sophisticated ships, such as containerships, roll-on/roll-off ferries and chemical carriers, which called for specialised equipment and skills.

British shipbuilders had traditionally looked to British owners as their primary source of orders. If the British merchant fleet had retained the 26 per cent world market share with which it started the post-war period, this might have been a viable policy. But the British share declined even more precipitately than it had done before the war; by 1970 it was down to 11 per cent as other nations, principally Greece, Japan, Germany and Norway, built up their merchant fleets. Some of the trades in which British operators specialised were in slow-growing sectors of the market. Passenger traffic across the Atlantic, for example, was badly affected by the rising popularity of air travel. There was also a continuing decline in coal exports. But the shipowners responded sluggishly to new opportunities. For example, the 1950s saw a spectacular rise in the volume of oil shipments from the Middle East to the consuming countries of Western Europe, the US and Japan. The oil companies relied even more than before the war on independent tanker owners with whom they negotiated time charters, usually lasting for seven or fourteen years. The charter agreement provided the security on which owners raised loans to finance the construction of new ships. This market was open to British owners, but most of them regarded it as too risky. The Norwegians and the Greeks, as well as Chinese entrepreneurs based in Hong Kong, had no such inhibitions.[20]

A marketing strategy geared to the requirements of domestic owners was becoming obsolete, and the same was true of the industry's production methods. For the transport of oil and bulk commodities such as iron ore the trend was towards larger, simpler and more economical vessels. In the early post-war years tankers were between 10,000 and 15,000 gross registered tons, but by the middle of the 1950s there were 50,000-ton ships on order. The closure of the Suez Canal in 1956, forcing operators to re-route their tankers round the Cape, led to a surge of orders for 100,000-ton vessels. With increasing scale came greater standardisation. The idea of 'mass-producing' ships on a flow-line basis had originated in the US during the First World War, but the big advance, made possible by the introduction of welding and prefabrication, came in the Second World War; some 2,600 Liberty ships – standard dry cargo vessels of 11,000 deadweight tons – and nearly 600 16,000-ton tankers were built in the US between 1941 and 1945. After the war other countries drew on US experience to rethink their approach to ship design.

Flow-line production called for a higher degree of mechanisation than under the traditional British system, and could be applied only in yards which specialised in a narrow range of ships. It also put a premium on planning and organisation. Instead of relying on the initiative and independence of skilled craftsmen, responsibility shifted to the drawing office, and the task of management was to ensure that plans were carried out precisely; a disciplined approach to the control of labour was required. British shipbuilders had difficulty in adjusting to these changes.[21] Some yards were too small to accommodate the larger vessels now in demand, and specialisation did not come easily to firms which prided themselves on their ability to produce a wide variety of different ships. The resource which had underpinned this flexibility, an ample supply of self-reliant skilled labour, was no longer a competitive advantage.

New entrants, unencumbered by tradition, were quicker to exploit these opportunities, and the most spectacular winner was Japan. For the first few years after the war Japan's maritime industries were subjected to restrictions by the US occupation authorities, but, as relations with the Soviet Union deteriorated, US policy shifted towards the development of Japan as a prosperous and economically independent nation. This called for a rapid expansion of Japanese exports, and to this end it was necessary to rebuild and enlarge the Japanese shipping and shipbuilding industries. The Programmed Shipbuilding Scheme, introduced in 1947, gave subsidies to owners to place orders with domestic yards, and Japanese shipping lines were allowed to re-establish overseas routes which they had operated before the war. The Korean War, which broke out in 1950, was a turning-point, since it prompted a wave of demand for new ships which European yards, already operating at full capacity, were unable to satisfy. This was the main stimulus for a modernisation of the Japanese shipbuilding industry, which increasingly focused its attention on exports. In 1950 new orders in Japanese yards amounted to 310,000 tons, of which 16 per cent was for foreign registration; the corresponding figure in 1955 was 2.7m tons, of which 86 per cent was for export.[22]

Japan was a new shipbuilding nation, and there was an enthusiasm for expansion and for new technology, just as there had been in Britain a century earlier. In 1956 Japan overtook Britain in shipbuilding output, and in the same year shipbuilding displaced textiles as Japan's largest export industry. The diffusion of modern production methods was assisted by the presence in Japan of an American company, National Bulk Carriers, which had been active in the Liberty ship programme during the war. This company leased the former naval yard at Kure, and the fifty-two ships which it built during the 1950s were based on production methods blending American know-how in welding and prefabrication with a novel Japanese approach to flow-line assembly. The Japanese chief engineer at Kure installed a production plan-ning system which stemmed from his experience in the aircraft industry during the war.[23] Other shipbuilders studied Kure's methods and applied them in their own yards. Productivity rose rapidly, and the Japanese industry was well placed to profit from the boom in orders which followed the closure of the Suez Canal in 1956.

Within Western Europe the most successful shipbuilding nations during the 1950s were Sweden and West Germany. Oil tankers were a Swedish speciality, and leading yards like Kockums in Malmo and Gotaverken in Gothenburg had a close relationship with Norwegian owners. Substantial investments were made in welding and prefabrication; in 1950 nearly 40 per cent of Swedish launchings were of all-welded vessels compared with only 4 per cent in Britain. The American approach to mass production was much admired in Sweden, and in 1959 Gotaverken decided to apply assembly-line principles to shipbuilding on a greenfield site at Arendal. Although the Arendal project later ran into difficulties, it was regarded at the time as the most advanced shipyard in the world.

As long as British yards had plenty of orders and were making good profits, the loss of market share was not a matter of pressing concern. But as Britain's lag became more evident, especially in the construction of larger ships, several companies committed themselves to ambitious re-equipment schemes. Capital investment rose sharply after 1956, and, as if to confirm the warnings of the Cassandras, these schemes came on stream just as the world shipping market entered its first serious post-war downturn. The reopening of the Suez Canal in 1957, together with the US recession in that year, led to a sharp fall in freight rates. In Britain new orders fell from 5.4m tons in 1956 to just over 2m tons in 1962.

The response to this setback showed how deeply pre-war experience had influenced the thinking of the industry. The view of senior managers was defensive, as it had been in the 1930s. Capacity should be reduced in line with the lower level of demand, and, in assessing how much capacity would be needed, the primary consideration was the likely size of the British merchant fleet.[24] If an industry-wide capacity reduction scheme was to be instituted, the approval of the government was necessary. The reaction of ministers was unenthusiastic. They believed that the industry's problems were mainly of its own making: the shipbuilders had failed to modernise as effectively as the Japanese and the Swedes had done. This diagnosis was confirmed by a critical report published in 1960 by a government agency, the Department of Scientific and Industrial Research (DSIR).[25] Its analysis drew attention to managerial weaknesses in British shipbuilding, including a primitive approach to production control and an old-fashioned approach to labour relations. An ominous sign of declining competitiveness was the increase in the number of orders placed by British shipowners with overseas yards.

Belatedly the industry began to put its house in order. In 1959 a joint delegation of employer and union representatives visited Swedish shipyards. They concluded that Sweden's superior productivity was due to the careful planning of the production process and the flexibility with which labour could be deployed. The absence of demarcation between trades made it easier for Swedish yards to maintain a stable labour force.[26] This visit was followed in 1961 by a more extensive study of production methods by a committee of industry experts, and this report also highlighted deficiencies in planning and supervision as major causes of low productivity.[27]

The Conservative government which held office until 1964 was concerned about the industry's performance, but reluctant to intervene directly. In the discussions over the capacity reduction scheme (which was eventually abandoned) the Minister of Transport, Ernest Marples, suggested that the industry might create a small number of multi-yard groups. This would facilitate the closure of uneconomic capacity and allow yards to specialise in work for which their equipment and skills were best suited. But a collective solution of this kind did not find favour with the shipbuilders. They claimed that they were losing orders from domestic owners because foreign yards offered more generous credit terms. The government commissioned a report from Peat Marwick, the chartered accountants, which showed that credit was much less important than price and delivery. But the government's non-interventionist line was hard to sustain as the continuing recession led to yard closures and unemployment. Between 1958 and 1963 employment in merchant shipbuilding fell from 78,000 to 48,000.

In 1963, with an election looming, the government announced a £30m scheme to help finance new orders from British shipowners for British shipyards. This was presented as a temporary measure to help the industry through its difficulties, but it marked the start of a more interventionist policy which was to be taken much further by the Labour government after 1964.

State-directed Modernisation

The new government was strongly committed to industrial modernisation, and shipbuilding was high on the list of industries which needed attention. Shortly after the election a committee was appointed under Reay Geddes, chairman of Dunlop Rubber Company, to examine what changes were necessary. While the committee was still taking evidence, the government was faced with a crisis at Fairfield, one of the largest yards on the Upper Clyde. This company had modernised its facilities and built up a substantial order book, but its debts were high and it had incurred serious cost over-runs on a luxury car/passenger ferry being built for an Israeli line. After making heavy losses in 1963 and 1964, the company declared itself bankrupt in October 1965. The attempted rescue, which became known as the Fairfield experiment, has been seen by some observers as one of the greatest missed opportunities in the history of British shipbuilding.[28]

The prime mover was Iain Stewart, a Scottish industrialist who had been arguing for some years that insecurity of employment lay at the heart of the industry's poor labour relations. He believed that Fairfield could be used as a laboratory for a new approach based on a constructive partnership between employers and trade unions. If Fairfield could be saved by these means, it would set an example to other shipbuilders. For the plan to be put into effect, an immediate injection of funds was necessary, and it could come from only the government. Stewart's request for help came at an opportune time, since ministers were anxious to avoid a major yard closure before the

Geddes committee had reported. A £1m loan was made available in November 1965, and the government took a 50 per cent stake in the new company which was formed to take over the Fairfield assets.[29]

The Fairfield experiment lasted for just under two years. During this period progress was made in relaxing demarcation barriers between trades and in introducing a job evaluation scheme as the basis for a more rational wage structure. A consultative council was established on which all the unions were represented, and shop stewards were given the right to participate in matters which had previously been the preserve of management. Stewart and his colleagues were also firmer than their predecessors in only taking orders which offered a realistic prospect of profitability. But Stewart's vision of using the yard as an example for other shipbuilders had to be abandoned in 1967 when the industry was restructured in line with the recommendations of the Geddes committee.

Much of the Geddes report went over familiar ground – the need for more stable industrial relations, more attention to research and development, and better yard management.[30] The novel recommendations were, first, that the shipbuilders should focus more strongly on the world market, and, second, that the industry should be reorganised, with government financial support, into four or five large groups. These groups, the committee argued, would be able to reduce costs by allowing each yard to specialise in a particular type of vessel. The committee recommended that within each group naval work should be clearly segregated from merchant shipbuilding.

Although the Geddes committee did not quantify the benefits which would accrue from the creation of large groups, its proposals were quickly accepted by the government. A new government agency, the Shipbuilding Industry Board (SIB), was set up to implement the scheme. The availability of public funds was a strong incentive for companies to co-operate, especially those which were in a weak financial condition or, like John Brown, wished to reduce their commitment to shipbuilding. It was difficult for the SIB to exclude yards which wanted to take part, even if their prospects of commercial viability were doubtful.

The most fragile of the new groups was Upper Clyde Shipbuilders (UCS), which brought together the Stephen, Connell, Fairfield, John Brown and Yarrow yards. The last of these, a warship specialist, participated with great reluctance and insisted on being treated as a separate, autonomously managed subsidiary. The finances of UCS were under pressure from the start. This was partly due to losses on inherited contracts, but the management also decided to keep the labour force stable and to give the highest priority to winning new orders. The cost savings which had been anticipated at the time of the merger did not materialise, and further support from the SIB was necessary to keep the business alive. Yarrow withdrew from the group in 1971, leaving it entirely dependent on merchant shipbuilding.

The other large groups formed as a result of the Geddes report were Scott Lithgow on the lower Clyde and the Swan Hunter group in the north-east. On the Wear the SIB tried without success to promote a merger between the three leading companies, Doxford & Sunderland, Austin & Pickersgill, and James Bartram. (The smallest of the three, Bartram, was later acquired by Austin & Pickersgill without SIB intervention.) On the other side of the country merger discussions were held between Vickers at Barrow, Cammell Laird at Birkenhead and Harland & Wolff at Belfast, but no agreement was reached.

These structural changes coincided with an upturn in the world shipping market, and the price competitiveness of British yards was improved by the devaluation of sterling in 1967. But although the workload increased, profitability was undermined by rising inflation and inadequate control of costs.[31] Apart from the problems at Upper Clyde Shipbuilders, two other companies were in severe financial difficulties by the end of the decade. Harland & Wolff made big losses in 1965 and 1966. This company was the largest employer in Ulster, and it had a special political importance at a time when civil unrest in the province was mounting. The decision by the Northern Ireland Ministry of Commerce to guarantee a £1.5m loan in 1966 was the first step towards a transfer of control to the government.[32] Cammell Laird was hit hard by cost over-runs and had to be bailed out by the government in 1970.

What had started as a programme of modernisation and rationalisation was turning into a series of rescues, and little progress was made on other aspects of the Geddes report. Several companies tried to buy out restrictive practices with higher wages, using the newly fashionable technique of productivity bargaining.[33] This was a technique pioneered by Esso, the American oil company, at its Fawley refinery in 1960, and it was widely applied in other industries during the 1960s. But most productivity agreements gave away more in wages than was gained in greater efficiency. In shipbuilding, the willingness of the government to subsidise loss-making yards reduced the incentive on both sides to reform long-established working practices.[34]

When the Conservatives were returned to power in 1970, their intention was to leave uncompetitive industries like shipbuilding to find their own salvation, and when UCS went into liquidation in the summer of 1971, the government at first refused to provide further funds. The decision provoked furious protests on the Clyde, and the unions organised a 'work-in' to keep the yards in operation. By the end of the year, the government was in retreat, agreeing to inject public funds into a new company, Govan Shipbuilders, which would take over three of the four yards; the fourth, John Brown's yard at Clydebank, was sold to an American oil company for building oil rigs. After this climb-down government policy towards shipbuilding was not much different from what it had been under Labour. The three 'lame ducks', Cammell Laird, Harland & Wolff, and UCS, continued to receive subventions from the taxpayer. The shipbuilding industry was becoming almost a ward of the state.

The most successful yard was one which had deliberately steered clear of government involvement. Austin & Pickersgill, a medium-sized firm on the Wear, had traditionally built general-purpose cargo vessels for tramp operators. In 1957 it was acquired by a London-based consortium of ship-owners and ship-brokers. The largest shareholder was London and Overseas Freighters (LOFS), founded by two Greek ship-owning families. The yard was extensively rebuilt in the early 1960s, before the Geddes committee was set up, and the managing director, Ken Douglas, conceived the idea of concentrating production on a standard bulk carrier which would meet the needs of the yard's traditional customers at the lowest possible cost. The new design, known as the SD14, was planned as a replacement for the US-built Liberty ships which were nearing the end of their lives. First launched in 1968, the SD14 proved to be a great success, competing effectively against the Japanese and Germans until the late 1970s.

The Austin & Pickersgill case showed that survival depended, not on size, but on a sound product and marketing strategy, backed up by low-cost manufacturing methods. It also showed that the problem of disorderly labour relations could be overcome by competent management. The transition which Austin & Pickersgill had to make in the 1960s was in some ways less difficult than the situation facing other shipbuilders. There was a long tradition on the Wear of supplying predominantly small shipowners with economical cargo vessels. The SD14, though innovative in concept, was a natural evolution from the vessels which Austin & Pickersgill had been building before.[35]

The other major Wearside builder, Doxford & Sunderland, was also taken over by an outsider. Court Line had originally operated a small fleet of tramp vessels, but moved into the tanker market during the 1960s and then diversified into aviation, package holidays and hotels. Its Appledore yard in Devon had been developed to produce small cargo ships on a flow-line basis, and Doxford & Sunderland was seen as an opportunity to apply the same technique to larger ships, principally gas carriers. After the take-over in 1972 extensive modernisation was carried out. The reconstruction was more costly than Court Line had hoped and several of the orders were unprofitable. But the subsequent collapse of the company (see below) was due to problems in other parts of the group. During its period of ownership Court Line modernised the Sunderland yards on a scale which the old management could not have contemplated. As one historian has commented, 'whatever faults Court Line had, it did not lack the drive and vision which would have been so useful to the UK shipbuilding industry before 1972'.[36]

These partial successes showed the value of new thinking in a highly traditional industry. They were, however, exceptions, and it was clear when Labour took office again in 1974 that the prescriptions offered by the Geddes committee had not worked. The new cure was nationalisation. The arguments for public ownership had been set out in 1973 in a document jointly produced by the Labour Party and the trade unions. This document noted that the industry had failed to grow despite the expanding world market, had failed to modernise despite receiving more support from the government than any other industry apart from aircraft, and had failed to reform its labour relations. A co-ordinated national strategy was essential, the document argued, and this required public ownership.

Before the nationalisation bill could be presented to Parliament, the outlook for the industry deteriorated. The oil crisis at the end of 1973 brought the long post-war boom to an end, and the downturn was aggravated by the over-ordering which had taken place in the five preceding years. World launchings of merchant ships, which reached a peak of 36m tons in 1975, fell to a low point of 17m tons in 1981. The British government was immediately plunged into a series of fire-fighting operations. Court Line, owners of Doxford & Sunderland, had over-extended itself through its ventures in aviation and hotels, and in June 1974 the company was on the brink of collapse. The government decided to take over its shipbuilding and ship-repairing interests. This move was justified on the grounds that it would safeguard £133m of shipbuilding orders and 9,000 jobs. Further short-term intervention was necessary at the three companies which were already wholly or partly owned by the government – Cammell Laird, Harland & Wolff, and Govan Shipbuilders. In February 1977 the government set up a shipbuilding intervention fund, with an initial allocation of £65m, to subsidise orders on a selective basis.

The progress of the nationalisation bill through Parliament was delayed by legal and procedural objections, and it did not become law until June 1977. The new state corporation, British Shipbuilders, began life on 1 July. An unfortunate consequence of the delay was that the chief executive-designate, Graham Day, withdrew from the post. Day was a Canadian, formerly a lawyer with Canadian Pacific, who had impressed the government while serving as managing director of Cammell Laird from 1971 to 1974. His place was taken by Michael Casey, a senior civil servant in the Department of Industry.

The immediate task for Casey and his colleagues was to secure new orders, but the few large contracts which were won required substantial support from the government's intervention fund. The first accounts covering the period up to March 1979 showed a loss of over £100m, partly because of provisions for losses on contracts taken before nationalisation; the losses would have been much higher had it not been for the profits earned by the warship builders. There were disturbing similarities between British Shipbuilders and Upper Clyde Shipbuilders a decade earlier – the lumping together of disparate yards, some of which were virtually bankrupt, and a desperate search for business to keep the workforce employed.[37]

The Labour government hoped to use nationalisation as a means of promoting the fuller involvement of the trade unions in solving the industry's problems. This meant a larger role for the Confederation of Shipbuilding and Engineering Unions. In 1978 a new procedure was agreed for settling wages at the national level, replacing 168 separate bargaining arrangements in individual yards, and in the following year provision was made for local productivity agreements within guidelines set at the centre. A few months later the Confederation accepted that jobs could be reduced as long as there were no compulsory redundancies. The effect of nationalisation was to give the Confederation more influence over the industry's affairs, but the centralisation of collective bargaining caused resentment among shop stewards in the yards. The national unions were in the awkward position of collaborating with management in policies which would inevitably lead to fewer jobs.

In the first two years after nationalisation the scale of redundancies was small enough to be manageable, but in 1978, with the order intake showing no sign of improvement, British Shipbuilders was forced to consider more drastic measures. In presenting the corporate plan to the government at the end of that year the company forecast that merchant shipbuilding capacity would be reduced from 631,000 tons to 430,000 tons by 1980–81, with a reduction in employment from 33,300 to 21,000. Although the corporate plan was not published and the government decided not to respond to it until after the general election, rumours of impending redundancies provoked anxiety among the unions.

The Government Opts Out

The Thatcher government, elected in May 1979, believed that loss-making state-owned enterprises were a burden on the economy which should be removed as soon as possible. In the case of British Shipbuilders privatisation was not feasible until the profitability of the company had improved, and there were no immediate steps to withdraw financial support. The corporate plan which had been prepared before the election was approved, and the government agreed to establish an intervention fund of £120m to cover the next two years. The management of British Shipbuilders was strengthened by the appointment as chairman of Robert Atkinson, an experienced businessman who had considerable knowledge of the engineering and shipbuilding industries. One of his first moves was to tighten financial control at the centre while putting stronger pressure on yard managers to increase productivity; he also brought a tougher line to the conduct of industrial relations. By the end of 1980 the order book was looking healthier, and the losses were reduced. Atkinson believed that break-even would be possible by 1983/4.

Employment continued to fall rapidly. The willingness of shipyard workers to accept voluntary redundancy angered some union leaders, but the combination of generous severance payments and the bleak outlook for the industry made it difficult to mobilise resistance. By the start of 1983 some 26,000 jobs had been lost since nationalisation, and in April of that year Atkinson announced plans for a further 9,000 redundancies. This prompted a strong reaction from union leaders, who threatened a campaign of yard occupations along the lines of the UCS sit-in. Implementation of the redundancy plan was deferred until after the election of June 1983, but the convincing Tory victory made it clear that there would be no softening in Mrs Thatcher's hard line. Unlike the miners, who began their ill-fated battle with Mrs Thatcher in 1984, few shipyard workers relished the prospect of an all-out fight with the government.[38]

Relations between Atkinson and the government were uneasy, mainly because of disagreements over the privatisation of the warship yards. Atkinson believed that the politicians were determined to get British Shipbuilders off their hands as quickly as possible, even at the cost of decimating an industry which, in his view, was capable of being rehabilitated, albeit on a smaller scale. Atkinson was succeeded after the 1983 election by Graham Day, the government's original choice to head British Shipbuilders, and privatisation was set in train. By the middle of 1986 Vickers in Barrow, Yarrow on the Clyde and Vosper Thornycroft in Southampton had been sold. Swan Hunter, which since the early 1980s had concentrated mainly on naval vessels, was sold in a management buy-out. National union leaders opposed these sales, but they had little support at the local level. Most workers in the warship yards felt that nationalisation had been a disadvantage for them, since it held wages in the industry below what the naval yards on their own could have justified.

The future of the merchant yards depended on reducing costs and improving productivity. As Day put it, 'The craft basis on which British Shipbuilders has operated – rigid demarcation lines, fierce protection of skills and the like – has to be altered. We've got to get from a craft to a system basis'.[39] With the unions weakened by rising unemployment and a general sense that the continued decline of the industry was inevitable, managerial control over the pace and allocation of work was tightened. At the end of 1983 the Confederation signed an agreement which showed how far the principle of craft control had been eroded. The terms of the agreement provided that 'all employees must be prepared to acquire new skills and to remove customary practices where they are no longer appropriate', and that 'all levels of staff will be interchangeable as required according to their individual skills and experience'.

The reaction of most union members to these changes was resigned acceptance. They recognised that their job security now depended not on their union, but on the commercial viability of the yard where they worked. The two features of the labour relations system that had persisted since the nineteenth century – sectionalism and craft control – were finally crumbling. But the reforms could do little to protect the industry in a market dominated by huge excess capacity. In 1986, when world merchant shipbuilding capacity was estimated at 18m tons, new orders totalled only 9m tons, of which the British share was 2 per cent. There was no prospect of improvement until 1990 at the earliest.

For the Thatcher government, these figures underlined the pointlessness of ploughing money into an industry which seemed likely to make heavy losses for the indefinite future. The remaining merchant yards, the government decided, had to be sold or closed. The Govan yard was bought by the Norwegian Kvaerner group, and Harland & Wolff was sold in a management buy-out, with financial support from Fred Olsen, a leading Norwegian ship-owner. No buyer could be found for North East Shipbuilders (including Austin & Pickersgill), which was closed at the end of 1988.

Subsequent events at Govan provided an interesting commentary both on the industry's earlier history and on the state of the world shipbuilding market in the 1990s. The Norwegian owners brought two things which had been lacking in the yard, and in much of the rest of the industry, throughout the post-war period: a clear product and marketing strategy, and a rigorous approach to the management of labour. The owners were prepared to co-operate with the unions and shop stewards, but only as long as 'the account-ability of the unions and their representatives was properly defined by procedures acceptable to management'.[40] The shop stewards had to recognise that they were 'first and foremost shipyard workers who were under the direct control of supervisors, and, in such a role, they had no authority to control the workforce'. Govan had survived as a loss-making yard for the preceding twenty years, thanks to government support, and it took some time for competitive realities to sink in. In 1991 a strike over three-shift working, called against the advice of the shop stewards, was seen as a last-ditch effort to turn the clock back. The collapse of the strike was a watershed for Kvaerner's labour relations strategy. Meanwhile orders had been secured for four gas carriers. The first of these ships took 2.3m man-hours to build; the fourth took 1m hours, roughly in line with comparable yards overseas.

Yet despite these improvements Govan was competing in an over-supplied market in which fierce competition between Korean and Japanese yards was constantly tending to drive prices down. In 1999 Kvaerner, which had over-extended itself through an ambitious programme of acquisitions in engineering, construction and other industries, decided to put all its European shipyards, including Govan, up for sale. While the withdrawal from shipbuilding was largely due to the internal problems of the Kvaerner group, it was also an indication of the extreme difficulty faced by all the remaining European shipbuilders in building merchant ships at a profit. It is conceivable that if the changes in working practices instituted at Govan in the 1990s had occurred twenty years earlier the yard would have had better prospects of survival, but, as experience in Sweden and other European countries showed, harmonious labour relations were no guarantee of com-mercial success.

Could the Decline Have been Halted?

The shipbuilding story has some similarities to that of cotton textiles described in Chapter 3. Both were large and once-dominant industries. Both faced a disruptive change in their trading environment after the Second World War, arising in one case from the growth of low-cost imports from the developing countries, in the other from the rise of Japan. In both cases memories of the inter-war slump engendered a defensive attitude which discouraged investment and inhibited innovation in design and production methods.

Could the government have done more to help? The first Labour government under Clement Attlee has been criticised by some historians for not doing enough to modernise British industry. But even if the political conditions of the time had been conducive to large-scale government intervention, it was far from clear what form modernisation should take. Civil servants did not have the knowledge or experience to formulate a comprehensive plan for the industry; if they had tried it, the result might well have been misdirected investment on a substantial scale.

A more valid criticism is that when governments did intervene in the 1960s and 1970s, the effect was to delay change. The Geddes committee assumed too readily, in line with the fashion of the time, that the consolidation of the industry into larger groups would improve efficiency. As with the Courtaulds plan for reorganising the textile industry, the committee and the government exaggerated the advantages of size and under-estimated the difficulties of making mergers work. Following the Geddes report, government subsidy was used to preserve existing yards and existing jobs. In the case of the Govan yard, it took the imminent prospect of liquidation and the arrival of new owners to initiate the necessary reforms. It is possible that if British shipbuilders had been faced with a starker choice between adjustment and extinction twenty years earlier, they might have been quicker to tackle their internal inefficiencies and rethink their product and marketing strategies.

The Thatcher government has been attacked on the opposite grounds, that it was too ruthless in denying the industry support and that it failed to consider ways of preserving a small but viable core of merchant shipbuilding capacity. Other European countries, including Germany and France, subsidised their shipbuilding industries during the 1980s and 1990s to a greater extent, and their share of the world market, though far below that of Japan and South Korea, is greater than Britain's. However, these subsidies were largely a response to local political pressures, and there is no indication that they will produce in the long run a commercially successful industry.[41]

Of the three institutional weaknesses referred to in Chapter 1, the financial system and the education system seem largely irrelevant in this case. Labour relations, on the other hand, have been widely regarded as a principal factor in the industry's decline. It is certainly true that the old-established system of craft control was an obstacle to modernisation, and that shipbuilding suffered more than most other British industries from the sectionalism of the trade union movement. But even if labour relations had been drastically reformed in the 1950s – perhaps a move to a single union for all shipyard workers and an end to demarcations between trades – it is far from certain that the industry would have done much better. The fundamental reason for the industry's failure to profit from the boom in world shipping in the 1950s and 1960s lay in the inability of management to adapt their product and marketing strategies to the changed conditions of the post-war world. A few companies, such as Austin & Pickersgill, did adapt successfully, and the trade unions did not prevent them from doing so. Bad labour relations were a contributory factor in the industry's decline, not its central cause.

—•○•—

Steel: The Thatcher Effect

The last chapter described how, in the 1960s and 1970s, successive British governments intervened in an attempt to save the shipbuilding industry from decline. In steel, a much larger industry than shipbuilding and traditionally regarded as even more vital to the economic health of the nation, government intervention was more continuous, and had a more pervasive influence on performance. Nationalised twice and privatised twice, steel was meddled with by politicians to a greater extent than any of the other industries discussed in this book, with the possible exception of aerospace. These were not the best conditions in which to build an efficient, internationally competitive industry, and at the end of the 1970s steel-making in Britain was in a parlous state; the productivity gap between Germany and Britain was wider in steel than in any other major industry.[1] Fortunately the damage was not irreparable. This is a case of an old industry which, unlike shipbuilding, did not fade away, but survived into the 1990s in surprisingly good shape.

1870–1914: An Entrepreneurial Failure?

The early history of the iron and steel industry has some parallels with that of textiles and shipbuilding. But whereas in those two industries British entrepreneurs retained their dominant position in world trade up to the First World War, the steel-makers were overtaken after 1870 by fast-growing competitors in the US and Germany. This is sometimes seen as a classic instance of British industrial failure, attributable to weaknesses which persisted into the inter-war years and beyond.[2]

The story begins with iron-making. Until the invention of the Bessemer converter in 1856, steel was an expensive material which could only be made in small quantities. British inventors led the way in iron-making technology, and in the middle of the nineteenth century Britain was overwhelmingly the largest producer and exporter of iron. But steel was a more resilient, more tenacious and more elastic material, and once the Bessemer converter was fully operational, it began to displace iron in rails, construction and machinery of all kinds. Two other innovations followed: the Siemens-Martin or open-hearth furnace (1867), which was more suitable than the Bessemer converter for making high-quality steel such as shipbuilding plate, and the Thomas or basic process (1879), which eliminated one of the drawbacks of the other two methods, that they could only be used with non-phosphoric iron ore. There were large deposits of phosphoric ore in Continental Europe, notably in Lorraine, and the Thomas process made it possible to exploit this resource.[3]

The arrival of cheap steel came at a time when industrialisation in the US and Germany was gathering pace. Entrepreneurs in these countries, having already mastered the technology of iron-making, had the necessary skills to take up the new steel-making processes. They were also at least as well placed as their British counterparts for raw materials. Germany's Ruhr valley, in Westphalia, contained the richest concentration of coking coal in Continental Europe, and there were other substantial deposits in Upper Silesia and the Saar. After Germany's annexation of part of Lorraine in 1871, following the war with France, German steel-makers also controlled large iron ore reserves. Since these raw materials were even more plentiful in the US, the conditions were ripe in both countries for a rapid increase in steel production.

Domestic demand for steel in Britain was growing more slowly during this period; the British railway network, for example, was largely complete by 1870. The US and Germany were bigger countries and industrialising fast, so it was not surprising that their steel production soon exceeded that of Britain (TABLE 6.1). The only way in which British steel-makers might have retained their lead was by increasing their exports. But access to the two largest and most dynamic markets, those of Germany and the US, was restricted by tariffs, and demand in the rest of the world was too small to compensate.

The German steel industry adopted an aggressive export policy, based on a combination of tariffs and cartels, which British producers were unable to counter. Some regional cartels had been formed in the German iron industry in the 1860s, but as long as imports were allowed in freely it was difficult to maintain pricing discipline among cartel participants. The introduction of tariffs in 1879 partially insulated German steel-makers from import

TABLE 6.1 *Steel production 1880–1913*

(millions of tons)

	Britain	Germany	US
1880	3.9	1.9	4.0
1890	6.2	3.1	7.7
1900	6.5	5.7	13.2
1910	7.9	9.8	28.8
1913	9.4	17.8	34.1

Source: Wirtschaftsvereinigung Stahl, *Statistical Yearbook*, 1992.

competition, and allowed them to establish stronger cartels. The purpose was to keep domestic prices high and stable, so that profits made in the home market could subsidise exports at lower prices.[4] These tactics were greatly resented by British steel-makers, who found themselves losing business to cheap German steel in their home market as well as overseas. But Britain was a free-trading country, and the complaints of the steel-makers did not carry sufficient weight to persuade the government to change course. An increase in steel imports was a small price to pay for preserving the liberal trading order on which the British economy as a whole depended.

In these circumstances a decline in Britain's share of world steel production and exports was unavoidable.[5] Was the decline steeper than it needed to have been because of managerial mistakes? A leading historian of the industry, Duncan Burn, argued that British steel-makers should have followed the German example in making more use of the Thomas process, and that their failure to do so was indicative of the industry's technical incompetence. Burn believed that the reserves of phosphoric ore in the East Midlands were sufficient to support a large steelworks comparable to those being erected by German firms in Lorraine and the Ruhr. If such a works had been built, he claimed, production costs would have been lower, and the industry would have been better equipped to withstand German competition.[6] Subsequent research, however, has shown that metallurgical problems associated with this ore would have made any such project unviable.[7] It was only when these problems had been solved, during and after the First World War, that steel-making on the East Midlands ore field became economic.

The charge of technical backwardness is hard to sustain in view of the British steel industry's continuing prowess in high-quality steels. German shipbuilders preferred to buy British steel plate, despite the tariff, because of its superior quality.[8] In the production of alloy steels, British manufacturers had a technical lead over the US and Germany which persisted until well after the First World War. Robert Hadfield, who invented manganese steel in 1882, was one of several entrepreneurs who helped to give Sheffield an unrivalled reputation in this field.[9] Technical progress was helped by close co-operation with the metallurgy department of Sheffield University, one of the new civic universities which were set up in the closing decades of the nineteenth century to serve the needs of local industry.[10]

The German and American steel industries were younger and growing faster, and more of their investment took place on 'greenfield' sites, whereas expansion in Britain usually took the form of piecemeal additions to existing plants. They were also more likely to integrate the three main manufacturing operations – iron-making, steel-making and steel-rolling – on the same site. Partly for this reason, the leading companies such as Krupp and Thyssen in Germany and Carnegie in the US were bigger than their British counterparts. In the US, though not in Germany, competition law had the paradoxical effect of encouraging the creation of larger companies. The Sherman Anti-trust Act of 1890, by making cartels illegal, stimulated a wave of mergers which transformed the structure of several major industries. In steel Carnegie and several other companies came together in 1901 to form United States Steel Corporation, accounting for two-thirds of the industry's capacity. Most British steel-makers during this period were small and family-owned, and the few mergers which took place generally left the founding families in control. But, as the Sheffield example shows, small size and family ownership did not imply technical or managerial backwardness. Moreover, the nature of the British market, with its requirement for a variety of different sizes and shapes of steel, did not lend itself to giant plants and companies on the US model.

Another aspect of management which some historians see as a source of weakness was the way in which production was organised within the works. Like the textile manufacturers and the shipbuilders, the early British iron-masters delegated to experienced workers responsibility for part of the production process in return for a lump sum based on output. The contractors were the first to organise a strong trade union – the Ironworkers Union, formed in 1868.[11] The contract system was dying out by the end of the nineteenth century, partly because of opposition from a rival union, the Smelters, which represented the underhands (the two unions came together in 1917 to form the Iron and Steel Trades Confederation). But the management of production through self-supervising teams remained a characteristic feature of British steel-making. A two-tier wage structure was negotiated, consisting of a basic wage, linked by a sliding scale to average steel prices, and a tonnage bonus related to the output of individual plants. The bonus enabled the production workers to benefit directly from improvements in productivity, and they became one of the highest paid groups in the country.[12] These arrangements did not include craftsmen engaged on maintenance duties, or unskilled workers, who were paid a fixed daily wage.

Employers liked the sliding scale because it enabled them to reduce wages during business downturns, while the tonnage bonus varied according to each company's ability to pay. The outcome was a stable relationship which helped to make steel an unusually strike-free industry; both sides had a strong interest in maintaining continuity of production. On the other hand, the tonnage bonus, which varied according to the efficiency of each plant, may have made it easier for high-cost producers to survive; if the union had pressed for the equalisation of wages across the industry, obsolete plant might have been closed down more quickly.[13] A more important consequence in the long run was the weak control which employers exercised over the deployment of labour. The seniority system for the process workers was administered by the trade unions, and when new equipment was introduced it was customary to seek the union's prior agreement to manning levels and pay rates.[14]

These practices may have been storing up trouble for the future, but they were not unreformable, and the labour relations system which took shape in iron and steel between 1850 and 1914 was not a block on technical progress. A German historian has concluded that if British steel-makers are to be criticised during this period, it is not for managerial shortcomings, but for their failure to press the government for a firmer response to the protectionist policies of their competitors.[15]

The Inter-war Years

In the years leading up to the First World War the British steel industry was exporting some 40 per cent of its production, and its prosperity was linked to the continued expansion of world trade. In the aftermath of the war prospects for demand at home and abroad looked good, and competition from the Continent seemed likely be less severe than before the war. The return of Lorraine to France under the terms of the Versailles treaty deprived the German steel industry of most of its ore mines and part of its steel-making capacity; it would take several years before production and exports got back to pre-war levels. But the brief post-war boom collapsed in 1921, and the British steel industry was plunged into one of the worst recessions it had ever experienced. Moreover, at a time when protectionist pressures were spreading around the world, Britain was still a free-trading country, and a natural outlet for steel which Continental and American producers could not sell at home.

By the mid-1920s it was clear that steel-making capacity in Britain was far in excess of likely demand. Rationalisation, involving the closure of smaller works and the concentration of production in more modern facilities, was widely agreed to be necessary. A few amalgamations had already taken place – the most important was the creation of United Steel Companies in 1920, bringing together a group of firms based in Sheffield, Lincolnshire and Workington – and merger activity quickened in the late 1920s as the outlook for demand worsened. As in the case of cotton textiles, Montagu Norman, governor of the Bank of England, took an active interest in the reorganisation of the steel industry, partly because he was anxious to avoid direct intervention by the government.[16] In 1927 the Bank helped to set up English Steel Corporation, which pooled the steel-making interests of the three major armaments manufacturers, Vickers, Armstrong-Whitworth and Cammell Laird. Several more ambitious proposals were canvassed, but the companies concerned were reluctant to give up their independence. In the north-east, for example, the logic of combining Dorman Long with its near neighbour on the River Tees, South Durham, was accepted by both sides, but the financial complexity of the proposed merger, together with the difficulty of reconciling a large number of sectional interests, proved an insuperable obstacle.

The issue of rationalisation was closely bound up with protection. The steel-makers argued that there was no incentive to modernise and re-equip as long as other countries were free to dump their surplus steel in Britain. This case was considered in 1929 by a government committee chaired by Lord Sankey. The committee agreed that rationalisation was needed, but rejected protection on the grounds that it would keep inefficient producers alive; the pressure on firms to participate in mergers would be reduced if a tariff was introduced.[17] However, by the time the committee reported, the world depression was deepening and demands for protection were becoming irresistible. A general tariff of 10 per cent was introduced in 1932, but steel was deemed to be a special case, justifying a higher duty of 33⅓ per cent.

The government hoped that the introduction of the tariff would produce a more stable environment in which industries which were suffering from excess capacity could reorganise themselves. A committee of civil servants, the Import Duties Advisory Committee (IDAC), was set up to supervise the industries concerned and to ensure that rationalisation took place. This was a new departure in government policy, a shift from Victorian *laissez-faire* to regulated competition based on a partnership between the state and industry. To make the partnership work, stronger trade associations were needed to exert tighter control over individual firms and to act as interlocutors with the government. The British Iron and Steel Federation was formed in 1934 to take over some of the authority previously exercised by regional trade associations. One of its tasks was to operate a price maintenance scheme under the supervision of IDAC. In 1935 the government encouraged the Federation to join the International Steel Cartel, which had been formed by the leading Continental steel-makers two years earlier.

Part of the purpose of these arrangements was to facilitate rationalisation, but neither the Federation nor IDAC had the power to enforce mergers, and only limited progress was made. In Scotland Colvilles acquired several smaller firms and by the end of the 1930s this company controlled about 80 per cent of the region's steel-making capacity.[18] There was also some consolidation in the South Wales tinplate trade under the leadership of William Firth, chairman of the largest producer, Richard Thomas. But these moves fell short of the sweeping reorganisation which many observers felt was necessary, and by the time of the Second World War the industry was only slightly less fragmented than it had been twenty years earlier. The three largest firms – United Steel, Colvilles and Dorman Long – each accounted for 12–13 per cent of the industry's production.

The slow pace of rationalisation appeared to confirm the views of those who had warned that the reduction of competition, through tariffs and cartels, would preserve the status quo. But the steel-makers were not necessarily wrong to take a cautious view of what mergers could achieve. To have embarked on large-scale amalgamations in the depths of the Depression would have been extremely risky; it was impossible to predict the revival of demand that occurred, mainly because of rearmament, in the second half of the 1930s.[19] Moreover, the industry's inter-war performance cannot be judged simply on the basis of how many mergers took place. The most encouraging development was the willingness of several firms to launch ambitious investment projects. Stewarts & Lloyds, the steel tube manufacturers, built a large integrated works at Corby in Northamptonshire to exploit the East Midlands ore fields. Richard Thomas installed Britain's first continuous wide strip mill at Ebbw Vale in South Wales. This was a new process which had been developed in the US to produce sheet steel on a large scale, principally for cars, domestic appliances and the canning industry. The British motor industry grew rapidly during the 1920s, partially offsetting the decline in traditional steel-using industries such as shipbuilding, and William Firth believed there was sufficient demand to support at least one wide strip mill; his persistence eventually overcame the opposition of other steel-makers to the project.[20] Work on a second strip mill, at John Summers' Shotton works in North Wales, began in 1939.

These projects contributed to a partial modernisation of the industry. There was modernisation, too, in management and organisation. Although many of the leading firms continued to be controlled by the owning families, professional managers were playing a larger role. For example, Robert Hilton, appointed managing director of United Steel in 1928, was a capable engineer who reorganised what had previously been a loosely run group, and under his direction United Steel became the best-managed firm in the industry; Hilton had previously been in charge of Metropolitan Vickers, one of the leading electrical equipment manufacturers. Another outstanding manager was Allan Macdiarmid, who joined Stewarts & Lloyds as a chartered accountant in 1909, was appointed company secretary, and worked his way up to become chairman. He steered Stewarts & Lloyds into a dominant position in the steel tube trade, supported by low-cost steel-making at Corby.[21] Macdiarmid was one of several ex-accountants who rose to senior positions in industry during this period.[22]

Meanwhile the German steel industry, which had been a formidable rival in export markets before the war, faced great difficulties in the inter-war years. To make up for the loss of Lorraine, a large capital spending programme was set in train in the Ruhr, but the expansion went too far, and by the mid-1920s action was needed to reduce surplus capacity. In 1926 twelve firms came together to form a giant steel trust, Vereinigte Stahlwerke (Vestag), controlling about half the industry's production. Thyssen was the prime mover behind this enterprise, which was modelled on United States Steel Corporation and partly financed by American capital.[23] The aim was to cut out duplication and close down obsolete plant. But, although some rationalisation was carried out after the merger, the concentration of the industry did little to improve its competitiveness. With fewer firms to keep in line, cartels were easier to enforce. The absence of price competition, together with continuing protection against imports, weakened the incentive for firms to specialise in the products where they had the lowest costs. When demand recovered in the second half of the 1930s, the priority was to maximise production from existing plant. Of the 418 rolling mills which were operating in Germany at the end of the decade, 300 had been built before the First World War; only one wide strip mill was built, at Dinslaken in the Ruhr.[24]

The inter-war period checked the advance of the German steel industry and allowed British steel-makers to recover some of the ground they had lost before 1914. Although the average size of German plants was slightly larger than in Britain, there was no great difference between the two industries in terms of overall productivity.[25] The productivity leader, by a wide margin, was the US. Not only was the US the largest steel-making nation (TABLE 6.2), with opportunities for economies of scale which were not available in Europe, but American steel-makers also benefited from the

TABLE 6.2 *Steel production 1913–39*

(millions of tons)

	US	Britain	Germany	France
1913	34.1	9.4	17.8	5.1
1920	44.7	9.9	8.6	3.8
1925	47.1	7.8	12.2	9.1
1931	26.4	5.3	8.3	9.4
1939	47.9	13.4	23.3	8.0

Source: Wirtschaftsvereinigung Stahl, *Statistical Yearbook*, 1992.

presence of a dynamic, technically demanding and fast-growing customer, the motor industry. By the end of the 1930s there were twenty-eight continuous wide strip mills in operation in the US.

To get closer to the American level of efficiency, European steel-makers needed a market as large and competitive as that of the US. As it was, the proliferation of cartels and tariffs limited the scope for intra-European trade in steel, and made the larger European industries more dependent on their domestic markets. In the British case, thanks to the system of imperial preference introduced after the Ottawa conference in 1932, the steel-makers had access to partially protected Empire and Commonwealth markets; this provided a useful addition to demand, although exports amounted to only 12 per cent of production during the 1930s. The British steel industry was largely insulated from international competition, but this was also true of Germany, where there was a much longer tradition of tariffs and cartels.

Steel is not an industry where the legacy of the past imposed a uniquely heavy burden on British manufacturers. All the European steel-making countries would have an equal opportunity to narrow the productivity gap with the US when the external environment became more favourable. How quickly they did so would depend, not on history, but on the policies adopted by companies and governments after 1945.

1945–60: The Post-war Boom

For the first fifteen years after the Second World War European steel-makers enjoyed a period of unprecedented prosperity in which demand for steel persistently outran supply. The priorities were to tackle the backlog of underinvestment which had been left by the war, and to raise productivity closer to the US level. With the rapid growth in demand for cars, there was greater scope for introducing the wide strip mills which had been pioneered in the US. An additional stimulus to investment in the second half of the 1950s was the invention of a new steel-making process, the basic oxygen furnace, which used less fuel, less capital and less labour than the older steel-making techniques. Basic oxygen steel-making was well suited for large-scale production, and its introduction hastened the closure of smaller plants.

Of the leading European steel-making nations, Britain seemed at the end of the war best placed to exploit these opportunities. The industry had suffered little damage from bombing; the new plants built in the 1930s were in good working order; and detailed planning for the post-war development of the industry was under way. In Germany the revival of steel production was delayed by political and economic uncertainty; it was not until the early 1950s that the structure and ownership of the steel industry in what had become West Germany were settled. The French steel-makers were quicker to get back into full production, but France had been a laggard in this field before the war; a notoriously conservative industry had to be shaken out of its old ways.

When Winston Churchill's coalition government began examining the future of the steel industry in 1943, a central issue was whether the regulatory arrangements which had been put in place in the 1930s should be retained. Some economists in Whitehall argued that cartels and protection were a recipe for inefficiency, and that competition should be given freer rein. But this was a minority view. The advantages of co-operation between industry and government had been reinforced by the war. Central planning worked well, and the British Iron and Steel Federation acquired more authority over member firms. The main debate was between those, including the leaders of the Federation, who favoured self-regulation under government super-vision, and those who wanted a stronger role for the government.[26] The Labour Party's position – and that of the principal trade union, the Iron and Steel Trades Confederation – was that the industry should be brought into public ownership. A joint study carried out by the Board of Trade and the Ministry of Supply at the end of 1944 accepted the Federation's view that the industry should be protected against imports for at least the first five years after the war and that price controls should be retained. In reaching this conclusion the civil servants were impressed by the apparent eagerness of the industry's leaders to press ahead quickly with modernisation. The Federation was then asked to prepare a development plan, which was pre-sented to the newly elected Labour government at the end of 1945 and approved a few months later.

The plan called for an expenditure of £168m over a seven-year period to renew some 40 per cent of the industry's capacity.[27] A third strip mill, in addition to the existing mills at Ebbw Vale and Shotton, was to be built at Port Talbot in South Wales by the newly formed Steel Company of Wales, in which Richard Thomas & Baldwins[28] and several other sheet and tinplate producers were shareholders. Two other integrated works were proposed for the East Midlands and Scotland, and several of the rationalisation schemes which had been left outstanding from the 1930s were revived. The plan was put together by the Federation out of projects submitted by its member companies. However, the companies were not necessarily committed to the projects contained in the plan. Some of the rationalisation proposals involved difficult negotiations between long-standing local rivals. Moreover, steel was in short supply, and the quickest way to raise output was to patch and mend existing plant.[29] The Federation had no powers of compulsion, and it could not prevent investment from being spread over a larger number of sites than had been envisaged in the plan.

Meanwhile the industry was engaged in a political battle over public ownership. Because of the complexity of steel nationalisation, the government excluded it from the first wave of nationalisation measures which covered coal, gas, electricity and the railways. As an interim measure an Iron and Steel Board was set up in 1946 to advise the government on the progress of the development plan, working closely with the Federation. Early in 1947, when the nationalisation bill was about to be put before Parliament, the Federation suggested a compromise, whereby the Board would be strengthened and given the power to acquire shares in individual steel companies. Some senior members of the Cabinet had been uneasy about steel nationalisation from the start, and they welcomed the Federation's proposal as a way of ensuring effective state control without the cost of a full-scale take-over. However, pressure from the left of the party, which regarded steel nationalisation as a test of the government's commitment to socialism, proved too strong for any halfway house to be acceptable.[30]

The nationalisation bill, after lengthy delays in the House of Lords, was enacted in 1949. Implementation was delayed until after the 1950 election, which Labour won with a much reduced majority, and the Iron and Steel Corporation of Great Britain began operations early in 1951. The chairman, Steven Hardie (former chairman of the British Oxygen Company), intended to reorganise the industry into seven regional groups, but the life of the Corporation was too short for any such plan to be put into effect.[31] Within less than a year another election was held, which the Conservatives won, and they promptly set about denationalising the industry.

The political battle over nationalisation was fought with much passion, but there were fewer differences between the parties than the rhetoric suggested. Both sides accepted the steel-makers' argument that steel was not a normal industry; with its large, capital-intensive plants, and its vulnerability to ruinous price competition when demand was weak, some form of regulation was thought to be unavoidable. The issue was whether regulation would be more effective under public or private ownership. Thus in 1950, when Britain was invited to join the European Coal and Steel Community

(ECSC), the idea of exposing steel to competition in a wider European market held no appeal for the government.[32] The steel-makers had no interest in Ruhr coking coal or Lorraine iron ore, and most of their export trade was with the Commonwealth; closer links with Europe were at best irrelevant and at worst disruptive. When another opportunity for closer association with the ECSC came up in 1954, the Conservative government's position was much the same as that of its Labour predecessor.[33]

The return of the steel companies to private ownership began in 1953 and was largely complete by 1957.[34] The only major producer left in the public sector was Richard Thomas & Baldwins; this firm was planning a large new steelworks and its shares were not easily saleable. Denationalisation did not involve any significant changes in the structure of the industry, although two small plants were bought by a newcomer to steel-making – Tube Investments, an engineering group – and the Steel Company of Wales was detached from its original shareholders as an independent quoted company. The Conservatives set up a new Iron and Steel Board to control prices and monitor the capital spending programme. The Board set maximum prices on a selected range of products, mainly semi-finished steel; price-fixing agreements ensured that these were normally the prices charged. On capital investment, the Board's prior approval was required for schemes costing more than £100,000, but it could not force companies to do things which they did not want to do.

This controlled environment, together with the seller's market for steel which prevailed for most of the 1950s, did nothing to encourage radical change in the way the industry was run. The focus was on increasing production rather than reducing costs. The patch-and-mend policy which had been adopted by several firms in the early post-war years meant that a number of older, poorly located plants had been expanded, and less rationalisation took place than had been envisaged in the Federation's 1946 development plan. Everyone was aware that productivity in British steel-making fell far short of the US level, and this was confirmed in 1952 when a team of managers and employees visited American steel companies under the auspices of the Anglo-American Council on Productivity.[35] Their report showed that output per man was between two and three times higher than in Britain, mainly because the average size of plant was larger. While recognising that the smaller domestic market imposed limits on how far British steel-makers could go in the American direction, the team set down minimum sizes for blast furnaces and steel-making equipment to guide future investment decisions. But to put these recommendations into practice would require the closure of smaller plants, many of which had been partially modernised since 1945 and were making money for their owners. There was no incentive for these firms to abide by the productivity team's guidelines.

The American advantage derived not just from larger plants, but also from lower manning levels. When Steel Company of Wales managers visited Inland Steel in Chicago in 1955, they saw 'many instances of one man doing what our trade unions would require three to do, and each craftsman assigned to departmental maintenance was able to turn his hands to fitting work, electrical repairs, welding and so on as required'.[36] But the chairman of the company declined to act on their report for fear of opposition from the trade unions. This was not because the steel unions were especially militant. On the contrary, the stability which had characterised the industry's labour relations since the nineteenth century continued throughout the Second World War and into the 1950s. But it was a stability based on a privileged position for the production workers' union, the Iron and Steel Trades Confederation. Other unions, representing craftsmen, blastfurnacemen and unskilled workers, resented the ISTC's high wages, and the employers had no wish to exacerbate these tensions. As long as they could sell all the steel they could make, it was better to leave the status quo on the shop floor undisturbed. Booming demand and persistent labour shortages put the unions in a strong bargaining position, and the employers were willing to make concessions on pay and manning levels in order to keep production going. The Port Talbot strip mill, in particular, which began full production in 1951, was notoriously overmanned; it was regarded by the unions as 'a treasure island with a permanently filled pot of gold'.[37]

The political climate of the 1950s did not favour confrontation with the unions. The Conservative governments which held office from 1951 to 1964 attached a high priority to full employment and social peace. Ministers were particularly concerned with the so-called depressed areas, which had suffered badly from high unemployment in the inter-war years. When plans for a fourth strip mill were being considered in 1957, a choice had to be made between two rival schemes, one from Colvilles in Scotland and the other from Richard Thomas & Baldwins in South Wales. The government was directly involved, partly because of regional policy considerations, partly because it was being asked to provide part of the finance. Richard Thomas was still state-owned, and the project was too big for Colvilles to finance entirely out of its own resources. The outcome was a Solomon-like judgement by Harold Macmillan, the Prime Minister, to split the project between Ravenscraig, adjacent to Colvilles' existing works, and a coastal site at

Llanwern, near Newport, in South Wales. The Ravenscraig mill was linked to the planned development of steel-using industries in Scotland, including a car assembly plant.[38]

The strip mill decision appeased the regional lobbies at the cost of depriving the industry of the economies which a single works would have provided. As one commentator wrote, 'the greatest economic advantage would be sacrificed deliberately in the interests of immediate social comfort and convenience'.[39] It was to some extent a repetition of the political battle which had taken place in the 1930s over the location of the first strip mill. Firth's original plan had been to build the works at Immingham in Lincolnshire, but he came under intense political and trade union pressure not to desert South Wales, where Richard Thomas was a large employer. Ebbw Vale was an awkward, inland site which had many disadvantages compared to Immingham.

Thus the partnership between industry and government which was re-established after denationalisation did nothing to alter the insularity of steel policy in Britain. Yet there was no sense at the end of the 1950s that the steel-makers were failing the nation. Prices were lower than on the Continent and the problem of shortages was easing. Even if the objectives set out in the first development plan had not been fulfilled, a substantial investment programme had been carried through, and it included some impressive projects – among them the Port Talbot strip mill, Dorman Long's universal beam mill at Lackenby on Teesside, and a major iron-making expansion by United Steel at Scunthorpe in Lincolnshire.[40] But, apart from the brief interlude of nationalisation, the organisation and management of the British steel industry, the character of domestic competition and the pattern of overseas trade showed a high degree of continuity with the 1930s. In France and Germany there was a sharper break with the past.

For reasons explained in Chapter 3, the steel industry was central to the drive for industrial modernisation which began in France immediately after the war. The two priorities were to expand the industry's capacity and to prevent, or at least to delay, the revival of steel-making in the Ruhr. Thus France would have first call on German coal, and French steel-makers would take over markets that had previously been supplied from Germany.[41] Plans for the country's first wide strip mill, to be built at Denain in northern France, were announced in 1946 by two companies which later merged to form Usinor. In the following year, responding to pressure from Jean Monnet's Planning Commission (and from Renault, which threatened to build its own strip mill), several Lorraine firms, led by de Wendel, established a consortium called Sollac to build a second strip mill. By this time the Marshall Plan was in operation, and the Sollac project was one of the largest recipients of American aid.[42]

There was a long tradition of price-fixing in French steel, and the industry had been orientated almost entirely to the domestic market. The effect of the European Coal and Steel Community (which was opposed by most French steel-makers) was to break down the parochialism of the industry and force it to plan for a wider European market. The new strip mills, for example, supplied large quantities of sheet steel to the German car-makers during the 1950s. The ECSC also adopted the American 'basing point' pricing system, which allowed greater scope for price competition than the controls exercised by the Iron and Steel Board in Britain.[43] On the other hand, structural change in French steel-making proceeded more slowly than the planners had hoped. A few mergers took place after the Community was formed, but they did not lead to much physical rationalisation; as in Britain, many firms preferred to patch and mend rather than instal new equipment.[44] There was also a growing problem arising from the high cost of Lorraine iron ore. During the 1950s low-cost deposits of coking coal and iron ore were opened up in countries such as Australia and Brazil, and steel-makers in Europe and elsewhere began to shift from inland locations to coastal sites where they could use imported raw materials. Finsider in Italy, Hoogovens in Holland and Klöckner in Germany were among the first European firms to build large coastal works. In 1956 Usinor decided to follow their example, announcing plans for a new works at Dunkirk. For the Lorraine firms a move to the coast was much more difficult, since it would involve closures and redundancies in a region to which they had a long historical commitment, and where they were by far the largest employers.

A more serious weakness was the industry's dependence on the state for funds. The steel companies were under-capitalised at the end of the war, and modernisation was partly financed by the government. During the 1950s, when the industry should have been able to wean itself off state support, profitability was held back by price controls. Contrary to the rules laid down in the Treaty of Paris, the French government intervened in the industry's pricing decisions in order to keep inflation down, and this kept profit margins low.

While a partial modernisation of the French steel industry was getting under way in the late 1940s, the revival of steel-making in Germany was held back by the policies of the occupying powers. As part of the drive for deconcentration and decartelisation, the American occupation authorities were determined to break the pre-war colossus, Vestag, into smaller pieces.[45] The Federal government was equally anxious to ensure that the break-up was not so drastic as to make the successor companies unviable. The eventual compromise, which came during the negotiations over the Coal and Steel Community in 1950–1951, called for the division of Vestag into thirteen separate companies. Ten others made up the rest of the industry, and most of the vertical links between coal and steel were broken.[46] Subsequent mergers in the second half of the 1950s reduced the number of ex-Vestag companies to four – Thyssen, Phoenix-Rheinrohr, Rheinstahl and Dortmund-Hörde Hütten Union (DHHU) – which accounted for about 35 per cent of German steel production. Most of the remaining 65 per cent came from five other large companies – Hoesch, Klöckner, Mannesmann, Hüttenwerk Oberhausen and Krupp. This was a more competitive structure than had existed before the war, encouraging the companies to specialise in sectors of the market where they had a competitive advantage, rather than spread themselves across a wide range of steel products.[47]

Once the issues of structure and ownership had been settled, the steel companies were free to set in train a programme of expansion and modernisation. Apart from Klöckner's works at Bremen on the North Sea coast, which started up in 1958, this took the form of repairing and re-equipping existing works. Most of the industry's capacity survived the war intact, and there were few new projects on greenfield sites. The German steel-makers also received much less support from the Marshall Plan than their French and British competitors. Finance for modernisation came in part from a levy on steel-using industries, proposed by the steel users themselves and effected through the Investment Aid Law of 1952. This measure has been described as West Germany's equivalent of the Monnet Plan,[48] but it did not imply any continuing government involvement in financing the industry. The steel-makers were soon profitable enough to finance their investments without recourse to the state. Only one company, Salzgitter, which had been built under the Nazi regime to exploit the low-grade ores of Lower Saxony, was government-owned.

Of the three countries, it was West Germany, which, thanks in part to pressure from the US, went furthest in correcting the steel industry's pre-war weaknesses. It was also in West Germany that the government played the least intrusive role in the industry's affairs. In the short term these policies ensured that the industry made a full contribution to the German economic miracle; steel production increased at a spectacular rate from the early 1950s (TABLE 6.3). In the longer term the new order helped the German steel

TABLE 6.3 *Steel production 1950–60*

(million tons)

	Germany	Britain	France	Italy
1950	12.1	16.6	10.6	2.4
1955	21.3	20.1	15.8	5.5
1960	34.1	24.7	17.3	8.5

Source: Wirtschaftsvereinigung Stahl, *Statistical Yearbook*, 1992.

industry respond more effectively than its French and British counterparts to the more difficult market conditions of the 1960s and 1970s.

The 1960s and 1970s: Slowdown and Crisis

In the early 1960s, after a decade of almost uninterrupted expansion, the European steel industry entered a period of slower growth. Post-war reconstruction was over and steel-making capacity had caught up with demand. Outside Europe, the Japanese steel industry was emerging as a formidable competitor (TABLE 6.4). Lacking indigenous raw materials of their own, Japanese companies invested in large, coastal plants fed by imported coking coal and iron ore.[49] As a late-comer to industrialisation, Japan had less old equipment to scrap, and Japanese companies were quicker than their Western counterparts to take up basic oxygen steel-making and the new technique of continuous casting – a way of eliminating the ingot stage in steel-rolling. In 1965 more than half of Japan's steel was made by the basic oxygen method, compared with less than 20 per cent in the US and Western Europe. Developing countries such as South Korea and Brazil were also building up their steel industries during this period, adding to the surplus of world steel-making capacity. Some of this surplus found its way to Europe, putting downward pressure on prices.

In Britain return on capital in the fourteen largest companies dropped from 15 per cent in the late 1950s to an average of 6 per cent between 1961

TABLE 6.4 *Shares of world steel exports 1950–71*

(per centage of total exports from principal exporting countries)

	1950	1960	1969	1971
Britain	15.1	7.9	6.6	5.2
France	20.7	13.8	11.1	8.1
Germany	11.0	20.0	16.1	14.0
US	16.3	6.9	3.8	2.8
Japan	3.4	5.8	12.7	23.3

Source: French Ministry of Industry, *La Division internationale du travail*, 1976, vol. 1, p. 143, quoted in Diana Green, *Managing Industrial Change: French Policies to Promote Industrial Adjustment*, Department of Industry, HMSO, 1981.

and 1965.[50] The response was to look for ways of raising productivity, both by reforming work practices and by closing down obsolete plant more quickly. Several companies tried to tackle overmanning, a legacy of lax management in the 1950s, by using the technique of productivity bargaining that Esso had pioneered at its Fawley refinery in 1960. The Steel Company of Wales called in the American consultants who had worked on the Fawley agreement, and they recommended a thorough overhaul of the wage structure and manning arrangements. But the presence of several competing unions made negotiations slow and cumbersome, and only minor concessions were agreed.[51] Like some other British industries, the steel industry was finding that inter-union rivalry was an obstacle to change. A particular source of tension in steel was the resentment the craft unions felt over the superior status and pay of the production workers represented by the Iron and Steel Trades Confederation (ISTC). As employers sought to modify time-honoured work practices, the labour relations harmony on which the industry had prided itself began to fade.

The other way of reducing costs was to concentrate production on the most efficient plants, and this raised the old question of how best to promote inter-company rationalisation. During the 1960s mergers and take-overs were running at a high level in Britain, but steel was almost entirely unaffected. It was not an attractive industry for outsiders to enter, partly because of price control, partly because of the threat of re-nationalisation if Labour returned to power. For the same reasons, the established steel companies had little incentive to expand by acquisition. The Iron and Steel Board pressed the Macmillan government for additional powers to enforce rationalisation, but without success.[52]

The Labour victory in the 1964 election brought public ownership of steel back on to the political agenda. But Labour had an overall majority in the House of Commons of only four, and some of its MPs, notably Woodrow Wyatt and Desmond Donnelly, were strongly opposed to steel nationalisation. But if the steel-makers thought the issue would go away, they were disabused of this idea when Harold Wilson called a second election in 1966 and won a more convincing majority. Now the threat of nationalisation was real, and the British Iron and Steel Federation responded, somewhat belatedly, by commissioning Sir Henry Benson, a respected accountant, to examine ways in which the industry might be rationalised under private ownership.[53] The Benson report, published in July 1966, called for a concentration of bulk steel-making on the five largest and most modern works – Port Talbot and Llanwern in South Wales, Scunthorpe in Lincolnshire, Lackenby in the north-east and Ravenscraig in Scotland.[54] All these works would be equipped with basic oxygen steel-making, and some 9m tons of obsolete capacity would be closed down. This would involve a reduction in the labour force from 317,000 to 215,000 over a ten-year period. A second stage of the Benson committee's work, which was completed but not published, outlined the mergers and amalgamations which would be necessary in order to facilitate rationalisation.

The Federation hoped that these proposals might be the basis for a compromise, perhaps involving the state acquiring a stake in some or all of the new groups. But as in the 1940s the Labour Party's ideological commitment to nationalisation proved too strong for any halfway house to be acceptable. In 1967 the fourteen largest companies, accounting for 90 per cent of the industry's crude steel production, were nationalized to form British Steel. This time nationalisation was more than an interlude. Steel was to remain in the public sector for the next twenty years.

Lord Melchett, British Steel's first chairman, was a merchant banker who had no previous connection with steel. (His grandfather, Alfred Mond, the first Lord Melchett, was one of the founders of ICI). His deputy and closest colleague was Monty Finniston, a pugnacious Glaswegian whose background was in metallurgical research. Neither of these men had any experience of running large companies. As a starting-point for modernisation, Melchett accepted the Benson committee's view that bulk steel-making should be concentrated in the five existing large works, but in 1970 this 'heritage' principle was superseded by a more radical approach. Finniston visited Japan in that year, and he returned with a burning conviction that giant plants on the Japanese model would have to be built if Britain was to remain one of the leading steel-making nations. Other managers were sceptical, believing that Germany, with its older and more highly developed steel industry, was a more appropriate model. But Melchett shared Finniston's view and in 1971 British Steel produced a corporate plan which included provision for a new greenfield works with an eventual capacity of 12m tonnes a year. This was part of a massive investment programme which would increase capacity from 28m tonnes in 1971 to 35m tonnes in 1975 and 43m tonnes in 1980. In addition to the new works, a 'brownfield' works would be built at Redcar in the north-east, close to the existing Lackenby works, with a capacity of 6m tonnes. The five 'heritage' works would also be enlarged to provide a further 20m tonnes of capacity, and the remaining tonnage would come from the smaller alloy and special steel plants. It was a 'big bang' strategy, designed to make up for the under-investment of the pre-nationalisation years.

In 1970, while these plans were taking shape, the political climate changed with the election of a Conservative government under Edward Heath. The new administration was ideologically opposed to nationalisation, but decided that to privatise British Steel would be too disruptive at a time when a large capital spending programme was in prospect; only a few peripheral activities were sold off.[55] However, the Prime Minister and his colleagues had no great respect for British Steel's management – profits since nationalisation had been poor – and took a sceptical view of the expansion programme. After lengthy debate between the government and the company agreement was reached in 1973 on a ten-year development plan that accepted the broad thrust of British Steel's strategy.[56] Although the greenfield works was dropped, the new Teesside complex was approved, as were the plans to enlarge the five 'heritage' works. The aim was to increase capacity to 33–35m tonnes of steel by the late 1970s, rising to 36–38m tonnes in the first half of the 1980s. These increases hinged on the assumption that domestic demand for steel would grow faster in the 1970s than in the 1960s, and that British Steel would substantially increase its exports, especially in Europe. Britain had become a member of the EEC at the start of 1973, and a market which had previously been regarded as marginal was now seen as central to the industry's future.

The labour implications were far-reaching. British Steel would have to close a large number of obsolete works and ensure that manning levels in the plants which remained were in line with best international practice. The less well-sited integrated works would either be completely closed or, like Corby, Shotton and Ebbw Vale, converted into finishing mills; at Shotton the end of steel-making would mean the loss of some 7,000 jobs. The publication of the ten-year plan sparked widespread local protests, with several plants organising action groups to campaign against British Steel's proposals. The national unions were in an awkward position. The traditionally moderate ISTC argued that the unions should not stand in the way of modernisation, but should concentrate on securing the best possible terms for their members. The union's general secretary, Dai Davies, insisted that nationalisation should not be regarded as 'a formula for preserving the status quo'.[57] But the Transport and General Workers Union, representing semi-skilled and unskilled workers, rejected British Steel's strategy and urged its members to resist it.

A year after the publication of the development plan British Steel was faced with another swing of the political pendulum when Labour was returned to power in the 1974 election. The new Industry Secretary, Tony Benn, was on the left of the Party and close to the trade unions. Within a few months of taking office he asked one of his junior ministers, Lord Beswick, to review British Steel's closure programme. Lord Beswick recommended that several plants which had been earmarked for closure, including Shotton, should be kept open for a few more years and that decisions on some of the expansion schemes should be deferred.

For Monty Finniston, who had taken over as chairman after the death of Lord Melchett in May 1973, this was the start of a stormy relationship with the government, culminating in a much-publicised row with Benn in April 1975.[58] Finniston had just announced plans to reduce British Steel's labour force of 220,000 by 20,000; more provocatively, he indicated that in the long run the company would need only 50,000 employees to produce 37m tonnes of steel. While Benn refused to accept that redundancies were necessary on this scale, Finniston insisted that British Steel could not become viable as long as its productivity was so far out of line with that of its overseas competitors (TABLE 6.5). Although the productivity lag was mainly due to the long tail of obsolete plants, the five largest works were also seriously overmanned. British Steel sought the consent of the unions to improvements in working practices, but even when national agreements were reached,

TABLE 6.5 *Comparative labour productivity in 1975*

(tonnes of crude steel per man year)

Company	Country	Productivity
Nippon Steel	Japan	520
Thyssen	Germany	370
Kawasaki	Japan	350
National Steel	US	280
Arbed	Luxembourg	205
Bethlehem	US	180
Hoogovens	Netherlands	150
British Steel	UK	122

Source: British Steel Corporation.

further negotiations had to take place at the local level and little progress was made.

The overmanning issue was of particular urgency since the UK economy had moved into recession in 1974 and steel demand was falling away at an alarming rate. The recession was a worldwide phenomenon, caused in part by the doubling of oil prices by the Organisation of Petroleum Exporting Countries, and it hit the steel industry with exceptional force. Britain was not the only country where the steel producers were expanding their capacity, and much of the new plant came on stream in the second half of the 1970s, just as the world economy was slowing down. To make matters worse for British Steel, entry into the Common Market was exposing the industry to serious import competition for the first time.

Slowly the realisation dawned that the industry was experiencing something more than a cyclical downturn, and that the expansion plan agreed in 1973 would have to be rethought. In 1976 the government replaced Finniston with Charles Villiers, who was regarded as more sympathetic – he had served the previous Labour government as managing director of the Industrial Reorganisation Corporation. But by mid-1977, faced with escalating losses and no prospect of an early improvement in demand, Villiers reached the reluctant conclusion that 'dramatic decisions' were necessary.[59] The original target of more than 30m tonnes of capacity was slashed to 15m tonnes, and British Steel sought to make itself profitable at that level.

The era of wishful thinking was over. In 1976 the government had been forced by a balance of payments crisis to negotiate a rescue package with the International Monetary Fund and to impose strict curbs on public spending. Subsidies for loss-making nationalised industries had to be cut back. Eric Varley, a more pragmatic politician who had taken over from Tony Benn as Industry Secretary in the summer of 1975, authorised British Steel to negotiate the closure of plants that had been reprieved in the Beswick review. In March 1978 the government published a White Paper called 'The Road to Viability', which formally abandoned the 1973 development plan.[60] The focus of the White Paper was on improvements in operating efficiency. The trade unions were urged to co-operate in building 'a profitable, high-wage, high-productivity industry comparable to its major competitors'. This would require 'very substantial improvements' in working practices.

The initial batch of closures following the change of course was handled without much difficulty, mainly because of generous redundancy payments. But resistance at the bigger plants, especially Corby and Shotton, was likely to be tougher, and relations with the unions, at national and local level, were uneasy. British Steel was still incurring heavy losses, and viability was a long way off.

This was the legacy which Labour handed over to Margaret Thatcher's Conservative government in May 1979. Even allowing for the suddenness of the collapse of demand in the mid-1970s, the industry's record under public ownership had been poor. Although some useful modernisation was carried out in the first few years after nationalisation (notably the replacement of open-hearth furnaces by basic oxygen steel-making in the large works), Melchett and Finniston had put too much emphasis on big new plants at the expense of improving efficiency in existing ones. Like Frank Kearton's grand design for the textile industry, it was a technocratic, production-led vision which paid insufficient regard to the customer. Investment in finishing mills was neglected and there was an increasing number of complaints, notably from the car-makers, about quality; Ford switched some of its orders for steel sheet from British Steel to Hoogovens in Holland.

Nationalisation had also done little to improve labour relations. Soon after the corporation was established worker directors were appointed to each of the four regional groups, but British Steel was no more successful than the private-sector companies in dealing with the problem of labour productivity. The breakdown in the traditionally harmonious relationship between employers and unions was partly due to the changes in technology and plant configuration which took place during the 1960s, before and after nationalisation. These changes 'posed a real and bewildering personal threat to what had been regarded since the 1930s as employment in a secure and stable industry'.[61] Conflict between rival unions exacerbated the situation.[62] British Steel had to deal with no less than eighteen unions – the ISTC, the National Union of Blastfurnacemen, fourteen craft unions (grouped together in the National Craftsmen's Co-ordinating Committee) and two general unions.[63] The theoretical attractions of a single industrial union were obvious to all, but the weight of history was against it.

By the 1970s the number of labour disputes in steel was running at well above the average for manufacturing industry. An extreme example was a pay dispute in 1975 involving the ISTC and the Blastfurnacemen, which delayed the blowing-in of a new blast furnace for several months.[64] When Charles Villiers was appointed chairman, he proposed a wide-ranging 'steel contract' which would allow the unions to participate more fully in the company's decisions; the plan included a German-style supervisory board on which workers would be represented. But despite spending 'endless time and effort' on the contract, he failed to persuade the unions to accept it.[65]

Nationalisation almost certainly made the industry's adjustment to the post-1975 crisis more difficult than it would have been under private ownership. Yet France, following a middle way between nationalisation and the free market, did at least as badly. The performance of the French steel industry in the 1970s was a disaster for French industrial policy.[66]

At the start of the 1960s a partial modernisation was under way, but the industry was slow to take up basic oxygen steel-making, and many plants, especially in Lorraine, were far too small. Profitability in the industry was low, and the level of indebtedness to the government was uncomfortably high. In 1966 Jacques Ferry, the influential head of the steel producers' trade association, the Chambre Syndicale de la Sidérurgie Française, persuaded the government to put its relationship with the industry on a new footing. In return for long-term financial support from the state, the steel-makers committed themselves to a programme of modernisation which included, among other things, the concentration of the industry around two 'poles' – one in the north, based on Usinor, and the other in Lorraine, where the two leading producers joined forces to form Wendel-Sidelor (later Sacilor). The recovery in demand in 1968 gave the industry the confidence to embark on a series of new projects, of which by far the most ambitious was a coastal works to be built by Wendel-Sidelor at Fos, near Marseilles, which would have an eventual capacity of 10m tonnes.

Yet the industry's Achilles' heel was its continuing dependence on the government for finance. Sacilor took on a large amount of debt to finance the Fos project, and the fragility of its financial position was exposed in 1971 when demand for steel fell sharply and profits came under pressure. It was forced to look for partners to share the cost of the Fos project. One possibility was the German company Thyssen, which was interested in gaining access to a coastal works. However, political objections limited Thyssen's participation to 5 per cent (with the possibility of a later increase to 25 per cent), and Sacilor turned to its long-time rival in the north, Usinor. Since this company was also facing financial difficulties because of the Dunkirk project, further assistance had to be obtained from the government. When the steel crisis struck in 1975, both companies were heavily in debt, and in the throes of costly expansion programmes. Without further support from the state one or both of them would have gone bankrupt. Under a rescue plan adopted in 1978 the bulk of the two companies' debts were written off, and the government acquired a controlling interest in both of them. Although they were not formally nationalised, the government was now in the driving seat.

French-style 'concertation' between industry and government was no more effective than British-style nationalisation.[67] In Germany, on the other hand, where the steel companies had been largely left to fend for themselves, the industry's response to the crisis, at least in its first phase, was far more robust.

During the 1960s and early 1970s the German steel industry pursued a twin-track strategy of rationalisation and diversification. The number of major crude steel producers was reduced through mergers to six – Thyssen, Hoesch, Krupp, Klöckner, Salzgitter and Mannesmann. One member of this group, Hoesch, was also involved in a rare trans-national joint venture, with Hoogovens of the Netherlands. Hoesch's works at Dortmund in the eastern Ruhr was at a cost disadvantage because imported raw materials had to be trans-shipped from the Rhine. The logic of the joint venture (which in 1971 was converted into a full merger, Estel) was that the Dutch company would supply Hoesch with semi-finished steel from a new coastal works, while the German partner, situated close to Germany's big steel-using industries, would concentrate mainly on finished steel.

Diversification took the form of acquisitions of engineering companies, not so much to secure captive outlets for steel as to insure against a decline in the profitability of steel-making. By the mid-1970s Thyssen, Krupp and Mannesmann derived more than half their turnover from non-steel businesses, and this was a source of strength when steel demand fell in 1975.

Up to this point the Federal government had largely eschewed intervention in the industry's affairs. This did not preclude some departures from free-market principles. In 1967 Krupp, still controlled by the founding family, ran into a financial crisis caused by over-expansion, and the government agreed to guarantee some of the company's loans.[68] A more important intervention was the decision in 1969 to reorganise the coal industry in the Ruhr, which could no longer compete with cheap imports. A new company, Ruhrkohle AG, was created with state support, and it was given a subsidy to offset the difference between the price of German coking coal and the world market price.[69] As far as the steel industry itself is concerned, the first serious breach in the Federal government's non-interventionist stance came not in the Ruhr, but in the Saar. This region had been placed under French administration after the war and, although it was restored to German control in 1957, it had not participated fully in the German economic recovery. It was even more dependent than the Ruhr on coal and steel, and the companies there lacked the financial strength either to modernise their operations or to diversify out of steel. By 1977 two of them, Neunkircher Eisenwerke and Röchling-Burbach were close to bankruptcy. The Federal and Land governments, working closely with the employers and the trade unions, stepped in with a rescue package which led to the two firms being placed under the control of Arbed, the Luxembourg-based steel group. This could be defended as a private-sector solution, but it involved substantial financial assistance from the Federal and Land governments.[70]

That the Ruhr would also need support seemed less likely at this stage, but as the crisis deepened and larger job reductions became necessary, the consensual approach to industrial adjustment came under strain. A campaign by the industry's trade union, IG Metall, for work-sharing through shorter working hours led to a three-week stoppage in 1978, one of the most serious strikes in the history of the Federal Republic. There was also increasing concern in Dortmund about the employment implications of the Hoesch–Hoogovens merger.[71] IG Metall demanded a commitment from Hoesch that steel-making in Dortmund would continue, and began to look to the Federal government for solutions to the crisis.

If there had been a completely free market in steel during this period, the German steel companies would have been in a better position. As the most efficient producers in Europe, they stood to gain from the disappearance of high-cost steel-makers in other countries. But the market was not free. Not only were many of Germany's competitors heavily subsidised (TABLE 6.6), but the weaker national industries were putting strong pressure on the European Commission to stabilise the market in a way which placed the German industry at a disadvantage. Under the Treaty of Paris the European Commission had the power to establish minimum prices and mandatory production limits in the event of a 'manifest crisis' in the European steel market. The French trade association had been arguing since 1975 that such a crisis had arrived, and in the summer of 1980, after trying without success to curb over-production by voluntary means, the Commission acceded to this request. Under the Davignon Plan (named after the Industry Commissioner, Count Etienne Davignon), the normal rules of competition were suspended, to the detriment of those steel-makers, principally in Germany, which were least subsidised and most likely to benefit from an open market.

TABLE 6.6 *State aid to European steel industries*

(in millions of DM)

	1975–9	1980–91
Belgium	2,725	10,017
France	2,060	21,710
Britain	13,852	13,275
West Germany	922	6,058
of which:		
Saar Volklingen	891	2,378
Other companies	31	3,680
Italy	4,327	35,059

Source: Dr Ruprecht Vondran, President, German Steel Federation, Düsseldorf, 13 February 1992.

Up to 1980 the policies and institutions which had been put in place in the early 1950s had served the German steel industry well. Although the principles of the social market economy had been bent in ways which Ludwig Erhard would not have approved, the distortions had been far less than in

Britain and France, and the German steel industry was stronger than its French and British counterparts. The onset of the steel crisis had led to a politicisation of the industry which was beginning to affect West Germany as well as other European countries. What happened next, as the steel-makers tried to find a way out of the crisis, would depend as much on governments as on the companies themselves.

The 1980s and 1990s: The Rehabilitation of British Steel

When the Thatcher government entered office in May 1979, the immediate priority was to halt British Steel's losses. The chairman, Charles Villiers, was told that the company must break even in the 1979/80 financial year, and that any operating losses after that date would not be funded by the government. The management's response was to accelerate the closure programme and to look for other ways of cutting costs. The trade unions were faced with the prospect of job losses on a much larger scale than in the 1970s, and within their ranks support grew for a united stand against British Steel's strategy.[72] The last straw was the company's decision during annual wage negotiations in October 1979 not to award a general pay increase. Instead, the unions were offered a basic 2 per cent increase, representing the consolidation of a previously earned bonus, with the possibility of earning up to 10 per cent more through locally negotiated productivity agreements. The downgrading of national pay negotiations was a threat to the ISTC's *raison d'être*, and the union resented the fact that other public sector workers, notably the miners, had won much larger pay increases. For Bill Sirs, the ISTC general secretary, the time had come to make a stand. In January 1980 the union called its members out on strike. It was the first national stoppage in the industry since the General Strike of 1926.

The strike, which lasted for three months, was in some respects a precursor to the miners' strike of 1984–5. Mrs Thatcher regarded it as a direct challenge to her economic strategy. She refused to intervene, despite the anxieties of several ministers, and she supported the management's position, though she was not impressed with the way British Steel presented its case.[73] From the union's point of view, the strike was poorly timed. Demand for steel was low because of the recession that followed the second oil shock of 1979–1980, and the shortfall in supplies could easily be made up by imports. Thus although the strike was well supported by ISTC members and by other unions, it did not have the crippling effect on manufacturing industry which Sirs had expected. The strike ended in April when a Court of Inquiry recommended a slightly higher basic wage increase which was accepted by the union. British Steel achieved its main objective, which was to tie future increases in earnings to locally agreed performance targets.

The short-term costs of the strike were an increase in steel imports and a further worsening of British Steel's financial position. Far from achieving break-even in 1979/80, British Steel made the largest loss in its history of £1.8bn. But the strike gave management the confidence to press ahead with the closure programme and to tackle the problem of overmanning. The closures were eased by generous redundancy payments, for which continuing financial support from the government was essential. Yet Mrs Thatcher and her colleagues were determined that British Steel should be run on commercial lines, and, when the strike was over, they made the controversial decision to replace Villiers with Ian MacGregor, a 67-year-old Scottish-born American who had spent most of his career in the US mining industry. MacGregor already had some experience of Britain's industrial problems, having served on the board of British Leyland, the state-owned car manufacturer, since 1975. Sir Keith Joseph, Mrs Thatcher's Industry Secretary, saw him as a man who would bring private-sector disciplines into British Steel.[74] MacGregor had a more 'macho' image than Villiers and he had little time for trade unions; the worker-director scheme withered under his chairmanship. However, the substance of MacGregor's policy during the three years he was at British Steel – he moved in 1983 to become chairman of the National Coal Board – followed the direction set by Villiers.

For all the dedication of the Thatcher government to free markets, there was no question of letting British Steel go bankrupt. Between 1980 and 1985 the Conservatives committed £4.5bn to finance closures, redundancies and new investment, compared with the £3.1bn which Labour had provided over the preceding five years.[75] But the terms on which these funds were made available were strict. Tight cash limits were imposed, stringent financial objectives were set, and, with one important exception, social concerns were no longer allowed to take precedence over commercial imperatives.[76]

The exception was Ravenscraig, the Scottish plant which owed its existence to Harold Macmillan's 'judgement of Solomon' in 1958 and was still a sensitive issue for the Thatcher government. It was the smallest and least economic of the five 'heritage' works, and its rationale had been largely undermined by the closure in 1981 of the Rootes car assembly plant at

Linwood, which had been a major customer. However, the government was anxious not to provide further ammunition to anti-Conservative forces in Scotland, and instructed British Steel to keep the plant open. (Ravenscraig was eventually closed in 1992.)

With the ISTC weakened by the strike, British Steel had little difficulty in introducing new payment arrangements at local level. Bonus payments, amounting to up to 18 per cent of an individual steel-worker's earnings, were tied to agreed improvements in performance. These arrangements had some similarity to the tonnage bonus which had been traditional in the steel industry, but the pay increases were related not simply to production, but to cost, quality and other measures of performance. Moreover, the local agreements were negotiated on a multi-union basis, reducing the scope for the arguments over wage differentials between one union and another which had dogged the industry in the past. Progress was also made in relaxing demarcations between trades and in moving towards a form of team-working in which multi-skilled workers performed both production and maintenance tasks. In an industry with a long tradition of delegating the organisation of work to the unions, the balance of power had shifted to management.[77]

The rehabilitation of British Steel during the 1980s was not simply a matter of closing plants and cutting costs. There was also a greater emphasis on product development and marketing. In the field of construction, for example, British Steel had considerable success in promoting the use of steel rather than concrete for multi-storey buildings. As quality improved, relationships with important domestic customers, such as the car-makers, were rebuilt and British Steel recovered some of the ground which had been lost to imports. At the same time a more aggressive export policy was pursued in Continental Europe.

In 1983 MacGregor was succeeded by a part-time chairman, Robert Haslam (a former deputy chairman of ICI), and the main responsibility for improving British Steel's performance fell on Robert Scholey, the chief executive; he was appointed chairman after Haslam's retirement in 1986 and held the post until 1993. Unlike Melchett, Finniston and Villiers, Scholey had spent his entire career in the steel industry, having worked before nationalisation for United Steel, and he was more concerned than any of his predecessors with operating efficiency. He was determined to make the best of an array of plants which, though not ideal in terms of size and location, were capable of producing high-quality steel at low cost. In 1987 a leading industry analyst estimated that British Steel had lower costs, per tonne of steel produced, than any of the world's major steel-makers.[78] In 1988 the company was successfully privatised; in that year British Steel had 52,000 employees, compared with 142,000 at the start of the decade.

British Steel's strategy after privatisation was to continue the drive for lower costs and greater efficiency in Britain. The magnitude of the changes which had taken place since the 1970s is shown in TABLE 6.7, which highlights the improved performance at the Llanwern works in South Wales.

TABLE 6.7 *The transformation of Llanwern 1979–95*

	1979	1995
Liquid steel (000 tonnes)	1,632	2,358
Manning	9,353	3,624
Man hours/tonne steel	10.77	2.67
Overtime	8.0%	5.33%
Absenteeism	9.4%	3.44%

Source: British Steel Corporation, reported in *Financial Times*, 2 August 1996.

The rehabilitation of British Steel is widely regarded as a triumph for Thatcherism. Yet the changes in France, the most *dirigiste* of the three countries, were almost as remarkable. When François Mitterrand took over the presidency from Giscard d'Estaing in 1981 the steel industry was still in crisis, and the new Socialist government had no clear idea how to deal with it. The inclusion of Usinor and Sacilor on the list of companies to be nationalised was almost a formality, since they had been controlled by the government since 1978. A new '*plan acier*', adopted in June 1982, provided for a further injection of government funds into the two companies to finance expansion and modernisation. The plan, which forecast an increase in production from 18m tonnes in 1982 to 26m tonnes in 1986, contained a large element of wishful thinking. As Raymond Levy, president of Usinor from 1982 to 1984, wrote later, 'everyone knew the goals were unrealistic, but for political and psychological reasons the government simply chose not to propose more realistic alternatives'.[79] The conversion to economic orthodoxy came in 1983, when the government decided to keep the franc in the European Monetary System and to bring inflation down to the German level. The *plan acier* was radically revised, and the priority shifted from expansion to cost reduction. At the same time the first steps were taken to unify the management of Usinor and Sacilor. Francis Mer, appointed president of Usinor-Sacilor in 1986, set about a streamlining of the business on similar lines to what had already taken place in British Steel. Manpower was reduced from 102,000 to less than 60,000, and profitability improved to the point where, in 1995, the company could be successfully privatised.

Compared to the drastic measures which were adopted in France and Britain, the rationalisation of the German steel industry proceeded more sluggishly during the 1980s. By 1980 the plight of the Ruhr firms had worsened to the point where the Federal government felt obliged to intervene. The most vulnerable company, because of its location, was Hoesch. The industrial logic behind the Estel merger was sound, but its implications for employment in the Ruhr were unpalatable, and Hoesch came under intense pressure from the unions to commit itself to an investment in new steel-making facilities in Dortmund.[80] Relations with its Dutch partner deteriorated and in 1981 the marriage was dissolved. Krupp as well as Hoesch requested Federal support for modernisation, and since the two programmes appeared to duplicate each other, the government encouraged the firms to merge. Despite encouragement from the two companies' lead banks – Dresdner Bank in the case of Krupp, Deutsche Bank in the case of Hoesch – no agreement could be reached on how their assets should be valued and negotiations broke down. This was the first in a series of attempted rationalisation schemes, largely initiated by the Federal government, all of which foundered on the unwillingness of one or other participant to give up their independence.

In 1991 Gerhard Cromme, chief executive of Krupp, broke the log-jam by launching a hostile take-over bid for Hoesch. This was a controversial move in a country where contested take-overs were virtually unknown, and it was strongly opposed by Hoesch's management and employees. But Cromme was able to buy enough shares in the market – unlike most German publicly quoted companies, Hoesch's shares were widely held – to force the acquisition through. In 1997 Cromme announced an even more audacious move – a bid for Thyssen, the country's largest steel producer. Once again the political and trade union reaction was hostile, and Cromme was obliged to withdraw the bid. But the logic of what he was proposing was irrefutable, and, after the fuss over the take-over bid had died down, the two companies entered into discussions which led to an agreed merger, taking effect in March 1999.

Thus at the end of the 1990s Britain, Germany and France each had a major national steel company of roughly comparable size and roughly comparable levels of productivity – Thyssen Krupp, Usinor-Sacilor and British Steel (TABLE 6.8). They were no longer national champions in the old sense, but part of an increasingly integrated European industry which was largely though not completely free of government ownership and control. British Steel saw itself as an international company, growing through overseas acquisitions and joint ventures as well as by exporting from Britain. Its first major investment after privatisation was in the US, but Continental Europe was central to British Steel's strategy, and in 1999 it announced a merger with Hoogovens, the Dutch company which had been briefly allied to Hoesch of Germany in the 1970s. The combined group would be the largest steel-maker in Europe, just ahead of Usinor, which had acquired control of Cockerill-Sambre, the Belgian company, in 1998.

The world steel industry, traditionally the most nationalistic of all major industries, appeared to be in the early stages of globalisation – a process which other industries, such as cars, electronics and some parts of engineering, had

TABLE 6.8 *Leading European steel-makers in 1997*

Company	Country	Output (million tonnes of crude steel)
Thyssen Krupp	Germany	17.50
British Steel	Britain	17.00
Usinor	France	16.10
Riva	Italy	14.80
Arbed	Luxembourg	12.50
Cockerill Sambre	Belgium	6.80
Hoogovens	Netherlands	6.70
HKM	Germany	5.10

Source: *Metal Bulletin*, 12 March 1998.

gone through some years earlier. That British Steel would emerge as one of the global leaders could not have been realistically predicted at the end of the 1970s.

Delayed Convergence

The British steel industry is a case of delayed modernisation, and the main responsibility for the delay lies with governments. By preserving the regulatory regime which had been put in place in the 1930s, by rejecting membership of the European Coal and Steel Community and by intervening in the industry in ways which impeded change, successive governments contributed to the slow growth of productivity in the industry.

These errors were compounded by the decision to nationalise the industry in 1967. Steel nationalisation has been defended on the grounds that the companies were too weak in the mid-1960s to finance the capital investment which took place under public ownership; by getting over the 'hump' of modernisation, nationalisation created the conditions in which a profitable British Steel Corporation could be returned to the private sector twenty years later.[81] But the weakness of the industry was itself the consequence of misconceived government policies. If nationalisation had not taken place and the companies had been obliged to compete freely, it is likely that market forces would have brought about the necessary reorganisation of the industry, with the more efficient firms enlarging their share of the market and the less efficient going out of business or being acquired.[82]

The contrast with Germany is instructive. The success of the German steel-makers in the first thirty years after the war was intimately linked to the revival of the West German economy, but it was underpinned by the policy reforms and institutional changes which took place soon after the establishment of the Federal Republic – the shift from cartelisation to a more competitive industrial structure, the new legal framework to govern relations between employers and trade unions, and the creation of the Coal and Steel Community. France, on the other hand, made many of the same mistakes as Britain. As one close observer of the French scene has written, 'there is little evidence that state intervention successfully corrected the mistakes of the major industrial firms, and plenty of evidence to suggest that it encouraged the sluggishness with which they adapted to rapidly changing conditions'.[83]

The 1980s and 1990s were a period of convergence. While Britain and France were catching up, the German model of consensual change was less well suited to a situation of static demand, over-capacity and rising unemployment. The German steel industry found itself in the unfamiliar position of being criticised for rationalising too slowly, and it was only through the use of a highly unGerman device – the hostile take-over bid – that obstacles to change were overcome.

In this case, then, government policy made a bigger contribution to the British steel industry's poor performance before the 1980s than any of the three institutional weaknesses referred to in Chapter 1. During the periods when the industry was privately owned, there is no evidence that it was ill served by the financial system. The supply of skills also appears to have been adequate. The labour relations issue is more relevant since the fragmented structure of the trade union movement undoubtedly complicated the industry's attempts to make itself more efficient in the 1960s and 1970s. The reform of working practices which took place in the 1980s was a necessary condition for the rehabilitation of British Steel. But it was subsidiary to other changes resulting from the actions of the Thatcher government. The fundamental difference, compared to the 1950s and 1960s, was that the British steel industry was forced to compete.

——————•o•——————

The Globalisation of the Paper Industry

T he revival of the British paper and board industry in the 1980s and 1990s did not receive as much public attention as the dramatic events in steel described in the last chapter. Yet the transformation in this sector was in some ways even more impressive, involving as it did the construction of new mills and a sustained increase in production (FIGURE 7.1). Like steel, this was a case of delayed modernisation, but an important difference was in the role played by non-British companies. Of all the industries discussed in this book, paper illustrates most clearly the importance of foreign investment in the regeneration of British manufacturing.

FIGURE 71 *Paper and Board production 1955–1997*

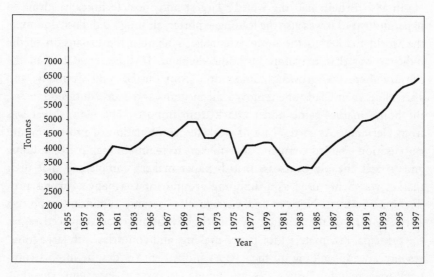

Source: Paper Federation of Great Britain

Paper-making in Britain before the Second World War

The modern paper industry was born at the end of the eighteenth century, when the old process of making paper by hand was replaced by the Fourdrinier machine. The inventor was a Frenchman, Nicholas Louis Robert, but the machine was commercialised in Britain and it was called the Fourdrinier after the firm of London stationers which was responsible for the first successful installation at their Frognal mill in Hertfordshire in 1804. Over the next fifty years the efficiency of the Fourdrinier machine was steadily improved, and many of the old hand mills were displaced.

During this period several of the firms which were to play a prominent role in the industry in the twentieth century were established. In 1809, for example, Robert Tullis, stationer, bookseller and printer, acquired a mill in Fife which today, as part of Tullis Russell, is one of the country's leading fine paper producers.[1] In the same year John Dickinson, another stationer, bought the Apsley mill in Hemel Hempstead; he later invented a rival machine to the Fourdrinier.[2] Stationers, paper-makers and rag merchants formed the 'triad' of the paper trade.[3] Rag was at that time the essential raw material in paper-making. The first stage of the manufacturing process involved the beating of cotton and linen rags into pulp, from which the cellulosic fibres were extracted and moulded into sheets.

In 1850 Britain had the world's largest and most technically advanced paper industry.[4] It was also the leading exporter, although it did not dominate the world market to the same extent as in textiles; the expansion of the industry was driven mainly by home demand. In the second half of the century there was growing competition from the US and Germany, and after 1861, when Gladstone removed the customs and excise duties on paper, the home market came under attack from imports. The main threat was from Germany. As in the case of steel, the combination of protection and cartelisation enabled German paper-makers to maintain high prices at home and to sell cheaply overseas. British paper-makers complained that their market was being used as a dumping ground for Germany's surplus production.[5] Sweden, Norway and Canada also became significant exporters after the turn of the century; by this time woodpulp had displaced rag as the principal raw material for paper-making, and countries with large forest resources were building up their paper industries. Yet despite import competition, demand in Britain was large enough to sustain a large and expanding domestic industry.

One of the fastest-growing sectors was the production of wrapping and packaging papers, needed in large quantity by manufacturers and distributors of mass-produced consumer goods. In 1902 American entrepreneurs built a mill at Purfleet in Essex, Thames Board Mills, to make cardboard for the packaging industry, using waste paper as the raw material; Unilever, a big user of packaging materials, later acquired a 50 per cent stake in this company. The rise of mass-circulation newspapers generated a big demand for newsprint. Some newspaper proprietors built paper mills of their own, either in Britain or overseas. Edward Lloyd, for example, owner of *Lloyd's Weekly News* and the *Daily Chronicle*, built a mill at Sittingbourne in Kent in 1876 which for some years was the largest paper mill in Britain. In 1905 the Harmsworth brothers (Lord Northcliffe and Lord Rothermere), owners of the *Daily Mail* and the *Daily Mirror*, invested in pulp and paper production in Newfoundland.[6] There was also scope for independent entrepreneurs in the newsprint business. Albert E. Reed, founder of what was to become one of the country's biggest paper-making empires, bought his first newsprint mill at Tovil, near Maidstone, in 1894.

The pressure of import competition eased after the First World War. Some grades were protected by tariffs under the Safeguarding of Industries Act of 1921, and the abandonment of free trade in 1932 extended protection to the whole of the industry. The only exception was newsprint, which continued to be imported free of duty, subject to limits on quantity. The government justified this on the grounds that most of the British newsprint mills were owned or controlled by the big newspaper proprietors, and imports were necessary to safeguard the interests of the smaller publishers.[7] Within this partially protected environment – imports amounted to 42 per cent of consumption in 1930, falling to 29 per cent in 1938 – the industry could invest with greater confidence.

Domestic paper consumption rose strongly during this period, from 1.8m tons in 1924 to 3.6m tons in 1938. New newsprint mills were built by Reed at Aylesford and by Edward Lloyd at Kemsley. They were joined in 1926 by an ambitious newcomer, Eric Bowater, one of the outstanding British entrepreneurs of the inter-war years. Bowater was a risk-taker on a grand scale, and his first venture into paper-making – a newsprint mill at Northfleet in Kent – almost ended in financial disaster. Rescued by the intervention of Lord Rothermere, Bowater launched himself on 'a career of growth, adventurously financed and extremely rapid, which has few parallels in the history of British business'.[8] In 1930 he built a second newsprint mill at Ellesmere Port in Cheshire, known as the Mersey Mill, to serve Manchester's growing newspaper market and then acquired his biggest competitor, Edward Lloyd. By 1936 Eric Bowater controlled 60 per cent of Britain's newsprint capacity.

Most of Bowater's production was based on imported pulp, and, to counter the power of the Scandinavian pulp cartels, Bowater bought pulp mills of his own in Sweden and Norway. He also had his eye on Canada, which was both a source of woodpulp and a potential competitor in newsprint. The growth of the Canadian newsprint industry during the 1920s had been driven by strong demand from the US. After the collapse of the US market following the Wall Street crash, the Canadians began to sell their surplus production in Britain. One of the companies engaged in this trade was Corner Brook in Newfoundland, owned by International Paper of the US. When the American parent put Corner Brook up for sale in 1938, Eric Bowater saw an opportunity to counter-attack, and with the help of the Bank of England he secured sufficient finance to make the purchase. Corner Brook gave him a captive source of Canadian pulp and a stake in the North American newsprint market.[9]

Bowater's nearest challenger among British newsprint producers was Albert E. Reed (now run by the founder's sons), in which the Rothermere interests held a minority stake. The Aylesford mill was enlarged in the 1930s to make other grades, including sack kraft for packaging, all of which, like newsprint, were based on imported pulp. Another large group was Inveresk, which had newspaper and magazine interests as well as a number of paper mills, mostly at the high-quality end of the trade.

Outside the newsprint sector one of the biggest companies was Wiggins Teape. Founded as a firm of wholesale stationers in 1761, it began acquiring paper mills before the First World War, and continued to do so in the inter-war years. By the end of the 1930s it controlled seventeen mills making a variety of grades including photographic base paper, greaseproof paper and printing and writing paper.

A large part of the industry consisted of small, privately owned firms, mostly operating from a single mill. Some of them, like Tullis Russell in Scotland, were well run and technically innovative, but there was a long tail of inefficient producers which had been saved from extinction by the tariff. They also benefited from the price-fixing agreements which spread widely in paper during the 1930s. As the trade association commented in 1937, 'at present there are more price agreements in operation in the industry than at any previous time in its history and this form of organisation has reached a stage from which it should be possible to progress in an atmosphere of unprecedented confidence'.[10]

Confidence there may have been, but the combination of tariffs and cartels insulated the paper-makers from competitive pressure and preserved a structure which was out of line with the changing economics of the world paper industry. The paper-makers were encouraged to believe that, because of Britain's lack of forests, they were entitled to protection against imports of finished paper while continuing to import their raw materials free of duty. This was the basis of the industry's prosperity in the inter-war years.

Post-war Protection

The dominant concern of the paper-makers at the end of the war was that the protective regime which had been established in the 1930s should be maintained. In its presentation to the Board of Trade in 1944, the British Paper and Board Makers Association laid out a vision of the future in which the domestic industry would satisfy the country's 'full requirements' for paper and board and provide them at an economic price. The association looked to the government for help in regaining export markets which had been lost during the war, and asked to be 'recognised as a key and vital industry as important to the body politic and economic as mining, shipbuilding or any of the great industries of this country'.[11]

For the first fifteen years after the war the industry got most of what it asked for. Imports were more tightly controlled than they had been in the 1930s. The tariff was reinforced by quotas, and, apart from a brief period of liberalisation in 1951 (promptly reversed when the balance of payments deteriorated), import penetration was kept below the 1938 level until the early 1960s. In the case of newsprint, the government relied on quotas rather than tariffs. In addition, domestic newsprint production was held back in order to save on imported woodpulp, and newspapers were restricted in the number of pages which they could produce.[12]

While there was no guarantee that these arrangements would last, the mood of the paper industry in the early 1950s was optimistic. Paper was in short supply throughout the world, and manufacturers were eager to press ahead with investments which had been delayed by the war. In newsprint, for example, Bowater installed new machines at its Mersey and Kemsley mills, and plans for a further doubling of capacity were announced in 1955. Eric Bowater was at the height of his powers, enlarging his empire in North America as well in Britain. His most ambitious move was the construction of a newsprint mill in Tennessee, making Bowater an even stronger force in the US newsprint market. At the same time the company was beginning to diversify its British operations away from newsprint, making its first foray into packaging materials and teaming up with Scott Paper of the US to make 'Andrex' soft tissues. Reed, too, was expanding vigorously during this period, commissioning a newsprint machine at Aylesford in 1957, and making several acquisitions in paper-making and packaging. Like Bowater, Reed turned to an American partner – Kimberly-Clark – to enter into the fast-growing soft tissue market.

Paper-making technology was advancing, and British mills were as alert to new opportunities as their overseas counterparts. St Anne's Board Mill in Bristol, a subsidiary of Imperial Tobacco, developed a new machine, known as the Inverform machine, to produce high-quality cartonboard for packaging; the invention was licensed to other board-makers in Britain and overseas.[13] Tullis Russell built the world's largest 'twin-wire' machine for making high-quality printing and writing papers.[14] Wiggins Teape spotted an opportunity in 'no carbon required' (NCR) paper, a new type of copying paper which had been developed in the US.

The paper-makers enjoyed a seller's market for most of the 1950s, and until 1956, when the Restrictive Trade Practices Act was passed, price-fixing agreements remained in force. There was also a small but profitable export trade with Commonwealth or ex-Commonwealth countries. But the economics of the world paper industry were changing. Producers in Canada and Scandinavia were investing in large, integrated mills, producing pulp and paper in a continuous operation. With their rich forest resources and access to cheap power, these companies had a cost advantage, amounting to 10 per cent or more of the final selling price, over mills which had to import their woodpulp. Some of this new capacity came on stream in the late 1950s when the seller's market was beginning to fade.

For British mills, the change in the balance between supply and demand coincided with a far greater shock – the end of protection. Once the principal trading nations had committed themselves to a programme of trade liberalisation through the General Agreement on Tariffs and Trade (GATT) in 1947, a gradual reduction in tariffs was expected, but the paper-makers were not prepared for the British government's decision, announced in 1959, to join with a group of other European countries, including Sweden and Norway, in the European Free Trade Association (EFTA). Finland was admitted as an associate member in 1961. The paper-makers regarded the EFTA agreement as a stab in the back, a clear rejection of their 1944 plea to be regarded as an 'essential industry'. One observer compared the situation to what had happened a hundred years earlier, when Gladstone eliminated import duties on paper. 'Then, as now, paper manufacturers were convinced that there was unfair discrimination against them. Then, as now, they made representations to the government which were received with amiable expressions of confidence in the future of the industry, but otherwise ignored.'[15] This time the threat was more serious, because the industry's overseas competitors were stronger.

The EFTA Shock

The immediate impact of EFTA was not as disastrous as had been feared. Domestic demand for paper and board was strong for most of the 1960s, and the reduction in tariffs was partially offset by other measures, including the temporary import surcharge which was in force between 1964 and 1966. Import penetration rose only gradually in the first few years of the agreement, and home production continued to increase, reaching a peak of 4.9m tonnes in 1969. From this point the industry began to decline at an alarming rate. During the 1970s paper consumption was virtually static, while import penetration increased rapidly (TABLE 7.1). The industry hoped that entry into the Common Market would bring some relief, since the Nordic producers would have to surmount the EEC's common external tariff. But the tariff was not high enough to have a significant effect, and British paper-makers found themselves under attack on a new front, from German, French and Dutch producers.

The most vulnerable mills were those which produced commodity grades of paper from imported pulp. These were the grades where the integrated mills in Canada and the Nordic countries had the biggest cost advantage. At the other end of the scale were the producers of high-quality or specialised paper which used a blend of pulps and suffered no cost penalty from non-integration. The more value which could be added to the paper, for example through coating, the more likely it was that a non-integrated mill could compete; with the growth of glossy magazines and weekly supplements in the newspapers, a substantial market for coated paper emerged during the

TABLE 7.1 *British paper and board production, consumption and imports 1960–80*

(figures in millions of tonnes)

	Consumption	Output	Imports	Imports as per centage of consumption
1960	5.3	4.1	1.4	26.4
1970	7.2	4.9	2.5	34.7
1980	6.8	3.8	3.5	51.4

Source: Paper Federation of Great Britain.

1960s. A switch into high-value-added grades was one possible strategy for the bulk producers. Another was to make more use of waste paper as a substitute for imported pulp. A third line of defence was to exploit home-grown timber resources. Supplies of wood were sufficient to support some pulp production in the 1950s, and, as earlier planting programmes bore fruit, these supplies increased during the 1960s and 1970s.

Among the larger companies, Bowater and Reed were in the most difficult position because they were heavily committed to commodity grades. Bowater was primarily a newsprint producer. Although newsprint had not been sub-ject to duty and so was not directly affected by EFTA, the viability of newsprint production in Britain, as long as it was based mainly on imported pulp, was fragile. The weakness had been offset before the war by the low price of woodpulp and in the early post-war years by the excess of demand over supply, but neither of these conditions applied in the 1960s.[16] This was the difficult legacy which Eric Bowater left to his successors when he died in 1962. Their response was to convert some of the machines from newsprint to either waste-based packaging grades or higher-quality printing papers. By the end of the 1960s a partial adjustment had been made to the post-EFTA world, but Bowater still had too much high-cost newsprint capacity in Britain.

Reed had more mills than Bowater and a broader portfolio of products, but a large part of its business was in newsprint and other commodity grades, most of which relied on imported pulp. The response to EFTA was, first, to diversify further into waste-based packaging materials and other grades less vulnerable to import competition, and, second, to invest on a large scale in a pulp and paper complex in British Columbia. Overseas expansion was taken further when Reed took over the Canadian mills owned by its principal shareholder, the International Publishing Corporation.

The pace of change was stepped up when Don Ryder was appointed managing director of Reed in 1963. A former financial journalist, Ryder was an energetic and ambitious manager, famous for his eighteen-hour working days. Like Frank Kearton at Courtaulds, he was an enthusiastic participant in the wave of mergers and acquisitions which transformed the structure of several industries during the 1960s. His strategy for Reed had three strands: the strengthening of the British paper business; international expansion; and diversification. The first involved the conversion of paper-making machines from woodpulp to waste paper, including for the first time the use of de-inked waste paper in newsprint production. The main thrust of Reed's overseas expansion was in Canada, and some grades which were no longer economic in Britain were supplied from Canadian mills. The third strand, diversification, took the form of several large acquisitions, taking the company into wallpaper, paint and building products.

Paper-making remained Reed's principal activity, and Ryder was eager to speed up the rationalisation which he believed was necessary. In 1967 he conceived the idea of a merger between Bowater and Reed. This would have monopoly implications, since the two companies would have a dominant share of some sectors of the market, and it would need the approval of the the competition authorities. At Ryder's suggestion the Labour government's merger-promoting agency, the Industrial Reorganisation Corporation (IRC), conducted a study of the industry to see whether rationalisation was necessary and, if so, how it might be brought about. The IRC concluded that mergers among medium-sized and smaller firms might be useful, but did not see how the problems faced by Reed and Bowater would be made easier if they were brought together in a single organisation. The merger idea was dropped, and the two companies went their separate ways, both of them looking for methods of reducing their dependence on British paper-making.

In Bowater's case this involved a bizarre merger with a commodity trading company partly owned by Jim Slater, a leading financial speculator. Slater had built up a considerable business empire by buying under-valued companies and either selling them on at a higher price or managing them himself. In 1972, having acquired a 12 per cent stake in Bowater, he engineered a merger with another company which he partly controlled, Ralli International. Ralli was primarily a commodity trader, with few links to the paper business, and the Bowater directors justifed the deal to their shareholders on the grounds that it would accelerate their diversification away from newsprint, and create 'a very large multinational manufacturing and trading organisation with substantial financial and management resources'. As with many other mergers during the 1960s, the synergies between the two companies proved to be non-existent, and the link with Ralli did nothing to ease Bowater's problems with its British paper-making business.

Reed diversified in a different way, merging in 1970 with its principal shareholder, International Publishing Corporation. This was in part a defensive merger – IPC was in a poor financial state and vulnerable to take-over – but it turned Reed International, as the merged group was called, into more of a conglomerate than a paper company. Ryder's acquisitions, together with his ambitious projects in Canada, had saddled the company with a heavy burden of debt, and it was not well placed to withstand the economic downturn which began after the first oil shock in 1973–4. When Ryder left Reed in 1974 to become chairman of the Labour government's National Enterprise Board, his successors had to take swift action to reduce the company's debts. The Canadian operations were sold, several mills were closed, and by 1980 British paper-making had been cut back to a small core of waste-based production, mainly located at Aylesford in Kent.

While Bowater and Reed were struggling to come to terms with the post-EFTA world, painful adjustments were being made in the rest of the industry. For the smaller firms diversification out of paper was not an option; they had to make the best out of their existing assets. Townsend Hook, for example, was a medium-sized newsprint manufacturer at Snodland in Kent. Two of the mill's three machines were converted to waste-based corrugating grades (for use in cardboard boxes) and the third to coated printing paper; newsprint production was discontinued. By the end of the 1970s the mill, producing 100,000 tons of packaging paper from waste, and 30,000 tons of coated paper from imported woodpulp, looked to have a viable future.[17]

Some companies tried to counter Nordic competition by investing in integrated pulp and paper production, using local timber. The most successful of these ventures was the board mill built at Workington in Cumbria by Thames Board Mills. This company, now wholly owned by Unilever, was the largest producer of waste-based packaging board, but demand from the food industry was shifting towards higher-quality cartonboard made wholly or partly from woodpulp. The Workington mill, which started production in 1966, enabled Thames to match the costs and quality of cartonboard imported from Canada or the Nordic countries.

Wiggins Teape already owned a small pulp mill near Bristol, and in the 1960s the growing availability of Scottish softwood encouraged the company to launch a more ambitious project – an integrated pulp and paper mill at Fort William, designed to produce high-quality printing and writing papers. There were technical problems with the pulping process which Wiggins Teape had adopted, and the pulp mill was never profitable. It was closed in 1980.

The failure of the Fort William project was not fatal for Wiggins Teape, since the bulk of its production consisted of grades which were not directly exposed to competition from integrated mills. It also had the financial backing of the tobacco company, British-American Tobacco (later BAT Industries), which bought a minority stake in 1965 and extended it to 100 per cent ownership in 1970.

Inveresk was in a similar position, since it no longer made newsprint or other bulk grades, but its seventeen mills contained a number of ancient machines which could not easily be modernised. Two bad mistakes – a pulp-making venture in the US and an ambitious move into coated paper – put the company into financial difficulty at the end of the 1960s. The coated paper mill, at Donside, near Aberdeen, was sold to a new company jointly owned by Bowater and Reed (Bowater later acquired full control), and the US pulp interests were sold. Several mills were closed during the 1970s, and in 1981 Inveresk was acquired by Georgia-Pacific of the US.

Some of the most resilient firms were medium-sized specialists which stuck to their last throughout the post-EFTA gloom. Tullis Russell in Scotland continued to invest in new machines for high-quality printing and writing papers, and maintained its position at the top end of the market. Another example was James Cropper in Cumbria, a publicly quoted company but one with a strong family interest. J. A. Cropper, appointed chairman in 1971, was the great great grandson of the founder. This company's strategy was to keep well away from commodity papers, focusing on technically demanding grades such as imitation bookcloth and coloured paper for corporate communications.

Specialisation was an appropriate response to EFTA competition, but not everyone could become a specialist. There were many mills which lacked the technical and financial resources to move in that direction, and their machines were not suitable for conversion to waste-based grades. These weaknesses were exposed as the economy deteriorated in the second half of the 1970s, and the pace of mill closures accelerated. By 1980 morale in the industry was at a low ebb. A partial adjustment to free trade had been made, but investment was falling and imports seemed likely to capture an ever-increasing share of the market. The commitment to the industry of the two biggest producers, Reed and Bowater, was waning.

The 1980s and 1990s: Transformation

The 1980s began on a gloomy note, with the decision by Bowater to close its Mersey mill. Strenuous efforts to make the mill economic had failed, and the losses rose to unacceptable levels during the overvaluation of sterling in 1980–81. Yet the decision was almost a blessing in disguise, since it set off a chain of events which was to transform the fortunes of the industry over the following twenty years. A year after the closure the mill was bought by a Canadian company, Consolidated Bathurst, which was looking for a way into the European market. Part of the purpose of the acquisition was to use the mill as an outlet for the company's Canadian pulp, but there was also scope for supplementing imported pulp with local wood and de-inked waste paper. The Canadians believed that, with new equipment and new working practices, the inefficiencies which had plagued the mill over the preceding decade could be removed. Newsprint production in Britain, it seemed, might have a future after all.

For Bowater and Reed, the die was already cast, and their next steps were not directly affected by what Consolidated Bathurst had done. After the sale of Mersey, Bowater was left with three mills – Kemsley and Sittingbourne in Kent, Donside in Scotland – making printing and writing papers and waste-based packaging materials. There was little in common between these activities and the much bigger newsprint operations in the US and Canada. Since Bowater did not have the financial resources both to expand a capital-intensive North American business and to modernise the British paper mills, it was logical to split the group into two. In 1984 Bowater in the US was floated as an independent company. Two years later the British paper mills were sold in a management buy-out, leaving Bowater to concentrate on packaging and building products; the separated company, UK Paper, was later floated on the stock exchange.

The management buy-out was a phenomenon of the 1980s. Large, diversified groups were under pressure from investors to focus on a narrower range of activities, and there was a ready supply of finance from venture capital firms to support enterprising managers who wanted to run their own business. In the case of UK Paper, independence did not last long, since it was bought in 1990, at a considerable profit to the original investors and managers, by a New Zealand group, Fletcher Challenge, which had ambitions to become a major international paper-maker.

Events at Reed followed a similar course. At the start of the 1980s Reed International had three main activities – paper and packaging, building and decorative products, and publishing. The management team which had taken over from Ryder regarded magazine publishing as the most promising avenue of growth, and in 1988 they put the paper and packaging operations up for sale. The winning bidder was a management buy-out team, led by Peter Williams, a Canadian who had worked for Reed in North America and had long experience of the international paper industry. Two years later the bought-out company, Reedpack, was acquired by SCA of Sweden. SCA already had a large stake in Britain as a supplier of pulp and paper, and was looking for ways of strengthening its position in packaging materials, where Reedpack was one of the market leaders. Another attraction was Reedpack's expertise in de-inked newsprint. At the time of the SCA purchase plans were well advanced for a new machine to be built at Aylesford with the capacity to produce 280,000 tonnes of newsprint a year entirely from recycled paper. SCA decided to go ahead with this project, sharing the cost with Mondi of South Africa, and the machine was commissioned in 1995. Aylesford newsprint was given the appropriate brand name Renaissance.

These divestments and acquisitions were part of an extensive reshuffle of ownership which took place during the 1980s and 1990s. The consequence was to put more of the industry's capacity into the hands of companies which were fully committed to paper-making. Unilever, for example, decided that it no longer needed a captive supplier of cardboard, and put Thames Board Mills up for sale. The Workington mill was bought by a Swedish company, and Purfleet by a British firm, BPB Industries (formerly British Plasterboard), which was already a large producer of waste-based board.[18] The changes in ownership are set out in TABLE 7.2, which also shows the impact of two new greenfield projects by foreign companies. One was a Finnish-owned newsprint mill at Shotton in North Wales, using a mixture of home-produced woodpulp and waste paper. The other was a Scottish mill, also Finnish-owned, which produced lightweight coated paper, using the same forest resources that had supported Wiggins Teape's pulp mill at Fort William.

TABLE 7.2 *Principal British paper and board producers in 1967 and 1997*

1967

Company	Ownership	Capacity (000 tonnes)
Reed	Quoted British	830
Bowater	Quoted British	800
Thames Board Mills	Owned by Unilever	450
Wiggins Teape	Part-owned by BAT Industries	195
Inveresk	Quoted British	160
Dickinson Robinson	Quoted British	158
St Anne's Board Mill	Owned by Imperial Tobacco	120
Davidson Radcliffe	Owned by BPB Industries	120
Peter Dixon	Quoted British	80
Associated Paper	Quoted British	76
Reed and Smith	Quoted British	72
Townsend Hook	Owned by News of the World	70
British Tissues	British consortium	60
East Lancashire	Quoted British	50

1997

Company	Ownership	Capacity
David S. Smith	Quoted British	1040
UPM-Kymmene	Finland	675
SCA	Sweden	660*
BPB Industries	Quoted British	500
Fletcher-Challenge†	New Zealand	470
Smurfit	Ireland	400
Abitibi-Consolidated	Canada	250
Arjo Wiggins Appleton	Anglo-French Quoted company	250
Kimberly-Clark	US	230
Fort James	US	230
International Paper	US	210

Company	Ownership	Capacity (000 tonnes)
Iggesund Paperboard	Sweden	190
RP Europe	Netherlands	160
Inveresk	Quoted British	160
Sappi	South Africa	145

*Includes 360,000 tonnes jointly owned with Minorco Mondi (South Africa).
† In 1997 Fletcher Challenge sold the Donside mill to a management buy-out team. In 1998 its two remaining British mills were sold to Metsä-Serla of Finland.

Source: author's estimates based on industry sources.

Note: The fourteen leading paper-making companies in 1967 were all British-owned. Only two of them, Davidson Radcliffe (owned by BPB Industries) and Associated Paper Mills (re-named API Industries), did not experience a change of ownership over the subsequent thirty years. Of the remaining twelve, two, Peter Dixon and St Anne's Board Mill, were closed. Reed and Bowater withdrew from UK paper-making. Thames Board Mills was sold by Unilever partly to Iggesund, and partly to BPB Industries. Wiggins Teape became part of an Anglo-French company, Arjo Wiggins Appleton. Inveresk was acquired by Georgia-Pacific of the US, then became independent again through a management buy-out and was floated on the Stock Exchange. Dickinson Robinson was acquired by Pembridge Investments; some of its mills were later sold to Sappi of South Africa. Reed and Smith was bought by St Regis of the US, then re-sold to David S. Smith. Townsend Hook was bought by Jefferson Smurfit. British Tissues went through several changes of ownership before being acquired by James River of the US, which in turn merged with Fort Howard of the US to become Fort James. East Lancashire was bought by British Syphon Industries, then resold to a management buy-out.

Of the companies on the 1997 list, only three are wholly British-owned. Most of the others are foreign companies which acquired or built paper mills in Britain. UPM-Kymmene owns the newsprint mill at Shotton and the lightweight mechanical printings mill in Scotland. SCA bought Reedpack, the management buy-out from Reed International. Fletcher Challenge bought UK Paper, the management buy-out from Bowater. Abitibi-Consolidated owns the former Bowater newsprint mill at Ellesmere Port. Kimberly-Clark acquired the tissue company which had been jointly owned with Reed, and in 1995 merged with Scott Paper of the US, which also had tissue interests in Britain through a joint venture with Bowater. Fort James, created by a 1997 merger between James River and Fort Howard of the US, owns tissue and fine paper mills in the UK. International Paper's main UK interest is the Tait fine paper mill in Scotland, which had been acquired by Federal Paper of the US in 1989; Federal was subsequently acquired by International Paper. Iggesund, now part of MoDo, bought the Workington board mill from Thames Board Mills. RP Europa, a joint venture between KNP and Buhrmann of the Netherlands, acquired Smith, Stone Knight, a manufacturer of corrugated case materials, in 1987.

The infusion of capital and technology from overseas made a big contribution to the regeneration of the industry, but another important ingredient was the entry of British entrepreneurs who took a more optimistic view of paper-making in Britain than some of the old-established companies. For example, Richard Brewster, a businessman who had no previous connection with the paper industry, bought a stake in a manufacturer of packaging materials, David S. Smith, in 1983, and used it as a springboard to create what was to become Britain's largest paper-maker. A series of acquisitions brought seven British mills into the group, all but one of which concentrated on waste-based grades, and these mills were then extensively modernised and re-equipped. Another entrepreneurial success story was Inveresk, bought from Georgia-Pacific by the management in 1990 and subsequently floated on the stock market. Operating from four mills instead of the seventeen it had owned in the early 1960s, Inveresk focused on high-quality and speciality papers, and built up a sizeable export business. In 1997 some 44 per cent of its revenues were earned outside Britain, and, with the purchase of another Scottish mill to broaden its range, Inveresk had become a major European force in its sector of the market.

Whether British-owned or foreign-owned, British paper-makers were becoming part of an international industry. This was reflected in a better export performance, with the Continent, rather than the Commonwealth, as the principal outlet (TABLE 7.3). There were also acquisitions and joint ventures involving European companies. David S. Smith, for example, bought a large French packaging company in 1992, and was looking hard for other acquisitions. Wiggins Teape, demerged from BAT Industries in 1989, joined with Arjomari to form Arjo Wiggins Appleton, an Anglo-French quoted company.

TABLE 7.3 *British paper and board exports, 1964 and 1997*

	1964	1997
Volume (000 tonnes)	170	1,438
Percentage of total production	4	22
Main markets	Australia, South Africa, New Zealand	France, Germany, Netherlands

Source: Paper Federation of Great Britain.

The industry was restructured in a way which reflected the comparative advantage of British and international paper-makers. Production of commodity grades such as newsprint and magazine papers was mostly controlled by Nordic and North American companies whose British mills benefited from the experience and technology they had accumulated in their home base. Similarly, the soft tissue market was dominated by American companies; it was in the US that this technology had originated and was most highly developed. British-owned firms had found a role for themselves as manufacturers of waste-based grades and high-value-added papers, both of which benefited from nearness to the customer. By the end of the 1990s, through inward investment and home-grown entrepreneurial effort, an impressive programme of rationalisation and modernisation had been carried out. Import penetration had stabilised, and maximum use was being made of home-produced raw materials (see TABLES 7.4, 7.5 and 7.6). An old industry had made a fresh start.

TABLE 7.4 *Structure of the British paper and board industry in 1967 and 1997*

	1967	1997
No. of companies	102	62
No. of mills	180	98
No. of machines	544	191
Output (million tonnes)	4.3	6.5

Source: Paper Federation of Great Britain.

TABLE 7.5 *Import penetration, 1960–97*

(imports as a per centage of apparent consumption)

1960	26.8
1970	34.9
1980	57.0
1990	60.8
1997	58.9

Source: Paper Federation of Great Britain.

TABLE 7.6 *Raw material consumption in British paper and board industry, 1967 and 1995*

(per centage of total in pulp equivalent)

	1967	1995
Imported woodpulp	62	29
Home-produced woodpulp	6	11
Waste paper	30	59
Other fibres/pulps	2	1

Source: Paper Federation of Great Britain.

Comparisons with Germany

The story of the paper industry raises questions which recur throughout this book. Why was modernisation delayed for so long? Why did the changes which took place in the 1980s not occur twenty or thirty years earlier?

A comparison with Germany provides part of the answer. As TABLE 7.7 shows, paper production and consumption rose much more rapidly in Germany between 1960 and 1980 than in Britain. This was, of course, mainly due to the faster growth of the German economy. But two other factors help to explain why the German industry was quicker to modernise than its British counterpart.

TABLE 7.7 *German and British paper and board industries, 1960–90*

(figures in millions of tonnes)

Britain

	Consumption	Output	Exports	Exports as per centage of output
1960	5.3	4.1	0.2	4.9
1980	6.8	3.8	0.5	13.2
1990	9.4	4.9	1.2	24.5

Germany

	Consumption	Output	Exports	Exports as per centage of output
1960	3.1	3.4	0.1	2.9
1980	9.7	7.6	1.7	22.3
1990	15.5	12.8	4.2	32.8

Sources: Paper Federation of Great Britain, Verband Deutscher Papierfabriken.

First, Germany was more open to paper imports in the early post-war years. Whereas import penetration in Britain remained below the pre-war level until the early 1960s, in Germany paper imports rose sharply from 6 per cent of consumption in 1950 to 24 per cent in 1960. 'The German paper industry was confronted at a very early stage with international competition in its home market and – in order to survive – was forced to invest heavily in the modernisation and rationalisation of the existing machines which remained after the war.'[19]

Second, Germany was a member of the Common Market from 1958, whereas Britain did not join until 1973. The great leap forward for the German paper industry came after 1960. Domestic paper consumption was rising strongly during this period, but so, too, were exports, and most of the increase came from neighbouring Common Market countries. At a time when the British paper industry was stagnating, German mills were investing in modern machines to serve an expanding European market. If Britain had joined the Common Market at the start, the paper industry would have avoided the sudden lurch from protection to free trade brought about by EFTA. It would also have been exposed at an earlier stage to competition in a large and dynamic market. Some of the modernisation and rationalisation which took place in the 1980s and 1990s might have occurred earlier. In addition, Common Market membership would have provided export opportunities for British mills. The expansion in exports which was achieved in the 1980s and 1990s might have started earlier.

The three institutional factors discussed in earlier chapters do not loom large in this story. The paper industry was not held back by a shortage of skills, and labour relations were less of a problem than, say, in shipbuilding or steel. A long-established system of industry-wide wage bargaining, supplemented by negotiations at the firm level, worked reasonably well throughout the post-war period. It is true that the industry was affected by the general deterioration in British labour relations during the 1960s and 1970s. The impact was mainly felt in mills close to large industrial centres, such as Purfleet and Mersey. Some of the restrictive practices for which the Fleet Street newspapers were notorious affected the paper industry; one of the main printing unions, the Society of Graphical and Allied Trades (SOGAT), had a large number of members in paper-making. In the early 1960s Bowater found that its Mersey mill was using 50 per cent more labour than its Corner Brook mill in Newfoundland.[20] The paper industry certainly benefited from the change in the British labour relations climate during the 1980s. But this did not involve a major confrontation of the sort which occurred in steel. Restructuring was achieved with the co-operation of the unions. Union membership remained high (86 per cent of all manual workers were unionised in 1992, compared with 91 per cent in 1976), and the national bargaining arrangements, modified to give individual firms greater flexibility, stayed in place.[21]

As for the financial system, there is no evidence that the industry was handicapped, before or after the EFTA agreement, by lack of support from the banks and financial institutions. When prospects for British paper-making improved in the 1980s, there were plenty of backers ready to support entrepreneurs who wanted to invest in the industry. At a time when changes in structure and ownership were needed, the financial system served the paper industry well.

The central problem for the British paper-makers was that an industry which had been enlarged in the inter-war years under favourable economic conditions faced a very difficult transition when those conditions changed. The adjustment was delayed by the continuation of protection for the first fifteen years after the war. The way in which protection was brought to an end, through the EFTA agreement, undermined confidence in the industry's future. The recovery that took place in the 1980s and 1990s was made possible by three factors: technical advances in the use of waste paper as a substitute for imported woodpulp; increasing competition in the world paper industry, prompting the leading international companies to build or acquire mills in their main markets, including Britain; and changes in the domestic political and economic environment, making Britain a more attractive location for foreign investors.

EIGHT

——•○•——

Engineering: From World Leader to
Niche Player

The last chapter described how the paper industry came to terms
with a disruptive change in its trading environment and, thanks in
part to inward investment, re-established itself on a viable basis in
the 1980s and 1990s. The engineering industry went through a similar experience, although in this case there was no single event comparable to the
EFTA shock. For most engineering firms the impact of international competition came later, reaching a peak of intensity in the late 1970s and early
1980s. But the result was the same: a process of specialisation and internationalisation as companies played to their strengths and searched for
defensible positions in the world market.

Engineering is a much bigger industry than paper, and it contains a large
number of sectors, from domestic appliances to earth-moving equipment,
which differ from each other in their economic and technical characteristics. The form which internationalisation took in the 1980s and 1990s
varied from sector to sector, as did the role played by inward investment.
This chapter explains why some parts of the industry performed better than
others.

The term 'engineering' is used here to refer to non-electrical and electrical
machinery, excluding electronics, which is the subject of Chapter 10. The
motor and aircraft industries are discussed in Chapters 9 and 11, although
this chapter makes some reference to motor and aircraft components.

Competition in Engineering before 1914

The Great Exhibition at Crystal Palace in 1851 was a showcase for the achievements of British engineers. No other country could match their prowess in designing and building the machines which had helped to drive forward the industrial revolution – steam engines and steam-powered machinery of all kinds, railway locomotives, textile machinery and machine tools. Over the next fifty years British hegemony in engineering came under attack from entrepreneurs in the US and Germany. The most striking British failure was in electrical engineering, which emerged as a distinct branch of the industry in the 1880s. In this field British manufacturers were outperformed from the start by American and German rivals; by the time of the First World War no British firm could match the size and technical strength of Siemens and AEG in Germany, or General Electric and Westinghouse in the US. The late-comers also gained ground in parts of mechanical engineering where British companies had previously been dominant. In machine tools, for example, Britain accounted for only 12 per cent of world exports in 1913, compared to Germany's 48 per cent and the US's 33 per cent.[1]

The progress of American entrepreneurs in engineering was closely linked to what became known as the American system of manufactures. In the early decades of the nineteenth century engineers in Federal armouries worked out a method of making rifles and other small arms in large quantity, using the principle of interchangeable parts.[2] The principle was not new, having originated in Europe in the eighteenth century, but American engineers converted it into a manufacturing system, developing high-output machine tools – milling machines, grinding machines, capstan and turret lathes – to make identical components in large volume and with great precision. These methods spread slowly into private industry, principally among manufacturers of light machinery for which there was a large, homogeneous demand. An early exponent was Isaac Singer, who began making sewing machines in the 1850s; by the 1880s his factory at Elizabethport, New Jersey, was turning out over half a million machines a year. The same techniques were applied to office machinery and harvesting equipment. The bicycle boom of the 1890s stimulated further innovations, notably the use of sheet steel stamping for bicycle components. This accumulation of experience prepared the way for the mass-produced automobile. The success of Henry Ford's Model T, launched in 1908, not only changed the way cars were made, but set a new standard for the management of high-volume, standardised production which could be applied to other industries.

British engineers observed these innovations with close interest. As early as 1853 Joseph Whitworth, doyen of Britain's machine tool builders, made a thorough study of US manufacturing practice and reported in detail on his findings. But the scope for imitation was limited by the market conditions which British firms faced. Home demand was smaller, and British manufacturers were supplying a range of overseas customers, many of whom wanted machinery tailored to their special requirements. For example, Platt Brothers, the largest British textile machine manufacturer, standardised its spindles and some other components, but the machines themselves were mostly built on a one-off or small-batch basis. Weir, a Scottish pump manufacturer, used US-type machine tools for making components wherever possible, but most of its pumps were manufactured to the specification of individual customers.[3]

Where American methods were appropriate, British businessmen were not slow to take them up. The introduction of the safety bicycle in the 1880s sparked off a surge in demand which was met at first by imports from the US, but British entrepreneurs soon learned how to make bicycles in the American way. Within a few years they were producing machines which were better suited to the local market.[4] The Raleigh Cycle Company, founded in 1888, equipped its Nottingham factory with American machine tools and some which the firm itself had designed; Raleigh was also one of the first to use stamping techniques for bicycle components.[5] By 1914 Britain was by far the largest bicycle exporter, with Germany a distant second. New entrepreneurs came into the machine tool business to serve the bicycle-makers, first borrowing American technology and then introducing their own designs. Alfred Herbert, for example, who was to become Britain's largest machine tool manufacturer, imported machines from the US before starting a manufacturing operation in Coventry in 1889. Herbert was one of the outstanding British entrepreneurs of the 1870–1914 period.[6]

The engineering unions, which until the end of the century were almost exclusively craft unions, viewed the spread of American techniques with anxiety. Their fear was that high-output machine tools operated by semi-skilled workers would damage the job prospects of their members and undermine their bargaining power. The use of semi-skilled 'handymen' had caused problems in the 1840s when an earlier generation of automatic lathes and drilling machines was introduced. There was a serious dispute over this issue in 1852, when members of the Amalgamated Society of Engineers, the principal craft union, were locked out for several months. But although the employers were victorious and recruited more semi-skilled workers, skilled craftsmen continued to make up the bulk of the industry's workforce, and the ASE, helped by the prosperous conditions of the 1850s and 1860s, was able to expand its membership.

The 'machine question' came to the fore again after 1870 when international competition began to bite and employers sought to reduce their costs of production. One tactic was to speed up the pace of work, using the piece-work method of payment instead of fixed hourly rates to elicit greater effort. Another was to hire more apprentices and use them as cheap labour. All these issues came to a head in the engineering lock-out of 1897–8 when the employers, newly united in the Engineering Employers Federation, inflicted a crushing defeat on the ASE. As part of the settlement, the employers won the right to place any suitable worker on any machine at a mutually agreed wage.[7] However, this outcome did not lead to the Americanisation of British engineering. Most British engineering firms continued to produce specialised machinery in small batches, and the skilled craftsman was a resource they could not do without. Partly for this reason they were more willing than their American counterparts to tolerate the existence of unions.[8] Although labour relations in engineering remained uneasy up to the First World War, trade union resistance did not prevent employers from using American-type machine tools if they chose to do so.

German competition in mechanical engineering took a different form. In this and other industries, as explained in Chapter 2, German entrepreneurs looked for high-value, low-volume sectors of the market where they could win customers through superior technical performance. This strategy put a high premium on workforce skills. While most training took place in the factory or workshop, as in Britain, German employers made increasing use of 'continuation schools' – some of them financed by city or state governments – to supplement on-the-job training. Germany's much admired 'dual' system of apprentice training, combining factory-based and school-based instruction, took shape towards the end of the century.[9] There was also an ample supply of graduate engineers from the technical high schools which had been established in most German states before unification; these institutions were later raised to the status of universities.[10]

Much of the dynamism of German mechanical engineering came from small and medium-sized enterprises located in states such as Baden and Württemberg which had long-established craft traditions. A network of local institutions, including training schools and chambers of commerce, provided common services which individual firms could not afford on their own.[11] The larger engineering companies which flourished in other parts of Germany, such as Deutsche Maschinenfabrik AG (DEMAG) and Maschinenfabrik-Augsburg-Nuremberg AG (MAN), also concentrated on complex machinery produced in small batches. With a few exceptions such as Robert Bosch, who made ignition equipment and other electrical components for cars, German entrepreneurs were no more advanced than the British in US-style high-volume production before the First World War.

The impact of German and American competition on world trade in machinery is illustrated in TABLE 8.1. By 1913 British firms had lost ground in some sectors of the industry, such as agricultural machinery and machine tools, but lessons had been learned from American experience and applied where it was economic to do so. Jonathan Zeitlin, a historian of the engineering industry, praises the 'resourcefulness and commercial success' of British engineers in appropriating selective elements of American practice without

TABLE 8.1 *Exports of mechanical engineering products in 1913*

(£m)

	UK	US	Germany
Agricultural machinery	3.0	6.7	2.5
Boilers and prime movers	7.0	1.9	5.5
Machine tools	1.0	2.9	4.0
Locomotives	3.4	1.2	3.9
Sewing machines*	2.4	2.4	2.8
Textile machinery	8.3	0.3	2.9
Miscellaneous	9.7	14.2	15.7
TOTALS	34.8	29.6	37.3

*The biggest British exporter of sewing machines was the American company, Singer, through its Glasgow factory.

Source: Committee on Industry and Trade, Survey of Industries, no. 4, pp. 138–206, quoted in S. B. Saul, 'The engineering Industry', in D. H. Aldcroft (ed.), *The Development of British Industry and Foreign Competition, 1870–1914*, Allen & Unwin, 1968.

losing the flexibility which they needed to serve a wide range of different customers.[12] In the long run the threat from Germany was to be more serious, but at this stage there were no grounds for concern about the technical competence of British firms. If technical education was more highly developed in Germany, the British apprenticeship system was in good working order, and the supply of shop floor skills was adequate.

In electrical engineering the performance of British firms was much less satisfactory. In the first phase of this new industry – the introduction of the electric telegraph in the 1840s – British firms were as advanced as any of their competitors. The cable-makers, in particular, established a strong position, which they retained for the rest of the century. But the growth of the industry accelerated after the invention of the incandescent lamp in 1878–9, and at this point British firms fell behind.[13] The lamp was invented by Thomas Edison in the US, followed almost immediately by Joseph Swan in Britain. A patent dispute between the two men was resolved in 1883 by the formation of a joint British company, Edison and Swan United Electric Light Company, soon shortened to Ediswan. But if the two countries were on a par in terms of invention, exploitation was much faster in the US.

Edison saw that an integrated system for generating and transmitting electricity was essential if the full potential of the incandescent lamp was to be realised.[14] In addition to lamps, Edison made generators and other electrical equipment, and organised utility companies to build and operate power stations. Financing all these enterprises posed considerable problems, and Edison faced competition in lamps and electrical equipment from two strong rivals, Thomson-Houston and Westinghouse. In 1891 the company which Edison had formed to manage his manufacturing operations, the Edison General Electric Company, merged with Thomson-Houston to form the General Electric Company (GE). General Electric and Westinghouse became the dominant suppliers of electrical equipment in the US.

In Germany the pioneering role in the electrical industry was played by Werner Siemens. After training as an engineer in the Prussian army, he became interested in electric telegraphy, and together with a partner, Johann Georg Halske, founded Siemens and Halske in 1847 to make telegraphic equipment. Siemens was an avid inventor, and in 1866 he worked out a more efficient way of converting mechanical energy into electricity through the dynamo converter.[15] He was surprisingly slow to see the importance of the incandescent lamp, and the rights to exploit the Edison patents were obtained by Emil Rathenau, whose company, Allgemeine Elektricitäts-Gesellschaft (AEG), threatened to topple Siemens from its leadership of the German electrical industry. A series of mergers just before and after the turn of the century gave these two companies, Siemens and AEG, a similar duopolistic position in the German market to that of General Electric and Westinghouse in the US.

In Britain progress was slower. This was not because of any lack of innovative skill on the part of British engineers. In addition to Joseph Swan's work on the incandescent lamp, Charles Parsons invented the steam turbine, a major advance over the reciprocating engine in the technology of power generation, and Sebastian de Ferranti, born in Britain of an Italian father, made original contributions to the design of transformers.[16] But the companies which these men set up came nowhere near matching the German and American leaders in size and all-round technical competence, and the same was true of the other British firms which came into the industry in the 1870s and 1880s.

Alfred Chandler sees this as an example of a persistent British weakness in management and organisation.[17] William Kennedy, a British economic historian, believes that when the industry was in its formative stage, the London Stock Exchange was poorly organised to give entrepreneurs the financial backing they needed.[18]

But there was another factor which may have been more important. Unlike the two late-industrialising countries, Britain was already an urbanised country when the incandescent lamp was invented, and a substantial investment had been made in gas lighting systems, most of which were owned and operated by the local authorities. These bodies had no incentive to promote the rapid expansion of electricity, which was more expensive than gas in the early years.[19] Under the Electric Lighting Act of 1882 privately owned electricity undertakings were subject to price controls and limited in the area they could cover; the Act also provided for the purchase of these undertakings by local authorities after twenty-one years. Although the rules were partially relaxed in 1888, the suppliers were still confined to a single local authority area. London was supplied by sixty-six generating stations with an average output of 3,000 horsepower, while comparable cities in the US had single generating stations of up to 70,000 horsepower.[20]

American and German manufacturers benefited from more favourable conditions in their domestic markets, and the manufacturing experience which they gained at home put them in a strong position to supply the

British market when demand began to increase at the end of the century. Westinghouse opened a large works at Trafford Park, near Manchester, in 1902, partly financed by raising funds from British investors. General Electric followed suit with a factory at Rugby; a British company, British Thomson Houston, was formed to run this business. Siemens, which had been manufacturing cables at Woolwich since 1863, built a works at Stafford to make electrical equipment. The British market was becoming almost a colony for foreign manufacturers.

The most progressive of the British-owned companies in the years leading up to the First World War was General Electric Company (GEC) – this firm was not related to its namesake in the US. Founded in 1880 as a wholesaler of electrical products, GEC acquired manufacturing interests, first in electrical accessories and then, after the Edison/Swan patents ran out in 1893, in lamps. The driving force behind GEC's growth was Hugo Hirst, German-born but fiercely patriotic towards his adopted country. 'Notwithstanding my origin,' he wrote, 'I was the only one in the electrical industry who could stand up against the Germans and who delighted in doing so.'[21] Hirst's aim was to make 'everything electrical', and in 1900 GEC, now a publicly quoted company, built a factory at Witton, near Birmingham, to manufacture dynamos, motors and switchgear. In 1905 Hirst negotiated a joint venture with a German company, Auer, which had invented a tungsten filament lamp, a more efficient device than the carbon filament used by Edison and Swan. GEC set up the Osram Lamp Works at Hammersmith, and ownership was shared equally with the German partner.[22]

By moving early into this new technology, Hirst strengthened GEC's position in the most profitable part of the electrical business. GEC, British Thomson Houston and Siemens were the three leading lamp producers at the time of the First World War (Ediswan having slipped behind), and they were linked together in a cartel that kept prices high. Price-fixing and market-sharing agreements were not yet as common in Britain as in Germany, but the electrical industry, dominated by a small number of companies in each country, provided a fertile environment for cartels, and they were extended more widely after the war.

Apart from GEC, there were some other promising British ventures in the electrical industry before 1914. Dick Kerr, a Scottish company, was active in tramway electrification and built a factory at Preston to make electric motors which was described as 'a harmonious blend of American skill and experience with British financial expertise'.[23] An Italian engineer, Guglielmo Marconi, came to Britain in 1898 to exploit his invention in wireless communications, and, despite competition from Siemens and AEG, his company was the leader in this field at the time of the First World War (see Chapter 10). Although Britain was still a poor third in the electrical industry behind the US and Germany, the beginnings of a fight-back were visible.

The Inter-war Years

The effect of the First World War and the disturbed economic conditions which followed it was to shift the competitive balance among the three leading machinery-exporting nations in favour of the US. Motor vehicles, sewing machines, typewriters, agricultural equipment and other products of the American system spearheaded a rapid increase in US exports during the 1920s (TABLE 8.2).

TABLE 8.2 *Shares of world exports of machinery and transport equipment 1913–37*

per cent

	1913	1929	1937
US	20.2	41.3	36.2
Germany	31.7	19.5	23.3
UK	29.1	19.8	20.5

Source: H. Tyszynski, *World Trade in Manufactured Commodities, 1899–1950,* Manchester School of Economic and Social Studies, no. 19, 1951.

The experience of the British engineering industry in the inter-war years was mixed. Older branches of the industry which had been heavily dependent on exports were hard hit by the depression in world trade. The textile machinery manufacturers, for example, which had exported 60 per cent of their production before the war, were faced at the end of the 1920s with serious over-capacity as overseas markets dried up. In 1931 six of the leading firms, led by Platt Brothers, came together to form Textile Machinery Manufacturers, with a view to cutting costs and eliminating surplus plant. They also negotiated a cartel agreement with the principal European producers, and this helped to stabilise prices. As a response to the Depression the merger was effective, and a good deal of rationalisation was carried out, but, with growing competition from Germany, Switzerland and Japan, the British textile machinery makers were no longer as dominant in world markets as they had been before the war.[24]

The machine tool makers also went through a difficult time. Although their exports increased after the war when the German economy was in disarray, the improvement was not maintained. By the mid-1930s their share of world markets was even lower than it had been in 1913. British manufacturers were squeezed between competition on two sides – from the Germans in high-precision machine tools suitable for small-batch production and from the Americans in special-purpose equipment for mass production. There was a tendency, also visible in other branches of the industry, for British firms to concentrate on simpler equipment for Empire and developing-country markets, while importing more advanced machine tools from the US, Germany and Switzerland.[25]

The newer branches of the engineering industry, especially those linked to the fast-growing motor industry, made better progress. The vehicle component sector benefited from an inflow of American capital and technology, but there was also plenty of indigenous entrepreneurial activity. Joseph Lucas, a Birmingham firm which had originally made bicycle lamps, became the leading supplier of car lighting, starters and other electrical equipment. Some of its technology came from Bosch – a joint company was formed to make diesel fuel injection equipment – and the two companies agreed not to compete with each other in overseas markets. There was also a promising start in the new field of high-speed diesel engines. Frank Perkins, scion of a long-established family business making agricultural machinery in the East Midlands, set up a factory in Peterborough in 1932 to make engines for commercial vehicles and farm tractors; by 1939 he was producing more than 1,000 engines a year.

In electrical engineering the prospects for British manufacturers improved after the reorganisation of the supply side of the industry. In 1926 the government set up a state-funded body, the Central Electricity Board, to co-ordinate the planning of electricity generation, and to build a national grid of high-tension transmission lines. This led to larger and more efficient power stations, and lower prices for the consumer; by the mid-1930s electricity consumption per head was about equal to that of other countries with similar income levels.[26] Demand for generating and transmission equipment, and for electrical appliances such as refrigerators, rose rapidly, giving the manufacturers confidence to invest in new capacity.

There were also changes in the ownership of the industry.[27] Following the expropriation of German-owned properties during the First World War, GEC acquired full control of the Osram lamp company, and the Siemens works at Stafford was sold to a newly formed British group, English Electric, which included Dick Kerr and several other firms. The other Siemens interests in Britain were floated as a public company, owned by British investors.

Hugo Hirst at GEC was now at the height of his powers and eager to enlarge his empire. In 1917 he came close to buying British Westinghouse when it was put up for sale by its American owners, but he was overruled by his fellow directors, who took a more cautious view of how fast GEC should expand. A year later British Westinghouse was sold to Vickers, the armaments manufacturer, and Metropolitan Carriage Wagon and Finance, a Midlands engineering company. The latter was the creation of Dudley Docker, an ambitious industrialist who, like Hirst, was determined to build a stronger British presence in the electrical industry; he hoped that the newly acquired company, which was renamed Metropolitan Vickers, would become a serious rival for Siemens and AEG.[28] However, Vickers ran into financial difficulties in 1927 and was forced to withdraw from the electrical industry. Metropolitan Vickers was sold in 1928 to General Electric of the US, which linked it with British Thomson Houston to form Associated Electrical Industries (AEI).

This transaction was masterminded by Gerard Swope, a shrewd negotiator whose aim was to preserve General Electric's dominant position in the world electrical industry through cartels, mergers and other inter-company agreements. Buying control of Metropolitan Vickers was part of a grand plan to merge all the major British electrical companies into a single enterprise, just as Alfred Mond and Harry McGowan had done in the chemical industry with the formation of Imperial Chemical Industries in 1926 (see Chapter 12). In 1929 Swope's managers had merger talks with Hirst at GEC, but Hirst was adamant that British interests must have majority control in any new group, and the negotiations broke down. Meanwhile, English Electric, after a difficult start, took its place during the 1930s as one of the 'big three' electrical manufacturers, along with AEI and GEC. It was capably led by George Nelson, an engineer who, like Robert Hilton at United Steel (Chapter 6), had been a senior manager at Metropolitan Vickers. In electrical engineering, as in other British industries, professional managers were coming to the fore.

By 1939 the technical gap between the British electrical industry and its German counterpart was narrower than before the First World War. The leading companies were committed to scientific research, and taking a keen interest in the new field of electronics. The start of broadcasting in 1921 had opened up a big market for radio sets, and most of the established electrical companies, as well as many new entrants, were participating in this business. There was also a growing demand for electrical appliances such as refrigerators and vacuum cleaners. American companies with factories in Britain (such as Hoover) met much of this demand, but British entrepreneurs, most of them new to the industry, were also making their mark.[29]

Thus both the electrical and mechanical sides of the engineering industry went through a partial modernisation during the 1920s and 1930s. There was also a trend towards larger companies, brought about by mergers and acquisitions (TABLE 8.3). Some of the mergers, as in textile machinery, were a response to over-capacity. Others involved expansion by companies which wanted to diversify into the faster-growing sectors of the industry. For

TABLE 8.3 *Leading engineering employers in 1935*

Company	No. of employees
Vickers	44,162
Associated Electrical Industries	30,000
Guest Keen & Nettlefolds	30,000
Textile Machinery Makers	24,600
General Electric Company	24,000
Joseph Lucas	20,000
Austin Motor Company	19,000
Tube Investments	15,000

Source: Drawn from David Jeremy, 'The Hundred Largest Employers in the UK, in Manufacturing and Non-manufacturing Industries, in 1907, 1935 and 1955'. Reprinted by permission from *Business History*, vol. 33, no. 1, published by Frank Cass & Company, 900 Eastern Avenue, Ilford, Essex, England. Copyright Frank Cass & Co Ltd.

example, Guest Keen & Nettlefolds (GKN), a Midlands-based group which had been formed in 1902 by bringing together a steel-maker (Guest), a manufacturer of nuts and bolts (Keen), and a manufacturer of screws and fasteners (Nettlefolds), made a number of acquisitions in the inter-war years, including John Lysaght, a supplier of steel stampings and pressings to the motor industry. Another acquisitive Midlands firm was Tube Investments, founded in 1919 as an amalgamation of two steel tube makers with two of their principal customers. Further purchases took Tube Investments into bicycles, electrical appliances and a range of other products.

Taking the whole period from 1870 to 1939, the British engineering industry had made a respectable showing in the face of German and American competition. There were weaknesses where the two late-comers were strong – skill-intensive machinery on one side and scale-intensive machinery on the other – but that left a large middle ground where British firms were competing strongly. In addition to the firms listed in Table 8.3, there were numerous specialists such as Weir, the Scottish pump manufacturer, which were holding their own in world markets.

An important difference from Germany, reinforced by the introduction of protection in 1932, was the bias towards the Empire in the industry's export trade. In the case of electrical engineering, for example, the largest export markets in 1938 were Australia, South Africa, India and New Zealand; these four countries together accounted for 50 per cent of the industry's exports. The international cartels in which many British firms participated usually allocated Empire markets to the British members, leaving the Continent to the Continental manufacturers.

These arrangements may have been storing up problems for the future, but there was no unbridgeable gap, technical or managerial, between the British engineering industry and its German and American counterparts. Nor can it be said that other institutional weaknesses inherited from the past – for example, in the field of labour relations – condemned the industry to inevitable decline. There had been some serious disputes over wages and conditions before and after the First World War, culminating in another lock-out in 1922 in which the Amalgamated Engineering Union (formed in 1920 by a merger between the Amalgamated Society of Engineers and several smaller craft unions) suffered a crushing defeat. After this episode labour relations in engineering were generally stable, and bargaining procedures between the Engineering Employers Federation and the unions were improved. There is no evidence that trade unions obstructed technical change in engineering in the inter-war years.

1945–60: Retreat from Europe

During the war the resources of the engineering industry were largely devoted to the needs of the military. Some of the bigger companies participated in the so-called Shadow factory scheme; these were factories built by the government and managed by private firms to supplement production of war-related goods. English Electric, for example, became a substantial manufacturer of aircraft and aero-engines, and decided to stay in this field after the war. The electrical companies were also involved in the manufacture of radar and other electronics-based equipment; defence electronics was to become an important part of their business after the war.

The Labour government elected in 1945 looked to the engineering industry for a major contribution to the export drive. In this case, unlike cotton textiles, officials were reasonably satisfied – except for one or two weak sectors – with the way the industry was organised and managed, and engineering firms achieved an impressive increase in exports in the first five years after the war. However, this was more a short-term response to the weakness of the balance of payments than a planned programme of market development. It was directed mainly at customers in the sterling area and North America who had the money to pay for imports, rather than the soft currency markets of Continental Europe. This was a rational decision in the aftermath of the war when the Continental economies were in disarray and the need to earn hard currency was urgent. But the neglect of Continental Europe as an export market continued after its recovery in the 1950s. This was to prove a serious error.

At the end of the war, when Allied policy towards Germany was in its punitive phase, it seemed likely that German industry would be shackled and that British manufacturers would take over some of its markets. But the US government's decision in 1947 to integrate West Germany into the Western alliance meant that, except in a few militarily sensitive areas such as aircraft, German industry was free to rebuild its productive capacity and its exports, most of which had traditionally gone to neighbouring European countries. Faced with this prospect, most British engineering firms chose to concentrate their efforts on non-European markets, principally the Commonwealth and the US, rather than engage in a head-on fight with the Germans in Continental Europe.[30]

This had two unfortunate consequences. First, British machinery exports increased more slowly than those of Germany, France and Italy. Economic growth in the Commonwealth was more sluggish than in Continental

Europe, and some of the larger countries, notably Australia, were beginning to restrict imports of manufactured goods in order to build up their own industries. Some British firms, notably the motorcycle manufacturers, did well in the US during the 1950s, but the American market was difficult and volatile; to establish a strong position against powerful domestic rivals was a formidable task.

Second, the choice of more familiar and (apart from the US) less demanding markets deprived the British engineering industry of the stimulus which would have come from fuller participation in intra-European trade. During the 1950s Germany became the hub of a fast-growing and increasingly integrated European market. The German economic miracle was crucially dependent on the growth of exports, and capital goods, for which there was a huge demand as European countries rebuilt their economies, set the pace. Machinery accounted for a fifth of Germany's exports in the early 1950s, and more than two-thirds of this trade was with other European nations.[31] But Germany's role as an importer was no less important. Whereas the protectionist Third Reich had exported manufactured goods in exchange for food and raw materials, the Federal Republic was committed to free trade, and imports of machinery into Germany grew almost as fast as German exports. The size and openness of the German market gave a powerful boost to the previously backward French and Italian engineering industries. As Alan Milward has written, 'German manufactured exports grew in a modernising symbiosis with the exports of other western European economies to Germany; the German market was as important to modernisation as German supply.'[32] The British engineering industry was not part of this network. Its share of world exports, roughly equal to Germany's in the mid-1950s, fell sharply over the subsequent decade (TABLE 8.4).

TABLE 8.4 *Shares of world machinery exports, 1955–65*

figures in per cent of world total

	Britain	Germany	US	Italy	France	Japan
1955	19.6	19.2	36.5	3.0	4.6	na
1965	14.5	22.5	30.1	5.9	5.9	3.7

Source: VDMA, Frankfurt, *Statistical Yearbook.*

The focus on traditional markets allowed many engineering firms to coast along comfortably with product designs and manufacturing methods which had served them well before the war. In the case of machine tools, for example, most manufacturers could make good profits by continuing to sell the simpler types of machine to the Commonwealth and other developing countries. At the end of the 1950s a committee of inquiry set up by the Board of Trade criticised the industry for failing to compete effectively against German, Swiss and American manufacturers in the market for advanced machine tools, and called for a more intensive development effort.[33] Some reforms were instituted as a result of the committee's report, but by that time the gap between the British industry and its main European competitor was as wide as it had been before the war.

The Germans were re-establishing their traditional leadership in skill-intensive machinery, and extending it into areas where British firms had previously been strong. In textile machinery, for example, German manufacturers were quicker than their British counterparts to take advantage of a wave of technological innovation that began in the 1950s. Platt Brothers was still a successful exporter, but it was no longer at the forefront in technology.

If Britain was losing ground in the 1950s at the skill-intensive end of the product spectrum, the situation was more promising in the scale-intensive branches. The motor industry was growing fast, and component-makers such as Lucas were building up their skills in high-volume production. There was also an inflow of investment from the US, strongly encouraged by the government. In construction equipment, for example, Caterpillar and several other American companies built factories in Britain as a base for supplying European and Commonwealth markets. In agricultural machinery, Ford had been making tractors at Dagenham since 1933, and this part of the industry was enlarged after the war. Standard Motor Company, a car manufacturer, used its wartime Shadow factory in Coventry to make tractors designed by Harry Ferguson, an Ulsterman who had invented a novel hydraulic mechanism for controlling implements mounted on the tractor. This operation was later acquired by Massey-Harris, a Canadian farm machinery group, which changed its name to Massey-Ferguson. By the end of the 1950s Ford and Massey-Ferguson were the world's leading tractor exporters, and Britain's share of world exports in this sector was far larger than that of West Germany (TABLE 8.5). Massey-Ferguson also acquired Perkins, the diesel engine manufacturer, and this sector, too, was highly successful in export markets. Cummins, the American diesel engine company, built its first British factory in 1957.

TABLE 8.5 *Export performance in selected products in 1960*

(per centage share of world exports)

	Britain	West Germany
Machine tools	11.2	34.3
Printing machinery	17.0	45.7
Textile machinery	19.8	25.5
Tractors	36.4	9.3
Construction machinery	14.5	11.3
Internal combustion engines	19.3	18.6

Source: VDMA, Frankfurt, *Statistical Yearbook*.

While inward investment was a source of strength in this part of the industry, indigenous entrepreneurs also played an active part. Joseph Bamford launched the first of the JCB range of excavators in 1953. With his flair for marketing and his determination to build a construction equipment factory which would be as well-equipped as Caterpillar's plants in the US, Bamford built a business capable of holding its own against much larger American competitors. In fork-lift trucks, Emmanuel Kaye and J. R. Sharp, joint owners of Lansing Bagnall, competed strongly against American companies and built a large export business from their Basingstoke factory. Production of lift trucks nearly trebled between 1951 and 1961.

Throughout the 1950s demand for machinery was booming, the home market was protected against imports, and order books were generally full or over-full. The same conditions prevailed on the electrical side. New power stations were under construction to make up for the under-investment of the war years, and demand for household appliances was buoyant. The 'Big Three' – English Electric, AEI and GEC – were all making healthy profits.

The best managed of the three was English Electric, where George Nelson was still at the helm; he remained chairman until his death in 1962 at the age of seventy-five. His strategy was to reduce the company's dependence on heavy electrical equipment by building up the aircraft business – a strong design team was established soon after the war – and by pushing more vigorously into electronics. English Electric bought Marconi when it was put up for sale by the government in 1946,[34] and it was one of the first British firms to venture into computers (see Chapter 10). Nelson also tried to buy Siemens Brothers, which would have provided an entrée into telecommunications – Siemens was one of the five companies which supplied telephone exchanges to the Post Office – but he was outbid by AEI.[35]

AEI became a wholly British company soon after the war when General Electric of the US sold its shareholding. It was run from 1954 to 1963 by an Old Etonian businessman-politician, Oliver Lyttelton (later Lord Chandos), who had been a close associate of Winston Churchill during the war. With his excellent City connections, Chandos had no difficulty in raising funds for an ambitious programme of expansion both at the heavy end of the industry and in consumer goods. But AEI suffered from the failure to integrate the two main subsidiaries, Metropolitan Vickers in Manchester and British Thomson Houston in Rugby, which were allowed to operate as separate fiefdoms. The acquisition of Siemens Brothers made AEI's internal structure even more complex. Chandos finally eliminated the old company names in 1959, but AEI remained a somewhat cumbersome, slow-moving organisation.

At GEC Harry Railing, a long-time colleague of Hugo Hirst, took over as chairman after the latter's death in 1942, and he, too, invested in new ventures after the war, including an expensive commitment to nuclear power. GEC was not well organised to manage this expansion and profit margins declined in the second half of the 1950s. Leslie Gamage, Hirst's son-in-law, took over as chairman in 1957 at the age of seventy, and the company's performance continued to deteriorate. When Prudential Assurance, GEC's largest shareholder, was asked in 1959 to subscribe to a new issue of loan stock, it declined to do so, indicating its unease at the way the company was managed. This led to the removal of Gamage from the chairmanship and his replacement by Arnold Lindley, an engineer who had previously run GEC's South African company.[36]

Until the mid-1950s the electrical industry was extensively cartelised, as it had been before the war. In 1956 the Restrictive Trade Practices Act made price-fixing agreements illegal, and in the following year the Monopolies Commission published a critical report which revealed the high profits being earned on electrical machinery. Even before the break-up of the cartels, the 'Big Three' had been facing competition from newer, entrepreneurial firms that were not part of the electrical establishment. One of them was Thorn Electrical Industries, the creation of Austrian-born Jules Thorn, who had come to England in 1923 as a sales representative for an Austrian manufacturer of gas mantles; he later imported lamps from Tungsram in Hungary. Thorn moved into manufacturing during the 1930s, first making lamps and then radio and television sets; he bought an existing company, Ferguson Radio Corporation, and used the Ferguson brand name for his sets. Thorn was not an engineer, but he had a shrewd appreciation of what technology could offer, and soon after the war he persuaded an American company, Sylvania, to share its know-how in fluorescent lighting in return for a shareholding in the British company. The fluorescent tube was the first major technical advance since the incandescent lamp, and it gave Thorn a weapon with which to attack the lamp cartel.[37]

Another outsider was Michael Sobell, who had emigrated to Britain from Poland in the 1930s. Having started in the radio set business in the 1930s he took over a government shadow factory at Hirwaun, near Aberdare, after the war to make electrical equipment, and began making television sets in 1952. Sobell's company, Radio & Allied Industries, became one of the most profitable and efficient manufacturers in the industry; it was floated on the Stock Exchange in 1958.

Sobell had been joined four years earlier by his son-in-law, Arnold Weinstock, who was to become one of Britain's most successful industrialists. Trained in statistics at the London School of Economics, Weinstock brought greater financial discipline to the business and an obsessive antipathy to waste. According to one account, 'he was almost fanatical about costs and would go round the factory inquiring why this component could not be bought for a halfpenny less, or why it was not more efficient to assemble this before that'.[38] By the end of the 1950s Sobell and Weinstock were looking for ways of diversifying away from the volatile television set market into other parts of the electrical industry.

The electrical industry was ripe for restructuring. Too much capacity had been installed in heavy electrical equipment, and with the end of cartels prices and profit margins were under pressure. At the same time the industry found itself under attack from imports. While British manufacturers had been preoccupied with their traditional domestic and Commonwealth customers, an integrated European market was emerging on the other side of the Channel, encouraging firms to adopt Europe-wide manufacturing and marketing strategies.

An early example was the rise of the Italian domestic appliance industry. This was led, not by established electrical manufacturers, but by new firms such as Zanussi, Indesit and Ignis. Taking advantage of advances in compressor design which facilitated mass production, they achieved economies of scale which none of the established producers were able to match and rapidly increased their exports to neighbouring European countries. Although Britain was protected by tariffs, imports of Italian refrigerators and washing machines rose sharply in the second half of the 1950s.[39]

This was a foretaste of what was to happen in other parts of engineering during the 1960s and 1970s as tariff barriers came down – first under the successive GATT rounds of trade negotiations and then through Britain's accession to the EEC in 1973. Imports from the Continent were not the only threat. The Japanese assault on Western markets, already causing problems in shipbuilding and steel, was spreading to other sectors such as motorcycles and television sets. Another source of anxiety was the drive by American companies to enlarge their share of the European market, often by acquisition; there were fears that smaller British firms would be overwhelmed by superior technical and financial resources. All this coincided with a general awareness, in government and in industry, that British economic performance was lagging behind that of the leading Continental countries, and that new initiatives were needed, in government and in industry, to halt the decline. British engineering firms had to shift into a higher gear.

1960–80: The Search for an International Dimension

The impact of these pressures varied from sector to sector, depending on the timing and severity of the challenge which they had to face and on how much ground had already been lost. An extreme case was that of the motorcycle industry. During the 1950s British manufacturers established a lucrative niche in the US, concentrating on the high-performance, sporty bikes which had been a British speciality before the war. American demand was large enough to keep the factories fully employed even though domestic sales were static. As Bernard Docker, chairman of BSA, the largest manufacturer, told his shareholders in 1951, the primary challenge for the company was 'production and still more production'.[40] But BSA, in common with the rest of the industry, was so busy selling its traditional heavy bikes that it neglected the potential demand for lightweight machines. When Vespa and Lambretta scooters began arriving in Britain from Italy in the mid-1950s, they were not taken seriously as a competitive threat. But the Italians and later the Japanese saw that the lightweight bikes which they had developed for their domestic markets as a cheap form of transportation were exportable to richer coun-tries. The Japanese export drive was supported by modern, well-equipped factories, producing on a scale far in excess of the British manufacturers. Honda and the other leading Japanese firms steadily extended their range into heavier bikes, and by the early 1970s they had almost eliminated the British motorcycle manufacturers from the US market. BSA collapsed in 1975, although remnants of the company survived for a few more years, with government help, in the form of the worker-owned Meriden co-operative.[41]

This was, in part, a story of blinkered management, unable to break away from a concept of the motorbike which had given the industry many years of prosperity before and after the war. BSA had been badly run for years. Bernard Docker, chairman from 1940 until he was he was ousted by the Board in 1958, became notorious for his erratic behaviour and lavish life-style.[42] But the motorcycle industry had the misfortune of being in the direct line of fire when the Japanese manufacturers began their attack on Western markets. Although a few Continental manufacturers, including BMW in Germany, survived the attack better than BSA, none of them came close to matching the scale and efficiency of the Japanese. In 1975 Japan accounted for nearly three-quarters of the world's exports of motorcycles. (A limited British revival took place in the 1990s, when production of Triumph motorcycles was restarted in Hinckley, Leicestershire. By the end of the decade the factory was turning out some 20,000 high-performance machines a year, 80 per cent for export.)

If the motorcycle industry was something of a special case, a more serious failure was in a sector where other European countries, especially Germany, were strong – machine tools. Alfred Herbert, the largest and once the most dynamic British machine tool manufacturer, enjoyed long order books dur-ing the 1950s and early 1960s, but it did little to modernise its designs or its manufacturing methods. Many of the machines in use in its factories were more than thirty years old, and almost nothing was spent on market research. This complacency was all the more dangerous because technological change in machine tools was accelerating. Numerical control, an electronics-based system for improving the accuracy of the metal-cutting process, had been developed in the US for the machining of complex aircraft parts, and was beginning to spread to other applications. Manufacturers had to rethink their approach to machine tool design and learn new skills.

In 1966 the directors of Alfred Herbert recognised the need for change and appointed a new chairman from outside the industry, R. D. Young, a senior executive from Tube Investments. By then the decline may have gone too far to be arrested. Alfred Herbert had diversified into a wide range of machine tools, and, shortly before Young's arrival, negotiated an agreement with an American company, Ingersoll, to build special-purpose machine tools which had previously been imported from the US. At this point the fate of the company became entangled with the industrial policies of the Labour government which entered office in 1964. Harold Wilson, the Prime Minister, had made industrial modernisation a central theme in the election campaign. He believed that the government should play an active role in upgrading the technological capabilities of British industry. Two new instruments were created for this purpose – the Ministry of Technology and the Industrial Reorganisation Corporation (IRC), charged with promoting mergers in industries which were too fragmented to compete effectively in world markets.

Both these agencies took a close interest in machine tools, which was seen as one of the weakest sectors of engineering. The IRC looked at ways of helping the two largest firms, Alfred Herbert and Staveley Industries. One possibility was for Herbert to sell some of its machine tool interests to other companies, but nothing came of this idea. In 1969, when the Herbert–Ingersoll joint venture needed money to expand its factory, the IRC agreed to provide a £2.5m loan, but orders for the new machines were far below expectations, and heavy losses from this operation threatened the viability of Alfred Herbert itself.

In 1975 Alfred Herbert was close to bankruptcy, and taken over by the National Enterprise Board, the successor body to the IRC. The company remained in public ownership until it was liquidated and broken up in 1980.

The decline of Alfred Herbert was part of a broader British failure in machine tools which government intervention did nothing to arrest. The IRC encouraged companies from outside the industry to take over some of the weaker producers, but size was not a competitive advantage in this field. The German machine tool industry, the strongest in Europe, consisted mostly of small, specialised firms, employing less than 500 people. Britain's share of world machine tool exports fell sharply in the 1960s and 1970s. This was a period in which, as TABLE 8.6 shows, the Japanese machine tool industry was emerging as a major force. Firms such as Yamazaki, Okuma and Mori Seiki pioneered the development of flexible, computer-controlled lathes and machining centres which were well suited to the needs of small engineering firms.[43]

As the table shows, British firms were falling behind even more precipitately in textile machinery. This was another skill-intensive branch of engineering in which British firms were out-performed by German, Swiss and Japanese competitors. Platt Brothers (which in 1958 became a subsidiary of

TABLE 8.6 *Export performance in machine tools and textile machinery, 1960–80*

(per centage share of total world exports)

	Machine tools		Textile machinery	
	1960	1980	1960	1980
Britain	11.2	8.2	19.8	8.5
Germany	34.3	32.4	25.5	29.0
Japan	1.0	14.5	6.6	13.0
US	28.2	11.1	15.5	6.4

Source: VDMA, Frankfurt, *Statistical Yearbook*.

Stone-Platt Industries, a diversified engineering group) made strenuous efforts to regain its technical leadership during this period – in the new technology of open-end spinning it had a joint development programme with two German and Swiss companies – but here, too, it was overtaken by German and Japanese competitors.

British firms seemed more strongly placed at the start of the 1960s in the scale-intensive, US-influenced sectors of engineering. Exports of farm tractors, construction equipment and diesel engines were going well. But because of the relatively slow growth of the British economy, and the industry's lack of involvement in intra-European trade, an increasing number of British manufacturers were falling behind their Continental counterparts in the scale of their production. This was particularly true of sectors linked to the motor industry; British car production increased much more slowly than in Germany and France during the 1960s and 1970s. Vehicle component makers found that they could not survive on the British market alone; they had to sell more to Continental car and truck assemblers. One way of doing so was to build or acquire factories on the Continent. Lucas built a brake plant in Germany, and formed a joint venture with a French company, Ducellier, to make lighting and other electrical equipment. Another option, pursued by Dunlop, the tyre manufacturer, was to merge with a Continental company. The 1970 union with Pirelli, the Italian tyre manufacturer, was hailed as an imaginative step in European collaboration, but the partnership was plagued by misunderstandings and conflicts of interest, and was unwound in 1980 three-years later; Dunlop sold its European tyre business to Sumitomo Rubber of Japan.

Part of the purpose of the Dunlop–Pirelli merger was to achieve economies of scale. Other British firms pursued the same objective by merging among themselves, and in some cases the IRC lent a helping hand. But mergers were no panacea, as the case of the ball bearings company, Ransome & Marles, makes clear. Although it was the leading British producer of ball bearings, it was small by international standards and had little business outside Britain and the Commonwealth. In 1968 the directors decided to seek an alliance with SKF of Sweden, the world's largest ball bearings manufacturer. The IRC then intervened, believing that the ball bearings industry was too important to be allowed to pass into foreign control, and promoted a merger between Ransome & Marles and two smaller British firms. The IRC hoped that the new group, Ransome Hoffman Pollard, would be big enough to compete on the international stage, but its starting-point – with a 2 per cent share of the world market and only 20 per cent of its sales outside Britain – was poor.[44] Despite valiant efforts over the next twenty years Ransome Hoffman Pollard never succeeded in lifting itself into the top rank of ball bearings companies. In 1990, after several changes of ownership, it was sold to a Japanese company, NSK.

This story illustrates the difficulties that many British firms experienced during the 1960s and 1970s as they tried to reduce their dependence on domestic and Commonweath markets. If Ransome & Marles had Europeanised itself much earlier, as SKF did, it might have had a better chance of surviving as an independent firm. As it was, the task may have been impossible.

The same forces were at work in electrical engineering. Here the initial stimulus for the reorganisation of the industry came not so much from international competition as from managerial weaknesses in some of the leading companies. The first step came in 1961, when Radio & Allied Industries, of which Arnold Weinstock was now managing director, merged with GEC. The attraction of the deal for GEC was that it acquired an able manager who could re-invigorate its poorly performing consumer products businesses. But the GEC board soon saw that Weinstock's talents were needed in running the group as a whole. In 1963 he was appointed managing director, a post he was to hold for the next thirty-three years.

Aided by his finance director and close colleague, Kenneth Bond, Weinstock developed a style of management which owed a great deal to his earlier experience at Radio & Allied. He looked on GEC with the eye of an owner – he had a sizeable personal shareholding in the company as a result of the merger – and he believed in tight financial control from a small head office, combined with a high degree of autonomy for the heads of the operating businesses. The usual appurtenances of a large corporation – a palatial head-quarters filled with advisory and support staff – were entirely alien to Weinstock's thinking. In the three years following his appointment as managing director GEC's pre-tax profits increased from £6m to £17m, the share price rose strongly, and Weinstock acquired a reputation as one of the handful of able and ambitious managers who were dragging British industry into the modern world.

Not surprisingly, when the IRC began examining ways of rationalising the heavy electrical industry, GEC under Weinstock was considered a poss-ible leader. In 1967 the IRC tried to arrange a friendly merger between GEC and AEI, but AEI resisted, and Weinstock, supported by the IRC, launched a hostile take-over bid. A hard-fought battle ensued, but AEI had dis-appointed its shareholders for too long, while GEC under Weinstock had become a City favourite. The result was a narrow victory for GEC.

Less than a year after the GEC–AEI merger the third member of the 'Big Three', English Electric was the subject of an unsolicited take-over approach from Plessey. Plessey was primarily an electronics company; it was interested in English Electric's Marconi subsidiary and in its stake in the recently formed computer group, International Computers Limited. English Electric, now chaired by George Nelson's son (also called George), could see no merit in Plessey's proposal and turned instead to Weinstock at GEC. Once again the IRC used its influence on Weinstock's behalf, and the outcome was an agreed merger. Nelson became chairman of the combined group and Weinstock continued as managing director.

Weinstock's record at GEC has been the subject of some controversy, especially in relation to the electronics industry, which is discussed in Chapter 10. As far as heavy electrical plant is concerned the GEC/AEI/English Elec-tric mergers were unquestionably successful. Weinstock welded the three businesses together and established GEC as a credible member of a world oligopoly in which German and American companies were no longer as dominant as they had been before the war. Of the four pre-war leaders, AEG in Germany was in the throes of a prolonged decline, while Westinghouse was slipping further behind its American rival, General Electric. Within Europe France's Compagnie Générale d'Electricité had emerged, following a govern-ment-induced reorganisation of the French electrical industry, as a strong contender. GEC was on a par with these companies in terms of technical and financial strength.

The market for heavy electrical plant differed from most of the rest of electrical engineering in that it was unaffected by European economic integration. In the larger European countries, the electricity supply companies, whether state-owned as in Britain and France or privately owned as in Germany, bought their equipment exclusively from domestic suppliers, and cross-border trade was minimal. The battle for export business was fought in developing countries, which did not have their own manufacturing industries, and to some extent in the US.

At the consumer end of the industry, on the other hand, intra-European trade was well established, and here GEC was less well placed. Its Hotpoint brand was virtually unknown on the Continent, and the scale of its production was far lower than that of the big Italian manufacturers. Similarly in lamps, GEC's Osram subsidiary was profitable, but its use of the Osram name was limited to Britain and the Commonwealth, and it was a minnow compared to the giants of the lamps business – Siemens, Philips of the Netherlands and General Electric of the US. In these businesses, even after the mergers with AEI and English Electric, GEC was not yet a world player.

The same was true of Thorn, the other star of the British electrical industry. During the 1960s Thorn had the largest share of the British television set market and was second to GEC-Hotpoint in domestic appliances; it had also bought AEI's lighting interests before the merger with GEC, consolidating its leadership in this field. But Thorn was not yet a world leader in any of these businesses, and, in one of them, television sets, it faced growing competition from the Japanese. In the closing years of Jules Thorn's chairmanship (he retired in 1976), the company diversified into a range of industrial products and was beginning to acquire the character of a conglomerate. The task for Thorn's successors was to give the company the international dimension that it lacked.

This was the strategic issue facing many of the other large engineering companies that had expanded by acquisition during the 1960s and 1970s (TABLE 8.7). Tube Investments, for example, had spread itself over a wide range of activities, including bicycles, domestic appliances, steelworks plant, aluminium and machine tools as well as its original business in steel tubes. Most of this expansion had taken place in the first fifteen years after the war under Ivan Stedeford, chairman from 1939 to 1962; one of his biggest acquisitions was that of Raleigh, making Tube Investments the world's largest bicycle manufacturer. His successor, Edwin Plowden, was a distinguished civil servant who brought a more orderly style to the running of the company, but he did nothing to narrow the company's diverse range of activities; he even extended it with an unsuccessful venture in machine tools. By the mid-1970s weaknesses were appearing in several parts of the group. Raleigh was facing strong competition from bicycle-makers in Taiwan and other developing countries.

TABLE 8.7 *Leading British engineering employers in 1974*

Company	No. of employees
GEC	200,000
Guest Keen Nettlefolds	120,340
Thorn	87,000
Hawker Siddeley*	86,700
Lucas	84,312
Tube Investments	82,100
BICC†	57,000
Vickers	40,543

*Hawker Siddeley was primarily an aircraft manufacturer (until the nationalisation of the aircraft industry in 1977), but had diversified into mechanical and electrical engineeering.
†BICC was the principal British cable manufacturer.

Source: *Fortune*, August 1975.

The second half of the 1970s was a critical period for many of these firms. European competition was hotting up following Britain's entry into the Common Market; Japanese firms were advancing strongly in some parts of the industry such as machine tools and construction equipment; developing-country producers, as in bicycles, were starting to make an impact; and the world economy was slowing down. British companies had to find a defensible position in what had become a more open and more crowded world market.

The 1980s and 1990s: Looking for Niches

A symbolic event at the start of the 1980s was the collapse of Platt Brothers, once the undisputed world champion in textile machinery. As part of Stone-Platt Industries, Platt Brothers had broadened its range of products, acquired other textile machinery makers in Britain and the US, and tried hard to catch up with its German and Swiss rivals in technology. But the Lancashire factories were overmanned, the parent company had diversified too widely, and its debts were dangerously high. When the British economy entered a severe recession in 1980, Stone-Platt was plunged into a financial crisis. New managers, appointed at the behest of the banks, made strenuous efforts to save the company. Following unsuccessful attempts to sell the textile machinery business to overseas buyers, the company went into receivership in 1982. Some of the subsidiaries were bought from the receivers and prospered under new ownership, but new American owners failed to resuscitate the Platt Brothers business, and in 1993 it went into receivership again.

Several other engineering companies, such as Weir, came close to bankruptcy during the 1980–81 recession as the overvalued pound undermined the profitability of their exports.[45] But the least likely firms to survive were those which did not have a core business that could be made internationally competitive. Stone-Platt's failure, like that of Alfred Herbert in machine tools, can be linked to a persistent British weakness, especially in relation to Germany, in complex, skill-intensive machinery. As TABLE 8.8 shows, Britain's share of world exports of machine tools and textile machinery continued to decline in the 1980s and 1990s.

The contraction in these two sectors was part of a drastic restructuring of the British engineering industry which took place during these two decades. This involved changes in ownership, and changes in strategic direction on the part of many of the leading companies. The scale-intensive sectors of the industry, producing standard machinery in relatively long runs, were affected by the increase in cross-border investment – the phenomenon known as globalisation. The world's leading companies sought to strengthen their position by building or acquiring factories in their principal overseas markets and organising their production and distribution on a worldwide basis. Globalisation was generally led by companies from the three largest industrial countries – the US, Germany and Japan.

British firms operating in these sectors had a difficult choice to make. Were they big enough to compete against the world leaders, should they sell

TABLE 8.8 *Export performance in machine tools and textile machinery 1980–95*

(per centage share of total world exports)

	Machine tools		Textile machinery	
	1980	1995	1980	1995
Britain	8.2	3.8	8.5	3.4
Germany	32.4	20.2	29.0	30.5
Japan	14.5	28.2	13.0	19.7
US	11.1	9.5	6.4	4.4

Source: VDMA, Frankfurt, *Statistical Yearbook.*

out and become part of a non-British company's global network, or should they specialise in niches where they would not be at a disadvantage because of their small size? The fate of Ransome & Marles, the ball bearings company, has already been described – a long struggle to establish a British-owned world leader, and the eventual sale to a Japanese company. In the case of fork-lift trucks, the leading British manufacturer, Lansing Bagnall, was acquired by Linde of Germany in 1990, and the Basingstoke plant was integrated into the German company's European manufacturing organisation.

In construction equipment, J. C. Bamford followed a different path. This sector was dominated by American and Japanese companies such as Caterpillar and Komatsu which manufactured a wide range of machinery on a large scale, and it would have been difficult if not impossible for Bamford to compete against them across the board. It chose to concentrate on the product on which the firm's early success had been built – the backhoe loader – and to support it selectively with other machines, such as telescopic handlers and rough-terrain lift trucks, where it was not at a scale disadvantage. Bamford survived into the 1990s as a profitable construction equipment manufacturer.

When Trevor Holdsworth was appointed chairman of Guest Keen & Nettlefolds in 1979, he and his colleagues realised that the existing portfolio of businesses was wholly unsuited to the competitive conditions now in prospect. Holdsworth had been trained as an accountant, and, perhaps because he had not spent his entire career with GKN, could see more clearly what had to be done. 'We had no unique technology or proprietary products: we were really a large sub-contractor. And we were almost wholly dependent on the British motor industry which was in severe decline. We had to find new products, new technology and we had to spread internationally.'[46] Fortunately, one of the companies which GKN had acquired in the 1960s, Birfield, contained a 'jewel' on which an international business could be built. This was the Hardy Spicer constant velocity joint, a key component for front-wheel-drive cars. Birfield was also part-owner of a German company operating in the same field. By exploiting these two assets with great skill, GKN reinvented itself as an internationally competitive vehicle component manufacturer, with a large share of the European and American markets. The commitment to steel-making, which had been at the heart of the group since its creation in 1902, was reduced and eventually eliminated, and most of the companies which had been bought in the 1950s and 1960s were disposed of.

A similar transformation took place at Tube Investments under Christopher Lewinton, a newcomer who had spent most of his career in the US. Lewinton believed that the company's distinctive strength lay in specialised engineering, not in consumer products, and investment should be concentrated in areas where the group's technology was strong or potentially strong. A series of disposals and acquisitions took place, aimed at giving Tube Investments a world-leading position in three areas – mechanical seals, specialised tubing supplied mainly to the motor industry, and aircraft components. Bicycles, domestic appliances, machine tools and aluminium were all sold off. Like GKN, Tube Investments (renamed TI Group) became a smaller, more specialised and more profitable company.

Companies supplying components to the motor industry had to adapt to a change in purchasing policy on the part of the vehicle assemblers. In order to reduce the cost of bought-in materials, the assemblers restricted their purchases to a small number of suppliers in each product category, and delegated to them the responsibility for providing systems or sub-systems rather than discrete components. These 'first-tier' suppliers were expected to operate on as global a scale as the assemblers themselves. To compete at this level component-makers needed technical strength, a high volume of sales in their chosen field, and the financial and managerial capacity to run an international network of factories.

The 1990s saw an increasing number of trans-national mergers among these companies. Lucas, for example, hit hard by the decline of the British motor industry in the 1970s and 1980s, was forced to accept a merger proposal – in effect, a take-over – from an American brake manufacturer, Varity.[47] Two years later the merged company, Lucas Varity, was itself taken over by another American company, TRW. Another large British component manufacturer, T & N (formerly Turner & Newall), was bought by Federal Mogul of the US in 1997.

Without the kind of technical advantage which GKN enjoyed in constant velocity joints, it was hard for British-owned firms to compete on an international scale in this sector. An alternative strategy, followed by Smiths Industries, was to shift into a different field. This company, famous for its clocks and watches, had been the principal supplier of instruments to the British motor industry since the 1920s. At the end of the 1970s it was suffering, like Lucas, from the decline of car and truck production in Britain. Roger Hurn, appointed managing director in 1979 after twenty years with the company, concluded that a radical break with the past had to be made. 'We had virtually no presence on the Continent, and we faced the prospect of a large investment in new products as electronics took over the instrument business.'[48] Between 1980 and 1982 Smiths withdrew from vehicle instruments and from clocks and watches, in order to specialise in aircraft components. This was a sector in which Smiths had advanced technology, and, because of the size of the British aircraft industry, a healthy home market.

Many of the surviving British-owned engineering companies were ones which specialised in the middle ground between the skill-intensive and the scale-intensive end of the product spectrum. When Weir, the Scottish pump manufacturer, reviewed its strategy after surviving its financial crisis in 1981, it concluded that its future lay in 'making products which were difficult to design or difficult to make and which were probably not produced in large quantities'.[49] Over the subsequent decade it modernised its main Glasgow factory, acquired other businesses related to pumps and expanded internationally, buying a large pump manufacturer in the US in 1994. When Imperial Metal Industries (IMI), formerly a subsidiary of ICI, was floated as an independent company in 1978, it was tied to the British economy and low-technology metal businesses; since then it has turned itself into a group of 'clearly defined, global businesses with technical and market leadership', with less than a third of its sales in Britain.[50]

One of the most successful British engineering companies during the 1980s was BTR. Built up by Owen Green, it concentrated on medium-technology businesses operating in niche markets which benefited from BTR's strict financial controls and rigorous attention to manufacturing efficiency.[51] Much of its growth was based on acquisitions, including that of Dunlop in 1985 and Hawker Siddeley in 1991. But BTR stumbled after Green's retirement in 1993 and, as international competition increased, the need for greater specialisation became evident. A refocusing of the business began under new management in 1996, but BTR continued to perform poorly. In 1998 it merged with Siebe, another large engineering group which had also expanded by acquisition, principally in the field of industrial automation and controls. The merged company, which was renamed Invensys, made clear its intention to compete in a smaller number of sectors where it could build a sizeable share of the world market.

Globalisation came later in electrical engineering, and took a different form. At the start of the 1980s the European market for heavy electrical equipment was still nationally based; the electricity supply authorities bought exclusively from their domestic suppliers. These arrangements began to break up as the utilities, for environmental and cost reasons, switched from coal-fired and nuclear power stations to smaller, more flexible installations, based on gas turbines. At the same time, some governments, led by Britain, introduced greater competition into the electricity market.[52] After the privatisation of the British electricity supply industry in 1987, the private-sector generating companies were no longer committed, as their state-owned predecessors had been, to buying British. Other European governments, under pressure from the European Commission, were also opening up their markets. This precipitated a series of mergers and joint ventures among the equipment manufacturers, starting with the link between Asea of Sweden and Brown Boveri of Switzerland in 1988. In the following year Weinstock negotiated a partnership with Alcatel-Alsthom (formerly Compagnie Générale d'Electricité) in France. This was primarily motivated by GEC's need to get access to the French company's gas turbine technology, but by joining forces with the French Weinstock also preserved a strong British presence in a rapidly consolidating industry (TABLE 8.9).

Despite the general trend towards globalisation, there was still scope for nationally based strategies in some areas. In domestic appliances, the rise of the Italian manufacturers was checked during the 1980s by a shift in consumer tastes away from standardised, low-price products towards greater variety. While some manufacturers, notably Electrolux in Sweden, sought economies of scale by buying appliance firms in Europe and the US and integrating them into a worldwide manufacturing system, GEC-Hotpoint continued to concentrate almost exclusively on the British market, and its profits were a good deal better than those of the globalisers.[53]

TABLE 8.9 *Consolidation in the heavy electrical industry, 1967–99*

1967	GEC buys AEI
1968	GEC buys English Electric
1968	C. A. Parsons merges with A. Reyrolle to form Reyrolle Parsons
1968	Siemens and AEG form Kraft-werk Union, joint venture in turbine generators
1969	Regrouping of French heavy electrical industry under CGE (later renamed Alcatel-Alsthom)
1976	AEG sells its half-share in KWU to Siemens
1977	Reyrolle Parsons merges with Clark Chapman to form Northern Engineering Industries (NEI)
1988	Asea (Sweden) merges with Brown Boveri (Switzerland) to form ABB
1989	GEC and Alcatel-Alsthom form joint venture, GEC-Alsthom
1989	Rolls-Royce buys NEI
1996	Rolls-Royce puts NEI up for sale
1997	Siemens buys Parsons Power Generation Systems from Rolls-Royce
1997	ABB buys Westinghouse's power-generating interests in the US
1998	GEC-Alsthom, renamed Alstom, floated on stock market
1999	Alstom and ABB merge their power-generating equipment businesses

Note: Following the AEI/GEC/English Electric mergers, the only other British turbine-generator manufacturer, C. A. Parsons, sought to safeguard its position, first by merging with Reyrolle, a switchgear manufacturer, and then with Clark Chapman, a boiler manufacturer, to form Northern Engineering Industries. But it remained much smaller than the leading international electrical manufacturers, and its problems were not solved during the period when it was owned by Rolls-Royce. By the end of the 1990s, as a result of the mergers and acquisitions listed above, the industry was consolidated around Siemens and ABB-Alstom in Europe, General Electric in the US, and Toshiba, Hitachi and Mitsubishi Electric in Japan.

Meanwhile Thorn, after the retirement of its founder in 1976, had embarked on a strategy that took the company more deeply into electronics, starting with the acquisition of EMI in 1980. The failure of that strategy, which led to Thorn's withdrawal from virtually all its manufacturing activities, is described in Chapter 10. But Thorn had one electrical business, lamps, that seemed capable of being given an international dimension. This was the view of Colin Southgate, a former computer software entrepreneur who joined the company in 1982 and became chief executive in 1987. Southgate set in train a strategy of expansion, buying several European light fittings companies to support a sales drive on the Continent. However, Thorn had great difficulty in prising wholesalers and distributors away from their established suppliers, principally Siemens and Philips. After various attempts to form joint ventures with other companies had failed, Thorn's lamps business was sold to General Electric of the US in 1991.[54] Following GEC's decision to sell its Osram subsidiary to Siemens, the participation of British-owned firms in what had once been the most lucrative part of the electrical industry came to an end.

A Restructured Industry

Out of the changes in structure and ownership which took place in the 1980s and 1990s emerged a smaller but more internationally competitive engineering industry, with a share of world exports roughly comparable to that of its Italian and French counterparts (TABLE 8.10).

Why did integration into the world market take the form it did? Although it is difficult to generalise about so large and complex an industry, three trends are discernible: a contraction in the skill-intensive sectors of the industry

TABLE 8.10 *Shares of world machinery exports 1960–95*

(per cent of total)

	1960	1980	1995
Britain	16.7	10.2	7.1
Germany	21.9	21.8	16.1
Italy	5.1	7.7	7.7
France	5.6	7.6	5.6
US	32.7	23.7	16.5
Japan	2.1	10.5	18.3
Others	15.9	18.5	28.7

Source: VDMA, Frankfurt, *Statistical Yearbook*.

such as machine tools and textile machinery; an increase in foreign ownership of the scale-intensive sectors; and a tendency for the surviving British-owned firms to specialise in niches which fall in the middle ground between skill and scale.

The weakness at the skill-intensive end of the spectrum had been evident long before the Second World War, and was not corrected after the war. It was not, however, a uniquely British weakness. The French machine tool industry did even less well than its British counterpart, and attempts by the government to revive it were no more successful than in Britain. Both countries – and the same was true of the US – lacked the infrastructure of craft skills and supportive local institutions on which the technical strength of the German machine tool industry depended. Partly because of the importance of local factors as a source of competitive advantage, these sectors of the engineering industry still consist predominantly of relatively small firms which export from their home base. There has been some cross-border investment in machine tools – Yamazaki, for example, a leading Japanese manufacturer, built a large factory in Worcester in 1987 – but the trend towards globalisation has been much less marked than, for example, in vehicle components.

In the scale-intensive sectors of the industry Britain has benefited throughout the post-war period from the inflow of foreign and especially American investment. Some of the most successful exporting sectors at the end of the 1990s are those, such as farm tractors, construction equipment and diesel engines, in which American companies built or acquired British factories soon after the war (TABLE 8.11). Britain has been a good global platform for these branches of the industry, even though the participation of British-owned companies has diminished. The relatively poor showing by British firms is partly due to to their failure, with some notable exceptions, to internationalise and Europeanise their operations in the first 10–15 years after the war. When they started to do so, in the 1960s and 1970s, it was often too late to recover the ground which had been lost.

The weakness in skill-intensive sectors reflected a long-standing deficiency, especially in relation to Germany, in the supply of craft skills. Neither of the other institutional weaknesses discussed in earlier chapters, the labour relations system and the financial system, played a central part in this story. Although the engineering industry suffered from the general deterioration in labour relations during the 1960s and 1970s, the sectors that declined most precipitately, such as machine tools and motor cycles, did so for reasons that had little to do with strikes or restrictive practices. Equally, there is no evidence that the industry suffered from inadequate support from banks and financial institutions, or that it was damaged by excessive take-over activity.

TABLE 8.11 *Leading British engineering exporters in 1997*

Company	Ownership	Exports (£m)
GEC	British	2052
Lucas Varity	British	854
New Holland UK*	Italy	798
J. C. Bamford	British	575
Cummins UK	US	512
Caterpillar	US	476
GKN	British	475
BICC	British	379
Vickers	British	282
Smiths Industries	British	273
IMI	British	220
Delta	British	209
Siebe	British	179
Weir	British	141

*New Holland, controlled by Fiat of Italy, acquired Ford's UK tractor business in 1991.

Source: *Financial Times*, 17 December 1998.

—————————•○•—————————

NINE

The Motor Industry:
An Avoidable Disaster

In 1960 British Motor Corporation (BMC) was one of the world's leading car makers. It held nearly 40 per cent of the British market and produced more cars than any other European company except Volkswagen. Fifteen years later, as the largest constituent of British Leyland Motor Corporation, it was on the brink of bankruptcy and taken over by the government. Fifteen years later still, having changed its name to Rover, it was back in the private sector as a subsidiary of British Aerospace, but too weak to survive without an alliance with a larger car manufacturer. In 1994 Rover was sold to BMW of Germany.

The BMC/British Leyland/Rover saga is part of Britain's most serious post-war industrial failure. Among the industries discussed in this book the motor industry is exceptional in three respects: the amount of ground that was lost to Continental competitors in the first thirty years after the war; the damage caused by government intervention in the 1960s and 1970s; and the role played by non-British companies in the partial recovery which took place in the 1980s and 1990s. At the end of the century Britain was the only one of the larger European countries not to have a major nationally owned car company. Germany had three (Volkswagen, Daimler-Benz and BMW), France two (Renault and Peugeot) and Italy one (Fiat). Even Rolls-Royce Motors, the epitome of Britishness, was sold to Volkswagen in 1998. How did this situation come about?

The British Motor Industry before 1939

The world's first motor cars were built in the 1880s by Gottlieb Daimler and Carl Benz, working independently of each other in Stuttgart and Mannheim. But the two pioneers were slow to market their inventions, and the technology was quickly taken up by a group of enterprising French manufacturers, including Armand Peugeot, a bicycle manufacturer.[1] France, especially Paris, provided a more receptive market for luxury consumer goods, and until 1905, when it was overtaken by the US, France had the world's largest motor industry; it remained the European leader until the First World War (TABLE 9.1).

TABLE 9.1 *Car production 1903–13*

(in units)

	France	Britain	Germany	US
1903	14,100	2,000	1,450	11,321
1908	25,000	10,500	5,547	65,000
1913	45,000	34,000	20,388	485,000

Source: James Laux, *The European Automobile Industry*, Twayne, 1992, p. 8.

British entrepreneurs lagged behind at the start – the first British cars were adaptations of French and German models – but, as the potential size of the market became clearer, a substantial industry took shape. Some of the early British car makers, such as Rover, Singer and Humber, came from the bicycle trade. Others were independent entrepreneurs with an engineering background. Henry Royce, for example, having served an apprenticeship with the Great Northern Railway Company, started a company in Manchester to make electrical equipment, then switched to cars in 1904 in partnership with Charles Rolls, who had a car dealership in London. The market also attracted established engineering firms, including the armaments manufacturers Vickers and Armstrong Whitworth.

The involvement of Vickers came about through the intervention of

Herbert Austin, who was to become one of the country's leading car manufacturers. Austin was born and educated in England, but served an apprenticeship in Australia, where he worked for the Wolseley Sheep Shearing Machine Company. When this company moved to England in 1889 and set up a workshop in Birmingham, Austin was appointed general manager. He persuaded the directors to let him experiment with car manufacturing, but the company's financial resources were limited, and Austin looked for a new sponsor. In 1901 Vickers took over Wolseley's car business and put Austin in charge. Four years later Austin left Wolseley to set up on his own, establishing a car factory at a disused printing works in the village of Longbridge, south-west of Birmingham.[2]

Britain, the richest country in Europe and still committed to free trade, was a large importer of cars and components up to the First World War, but the efforts of Austin and others gradually reduced the industry's dependence on French and German technology. All the European firms were producing cars in small numbers – rarely more than a few hundred a year – for an affluent minority of the population. There was little standardisation of design or of components, and the production process relied on craft skills, in line with traditional engineering practice.

In the US, where the market was potentially far larger, the industry took a different form. In 1902 Randolph Olds produced a light-weight car, the Oldsmobile, selling for less than $1,000, and it was an immediate success. Over the next few years Henry Ford and a group of talented engineers around him evolved a novel approach to making cars which marked a radical departure from craft techniques. Determined to produce a car which ordinary people could afford, Ford aimed for simplicity of design, ease of manufacture and, above all, standardisation. Special-purpose machine tools were linked together in a synchronised manufacturing system which achieved massive economies of scale. The Model T Ford was launched in 1908, and a new factory devoted to this model was built at Highland Park, Detroit. In 1913, when the moving assembly line was in full operation, 300,000 cars were produced, more than the whole of the European motor industry put together. In contrast to the production methods used in Europe, 'Fordism' depended on tight supervision of predominantly unskilled employees, each of whom was given a precise, repetitive task.

The Model T was designed for the US market, but it was also successful overseas. The biggest export market was Britain, and in 1911, in order to reduce shipping costs, an assembly plant was opened at Trafford Park in Manchester. Ford was soon the market leader, selling 6,000 cars in 1913, twice as many as Wolseley, its nearest competitor. None of the British firms had yet adjusted to the revolutionary implications of what Ford had done.[3] The first to do so was William Morris, a self-taught mechanic who had run a bicycle repair shop in the village of Cowley, south of Oxford.[4] With the help of a wealthy patron, the Earl of Macclesfield, Morris started assembling cars in 1912, and launched the Morris Oxford in the following year. Priced at £180, the Oxford was £45 more expensive than the Model T, but it was more comfortable and offered more features. It was followed in 1915 by the slightly larger Morris Cowley. To keep costs down, Morris relied on outside suppliers for most of his components, including the engine.

During the First World War the government imposed a 33⅓ per cent tariff on imported cars and components. This was an emergency measure to save shipping space, but the manufacturers pressed for the tariff to be retained after the war, and it remained in place, apart from a brief suspension in 1924–5, until 1956. Morris, who had planned to use American engines in his Cowley model, had to turn to British manufacturers. Ford, too, was obliged to develop a network of local component suppliers instead of importing from the US. One of the consequences of protection – and this was also true of France and Germany – was to stimulate American companies to invest directly in Europe, either by building their own factories, which was Ford's policy, or by acquisition. General Motors, Ford's principal competitor in the US, bought Vauxhall in Britain in 1925 and Opel in Germany in 1929.

The brief post-war boom in Britain encouraged scores of hopeful entrepreneurs to try their hand at car making, but the recession which began in 1920 led to a shake-out in the industry; the number of car manufacturers fell from 88 in 1922 to 31 in 1929.[5] Boldly cutting prices when demand fell, William Morris increased his share of the market, and overtook Ford as the country's largest manufacturer. In 1925 just over 50,000 Cowleys and Oxfords were produced, representing 41 per cent of the industry's output. Austin also gained ground during this period, despite a financial crisis at the start of the decade which briefly put the firm into the hands of a receiver. The turning-point was the launch of the 8 hp Austin Seven in 1922. Smaller and cheaper than the Cowley and the Model T, it became the best-selling British car of the inter-war years.

Even after this success Austin's finances remained fragile and in 1924 he responded favourably to a suggestion, put forward by Dudley Docker on behalf of Vickers, that Austin, Morris and Wolseley should merge into a single enterprise. When Morris rejected the idea – he did not wish to relinquish personal control over his business – Austin turned to General Motors of the US. Terms for the sale of Austin to General Motors were agreed, but the proposal was vetoed by Austin's fellow directors, who believed that the company had a promising future on its own. By 1926 Austin's finances had recovered sufficiently for him to try to buy Wolseley when it was put up for sale by Vickers, but he was outbid by Morris.

Although the advent of cheaper cars enlarged the market, Britain, unlike the US, was still predominantly a middle-class rather than a mass market, and competition was based more on specification than price. Morris and Austin understood this better than Ford, and they offered a range of well-designed cars, less spartan than the Model T, to suit different customer tastes.[6] Henry Ford refused to allow his managers to adapt the Model T for the British market or to develop a smaller car. By 1930 the American company's share of the British market was down to 6 per cent, far behind Austin and Morris and only marginally ahead of Vauxhall, Rootes and Standard (TABLE 9.2).

TABLE 9.2 *Leading British car producers, 1930 and 1938*

(per centage of total car output held by each company)

	1930	1938
Morris	34.4	23.6
Austin	32.2	20.4
Ford	6.1	17.5
Vauxhall	5.1	10.4
Rootes	4.8	10.2
Standard	4.4	9.9
Others	13.0	8.0

Source: D. G. Rhys, 'Concentration in the Inter-war Motor Industry', *Journal of Transport History*, vol. 3, no. 4, September 1976.

Ford's decline in Britain, together with increasing competition in other European countries from General Motors and from local firms such as Citroën and Fiat, finally convinced Henry Ford that the company's international operations needed to be reorganised. A new British company was formed to co-ordinate all Ford's European activities, and a factory was built at Dagenham in Essex to replace the Manchester assembly plant; production began in 1932. Partly financed by the sale of shares in Ford's British company to British investors, Dagenham was a smaller version of the giant River Rouge plant in Detroit, which had opened in 1921. Equipped to make 120,000 vehicles a year, far more than any other British factory, it was intended to be a source of components and vehicles for Ford's associated companies on the Continent. This early attempt at a European manufacturing strategy was frustrated by the general retreat into protectionism throughout Western Europe, and Dagenham operated well below its capacity.[7] Within Britain, however, Ford's market position improved after the launch of the 8 hp 'baby Ford', the first Ford car designed and built in Britain for the British market. It competed directly against the Austin Seven and the Morris Minor.[8]

By the end of the 1930s Morris, Austin and Ford together accounted for just over 60 per cent of British car production. The number of independent car makers had dwindled to about twenty, but there was still a demand for a variety of models in different price categories, and the British industry remained more fragmented than its American counterpart. The three leaders faced vigorous competition from Vauxhall, Standard and Rootes, each of which held about 10 per cent of the market. Outside the 'Big Six' there were several successful specialist firms. Rover, after nearly going bankrupt in 1930–32, had abandoned low-priced cars in order to concentrate on the semi-luxury end of the market, where it built a reputation for solid, well-engineered vehicles.[9] A new entrant, William Lyons, began making roadsters and sports cars under the name of Swallow in 1931; the name was changed to Jaguar in 1936.

The British motor industry was by now the largest in Europe, although the gap with the US was even bigger than before the First World War (TABLE 9.3). The French manufacturers had failed to build on their earlier lead, partly because of the poor performance of the French economy, but also because of management mistakes. André Citroën was the most adventurous of the French manufacturers, but his finances were always precarious: he nearly sold out to General Motors in 1919, and in 1935, the year of his death, the company was again on the brink of liquidation. Control passed to Michelin, the tyre manufacturer, one of Citroën's largest creditors.[10] Renault and Peugeot were managed more cautiously and came through the Depression in better shape.

The German industry, slow to break away from craft methods, performed

TABLE 9.3 *Motor vehicle production in selected countries, 1933 and 1938*

(in thousands of units)

	1933	1938
USA	1,920	2,489
Britain	286	447
Germany	118	340
France	189	227
Italy	40	67

Source: Society of Motor Manufacturers and Traders, *The Motor Industry of Great Britain 1938*, 1939.

poorly in the 1920s. Daimler and Benz came together in 1926 (after the death of the two founders), and the merged company specialised in high-priced vehicles produced in small numbers. The bankers who arranged the Daimler-Benz merger (principally Deutsche Bank) had hoped to create a larger group embracing Opel, the most Fordist of the German manufacturers, but the Opel family declined to participate and sold their business to General Motors in 1929.[11] By the mid-1930s Opel and Ford, which had built an assembly plant in Cologne in 1931, were the market leaders. The industry was then given a powerful boost by Hitler's 'motorisation' programme, of which the centrepiece was the Volkswagen or 'people's car', designed by Ferdinand Porsche.[12] This car was to be manufactured in a giant factory at Wolfsburg in Lower Saxony. The plan was for an initial output of 150,000 cars in 1940, rising eventually to the extraordinary figure of 1.5m cars a year. Construction went ahead as planned, but by the time the factory was built, the war had started and the factory was given over to military vehicles.

In comparing British, French and German car manufacturers at the time of the Second World War, it is hard to detect signs of technical or managerial weakness in the British industry which might account for its poor performance after 1945. Two of the men who worked closely with Morris, A. A. Rowse and F. G. Woollard, were well-trained and creative engineers, as was Carl Engelbach at Austin. Woollard's role in adapting American flow-line techniques to British conditions has been compared in originality to that of

Taichi Ohno, architect of Toyota's famous 'lean production' system in the 1950s.[13] Another capable engineer, Leonard Lord, was hired by Morris to reorganise the Wolseley factory and later moved to the main Cowley works, which he transformed into one of the most efficient car factories in Britain.[14] The fact that the Austin Seven was made under licence in Germany and France suggests that British car manufacturers were well to the fore in small car design.[15]

Herbert Austin and William Morris were outstanding entrepreneurs, comparable to André Citroën and Louis Renault in France, and their firms ranked among the largest European manufacturers (TABLE 9.4). Morris, who was elevated to the peerage in 1934 as Lord Nuffield, had his most creative period in the 1920s.[16] Thereafter he partially withdrew from the business, but was reluctant to delegate, and failed to create a cohesive management team. The resignation of Leonard Lord after a disagreement in 1936 was a serious blow, especially as Lord transferred his loyalties to Austin. Lord went to Longbridge as works manager, became joint managing director in 1942 and chairman in 1945. But the erratic founder-entrepreneur was not a uniquely British phenomenon. The idiosyncrasies of Henry Ford were even more damaging, bringing the Ford Motor Company close to collapse at the end of the war.

TABLE 9.4 *Leading European car-makers in 1937/38*

Company	No. of vehicles	Year
Opel	140,580*	1938
Ford, England	94,165*	1937
Morris	90,000 (est.)	1937
Austin	89,745*	1937
Citroën	66,723	1938
Fiat	64,157*	1937
Renault	58,396*	1938
Peugeot	47,213	1938

*including trucks.

Source: James M. Laux, *The European Automobile Industry*, p. 120.

Some historians believe that a distinctively British weakness lay in the inability or unwillingness of the British-owned manufacturers to adopt a Fordist approach to the management of labour. Instead of following Ford's practice of paying a fixed hourly wage for a specified amount of work, British employers allowed the pace of work on the shop floor to be determined by the workers themselves, through the operation of the piecework system of payment.[17] The consequence was an abdication of control over the organisa-tion of work to employees and their trade union representatives. These arrangements worked well enough in the inter-war years when the trade unions were weak, but were storing up trouble for the future. According to this view, the labour relations strategies adopted by British employers in the inter-war years led directly to the crises of the 1960s and 1970s, when the industry was struggling to cope with chronic disorder on the shop floor.

The difficulty with this argument is that in the inter-war years Fordist methods as practised by Ford did not work well in Britain. In the US cars such as the Model T could be produced in long runs, and standardisation made possible the precise allocation of tasks to individual employees; tight supervision by management was essential. In Britain the demand was for a greater variety of models, and manufacturers needed the flexibility to switch quickly from one to another. In these circumstances piecework was an appro-priate system for motivating and rewarding employees.[18] Moreover, the reliance of British employers on piecework did not imply a surrender of management control. The manufacturers insisted on setting pay rates and work standards without interference from trade unions. Neither Ford nor Vauxhall recognised trade unions before the Second World War, and the Austin and Morris factories were largely union-free.

Labour relations did become more problematic in the second half of the 1930s as unemployment fell and union membership increased. Both the Amalgamated Engineering Union, representing mainly craftsmen, and the Transport and General Workers Union, representing semi-skilled and unskilled workers, mounted successful recruiting campaigns, and in some factories, especially in Coventry, began to build up an effective shop floor organisation. Inter-union rivalry had the effect of enhancing the power of shop stewards, whose task was not only to bargain with the employer, but also to protect the interests of their work group against incursions from other unions. The labour relations system in the British-owned car companies was beginning to acquire some of the characteristics which became so promi-nent in the 1950s and 1960s.[19] But the employers cannot be blamed for failing to anticipate problems which arose in the very different economic circumstances of the post-war period. Their labour relations policies suited the conditions of the time, and cannot be regarded as a fatal flaw that condemned the industry to decline after the war.

The British, French and German motor industries were at a similar stage of development in 1939. All three were far behind the US in scale and productivity. Unlike their European counterparts, American manufacturers had access to a large, tariff-free internal market which provided ample scope for high-volume production. European demand was not only smaller in aggregate, but also segmented by tariffs. There was little scope for intra-European trade, and the prosperity of the manufacturers depended primarily on sales within their domestic markets. After 1932 British firms had the advantage of imperial preference, giving them privileged access to Empire markets, but the volume of exports was small; in 1938 only 44,000 British cars were exported, representing 15 per cent of the industry's production.

If the productivity gap with the US was to be closed, the protective barriers within Europe would have to be dismantled, giving European manufacturers the same opportunities for economies of scale as were available in the US.

1945–60: Continuity

During the Second World War the British motor industry's energies were devoted almost entirely to serving the needs of the armed forces. Several firms managed Shadow factories on behalf of the government; most of these plants were acquired by the vehicle makers after the war, providing a useful addition to capacity. A more important long-term consequence of the war was to alter the character of the industry's labour relations. As part of the drive to increase production and minimise labour conflict, the government promoted the extension of collective bargaining, so that firms which had hitherto refused to recognise unions came under pressure to do so. Ford reluctantly signed a recognition agreement with its unions in 1944, although it did so in a way which preserved as much as possible of its managerial authority. Like Vauxhall, which also recognised unions during the war, Ford stayed outside the Engineering Employers Federation, to which most of the British-owned manufacturers belonged.

Trade union membership increased during the war, and in some factories, principally in the Midlands, shop stewards acquired greater authority. The

exigencies of war called for numerous changes in the organisation of production, and these arrangements were usually negotiated with shop stewards
rather than full-time union officials.[20]

Apart from some bomb damage in Coventry, the industry came out of
the war with its manufacturing capacity intact. Although there was a huge
domestic demand waiting to be satisfied, the government restricted home
sales in order to facilitate an expansion of exports. The wartime controls
over raw material supplies remained, and allocations of steel were tied to the
fulfilment of export quotas. These were set at 50 per cent of each company's
production, rising to 75 per cent in 1948 and 80 per cent in 1950. This was
an emergency response to the balance of payments crisis rather than a
planned programme of market development. Most manufacturers met their
export obligations by making maximum use of existing models, however
unsuitable they were for overseas customers. In some markets British cars
acquired a reputation for unreliability which proved difficult to shake off.[21]
In the short term, however, the export drive was extremely successful. With
their main European competitors still recovering from the war, and the
Americans preoccupied with their domestic market, Britain's share of world
car exports rose to 52 per cent in 1950, compared with 15 per cent in 1937.

When the export quotas were removed by the Churchill government in
1953, the proportion of cars sold abroad declined, although it remained at
about 45 per cent for the rest of the decade. The Continental manufacturers
were by then back in full production, and most British firms chose to
concentrate their exporting efforts on Commonwealth markets. As in the
case of engineering discussed in the last chapter, British car manufacturers
assumed that Continental markets would be served mainly by Continental
manufacturers, and that a head-on fight with the Germans, French and
Italians on their home ground was unlikely to be rewarding. There were, in
addition, high tariff barriers to overcome, especially in France and Italy.

Apart from the Commonwealth, the other high-priority market was
North America. For a brief period in the second half of the 1950s British
cars sold well in the US, filling a gap at the bottom end of the market, but
in 1959 the domestic US manufacturers introduced their own 'compact' cars,
and imports of all European small cars fell sharply.

Thus despite the higher level of exports the pattern of trade in the 1950s
was not very different from what it had been before the war. The home
market was still protected by the 33⅓ per cent tariff (reduced to 30 per cent
in 1956), and the bulk of the industry's exports went to markets in which,
thanks to imperial preference, British manufacturers had a price advantage

over their competitors. Moreover, although domestic demand for cars rose rapidly, the British market continued to be orientated towards quality and variety rather than the lowest possible price. It was not yet a mass market in the American sense, and companies needed to offer a range of vehicles produced in relatively short runs.[22]

Of the three pre-war market leaders, Ford was in the best position to profit from the post-war boom. Dagenham, larger and better equipped than Austin's factory at Longbridge and the main Morris factory at Cowley, could now be used to its full capacity. With a range of attractive models – the Anglia, Prefect and Popular at the cheaper end of the market, and the medium-sized Consul and Zephyr – Ford raised its share of British car production from 14 per cent in 1946 to 27 per cent in 1953.

Ford was a more professionally managed company than Austin or Morris and more systematic in its approach to product planning. This was partly due to the influence of its American parent, which went through a much-needed modernisation after the war under the chairmanship of the founder's grandson, Henry Ford II. But the British subsidiary also had an outstandingly able leader in Patrick Hennessy, who recognised the importance of building up a cadre of well-trained junior and middle managers. Ford was a large employer of graduates; a training at Ford came to be regarded as almost equivalent to a course at an American business school.

Competition from Ford was one of the factors which led in 1952 to the merger of Austin and Morris to form British Motor Corporation (BMC). Austin, the more profitable company, was the senior partner, and Leonard Lord took over as chairman of the merged group. (Lord Nuffield was made honorary president, but played no part in the management; he died in 1963.) The merger was followed by a partial integration of the two companies. BMC continued to offer a wide range of models, sold under the Austin, Morris, Wolseley, Riley and MG marques, but engines and other components were rationalised.[23] Lord has been criticised for not integrating the two companies more completely – Austin and Morris continued to have separate boards of directors and separate dealer organisations – but BMC held its market share against Ford (TABLE 9.5), and profits up to the early 1960s were satisfactory.

One of BMC's assets was a talented designer – Alec Issigonis, who had previously worked for Morris. The new Morris Minor, launched in 1948, was the best-selling small car in Britain in the 1950s. Issigonis left Morris after the BMC merger, but he was re-hired by Lord in 1955 and began work on the most famous of all Britain's post-war cars, the Mini. Launched in

TABLE 9.5 *Shares of the British car market held by principal*
manufacturers in 1955 and 1964

(per cent)

	1955	1964
BMC	39.0	37.0
Ford	26.5	28.5
Vauxhall	8.5	13.0
Rootes	11.5	12.0
Standard	9.5	6.5
Others	5.0	3.0

Source: A. Silberston, 'The Motor Industry, 1955–64', *Oxford Bulletin of Economics
and Statistics*, vol. 27, no. 4, November 1965. Blackwell Publisher Ltd/Institute of
Economics and Statistics.

1959, the Mini was a front-wheel-drive car with a transverse-mounted engine,
a new concept in small car design which was widely imitated overseas.[24]

The 1950s were years of prosperity for the British motor industry,
although two of the pre-war leaders, Standard and Rootes, faced financial
strains as they tried to keep pace with their larger and better-financed competitors. Apart from a recession in 1956, following the Suez crisis, home
demand was strong and export volumes held up well. At the end of the
decade all the leading firms were planning a further expansion of capacity,
most of which, at the government's request, was directed to areas of high
unemployment, away from the traditional car-making centres. Ford and
Vauxhall went to the north-west, building assembly plants at Halewood and
Ellesmere Port, while BMC built a factory at Bathgate in Scotland to make
commercial vehicles and tractors. Rootes also went to Scotland to manufacture a new small car, the Hillman Imp, in Linwood, using sheet steel from
the Ravenscraig strip mill (Chapter 6).

The one blot on the industry's record was the deterioration in labour
relations. The manufacturers had failed to respond adequately to the accre-
tion of shop steward power which had taken place during and after the war.
Most of the British-owned companies continued to pay their employees on
a piecework basis, and it was customary for piece rates to be fixed by

negotiation. This was the principle of 'mutuality', which had long been a feature of labour relations in engineering. The shop steward was at the centre of these negotiations, and, at a time of booming demand, factory managers were often tempted to make concessions in order to keep the production line moving. Shop stewards were increasingly willing to back their demands by calling their members out on strike, knowing that they were likely to win most of their demands. The number of strikes in the industry increased in the second half of the 1950s. Most of them were unofficial and unconstitutional – that is, not approved by the union and not in accordance with the procedures agreed between the Engineering Employers Federation and the unions for handling disputes.

Ford, unlike the British-owned firms, continued to pay its workers a fixed hourly wage. It also insisted that wage negotiations, and all other labour relations issues, should be handled exclusively by union officials. This did not prevent the emergence during the 1950s of a militant shop steward movement which constantly battled to establish bargaining rights.[25] The other American-owned company, Vauxhall, took a more conciliatory line, setting up a Management Advisory Committee, on which shop stewards were represented. Vauxhall's British management was regarded as forward-looking and constructive in its approach to industrial relations; its strike record was better than that of Ford or BMC during the 1950s.[26]

Worrying though these problems were, there was no sense at the end of the 1950s that they were putting the industry's future at risk. Production losses caused by unofficial strikes were quickly recouped.[27] A more serious source of anxiety was the fact that Continental car manufacturers were growing much faster, and gaining ground in export markets. It was, of course, inevitable that Britain's abnormally high share of world car exports in the early 1950s would be eroded as the European economies recovered. But the Continental manufacturers did more than catch up. By 1960 the German share of world car exports was well ahead of Britain's, and the French were not far behind (TABLE 9.6).

The principal reason for their superior performance – as in the case of the engineering industry as a whole – was that the export markets on which the Continental manufacturers concentrated were growing faster than the sterling area which absorbed the bulk of Britain's car exports. When the German motor industry began exporting again in the early 1950s, it had no alternative but to sell to neighbouring European countries. Since the French and Italian markets were virtually closed by high tariffs, the first targets were smaller countries, principally Belgium, Austria, Sweden and Switzerland;

TABLE 9.6 *Car production and exports in Britain,*
France and Germany 1950–60

(in thousands of units)

	Britain		France		Germany	
	Output	Exports	Output	Exports	Output	Exports
1950	523	399	257	89	219	69
1955	898	373	561	133	762	320
1960	1,353	570	1,175	492	1,817	865

Source: Society of Motor Manufacturers and Traders, *The Motor Industry of Great Britain*, 1965.

in 1954 these four countries accounted for 45 per cent of German car exports.[28] The French manufacturers, for their part, took advantage of relatively low German tariffs to boost their sales in what was becoming, thanks to the 'economic miracle', the largest and fastest-growing car market in Europe. As trade barriers came down in the second half of the decade, intra-European trade expanded more rapidly, and the signature of the Treaty of Rome in 1957 gave a further fillip to this process. In 1959, well before the tariff-cutting provisions of the Treaty had taken effect, nearly a quarter of French car exports went to the Common Market countries; the corresponding figure for the British motor industry was 6 per cent.

There was another important difference, less easy to quantify, between the British motor industry and its German and French competitors. Whereas Austin and Morris, and later BMC, were managed by the same people and in much the same style as before the war, the two leading nationally owned companies in Germany and France, Volkswagen and Renault, represented in different ways a break with the past.

Volkswagen was, in effect, a new entrant since it had produced no passenger cars before the war. After a period of confusion over whether its factory should be dismantled, shipped out of Germany or merged with one of the other German manufacturers, Volkswagen was recognised by the Allies as a valuable asset which could contribute to the revival of the German economy.[29] The plant, which had suffered little damage from bombing, restarted production in 1946, and two years later the British authorities appointed Heinrich Nordhoff as managing director. Nordhoff had worked for Opel, the General Motors subsidiary, before the war and was familiar with American production methods. The Volkswagen 'Beetle' proved to be ideally suited for the German market, playing almost the same role in the German motor industry as the Model T had done in the US forty years earlier. By concentrating on a single model, Nordhoff achieved levels of productivity that none of the other German manufacturers could match. By the mid-1950s Volkswagen had overtaken Ford and Opel in the German market, and was the pace-setter in exports. The rise of Volkswagen was to some extent a historical accident stemming from a political decision taken by Hitler before the war, but the effect was to inject mass-production capability into an industry in which the craft ethos had previously been dominant.

In France there was no new entrant, but the changes that took place in Renault amounted to almost the same thing. This company was nationalised in 1945 because of its collaboration with the Pétain régime during the war. The new chief, Pierre Lefaucheux, was a businessman with no previous experience of the car business, but he had a burning desire to convert Renault into a mass producer and to lift the French motor industry as a whole into a higher league. Lefaucheux has been described as the 'French Ford', the role that André Citroën had wanted to play before the war.[30] By launching a small car, the 4CV, in 1947 he opened up a new sector of the market just as Volkswagen had done in Germany. Renault soon overtook Citroën as market leader, and it was the first of the French companies to attack the American market.

Volkswagen and Renault helped to set the German and French industries on a new path after the war. The contrast with BMC illustrates the theme of continuity and change which was discussed in Chapter 3. Yet it was not predictable at the end of the 1950s that the British motor industry was about to enter a period of decline from which it would never fully recover. BMC and Ford were two of the largest car manufacturers in Europe, and, if there were doubts about the viability of Standard and Rootes as high-volume producers, the two specialists, Jaguar and Rover, seemed in excellent shape. In addition to its up-market saloon cars, Rover had scored a great success with the Land Rover, a rugged cross-country vehicle introduced in 1948 partly as a way of getting round the steel shortage; the chassis was made out of aluminium. The Land Rover was exported all over the world to armies and police forces, which valued its reliability and ease of maintenance. In commercial vehicles Ford and Vauxhall (through its Bedford subsidiary) were the largest manufacturers of medium-weight trucks in Europe, while Leyland, having bought up several of its competitors, was well placed at the heavier end of the market.

When two economists, George Maxcy and Aubrey Silberston, examined the industry in 1959, they took an optimistic view. 'As far as productive efficiency is concerned,' they wrote, 'there is no reason to believe that the British industry is inferior to its competitors, and if at present design and sales efficiency seem to be at a comparative disadvantage, these are matters which can be remedied within a short span of years.'[31] Their main concern was that, despite the BMC merger, the industry was still too fragmented. They pointed out that whereas the Volkswagen was being produced at a rate of 400,000 cars a year and the Renault Dauphine (successor to the 4CV) at about 200,000, no British model achieved volumes of more than 100,000 a year. The industry, in their view, needed fewer models produced in longer runs, and that would require mergers, not only among the smaller companies, but also among what had become, since the creation of BMC, the Big Five.

This prescription came at a time when competition in Europe was increasing. Although the British government had not yet decided to apply for Common Market membership (that came in 1961), trade barriers within Europe seemed certain to come down, putting pressure on smaller and less efficient companies. The British motor industry was not obviously less well equipped to meet these challenges than its German and French rivals. Despite the success of Volkswagen and Renault, their industries contained a number of smaller firms whose ability to survive in an integrated European market was open to question.

1960–80: Decline

In Britain the merger movement began with the absorption of the two smallest members of the Big Five, Rootes and Standard-Triumph.[32] Rootes was a collection of companies put together by the Rootes brothers, William and Reginald. William had started in business before the First World War as a motor dealer, but moved into manufacturing by buying Humber in 1928, followed over the next few years by the purchase of Hillman, Sunbeam and Talbot. The last major acquisition, that of Singer, came in 1955. Rootes had ambitions to catch up with BMC, and in 1963 launched a small car, the Hillman Imp, to compete with the Mini. This was an unproven design made by an inexperienced labour force in a new Scottish factory, and the Imp suffered from severe teething problems.[33] The Rootes brothers were forced to look for a rescuer, and in 1964 they sold a minority stake in the company to Chrysler of the US, subsequently extended to majority control. Chrysler had already bought Simca in France and planned to use the two companies as the basis for a European organisation comparable to those of Ford and General Motors.

Standard-Triumph, like Rootes, was struggling to compete in the mass market with inadequate financial resources. In 1961 its board accepted a take-over offer from Leyland Motors. This first move into cars by Britain's leading heavy truck manufacturer was prompted by the belief that a wider range of vehicles would yield advantages in overseas markets.

The two specialist companies, Jaguar and Rover, also gave up their independence during the 1960s. Jaguar, still controlled by its founder, Sir William Lyons, was a profitable manufacturer of luxury and sports cars, selling half its production to the US. Lyons decided to sell out to BMC in 1966 partly for family reasons – he had no heir to whom he could hand over the business – and partly out of fear for the long-term future of the company in an industry which appeared to be coalescing into a few large enterprises. Rover's directors felt the same way. This company had considered a possible merger with Standard-Triumph in the 1950s, but it was the success of the Rover 2000 saloon, launched in 1963, which convinced the board that an alliance with a stronger company was essential. Selling at a rate of 60,000 a year, this car brought Rover to the fringes of the mass market and the directors doubted whether the company had the financial strength to compete at this level. Following the sale of Jaguar to BMC, they felt 'alone, exposed and vulnerable', and willingly accepted a take-over approach from Leyland.[34]

The least likely merger candidate at the start of the 1960s was BMC. When George Harriman, a production engineer, took over the chairmanship from Leonard Lord in 1961, the company seemed in a sound condition. Some commentators criticised its old-fashioned management style. 'Compared with Ford,' The Economist wrote in 1962, 'it lacks the set of bright young graduates in their thirties which now forms the nucleus of that company's middle and sometimes its top management.'[35] But there was no disputing the innovativeness and popular appeal of its models. Issigonis came out in 1963 with another front-wheel-drive car, the 1100/1300 model, which Ford regarded as a more serious threat than the Mini. These two cars between them gave BMC nearly a quarter of the British market; both of them were produced at a rate of more than 200,000 cars a year.

In the Mini BMC at last had a car which was popular in Continental Europe. This was important because, by the early 1960s, the company had recognised that it could no longer rely on the Commonwealth as its prime export market. Several of the larger countries, notably Australia and South Africa, were building up their own car production behind tariff barriers, and, with the general shift towards freer trade, imperial preference was a wasting asset. Selling in the US was always likely to be difficult because of the strength of the domestic industry; after the collapse of American demand for small European cars, only sports cars and high-quality saloons like the Jaguar continued to sell well. The only accessible large market for mass-produced cars was Continental Europe, and BMC hoped to use the Mini to establish itself in a market which it had neglected in the 1950s. By the mid-1960s, despite the tariff barrier (TABLE 9.7), about 40 per cent of BMC's exports were going to Continental Europe.[36]

TABLE 9.7 *Tariffs on imported cars 1956–78*

(per cent)

	Britain		Germany		France	
	World	EEC	World	EEC	World	EEC
1956	30		17		30	
1962	28		19	10	28	15
1965	26		20	3	25	9
1970	15		15	0	15	0
1972	11		11	0	11	0
1978	11	0	11	0	11	0

Source: Nicholas Owen, *Economies of scale: Competitiveness and Trade Patterns within the European Community*, Oxford, 1983, p. 62. By permission of Oxford University Press.

In 1965 BMC made 846,000 vehicles, compared with 440,000 in 1955. But higher volume was not translated into higher profits.[37] The Mini and the 1100/1300 were expensive to make and under-priced, a reflection of BMC's somewhat primitive approach to cost control and pricing. The larger and potentially more profitable member of the Issigonis front-wheel-drive family, the 1800, never achieved the level of sales that had been hoped for. BMC also suffered from the fact that the Longbridge and Cowley factories were less highly mechanised than Dagenham. With a labour-intensive mode of production, an expansion of output did not produce a commensurate increase in productivity.[38] Even in good years profitability barely reached the level achieved in the mid-1950s, and by 1966 commentators were expressing concern about the company's future.

This concern was shared by one of BMC's principal shareholders, Prudential Assurance, which was uneasy about the managerial ability of Harriman and his colleagues. One possibility would have been to press for management changes, as the Prudential did in the case of GEC at the end of the 1950s (Chapter 8). But the influence of the Prudential and other institutional investors was limited by the fact that the largest shareholder in BMC was the Nuffield Foundation, a charitable trust set up by Lord Nuffield. A representative of the trust sat on the BMC board and supported the incumbent management. The alternative course was to promote a merger between BMC and a stronger company, and by 1967 the Prudential reached the conclusion that this was the best option.[39]

At this point the Labour government under Harold Wilson enters the story. As earlier chapters have shown, Labour's recipe for strengthening the competitiveness of British industry was the creation of larger companies through mergers. The Industrial Reorganisation Corporation was created for this purpose in 1966. In the case of the motor industry, ministers were concerned about the weakness of British-owned companies in the face of powerful American competitors – a concern which had been underlined by the Rootes–Chrysler deal. The IRC was involved, somewhat reluctantly, in this transaction, taking a small shareholding in Rootes in order to preserve a semblance of British ownership. While the discussions on Rootes were under way at the end of 1966, Tony Benn, Minister of Technology, told the IRC that the government favoured a merger between Leyland and British Motor Holdings (this was BMC's new name following the acquisition of Jaguar). The Prime Minister had already made this clear to the chairmen of the two companies.[40]

The logic behind the proposal was that Leyland, after the take-over of Standard-Triumph and Rover, was now a substantial car manufacturer with an impressive profit record, and Donald Stokes, its chairman, was a strong leader who seemed capable of breathing new life into BMH. Stokes had joined Leyland in 1930 as a student apprentice, and after qualifying as a mechanical engineer he was assigned to work on the design of specialist vehicles such as railcars and trolley-buses. He soon developed a remarkable talent for sales and marketing, and after war service he returned to Leyland as export manager. During the 1950s and 1960s he won a considerable reputation as one of Britain's foremost overseas salesmen. The acquisition of Standard-Triumph had also gone well; the model range had been shifted towards up-market saloons and sports cars, away from direct competition with BMC and Ford.

The IRC took on the task of promoting the merger between BMH and Leyland, with the clear understanding that Stokes would be in charge of the combined group. Despite resistance from some BMH directors, who resented playing second fiddle to Leyland, terms were agreed in January 1968, and the new company, British Leyland Motor Corporation, was launched four months later.

The merger posed a huge management challenge for Stokes and his Leyland colleagues. It involved a leap into high-volume car production, very different from their experience at Rover and Standard-Triumph. Some Leyland managers opposed the merger for that reason, believing that it would be better to build Standard-Triumph and Rover into a strong, specialist car group instead of taking on the mass-producers. The merger also called for organisational skills of a high order. Both Leyland and BMH were products of recent mergers which had not been fully digested. If the hoped-for economies were to be achieved, extensive rationalisation of products and factories would be necessary, and this would require co-ordination from a powerful head office. Stokes had no experience of large-scale organisation at this level; the Leyland group had consisted of a collection of relatively small car and truck companies which were run independently.

The two immediate priorities were to devise a coherent programme of new model development and to establish a clear management structure for the group. The main weakness lay in what was now called the Austin Morris division (the old BMC), centred on Longbridge and Cowley. The only new model ready to be launched was the 1.5 litre Austin Maxi, and this car, introduced in 1969, was the least successful of the Issigonis front-wheel-drive models. Successors were needed for the Mini and the 1100/1300, and there was a serious gap in the company car segment, a part of the market which had been artificially boosted by the government's tax and wage restraint policies. Companies found it economical to buy fleets of cars and lease them to managers as a perk, instead of giving them a salary increase.[41] The Ford Cortina, launched in 1962 and replaced with a new version in 1966, was precisely targeted at this segment, and British Leyland had no competitor.

The specialist car division, incorporating Jaguar, Triumph and Rover, was in a healthier state. The Jaguar XJ6 saloon was launched a few months after the merger to considerable acclaim, and Rover was well advanced with the Range Rover, a luxurious version of the basic Land Rover. Nevertheless, Rover and Triumph were a long way behind their European competitors – principally Mercedes-Benz, BMW and Volvo – in executive cars. The Rover 2000 and the Triumph 2000 had done well in Britain, but neither marque was well established on the Continent.

An early decision was to make a clear distinction between Austin and Morris, which, under the 'badge engineering' policy pursued by the BMC management, had sold similar or identical cars under different marques. Under the new policy, Morris was to compete directly with Ford with rear-wheel-drive cars, while Austin continued the Issigonis front-wheel-drive philosophy. But the first new models to emerge from this strategy were disappointing. The Morris Marina, launched in 1971, never came near to catching up with the Ford Cortina, and the Austin Allegro (1973), with its much-derided square steering-wheel, was far less successful than the 1100/ 1300 range which it replaced.

The programme was almost certainly too ambitious for the limited design and engineering resources at British Leyland's disposal. John Barber, a former Ford executive who was appointed finance director of British Leyland shortly after the merger, thought it was a mistake to launch a frontal attack on Ford. He wanted to move Austin and Morris somewhat up market in quality and styling, drawing on the skills of the specialist car companies, even at the cost of some loss of market share.[42] But that would have required a more integrated approach to product planning and engineering across the entire range of cars.

British Leyland suffered badly from organisational uncertainty, reflecting unresolved tensions between ex-Leyland men from a small-company background and ex-Ford managers (most of them recruited by Barber) who brought a different conception of how a large car manufacturer should be run. These conflicts contributed to one of British Leyland's most serious model failures during the 1970s – the new Rover saloon. In 1971 the replacements which Rover had planned for the Rover 2000 were cancelled in favour of a new model, to be built at a new factory at a rate of 150,000 cars a year. This was a decision imposed on Rover by the central staff, and it marked a sharp break from the 'cautious pursuit of engineering excellence within a limited market niche' which had guided the company since the 1930s.[43] The consequent strains, especially in labour relations, had a bad effect on quality and reliability. The new Rover never came near to meeting its sales targets.

These model failures came at a time when the British market was under attack from imports for the first time since the war. In 1968, when Britain's tariff on imported cars stood at 22 per cent, imports amounted to only 8 per cent of domestic sales. As soon as Britain's entry into the Common Market had been agreed in 1972, it was inevitable that import penetration would rise nearer to the levels already reached in Germany and France (TABLE 9.8). But the Continental manufacturers had been operating for more than a decade in an integrated European market, and were manufacturing a range of models produced on a large scale to suit European customers. British Leyland had little that could be shipped in the reverse direction. In the Austin Morris division, only the Mini was selling well on the Continent.

There were ominous signs of weakness, too, in the truck and bus division. During the 1960s imports of heavy trucks from Volvo and Scania in Sweden had been rising, partly because of tariff reductions within the European Free Trade Association, of which both Sweden and Britain were members. Leyland was slow to develop models suitable for long-distance haulage on European motorways, and its dealer network on the Continent was weak.

If British Leyland's new model strategy was disappointing, the same was true of its approach to rationalisation. Whereas Weinstock at GEC had moved quickly after the mergers with AEI and English Electric to cut out

TABLE 9.8 *Import penetration in Germany and Britain, 1955–80*

(per centage of car sales supplied by imports in each country)

	Britain	Germany
1955	2.2	4.1
1960	7.1	19.0
1965	5.0	18.1
1970	14.4	31.3
1975	33.2	36.5
1980	56.7	42.3

Source: SMMT, Verband der Automobilindustrie (VDA).

unnecessary duplication and close down surplus capacity (Chapter 8), Stokes took a more cautious line. He was by nature an optimist, and he preferred to keep the existing labour force fully employed by expanding sales. To a critic who questioned his strategy, he replied: 'We shall produce 1.5m vehicles a year and with the same number of people, and sucks to you and everyone else.'[44] Stokes was also anxious to avoid large-scale redundancies when the company was engaged in difficult negotiations with the trade unions over pay.

At the time of the merger the problem of unofficial strikes was getting worse, and there was a growing conviction among the Midlands companies that the prime source of the problem lay in unregulated shop floor bargaining over piece rates.[45] Employers were losing control over a payment system which had been an effective means of relating pay to effort when the unions were weak, but was now a fertile source of discontent. British Leyland decided to replace piecework with measured day work along Fordist lines. On paper the new system had clear advantages. It would remove control over the pay-effort bargain from the shop stewards and permit the establishment of appropriate performance standards for each job. But implementing the reform was fraught with difficulties. The new system was installed before foremen and supervisors had been fully trained for their new responsibilities. Moreover, the principle of 'mutuality' – that changes in pay and working arrangements should not be introduced without union agreement – was left intact. Since pay was now fixed, shop stewards turned their attention to other issues – manning levels, worker effort and security of earnings. The incentive to work hard was less than under piecework, and there was just as much scope as before for sectional bargaining, and just as many disputes.[46]

By 1972 it was clear to outside observers, and to many people inside the company, that the merger was not working. In that year Lewis Whyte, a City financier who had been on the Leyland board before the merger and was now a non-executive director of British Leyland, suggested that McKinsey, the management consultants, should be brought in to advise on how the company might be reorganised. This was vetoed by the executive directors. Another of Whyte's proposals, also turned down, was that the truck and bus division and the specialist car division should be hived off into a separate company, leaving Austin Morris to be run by a dedicated management team. Whyte later regretted that he did not resign when the board rejected his advice.[47]

Although profits improved in 1973 in response to a boom in domestic car sales, the company's cash position was weak, and when the market collapsed in 1974 after the rise in oil prices, it was desperately short of funds (TABLE 9.9). In view of the company's poor record since 1968, the banks refused to provide more loans, and Stokes was obliged to turn to the government for help.

TABLE 9.9 *British Leyland sales and profits, 1968–75*

	Sales (£m)	Pre-tax profit (loss) (£m)
1968	907	38
1969	970	40
1970	1,021	4
1971	1,177	32
1972	1,281	32
1973	1,564	51
1974	1,595	2
1975	1,868	(76)

Source: British Leyland Annual Reports.

Following Labour's election victory in March 1974, the same ministers were in charge – Harold Wilson in Downing Street, Tony Benn at the Department of Trade and Industry – who had promoted the creation of British Leyland six years earlier. The choice was between a private-sector reconstruction of the company, which would have involved factory closures and the sale of some subsidiaries to raise cash, and a government rescue. The employment implications of the first course were politically unacceptable, and at the end of 1974 the government announced that it would stand behind British Leyland's borrowings while a committee led by Don Ryder (formerly chairman of Reed International, and soon to be head of Labour's National Enterprise Board) examined the company's future.

The Ryder report, published in 1975, concluded that British Leyland's internal weaknesses were not irremediable, and that, with support from the government, the company could be re-established as one of the world's leading car and truck manufacturers.[48] A central recommendation was that British Leyland should continue to compete in volume as well as specialist cars. Ryder feared that if British Leyland abandoned the bottom end of the market, the gap would be largely filled by imports. A decision not to replace the Mini would also be damaging for exports, since the Mini represented about two-thirds of the company's sales in Continental Europe. Some managers, including John Barber, argued that it was no longer realistic for British Leyland to compete in the mass market; it would be better to sell fewer cars at higher margins. The House of Commons Expenditure Committee, which investigated British Leyland's situation after the Ryder report, agreed with this view. The committee warned that if British Leyland tried to compete in mass-market and specialist cars, it might fail in both.[49]

The government ignored these warnings and accepted the Ryder report as the basis for a massive injection of public funds – £900m over an eight-year period – most of which was provided in the form of equity. The existing shareholders were bought out, and British Leyland became a state-owned company. Stokes was replaced by a non-executive chairman, Ronald Edwards, former chairman of Beecham, and the former finance director, Alex Park, was appointed managing director. The National Enterprise Board, chaired by Ryder, was given the responsibility for monitoring British Leyland's progress.

The Ryder report was criticised at the time for being over-optimistic, and this applied not only to its sales projections, but also to its proposals on labour relations. The committee's main recommendation in this field was that employees should be given a larger say in the company's affairs. An elaborate, three-tier structure of worker participation was proposed, but it was not linked to any clear plan for tackling the sources of British Leyland's labour problems – fragmented wage bargaining, ill-defined work standards, and shop steward autonomy.[50] The trade unions were willing to participate in the new structure, but that did not imply any commitment on the shop floor to changes in working practices.

In the two years following the Ryder report British Leyland's share of the UK market continued to decline, exports fell, and there was no improvement in labour relations (TABLE 9.10). When Ryder resigned from the NEB in August 1977 (for reasons unrelated to British Leyland), he was succeeded by Leslie Murphy, a merchant banker who saw that management changes were necessary. In November 1977, he appointed Michael Edwardes, a

TABLE 9.10 *The decline of British Leyland 1970–80*

	Output of cars (000s)	Exports of cars (000s)	British market share (per cent)
1970	789	368	38.1
1975	605	257	30.8
1980	396	158	18.2

Source: Karel Williams, John Williams and Colin Haslam, *The Breakdown of Austin Rover*, Berg, 1987, pp. 125–6.

newcomer to the motor industry, as executive chairman. The partial rehabilitation of British Leyland which took place under Edwardes' leadership is described later in this chapter.

The failure of the national champion would have been less serious if the US-owned manufacturers had performed better. But they, too, went through a bad period in the 1970s. The decline of Ford was particularly damaging because the British subsidiary had traditionally been the largest and most profitable constituent of the American company's European empire. Like BMC, Ford had entered the 1960s in an expansionist mood. The assembly plant at Halewood, with a capacity of 200,000 cars a year, opened in 1963, and the new models coming out of Ford's well-organised product planning department were successful. The Cortina was a triumph in the company car segment, and the Escort, a smaller car introduced in 1968, was soon offering strong competition to BMC's 1100/1300 range. But during this period the status of the British subsidiary went through a significant change. The creation of the Common Market, and the prospect that Britain would sooner or later become a member, prompted Ford in 1967 to unite its British and German subsidiaries in a single organisation, Ford of Europe. Although the new company had its headquarters in Essex, not far from Dagenham, decisions about new models and the location of new investment would in future be taken on a European basis.

As part of this new policy, the relative efficiency of the British and German factories came under closer scrutiny. The most obvious difference was that while Dagenham and Halewood were plagued by unofficial strikes, the German plants were virtually strike-free. Ford's British management continued to insist on dealing only with national union officials and on excluding shop stewards from any role in collective bargaining. This produced mounting frustration on the shop floor, with Communists and other militants playing an active role in mobilising discontent. In 1969, after a major strike, Ford finally conceded a role for the shop stewards in its bargaining arrangements, and labour relations policy began to shift from confrontation towards what was intended to be a constructive dialogue. But this did not involve any surrender of managerial control, and disputes over pay and working practices continued at a high level. Persistent labour disruption led to poor quality and unreliable delivery, and increasingly Ford chose to supply export markets from Germany rather than from Britain. In addition, German-built cars were imported into Britain to make up for shortfalls in British production, and by the end of the 1970s these captive imports accounted for nearly half Ford's sales of cars.

Vauxhall fared even worse. Here, too, the 1960s had begun promisingly. The Ellesmere Port plant opened in 1964 and a new small car, the Viva, competing against the Escort and the 1100/1300, sold well. But Vauxhall's larger cars were less successful, and its market share began to slip. Ellesmere Port was in a region which had a long tradition of trade union militancy, and shop stewards there were less willing to participate in the consultative arrangements which had been operating in Vauxhall's main plant at Luton. Shop floor disputes, many of them linked to pay differentials between different work groups, increased during the 1970s. By the end of the decade Vauxhall's plants were almost as strike-prone as those of Ford and British Leyland.[51] Like Ford, Vauxhall began to import German-built cars into Britain, and exports dwindled almost to vanishing point.

The weakest of the three American companies was Chrysler, which badly under-estimated how difficult it would be to revive Rootes and integrate it with Simca in France. In 1974, following the collapse in US car sales after the oil price increase, Chrysler was in financial trouble at home and forced to bring its European adventure to an end. In Britain this led to an extraordinary episode in which Chrysler managers informed the government that without support from public funds they would close down all their British manufacturing operations. Ministers, influenced mainly by the desire to avoid the closure of the Linwood factory in Scotland, gave in to this ultimatum despite a warning from the government's think tank, the Central Policy Review Staff (CPRS), that to preserve Chrysler's uneconomic plants would damage the health of the rest of the industry.[52] The plants were propped up by the government until 1978, when the whole of Chrysler's European operations were acquired by Peugeot.[53]

By 1980, as TABLE 9.11 shows, the British motor industry had fallen a long way behind its European competitors in production and exports. One of the consequences was a rapid increase in imports: the balance of trade in motor vehicles went from a surplus of £206m in 1960 to a deficit of £1.3bn in 1980. Yet German and French companies also had to make the transition from protected national markets to an open European market. They, too, had to navigate their way through the recession which followed the increase in oil prices in 1973. What did they get right which the British got wrong?

TABLE 9.11 *Car production and exports 1960–80*

(000 units)

	Britain		France		Germany	
	Output	Exports	Output	Exports	Output	Exports
1960	1,353	570	1,175	492	1,817	841
1965	1,722	628	1,423	487	2,734	1,434
1970	1,641	690	2,458	1,061	3,528	1,934
1975	1,268	516	2,546	1,233	2,908	1,500
1980	924	359	2,939	1,373	3,521	2,108

Source: Society of Motor Manufacturers and Traders.

Part of the answer is that Germany and France were inside the Common Market from 1958 and Britain was not. As TABLE 9.12 shows, the great surge in German and French exports to other European countries occurred in the 1960s, when the trade-creating momentum of the European Economic Community was running at its strongest. British car exports to Continental Europe also increased during this period, but from a much lower starting-point, and in selling to EEC countries British firms had to surmount the common external tariff. The importance of intra-European trade is particularly striking in the case of France; in 1970 more than 70 per cent of the industry's overseas sales were in Europe (TABLE 9.12). In Germany the proportion was lower – just over 50 per cent in 1970 – because of Volkswagen's success in the US. Volkswagen's American sales fell in the 1970s as Japanese competition increased, and by 1980 the German motor industry was nearly as dependent on Europe as its French counterpart.

TABLE 9.12 *Exports of cars to other European countries from Britain, France and Germany, 1960–80*

(000s of units)

	1960	1970	1980
Britain	142 (27.3)	346 (46.4)	143 (31.81)
France	243 (51.5)	834 (71.2)	1,020 (81.5)
Germany	434 (69.3)	1,090 (55.7)	1,657 (68.2)

Note: The figure in brackets refers to the per centage of each country's total car exports going to European markets.

Source: Society of Motor Manufacturers and Traders.

The second factor was a British 'own goal' – the creation and subsequent mismanagement of British Leyland. Although mergers took place in Germany and France, there was no attempt in either country to create a single national champion. In Germany Borgward, one of the smaller firms, went bankrupt, and Volkswagen acquired Auto-Union and NSU. BMW narrowly avoided being taken over by Daimler-Benz after a financial crisis in 1960, but escaped with the aid of a wealthy private investor, Herbert Quandt, and recovered to become a formidable competitor to Mercedes at the high-quality end of the market. Thus three strong, nationally owned companies survived.

In France Peugeot and Renault formed a joint venture in 1966 to make engines and other components, but this was never likely to lead to a full merger. The Peugeot family, which retained a controlling interest in the company, was determined to maintain its independence and its private-sector status. This was an important consideration in Peugeot's decision to acquire Citroën in 1974. Both Michelin, the controlling shareholder in Citroën, and the Peugeot family were anxious to prevent a take-over of Citroën by the state-owned Renault or by a foreign company. The next big merger came in 1978 when Peugeot bought Chrysler's European operations. This was an expensive and risky undertaking which brought Peugeot close to disaster in the early 1980s, but even this merger did not compare in size and complexity with the task that faced Donald Stokes and his colleagues at British Leyland.[54]

The Continental motor industries were, of course, affected by the downturn in the market which followed the 1973 oil shock, and this was the moment at which Volkswagen faltered for the first time since the war. For a brief period its position looked almost as precarious as that of British Leyland. The source of the crisis, which began in the late 1960s, lay in the company's over-dependence on a single model, the Beetle. The company had also allowed wage costs to escalate at a time when the strength of the Deutschmark was undermining the profitability of exports. The resolution of the crisis, which called for a reduction in the labour force of some 33,000 (achieved partly by terminating contracts with foreign workers), involved co-operation between the trade unions, the banks and the government.[55] The Federal government and the state of Lower Saxony each held 20 per cent of the shares, but the Chancellor, Helmut Schmidt, unlike Harold Wilson in Britain, was determined to avoid a public-sector bail-out for a company which had become a symbol of the German economic miracle. There was never any possibility that the crisis would lead to nationalisation.

The third difference between the British motor industry and its French and German competitors in the 1960s and 1970s concerns labour relations. The clearest contrast is with West Germany, where the legal framework for collective bargaining established in the 1950s (described in Chapter 3) was working well. Strikes were rare, and the generally constructive relationship between management and labour contributed to the peaceful resolution of the Volkswagen crisis. In France attitudes were more adversarial and strikes more frequent, but, with the partial exception of Renault, where the Communist-controlled CGT enjoyed a privileged relationship with management, union membership in the car factories was low. At the shop floor level French unions never wielded the same influence as their British counterparts.

These three issues – non-integration into Europe, the British Leyland blunder and defective labour relations – lay at the heart of the British motor industry's poor performance between 1960 and 1980. At the end of the period continued decline seemed inevitable.

The 1980s and 1990s: Rehabilitation

When Japanese manufacturers began exporting cars to the West in the early 1970s, their success was at first attributed to low wages and an undervalued exchange rate. As Japanese production methods were studied in more detail, it became apparent that they had invented a way of designing and making cars which combined the efficiency of Fordism with higher quality, greater speed in bringing new products to the market and greater flexibility in switching assembly lines from one model to another.[56] Pioneered by Taichi Ohno at Toyota in the 1950s, this system came to be known as 'lean production'. The 1973 oil price rise, by shifting demand towards smaller and more fuel-efficient vehicles, created an opportunity for Japanese manufacturers to increase their sales in the US. The Japanese share of the American market rose from 4 per cent to 23 per cent between 1970 and 1980, and some Japanese firms built their own car factories in the US.

In Europe protectionist sentiment was stronger, and several countries, including Britain and France, imposed formal or informal quotas on Japanese imports. But import controls were not a long-term solution to what was gradually recognised as a threat to the survival of Western car manufacturers. American and European companies had to learn how to make cars in the Japanese way.

The new era of 'Toyotaism' coincided with a change in the political environment in Britain. The election of Margaret Thatcher's Conservative government in May 1979 marked a break with the past in the conduct of industrial policy. Pumping money into a chronically loss-making car company was abhorrent to the Prime Minister, and she was anxious to return British Leyland to the private sector as soon as possible.

The days of national champions were over (at least outside the defence and aerospace industries) and the apparatus of state intervention which had been erected by Labour was quickly dismantled. There was, however, one aspect of industrial policy, the promotion of inward investment, to which the government attached considerable importance. Mrs Thatcher wanted foreign companies to come to Britain, especially in industries where British firms were weak. The Japanese car makers, already planning the construction of assembly plants in Europe as they had done in the US, were an obvious target. The Prime Minister played a direct part in persuading Nissan to come to Britain in 1984.[57]

The immediate task was to deal with the problem of British Leyland, which Michael Edwardes was battling to revive. A combative South African, Edwardes had spent twenty-six years with Chloride, the battery company, starting as a management trainee and rising to the post of chief executive in 1971. The impressive rise in Chloride's profits during the 1970s boosted Edwardes' reputation, and in 1975 he was invited to join the National Enterprise Board. He accepted with some reluctance, being philosophically opposed to government intervention in industry, but felt that the presence of a 'free enterprise' man on the NEB might have some restraining effect.[58]

Once established at British Leyland, Edwardes had to grapple with the same problems that had faced Donald Stokes in 1968 – uncompetitive models, low profitability, and disorderly labour relations. But the political climate was different. During the last two years of the Labour government, job preservation at all costs – as reflected in the Chrysler rescue – had given way to a more hard-headed industrial policy. Open-ended support for British Leyland was no longer acceptable, and ministers raised no objection when Edwardes, a few months after his appointment, shut down the Standard-Triumph assembly plant at Speke, near Liverpool. The main reason for the closure was that British Leyland had too much manufacturing capacity – the TR7 sports car could be produced more economically in Standard-Triumph's main Coventry plant – but the Speke factory had also been badly affected by strikes.

To make British Leyland profitable at the level of sales now in prospect, Edwardes needed fewer factories run more efficiently. Against a theoretical capacity of 1.2m cars a year, forecast sales in 1978 were just over 800,000. When the appreciation of sterling in 1980 undermined the profitability of the company's exports, even more drastic capacity reductions were necessary. This was the context in which Edwardes set about what he regarded as his most important task – the re-establishment of management control over the shop floor. Some progress had been made before he arrived on centralising pay bargaining and establishing a more rational wage structure throughout the company. But shop stewards were still resisting any diminution in their authority, and 1977 was the worst year for disputes in British Leyland's history.

The recovery plan worked out by Edwardes in 1979 envisaged the loss of some 25,000 jobs and the closure of several factories. It was immediately opposed by the shop stewards, but when the plan was put to the employees in a ballot, 87 per cent of those voting supported it. Subsequent attempts by the stewards at Longbridge to organise resistance to the plan led to a celebrated confrontation between Edwardes and the senior AEUW shop steward, Derek

Robinson – known as 'Red Robbo' because of his Communist Party membership. Robinson's dismissal in November 1979 was a demonstration of the tougher management style which Edwardes brought to the company. Even after this episode there was still opposition from union officials and shop stewards to the proposed changes in working practices. Fruitless negotiations continued over several weeks. Edwardes then announced that the new arrangements would be implemented without union agreement, and that any employee who turned up for work on 8 or 9 April 1980, would be deemed to have accepted them. As resistance crumbled, Edwardes wrote later, 'thirty years of management concessions, which had made it impossible to manufacture cars competitively, were thrown out of the window and our car factories found themselves with a fighting chance of being competitive'.[59]

While these battles were under way, crucial decisions had to be taken on the new model programme. Plans were well advanced for a Mini replacement, but Edwardes decided, in the light of discouraging tests of customer reaction, to go for a slightly larger and potentially more profitable car, the Metro. Launched in 1980, it was an improvement on British Leyland's earlier mass-market cars such as the Allegro and the Marina, but it was competing in a crowded market. Besides competition from Renault, Volkswagen and Fiat, Ford and General Motors had entered the 'supermini' sector for the first time, with the Ford Fiesta and the Vauxhall Nova. The Metro was never able to reach the market share which the Mini had achieved.

The Allegro and Marina had been outsold in Britain by Ford's Escort and Cortina and had made little impact on the Continent. The replacement models, the Maestro and the Montego, could not be launched any earlier than 1983. As a stopgap, Edwardes negotiated a licence to manufacture a Honda car, sold in Britain as the Triumph Acclaim. In 1982 the Acclaim secured just over 2 per cent of the British market, compared to 11 per cent for the Escort.

The fundamental problem was the one which John Barber had highlighted at the time of the Ryder report. Could British Leyland, having lost so much ground since 1968, realistically expect to compete in the mass market, and, if not, could it reinvent itself as an up-market manufacturer comparable to BMW in Germany? With sales in 1980 and 1981 running at not much more than 600,000 cars a year, the concept of separate volume car and specialist car divisions no longer made any sense. Edwardes decided to bring together Austin Morris, Rover and Triumph in a single division to form Austin Rover, while Jaguar was given greater autonomy as a free-standing subsidiary.

Throughout this period Mrs Thatcher was pressing for privatisation. Since there was no prospect of selling the company as a whole, still less of floating it on the stock market, privatisation had to be done piecemeal. Land Rover was a candidate for disposal, but Edwardes insisted that it should be retained in order to sweeten a future sale of the truck and bus operation. Another possibility was Jaguar. Jaguar had suffered from the incoherence of British Leyland's management before and after the Ryder report, and the quality of its cars had deteriorated. But it had a well-defined niche in the market, which provided the basis for its rehabilitation. In 1984, to Mrs Thatcher's great delight, it was separated from British Leyland and privatised; when the shares were floated on the stock exchange, they were heavily over-subscribed.

The company's central weakness lay in Austin Rover, which lacked an attractive range of models and a clear image. Edwardes' aim was to move up-market, offering 'a better than average specification, an Austin with a pinch of Wolseley and a drop of Riley'.[60] But it was not easy to graft the exclusive image of a BMW on to a company which had long been seen, at least in Britain, as a rival to Ford in the mass market. A partial answer was to extend the Honda alliance. The two companies agreed in 1981 to develop jointly an executive car, launched in 1986 as the Rover 800.

Edwardes left the company in 1982 on completion of his five-year term, and was succeeded by a non-executive chairman, Austin Bide, former head of Glaxo. Two ex-Ford men, Ray Horrocks and David Andrews, were given responsibility for cars and trucks respectively. Although substantial progress had been made on labour relations under Edwardes' chairmanship, financial viability seemed as far away as ever. Relations with the government were poor. The post-Edwardes management team was soon embroiled in an argument over whether the company should be given the funds to develop a new range of engines for its small cars, or, as Mrs Thatcher wanted, buy engines from Honda. The management insisted that engine technology was a 'core competence' without which the value of the company in any subsequent privatisation would be reduced, and this argument narrowly won the day; work on the K-series engine began in 1985.[61]

In 1986 General Motors expressed interest in buying the Leyland truck business, together with Land Rover. This deal might have gone through had not the government also initiated separate negotiations to sell Austin Rover to Ford. When news of both sets of talks leaked out, senior Conservative members of Parliament expressed deep concern about the loss of British control over such a large slice of the motor industry. The government, weakened by a political row over the possible sale of Westland, the helicopter maker, to an American firm, was forced to break off the discussions. The episode greatly irritated Mrs Thatcher and made her even more impatient for privatisation.[62] The government's frustration was understandable. Although the Metro had done well and the Maestro and Montego were improvements on their predecessors, market share in Britain had continued to decline. The export record was even worse. Sales of British Leyland cars on the Continent fell from 170,000 in 1977 to 70,000 in 1984. The once profitable truck and bus division had been hit hard by the collapse of its traditional customers in the developing countries, and it was still weak in Continental Europe. Only Land Rover was well placed, mainly because of a determined effort, starting in the early 1980s, to redirect its marketing effort away from developing countries to Western Europe and North America. Land Rover was the only part of Austin Rover which could be regarded as a truly international business.

At the end of 1986, shortly after the talks with Ford and General Motors had been terminated, the government brought in a new executive chairman: Graham Day, who had earlier presided over the dismantling of British Ship-builders (Chapter 5). Day's first step was to define what he saw as the core of the company – Austin Rover and Land Rover – and to dispose of every-thing else. No longer included in the core was the truck and bus division, which was sold in 1987 to DAF of the Netherlands. Day also changed the name of the company to Rover, indicating his intention to give the business a clearer image as a manufacturer of high quality cars. 'Rover was the oldest and most respected name available to us,' he said, 'and market research confirmed its appeal.'[63] The aim was to establish a viable car business with an annual output of some 500,000 cars a year, and to do so in close collabor-ation with Honda. On the earlier joint projects Rover engineers had been reluctant to accept a subordinate position, but by 1987, when the fourth project was started, there were no illusions on the British side about how much could be learned from Honda in terms of quality, productivity and speed of new model development.[64] While Rover continued to make its own engines, the new models which were introduced over the next few years were Honda designs with minor modifications.

In 1987 Volkswagen showed some interest in acquiring Rover, but on terms which the government found unacceptable.[65] In the following year an unexpected opportunity arose to sell the company to British Aerospace, the aircraft manufacturer which had itself been privatised in 1985. The govern-ment was enthusiastic. As Lord Young, Mrs Thatcher's Secretary of State for

Trade and Industry, wrote later, 'the prize of disposing of Rover Group as a whole to a politically acceptable purchaser seemed too good to be true'.[66] While there were no savings to be achieved by putting the two companies together, the change of ownership gave Rover the stability in which it could pursue its up-market strategy and deepen its relationship with Honda. The Japanese company bought a 20 per cent stake in Rover, and Rover acquired a similar shareholding in Honda's British subsidiary. By the early 1990s three of Rover's four principal models – the Rover 200/400 series, the 600 and the 800 – were based on Honda technology, leaving only the Metro, now marketed as the Rover 100, as an all-British car. The Mini was still in production at a rate of some 20,000 vehicles a year.

This period of stability came to an end in 1993 when British Aerospace ran into a financial crisis, and Rover was up for sale again. The most likely buyer seemed to be Honda, but the Japanese company had built its own assembly plant at Swindon and had no need for additional capacity. One possibility briefly considered was that Rover should be jointly owned by Honda and British Aerospace (with the management also holding a small stake) prior to a flotation of the company on the Stock Exchange. But British Aerospace wanted an outright sale and, in January 1994, it accepted an offer from BMW. The German company paid £800m for British Aerospace's 80 per cent stake, and subsequently bought the remaining 20 per cent from Honda.

BMW bought Rover in order to acquire assets which it did not possess – technical competence in small, front-wheel-drive cars and a strong international position in four-wheel-drive vehicles through Land Rover. In addition, Rover provided a manufacturing base in a country which had lower labour costs than Germany and, thanks to the Thatcher government's reforms, a stable labour relations climate. A year after the take-over the chairman of BMW, Bernd Pischetsrieder, declared that Britain had become the most attractive location in Europe for car production.

BMW's strategy, according to Pischetsrieder, was to re-establish Rover as 'the premium British marque with its own identity linked to the great tradition of the British motor industry'.[67] This involved a programme which would, over time, eliminate all traces of Honda and give Rover cars an up-market image complementary to, but distinct from, that of BMW itself; the two ranges would share some common components, including engines. At the lower end of the market the Mini replacement would be used as the basis for a range of small cars, separate from Rover and BMW. However, the revival of Rover proved to be far more difficult than BMW had expected. The company continued to lose market share in Britain (down to 5.6 per cent at the end of 1998, compared to 13 per cent five years earlier), and the appreciation of sterling which began in 1997 eroded profit margins on exports.

The first new model to be launched after the BMW take-over was the R75, an executive car which replaced the Rover 600 and 800; it was built at Cowley, the smaller of Rover's two assembly plants. But by 1998, with Rover still making heavy losses, some BMW directors were questioning the wisdom of ploughing more money into their British subsidiary. The issue was whether BMW could justify the investment needed to develop the Longbridge factory and introduce replacements for the higher-volume Rover 200 and 400 cars. Dissension on the BMW board led, in February 1999, to the resignation of Bernd Pischetsrieder, who had been the principal instigator of the Rover purchase. In April, however, the company announced that it would, after all, go ahead with the Longbridge investment, with financial support from the British government.

Fortunately the British motor industry was no longer as dependent on Rover as it had been twenty years earlier. While Edwardes and Day had been struggling to revive the old national champion, three Japanese companies were giving the industry a fresh start. Nissan's Sunderland factory, opened by Mrs Thatcher in 1986, set a new benchmark for the British motor industry in labour productivity. The Japanese company sought to engender in its British workforce the same commitment to quality, flexibility and teamwork that it expected from its Japanese employees. A single-union agreement with the Amalgamated Engineering Union provided for binding arbitration in the event of disputes, making strikes unlikely though not impossible; the power of the union was reduced by the establishment of a Company Council, elected by all employees, to act as a consultative forum, as the final decision-making body in the in-house grievance procedure, and as the institution for negotiating pay and conditions.[68] A similar approach was followed at the other Japanese factories – Toyota at Burnaston, near Derby, and Honda at Swindon. In 1997 the three companies accounted for just under 40 per cent of Britain's total car exports (TABLE 9.13). Although Toyota announced in 1998 that it would build a second assembly plant in northern France, Britain seemed likely to remain the principal European production base for the Japanese manufacturers.

While the arrival of the Japanese was the most spectacular change in the

TABLE 9.13 *British car production and exports in 1997*

	Total production (000s)	Exports (000s)
Rover (incl. Land Rover)	488	255
Ford	302	104
Vauxhall	259	157
Nissan	272	207
Honda	108	76
Toyota	105	84
Peugeot	85	23
Jaguar	44	34
IBC*	25	18
Others	10	4
Total	1,698	962

*IBC was a joint venture set up by General Motors and Isuzu of Japan in Luton in 1987 to make four-wheel-drive vehicles. In 1997 General Motors announced plans to make vans at the plant in association with Renault. Isuzu's shareholding was subsequently bought out by General Motors.

Source: SMMT.

British motor industry during the 1980s, a partial renaissance was under way at the other foreign-owned companies – and Japanese competition was the spur.

When Bill Hayden, head of manufacturing in Ford of Europe, visited Japan in 1978, he was 'shattered' by what he found. 'I could not believe the magnitude of the productivity gap.'[69] Hayden saw that the Japanese advantage lay not in low labour costs, but in a different approach to the organisation of production. Instead of the rigid job classifications and tight managerial control which were characteristic of Fordism, the Japanese system relied on teams of workers capable of carrying out a variety of different tasks and committed to a constant drive for better quality and higher productivity. There were many other lessons to be learned – in relations with suppliers, in closer links between engineering and manufacturing to speed up new model introductions, and in using assembly lines more flexibly to accommodate a greater variety of low-volume cars.[70] But labour relations reform was a central part of the 'After Japan' (AJ) programme instituted by Hayden in 1980.

The programme got off to a bad start with a clumsy attempt to introduce Japanese-style quality circles; this device – small groups of workers who meet regularly and voluntarily to improve quality and efficiency in their areas – was alien to the Ford culture.[71] Nevertheless, the principle of 'employee involvement', already accepted in Ford's American factories, gradually won support among managers and on the shop floor. The 1985 Pay and Working Practices Agreement provided for unprecedented flexibility among craft and production operatives. The number of separate job titles was reduced from 500 to 50, and assembly-line workers were expected to carry out tasks which had previously been performed by skilled craftsmen from the maintenance department. Given Ford's long history of authoritarian management, no sudden conversion to a high-trust relationship with employees could be expected, but the 1985 agreement laid the foundations for an improvement in productivity and a reduction in the number of disputes. The improvement was maintained during the 1990s and in 1999 Ford announced plans for increasing the capacity of the Dagenham plant from 272,000 vehicles a year to 450,000 vehicles a year – the first major expansion after two decades of retrenchment. The unions at Dagenham had co-operated in bringing about what was described as a revolution in production methods, including the removal of demarcation lines, a reduction in absenteeism, flexible use of contract labour, staggered holidays, and the introduction of new forms of shift working.[72]

Ford's commitment to Britain increased when it bought Jaguar in 1989. This company had done well in the early years after privatisation, but its dependence on the US market made it vulnerable to currency fluctuations. Like BMW and Mercedes, it also faced strong Japanese competition as Toyota, Nissan and Honda introduced luxury cars. Ford had the resources to invest in modernising the Coventry plant and to broaden the model range. The first step was the announcement of a new mid-range car, the X400, to be built at a new plant near Birmingham, and this was followed in 1998 by the decision to launch a smaller car, X200, to compete with the BMW 3-series. Ford's decision to build the X200 at Halewood was a reflection of the improvements in quality and productivity which had been made at this once strike-prone factory.

At General Motors, the future of the two British assembly plants had looked uncertain at the start of the 1980s, but the European operation as a whole, now fully integrated in General Motors Europe, was in the throes of a product-led revival, based on the German-designed Astra and Cavalier. Facing the same Japanese pressure as Ford, Vauxhall improved its productivity to the point where new investment could be justified. Like Ford, Vauxhall was able to resume exports of British-made cars to Continental Europe, and in 1996 it announced a £300m expansion programme at Ellesmere Port to increase output from 135,000 to 200,000 vehicles a year.[73]

Peugeot went through a very difficult period in the early 1980s, mainly because of the financial strains arising from the Chrysler acquisition, and there was a possibility that its British manufacturing operations would be closed down. However, although the Linwood plant in Scotland was shut, Peugeot continued to invest in the main works at Ryton, Coventry, and by the end of the 1990s this factory was producing the Peugeot 206 as efficiently as its sister plants in France. In March 1999, the company announced that the Ryton factory would start working a seven-day week, the first European assembly plant to do so, and that production would increase to 155,000 cars a year, of which about 100,000 would be exported.

As a result of these changes – the partial rehabilitation of Rover, the entry of the Japanese, and the improvements in the other foreign-owned factories – the long decline in the British car industry came to an end. As FIGURE 9.1 shows, from the mid-1980s to the mid-1990s production of cars was on a rising trend, and although the recovery was checked by the appreciation of sterling in 1997 and 1998, there seemed every prospect that the improvement would be maintained.

The recovery did not extend to trucks. Both General Motors and Ford tried during the 1970s to develop a range of trucks for the European market, but neither was successful. In 1987 General Motors sold its Bedford subsidiary to a British entrepreneur, David Brown, but he was unable to build a viable business, and Bedford was put into liquidation in 1992. Ford's truck operation was stronger, but a large investment was required to give it the European dimension it needed. In 1986 Ford put its UK truck business into a joint venture with Iveco, the Italian truck manufacturer, but demand for the medium-weight trucks made at Ford's Langley factory, near Slough, declined during the 1990s. The factory was closed in 1997. The withdrawal of General Motors and Ford left Leyland as the only substantial British truck manufacturer. Its future, as Graham Day had recognised, lay in an association with another truck company, preferably one which could provide the European distribution that Leyland lacked. That was the rationale for the sale of the

FIGURE 9.1 *Production of the British motor industry, cars and commercial vehicles, 1940–95*

☐ Cars   ▽ Commercial Vehicles

Source: Society of Motor Manufacturers and Traders.

business to DAF of the Netherlands in 1986. But DAF, too, was a relatively small company competing in an over-supplied market, and could not survive the deep recession which struck the European truck industry in the early 1990s. It went into liquidation in 1993, dragging Leyland down with it. The Dutch government then stepped in to keep the Dutch operation alive, while the Leyland side was bought from the receivers by a team of managers; it continued to make trucks for sale on the Continent through DAF's dealer network. In 1996 DAF was acquired by Paccar, an American heavy truck manufacturer which also owned Fodens, a specialist British truck-maker; two years later Paccar bought Leyland. There seemed a reasonable prospect that, as part of Paccar, Leyland would be able to increase its production and exports, and this was a better outcome than had seemed likely in the early 1980s. But the decline of Leyland has to be seen as an avoidable disaster, largely attributable to the failure to Europeanise the business in the 1950s and 1960s.

The Search for Culprits

The motor industry illustrates in an extreme form a familiar pattern in Britain's post-war industrial history: continuity, decline and partial rehabilitation. Why was the decline so steep in this case? Comparisons with Germany and France highlight three factors that provide at least part of the explanation.

First, the motor industry was damaged more than most other industries by Britain's failure to participate in the expansion of intra-European trade that took place between the 1950s and the mid-1970s. The emergence in Europe of a homogeneous, fast-expanding and highly competitive mass market enabled companies such as Renault, Volkswagen and Fiat to narrow the productivity gap with the American manufacturers, which had been competing in a similar market since the 1920s. The fact that British firms were not part of this process was largely due to an understandable but ultimately disastrous decision to give a low priority to Continental Europe as an export market in the first fifteen years after the war. When Britain entered the Common Market in 1973, the post-war boom was nearly over and the trade-generating effects of European integration were less powerful than they had been fifteen years earlier. It would be absurd to claim that all the industry's subsequent problems would have been avoided if it had chosen Europe rather than Empire in the first few years after the war, and if Britain had entered the Common Market in 1958 rather than in 1973. But in view of the progress made by the French car manufacturers after the mid-1950s it is reasonable to believe that earlier exposure to Europe-wide competition would have been a stimulus to change in product design, in manufacturing methods and perhaps in the management of labour.

Second, the British-owned part of the industry was seriously damaged by the British Leyland merger. This was a mistake both in concept and in execution, reflecting a naïve belief in the advantages of size and in the ability of charismatic individuals to revive declining companies. The merger made BMC's problems harder to solve and damaged the healthier parts of the British Leyland group. The Leyland truck operation was neglected at a time when there was still a chance of converting this business into one of the European leaders in its field. If there had been no merger, it is possible that Rover and Triumph could have been developed by Leyland into a viable, medium-sized specialist car manufacturer, comparable to BMW or Volvo. BMC would have been forced to slim down, perhaps concentrating volume car production at one rather than two assembly plants and developing a distinctive model range out of the Mini/1100 family. The blame for the British Leyland merger must be shared between Harold Wilson's Labour government, which promoted it, and the Leyland management which went along with it. The mishandling of the 1975 rescue, on the other hand, was the fault of government alone. The Ryder report was an exercise in wishful thinking which delayed necessary changes in the company, at considerable cost to the taxpayer.

The British government was not alone among European governments in regarding the motor industry as too important to be left to the market. It is sometimes argued that, in France, intervention was more constructive because of the closer rapport between government officials and senior industrial managers.[74] Yet it is doubtful whether the post-war success of the French motor industry can be attributed to government industrial policy. There was certainly intervention – including the nationalisation of Renault and financial support for the Peugeot-Citroën and Renault-Berliet mergers – but there was no overall plan for the industry as there was, for example, in electronics. The productivity gains which the French industry achieved during the 1960s and early 1970s were due more to Europe-wide competition than to government support.[75]

Third, the British motor industry, because of the nature of the production process, was peculiarly vulnerable to two of the institutional weaknesses in the British labour relations system – multiple unionism and sectional shop floor bargaining. Managers and unions were at fault for allowing this situation to deteriorate in the 1950s and 1960s. The fact that they did so suggests that the pressure for reform, in conditions of full employment, booming demand and a protected domestic market, was not as great as it became in the 1970s. By that time the two sides were locked into rigid positions, and it was not until the 1980s, under the impact of the Thatcher shock and intense international competition, that the barriers were broken.

Turbulent labour relations complicated the task of management at BMC and British Leyland, and they were an important factor in inducing the American-owned companies to shift more of their production to the Continent. The partial rehabilitation of the industry in the 1980s and 1990s could not have occurred without an improvement in labour relations. On the other hand, trade unions and shop stewards were not responsible for the commercial and managerial errors made by British Leyland after the 1968 merger. Moreover, the decline of the commercial vehicle side of the industry, which was more precipitate than in cars and not reversed in the 1980s, had very little to do with labour relations; the truck factories were smaller and less strike-prone than the big car assembly plants. As in the case of shipbuilding discussed in Chapter 4, labour relations contributed to the decline of the British motor industry but were not its central cause.

—————————•○•—————————

TEN

Electronics: A Shared European Failure

E lectronics has been the most glamorous of the science-based industries in the post-war period. A never-ending stream of innovations, starting with the transistor in 1947, has generated a host of new products – personal computers, mobile telephones, video recorders and many more – which have profoundly altered the way people live and work. Electronics-based technologies have also had a pervasive influence on other industries. The performance and reliability of cars and aircraft, for example, have been transformed by the use of electronic components and systems.

These developments created huge commercial opportunities for firms which had the skills and resources to take advantage of them. But the role played by European companies has been disappointingly small. Most of the fastest-growing sectors of the market have been dominated by American or Japanese manufacturers. Why did European firms fall behind, and, within this general picture of European failure, did the British electronics industry perform better or worse than its German and French counterparts?

Origins

The origins of the electronics industry lie in the invention of wireless telegraphy at the end of the nineteenth century. In 1896 an Italian engineer, Guglielmo Marconi, demonstrated the first practical system for sending and receiving signals by means of electro-magnetic waves. After conducting his early experiments in Italy Marconi came to England to patent his invention, setting up the Wireless Telegraph and Signal Company in 1897 (it was renamed Marconi's Wireless Telegraph Company in 1900). The first applications were for ship-to-ship and ship-to-shore communications, but in 1901 Marconi transmitted signals across the Atlantic, showing that wireless could be an alternative to cable for long-distance international communications.[1]

Other inventors were working in the same field, and Marconi soon faced strong competition. In Germany two systems were developed, one backed by Siemens, the other by AEG. In 1903 the two electrical companies pooled their wireless interests in a jointly owned subsidiary which they called Telefunken. The merger was prompted by the government's concern that Germany's position in wireless communications, a technology which had obvious military value, would be weakened if the industry was split into hostile factions.[2]

In the US General Electric and Westinghouse took a close interest in wireless from the start, as did American Telephone and Telegraph Company (AT&T). AT&T's network, the Bell System – so called because the original company had been founded by Alexander Graham Bell, the inventor of the telephone – was based on electrical communication across wires; it could not afford to ignore a technology which might pose a competitive threat.

To realise the full potential of wireless, transmitting and receiving apparatus had to be made more powerful. The search for more efficient signal detectors led to the invention of the thermionic valve. The first version was the diode, invented in 1904 by Ambrose Fleming, professor of electrical engineering at University College London, and Marconi's technical adviser. Two years later an American, Lee de Forest, working for the Federal Telegraph Company in Palo Alto, California, developed the triode, a more powerful device which could be used as an amplifier. The manufacturing process for valves was similar to that used in lamps, and several of the established lamp producers, such as Ediswan in Britain, entered the valve-making business.

During the First World War valves were needed in large quantity for military communications equipment. As manufacturing techniques improved and valves became more reliable, new applications became possible. In 1916, David Sarnoff, contracts manager for Marconi's American subsidiary, suggested the use of wireless as a medium of entertainment, transmitting speech and music to the home. The world's first regular broadcasting service was launched by Westinghouse just after the First World War. At that time US companies with an interest in wireless, including American Marconi, were engaged in litigation over patents. There was also fierce rivalry between General Electric and AT&T, both of which sought to control radio broadcasting, or to prevent the other from doing so.[3] The outcome in 1919 was a patent-pooling agreement and the creation of Radio Corporation of

America (RCA), in which Westinghouse, AT&T and General Electric were shareholders; American Marconi was then absorbed by RCA.[4] In 1930 the US antitrust authorities broke up these arrangements and RCA became an independent company.

In Britain Marconi broadcast for the first time from its transmitters at Chelmsford in 1920. In order to avoid the free-for-all which was emerging in the US, the government encouraged the manufacturers which had an interest in radio to form a consortium. The British Broadcasting Company was set up in 1922 by a group of six companies, which, in addition to Marconi, included three leading electrical companies, GEC, British Thomson Houston and Metropolitan Vickers. Another founder member was Western Electric, the British subsidiary of AT&T. (In 1925 AT&T, in order to concentrate on its domestic business, sold all its overseas manufacturing subsidiaries to another American company, International Telephone & Telegraph; the British operation was renamed Standard Telephones and Cables.[5]) In 1926 the British Broadcasting Company was converted into a public corporation, financed by a licence fee paid by radio-set owners.

The market for radio sets increased rapidly – production reached nearly 2m in 1936 – and attracted many new entrants. Some of them, like Ferranti, had a background in electrical engineering and made components as well as complete sets.[6] Others were assemblers, building sets from bought-in components.[7] The largest supplier of valves to the independent set makers was Mullard, founded by a British engineer, Stanley Mullard, who had worked on valves for the government during the First World War; this company was later acquired by Philips, the Dutch lamp-maker. Another component maker was Plessey, which had originally been a manufacturer of pianoforte actions. Taken over by an American, B. G. Clark, in 1921, Plessey made radio sets under contract for Marconi and later concentrated on making components for other set-makers. Clark's son, Allen, an outstanding salesman, was responsible for Plessey's rapid growth in the 1930s, and he continued to dominate the company until his death in 1962.[8]

As competition in radio sets increased, the Marconi Company lost ground. Its manufacturing skills lay more in capital equipment than in mass-produced consumer goods, and it was also deeply involved in international wireless communications, with a network of subsidiaries around the world. These commitments caused financial strains, and Guglielmo Marconi was not in a strong position to resist a government-induced merger which led to the loss of his company's independence. The authorities in Britain and the Dominions were concerned that communications within the

Empire were being hampered by wasteful duplication between wireless and cable. In 1929 Marconi and the Associated Cable Companies were persuaded to join forces in a new company, Cable and Wireless.[9] Guglielmo resigned from the chairmanship, although he remained active on the scientific side of the company; he died in 1937.

As part of Cable and Wireless, the Marconi Company continued to conduct research in wireless, and it played an important part, together with Electrical and Musical Industries (EMI), in the development of television. EMI was a British company with American roots.[10] Formed in 1931 by a merger between two US-controlled recording firms, the Gramophone Company and the Columbia Gramophone Company, it needed new products to offset the inroads which radio had made into the market for gramophone records. The feasibility of television had already been demonstrated by John Logie Baird, a Scottish inventor, but his system, based on mechanical scanning, produced a fuzzy, flickering picture which was not suitable for public broadcasting. A team of EMI engineers, led by Isaac Shoenberg (who had previously worked for Marconi), set out to develop a superior system, using the cathode ray tube and the photo-electric cell to develop an electronic scanning camera, the 'emitron'. EMI's achievement was 'not so much the invention of radically new technology, but the design and integration of all the elements – from cameras to receivers and all the complex circuits in between – necessary for a practical television system'.[11] Marconi, which had complementary skills in the design of transmitting apparatus, was brought in as a partner, and the Marconi-EMI system was adopted by the BBC in 1936 for the world's first regular television broadcasting service.

British electronics firms established close links with academic scientists and government laboratories, and this co-operation was put to good use before and during the Second World War.[12] EMI developed the world's first airborne radar, and other firms which had previously been concerned with consumer electronics, such as Decca, turned their attention to the military field. The Decca Navigator, a position-fixing aid, was widely used in merchant and naval vessels during and after the war.

In contrast to the early days of the electrical industry, described in Chapter 8, the performance of the British electronics industry in the inter-war years compared favourably with that of its German and American counterparts. Germany's progress was unspectacular, partly because of a confusion of responsibilities between Siemens, AEG and their jointly owned subsidiary, Telefunken.[13] In 1940 Siemens sold its half-share to AEG in order to develop an electronics capability of its own.[14] The American electronics industry was bigger, and devoting more resources to research. AT&T's research arm, Bell Laboratories, was emerging as one of America's foremost research organisations. But the quality of British science was high, and it was exploited well. As one historian has commented, 'Britain was responsible for some of the main inventions in radio, television and radar, and it cannot be said that these were subsequently neglected and left to the foreigner to take up.'[15]

It could not have been predicted at the time of the Second World War that American electronics manufacturers would surge ahead of their British competitors as they did in the 1950s and 1960s. That they did so was primarily due to two innovations, the transistor and the computer, which altered the character of the electronics industry.

US Leadership after the Second World War

The invention of the transistor was the culmination of a long search for a more efficient amplifier than the thermionic valve. The disadvantage of the valve was that it was bulky and gave off a large amount of heat. The properties of semiconductor materials – that is, materials which were neither good conductors of electricity, like copper, nor good insulators, like rubber – had been investigated on both sides of the Atlantic before the war. AT&T was at the forefront of this research because of its relevance to telecommunications, and a team of scientists at Bell Laboratories, led by William Shockley, invented the transistor in 1947; it was introduced commercially four years later.[16]

The transistor turned out to be far more than a replacement for the valve. It opened up a new line of research into semiconductors which proved immensely productive. Most of the major innovations took place in the US, not because American scientists were cleverer than their counterparts in Europe or Japan, but because conditions in the US were more conducive for the exploitation of the new technology.

AT&T adopted a liberal licensing policy for its know-how in transistors. It was engaged in an antitrust suit with the US Justice Department; to have appeared as a greedy monopolist would have strengthened the government's case for a break-up of the company.[17] The consent decree signed in 1956 left the structure of AT&T intact, but imposed an obligation on the company to make its patents available to other American companies free of royalty;

it was also prohibited from selling semiconductors on the open market, although it could make them for its own use and for the government.

By this time most of the American valve producers, including General Electric and RCA, were making transistors under licence from AT&T and conducting research of their own into semiconductors. The market also attracted firms, such as Texas Instruments, that had not previously made valves but had relevant manufacturing skills. Another type of new entrant was the start-up firm, founded by scientist-entrepreneurs to compete in the semiconductor field. A seminal event in the history of the electronics industry was the decision by William Shockley to leave AT&T in 1954 and set up his own firm in Palo Alto, California – the same town in which Lee de Forest had invented the triode some fifty years earlier. The team of scientists which Shockley recruited included two men, Robert Noyce and Gordon Moore, who were to make a major contribution to semiconductor technology over the subsequent twenty years – first at Fairchild, which they helped to set up when they broke away from Shockley in 1957,[18] then at Intel, which they founded in 1968.

Many of these new firms congregated around Palo Alto in what came to be known as Silicon Valley. One of the attractions of the area was its proximity to Stanford University, which had been America's leading academic centre in radio engineering before the war and an 'incubator' for high-technology firms. Financial backing came from a growing community of venture capitalists, who supported new firms in the hope that the successful ones would subsequently be floated on the stock exchange. The initial capital requirement was not large, and the rewards could be spectacular. Success bred success, and it was common practice for engineers with a promising idea to leave their employer and start up on their own.

Most of the new entrants were 'merchant' producers, making transistors for sale on the open market rather than for use in their own equipment. Perhaps because they had no commitment to the older valve technology, they proved to be a prolific source of innovation. Fairchild and Texas Instruments were responsible for two breakthroughs at the end of the 1950s – the planar process, which made possible the large-scale production of transistors, and the integrated circuit, which allowed transistors to be packed together on a single silicon wafer or chip.[19]

During this formative period of the industry, the largest and most demanding customer was the military. The US government was engaged on an ambitious missile and space exploration programme. Missile guidance and control systems depended on reliable, miniaturised electronic circuitry, and transistors met this requirement precisely. Eager to push the technology forward, the Defense Department placed development contracts for advanced semiconductor devices, often with new firms.[20] If the development was successful, production orders followed. The semiconductor industry was characterised by large 'learning economies': as sales volumes increased, production techniques improved and costs fell. Manufacturers had a powerful incentive to develop new products quickly and to establish a cost advantage which others would find hard to match.

The invention of the electronic computer, unlike the transistor, was not a single, isolated event. Its origins lay in the work on calculating machines carried out by scientists in Britain, Germany and the US before and during the war. Britain's Colossus code-breaking machine, built at Bletchley Park in 1943, incorporated some of the technology which was used in computers after the war, and similar work was done in the US. At the end of the war the main applications for computers were expected to be in the military field, and the US Navy funded a number of computer projects, carried out in universities and in industrial firms. Two of the men involved in this programme, J. Presper Eckert and John W. Mauchly at the Moore School in the University of Pennsylvania, were among the first to see that computers could be used to perform data-processing tasks in business. Their first computer, the ENIAC, completed in 1945, was made for the US Army, but in the following year they set up on their own to make computers for commercial use.[21]

The Eckert-Mauchly company was not a success, and in 1950 it was sold to Remington Rand, a manufacturer of typewriters and office machinery.[22] This was the crucial link, between office machinery and electronics, which made possible the birth of the computer industry. Office machinery was an industry in which American firms such as Remington Rand, National Cash Register and International Business Machines (IBM) had built a strong position in the inter-war years. Their business, based on electro-mechanical technology, was the handling of large amounts of data; the computer made it possible to perform these tasks more efficiently.

While Remington Rand got into the computer business by acquisition, IBM, the leading producer of punched card equipment, relied at first on contracts secured from the Federal government. The first IBM electronic computer, the 701 Defence Calculator delivered in 1953, was designed for military work, and it was followed by a bigger contract for the SAGE air defence system.[23] From this starting-point IBM began to invest its own resources in research and development, and, under the brilliant leadership of Thomas J. Watson Jr (who succeeded his father as president in 1952) turned itself into a high-technology company. By the end of the 1950s advanced research was under way into semiconductors, and IBM later became a large manufacturer of integrated circuits for its own use. Watson's achievement was to blend these newly acquired electronics capabilities with IBM's long-established strength as a solver of data-processing problems in business. Unlike electronics companies such as General Electric and RCA, which also entered the computer field, IBM had the advantage of a large customer base and an established dealer organisation.

These two new branches of the electronics industry, computers and semiconductors, were intimately linked. The early computers were based on valves, but as semiconductor technology improved valves were replaced by transistors and later by integrated circuits. The most widely used type of integrated circuit was the Dynamic Random Access Memory (DRAM), used as a data storage device inside the computer. The performance and reliability of these components were critical for the computer makers, and semiconductor firms vied with each other to develop faster and more powerful chips. After the planar process and the integrated circuit, the next big advance was the microprocessor, which performed all the functions of the computer's central processing unit. Invented by Intel in 1971, it paved the way for the personal computer and a raft of new applications in which, as before, American entrepreneurs such as Steve Jobs at Apple – another product of the Silicon Valley network – set the pace.

The European Response

The post-war history of the European electronics industry can be seen, in part, as a series of attempts by European manufacturers, mostly unsuccessful, to catch up with the Americans in computers and semiconductors. In the 1970s a new threat appeared in another branch of the industry. Japanese firms such as Sony and Matsushita established a competitive advantage in mass-produced consumer products – radio sets, television sets and video recorders. Other Japanese companies, principally Fujitsu, Hitachi and Nippon Electric Corporation (NEC), later acquired capabilities in computers and semiconductors, although Japanese industry was never as strong in these fields as in consumer electronics.[24]

Among the larger European countries, the British electronics industry seemed in the 1950s to be well equipped to respond to these challenges. The industry consisted of a large number of companies, some of which, like AEI, English Electric and GEC, made a wide range of components and equipment. These three had expanded their interests in electronics during the war, and were keen to go further. As described in Chapter 8, George Nelson at English Electric bought Marconi in 1946 when it was put up for sale by the government, while AEI bought Siemens Brothers, a manufacturer of telecommunications equipment. Another electrical company, Ferranti, had worked on advanced electronic systems in the war, and was involved in the early development of guided missiles. EMI (which bid unsuccessfully against English Electric for Marconi) had become a diversified electronics manufacturer with interests in military equipment as well as television; music recording remained a substantial part of its business.

Firms which had previously been involved mainly in consumer products – radio and TV-set makers like Decca and Pye, component makers like Mullard and Plessey – had also enlarged their electronics capabilities during the war. Mullard was still owned by Philips of the Netherlands, one of the two major foreign-owned firms in the industry. The other was the ITT subsidiary, Standard Telephones and Cables (STC). Its main business was the supply of switching and transmission equipment to the Post Office, but it also made valves and television sets, and had access to technology from other ITT subsidiaries in Europe.

Behind these companies stood the government, more aware as a result of the war of the strategic importance of electronics and anxious to ensure that British firms stayed abreast of the latest technology. Although direct intervention remained modest until the 'national champion' era of the 1960s, the Ministry of Defence was a useful source of orders and research support. In 1949 the Labour government set up the National Research Development Corporation to promote the commercialisation of publicly funded research, and this agency took an active interest in computers.

The German electronics industry, still dominated by Siemens and AEG-Telefunken, was slow to recover from the war, and technical progress was held back by the Allied ban on military-related research. In France the two big electrical equipment manufacturers, Thomson and Compagnie Générale d'Electricité (CGE), had only minor interests in electronics in the 1950s. The only French company with a tradition of independent research in this field was Compagnie Générale de Télégraphie sans Fil (CSF). This firm had been a pioneer in the early days of radio, and it helped to develop the French TV broadcasting system, SECAM, which was installed in 1956. In 1968, as part of a government-inspired restructuring of the industry, CSF was absorbed by Thomson. Thomson-CSF and CGE became France's national champions in electronics, the latter concentrating mainly on telecommunications.

The next four sections describe how the British manufacturers played their cards in four branches of the industry – computers, semiconductors, consumer electronics, and telecommunications equipment – and compares their performance with that of their German and French counterparts.

Computers

In the late 1940s, thanks to the work which had been done on code-breaking during the war, computer technology in Britain was roughly on a par with the US.[25] The world's first fully operational computer, the EDSAC, was commissioned at Cambridge University in 1949, and other projects were under way at Manchester University and at the government's National Physical Laboratory. Ferranti and English Electric participated in these projects, and used the experience to develop their own computers – the Ferranti Mark I, delivered to Manchester University in 1951, and the English Electric DEUCE, introduced three years later. Both these machines were designed for high-level scientific computation, for which there was expected to be a limited but potentially profitable demand in industry, government and academia. Another early entrant was Elliott Brothers, an instrument manufacturer which had made control systems for ship-mounted gunnery during the war and saw an opportunity for using computers to control industrial processes.

One of the first firms to show an interest in commercial data processing was J. Lyons, a food manufacturer well known for its tea shops. Recognising that the new computational techniques could be applied to clerical operations, Lyons designed and built its own computer, the LEO (standing for Lyons Electronic Office), in collaboration with the Cambridge scientists who had worked on the EDSAC machine. Leo Computers was set up as a separate subsidiary in 1955.[26]

Most of the early research on computers was financed directly or indirectly by the government, and hence of interest to the National Research Development Corporation (NRDC). Lord Halsbury, the NRDC's managing director, was an Eton-educated hereditary peer who had taken a degree in mathematics and chemistry and had spent most of his career in industrial research; he was director of research at Decca before taking up the NRDC post in 1949.[27] Halsbury was well aware of the progress being made by IBM and Remington Rand in the US, and he saw that closer links between electronics companies and office machinery manufacturers were essential.

Halsbury's first move was to encourage Ferranti to work with the leading manufacturer of punched-card equipment, the British Tabulating Machine Company (BTM). BTM had been a licensee of IBM for many years and had obtained most of its technology from the American company. In 1949, following a series of disagreements, the licensing agreement was terminated. IBM was now free to attack the British market, while the British company had to develop a research capability of its own.[28] A link with Ferranti, the most advanced of the British computer makers, was logical, but the two firms were unable to work out a satisfactory basis for collaboration. In 1956 BTM formed a joint venture with GEC, a company which, like Ferranti, had electronics expertise but did not wish to enter the computer market directly.

Partly as a result of Halsbury's efforts, several other electronics companies, including EMI, entered the computer business. But the market was much smaller than in the US, and British manufacturers received only modest financial support from the government. The value of military development contracts for the American computer industry between 1949 and 1959 has been estimated at about £350m, compared with not much more than £10m in Britain, to which can be added loans and guarantees from the NRDC amounting to some £2m.[29]

The size of the US market gave the American manufacturers a competitive advantage, which they were able to exploit overseas. IBM opened a factory at Greenock in Scotland in 1954 and rapidly increased its share of the British market. The IBM 1401 computer, launched in 1959, set a new standard in price and performance, and British computer manufacturers became aware of how difficult it would be to stay in the race.[30]

BTM had no alternative but to invest in the new technology, since its survival depended on it. Although it was not yet clear how soon conventional punched-card equipment would be displaced by computers, there was no doubt that demand for computers from BTM's customers would rise. The need to devote larger resources to computer development was one of the factors which led BTM to take over Powers-Samas, its main British competitor in punched-card equipment, in 1959; the merged company was called International Computers and Tabulators (ICT). For most of the other British manufacturers computers were a more marginal activity, and they did not relish a head-on fight with IBM. In 1962 EMI sold its computer interests to ICT and in the following year Lyons sold its LEO subsidiary to English Electric. Ferranti, still a family-owned company, did not have the financial resources or the marketing skills to compete in office computers against IBM; this side of the business was sold to ICT in 1963.

By 1964 the only British survivors in computers were ICT, English Electric and Elliott-Automation (the renamed Elliott Brothers); the last of these concentrated mainly on process control machines. In that year the extent of American superiority was underlined by the launch of IBM's System 360. This was a family of compatible machines which allowed customers to progress easily from small to large computers without making obsolete their existing investment in software and technical support. System 360 incorporated the latest transistorised technology, and marked a step forward in computer design which took all IBM's competitors by surprise. ICT's reaction was to speed up the development of its new range of computers, the 1900 series, which was announced in the autumn of 1964. English Electric collaborated with one of IBM's American competitors, RCA, in the development of System 4, which, unlike ICT's 1900 series, was compatible with IBM's System 360.

After Halsbury's retirement from the NRDC in 1959 official interest in computers had waned and the Conservative government was not involved in the restructuring of the industry which took place between 1959 and 1964. The political climate changed with Labour's victory in the election of October 1964. Harold Wilson, the Prime Minister, was determined to strengthen Britain's position in high-technology industries, and computers had a special importance. As Wilson saw it, ICT and English Electric were rapidly losing ground to IBM, and, if nothing was done, Britain might soon have no indigenous computer industry. Wilson told the new Minister of Technology, Frank Cousins, immediately after the election that he had 'about a month' to save the industry and this must be his first priority.[31]

The government's favoured solution, in line with the fashion for mergers which was running strongly at that time, was to bring together the three remaining companies in a single organisation. But ICT and English Electric were in the throes of launching new and wholly incompatible computers, and they could see no advantage in getting together. It was not until 1966, when Tony Benn had replaced Cousins as Minister for Technology, that merger discussions began. In June 1966 English Electric acquired Elliott-Automation. Detailed negotiations then got under way between ICT and English Electric, spurred on by the promise of government financial support.

An unexpected complication arose when Plessey informed ICT that it was interested in making a bid for the company. Plessey, now run by Allen Clark's son, John, had diversified from its original business in components to become a diversified electronics manufacturer, with interests in defence and telecommunications equipment. Clark believed that there was a technological link between computers and communications and that the combination of ICT and Plessey would create a powerful force in computer networks.[32]

The Ministry of Technology persuaded Plessey to hold off while the talks between ICT and English Electric continued, and merger terms were agreed in March 1968. A new company, International Computers Ltd (ICL), was formed, in which the government, through the Ministry of Technology, held a minority stake (TABLE 10.1). In addition, the Ministry provided a grant of £13.5m for the development of a new range to replace the ICT 1900 and the English Electric System 4, and all government departments and agencies were encouraged to buy computers from ICL in preference to IBM and other non-British suppliers.

TABLE 10.1 *Principal shareholders of ICL in 1968*

	Percentage of ordinary shares
Existing ICT shareholders	53.5
English Electric	18.0
Plessey	18.0
Ministry of Technology	10.5

Note: Plessey obtained its shareholding in exchange for a cash investment of £18m. The English Electric shareholding passed to GEC after the merger between these two companies later in 1968.

The creation of ICL marked the start of a twenty-year battle to preserve a British national champion in computers. The objective was to establish a British counterweight to IBM, but IBM was a far bigger company, and ICL's ambitions persistently outran its resources. The first crisis came in 1971. A recession in the US prompted a wave of price-cutting, and competition became even more intense after the launch of the IBM System 370, which offered more computing power at a lower price than the System 360. The pace was getting too hot for some of IBM's US competitors; both General Electric and RCA withdrew from the computer business.[33] ICL's profits fell, and, having already used up the £13.5m provided in 1968, it was forced to turn to the government for help.

The new Conservative government under Edward Heath was opposed on principle to the interventionist policies of its Labour predecessor. But the computer industry was still thought to have a strategic importance which justified special treatment. Half-hearted attempts were made to promote a merger between ICL and another European company, but ministers did not want to see control pass out of Britain, and in 1972 they agreed to provide £14.2m (later increased to £40m) to support the development of a new range of computers. Support was made conditional on a change of management. Geoffrey Cross, who had held senior posts with Sperry Rand, one of IBM's American competitors, was brought in as managing director.

The first computers in the new range, the 2900 series, were announced in October 1974, and over the next few years ICL's financial position improved. GEC and Plessey sold their shares at a profit, and under the Labour government of 1974–9 ICL acquired a new sponsor, the National Enterprise Board (NEB). The NEB took over the government's stake in ICL and bought additional shares from GEC and Plessey, bringing its holding to 25 per cent. But the fundamental problem remained: could ICL generate sufficient revenue and profit to compete with IBM and the other big American companies as a full-line computer manufacturer? The five-year plan presented to the ICL board in 1978 by Cross's successor, Chris Wilson, posed a choice between two strategies – one based on modest growth targets, cutting back the product range and restricting expenditure on research to 7 per cent of revenue, the other aiming for an annual growth in sales of 20–25 per cent and a much higher level of research spending. The board chose the latter course, with the full support of the Labour government.[34]

The revenue projections on which this strategy depended turned out to be far too optimistic. In 1979 a price war broke out between IBM and the fast-rising Japanese computer manufacturers. At the same time the overvaluation of sterling in 1980 undermined the profitability of ICL's exports. The company was faced with a Conservative administration under Margaret Thatcher, deeply unsympathetic to bailing out 'lame ducks'. One of the new government's first acts was to close down the NEB and sell off its shareholdings, including the stake in ICL. But ICL's bargaining position was not as weak as it appeared. If the company collapsed, this would jeopardise the government's plan to promote the diffusion of computer technology throughout British industry; a new Ministry of Information Technology was formed for this purpose within the Department of Trade and Industry. The government agreed to provide loan guarantees (rather than loans or grants) to tide the company through the crisis, and, as in 1972, the top management was replaced.

The two key appointments were those of Robb Wilmot as managing director and Peter Bonfield as director of marketing; both men had previously worked for Texas Instruments, the US semiconductor manufacturer. Wilmot and Bonfield recognised that, without open-ended support from the government, ICL could not hope to compete on all fronts against IBM. As Bonfield put it later, 'We were obviously relatively large in European terms, but not in international terms and we had to come to terms with that ... Rather than try to compete with the big US multinationals across the board, we would only compete with them in very specific areas.'[35] This meant cutting back research and development to levels which ICL could afford, and filling the gaps by alliances with other companies. In 1981 an agreement was reached with Fujitsu, whereby the Japanese company made available its semiconductor technology for use in ICL's computers.

After nearly fifteen years of wishful thinking, ICL was adapting to the realities of its position in the world computer industry. Without government tutelage, it was free to make its own commercial decisions. In 1984, Kenneth Corfield, chairman of Standard Telephones and Cables (STC), announced his intention to make a take-over bid for ICL. STC's main business was in telephone switching and transmission equipment, and Corfield believed, as did many people in the computer industry at that time, that the technologies of computing and telecommunications were converging. Another reason for the bid was that STC had been excluded by British Telecom from the consortium which was manufacturing the new digital telephone exchange, known as System X (see below). Corfield was looking for a new avenue of growth, and the merger with ICL appeared to provide it.

Wilmot and his colleagues agreed with the logic behind Corfield's proposal, and after some haggling over terms the merger went through amicably. However, the convergence concept, whether through faulty implementation or because the concept itself was flawed, did not produce the benefits which Corfield had hoped for. When the performance of the STC side of the business started to deteriorate not long after the merger, his position as chairman came under threat. In 1985 he was replaced by Arthur Walsh, a senior executive from GEC, who was not committed to the convergence idea. He regarded telecommunications equipment and computers as separate businesses which did not have to be kept under the same roof. In 1990 he sold a controlling interest in ICL to Fujitsu of Japan, which was seeking to enlarge its stake in the European computer market. Three years later STC itself was acquired by Northern Telecom of Canada.

The sale of ICL came at a time when the world computer industry was in the throes of another upheaval, precipitated by the rise of the personal computer. The dominance of the mainframe was at an end, forcing all the established manufacturers, including IBM, to rethink their strategies. In the course of the 1990s ICL abandoned the manufacture of hardware in order to concentrate on the supply of information systems; by the end of the decade a successful transition had been achieved. Fujitsu planned to refloat ICL on the stock exchange in 2000, while retaining a controlling interest in the company.

The ICL story is often regarded as an example of bad industrial policy, comparable in some respects to British Leyland – the same exaggerated faith in mergers as the cure for competitive weakness, the same reluctance to accept that the national champion could do anything less than compete on all fronts against the world leaders. But, whereas the demise of British Leyland was a uniquely British disaster, in computers other European countries made many of the same mistakes as Britain, and the results were not much better.

In France, as in Britain, the stimulus for government intervention was the fear of American domination in what was seen as a strategically important industry.[36] By the early 1960s IBM had established a commanding position in the French computer market. Its principal French rival was Bull, a manufacturer of punched card equipment, which had made a promising start in computers but lacked the financial resources to compete with IBM. In 1964 this company, having over-extended itself in the development of a large scientific computer, was in financial difficulty, and, despite last-minute efforts by the government to engineer a 'French solution', was taken over by General Electric of the US.[37] This episode, followed shortly afterwards by the refusal of the US government to authorise the export of an advanced computer ordered for the French nuclear weapons programme, galvanised the French authorities into action. In 1966 they launched the 'Plan Calcul', an ambitious programme to create a French-owned computer company which would be strong enough to withstand American competition. Three firms which had small computer subsidiaries – CGE, CSF and Schneider – were induced to merge them into a new company, Compagnie Internationale pour l'Informatique (CII), which was to become the national champion.

Like ICL, CII was supported by subsidies and preferential procurement, but it was too small to fulfil the goals which the government had set for it, and its share of the French market remained far below that of IBM. A possible solution emerged in 1973 in the form of collaboration between CII and two other European companies, Philips and Siemens. Philips was losing money on its computer operations, and interested in putting them into a larger group. Siemens had been manufacturing computers under licence from RCA; when RCA decided to abandon the computer market in 1971, the German company needed a new partner. A jointly owned computer company, Unidata, was formed in 1974, but the conflicts of interest between the three partners proved impossible to reconcile, and the French government decided to explore a different route.[38]

Honeywell, the American firm which had taken over General Electric's computer interests, including Bull, in 1970, was persuaded to participate in the creation of a new company, CII-Honeywell Bull, partly owned by the French government. For a brief period this arrangement appeared to work well, but in 1981 the new Socialist government under François Mitterrand nationalised all the leading electronics companies and set in train an ambitious industrial strategy in which Bull, no longer linked to Honeywell, was given a starring role.

The outcome was a financial disaster. By the early 1990s Bull's losses were so high that even a socialist government was forced to scale back its ambitions. The issue was no longer one of preserving a national champion, but of finding some way of lifting a financial burden from the shoulders of the French taxpayer. Since there was no prospect of floating the company on the stock market, privatisation took the form of encouraging other computer manufacturers, Japanese and American, to take minority stakes in the business. By 1999 the government shareholding in Bull had ben cut to 17 per cent.

In Germany government intervention was not as extensive or as continuous as in Britain and France, and it was motivated less by political concerns than by the desire to upgrade the technological capabilities of German industry. Support for the industry began in the 1960s, and took the form of grants for research and development, most of which went to Siemens and AEG; AEG subsequently sold its computer interests to Siemens. Yet by the mid-1970s Siemens had only 17 per cent of the German computer market, compared to IBM's 62 per cent, and its position outside Germany was weak.

The most successful German computer company during this period was a new entrant, Nixdorf, which had targeted the market for small business systems, where competition from IBM was less severe. During the 1980s, however, Nixdorf expanded too fast and failed to adjust to the shift in the computer market from proprietary to open standards. In 1989 it was on the brink of bankruptcy and taken over by Siemens. Over the next few years the merged company, Siemens Nixdorf Information Systems (SNI), made heavy losses, contributing to the poor financial performance of Siemens as a whole. SNI began to make a modest profit in the second half of the 1990s, partly by putting more emphasis on systems integration and other services than on the manufacture of hardware. In 1999 Siemens put its European computer operations into a 50/50 joint venture with Fujitsu. While the stated purpose of this deal was to secure economies of scale, some analysts saw it as a precursor to Siemens' eventual withdrawal from the personal computer business.[39]

Why did ICL, Bull and Siemens not do better? Part of the answer is that these companies, encouraged by their governments, devoted most of their efforts to sectors of the market where IBM was overwhelmingly strong. 'With a few notable exceptions, European industry ignored other strategies that were successful when tried in the US, like targeting specialised niches and new applications and going after the high and low ends beyond the IBM product range.'[40] The European industry might have done better if governments, instead of nurturing and protecting national champions, had concentrated on widening the market for computers. This would have called for more emphasis on promoting the diffusion of computer technology and encouraging new computer applications.[41] As it was, nationalistic, producer-orientated policies, discriminating in favour of chosen domestic suppliers, exacerbated Europe's most serious weakness *vis-à-vis* the US, the small size of the market.

Semiconductors

The progress of the semiconductor industry after the invention of the transistor in 1947 in some respects resembles what happened in computers: an early American lead, followed by a prolonged and generally unsuccessful effort on the part of European manufacturers, supported in some cases by their governments, to catch up.

The starting-point in Britain was a group of established valve-makers which quickly appreciated the significance of Bell's invention. By the mid-1950s production of transistors, under licence from Bell and other American firms, was rising strongly. At this stage, although the US market was larger, there was little if any technological gap between American and British manufacturers.[42] But the introduction of the planar process and the integrated circuit at the end of the 1950s called for a higher level of technical skill in design and manufacture. The first American companies to exploit these innovations – principally Fairchild, Texas Instruments and Motorola – gained a technical lead which later entrants found hard to match.

As competitive pressure mounted during the 1960s, European firms faced a dilemma that was to dog them for the next twenty years: should they try to compete head-on with the Americans, form partnerships with them, look for specialised sectors of the market where competition was less severe, or withdraw from the race?

Among the leading British firms, GEC virtually opted out in 1962 when it put its semiconductor interests into a joint venture with Mullard, retaining only a one-third stake. When Arnold Weinstock became managing director of GEC in 1963, he did not regard semiconductors as a high priority for investment, and did not seek to re-establish an independent position. English Electric and AEI, on the other hand, continued to manufacture semiconductors for their own use and for outside sale, and when these two companies merged with GEC at the end of the 1960s, Weinstock found himself in control of a substantial part of the British-owned semiconductor industry. He took the view that there was little future in competing head-on against the Americans, and did not regard a semiconductor capacity as essential to GEC's electronics business. He therefore cut back semiconductor production, retaining a small facility at Lincoln to make specialised devices.

Outside the GEC empire the principal British producers of semiconductors were Ferranti and Plessey. Ferranti, true to the innovative traditions of the founder, had introduced the first British-designed integrated circuit in 1962 and by the end of the decade it was selling these devices to ICL and other computer makers as well as using them in its own equipment. But Ferranti was also engaged in a variety of other high-technology businesses, which strained its financial and managerial resources. In 1974 a combination of problems, including heavy losses in the transformer division, brought on a financial crisis. When the banks refused to provide further loans Sebastian Ferranti, the chairman, turned for help to the Labour government's National Enterprise Board. The company was refinanced, with the NEB taking a

62.5 per cent stake in the equity, and a new managing director, Derek Alun-Jones, was appointed; family control came to an end.

While Ferranti was in the NEB's care, there were talks with Plessey over a possible merger of the two companies' semiconductor operations. No agreement was reached, but the NEB continued to take a close interest in the semiconductor industry and looked for ways of strengthening it against competition from the increasingly dominant American manufacturers; in 1977 British-owned firms accounted for less than 20 per cent of the British semiconductor market.

Up to this point the semiconductor industry had received much less support from public funds than the computer industry, and there had been no attempt to create a national champion like ICL. But there was a growing feeling in government and in some parts of the industry that excessive reliance on non-British semiconductor suppliers could be dangerous. The performance of electronic equipment such as computers depended crucially on the semiconductor devices – principally memories and microprocessors – that went into them. The argument was that without an indigenous source of these components, the British electronics industry would be at a disadvantage against Japanese and American competitors, which had access to state-of-the-art semiconductor technology on their doorstep.

Since none of the established semiconductor producers – GEC, Ferranti and Plessey – seemed able or willing to compete against the Americans and Japanese in standard memories and microprocessors, the NEB reacted positively to a proposal put to it in 1977 by a group of British and American entrepreneurs.[43] This group had developed advanced technology which, they claimed, offered the prospect of leapfrogging current American designs and re-establishing Britain in the forefront of semiconductor development. With the approval of the government, the NEB agreed in 1978 to finance the new venture, which was called Inmos; the initial capital was £25m, with the promise of a further £25m at a later stage.[44] The plan was to start with memories, to be made at a new plant in Colorado and later in the UK, then to move into microprocessors.

Meanwhile Arnold Weinstock at GEC was being urged by his colleagues in GEC-Marconi to secure access to the latest semiconductor technology by forming an alliance with one of the leading American firms. In 1978 GEC and Fairchild announced that they would jointly build a semiconductor plant in Britain. Before this deal could be completed, however, Fairchild was taken over by another company, and the new owners withdrew from the British venture. Weinstock's response, after briefly considering a possible take-over of Inmos, was to build up GEC's existing semiconductor capacity, based at Marconi's plant in Lincoln.[45]

As a state-supported venture, Inmos was regarded with suspicion by the new Thatcher government. Although it reluctantly agreed to provide the second tranche of £25m which had been promised by the NEB, Mrs Thatcher was anxious to sell Inmos to the private sector as soon as possible. In 1984 it was sold to Thorn-EMI, then resold three years later to the Franco-Italian group, SGS-Thomson. This left Ferranti and Plessey as the two remaining British-owned semiconductor-makers. Ferranti, having been resuscitated by the NEB and returned to the private sector (the shares were floated on the stock exchange in 1978), had developed a strong position in 'semi-custom' integrated circuits and for a brief period was the world's leading producer of devices known as Uncommitted Logic Array – integrated circuits that could be modified to suit particular customer requirements. However, this market was invaded in the mid-1980s by American and Japanese semiconductor producers, and prices fell sharply. As Alun-Jones explained later, 'There was no patent protection and the big American and Japanese companies started pumping capital into the business and cutting prices . . . People urged us to put up plants all over the world and exploit our market position, but there was no way of doing that on any terms that would have made money.'[46] Ferranti sold its semiconductor business to Plessey in 1988.

Plessey, after going through a difficult period in the 1970s, regarded semiconductors as one of its core businesses. In 1980 Doug Dunn was recruited from Motorola to run the division, and he believed that Plessey could be a viable producer of 'application-specific' integrated circuits (ASICs), especially if it could acquire the other British-owned businesses operating in the same field. The purchase of Ferranti's semiconductor division was part of this strategy, and Dunn also tried to buy Inmos from Thorn-EMI. However, the future of Plessey was thrown into doubt in 1989 when it was taken over by GEC and Siemens.[47] The main purpose of the take-over, from GEC's point of view, was to bring together the two companies' defence electronics and telecommunications interests, while Siemens wanted to establish a foothold in the British telecommunications market. The plan for semiconductors was that Plessey's activities and those of GEC should be brought together under the joint ownership of GEC and Siemens, and that Siemens – which had a large semiconductor operation of its own in Germany – would be responsible for managing it.[48] After the merger went through, however, Siemens withdrew from this arrangement, leaving GEC to carry on with semiconductors alone.

Thus what was left of the British-owned semiconductor industry was in the hands of a man who had always been dubious about committing large sums of money to the business. Although the newly merged GEC-Plessey semiconductor operation sold part of its output to other GEC divisions, Weinstock was not convinced that having an in-house supplier gave these divisions any competitive advantage. Several attempts were made to dispose of the business, and it was eventually sold in 1998, after Weinstock had retired from the company. In announcing the sale to Mitel, a Canadian electronics group, George Simpson, Weinstock's successor, regretted that the last remaining British-owned semiconductor maker was passing into foreign hands, but claimed that it was the sensible thing to do. 'If we hung on to it,' he said, 'we wouldn't have the critical mass to succeed.'[49]

At the end of the 1990s virtually the whole of the British semiconductor market was supplied by non-British companies, several of which had built or acquired factories in Britain. Some commentators deplored this outcome, arguing that the loss of an indigenous technological capability in semiconductors would inflict long-term damage on the British economy.[50] Others saw it as a rational decision to retreat in the face of superior opposition. What is clear is that other European countries also had great difficulty in preserving a nationally owned semiconductor producer and that government intervention had generally disappointing results.

As in computers, the most *dirigiste* of the European countries was France. The chosen instrument in semiconductors was Thomson-CSF, whose semiconductor subsidiary, Sescosem, was given substantial subsidies during the 1960s and 1970s. After nationalisation in 1981 Thomson was encouraged to broaden its range of products and compete directly against the big Japanese and American companies. But despite large subventions from the state, Thomson failed to achieve the objectives the government had set for it, and the semiconductor business became a financial burden on the rest of the group. In 1987 Thomson's semiconductor subsidiary was put into a joint venture with an Italian state-owned semiconductor firm, SGS. Over the subsequent decade SGS-Thomson, run by an Italian, Pasquale Pistorio, who had previously worked for Motorola, gradually established a defensible position in the world market, concentrating on semi-custom devices. The link with Thomson became increasingly distant, and in 1997 the French company sold its remaining shares in SGS-Thomson. What had originally been envisaged as a French national champion in semiconductors had become part of a specialised supplier focusing on market niches rather than high-volume commodity chips.[51]

In Germany events followed a different course. From the start of the transistor era Siemens, unlike GEC, took the view that an in-house capability in semiconductors was essential to the competitiveness of its electronic products – computers, telephone exchanges and other equipment. This strategy called for substantial investments, not merely in application-specific semiconductors, but in standard memories and microprocessors. Although Siemens took steps to reduce the size of its expenditure through partnerships with other companies, it stuck to the principle of retaining control over what it regarded as a strategic technology. This policy of vertical integration exposed the company to losses whenever the semiconductor market went through one of its periodic downturns; a financial analyst commented in 1991 that the loss-making semiconductor division 'continues to be a painful example of how the Siemens style of running a business can leave the group with a burden no competitor would countenance'.[52]

In the second half of the 1990s, when Siemens was being criticised by investors for its poor financial performance, the semiconductor strategy came under more critical scrutiny within the company. In 1997, partly because of the economic crisis in Asia, semiconductor prices fell sharply and all the leading producers of commodity chips, including Siemens, suffered heavy losses. In August 1998, Siemens announced that a recently opened semiconductor plant in Britain would be closed; the plant was reported to be losing £150m a year.[53] Three months later the company announced that the whole of the components division, employing some 47,000 people, would be hived off as an independent company and that Siemens would in future obtain its semiconductors from outside suppliers. This marked the recognition, apparently forced on the company by shareholder pressure, that Siemens could not afford to subsidise a chronically loss-making business from profits made elsewhere in the group. The chief executive, Heinrich von Pierer, said he could no longer inflict the ups and downs of the semiconductor cycle on investors. 'We have learned from the experience and are drawing the consequences.'[54]

Thus neither Britain nor France nor Germany was able to foster a strong, nationally owned semiconductor producer – and for much the same reasons as in computers. The fundamental problem was the absence of the favourable market and institutional conditions from which American companies benefited during the formative period of the industry in the 1950s and 1960s. Intervention by governments did little to remedy this weakness.

Consumer Electronics

In consumer electronics international competition did not bite hard until the 1970s, and the challenge for European manufacturers came, not from the US, but from Japan. The post-war growth of the Japanese electronics industry was driven by demand for consumer products – first transistor radios, of which Japan became by far the largest producer and exporter, and then television sets. As in the case of cars discussed in Chapter 9, Japanese companies such as Sony and Matsushita developed a novel approach to the design and manufacture of television sets which enabled them to combine economies of scale with exceptionally high quality and reliability. Fewer components were used than in European or American sets, and new techniques of automatic insertion reduced the scope for human error during assembly.[55]

When colour television began in the 1960s, Japan adopted the same broadcasting system – NTSC (National Television System Committee) – as the US. Japanese sets needed no modification to be saleable in the US, which became almost an extension of the Japanese home market. Penetrating the European market was more difficult because of the existence of two incompatible formats – SECAM in France, and PAL, adopted in Germany, Britain and most other countries. It was not until the early 1970s that exports from Japan began to pose a serious threat to domestic manufacturers.

Partly because of incompatible broadcasting systems, intra-European trade in television sets did not develop as rapidly as in cars or domestic appliances, and until the 1970s the European consumer electronics industry had a strongly national character. A few locally owned companies, such as Grundig and AEG-Telefunken in Germany and Thomson-Brandt in France, dominated the market in each country. The Dutch company, Philips, which had long-established valve-making and set-making operations in Britain, France and Germany as well as in the Netherlands, was the only genuinely European company, but its subsidiaries were run autonomously, and there was little attempt to obtain economies of scale through Europe-wide factory rationalisation.

At the end of the 1960s about 75 per cent of Britain's TV-set production was in the hands of four companies – Thorn, GEC, Philips and Rank. Import penetration was minimal, and exports amounted to less than 5 per cent of the industry's production. Over the next few years demand for colour sets increased rapidly, especially during the so-called Barber boom of 1973. Tax cuts announced by the Conservative Chancellor of the Exchequer, Anthony Barber, in his 1972 Budget stimulated a surge in consumer spending, and the TV-set manufacturers found themselves short of capacity. Imports from Japan poured in to fill the gap, giving dealers and consumers an opportunity to appreciate the superior quality of Japanese sets. When the boom collapsed, Japanese manufacturers had established a bridgehead in the market from which they could not easily be dislodged.

The domestic manufacturers clamoured for protection, and with support from the government negotiated an agreement whereby the Japanese firms would limit their exports of colour sets to 10 per cent of the British market. To get round these restrictions Sony and Matsushita decided to manufacture TV sets in Britain; as long as 50 per cent of their components were British-made, these sets would count as British and not be subject to the 10 per cent limit. In 1974 a third Japanese manufacturer, Hitachi, announced plans for a TV set factory in the north-east, promising that up to 70 per cent of its components, including tubes, would be bought locally, and that half of the production would be exported. This was warmly welcomed by the newly elected Labour government, but the domestic industry protested that there was already too much capacity in the industry and that the Hitachi investment would disrupt the market. The Japanese companies were then encouraged by the government to form partnerships with local firms, in the hope that the British manufacturers would learn how to make sets as efficiently as the Japanese. A report commissioned by the National Economic Development Office showed that the number of man-hours needed per set was far lower in Japan than in Europe (TABLE 10.2).

In 1978 GEC formed a joint venture with Hitachi, and Rank followed suit with Toshiba, but both partnerships were dogged by conflicts of interest and the Japanese companies subsequently acquired full control. Thorn, the biggest of the British manufacturers, was confident that it had the skills and resources to go it alone. In the second half of the 1970s Thorn's management embarked on a determined effort to match Japanese quality and efficiency. By the early 1980s the quality gap had been largely closed, but Thorn was still some way behind in terms of scale, making less than 1m TV sets a year, while the leading Japanese companies were making 2m or more. During this period Thorn had been going through a difficult management transition. The founder, Jules Thorn, retired in 1976, and his successor, Richard Cave, believed that the company needed to acquire a stronger research capability. An unexpected opportunity to do so arose in 1979 when EMI was put up for sale and Thorn decided to buy it.[56] EMI was widely regarded

TABLE 10.2. *The costs of making a television set in 1978*

Direct labour costs per set

	Britain	Japan	South Korea	West Germany
Average man-hours per set	6.1	1.9	5.0	3.9
Employment costs (£ per hour)	1.74	3.00	0.30	3.85
TOTAL (£)	10.60	5.70	1.50	15.00

Total costs per set

Direct Labour (£)	10.60	5.70	1.50	15.00
Material (£)	126.00	100.00	113.00	119.00
Plant overhead (£)	20.00	11.00	2.00	17.00
TOTAL (£)	156.60	116.70	116.50	151.00

Source: National Economic Development Office, quoted in *Financial Times*, 3 November 1979.

as Britain's most innovative electronics company, and Cave believed that its skills would complement Thorn's strengths in manufacturing and market-ing.[57] His plan was to turn Thorn into a broadly based, high-technology concern, with interests in industrial as well as consumer electronics. EMI's interests in music publishing, records and films, Cave argued, fitted well with Thorn's skill as a manufacturer of TV sets and other consumer products.

This strategy was regarded sceptically by outside commentators, and they became even more dubious in 1984 when Thorn-EMI took over Inmos, the semiconductor-maker, and then tried to merge with British Aerospace. By 1985 profits were falling and investors were losing confidence in Thorn's manage-ment. A new managing director, Colin Southgate, was appointed, who took a more realistic view of Thorn's competitive position in electronics. He saw Thorn's TV-set operation as 'a national business in a global market'[58] and in 1987 sold it to Thomson of France. This deal has been described by the historian of the company as 'probably the most critical one in the remaking of Thorn-EMI and one of Southgate's greatest personal coups'.[59] Over the next few years Thorn-EMI disposed of most of its manufacturing operations in order to concentrate on TV rental, through Thorn, and recorded music, through EMI; the two sides of the company were demerged in 1996.

Thomson was more interested in Thorn's share of the market than in its manufacturing capacity, and the British plants were shut down not long after the take-over. Philips, too, closed its British TV-set factories, and, like Thomson, supplied the British market from the Continent. By the mid-1990s the British consumer electronics industry was almost entirely in the hands of Far Eastern producers (TABLE 10.3). Successive British governments made no attempt to prevent this transfer of control. On the contrary, the Conservative government welcomed inward investment as a way of strengthening the British electronics industry and improving its export performance. As the main European manufacturing base for Japanese and Korean consumer electronics companies, the UK became Europe's largest producer and exporter of TV sets, with a healthy trade surplus.[60]

TABLE 10.3 *British production of TV sets in 1996*

Company	Nationality	Output (millions)
Sony	Japan	1.5
Matsushita	Japan	1.0
Samsung	South Korea	0.7
Toshiba	Japan	0.7
Mitsubishi*	Japan	0.4
JVC	Japan	0.4
Hitachi	Japan	0.3
Tatung	Taiwan	0.3
Others		0.9
TOTAL		6.2

*The Mitsubishi factory, in Scotland, was closed in 1998.

Source: *Financial Times*, 15 April 1997.

Successive French governments, by contrast, believed that, without a nationally owned consumer electronics manufacturer, the French electronics industry as a whole would be weakened. As in semiconductors, the chosen instrument was Thomson, which after a series of mergers and acquisitions had emerged by the early 1970s as the largest French-owned TV-set manufacturer. Most of its business at that time was in France, but the management was aware that if they were to have any prospect of competing against the Japanese, the company needed to become bigger and more international. Two small German manufacturers were acquired as a means of building up a distribution network in Germany for French-built TV sets. But the big push for internationalisation came after Thomson had been nationalised in 1981. The French authorities wanted Thomson to be the nucleus of a strong European consumer electronics group, and proposed that Thomson and Philips should jointly take control of Grundig, the leading German TV-set manufacturer. Philips was already allied to Grundig, supplying tubes and other components and holding 24.5 per cent of its shares. Negotiations on a three-way link-up began, but the German Cartel Office objected to it on competition grounds. Thomson then turned to the second largest German manufacturer, Telefunken, which its owner, AEG, was anxious to sell.[61] This was the start of a highly ambitious strategy of global expansion. The most spectacular move was the take-over in 1987 of RCA, once the largest and most innovative consumer electronics manufacturer in the US. RCA had been no more successful than European firms in resisting the Japanese invasion, and by 1985, when it was taken over by General Electric, it was making heavy losses; General Electric was relieved to be able to sell the company to Thomson.

France now had its world leader in consumer electronics (TABLE 10.4), but as a collection of recently acquired businesses Thomson Consumer Electronics (later renamed Thomson Multimedia) lacked the coherence of the big Japanese groups. Unlike Sony or Philips, it had no internationally recognised brand, and was saddled by the burden of debt incurred in making its overseas acquisitions. As a chronic loss-maker, the TV set business was a complicating factor in the attempts by non-socialist governments, after François Mitterrand's defeat in the 1995 presidential election, to privatise Thomson. The solution arrived at in 1996 was to sell the Thomson group as a whole to a privately owned French electronics firm, Lagardere, which would then sell Thomson Multimedia to Daewoo, one of the leading Korean consumer electronics firms. This plan was subsequently abandoned in the face of strong

TABLE 10.4 *World's leading consumer electronics companies in 1995*

Company	Nationality	Percentage share of world sales by value
Sony	Japan	17.9
Matsushita	Japan	12.6
Philips	Netherlands	8.6
Sharp	Japan	6.0
Thomson Multimedia	France	5.5
LG Electronics	South Korea	4.4
Pioneer	Japan	4.4
Sanyo	Japan	3.8
Daewoo	South Korea	3.6
Samsung	South Korea	3.6

Source: *The World Market for Consumer Electronics*, Euromonitor, 1997.

political opposition, and the French government set about privatising Thomson Multimedia on a gradual basis, as it had done with Bull, by inviting other companies to take a minority stake in it.

Japanese competition was too strong for all the European TV set makers, including the Germans. This was one part of the electronics industry which Siemens chose not to enter; it was also one in which the Federal government did not intervene to support the domestic industry. Following the purchase of Telefunken by Thomson, the principal German manufacturer was Grundig, partly owned by Philips, but its market position deteriorated badly during the 1990s and Philips cut its ties to the company in 1996. In the following year a group of Bavarian banks intervened to save Grundig from collapse.[62] By 1999 it was back in profit, but only a marginal player in the world market.

If there is any consolation for Europe in this story, it is that in consumer electronics, unlike computers and semiconductors, American manufacturers did at least as badly. What distinguished Britain from France and Germany was that admission of defeat came earlier, and investment from Japan and South Korea was strongly encouraged. In view of the French experience with Thomson Multimedia, it is not obvious that this was a mistake.

Telecommunications Equipment

In computers, semiconductors and television sets European manufacturers were on the defensive against American and Japanese competitors from the 1960s onwards. In telecommunications equipment, because of the greater influence of governments and their agencies as customers for the industry's products, competition took a different form. This applied particularly to the supply of public switching and transmission equipment for telephone networks. Until the 1980s, when the trend towards privatisation and deregulation began to open up the market, national telephone administrations such as the Post Office in Britain and the Bundespost in Germany bought their telecommunications apparatus almost exclusively from domestic manufacturers. In Europe these administrations were directly or indirectly controlled by governments. The US was exceptional in that the network operator, AT&T, was a private-sector company and obtained its equipment from a wholly owned manufacturing subsidiary, Western Electric. Because these large markets were closed to non-domestic suppliers, competition for export business was largely confined to smaller or less developed countries which did not have an indigenous source of telecommunications equipment.

At the start of the post-war period telephone switching systems were based on electro-mechanical technology. The British Post Office, in common with many other telephone administrations, had adopted in the 1920s the American-designed Strowger automatic switching system, which used mechanical selectors, and it continued to rely on this equipment up to the Second World War. An alternative to Strowger, invented at Bell Laboratories, was Crossbar, based on a relay selector which had fewer moving parts and a shorter operating cycle. This system was improved in the inter-war years by Bell and other companies, notably ITT (through its French subsidiary) and Ericsson in Sweden, and by the 1950s Crossbar was beginning to displace Strowger in a number of markets. A much bigger change, beginning tentatively in the 1950s but not fully completed until the 1980s and 1990s, was the transition from electro-mechanical to electronic switching techniques. In Britain this transition was badly handled, with damaging consequences for the international competitiveness of the equipment manufacturers.

The structure of the industry in Britain had been established in the 1920s when the Post Office formed a special relationship with a 'ring' of five companies – GEC, Siemens Brothers, the ITT subsidiary Standard Telephones and Cables (STC), Automatic Telephone & Electric and Ericsson Telephones. Orders were shared out among these companies on a non-competitive basis, with the Post Office taking overall responsibility for system design. Although the Post Office was by far their largest customer, the manufacturers also built up a sizeable export business in Strowger equipment, especially among Empire or ex-Empire countries, which generally followed the Post Office's technical lead.

The issue which faced the Post Office after the war was how best to replace its ageing Strowger network. Crossbar was an obvious alternative, but Post Office engineers believed that the more logical next step after Strowger was electronic switching, based on the same techniques which had been used in the Colossus computer during the war.[63] In 1956 a joint electronic research committee was set up with the five suppliers. By 1959 an electronic switch had been developed, and three years later it was installed in the Highgate Wood exchange in London. But what was intended to be a great leap forward into the electronic age turned out to be a technical disaster. The electronic exchange failed to work effectively and had to be closed down after a few months of operation. A major problem was the excessive heat generated by the large number of valves within the switching system; the switch was designed at a time when reliable transistors were not yet available in quantity.

The Highgate Wood fiasco left the Post Office with difficult decisions on switching systems. One possibility was to take up Crossbar, and this course was strongly urged by the manufacturers. Many of the countries which had traditionally bought their telecommunications equipment from Britain were moving to Crossbar, and it was difficult for British firms to compete without a base load of orders from their domestic customer. The Post Office placed some Crossbar orders during the 1960s, but its main priority was to chart a path which would lead to the ultimate goal of an electronic system. As an intermediate step a semi-electronic system was developed, but neither this system nor Crossbar could be introduced quickly enough to meet the rapidly expanding domestic demand for telephones, and the Post Office was forced to order more Strowger equipment.

During this period the structure of the industry was altered by a series of mergers and take-overs (TABLE 10.5), and the number of suppliers was reduced from five to three – GEC, Plessey and STC. Relations between these companies and the Post Office were becoming fractious, partly because of disagreements over the choice of switching systems. The Post Office was also dissatisfied with the industry's poor delivery performance, and in 1969, in place of the old arrangement whereby orders had been shared out among members of the 'ring', a new system of competitive tendering was introduced. A further slap in the face for the manufacturers came in 1971, when Ericsson was awarded a contract for an international exchange. The aim was to sharpen up the British manufacturers by bringing in a well-regarded overseas supplier.

TABLE 10.5 *Principal suppliers of switching equipment to the Post Office*

Company	History
Standard Telephones and Cables (STC)	Subsidiary of ITT from 1925 to 1982, when ITT reduced its stake to 35 per cent. Merged with ICL in 1984. Sold to Northern Telecom of Canada in 1993.
Ericsson Telephones* Automatic Telephone and Electric	Both companies were acquired by Plessey in 1961. In 1987 Plessey merged its telecommunications interests with GEC to form GEC-Plessey Telecommunications (GPT).
Siemens Brothers	Acquired in 1954 by AEI, which in turn was acquired by GEC in 1967.
General Electric Company (GEC)	Merged its telecommunications interests with Plessey in 1987 to form GPT. Sold 40 per cent in GPT to Siemens in 1989, bought the stake back from Siemens in 1998.

*Ericsson Telephones was originally a subsidiary of L. M. Ericsson, but the Swedish company's holdings were progressively reduced, and in 1951 it ceased to be a shareholder.

Meanwhile the Post Office was continuing to work on the development of a fully electronic exchange, and in 1974 the decision was taken to re-equip the network with what became known as System X; the first development contracts were signed in 1977. The Post Office decided that, despite its earlier attempt to promote competition, System X would be handled on a co-operative basis, with each of the three companies being allocated part of the system and the Post Office itself taking responsibility for the overall co-ordination of the programme. There was probably no alternative to this arrangement, since none of the three firms had the technical resources to undertake the entire project on its own.[64] But the collaborative approach aggravated the problems of managing a highly complex and technically demanding project. The three companies did not find it easy to work together. Relations between GEC and Plessey were notoriously poor, and both companies were suspicious of the American-owned STC, which they feared might leak confidential information to its parent ITT, although there is no evidence that it ever did so. (In an effort to enhance its Britishness, ITT floated 15 per cent of its STC shares on the stock exchange in 1979). The Post Office would have preferred two suppliers rather than three, but an attempt to persuade Plessey and STC to pool their telecommunications interests was resisted by the two companies.[65]

By 1981, when the Thatcher government converted the telecommunications side of the Post Office into British Telecom (BT), the System X project was running badly behind schedule. In 1982 BT announced its intention to place all orders for the system with a single company and to put 30 per cent of its switching business out to international tender. This led to a furious bout of lobbying among the manufacturers, the outcome of which was the appointment of Plessey as prime contractor, with GEC as the principal sub-contractor. STC was dropped from the programme. In 1987 GEC and Plessey merged their telecommunications interests in a joint company, GEC-Plessey Tele-communications (GPT), which became the sole supplier of System X; two years later, following the successful joint bid for Plessey by GEC and Siemens, the German company became a 40 per cent shareholder in GPT.

System X had two objectives – to modernise the British telephone net-work and to enable the British equipment manufacturers to regain lost ground in export markets. The first was achieved, but the second was not. By the time the new exchanges were ready for delivery to overseas customers in the mid-1980s, several competing electronic systems were well established and GPT was unable to win more than a modest share of the world market (TABLE 10.6).

The blame for this outcome has to be shared between the Post Office and the manufacturers. The premature leap into electronics was unfortunate, leading as it did to a period of uncertainty over switching technology. More fundamental was the inability of the Post Office to find a satisfactory replacement for the non-competitive system of procurement which had operated between the 1920s and the 1960s. The instability in supplier-customer relations during the 1970s had a damaging effect on the System X programme.

TABLE 10.6 *Shares of world public switching market in 1989*

Company	Country	System	Market share (per cent)
Alcatel	France	E10/System12	20
AT&T	US	5ESS	17
Northern Telecom	Canada	DMS	12
Siemens	Germany	EWSD	12
NEC/Fujitsu/Hitachi	Japan	NEAX/FETE X/D60/D70	12
Ericsson	Sweden	AXE	11
GPT	Britain	System X	6
Others			10

Source: Alfonso H. Molina, 'The Development of Public Switching Systems in the UK and Sweden: The Weight of History', Programme on Information and communication technologies, Edinburgh University, Working Paper, no. 19, 1990. Based on figures in Datapro Report on International Telecommunications, McGraw Hill 1989.

As TABLE 10.6 shows, the surprise winner in international competition was Alcatel of France (formerly Compagnie Générale d'Electricité). The French company's success was all the more remarkable in view of the backward state of French telecommunications in the 1950s and 1960s. At that time the supply of switching equipment was almost entirely in the hands of ITT and Ericsson subsidiaries. There was, however, an independent source of technical expertise in a government research organisation, the Conseil National d'Etudes des Télécommunications (CNET), founded in 1944. Researchers at CNET observed the work on electronics which was taking place in Britain and the US, and during the 1960s developed two prototype electronic exchanges. One of them was a fully digital exchange, the E10, and CNET arranged for it to be manufactured by CIT-Alcatel, a subsidiary of

Compagnie Générale d'Electricité (CGE). The development of the E10 by CNET proceeded more smoothly than the System X project in Britain. This was due to the choice of a relatively simple initial design and the clear allocation of responsibilities between the research laboratory, the network operator and the equipment manufacturer.[66] The E10 was first installed in 1970, and it formed part of a comprehensive programme for modernising the French telephone network.[67] The programme involved the transfer of technology from ITT and Ericsson to Thomson, which was to become the second supplier to the French telephone administration, competing against CIT-Alcatel. However, in 1983, after both companies had been nationalised, Thomson ceded its telecommunications assets to CGE.

CGE was now securely placed as the monopoly supplier in France, but not yet a strong force in the world market. The company was aware that, under pressure from the European Commission and from liberalising governments like that of Britain, barriers to trade in telecommunications equipment were likely to come down. An opportunity for CGE to acquire a greater international dimension arose in 1986, when ITT decided to sell all its European telecommunications interests, including its large German subsidiary, Standard Elektrik Lorenz. CGE proposed to make a joint offer for the ITT assets with other European companies, but the eventual deal gave the French company majority control, with ITT retaining a minority stake; this stake was bought out by CGE six years later.[68]

The effect of the acquisition was to lift CGE into the front rank of telecommunications equipment suppliers, not far behind AT&T in the US. CGE was privatised in 1987 and re-named Alcatel-Alsthom in 1990. During the 1990s the deregulation of telecommunications markets, together with the rapid growth of mobile telephone networks, posed awkward challenges for a group which had traditionally relied on a privileged relationship with the French state. Nevertheless, by the end of the 1990s it appeared to have adjusted successfully to the new environment. In contrast to the three branches of electronics discussed in earlier sections, telecommunications was a success for French industrial policy.

The survival of Siemens as a major international supplier of telecommunications equipment was less surprising, since it had always been a technical leader in this field. It also benefited from a stable relationship with its domestic customer, the Bundespost. Unlike its counterparts in Britain and France, the Bundespost did not have large research laboratories of its own and was content to rely on the expertise of its principal supplier. Siemens had several competitors, of which Standard Elektrik Lorenz was the most important, but the Bundespost's policy was to standardise on one system. All the manufacturers were licensed to make Siemens-designed equipment.[69] This policy was modified in the early 1980s when the Bundespost ordered System 12 from ITT as well as the EWSD electronic switch from Siemens, but the change did not seriously damage Siemens' competitive position; it may even have been helpful since Siemens had to ensure that the exchanges which it developed for the Bundespost were also suitable for overseas customers.[70]

The consequence of the System X delays was to weaken GEC's position in the world market for public switching equipment *vis-à-vis* its main European rivals. There was speculation in the closing years of Weinstock's tenure as managing director that GEC might withdraw entirely from the sector by selling its 60 per cent stake in GPT to Siemens. However, in the review of strategy which took place after Weinstock's retirement in 1996, the new management decided that GEC could re-establish itself as a strong force in telecommunications by taking advantage of new technological opportunities. The first step, in June 1998, was to buy out Siemens's 40 per cent stake in GPT.[71] Then, in January of the following year, came the unexpected decision to sell the GEC-Marconi defence electronics business, the largest and most profitable part of GEC, to British Aerospace for £7bn. George Simpson, Weinstock's successor as managing director, made it clear at the time that he saw GEC's future as lying primarily within the telecommunications field. 'At the moment,' he said, 'we are still an ugly duckling in the telecoms market, but I believe in five years' time we will emerge as a beautiful swan.'[72] In the course of 1999 GEC made two large acquisitions in the US – the purchase of Reltec for $2.1bn and Fore Systems for $4.2bn – which were designed to position GEC in the fast-growing markets for high-speed data switches and networking equipment. The old days of national champions supplying equipment on an exclusive basis to national telephone authorities were over, and many analysts believed that, despite the disappointments over System X, GEC had the technical and financial resources to compete effectively in the new markets which were emerging at the end of the 1990s.

The Performance of the British Electronics Industry

The performance of British-owned electronics companies in the four branches of the industry which have just been described can only be regarded as poor. Except in telecommunications, however, their record was not significantly worse than that of their German and French counterparts. All three industries faced the same problems in coping with American and Japanese competition, and none of them made a very good job of it. If performance is measured by exports and imports, then Britain was not out of line with Germany and France (TABLE 10.7). Nevertheless, many people believe that British firms should have done better. Were opportunities thrown away, and, if so, does the blame lie with the industry's managers or with the institutional environment within which they were operating?

TABLE 10.7 *Electronics exports and imports in six countries in 1995*
($bn)

	Exports	Imports	Balance
Japan	121.0	46.8	+74.2
US	98.8	144.0	−45.2
UK	37.7	42.4	− 5.7
Germany	43.8	51.1	− 7.3
France	26.4	30.0	− 3.6
Italy	13.3	19.5	− 6.2

Source: *Yearbook of World Electronics Data*, Reed Electronics Research, 1998.

Of the eight major firms which constituted the core of the industry in the mid-1970s, only two, GEC and Racal, existed as independent, British-owned electronics manufacturers twenty years later (TABLE 10.8). The others were either taken over (Plessey, EMI, ICL, STC), or went into receivership (Ferranti), or withdrew from electronics manufacture (Thorn-EMI). Avoidable mistakes undoubtedly contributed to this outcome. Two well-known examples were EMI's mishandling of the scanner,[73] and Ferranti's disastrous merger with an American defence contractor, International Signal, in 1987; two years after the merger International Signal was found to have defrauded its shareholders on a massive scale, and the consequent financial crisis brought Ferranti down.

TABLE 10.8 *Leading British electronics companies in 1975 and their status in 1999*

Company	Outcome
GEC	Survived
Racal	Survived
Plessey	Taken over by Siemens and GEC in 1989
EMI	Taken over by Thorn in 1979
Thorn-EMI*	Withdrew from electronics and other manufacturing activities
ICL	Merged with STC in 1984, sold to Fujitsu in 1990
STC	Taken over by Northern Telecom in 1993
Ferranti	Receivership in 1993

*Thorn-EMI was split into two separate companies in 1996. Two years later Thorn was bought by Nomura International.

Of the two survivors, Racal was greatly admired for its nimbleness in targeting opportunities which generally lay outside the mainstream of the industry. It did not, for example, compete directly in any of the four sectors discussed earlier in this chapter, although it did briefly consider a take-over of Plessey. Racal was largely the creation of Ernest Harrison, who became chairman in 1966 and was still in that post in 1999. The early growth of the company was based on the supply of tactical radio sets to armies around the world; defence electronics, enlarged in 1980 by the purchase of Decca, had always been a sizeable part of Racal's business. But Harrison also looked for opportunities in commercial markets where the company could establish a strong proprietary position without heavy expenditure on research. He was an opportunist, willing to take large risks and to move in and out of businesses when market conditions changed. Judged by the criterion of increasing shareholder value, Harrison was extraordinarily successful between the 1960s and the 1990s.[74] One of his greatest triumphs was the creation of the Vodafone mobile telephone business, which was demerged from Racal in 1991.

The record of GEC, a much larger company, is more difficult to assess. Most commentators agree that Arnold Weinstock, its long-serving managing director, did an outstanding job in welding together GEC, AEI and English Electric after the mergers of the late 1960s (see Chapter 8). But he has also been criticised, especially in the latter part of his tenure, for failing to make full use of GEC's financial strength, for relying too much on partially protected defence and telecommunications markets, and for missing opportunities in riskier but faster-growing sectors of the electronics industry.[75]

Weinstock's policy was to allocate resources to businesses which he thought GEC was capable of managing well. One of these businesses was defence, where the UK provided a relatively large market, and Weinstock used this as the base from which to build a strong international business. In the course of the 1980s and 1990s the GEC-Marconi subsidiary was converted from a nationally orientated group of defence equipment companies into a world leader in defence electronics; at the end of the 1990s about 70 per cent of its sales were outside Britain.[76] It is not clear why Weinstock should be criticised for making good use of the opportunities which were available to him in defence. GEC was playing to its strengths, rather than plunging into areas such as computers and semiconductors where it had no competitive advantage. In view of the record of other European companies in these fields, Weinstock's caution seems eminently justified. As he once remarked, 'People wanted me to make things which have lost a lot of money for people who did make them.'[77]

Weinstock had a distinctive management style. A small head office, consisting of Weinstock himself and a few close colleagues, exercised tight financial control over the operating businesses, but did not attempt to develop an overarching strategy for the group as a whole. Some critics thought that the lack of strategic direction from the centre was a weakness; decentralisation to small units 'limited the scale of ambition to that of the units rather than the company as a whole'.[78] It has also been argued that if GEC had paid more attention to linkages between its various subsidiaries, it could have achieved more. It is true that when attempts were made to pull together different parts of the company to attack new markets, the results were sometimes disappointing. In 1979 GEC sought to link GEC-Marconi's electronics expertise with A. B. Dick, a US office-equipment maker, and Averys, the British manufacturer of weighing machines. The idea, GEC explained to the Monopolies Commission (which was investigating the acquisition of Averys), was to supply 'total information systems' by drawing on the skills and resources of all three companies. Other electronics firms, GEC told the Commission, were moving in the same direction, and GEC would probably need to acquire additional capabilities in such fields as mini-computers and cash registers.[79] In the event, the hoped-for synergies were not achieved. A. B. Dick and Averys were run as free-standing companies, and no further acquisitions in mini-computers and cash registers were made.

Weinstock was a better controller of existing businesses than a creator of new ones. On the other hand, in an industry as volatile as electronics, recognising one's limitations can be a strength. GEC's namesake in the US, General Electric, widely regarded as one of the world's best managed companies, also withdrew from computers, semiconductors and consumer electronics in the 1970s and 1980s, on the grounds that it did not have the capabilities which were needed to compete profitably in these industries. Commentators in the US did not regard these decisions as acts of cowardice, but as a sensible redeployment of resources. No doubt Weinstock did miss some opportunities, but to have maintained GEC as a consistently profitable enterprise at a time when several other European electronics companies (such as Philips and Olivetti) came close to financial disaster was a considerable achievement. He left a strong platform on which his successors can build.

GEC has often been compared unfavourably with Siemens, mainly on the grounds that Weinstock paid too much attention to short-term profit improvement and not enough to long-term strategic opportunities. According to one writer, 'the missed opportunities in new markets and retreats in old ones stem more or less directly from GEC's methods of enterprise calculation, grounded in financial criteria which favour relatively short-term profitability'.[80] Siemens increased its sales faster than GEC between the 1970s and the 1990s, but its profitability was much lower (TABLE 10.9). It is not easy to see what benefits accrued to shareholders in the company, or to the German economy, from Siemens' heavy investments, over a period of many years, in loss-making activities such as semiconductors. The company's recent decision to withdraw from semiconductors indicates that concern for shareholder value, usually associated with the Anglo-American financial system, is now spreading to Germany.

The merit of the Anglo-American financial system is that it forces firms to specialise in businesses where they have a realistic chance of competing

TABLE 10.9 *Sales and profits in Siemens and GEC, 1972–97*

	Siemens			GEC		
	Sales ($m)	Profits ($m)	Employees	Sales ($m)	Profits ($m)	Employees
1972	4,713	125	301,000	2,514	166	201,000
1983	15,724	296	313,000	7,731	649	178,000
1997	63,745	1,427	386,000	10,294	1,112	71,963

Source: *Fortune*, September 1973 and 20 August 1984.

Note: In 1997 GEC's return on assets was 11 per cent, compared with 3 per cent for Siemens.

profitably. The British stock market reacts quickly to management mistakes, and if investors lose confidence in a company's strategy, as they did at STC after the ICL take-over and at Thorn-EMI in the early 1980s, boards of directors come under strong pressure to change course. The fact that this has resulted in a large part of the British electronics industry being owned by non-British companies does not appear to have damaged the British economy.

A more legitimate criticism of the British financial system – although Germany and France were even less well served in this respect – was the absence of a venture capital industry as large and sophisticated as that of the US. This was certainly one of the factors which underpinned American success in computers and semiconductors. On the other hand, lack of financial support was not the main reason why there were no British counterparts to Apple Computer or Intel. There was a particularly favourable combination of institutional and market factors in the US which could not have been replicated in Britain, or in Germany and France.

As for the two other British institutions which have been considered in earlier chapters, neither labour relations nor training and education has much relevance in electronics. With the exception of some of the big telecommunications equipment factories in the 1960s and 1970s, electronics was not a strike-prone industry, and the influence of trade unions on the events described in this chapter was minimal. Similarly, the failure of British-owned firms in computers, semiconductors and TV sets was not due to an inadequate supply of skills, whether at the shop floor level or at the level of scientists and engineers.

ELEVEN

Aerospace: Partnership with Government

Measured by its trade performance, aerospace has been one of Britain's most successful industries throughout the post-war period. In 1997 about 75 per cent of its output was exported, and its trade surplus, at just over £3bn, was higher than that of Britain's other star performer, the chemical industry. During the 1990s, when several erstwhile national champions such as British Leyland and ICL were taken over by foreign companies, the two principal aerospace firms, Rolls-Royce and British Aerospace, held their position among the world leaders in the field. Yet there are many people inside and outside the industry who believe that it should have done better. According to the critics, too many opportunities were thrown away in the early post-war years when the industry lost ground, not only to the big American companies, but also to French manufacturers which were much weaker than their British counterparts at the end of the war. More recently the German aircraft industry has re-emerged as a strong force in the world market (TABLE 11.1).

Was the British aerospace industry's loss of market share avoidable, and, if so, does the blame lie with managers or with governments? To a greater extent than any of the industries discussed in earlier chapters, aerospace has depended on the state both as a customer and as a source of funds for research and development. Successive British governments have sought to preserve a large, nationally owned aerospace industry for a mixture of strategic, employment and balance of payments reasons, and as a symbol of national prestige. An assessment of the industry's performance has to take into account, not only how well or badly British companies were managed, but also whether relations between government and industry were handled better or worse in Britain than in other countries.

TABLE 11.1 *Aerospace turnover 1980–97*

(£m)

	1980	1997
UK	10,617	15,028
US	38,613	65,843
France	9,084	13,810
Germany	3,217	6,422
Japan	1,143	7,303

Source: Society of British Aerospace Companies.

The Aircraft Industry before 1939

Links between aircraft manufacturers and the government were established early in the industry's history, as soon as the aeroplane was reliable enough to be used as a weapon of war.[1] In Britain Richard Haldane, Secretary of State for War in the Asquith government, set up the Aeronautical Research Committee in 1909, and the Army Balloon Factory at Farnborough (renamed the Army Aircraft Factory) was given responsibility for aircraft development.[2] The Royal Flying Corps was created in 1912, and the first orders for military aircraft were placed in that year. Several of the entrepreneurs who were to play a distinguished part in the subsequent growth of the industry – Frederick Handley Page, Thomas Sopwith, Robert Blackburn, A. V. Roe and others – were already making aircraft, and they were joined by established engineering firms, including the armaments manufacturers Vickers and Armstrong Whitworth.

Military demand during the First World War converted what had been little more than a collection of workshops into an industry. Output rose from about 10 aircraft per month in 1914 to a peak of over 2,500 per month in 1918.[3] Some were built by what had become the Royal Aircraft Factory at Farnborough, but the government decided in 1917 that this institution – now called the Royal Aircraft Establishment – should concentrate on research, leaving production in the hands of private firms. By the end of the war the leading manufacturers had become substantial enterprises; the largest, Aircraft Manufacturing Company (Airco), employed 7,000 people. The war also gave a boost to the manufacture of aero-engines, where most British firms had previously been dependent on French or German technology. The Rolls-Royce Eagle, designed by Henry Royce, co-founder of the company, was the most successful of the water-cooled engines used during the war. Sir John Siddeley's Siddeley-Deasy,[4] which, like Rolls-Royce, was primarily a car manufacturer, took over work on air-cooled engines which had been started at Farnborough.[5]

At this stage the science of aerodynamics was more advanced in Germany than in Britain or France, thanks in part to the work of Ludwig Prandtl at the University of Göttingen. Prandtl was one of the first people to recognise the importance of streamlining, and the research centre which he headed from 1904 trained many of Germany's leading aircraft designers.[6] Hugo Junkers, professor at the Aachen technical high school and founder of one of Germany's most famous aircraft companies, saw that drag could be reduced by building aircraft out of metal rather than wood, and in 1915 he designed the first all-metal cantilever monoplane (the cantilever eliminated the struts which were used on single-wing aircraft to support the wing). Although the Junkers machine was too heavy to fly well, it pointed the way to the technical changes which were to transform the economics of aviation two decades later.[7]

However, this is not an industry in which British entrepreneurs could not be accused of technical backwardness, or a lack of interest in academic science. Most of the founders of the British aircraft companies were well-trained engineers, and aeronautical research of high quality was carried out at the Royal Aircraft Establishment and the National Physical Laboratory, and in several universities, principally Cambridge and Manchester.

After expanding rapidly during the war, the industry went through a painful contraction in the early 1920s. Airco was put into liquidation, and its chief designer, Geoffrey de Havilland, later set up his own business. Sopwith Aviation was wound up and its assets transferred to a new company, Hawker Engineering (named after Sopwith's chief test pilot, Harry Hawker), which 'built aircraft whenever there was a demand, and kept out of debt by making motorcycles and other things'.[8]

Some manufacturers, such as Handley Page, looked to civil air transport as an alternative market and helped to set up new airlines; the first regular London–Paris service was launched in 1919. But the promoters were over-optimistic about the operating costs of their aircraft, and by 1921 all of them had ceased operations. They were competing against subsidised Continental airlines, and the British government, though at first reluctant to follow suit, decided that to rely on foreign companies for air transport between Britain and the Continent was unacceptable. Subsidies were introduced in 1921, and three years later the competing airlines merged at the government's request to form Imperial Airways. This company was required to operate air services throughout the Empire as well as in Europe, and instructed to buy only British aircraft.[9] Orders for airliners were sparse, and most firms continued to obtain the bulk of their business from the military. An exception was de Havilland, which built mainly small aircraft for private aviators and flying schools; the de Havilland Moth was one of the most successful British aircraft in the inter-war years.

The industry's prospects improved in 1923 when the government announced plans to equip the newly created Royal Air Force with fifty-two squadrons of aircraft. In order to promote competition and to keep a reserve of design and production capacity in case of war, the Air Ministry spread its contracts among fifteen airframe and five engine manufacturers. Although the number of orders was small – an average of 646 aircraft per year between 1923 and 1930 – it was sufficient for the firms to keep their design teams together.

Most of them stayed independent, although some consolidation of the industry took place. Vickers took over Supermarine in order to acquire its flying boat expertise and the services of its chief designer, R. J. Mitchell. A financial crisis at Armstrong Whitworth in 1926 led to the sale of its airframe and aero-engine subsidiaries to John Siddeley; two years later Siddeley bought another of the pioneering firms, A. V. Roe. The biggest merger of the inter-war period came in 1935, when the Siddeley interests joined with Hawker to form Hawker Siddeley; the various subsidiaries of the group continued to design and build their own aircraft.

Technical progress consisted of incremental innovations, some of which, such as the variable pitch propeller and the slotted wing, originated in Britain. While the main sponsor of research was the Air Ministry, the popularity of air racing encouraged firms to use their own funds to develop high-performance aircraft, using more powerful engines and high-octane fuels. Mitchell of Vickers-Supermarine was to draw on this experience in the design of the Spitfire, the most successful British aircraft of the Second World War. For transport aircraft the preferred design, especially in Britain and France, was the biplane. Although the Germans made more use of monoplanes such as the Fokker Trimotor and the Junkers Ju 52, operating costs were not much lower than on a well-designed biplane. The breakthrough on this front came not in Europe, but in the US.

As in Europe, the Federal government had supported the aircraft industry from an early stage because of its military importance. The National Advisory Committee on Aeronautics (NACA) was set up in 1915 to carry out aeronautical research. But the military side of the industry grew more slowly than in Europe, and until the 1930s the leading American airframe and aero-engine builders were smaller than their European counterparts. The trigger for change was the growth of commercial aviation in the second half of the 1920s. The first successful American airliner was the Ford Trimotor, introduced in 1926; it was copied from similar aircraft built in Europe. Henry Ford's entry into the business alerted entrepreneurs to the possibility of a mass market for air travel. With the economy booming and popular interest in aviation boosted by Lindbergh's solo flight across the Atlantic in 1927, new airlines were formed, and several of them were floated on the New York Stock Exchange.

In contrast to Europe, where national governments protected their domestic airlines, the US was a big, uniform market which could sustain a number of competing carriers. Although the government assisted the airlines by providing airmail contracts at subsidised prices, the crucial difference with Europe was the intensity of competition among airlines to offer their customers a better service. Hence there was strong pressure on the manufacturers to develop more economical aircraft.

A year after the launch of the Ford Trimotor, Lockheed introduced a single-engined high-wing cantilever monoplane, the Vega, with a cruising speed of up to 150 mph. Though made out of plywood, the Vega was an advance in the streamlining of production aircraft, and it was followed by two low-wing monoplanes, the Northrop Alpha and the Boeing Monomail, which used a stressed-skin metal structure. In 1932 Boeing launched the 247, which, with two engines rather than three, was more economical than the trimotors and won an immediate order for sixty aircraft from United Airlines.

Trans World Airlines then invited other manufacturers to design an aircraft which would match the speed of the Boeing 247 but carry more passengers. The winner was Douglas, a company which had previously concentrated mainly on military aircraft. The prototype, the Douglas DC-1, flew for the first time in 1933, followed by the production version, the DC-2. The next version, the DC-3, was designed for American Airlines, which planned to use it for a coast-to-coast sleeper service. A wider and longer fuselage produced a more streamlined aircraft, with much lower operating costs than any of its competitors.[10]

The DC-3 was hugely successful both as a civil airliner and as a military transport; when the last DC-3 was rolled out in 1946, nearly 11,000 had been built. Its uniqueness lay not in any single technical breakthrough, but in its incorporation of all the innovations that had been made over the preceding decade into a well-balanced package. The twin- and four-engined cantilever monoplane became the dominant civil airliner design until the arrival of the jets in the 1950s.

The significance of what the Americans had done was slow to dawn on European airlines and aircraft manufacturers. Aircraft design was dominated by military requirements, and the subsidised airlines did not press as hard for lower operating costs as their counterparts in the US.

A salutary shock was the England–Australia race of 1934. Although the race was won by a de Havilland aircraft which had been specially built for racing, the Douglas DC-2 airliner came second, showing how far the Americans had progressed in improving the speed and performance of production aircraft. Douglas and Lockheed began exporting to Europe in the second half of the 1930s, exposing the inadequacies of the British-built biplanes on which Imperial Airways relied.

A second British airline, British Airways, was formed in 1935 to operate European routes; like Imperial Airways, it was subsidised by the government, but allowed to buy American and German aircraft. In 1939, following a government inquiry into the future of civil aviation, British Airways and Imperial Airways were combined in a single, state-owned enterprise, British Overseas Airways Corporation (BOAC), which was given a larger subsidy to finance the construction of new British airliners.[11]

Rearmament was by then in full swing, and civil airliner development in Britain was abandoned for the duration of the war. But the progress which the Americans had made in building all-metal, stressed-skin monoplanes was relevant to military as well as civil aircraft, and several British firms sent missions to the US to learn about the new techniques.[12]

The Impact of the Second World War

In 1935 British manufacturers produced 893 aircraft for the Royal Air Force; in 1941 more than 20,000 military aircraft were built. Over this six-year period employment in the industry rose from 25,000 to 395,000.[13] The transition from craft-based methods to mass production took place with remarkable speed. 'Old designers showed an unexpected ability to learn new techniques they had once regarded with suspicion, and abler men gained influence in the British government technical service.'[14]

The government enlarged the capacity of the industry by building Shadow factories, some of which were managed by engineering companies such as Austin, Ford and English Electric, but the main responsibility for the increase in production lay with the established manufacturers and with officials in the Ministry of Aircraft Production who co-ordinated the programme. Although some historians have criticised the industry's war-time performance,[15] it was in most respects superior to that of its German counterpart.[16] In 1940 Britain produced 71 per cent more aircraft than Germany, and 63 per cent more aero-engines. British firms also had the edge in quality, balancing the need for increased production with incremental improvements in performance. The weaknesses on the German side were mainly due, not to shortcomings on the part of the manufacturers, but to administrative incompetence. In contrast to Britain, where the Ministry of Aircraft Production, headed for most of the war by a Labour politician, Stafford Cripps,[17] was firmly in charge of the production programme, responsibility in Germany was spread among several agencies.

A recent historian has attributed the achievements of the British aircraft industry during the war to 'consistent and methodical plans for wartime production first proposed in the 1920s and finally implemented during the rearmament and early wartime years', together with 'sustained effort and innovation on the part of the leading firms'.[18] The most successful of the airframe builders were Vickers, Hawker Siddeley and de Havilland. Of the newcomers which had come into the industry through the Shadow factory scheme, English Electric did well, producing the Handley Page Hampden and Halifax bombers efficiently and in large numbers; towards the end of the war it was selected to assemble the de Havilland Vampire jet fighter. Among the engine manufacturers, Rolls-Royce and Bristol consolidated the leading position which they had established before the start of rearmament; over 80 per cent of the aero-engines produced during the war were designed by these two companies. Rolls-Royce, in particular, greatly enhanced its reputation for technical competence and reliability during the war. It had an outstanding leader in Ernest Hives, appointed general manager in 1937. 'A tough, highly pragmatic engineer, but not without a visionary streak, he had a powerful instinct for engineering development.'[19]

While the primary concern of the combatant nations was with maximising production, the war also stimulated advances in technology. In the field of airframe design, German engineers developed many of the concepts, including swept-back and delta-shaped wings, that paved the way for supersonic flight.[20] But most of this work came too late to affect the outcome of the war.

An even bigger breakthrough was the jet engine, and here British and German engineers were working on parallel lines. The key figure in Britain was Frank Whittle, who studied the problems of high-altitude, high-speed flight while serving as a cadet in the Royal Air Force. In 1929 he conceived the idea of using a gas turbine instead of the conventional piston engine as the source of power, and he applied for a patent in the following year. After several years of study and experimentation, including a two-year spell at Cambridge, where Whittle worked closely with B. M. Jones, Professor of Aeronautical Engineering, the first Whittle engine ran in 1937, and a 'demonstrator' aircraft, the Gloster-Whittle E-28/39, flew in 1941. The Gloster company, part of the Hawker Siddeley group, was commissioned to develop a twin-engined jet fighter, the Meteor, which flew in 1943. The development of the engine was far from smooth, not least because of an unhappy collaboration between Power Jets (the firm set up to exploit Whittle's invention) and the Rover car company. But progress was faster after the transfer of responsibility to Rolls-Royce, which became the principal repository of jet engine technology.

In Germany Hans von Ohain, a student of aerodynamics at Göttingen, produced an experimental jet engine in 1935, and the engine-makers at first showed little interest. One of von Ohain's professors persuaded Ernst Heinkel, whose company did not make its own engines, to take the young man on to its staff, and von Ohain's engine was used in the Heinkel He 178, which flew in August 1939, a few days before the outbreak of war. The established engine companies – Daimler-Benz, BMW and Junkers – were subsequently brought in to work on the jet engine. The most successful of Germany's jet-powered fighters was the twin-engined Messerschmitt Me 262, which was 100 mph faster than the Gloster Meteor, but this programme was delayed because of administrative muddles within the German High Command, and production did not begin until 1944.[21]

At the end of the war, with Germany barred from aircraft and aero-engine production, the British industry had a technical lead in jet engines. The established American engine builders, including Pratt & Whitney, had concentrated throughout the war, at the government's request, on increasing production of conventional piston engines. A Whittle engine and drawings were sent to the US in 1941, and a contract was placed with General Electric, the electrical company, which had relevant experience in industrial gas turbines. A General Electric jet engine was put into production before the end of the war, but it was inferior to the ones that Rolls-Royce was making.[22]

In civil airframes the British position was far weaker. Given the strength of the US in civil airliners, it was logical for British manufacturers to concentrate on fighters and bombers, while the US supplied the transport aircraft which the Allies needed. However, the British government had no intention of allowing this situation to persist after the war. The aircraft industry was seen as an instrument of national power and prestige; the aim, as a Cabinet minute put it, was 'to secure the production after the war of British transport aircraft, civil and military, of a scale and quality in keeping with our world position'.[23] In 1943 Lord Brabazon, a distinguished aviator and former Minister of Aircraft Production, was asked to prepare a plan for post-war civil aircraft development.

The assumption underlying the establishment of the Brabazon committee was that the aircraft industry, having grown to enormous size during the war, should not be allowed to decline precipitately.[24] Stafford Cripps looked to aircraft as one of the new industries which would take over from the old staples such as cotton and coal as the driving force in exports. Cripps believed that the government must be prepared to assist the industry in its conversion from war to peace, and to ensure that as much as possible of its manufacturing capacity and its skills was preserved. The concept of partnership between the aircraft industry and the state was broadly accepted by the coalition government and had a powerful influence on policy for the first two decades after the war.

1945–64: Britain Tries to Keep Up

In view of this background it is perhaps surprising that the Labour government did not nationalise the aircraft industry after the war. But public ownership would have been difficult to justify in view of the industry's outstanding performance during the war, and there were strong industrial arguments against it. Technical progress was thought to depend on competition between independent design teams; centralisation in the hands of a single public corporation was likely to be damaging.[25] In any case the government had other instruments for controlling the industry which were at least as effective as public ownership. The Ministry of Aircraft Production was merged with the Ministry of Supply in 1946, and this powerful department handled the ordering of aircraft on behalf of the Ministry of Defence and the state-owned airlines.

Although orders for military aircraft fell sharply after the war, the contraction in employment was less than it had been after the First World War. Employment fell to 179,000 in 1950 before rising again under the impact of the Korean War and rearmament to 279,000 in 1954, and staying around that level into the 1960s.[26] The government set in train a number of new military programmes designed to take advantage of the technical advances which had been made during the war. Two jet fighters, the Gloster Meteor and the de Havilland Vampire, were already in production, and development of more advanced successors – the Hawker Hunter and Supermarine Swift – began in 1948. All of these were subsonic aircraft; the armed services took a more cautious view than their American counterparts about manned supersonic flight. The English Electric Canberra, a subsonic jet bomber on which work had started during the war, came into service in 1949, and it was followed by the three long-range V-bombers – the Vickers Valiant, the Avro Vulcan and the Handley Page Victor – which carried the nuclear bomb. These four aircraft incorporated some of the advanced wing technology which had been developed in Germany during the war.

On the civil side the Labour government accepted the Brabazon committee's view that the British aircraft industry should compete in all main sectors of the market. The initial Brabazon proposals had called for four wartime aircraft to be converted into civil transports and for five new projects: a large piston-engined airliner for transatlantic routes; a DC-3 replacement for short-haul routes in Europe; a medium-range airliner for Empire routes; a mail-only jet transport capable of flying non-stop to the US; and a small feeder aircraft carrying 8–10 passengers. By 1945 these nine projects had expanded to sixteen – four conversions, four 'interim' aircraft and eight new aircraft.

The programme was worked out at a time of uncertainty about how soon the piston engine would be replaced in transport aircraft by the jet. An intermediate engine type, the propeller turbine or turboprop, was chosen for two of the Brabazon projects – the Vickers Viscount for short-haul routes and the Avro 693 medium-range airliner. The only pure jet in the programme was the mail carrier, for which the contract was awarded to de Havilland. The mail-only idea was quickly dropped in favour of a passenger-carrying aeroplane, and de Havilland, using the experience it had gained with the Vampire fighter, developed the 36-passenger Comet, the world's first jet airliner. The Comet flew for the first time in 1949 and entered service with BOAC three years later. Meanwhile several new projects were added to the Brabazon programme, the most important of which was the Bristol Britannia, a long-range turboprop airliner, conceived as an insurance against possible delays with the Comet.

Doubts about the industry's ability to handle so many projects began to surface in the late 1940s, and grew more insistent during the 1950s as several of the new programmes ran into difficulty. Some technical misjudgements had been made on the civil side, and three of the aircraft recommended by the Brabazon committee were abandoned as uneconomic before entering service (TABLE 11.2). The only real successes were the Vickers Viscount and the de Havilland Dove feeder airliner, both of which sold well overseas. But the biggest disaster was the grounding of the Comet in 1954 following a series of crashes caused by metal fatigue. The Conservative government, which had taken over from Labour in 1951, stepped in to save the company and helped to finance the redesign of the aircraft. The Comet 4, equipped with more powerful Rolls-Royce Avon engines (the earlier versions had used de Havilland engines), entered service with BOAC in 1958, but by then the American manufacturers, Boeing and Douglas, had developed their own jet airliners, and the British lead was lost.

From this point onwards, as orders flowed in from the world's airlines for the Boeing 707 and the Douglas DC-8, the British aircraft manufacturers were struggling to regain lost ground. Vickers secured a development contract from the government for the V-1000, planned as a dual-purpose civil and military transport, but the contract was cancelled in 1955 before the prototype had been completed, on the grounds that the aircraft would not be economic. Vickers then went ahead at its own expense with the VC-10, initially designed

TABLE 11.2 *The Brabazon civil airliner programme*

Name	Specification	Manufacturer	Number sold
Brabazon	Long-range piston-engined airliner	Bristol	Abandoned
Ambassador	Short-range piston-engined airliner	Airspeed	22
Viscount	Short-range turboprop airliner	Vickers	444
Apollo	Short-range turboprop airliner	Armstrong Whitworth	Abandoned
Avro 693	Medium-range turboprop airliner	A.V. Roe (Hawker Siddeley group)	Abandoned
Comet 1 and 2	jet mail carrier	de Havilland	37
Marathon	piston-engined feederliner	Miles	40 (inc. 28 military versions)
Dove	piston-engined feederliner	de Havilland	540

Source: D. J. Hickie, 'The Government and Civil Aircraft Production 1942–51', Ph.D. thesis, Birkbeck College, London University, 1988.

as a medium-range airliner for BOAC's Empire routes, but later enlarged to compete with the Boeing 707. For short-haul routes Vickers tried to build on its success with the Viscount by developing a larger successor, the Vanguard, which, like the Viscount, was powered by Rolls-Royce turboprop engines. This turned out to be a mistake, since the Vanguard was not competitive with the pure jets, including the French-built Caravelle, which entered service in the late 1950s.

Serious though these setbacks were, some 70 per cent of the industry's workload during the 1950s was military, and the manufacturers were busy on a variety of fighters and bombers, some of which, like the Canberra and the Hunter, were exported in considerable numbers. Work started on Britain's first supersonic fighter, the English Electric Lightning, and the success of this aircraft (which entered service in 1959) enhanced the reputation of English Electric's design team. In the second half of the decade, however, strategic thinking in the Ministry of Defence shifted away from manned aircraft towards a greater reliance on guided missiles. Duncan Sandys, Minister of Defence, announced in 1957 that no new high-performance fighters would be ordered after the Lightning and no new long-range bombers after the V-bombers. Only one major military aircraft project was envisaged, a replacement for the Canberra.

The change of policy brought to a head an issue which had been causing concern since the early 1950s – the fragmented structure of the industry. The government believed that one of the reasons for the industry's disappointing performance was that projects had been spread among too many companies, some of which were ill-equipped to handle the complexity of modern aircraft; in the mid-1950s there were thirty-one full members of the industry's trade association, the Society of British Aircraft Constructors, and only three firms had left the industry since the war.[27] The government could have reduced the number of companies by placing orders with its preferred suppliers, letting the others wither away. Instead, the decision was taken to force the industry to coalesce into larger groups.[28] In 1958 the contract for the Canberra replacement – the TSR-2 (tactical, strike, reconnaissance) – was awarded jointly to Vickers and English Electric, with the expectation that the companies would merge their aircraft operations. The engine contract went to Bristol, on condition that it worked with two of the smaller engine builders, Armstrong Siddeley and de Havilland Engines.

The merger process accelerated after the Conservative victory in the 1959 election. A new department, the Ministry of Aviation, was created to take over the procurement role of the Ministry of Supply as well as the regulatory responsibilities of the Ministry of Civil Aviation, and the Minister, Duncan Sandys, made clear his intention to reduce the number of competing firms to two airframe manufacturers and two engine builders. As a carrot for the companies to get together, a new system of 'launch aid' for civil airliners was introduced, whereby the government would pay a proportion of the development costs, with repayment by means of a levy on each aircraft sold. In the case of two aircraft which had been started as private ventures, the Vickers VC-10 and the de Havilland Trident, a short-haul jet for British European Airways, the aid was set at 20–25 per cent of the cost of development. For future projects launch aid was limited to a maximum of 50 per cent.

As a result of the changes in ownership that followed in 1960, the airframe side of the industry was concentrated in the hands of two groups: British

Aircraft Corporation, in which Vickers and English Electric each held 40 per cent and Bristol Aeroplane 20 per cent; and Hawker Siddeley, which acquired de Havilland and two smaller firms, Folland and Blackburn. The only significant airframe company to stay independent was Handley Page; despite receiving launch aid for the Herald turboprop airliner, it played a diminishing role in the industry and ceased trading in 1970.[29] A separate helicopter group was formed around Westland, which took over three smaller manufacturers. On the engine side, Rolls-Royce absorbed English Electric's aero-engine interests, while Bristol, which had already acquired Armstrong Siddeley, took over the engine interests of Blackburn and de Havilland.

Welding these companies together was not easy. In the case of British Aircraft Corporation, there was friction between the Vickers and English Electric design teams over the TSR-2, and this was one of the factors which made an exceptionally complex project hard to manage. There was also bickering over specifications between the Air Ministry and the Navy; the latter had been sceptical about the TSR-2 from the start.[30] Meanwhile defence policy shifted away from the philosophy embodied in the 1957 White Paper, and in 1962 development contracts were placed with Hawker Siddeley for two advanced military aircraft – the AW681 short take-off transport and the P1154, a supersonic vertical take-off fighter. This reflected the view within the North Atlantic Treaty Organisation that small, local wars were more likely than large ones and that the armed services needed a more versatile range of aircraft than had been envisaged in 1957.

The Conservative government was still committed to the view that the aircraft industry was a national asset which had to be nurtured and protected, and that, wherever possible, the armed services and the state-owned airlines would buy British-made aircraft. The failure of the Comet forced the government to modify this policy, and BOAC was allowed to buy Boeing 707s, powered by Rolls-Royce engines. But the airline was later forced to buy the Vickers VC-10, and all the aircraft which BEA operated during the 1960s – the Vanguard, the Trident and British Aircraft Corporation's BAC 1–11 – were British. But none of these aircraft, with the partial exception of the BAC 1–11, sold well overseas, and the industry continued to lose ground to the American manufacturers.

One way of catching up was for Britain to take the lead in what was expected to be the next major technical advance after the subsonic jet – the supersonic airliner. Scientists at Farnborough had begun examining the feasibility of such a project in the early 1950s, and in 1956 a Supersonic Transport Advisory Committee was set up, including representatives from the industry as well as the Ministry of Aviation. By 1959 the project had gained sufficient momentum for Bristol Aeroplane and Hawker Siddeley to be invited to submit proposals for two different versions of a supersonic airliner. Duncan Sandys, the Minister of Aviation, was a strong supporter of the idea; he is said to have argued in Cabinet that 'if we are not in the big supersonic airliner business, then it is really only a matter of time before the whole British aircraft industry packs up'.[31] However, the government recognised that the project would be enormously expensive, and that there was a strong case for sharing the cost with other countries. In 1960, after an initial approach to the US had been rebuffed, attention turned to France, the only other country seriously engaged in civil airliner development.

France was a more natural partner than the US, for political as well as industrial reasons. The Macmillan government was preparing its application for Common Market membership, and an Anglo-French supersonic airliner would be a useful demonstration of Britain's new European vocation. The French government was enthusiastic, seeing the supersonic airliner as a way of building on the success of the Caravelle and restoring France to its rightful position in world aviation. An inter-governmental treaty was signed in November 1962, committing Britain and France to develop the Concorde supersonic airliner. Sud-Aviation and BAC were selected as the airframe contractors, and the development of the engine, a version of the Olympus which had been ordered for the TSR-2, was assigned to Bristol Siddeley and SNECMA, the principal French aero-engine company.

The Concorde was a useful addition to the industry's workload, and one which, because it was wholly funded by the two governments, carried no financial risk for the manufacturers. But the situation in the industry as a whole in the early 1960s was far from healthy. Some of the military programmes, such as the Canberra and the Lightning, were going well, but there were ominous noises coming out of Whitehall about the escalating costs of the TSR-2. Some powerful figures in the armed services were known to be pressing for cancellation. On the civil side, the Americans, having established an apparently unassailable lead in long-distance jet airliners with the Boeing 707 and the DC-8, were extending their dominance into the short- and medium-range market (TABLE 11.3). Boeing, in particular, was building on the experience gained with the 707 to develop a family of airliners over which development costs could be spread. It was this family concept, together with long production runs for individual aircraft, which made it extremely difficult for Boeing's competitors, American as well as European, to keep pace.[32] Douglas lost money on the DC-8 and the smaller DC-9, and in

TABLE 11.3 *Civil aircraft deliveries 1958–84*

Aircraft	No. of deliveries
Boeing 707	969
727	1834
737	1070
Douglas DC-8	556
DC-9/MD-80	1166
Comet	112
Caravelle	279
Trident	117
VC-10	54
BAC 1–11	231

Source: Based on Richard Baldwin and Paul Krugman, 'Industrial Policy and International Competition in Wide-bodied Aircraft', in Robert E. Baldwin (ed.), *Trade Policy Issues and Empirical Analysis*, University of Chicago Press/National Bureau of Economic Research, 1988.

1967 was forced into a merger with McDonnell, a manufacturer of military aircraft.

By the time of the 1964 election, it was clear that the high hopes invested in the aircraft industry in 1945 had not been fulfilled. This was partly due to technical mistakes. The Britannia, for example, would have been more successful if it had entered service as planned in 1954; it was delayed for three years by difficulties with the engine. But mistakes of this sort were also made in the US, and the relatively poor performance of the British aircraft industry between 1945 and 1964 cannot be blamed on engineering incompetence. A bigger problem was that too many British aircraft, military and civil, had been designed narrowly for the needs of the British armed forces and the state-owned airlines without sufficient regard to the potential for overseas sales. Hence production runs were much shorter, on average, than in the US, and British manufacturers were at a severe cost disadvantage. The government, as the industry's patron, principal customer and source of funds for development, must bear a large share of the blame. It over-estimated the industry's capacity to manage a large number of projects, and made matters worse by a clumsy approach to procurement.[33] There may also have been a large element of wishful thinking, a failure to recognise that to compete with the Americans on all fronts was unrealistic.[34]

The outstanding performer during this period was Rolls-Royce, which had remained at the forefront in jet engine technology. Having been predominantly a manufacturer of military engines, it had made a successful transition to the civil market after the war. The Dart turboprop engine, which powered the Viscount, was widely sold overseas for other short-haul airliners, and Rolls-Royce introduced the first turbofan engine, the Conway, which was more economical than the earlier generation of axial-flow engines; the Conway was used on the Boeing 707s bought by BOAC and some other non-American airlines.

But competition from the US was getting stronger. The American aero-engine industry was now dominated by Pratt & Whitney and General Electric, both of which had caught up with Rolls-Royce in jet engine technology. They also benefited from a much bigger domestic market for civil and military aircraft. If Rolls-Royce was to maintain its position as one of the world's leading aero-engine builders, it needed to establish itself with American airlines as a credible alternative to the domestic manufacturers.

While the US aircraft industry was the dominant player in the world market, another rival was emerging closer to home. France was a country with a proud aeronautical tradition, and, although its aircraft industry had been badly damaged during the war, there were design and manufacturing skills on which post-war governments could build. General de Gaulle regarded a strong, nationally owned aircraft industry as indispensable if France was to re-establish itself as a world power, and this view was widely shared across the political spectrum. The principal airframe manufacturers were Dassault and Breguet, both privately owned, and three state-owned firms – Sud-Est, Sud-Ouest and Nord-Aviation; the first two of these were merged in 1957 to form Sud-Aviation, based in Toulouse. SNECMA, the engine manufacturer, was also state-owned.

France's first entry into the civil airliner market was the Caravelle, which entered service with Air France in 1958. The Caravelle, the design of which was influenced by the Comet, was sold in the US as well as in Europe, though not in sufficient numbers to make a profit. But the biggest French success came in military aircraft, through Dassault. The first Dassault jet fighter, the Ouragan 450, flew in 1949, followed in 1951 by the Mystère and in 1955 by the first of the Mirage series.

Although government policy towards the aircraft industry was as nationalistic as in Britain, France's short-term ambitions were more modest. There was no attempt, for example, to compete with Boeing and Douglas in long-range jets. But the ultimate goal was to catch up with Britain and the US, and for this purpose the revival of the German aircraft industry after 1955 was seen as an opportunity rather than a threat. The Germans, having been out of the business for a decade, needed help, and the French were keen that they, rather than the US, should provide it. Two Franco-German projects were initiated in the early 1960s – the Atlantic patrol aircraft, designed by Breguet with Dornier and several other German firms acting as sub-contractors, and the Transall troop transport, in which Weser of Germany was given project leadership, working with Nord-Aviation in France. Neither of these aircraft was a great commercial or technical success, but they provided experience which was to prove useful in later collaborative arrangements.

European collaboration held no great appeal for the British aircraft industry in the 1950s, and France was seen as a customer rather than a partner. Air France bought the Viscount, but there was no question of BEA buying the Caravelle even though it had Rolls-Royce engines and might have been more suitable than either the Vanguard or the Trident.[35] The Concorde treaty of 1962 indicated a change of attitude, at least on the part of the government, and it was followed by preliminary discussions about joint military projects. The issue of international partnerships acquired greater importance after the 1964 election, when the political environment for the British aircraft industry turned more hostile.

1964–79: A Choice of Partners – Europe or the US?

Harold Wilson and his colleagues in the new Labour government believed that the aircraft industry had absorbed too much of the nation's engineering resources and that the benefits for the rest of the economy had been meagre.[36] These attitudes were reinforced by the weak state of the government's finances, which demanded sharp cuts in public spending. The defence budget was an obvious target. An early decision was to cancel the AW681 and the P1154, followed a few months later by the abandonment of the TSR-2. The TSR-2, plagued by constant changes in specifications, had been looking shaky before the election, and many people in government and in the industry believed that cancellation was inevitable. It was, nevertheless, a huge blow for the manufacturers and for the suppliers of the electronic systems which the aircraft would have carried.

The government planned to replace the three cancelled aircraft by buying the General Dynamics F-111 and the McDonnell Phantom from the US, and by ordering more British-built Blackburn Buccaneers, which were already in service. The F-111 order was later cancelled, but the Phantoms, re-engineered to accommodate Rolls-Royce engines, went ahead. One of the few all-British military projects to survive the axe was Hawker Siddeley's subsonic vertical take-off fighter, the P1127, later known as the Harrier. The government also tried to withdraw from the Concorde, a course strongly recommended by the Treasury. Development costs were escalating at an alarming rate, and the French Ministry of Finance was known to be as worried about it as the British Treasury. However, the impact of withdrawal on Anglo-French relations, as well as employment considerations, persuaded ministers to let the project continue.[37]

While these decisions were being taken, the government was awaiting the results of an inquiry into the aircraft industry, which had been set up shortly after the 1964 election. Chaired by Lord Plowden, chairman of Tube Investments, the committee was asked to examine 'the future place and organisation of the aircraft industry in relation to the general economy of the country'.[38]

The committee, which reported in December 1965, was critical of the industry's performance, which it blamed on a proliferation of poorly planned projects and a failure to develop aircraft suitable for the world market. But the report argued against allowing the industry to decline. The production of aircraft, calling for a highly skilled labour force and a negligible amount of imported material, was 'exactly the sort of industry on which Britain should concentrate'. The problem was that production runs were too low to recoup the high costs of development. The answer, in the committee's view, lay in collaboration. The US was not an appropriate partner, since its aircraft industry was too big and powerful, and unlikely to want to rely on other countries. France, on the other hand, shared many of the same disadvantages as Britain, and a partnership between these two countries provided the basis for a viable European aircraft industry.

These conclusions were accepted by the government, which had already begun to explore the possibility of co-operation with France. In May 1965, agreement was reached with the French government on two military projects. One was a supersonic attack/trainer, the Jaguar, for which Breguet took the lead on the airframe, supported by BAC, while Rolls-Royce, working with

Turbomeca of France, was responsible for the engine. The other was a sophisticated multi-role combat aircraft, known as the AFVG (Anglo-French Variable Geometry), on which the lead contractor was BAC, supported by Dassault. SNECMA and Bristol Siddeley were to work together on the engine. The Jaguar project worked well; nearly 600 Jaguars were sold, more than either country could have achieved on its own. But the AFVG project fell apart in 1967 when it became clear that neither Dassault, nor the French government had any intention of playing second fiddle to the British in advanced fighter aircraft. Dassault broke away to develop its own variable geometry fighter, leaving the British to find other partners.[39] Two years later Britain, Germany and Italy agreed to develop the Multi-Role Combat Aircraft (MRCA), later known as the Tornado; the initial order was for some 800 aircraft – 385 for Britain, 324 for Germany and 100 for Italy. The main contractor on the British side was British Aircraft Corporation, and the Tornado provided a large part of the company's workload during the 1970s and 1980s.

The Plowden committee believed that the case for collaboration was equally pressing on the civil side. At the time of the committee's report Hawker Siddeley and BAC in Britain, and Sud-Aviation in France, were considering what aircraft should follow their existing short-range airliners – the Trident, the BAC 1–11 and the Caravelle. The availability of more powerful turbofan engines with a higher by-pass ratio prompted consideration of wide-bodied aircraft which would carry 300 passengers or more. Similar plans were under discussion in the US.

The first to take the plunge was Boeing, with the decision to launch the four-engined, long-range 'Jumbo Jet', the 747, powered by a Pratt & Whitney engine, the JT9D. Lockheed and McDonnell Douglas went for slightly smaller, but also long-range three-engined aircraft, the Lockheed L-1011 (or TriStar) and the Douglas DC-10.

In Europe, the requirement was for a wide-bodied aircraft for inter-city routes, and there was a flurry of activity as British and French manufacturers searched for the most appropriate specifications. The two governments, which were expected to provide part of the finance, were closely involved, and encouraged the companies to form consortia. The German aircraft industry, gaining in confidence and keen to re-enter the civil airliner market, also took part in these discussions. In 1965 five German companies – Bolkow, HFB, VFW, Messerschmitt and Dornier – formed the Studiengruppe Airbus to act as interlocutor with the British and French firms.[40]

The design which won favour at the end of 1966 was a twin-engined

300-seater, the A300 Airbus. A year later the three governments agreed to go ahead with detailed technical studies, with the British insisting that no prototype should be built until at least seventy-five firm orders had been received from the three national airlines, BEA, Air France and Lufthansa. The airframe was assigned to Sud-Aviation and Hawker Siddeley, which were each allocated 37.5 per cent of the work, with the Germans taking 25 per cent. The choice of engine was more contentious. The French preference was for the Pratt & Whitney JT9D which had been chosen by Boeing for the 747. An agreement was already in place for this engine to be manufactured under licence by Bristol Siddeley Engines and SNECMA. But the idea that an American engine might be used on the European Airbus was anathema to Rolls-Royce. It had competed unsuccessfully with Pratt & Whitney for the Boeing 747 contract; to lose the Airbus engine to Bristol Siddeley, acting as a Trojan horse for the Americans, was wholly unacceptable.[41] It was partly to frustrate Bristol's deal with Pratt & Whitney that Rolls-Royce launched a take-over bid for its British rival in June 1966. This was a costly acquisition which contributed to Rolls-Royce's subsequent financial troubles, but it consolidated the company's position as Europe's premier aero-engine manufacturer and increased its lobbying power in Whitehall. The British government insisted on the choice of a Rolls-Royce engine as a condition for its participation in the Airbus programme.

Keeping an American engine out of the Airbus was important for Rolls-Royce, but the US market remained a higher priority; there was, after all, no certainty that the European Airbus would ever be built, and the prospects of it competing successfully against the Americans were doubtful at best. When Lockheed and Douglas invited bids for engines for their wide-bodied airliners, Rolls-Royce launched a massive effort to win the business. The engine which it offered, the RB211, contained a number of innovative features, of which the most important was the three-shaft design, promising greater fuel economy and higher thrust than the two-shaft concept used by General Electric and Pratt & Whitney. In 1968 the RB211 was chosen by Lockheed for the L-1011, with Douglas opting for the General Electric CF6.

This was the biggest export order in the history of the British aircraft industry. The British government, delighted by Rolls-Royce's success, agreed to contribute 70 per cent, instead of the usual 50 per cent, to the development costs of the RB211, which were estimated at £66.5m. It was the largest amount of launch aid ever granted, justified on the grounds 'that the RB211 was essential to the future of Rolls-Royce and that an aero-engine industry was a vital national interest'.[42] The reaction in France and Germany was less enthusiastic. There was anxiety that Rolls-Royce's energies would be diverted from the Airbus to the Lockheed contract, although Rolls insisted that commonalities between the two engines made a dual programme feasible.

Meanwhile the Airbus itself was running into trouble. BEA wanted a smaller aircraft than the proposed A300, and was inclining to a new proposal from British Aircraft Corporation, the BAC 2–11. Even the French government appeared to be having second thoughts, agreeing to support a separate short-haul airliner project – the Mercure – put forward by Dassault, which had taken over Breguet and was keen to expand its non-military business. In March 1969, the British government pulled out, on the grounds that the Airbus did not meet BEA's requirements and that the project was unlikely to be economic. The Airbus still had powerful political and industrial backing in France and Germany, and the two governments agreed to go ahead on their own. Responsibility for the airframe was shared between Sud-Aviation (which was merged with Nord-Aviation in 1970 to form Aerospatiale) and the Deutsche Airbus consortium, in which the newly merged Messerschmitt-Bolkow-Blohm held 60 per cent, Dornier and VFW 20 per cent each. The two American engine builders, Pratt & Whitney and General Electric, were invited to compete for the engine. The General Electric CF6 was chosen, mainly because the American company was prepared to share a large part of the development work with SNECMA.[43]

Although withdrawal from the Airbus did not affect Britain's participation in joint military projects with France and Germany, the Labour government's enthusiasm for European collaboration had cooled since the Plowden report. As the collapse of the AFVG had shown, it was not easy for the armed forces of different countries to agree on specifications, and compromises had to be made which added to costs. Some joint projects turned out to be more expensive, and to take longer to complete, than national ones.[44]

Another committee of inquiry, under St John Elstub, reporting in 1969, pointed out that considerations of national prestige often weighed too heavily in joint projects. The report also warned that 'Britain's partners of today may become the competitors of tomorrow, when they have fortified themselves technically through contact with the most experienced aircraft industry in Europe'.[45]

The Airbus decision, nevertheless, left a big hole in the industry's civil programme. Hawker Siddeley negotiated a private arrangement to manufacture the Airbus wings; British wing technology was acknowledged to be the best in Europe, and the French were reluctant to delay the programme by switching to a Continental supplier.[46] British Aircraft Corporation still hoped to develop a family of aircraft to build on the BAC 1–11, and put forward a proposal for the BAC 3–11, a 245-seat wide-bodied aircraft with two RB211 engines. But the government, which had already made a large commitment to Rolls-Royce, deferred a decision on launch aid for BAC until after the 1970 election.

The new Conservative administration was in a difficult position. The Prime Minister, Edward Heath, was committed to British membership of the Common Market. To back the BAC 3–11, a competitor to the Airbus, would anger France and Germany. But to rejoin the Airbus consortium, as the French and Germans proposed, implied a large investment in an aircraft whose commercial prospects still looked doubtful. At the end of 1970 the government announced that it would not support the BAC 3–11 and would not rejoin Airbus. For BAC, this marked the end of the independent development of large civil airliners, and the company became even more dependent on military aircraft.

The attention of the Heath government was soon focused on Rolls-Royce. This company had taken on a considerable risk with the RB211 contract, since several features of the engine's design were unproven and development costs were inevitably uncertain. The first signs of impending trouble came in 1969, when Rolls-Royce asked the then Labour government for additional launch aid. In response the Ministry of Technology invited the Industrial Reorganisation Corporation to examine the company's financial position. The IRC team concluded that the situation was serious, mainly because of inadequate financial controls, and that Rolls-Royce's problems were much more fundamental than a short-term cash flow deficiency.[47]

The company reacted sceptically to the report, and was reluctant to make the management changes recommended by the IRC, but by the summer of 1970 it was clear that Rolls-Royce would need much more than the £10m loan offered by the IRC. In November the company was on the brink of bankruptcy. Denning Pearson, the chairman, resigned, as did David Huddie, who, as managing director of the Aero Engine Division, had negotiated the RB211 contract. The newly elected Conservative government agreed to provide additional launch aid of £42m, but it was not enough. In February 1971, receivers were called in.

The collapse of Rolls-Royce is often blamed on the dominance of the company by over-confident engineers, who refused to heed warnings from the financial staff.[48] It has also been argued that Rolls-Royce was taking too many technological leaps at one time. Defenders of the company point out

that the development of the RB211 was no more risky than similar programmes undertaken by the two American engine builders. The difference
was that, whereas in the US the development of high by-pass ratio turbofan
engines was funded largely by the military, Rolls-Royce was in a more
exposed position because its new engine was tied to a tightly drawn commercial contract with an American company.[49] What is not in doubt, as subsequent events were to show, is that the design of the RB211 was basically
sound.

The government's immediate concern after the receivership was to preserve those parts of Rolls-Royce which were essential to national defence. A
new company, Rolls-Royce (1971), was formed, with the state as sole shareholder, to take over the company's aero-engine assets; the car business was
sold in a public flotation.[50] The government entered negotiations with
Lockheed, and in September 1971 a new contract was agreed. The RB211
programme was back on course.

The Rolls-Royce affair, together with the cost over-runs on Concorde,
raised questions about the economic case for continuing to subsidise the
development of civil aircraft and aero-engines. A study carried out by a
government economist in the mid-1970s showed that the equivalent of £1.5bn
of public funds had been spent on civil aircraft and aero-engine programmes
since the war, of which less than £150m had been recovered; in only two
cases, the Viscount and the Rolls-Royce Dart engine, had the government
been fully reimbursed.[51] Yet the Heath government, like its predecessors,
was not prepared to abandon the industry. Some ministers, notably Michael
Heseltine at the Department of Trade and Industry, argued that despite
Concorde and despite the withdrawal from Airbus, European collaboration
was the best way forward.[52]

Opinion within the industry was divided. The strongest anti-European
line came from Rolls-Royce, its self-confidence gradually returning under
the leadership of a fiercely independent chairman, Kenneth Keith; Keith was
also chairman of Hill Samuel, a leading merchant bank, and an influential
figure in Whitehall. The company's strategy was the same as it had been
before the bankruptcy – to concentrate on the US market and to use the
RB211 and its derivatives as the basis for a vigorous attack on General Electric
and Pratt & Whitney. Collaboration in Europe, Keith suggested, was usually
in a one-way direction, 'with Rolls-Royce on the giving end'.[53]

On the airframe side, Hawker Siddeley had a foot in the Airbus camp
with its wing contract, but it was keen to retain an independent design
capacity. In 1973 it secured launch aid for a new regional airliner, the HS-146,

even though it was directly competitive with a German-Dutch project, the VFW-Fokker 614.[54] The government justified this non-European stance by arguing that the project was small enough to be financed on a national basis.[55] British Aircraft Corporation was well placed for military work, with the Jaguar in full production and the Tornado in development. It was also benefiting from a large order from Saudi Arabia for fighters, trainers and other equipment. But, apart from Concorde and the BAC 1–11, which was nearing the end of its life, no other civil work was in prospect.

These uncertainties were compounded in 1974 by the return of a Labour government committed to nationalising the industry. The arguments for nationalisation were mainly political; Labour claimed that the industry's dependence on public funds made private ownership anomalous. But it was also argued that, by bringing Hawker Siddeley Aviation (the aerospace division of the Hawker Siddeley Group) and BAC into a single organisation, unnecessary duplication would be eliminated. The nationalisation bill was strongly resisted by the industry, and by the Conservatives in Parliament. It was not until 1977 that the new state-owned corporation, British Aerospace, was formed.

One of the first issues that had to be resolved after nationalisation was the future relationship with the Airbus consortium. The A300 had flown for the first time in 1972 and entered service with Air France two years later. Further orders were obtained from Lufthansa and a few other European airlines, but airliner demand was sluggish after the oil shock of 1973. Five years after the maiden flight, the Airbus consortium had sold only fifty-three aircraft. But by then the world economy was recovering and, following the steep rise in fuel prices, airlines needed to re-equip their fleets with more fuel-efficient aircraft. The A300, a twin-engined, wide-bodied airliner, filled a gap in the market which the three American builders, Boeing, Lockheed and McDonnell Douglas, had neglected. In 1977 Eastern Airlines, one of the largest US carriers, leased the A300 on a trial basis and then placed a firm order. This was a boost to the credibility of the Airbus and orders began to flow in from other airlines. In 1978 the Airbus partners were planning a smaller version of the Airbus, the A310.

From the British point of view, these events increased the attractiveness of the Airbus as a partner, and the French and Germans were keen to have Britain back in. But it was not the only option. Boeing, having committed huge sums to the development of the 747, was looking for partners to share the cost of developing the next members of its family, the narrow-bodied 757, planned as a successor to the highly successful 727, and the wide-bodied

767, which would compete directly against the A300 and the A310. In 1978 the American company, having identified British Airways as a likely launch customer for the 757, proposed that British Aerospace should build the wings and Rolls-Royce the engines.[56] Rolls-Royce was enthusiastic about this idea: the 757 would be the first new Boeing airliner to be launched with a Rolls-Royce engine. British Aerospace preferred a link with Airbus, mainly on the grounds that under the Boeing plan it would be relegated to the status of a sub-contractor. The government was split. The Treasury, a long-time critic of subsidies for the aircraft industry, favoured the American connection, not least because British Aerospace would be forced to submit to Boeing's commercial disciplines. The Foreign Office, for reasons of European diplomacy, supported the Airbus.

A lengthy debate ensued, during which James Callaghan, who had succeeded Harold Wilson as Prime Minister in 1976, had talks with Boeing and other potential partners. Frustration mounted on the other side of the Channel, and there were threats to take the wing contract for the Airbus away from British Aerospace. The outcome was a compromise. Rolls-Royce's American strategy was endorsed, and £250m in launch aid was provided for a new engine, the RB211–535, to power the Boeing 757. At the same time British Aerospace was allowed to join the Airbus as a 20 per cent partner, with a £100m contribution from the British taxpayer towards the cost of the A310.

These decisions, made shortly before the 1979 election, resolved some of the strategic dilemmas which had dogged the industry since the war. For the airframe side of the industry, European collaboration was the way forward, at least for large civil and military projects. The next big military project after the Tornado was expected to be a new combat aircraft on which British Aerospace had already started design work; preliminary discussions were taking place between the British, German and French Defence ministries.[57] Rolls-Royce, for its part, continued on the path which it had set in the 1960s, focusing mainly on winning more business from the US.

The British Aerospace Industry in the 1980s and 1990s

The Conservative government under Margaret Thatcher was committed to reducing the role of the government in the economy, and, once the privatisation programme got under way, British Aerospace and Rolls-Royce were early candidates for sale. Both companies were profitable, and both had substantial order books. The government sold 52 per cent of its shares in British Aerospace in 1981 and the rest in 1985. Rolls-Royce was privatised in 1987. But the change of ownership did not imply that the government was washing its hands of the industry. Aerospace still had a privileged status, and there was no question of allowing either company to fall under foreign control. The government retained a 'golden share' in British Aerospace and Rolls-Royce after privatisation, and foreign shareholdings were restricted to a maximum of 15 per cent, later raised to 29.5 per cent.[58]

More surprisingly, at a time when subsidies for other industries were being cut back, Mrs Thatcher was willing to continue supporting civil aerospace projects.[59] In 1983, after much agonising, she authorised launch aid for a new member of the Airbus family, the narrow-bodied A320. This was a significant decision in view of the escalating political row between the US and Europe over the financing of the Airbus. The Americans complained that competition from the Airbus, based on government subsidies, was grossly unfair, and putting the American industry at a disadvantage.[60] The success of the A320 in the second half of the 1980s made the Americans even angrier. Lockheed withdrew from the civil airliner market, and McDonnell Douglas entered into a financial decline which was to lead, a decade later, to its absorption by Boeing. In 1987 the Thatcher government provided another tranche of launch aid for the A330/340 long-distance airliners.

The old arguments about the relative merits of European and American partnerships had not been entirely laid to rest, and they flared up again in the Westland affair of 1985. The helicopter company, in financial difficulty because of a dearth of orders, sought assistance from its long-time American licensor, Sikorsky; this involved the American company acquiring a 29.9 per cent stake in Westland. Michael Heseltine, now Defence Secretary, concerned at what he saw as the impending loss of Westland's technological independence, undertook an urgent search for a European solution. A consortium of French, German and Italian helicopter manufacturers was assembled, with GEC and British Aerospace, to put alternative proposals to Westland. The Cabinet was divided, with some ministers, including Mrs Thatcher, arguing that Westland must be left free to choose its partner without interference from the government. Infuriated by the Prime Minister's apparent indifference to Westland's fate, Heseltine resigned from the Cabinet and precipitated a political crisis which almost brought the government down.[61] Shareholders in Westland subsequently approved the Sikorsky proposals, which had been made more politically acceptable by the inclusion of Fiat in the rescue package.[62]

This bizarre episode did not presage a shift away from European collaboration in military aircraft. The government worked closely with British Aerospace in promoting what was to become one of the largest European collaborative projects, the European Fighter Aircraft (EFA). The partners were Britain, Germany, Italy and Spain. The French government again refused to participate, and Dassault went ahead with a rival fighter, the Rafale. Thus, in this aspect of industrial policy, the Thatcher government adhered closely to policies set by its predecessor.

Yet Thatcherism did make a difference. The aircraft industry was still a special case, but not quite so special as before. The Ministry of Defence adopted a tougher policy on procurement, putting more emphasis on competitive tendering and fixed price contracts, instead of the cost-plus environment of the 1960s and 1970s.[63] The Ministry was also more willing to open up the market to foreign suppliers. In 1986, for example, the early warning version of the Nimrod (a reconnaissance aircraft based on the Comet airframe) was cancelled in favour of buying the AWACS (Airborne Early Warning and Control System) from Boeing; the Nimrod project had been seriously delayed by technical problems with the radar equipment supplied by GEC. There was no commitment on the government's part to maintain the industry at its existing size, and no disposition to interfere in its commercial decisions. To a greater extent than in the past, the industry's future was in its own hands.

When British Aerospace was privatised, it had a healthy military order book, boosted by a large contract from Saudi Arabia for Tornados, Hawk trainers and other equipment. The civil side was more problematic. In addition to the supply of wings for the Airbus, British Aerospace had three businesses of its own at the lower end of the market – the 146 regional airliner, the Jetstream turboprop for commuter routes and the HS-125 business jet; all three aircraft were competing in a crowded market and barely profitable. They also involved large financial risks in the form of leasing contracts with airlines. To give British Aerospace the financial muscle which it lacked, a new management team, led by Professor Roland Smith, took over in 1987, and embarked on a series of acquisitions to enlarge the company's asset base.

Some of the acquisitions, such as the purchase of Royal Ordnance from the government, were logical additions to the company's existing interests, but the take-over of Rover, the car-maker, in 1988, took British Aerospace into unfamiliar territory. This deal was partly justified on the implausible grounds that there were synergies between aircraft and cars, but Rover needed capital for new model development and British Aerospace had little to spare.

Some of the other acquisitions were badly timed, and by 1990 the cash position was deteriorating. The launch of a £432m rights issue in the following year alerted investors to the depths of the crisis. This precipitated a change of top management, a reorientation of strategy, and a drastic streamlining of the business comparable to what many British engineering companies had gone through in the early 1980s. Most of the acquired businesses, including Rover, were sold off. The business jet operation was sold to Raytheon of the US; production of the Jetstream commuter aircraft was halted; and the 146 was made profitable at a production rate of about twenty-three per year. The core of the business would in future consist of military aircraft and missiles (amounting to about three quarters of the company's total revenue), and the Airbus.[64]

These events came at a time when the world defence industry was beginning to adjust to the end of the cold war. In the US, the defence contractors moved rapidly to consolidate into larger groups, but similar moves in Europe were hindered by the existence of national champions, protected and in some cases owned by governments. Everyone agreed that cross-border mergers were desirable, but governments in the three main countries – Britain, Germany and France – were reluctant to see their companies reduced to a subordinate role in any new European grouping. This was particularly true of France, where the aircraft industry had long been regarded almost as an arm of the state. In Germany, as in Britain, the industry was privately owned – all the leading aircraft makers had been brought together in the late 1980s under Daimler-Benz – but the Federal government remained closely involved in the industry's affairs.

At the end of 1998 British Aerospace came close to a full merger with the Daimler-Benz subsidiary Deutsche Aerospace SA (DASA), a move which would have left the French industry out on a limb. Much to the German company's surprise, however, British Aerospace opted early in 1999 for an all-British defence merger, buying the Marconi defence electronics business from GEC (see Chapter 10). How this would affect the prospects for Europe-wide rationalisation in military and civil aircraft was not certain at the time this book was written. But it was clear, even before the Marconi acquisition, that British Aerospace was in a strong bargaining position. Thanks to the changes that had taken place since the crisis of the early 1990s, this company had become, as one observer wrote, 'a world leader in airframes and far ahead of its European rivals as a low-cost manufacturer'.[65]

Rolls-Royce, too, greatly improved its competitive position during the 1980s and 1990s. The central issue, before and after privatisation, was how to keep up with its two American rivals without facing a repetition of the financial strains which had led to the 1971 collapse. One way of limiting the risks inherent in developing new engines was to share the costs with other manufacturers. During the 1970s Rolls-Royce had briefly collaborated on a new engine with Pratt & Whitney, but this agreement ended in 1977 when the British company decided to develop new versions of the RB211. In 1984 William Duncan, a former deputy chairman of ICI who had taken over from Kenneth Keith as chairman, negotiated a partnership with General Electric which had potentially far-reaching implications. The American company agreed to contribute to the cost of developing the RB211–535E4, an engine of about 40,000 lb thrust, while Rolls-Royce would do the same with GE's larger engine, the CF6–80C. This arrangement was described by Duncan as 'a watershed in the big engine market', and welcomed by outside observers as a necessary scaling-down of Rolls-Royce's ambitions.[66] But the agreement lasted no more than two years. Rolls-Royce continued to work on more powerful versions of its own engines and in 1986 the RB211–524G, capable of 50–60,0000 lbs thrust, was selected by British Airways in preference to the General Electric engine for the new versions of the Boeing 747s it was ordering. The agreement with GE was terminated amid considerable acrimony between the two companies.

Rolls-Royce managers welcomed this outcome, since they regarded the GE deal as an attempt by the American company to eliminate competition in large engines. Others regarded it as a high-risk gamble. But if it was a gamble, it paid off. Rolls-Royce continued to extend the RB211 family, the sixth and seventh generations of which, involving engines of 70,000–90,000 lbs thrust, were renamed the Trent. While Boeing remained Rolls-Royce's most important customer, these engines enabled the company to win business from the Airbus consortium; the Trent 500 was chosen in 1997 as the sole power plant for the A340-500/600 aircraft.

Despite the collapse of the agreement with General Electric, partnerships continued to be an important strand in Rolls-Royce's strategy. It is a participant, with Pratt & Whitney, in International Aero Engines, which makes a turbofan engine for short-haul airliners, the V2500; this consortium also has Japanese and German participation. At the lower end of the market Rolls-Royce set up a joint company with BMW in 1990 to make engines of 14,000–23,000 lb thrust. The aim in these and other arrangements was to compete in all sectors in the market in a way which did not impose unbearable financial burdens, and to retain control of the key technologies, especially in larger engines. By the end of the 1990s Rolls-Royce appeared to be securely placed, with a broad range of civil and military engines and a steadily increasing share of the world market. In 1998 it won 35 per cent of civil engine orders worldwide, compared with 50 per cent for General Electric/SNECMA and 15 per cent for Pratt & Whitney.

Both British Aerospace and Rolls-Royce, after the upheavals of the 1970s and 1980s, had emerged as profitable, internationally competitive manufacturers. In a world which was moving away from subsidies, and national champions (even Aerospatiale was privatised in 1991), they were well placed to hold their own in a demanding market.

Could the Industry Have Done Better?

At the end of the Second World War Britain had the world's second largest aircraft industry; in some areas of technology it was ahead of its American counterpart. In view of the special advantages enjoyed by the American manufacturers, it is not surprising that the gap with the US should have widened over the next fifty years. In civil airliners, it is conceivable that if the Comet had not had its accidents de Havilland could have established itself as a credible supplier to US airlines and developed the Comet into a family of airliners as Boeing and later Airbus did. But such an effort would have involved great financial and technical risks: all Boeing's domestic rivals – Convair, Lockheed and Douglas – eventually withdrew from the contest. This makes Rolls-Royce's achievement as an engine manufacturer all the more impressive. The culture of engineering excellence which was formed in this company during the 1930s and 1940s may have bred a certain arrogance, and this was one of the factors which contributed to the crisis of the early 1970s. But the shock of receivership appears to have had a salutary effect, and in contrast to the British Leyland case described in Chapter 9, the period of public ownership was used constructively to correct the company's management weaknesses.

The story on the airframe side is less happy. The industry was undoubtedly damaged by the twists and turns of government policy in the first thirty years after the war. Between 1945 and 1964, even allowing for technical uncertainty, serious mistakes were made in the procurement of military and civil aircraft. Too many military projects were launched without sufficient regard to potential overseas sales, and the use of the state-owned airlines as tied customers for civil aircraft was unhelpful. The lurch from manned aircraft to guided missiles and back again was disruptive. More generally, there were delusions of grandeur in the extent to which governments expected the British aircraft industry to compete with the Americans on all fronts. The most expensive folly was the Concorde, a waste of national resources on a gigantic scale.[67] After 1964 governments took a more realistic view of the industry's position in the world, but policy continued to veer between 'techno-nationalism' and a search for partners to share the costs of development. The hesitation over the Airbus was understandable given the doubtful economics of this programme, but the effect was to give the airframe side of the industry the worst of both worlds – neither a position of leadership in Europe nor a close link with the US. It was not until the second half of the 1970s that these dilemmas were resolved.

Did France play its cards better? Rebuilding a shattered industry was perhaps easier than scaling down an over-large one. There was no thought of matching the Americans in large civil airliners, and the French government was willing to accept a subordinate position for SNECMA in engines. Dassault's success in fighters was based on simple designs suitable for low-cost production. Each new model contained incremental improvements, based on proven materials and technology; there were no high-risk technological leaps of the sort which Britain attempted with the TSR-2. Dassault also insisted that its aircraft must be exportable, convincing the French Air Force to make design compromises in order to facilitate overseas sales.[68] Government policy towards the industry was less erratic than in Britain, reflecting a consensus across the political spectrum on the need to maintain a strong French position in this field. The Airbus programme, costly though it has been for the French taxpayer, benefited from a degree of consistency on the part of politicians, civil servants and managers which was notably lacking in French policy towards computers (Chapter 10). On the other hand, 'techno-nationalism' was at least as prevalent in France as in Britain. The record in civil airliners, before the Airbus, was poor, and the go-it-alone strategy in military aircraft became increasingly expensive as development costs increased. Some observers believe that the strength of the military-industrial complex had malign consequences for the French economy, leading to a concentration of technical resources in aerospace and other defence-related industries to the detriment of other sectors.[69]

The same point has been made about Britain, and it is certainly arguable that the money spent on a vain attempt to keep up with the Americans in the 1950s and 1960s could have been used more constructively in other ways. If the industry had not been supported by the government, it would have been forced to specialise in sectors of the market where it had a competitive advantage.[70] On the other hand, the industry which emerged from the war did represent a considerable national asset, and Stafford Cripps' view about the role which it could play in the post-war economy was not an unreasonable one. The fact that Cripps' hopes were not fulfilled was at least partly due to changes in the economics of the industry – the huge rise in development costs – and to the special advantages enjoyed by the American companies.

Government policy has been far more central to the post-war history of the aircraft industry than the three institutional weaknesses which have been discussed in earlier chapters. The industry was not held back by lack of support from the financial system. As for labour relations, the industry was affected by strikes and restrictive practices during the 1960s and 1970s, but this was not as big a problem as in cars or shipbuilding. It is also hard to argue that the industry suffered from defects in the training and education system. While there have been serious commercial misjudgements, the quality of engineering has been consistently high.

TWELVE

Chemicals: The Birth, Growth and Break-up of a National Champion

The chemical industry shares with aerospace the distinction of being a consistently positive contributor to the balance of trade throughout the post-war period. It also has an impressive record of technical innovation. Part of this success is due to the outstanding performance of the pharmaceutical sector, which, though part of the chemical industry, has evolved in a distinctive way and is examined separately in Chapter 13.[1] This chapter looks at Imperial Chemical Industries (ICI), which until the pharmaceutical division was split off as a separate company in 1993, was by far the largest and most diversified British chemical manufacturer; in the 1950s it accounted for about 40 per cent of the industry's output.

The post-war history of the world chemical industry, outside pharmaceuticals, falls into two distinct periods – growth and prosperity up to the mid-1970s, followed by maturity and decline thereafter. How well or badly did ICI respond to these two very different sets of circumstances? What were the advantages and disadvantages of Britain as a global platform for a chemical manufacturer?

1870–1926: Germany Takes the Lead

The chemical industry was not one of the pace-setters in the British industrial revolution, but it played a supporting role as a supplier of essential materials to other industries. The bulk of its output during the nineteenth century consisted of inorganic chemicals, principally alkalis and acids, which were manufactured by processing minerals such as salt, lime and sulphur; one of the biggest customers for alkalis was the textile industry, which used them in dyeing and bleaching. In the 1870s Britain was by far the largest producer and exporter of chemicals, accounting for nearly half the world's production of sulphuric acid, compared with 9 per cent in Germany and 14 per cent in the US.[2] Some of the technology on which British manufacturers relied originated outside Britain, the best-known example being the Leblanc soda process, invented in France in 1791. But the Leblanc process was greatly improved by British chemists, and until the closing decades of the century there were no grounds for concern about the technical competence of the industry. At this point a different sort of industry began to emerge, and leadership passed from Britain to Germany.

The starting-point for this transition was an advance in scientific understanding of the chemistry of organic compounds. These are compounds which contain carbon and hydrogen, and they were called organic because of the long-held belief that they could only come from living organisms, whether animals or plants.[3] In the 1820s German scientists showed how the properties of organic chemicals could be synthesised in the laboratory out of mineral substances. A central figure was Justus von Liebig, appointed professor at the University of Giessen in 1825. His systematic approach to teaching and research, based on teams of scientists working together in well-equipped laboratories, helped to give German universities a pre-eminent position in chemistry.[4] Such was Liebig's international prestige that when the Royal College of Chemistry was set up in London in 1845, he was invited to nominate the first director.[5]

Liebig recommended August Wilhelm Hofmann, who had been one of his colleagues at Giessen. Hofmann was interested in the chemical composition of coal tar, a by-product of the process used to make coal gas for town lighting. He encouraged his assistant at the Royal College, William Henry Perkin, to investigate whether aniline, a chemical derived from coal tar, could be used as the basis for synthesising quinine, an anti-malarial medicine. In 1856, in one of the most famous accidental discoveries in the history of chemistry, Perkin's experiments produced, not synthetic quinine, but a synthetic dye, later known as aniline purple. Most dyes at that time were derived from plants, some of them imported from distant countries. The invention of synthetic dyestuffs opened up the possibility of providing the textile industry with a wider range of colours than was available from natural sources, and at a lower price.

Perkin left the College to manufacture the new dye, and other entrepreneurs in Britain and on the Continent soon tried to match what he had done. In 1859 a French chemist synthesised a red dye called fuchsin, known in Britain as magenta, and over the next decade several German and Swiss entrepreneurs joined the race. As competition in synthetic dyestuffs increased, British firms seemed well placed to win the lion's share of the business. The huge textile industry provided an easily accessible market, and ample supplies of coal tar were available. But Germany had an asset which did not exist in Britain – an education system which, thanks in part to Liebig and his followers, was turning out well-trained chemists capable of understanding and applying the new techniques. Most of the men who founded the leading German dyestuffs firms – Hoechst in 1863, Bayer in 1864, Badische Anilin und Soda Fabrik (BASF) in 1865 and AG für Anilin-fabrikation (AGFA) in 1873 – were either chemists themselves or had close links with university chemistry departments. The same was true of the cluster of Swiss manufacturers – Ciba, Geigy and Sandoz – which made Basle a flourishing centre of dyestuffs production.[6]

Britain had no tradition of collaboration between industry and academia, and the study of chemistry in universities was still in its infancy. One of the few academic institutions to take chemical education seriously was Owens College in Manchester (forerunner of Manchester University), where Henry Roscoe, appointed professor of chemistry in 1857 after taking his Ph.D. at Heidelberg, taught courses based on the German model. But Manchester's output of chemistry graduates was tiny compared to that of the leading German universities. The Royal College of Chemistry attracted little support from the chemical manufacturers.

During the 1870s the German dyestuffs manufacturers, helped by more effective patent protection than was available in Britain, pulled ahead of their British competitors.[7] A small British dyestuffs industry continued to exist – the strongest firm was Levinstein, founded by a German immigrant in 1864 – but it received little encouragement from the British textile manufacturers, who were content to import their dyes from Germany or Switzerland.

The commitment to company-financed scientific research was at the heart of the German achievement in dyestuffs. The opening of Bayer's labora-tory in 1891 has been described as 'the end of a long period of experimentation on how best to employ science in the solution of industrial problems, and the beginning of the era in which industrial research was fully institutional-ised.'[8] The leading firms broadened their research beyond dyestuffs into other areas where the same intermediate chemicals and the same manufacturing processes could be used. The discovery that certain dyes had therapeutic properties led to the development, again in close co-operation with academic scientists, of more effective medicines.

Dyestuffs were only one part of the chemical industry, and there were other sectors where British firms were still competitive. Britain's share of world chemical exports declined only slightly, from 29 per cent to 22 per cent, between 1880 and 1913.[9] There were, however, signs of conservatism in the heartland of the industry, the production of alkali. In 1861 Ernest Solvay in Belgium invented a way of making alkali which was cheaper and cleaner than the Leblanc process, and it was quickly taken up by manufacturers in Germany and France. The British alkali industry had a great deal of capital sunk in Leblanc plants, many of which were relatively modern; rather than switching to the Solvay process, most of them concentrated on trying to make the Leblanc process more efficient. In an effort to keep prices up and to share the costs of modernisation, forty-eight alkali producers came together in 1890 to form the United Alkali Company (UAC), but they could not stave off the decline of the Leblanc process.[10]

It was left to a new-comer, an immigrant from Germany, to introduce the Solvay process into Britain. Ludwig Mond, who had studied chemistry at the universities of Marburg and Heidelberg and worked for alkali producers in Germany and the Netherlands, came to Manchester in 1862.[11] After working briefly for Hutchinsons, an alkali producer in Widnes, he formed a partnership with John Brunner to exploit the Solvay process. Brunner, whose parents were Swiss, had no technical training, but his commercial experience complemented Mond's scientific background. Brunner Mond was formed as a partnership in 1873 to manufacture soda ash at Winnington in Cheshire; it was converted into a public company in 1881. From the start Ludwig Mond insisted on hiring scientists and engineers of the highest calibre, and established close links with Henry Roscoe at Owens College.[12]

Brunner Mond was not the only modernising force in the British chemical industry during this period. Another new entrant, also with foreign connections, was British Dynamite, set up in Glasgow in 1871 as part of an international network put together by Alfred Nobel, the Swedish inventor of dynamite. This company, later renamed Nobel's Explosives, participated in the market-sharing agreements which Nobel organised in an attempt to maintain his grip on the world explosives industry. These activities were co-ordinated through the Nobel Dynamite Trust, which extended its influence to the US through an alliance with Du Pont, the leading American explosives manufacturer. After Alfred Nobel's death in 1889 the British company conducted much of the international diplomacy on the Trust's behalf. A rising star in Nobel's Explosives was Harry McGowan, who was to play a central part in the creation of ICI. McGowan, who joined Nobel's Explosives in 1894 at the age of fifteen, rose to become an assistant manager, and in 1909 he was given the responsibility for sorting out the relationship between American and European explosives makers in Canada. A new company was formed, Canadian Explosives, in which Du Pont and Nobel's Explosives were shareholders. This experience gave McGowan his first taste of international business negotiations; it also marked the start of a long association between Nobel's and Du Pont.

Before the First World War neither Brunner Mond nor Nobel's had any interest in dyestuffs, which remained a backward sector of the industry. This was not a matter of great concern to the government, or to the textile manufacturers. Given Britain's commitment to free trade, of which the textile industry was the foremost champion, it was rational to import dyes from the countries which made them most efficiently. This view of the world, like so many of the assumptions which governed British economic policy, was shattered by the war. The supply of dyes from Germany was halted and the government was forced to intervene, 'if only to see that soldiers got uniforms of the proper colour'.[13]

Despite opposition from free traders, a new company, British Dyes, was set up, sponsored by the government and partly financed by a reluctant textile industry, to take over existing dyestuffs manufacturers, rationalise production between them, and organise a research programme. Levinstein, the most technically competent dyestuffs producer, refused to co-operate, and the new company had a difficult start. But the formation of British Dyes was a significant event in relations between government and industry. The production of dyestuffs, and by implication other parts of the chemical industry, were seen to have a strategic value which justified intervention to override market forces. This was more than an emergency response to the war; the government indicated that imports of dyestuffs would be restricted after the war. In 1919, when British Dyes was refinanced and Levinstein agreed to participate in what became British Dyestuffs Corporation, the government retained a minority interest and voting control.[14]

The military importance of the chemical industry had been underlined by another development which took place just before the war. BASF in Germany succeeded in synthesising ammonia, an essential intermediate in the production of fertilisers and explosives. Fritz Haber, a professor at the

Karlsruhe technical high school, and Carl Bosch, an engineer at BASF, found a way of 'fixing' nitrogen in the atmosphere and reacting it with hydrogen gas under high pressure to produce ammonia. The process provided a substitute for the Chilean nitrates on which both Germany and Britain had relied for much of their fertiliser production. When supplies from this source were threatened by attacks from German submarines, the British government initiated research on the Haber-Bosch process, and built a factory for this purpose at Billingham in the north-east.

The unfinished plant was put up for sale after the war. The government was anxious that work on ammonia synthesis should continue, and looked to Brunner Mond as a likely purchaser. In 1919 a team of engineers from the company inspected BASF's Oppau works on the Rhine, where the Haber-Bosch process had been installed, and a year later Brunner Mond acquired the Billingham plant. With the help of two German engineers who had been trained at Oppau, the high-pressure technology was gradually mastered, and Brunner Mond built a research laboratory on the Billingham site. 'For the first time in the history of this country,' wrote F. G. Donnan, professor of chemistry at University College London, and a consultant to Brunner Mond, 'we have a technical and scientific laboratory which can bear comparison with anything to be found in Germany or the States.'[15]

This was a step forward for the British chemical industry, but in dyestuffs the gap with Germany was still alarmingly wide. The board of British Dyestuffs Corporation was made up of quarrelling representatives of formerly independent companies, and stronger leadership was badly needed. The need for action to shore up BDC's position became more urgent in 1925, when all the leading German dyestuffs-makers came together in a giant merger to form IG Farbenindustrie.* Like other industries such as iron and steel, the German chemical industry had been extensively cartelised since the 1880s, but some senior managers had been arguing that mergers on the US model would eliminate unnecessary duplication in research and production. This view carried more weight in the early 1920s as international competition increased. Countries such as Britain and the US, which had previously been major importers, were building up their dyestuffs production behind tariff walls. The German firms were also concerned about the financial resources which would be needed to continue the development of the ammonia syn-

---

*The founder members of IG Farben were Bayer, Hoechst, Badische Anilin und Soda Fabrik (BASF), AG für Anilinfabrikation (AGFA), Cassella, Kalle, Griesheim-Elektron and Weiler-ter-Meer

thesis process and to undertake the next major advance in high-pressure technology, the synthesis of oil from coal.

The motives behind the creation of IG Farben were primarily defensive. From the British point of view, however, what was impressive about the new company was its size and technical strength, threatening to perpetuate German domination in the most technologically advanced branches of the chemical industry. The immediate concern was the weakness of the dyestuffs sector, and in January 1926, Reginald McKenna, chairman of the Midland Bank, who had helped to refinance British Dyestuffs Corporation, suggested to McGowan, now chairman of Nobel's Explosives, that he should take it over. Nobel's had shown an interest in dyestuffs during the war, having bought a stake in Levinstein shortly before it became part of British Dyestuffs Corporation. Since then McGowan had been expanding in other directions – buying up most of his competitors in explosives, then turning his attention to non-ferrous metals. He saw great opportunities in the motor industry, and he wanted the company, now called Nobel Industries, to be a major supplier to the car manufacturers. Paint and lacquers were obvious areas of interest, since they used the same technology and raw materials as explosives, but McGowan also bought several vehicle component suppliers in the Midlands. Nobel Industries' biggest investment in the motor industry was the purchase of a stake in General Motors of the US, a company in which Du Pont, McGowan's long-time ally, was the largest single shareholder.[16]

McGowan's first reaction to McKenna's suggestion was that dyestuffs were not in his 'line of country'.[17] But he saw that a merger between British Dyestuffs and Nobel might make sense as part of a larger grouping, involving Britain's two other major chemical companies, Brunner Mond and UAC. A four-way merger would create a 'British IG', capable of being a serious rival to the Germans and negotiating from strength with the other rising force in the world chemical industry, the US.

Before the war the US had been as backward as Britain in synthetic organic chemistry, but the cut-off in German dyestuffs supplies prompted several firms, including Du Pont, to enter this field. There were also moves after the war to consolidate what had been a fragmented industry. A new giant, Allied Chemical and Dye Corporation, was formed in 1920 by a merger of five firms making dyes, alkali and synthetic ammonia.[18] Several other mergers took place in the US during the 1920s, and a group of strong companies – Du Pont, Allied Chemical, Union Carbide, Monsanto and Dow – emerged as the industry leaders.

McGowan's plan for a four-way British merger hinged on the co-operation of Brunner Mond, which was by far the strongest of the other three companies. Its chairman was the founder's son, Sir Alfred Mond, later Lord Melchett, who had returned to the business after a career in politics. (Ludwig Mond died in 1909.) At first Mond saw no attractions in a link with Nobel. His priorities were to develop fertiliser production at Billingham and to gain access to the oil-from-coal technology which was under development in Germany. Mond believed that IG Farben could be persuaded to make this technology available in return for access to the British dyestuffs market. To this end he conceived the idea of an international alliance which would embrace IG Farben in Germany, British Dyestuffs in Britain, Solvay in Belgium and Allied Chemical in the US. In September 1926, having held amicable discussions with representatives of Solvay and IG Farben, he travelled to New York to present the plan to Allied Chemical. McGowan, alarmed by what was going on, followed Mond to the US a few days later in the hope of averting what he saw as a threat to the independence of the British chemical industry.[19]

To McGowan's relief, the chairman of Allied Chemical rejected the scheme. Mond then considered a more limited agreement between Brunner Mond, British Dyestuffs and IG Farben, but McGowan convinced him that an all-British solution was preferable to a German alliance in which Brunner Mond would be the junior partner. As the two men and their advisers returned to England on the *Aquitania*, they worked out a scheme whereby the four principal British chemical companies – Brunner Mond, Nobel Industries, British Dyestuffs and UAC – would come together to form a single enterprise, to be known as Imperial Chemical Industries. Merger terms were agreed in October, and on 1 January 1927, ICI was ready for business, with Mond as chairman and McGowan as his deputy.

1926–45: The New Company Takes Shape

The creation of ICI was Britain's biggest-ever merger, bringing under single ownership most of the country's heavy chemical industry. But ICI was smaller and technically weaker than IG Farben (47,000 employees against 100,000), and head-on competition was not what Mond and McGowan had in mind. Part of the purpose of the merger was to enable them to negotiate with IG Farben about markets and technologies from a position of strength. In the course of 1927 they tried to persuade IG Farben to share its technology on dyestuffs, nitrogen and oil-from-coal, but the terms demanded by the Germans were too onerous to be acceptable.

Attention then turned to the US. Mond's first preference was to co-operate with Allied Chemical, which had a similar product range to ICI (and in which ICI, through Brunner Mond, had a shareholding), but McGowan was eager to build on Nobel's links with Du Pont, dating back to the days of the Dynamite Trust. In 1929 ICI and Du Pont signed a Patents and Processes Agreement, providing for an exchange of technical know-how and for the division of the world into 'exclusive licence territories'. The British Empire was reserved for ICI, North and South America, apart from Canada, for Du Pont. The jointly owned Canadian explosives company, renamed Canadian Industries Limited, was enlarged to make other ICI and Du Pont products.

The ICI/Du Pont agreement was designed to support the efforts which both companies were making to catch up with the Germans in technology. At the time of its formation in 1925, the constituent companies in IG Farben were pushing beyond dyestuffs and pharmaceuticals into polymer chemistry, which was to prove a fertile area of research in the inter-war period. As with the earlier development of dyestuffs, most of the theoretical advances in this field came from German scientists. They showed how natural and synthetic materials were made up of long chains of molecules linked by chemical bonds, and that new products – synthetic rubber, plastics and fibres – could be created by changing the way in which molecules were connected. But Germany no longer had a monopoly of expertise in this field: the US and Britain were catching up.

In the early post-war years Du Pont had little research capability of its own, and relied mainly on European technology. The dyestuffs venture made slow progress, and it was not until a group of German dye chemists had been recruited that the operation began to make modest profits. As in Britain, import protection was necessary to get an American dyestuffs industry off the ground.[20] Du Pont also acquired French know-how in rayon, which proved to be a great money-spinner during the consumer boom of the 1920s. In the second half of the decade the company instituted a more ambitious research programme, building new laboratories and staffing them with first-class academic scientists. Du Pont's greatest success came in polymer chemistry – first neoprene synthetic rubber and then nylon, the world's first laboratory-produced synthetic fibre. These achievements were the work of a research team led by Wallace Carothers, a brilliant scientist hired from Harvard University.

For ICI, the post-merger years were marred by a disastrous decision to expand ammonia capacity at Billingham, based on what was expected to be a rising demand for nitrogenous fertilisers in Britain and the Empire. As shown in TABLE 12.1, this side of the business attracted a large share of ICI's new investment between 1927 and 1932. By 1929 it was clear that the sales forecasts had been far too optimistic. Other countries, including Germany, were increasing their fertilizer capacity, and prices were falling even before

TABLE 12.1 *Capital employed in ICI's*
UK manufacturing activities 1927–32

(per cent of total)

	1927	1932
Heavy chemicals	50	37
Explosives	23	13
Fertilisers, hydrogenation, etc.	18	31
Dyestuffs, etc.	4	7
Paints, lacquers, leathercloth	1	4
Metals	4	8

Source: W. J. Reader, *Imperial Chemical Industries: A History*, vol. 2, Oxford, 1975, p. 446.

the onset of the world depression. In 1930 ICI negotiated a market-sharing agreement with IG Farben which helped to stabilise prices, but profits fell and spending on capital projects had to be curtailed throughout the group. This was an inauspicious start, but profits from other activities, principally the alkali business inherited from Brunner Mond, kept ICI afloat, and the company did not waver in its commitment to scientific research. The reward came with the invention of polythene in 1933, the result of speculative research into high-pressure chemical reactions by the Alkali Division. Polythene went into commercial production in 1939, and helped to make ICI a leader in plastics after the war. The other major discovery in the same field was methyl methacrylate, sold under the brand name Perspex.

ICI, like Du Pont, was emerging as a technically competent, broadly based chemical manufacturer, with a growing stake in the newer branches of the industry. Even the dyestuffs business, which had been regarded by Alfred Mond mainly as a bargaining chip to be used in negotiations with the Germans, was making progress, and ICI was beginning to follow the German route from dyestuffs into pharmaceuticals. The first major advance in this field came during the Second World War, with the invention of Paludrine, an anti-malarial medicine. Another wartime success for ICI was Gammexane, a powerful pesticide which was a substitute for derris, a vegetable substance imported from Malaya.

Synthetic fibres were a natural target for ICI's research, as they were for Du Pont, but in this field the British company was inhibited by its relationship with an important customer. Courtaulds was the dominant producer of rayon, and a large buyer of ICI's caustic soda and other chemicals. In 1928, when ICI was offered the rights to the French rayon process, the directors felt obliged to discuss the proposal with Courtaulds. The outcome was a non-aggression pact in which each company agreed to stay out of the other's territory.[21] Thus when ICI, under the terms of its agreement with Du Pont, was licensed to make nylon, it did so in partnership with Courtaulds. As described in Chapter 4, British Nylon Spinners, in which ICI and Courtaulds each held a 50 per cent interest, was formed in 1940. During the war, however, ICI initiated a research programme of its own into synthetic fibres. Work on an acrylic fibre was under way when ICI was offered the rights to manufacture a polyester fibre which had been invented by a British textile company, Calico Printers Association.[22] Polyester turned out to be almost as important a discovery as nylon, and ICI decided to keep the new fibre to itself; pilot production of polyester – sold under the brand name of Terylene – began in 1944.[23]

Du Pont's research was probably somewhat more productive than ICI's, but the margin of superiority was small, which was why the partnership worked well.[24] In management and organisation, too, ICI was not far behind its American ally. Du Pont was one of several large US companies which pioneered a new organisational form, the multi-divisional corporation. Central co-ordination by a powerful head office staff was combined with decentralised responsibility for the operating businesses.[25] ICI came nearer than most other large British firms to this model, converting the various businesses inherited from the founding companies into divisions, controlled by a head office in London.[26] A handsome headquarters was built at Millbank, near the Houses of Parliament – it opened in 1928 – and a large corporate staff was assembled.

ICI was conceived as an imperial company, and the focus on the Empire was reinforced by the numerous cartel agreements of which the company was a member; almost none of its exports went to Continental Europe or the US. It also inherited from Nobel Industries subsidiary or associate companies which manufactured explosives in Australia, South Africa and Canada. These companies were expanded after the merger to manufacture other ICI products, with the intention of making them as dominant in their local markets as ICI was in Britain.

In view of what happened after the Second World War it is tempting to regard ICI's imperial bias as a sign of weakness, but no alternative strategy was available in the cartelised world in which all the leading chemical companies were operating at that time. The importance of ICI in the context of this book is that by the end of the 1930s a British company had acquired the technical and managerial capabilities necessary to compete in an industry which was in the early stages of a productive period of innovation. The institutional weakness which had held British chemical companies back at the end of the nineteenth century – the lack of university-trained chemists – had been largely corrected, and if the number of scientists employed in ICI was less than in IG Farben the disparity between Britain and Germany was far less than it had been at the time of the First World War. Like the case of electrical engineering discussed in Chapter 8, this is a story of catch-up after an initial lag.

1945–75: The Golden Age

For the first thirty years after the Second World War the world chemical industry enjoyed a golden age of prosperity. Rising living standards and expanding international trade created favourable conditions for exploiting the technical advances which had been made before and during the war. Plastics gained ground at the expense of paper, steel and other traditional materials, while the three main synthetic fibres – nylon, polyester and acrylic – rapidly increased their share of the textile market. At the fine chemical end of the industry, the pharmaceutical makers were in the midst of what came to be called the therapeutic revolution, building on the success of penicillin and other antibiotics to generate a stream of 'wonder drugs'.

The large, research-based companies which had been formed before the war, including Du Pont and ICI, were well-equipped to exploit these opportunities. Although new entrants came into the market, they did not radically alter the structure and geographical location of the industry in the way that the Japanese did in shipbuilding, nor was there a disruptive technological breakthrough, like the invention of the transistor in electronics, which might have given newcomers a chance to topple the incumbents.

The one major technological change was the shift in the industry's raw material base from coal to oil. This had begun in the US before the war, and American companies took the lead in what became known as the petro-chemical industry. But the technology quickly spread to Europe, and firms such as ICI and the successors to IG Farben in Germany did not have great difficulty in making the switch. Thanks in part to the activities of US-based consulting firms and engineering contractors, there were no barriers to the transfer of petrochemical know-how from the US to Europe.[27]

Thus the main sources of innovation in chemicals continued to be the established companies in Germany, the US and Britain, and to a lesser extent in France. In contrast to some of the industries discussed in earlier chapters, Japanese firms have not been major players in the world chemical industry. Much of their technology came from outside Japan, and they failed to develop the close links with academic science which underpinned the success of the chemical industries in the West.[28]

The trading environment differed in one important respect from before the war: the break-up of cartels. This was largely due to the drive by the US to convert the rest of the world to the virtues of free enterprise. The principles which guided domestic antitrust policy were applied to international cartels, and the ICI–Du Pont agreement was an early target for attack. The US Justice Department started proceedings against the two companies in 1944, and although it took eight years before the agreement was finally declared illegal, the companies soon recognised that they had little chance of saving it.[29] The main Patents and Processes Agreement was terminated by mutual consent in 1948, and over the next few years the various joint ventures which had been set up before the war were dismantled. This removed the main prop in ICI's pre-war foreign policy, forcing the company to rethink its international strategy.

While the ICI–Du Pont case was going through the courts in the US, the Americans were applying the same approach with even greater vigour in Germany. As explained in Chapter 3, the deconcentration and decartelis-ation of German industry were seen as essential to the construction of West Germany as a liberal, democratic state. The US occupation authorities regarded IG Farben with particular hostility because of its co-operation with the Nazis during the war. The eventual settlement, reached in 1952, was less drastic than some of the more extreme trustbusters had hoped, providing as it did for the recreation of Bayer, Hoechst and BASF as separate companies. (Bayer also acquired a controlling interest in AGFA.) But the effect was to give the German chemical industry a structure similar to that of its American counterpart. Although the successor companies tried to avoid competing directly with each other, the existence of three separate centres of innovation, all pursuing different strategies, was a significant change for the German chemical industry.[30]

The end of cartels, together with the gradual movement towards free trade and the free flow of capital across national borders, meant that the leading companies could attack each other's markets, both by exporting and by direct investment, in a way that had not been possible before the war. Du Pont and several other American chemical manufacturers built factories in Britain and in Continental Europe during the 1950s and 1960s.

Another source of competitive pressure was the increasing involvement of the oil companies. The production of basic petrochemicals such as ethylene and propylene was a natural extension of their oil-refining operations, and some of them went further into plastics and other 'downstream' products, either on their own or in association with established chemical firms.

Because sales were rising so fast, there was room in the market for all these competitors, and the priority for ICI, as for its counterparts in Germany and the US, was to ensure that manufacturing capacity kept pace with demand. One of ICI's biggest projects after the war was the construction of a petrochemical complex at Wilton on the south bank of the Tees, a few miles from the Billingham works. ICI decided to build its own naphtha-cracking plant on this site, in preference to an earlier plan to form a joint venture with British Petroleum.[31] The Wilton works, which was opened in 1949, supplied intermediate chemicals to Plastics, Dyestuffs and other divisions, all of which were engaged in large capital-spending programmes of their own.

These projects put a strain on the company's finances. Before the war ICI had rarely gone to the capital market for funds, but in 1948 a £20m rights issue was launched and another £20m was raised through an issue of loan stock two years later. The finance director, Paul Chambers, who had been recruited from the Inland Revenue in 1947, brought a more disciplined approach to the control of capital expenditure, and a new board committee, the Capital Programme Committee, was set up to scrutinise the divisions' proposals more rigorously.

There was also concern among the directors about whether the range of ICI's businesses was too wide to be managed effectively.* 'As a unit of industrial organisation,' the Capital Programme Committee noted, 'the company does not appear to be very logical.'[32] One possibility briefly considered was to divide ICI into two or more independent firms, which would have had the additional advantage of making the company less vulnerable to the threat of nationalisation (Labour ministers made occasional threatening noises about taking over ICI, although the chemical industry was not seriously considered as a target for nationalisation). A candidate for divestment was the Metals Division, the product of Nobel Industries' diversification after the First World War, but the directors decided instead to hold on to it but to give it more autonomy. Generally, they concluded that because of the interdependence of the divisions, which supplied each other with intermediate chemicals, shared common services and drew on the same technologies, there was no advantage in hiving off parts of the business.

Following McGowan's retirement in 1950, the company was run for the rest of the decade by 'elderly Scotsmen of scientific rather than commercial inclination' – first John Rogers, then Alexander Fleck.[33] With demand booming in Britain and overseas, the focus of the company was on research, engineering and production rather than sales. As one senior manager later recalled, everyone assumed that 'if the chemistry was right and the engineering was right, the rest would look after itself – we did not believe in sordid things like marketing'.[34]

Most of the research was carried out in the divisions (a small central laboratory was set up in 1949), and several notable advances were made. In pharmaceuticals, for example, co-operation between the General Chemicals and Dyestuffs divisions led to the development of Fluothane, a successful anaesthetic. In 1957 the Pharmaceutical Division was given greater autonomy (it had previously been under the wing of Dyestuffs) and new laboratories were built at Alderley Park in Cheshire. James Black, a physiologist from Glasgow University and a future Nobel prize-winner, was recruited to work on heart drugs.[35]

As long as markets were strong and ICI was making healthy profits, there was no pressing need to tackle the organisational issues which had been left unresolved at the end of the war. But the seller's market faded in

---

*In 1952 ICI was made up of fifteen divisions: Alkali, Billingham, Central Agricultural Control, Dyestuffs, General Chemicals, Leathercloth, Lime, Metals, Nobel, Paints, Pharmaceutical, Plastics, Salt, 'Terylene' Council, Wilton Works.

the late 1950s and international competition increased. The board of ICI was sufficiently alert to these developments to recognise that change was needed, and in 1960 the unusual decision was taken to appoint the finance director, Paul Chambers, as chairman in succession to Fleck; Chambers was narrowly preferred to Ronald Holroyd, a distinguished scientist more in the ICI mould.

Chambers was articulate, self-confident and not afraid to impose his own views. He was described by a journalist as 'instinctively a reformer, an intellectual and a rationalist'. One of his main tasks, as he saw it, was to shift ICI from 'a narrow technical approach to a broad commercial approach'.[36]

ICI in 1960, according to one account, 'was internationally weak, technologically conservative compared to the Americans, and its organisation was both illogical and out of date'.[37] Chambers resolved to take action on all three fronts. He saw that the relationship between the head office in London and the divisions made for slow decision-making and unclear lines of responsibility. To the dismay of some of his colleagues, he brought in McKinsey, the American management consultants, to advise on ICI's internal organisation. This led to a number of changes, of which the most important were an increase in the authority of the divisional chiefs and some reduction in the bureaucracy at Millbank. The regional sales organisation, which had been run from the centre, was disbanded, and the functions of the executive directors in London were redefined, so that they provided advice and support to the divisions and no longer meddled in day-to-day matters. The divisional structure was also simplified (TABLE 12.2). The two big heavy chemical operations, Alkali and General Chemicals, were merged to form the Mond Division, and the Metals Division was detached from the rest of ICI as a free-standing (though still wholly owned) subsidiary, Imperial Metal Industries.

Another priority for Chambers was to raise ICI's labour productivity closer to that of its overseas competitors. Comparisons carried out with an American company in 1964 showed that for a selected group of comparable activities ICI employed three times as many people per unit of sales and more than twice as many people per unit of assets. Following the example set by Esso at Fawley, ICI embarked on an ambitious exercise in productivity bargaining, and, although only limited progress was made in breaking down demarcation barriers between craft unions, substantial savings in manpower were made.[38] At the same time Chambers encouraged the divisions to invest in larger plants. At Wilton, for example, giant ethylene crackers were built

TABLE 12.2 *ICI divisions in 1968*

Division	per cent of sales
Mond	19
Heavy Organic Chemicals	8
Agricultural	12
ICI Fibres	22
Plastics*	12
Dyestuffs	12
Paints	7
Nobel	5
Pharmaceuticals	3

*In addition to polythene, which had been invented by ICI, the Plastics Division made polyvinyl chloride (PVC) and polypropylene.

Source: Graham Turner, *Business in Britain*, Eyre & Spottiswoode, 1969, p. 140.

to supply intermediate chemicals for plastics and fibres, and, in an extension of the long-standing policy of vertical integration, an oil refinery was built. To make itself less dependent on the oil companies for supplies of crude oil, ICI also invested in exploration and production in the North Sea.

Chambers began the process of making ICI less 'imperial' and more international in its outlook. In 1958 the company had taken the first tentative steps to attack the heartland of its old partner, Du Pont, by forming a joint venture with Celanese Corporation to sell polyester fibre in the US. This operation was expanded during the 1960s, and ICI established its own American subsidiary.

Like most British companies, ICI had not been much interested in Continental Europe during the 1950s; its exports went mainly to Commonwealth countries. In 1960, responding to the establishment of the Common Market and the impressive growth of the Continental economies, ICI established a European Council, followed by the creation of a new subsidiary company, ICI Europa, based in Brussels, to work with the divisions in developing a European strategy. This involved direct investment as well as exports. Some of the divisional chairmen were distinctly unenthusiastic about diverting capital expenditure away from their British factories. They also feared that an assault on Continental markets would provoke a German counter-attack from which both sides would lose; the pre-war cartels had left their mark on the attitudes of ICI managers.

Some plants were built in Continental Europe during the 1960s, principally in the Netherlands, but by the time of Chambers' departure in 1968 the shift from Empire to Europe still had a long way to go. Two-thirds of ICI's sales were still in Britain or the Commonwealth. Like the rest of British industry, ICI participated to only a small extent in the expansion of intra-European trade that took place in the 1960s and early 1970s, and this was the main reason why the German chemical companies grew much faster than ICI during this period (TABLE 12.3).

TABLE 12.3 *Growth of ICI, Hoechst, Bayer and BASF, 1965–75*

	Sales in 1965 ($m)	Sales in 1975 ($m)
ICI	2,479	6,884
Hoechst	1,457	8,462
Bayer	1,385	7,223
BASF	1,177	8,152

Source: *Fortune*, 15 September 1967 and August 1976.

A setback for Chambers, described in Chapter 4, was the failed bid for Courtaulds, followed by a series of unproductive investments in the textile industry. Chambers also made the mistake of allowing the capital-spending programme to expand too quickly; the divisional chairmen were encouraged to think that finance would always be available for any worthwhile project. There were delays in bringing some of the new plants into operation, and ICI ran into a temporary cash crisis in 1966. Yet despite the flaws in his record Chambers gave ICI a much-needed shake-up at a time when many other British companies were stuck in their old ways.

None of the three men who held the chairmanship between 1968 and 1978 – Peter Allen, Jack Callard and Rowland Wright – impressed their personality on the company in the way that Chambers had done. Even if they had wanted to make radical changes, the fact that they held office for only three or four years each made it difficult for them to do so. ICI reverted to a consensual style of management, with the chairman acting as *primus inter pares* rather than as chief executive. (The term 'chief executive' was not used in ICI until the 1990s.)

To say that ICI stood still would be an exaggeration. Capital spending continued at a high level. For example, the Agricultural Division (formerly the Billingham Division) commissioned new methanol and ammonia plants based on natural gas from the North Sea. But ICI gave the impression of a great ship lumbering along on its own momentum, without much direction from the bridge. The allocation of capital between divisions tended to reflect the historical pattern; each divisional chairman felt entitled to the same share of the pot that he had received the previous year. ICI was still dominated by the traditional heavy chemical operations, and these divisions were the main profit earners. Mond Division and Agricultural Division accounted for 30 per cent and 25 per cent respectively of ICI's trading profits in 1978, compared to only 7 per cent for pharmaceuticals. The one black spot was the fibre business, which, after a period of exceptionally high profits in the 1960s, was suffering from over-capacity in the industry and a fashion shift back to natural fibres.

In 1972 a sense among some of the directors that the board was not providing effective leadership prompted the chairman, Jack Callard, to initiate a review of the board's operations, the first such study since the McKinsey exercise ten years earlier. Some radical changes were proposed, including a reduction in the size of the board and a greater focus on strategic issues. But they did not find favour with Callard or a majority of the directors. 'With the financial results as good as they were in 1973, there was no desire to rock the boat that fundamentally.'[39]

Some senior managers remained uneasy. In 1973 John Harvey-Jones, the most reform-minded of the divisional chairmen, joined the board. In a company dominated by scientists and engineers, Harvey-Jones was an unconventional figure. He had joined ICI at the age of thirty-one after some years in the Royal Navy, starting as a work study officer in the Petrochemical Division, before rising to personnel director and then chairman of the division. After joining the board in London he began to press for organisational changes. The divisional structure, in his view, had been made obsolete by technological change; he favoured a merger between Mond, Petrochemicals and Plastics to create a single heavy chemicals division. However, the only major structural change, taking effect in 1977, was the hiving-off of Imperial Metal Industries as an independent quoted company.

Outside Britain, the push into Continental Europe continued, and in 1978 the British divisions were made fully accountable for sales and profits on a pan-European basis, instead of sharing responsibility with ICI Europa. But ICI's European strategy was based on the belief that it could establish on the Continent a kind of mini-ICI which would have a similar spread of products to that of the parent company in Britain. In 1978 plans were announced for a petrochemical complex at Wilhelmshaven in Germany, to make, among other things, vinyl chloride monomer and PVC; this matched a similar investment made at the same time at Wilton. But in petrochemicals and plastics ICI was a late-comer in a market dominated by the three big German companies, and in these products it had no technical advantage which might have enabled it to take business away from the incumbents.

A quicker way into Europe might have been to acquire or merge with another chemical company, but few large firms were available for purchase – and memories of the failed Courtaulds bid had made ICI cautious about undertaking a large-scale take-over, especially if it was likely to be resisted. In the US acquisitions were easier, and in 1971 ICI bought Atlas Chemical Industries, a medium-sized manufacturer of chemicals and pharmaceuticals. This was intended to be a bridgehead into the US market and it was followed by the decision to invest in a petrochemical complex in Texas. But here, as in Europe, ICI was up against formidable domestic competitors, and catching up was bound to be a long and expensive process.

By the end of the 1970s about 20 per cent of ICI's sales were in Continental Europe and 14 per cent in North America, but most of its assets were still in Britain, and the home base generated about 80 per cent of the profits. The British economy performed poorly in the second half of the decade, but, despite the losses in fibres, ICI's profits held up well enough not to engender any sense of crisis; there was no pressure from shareholders for a change of direction. ICI was still very much an engineering-led company, confident that its technological prowess would keep it in the front rank of world chemical companies. As one senior manager recalls, 'we were still living in a technocratic age'.

Meanwhile the world chemical industry was in the early stage of a transformation which was to have profound implications for ICI and other leading companies. The heady growth rates of the early post-war decades had encouraged a large number of new entrants to come into the industry – there were forty producers of polythene in Europe in 1973, up from 23 in 1964.[40] Few of the newcomers had any technical advantage which might have given them an edge over the incumbents. There was a misplaced belief, encouraged by the engineering contractors, that scaling up plants to double or triple their previous size would yield large cost reductions.[41] At the same time the rate at which plastics and fibres were displacing natural materials was slowing down, and there were no blockbuster innovations on the horizon which might have given the market a new impetus. Much of the new capacity came on stream in the mid-1970s just as the world economy was entering a deep recession.

As earlier chapters have shown, the second half of the 1970s was a period in which some British companies – British Leyland being the extreme case – entered a downward spiral from which they never recovered. ICI was in a stronger position because it had made better use of the post-war boom; it still ranked among the top five chemical companies in the world, along with Du Pont in the US and the three big German firms. But it suffered from a number of disadvantages *vis-à-vis* these competitors, the most important of which was its continuing dependence on the slow-growing British economy. Although ICI had been quicker than most British firms to invest on the Continent, it was not yet fully integrated into the European market. Too many of ICI's businesses were relatively strong in Britain, but not competitive internationally. The maturing of the chemical industry exposed these weaknesses, forcing ICI to make a radical break with the past.

The Maturing of the Chemical Industry

Since the 1920s, when the modern chemical industry took shape, the leading companies had relied on in-house research to generate a stream of new products and processes which took them into a variety of different markets. As long as the underlying science was advancing rapidly and on a broad front, this diversity had made good strategic sense. The various divisions within ICI and the other big companies drew on common technologies, supplied each other with intermediate chemicals and made use of similar technical and managerial skills. Another characteristic of these firms was vertical integration – in ICI's case, stretching from the production of crude oil in the North Sea to the manufacture (through the textile companies in which it invested) of nylon stockings.

As the growth of the industry slowed down, this model became less appropriate. Some of the products which had powered the industry's expansion, such as petrochemicals, plastics and fibres, acquired the status of low-margin commodities. Success in these businesses, which tended to be cyclical and subject to fierce price competition, now depended less on scientific research than on scale, manufacturing efficiency, and access to cheap feedstocks. At the other end of the spectrum were research-intensive businesses such as pharmaceuticals and speciality chemicals, where volumes were lower and profit margins higher. Companies had to decide where their strengths lay: did they have a sufficiently strong market position to compete profitably in commodities, or should they concentrate on high-value-added chemicals?

The trend towards greater specialisation was reinforced by the increasingly global character of competition. The leading companies sought to exploit any advantage which they might have as widely as possible, building or acquiring plants in all their major markets.[42] While it was still possible to compete in some products on a local or regional basis, in others economies of scale in research, production and distribution were such as to compel firms to operate internationally, and to build strong market positions in the three main consuming areas – Western Europe, North America and Asia-Pacific.

This strategy of specialisation and internationalisation, which has been a recurring theme throughout this book, posed particular problems for ICI. For reasons of history – the four-way merger which created the company in 1926, and the subsequent diversification – it had an exceptionally broad range of products. The Allies did the German chemical industry a good turn after the war by breaking up IG Farben. Hoechst, Bayer and BASF had a narrower range of businesses than ICI and tended to specialise in particular sectors of the market. The same was true of the US. Du Pont, for example, had always focused strongly on synthetic fibres, although it also made plastics and a range of other chemicals.

ICI was widely spread geographically, with the new businesses in Continental Europe and North America tacked on to the long-established Commonwealth subsidiaries. The most important of the latter were in Australia, South Africa and Canada, and they had as wide a range of products as ICI itself. All three of them, moreover, had partners or minority shareholders whose interests had to be taken into account. The heads of these companies were powerful figures who constituted one of the three management layers – the other two being the divisional chairmen in Britain and the corporate headquarters at Millbank – in what had become a highly complex organisation.

The first major effort to face up to the changes in the world chemical industry came during the chairmanship of Maurice Hodgson, from 1978 to 1982. Hodgson had served as head of the planning department under Paul Chambers and later as chairman of the Petrochemical Division. He brought to the chairmanship a rigorously analytical mind and a determination to raise ICI's performance closer to that of its overseas competitors. He also wanted to make the company less dependent on the UK, probably by means of a major acquisition; one of his proposals, turned down by his colleagues, was to take over Celanese in the US, Du Pont's main competitor in synthetic fibres.

From the start of his term of office Hodgson pressed for improvements in labour productivity, and for reductions in working capital. But, as in so much of British industry, the pace of change was greatly accelerated by the recession of 1980–81. ICI's profits halved in 1980, and the dividend was cut for the first time in the company's history. The biggest loss-makers were petrochemicals, plastics and fibres, and these divisions bore the brunt of the job losses which took place under Hodgson's chairmanship. The number of ICI's British employees fell from 84,000 in 1980 to 62,000 in 1983.

Hodgson established a momentum of reform which was carried forward by his successor, John Harvey-Jones. The appointment of Harvey-Jones came as a surprise to the outside world, but, as the most consistent and articulate champion of reform over the preceding decade, he was the logical choice.[43] With his long hair, his garish ties and his willingness to speak out in public on controversial issues, he was an unusual leader of a company which had always been regarded as a pillar of the British establishment.

Like Chambers in the 1960s, Harvey-Jones made changes both in organisation and strategy. He reduced the size of the board, eliminated the post of deputy chairman and abolished the complicated system whereby each executive director had oversight of a division, a head office function and an overseas region. The aim was to sharpen the profit responsibility of the divisional chairmen, to lighten the bureaucracy at the Millbank head office and to make the board focus on the strategic direction of the company. Harvey-Jones also merged the Petrochemicals and Plastics divisions, as a precursor to a larger regrouping which took place towards the end of his chairmanship. Five divisions – Petrochemicals, Plastics, Agricultural, Mond and Fibres – were brought together in 1987 to form ICI Chemicals and Polymers.

Like Hodgson, Harvey-Jones wanted to make ICI more international, and he set up an acquisitions unit to develop a more active policy on take-overs – the inhibitions arising from the Courtaulds affair were finally discarded. Three large purchases were made in the US – Beatrice, a manufacturer of high-strength plastics and other advanced materials, Glidden, one of the largest American paint companies, and Stauffer, an agrochemicals manufacturer. The first of these turned out to be a mistake, and most of the Beatrice businesses were subsequently sold. The other two were successful, and helped to give ICI's paints and agrochemical interests a larger international dimension.

Part of the purpose of these acquisitions was to shift ICI away from heavy chemicals towards the lighter, high-value-added end of the market, sometimes referred to as 'effect' chemicals. In this context the Pharmaceutical Division, now emerging as a major contributor to ICI's profits (28 per cent of the total in 1982), had a special importance. Thanks largely to James Black's work on beta-blockers – Tenormin, launched in the mid-1970s, became the world's best-selling heart drug – the Pharmaceutical Division had the potential to become a world leader. An opportunity to double the size of the division arose when Beecham, another British drug manufacturer which had done well in antibiotics, became available for purchase in the mid-1980s. ICI came close to buying it, but some directors opposed the deal, arguing that organic growth in pharmaceuticals was preferable, and Beecham was subsequently merged with an American company, Smith Kline & French (Chapter 13). Some ICI managers believe this was a serious missed opportunity.

In heavy chemicals Harvey-Jones sought to withdraw from businesses that had no realistic chance of becoming internationally competitive. An early move, revolutionary by ICI standards, was to get out of polythene, a product which ICI itself had invented. Under an innovative deal negotiated in 1982, British Petroleum bought ICI's polythene business in exchange for its own PVC operations. Three years later ICI merged its PVC interests with those of Enichem in Italy; the joint company, EVC, was the largest PVC producer in Europe, and was floated on the Dutch stock exchange in 1990.

Polythene and PVC were typical of the kind of high-volume commodity chemical that was subject to periodic bouts of over-capacity and price-cutting. The only companies able to make money in these businesses were those that had the lowest costs, the best technology and a large share of the world market. Too many of ICI's commodity businesses did not meet these criteria. In polyester fibre, for example, ICI had had a huge success with Terylene in the 1960s, but, with the patents now expired, there were many producers on the market, and some of them were technically more advanced than ICI. Polyester fibre was one of several businesses that ICI divested during the 1980s.

One of the arguments for putting all the heavy chemicals into ICI Chemicals and Polymers was that this part of the company might in due course be hived off as a free-standing business – or possibly sold to an oil company. The rest of ICI would then be free to concentrate on the lighter end – principally pharmaceuticals and agrochemicals, paints, materials and explosives. No decisions on a break-up had been reached before Harvey-Jones retired from ICI in 1987, and the issue lost some of its urgency with the upturn in world chemical markets which was then under way; ICI Chemicals and Polymers was turning in handsome profits.

Harvey-Jones made ICI less bureaucratic, less inward-looking and more willing to contemplate radical change. But too few of ICI's businesses ranked as world leaders, and those that were potentially in that category, such as pharmaceuticals, needed a stronger push. Moreover, the US acquisitions had made ICI's internal organisation even more complex than before; the board of directors was trying to keep a large number of balls in the air at once. These were the issues which preoccupied Harvey-Jones' successor, Denys Henderson.

Like his predecessor, Henderson did not have a scientific background. He had trained as a lawyer in Scotland and rose to the top of ICI through the legal and commercial side of the company; he had been outstandingly successful as head of the Paints Division. Less flamboyant in his public image than Harvey-Jones, he was as determined as his predecessor, and his chairmanship proved to be the most eventful in ICI's history.

In his first two years Henderson continued the policy of pruning the heavy chemicals portfolio through divestments and joint ventures, and enlarging the lighter end of the business. An important step was the decision to sell ICI's stake in North Sea oil; the case for vertical integration was no longer compelling, and oil exploration was better left to the oil companies. The fertiliser business, once one of the largest and most profitable parts of ICI, was also sold. However, as the chemical market turned down in 1989 and another recession loomed, Henderson became increasingly convinced that more drastic measures were needed to lift ICI out of the pedestrian financial performance which it had achieved for most of the 1980s.

In the autumn of that year there were rumours that a predator might seek to 'unbundle' ICI. This technique, of which Sir James Goldsmith and Lord Hanson were well-known exponents, involved the take-over of diversified companies and the subsequent disposal of the constituent parts to other buyers. The attraction of ICI for a predator was that it contained one highly profitable business, pharmaceuticals, which, if floated separately on the stock exchange, would enjoy a much higher rating than ICI itself. ICI was valued in the stock market at less than the sum of its parts.

At this stage unbundling was not regarded as a serious threat, but Henderson was well aware that the loyalty of shareholders could not be taken for granted and that existing policies seemed unlikely to deliver the improvement in performance which they were looking for. In the course of 1990, after commissioning two internal task forces on strategy and organisation, he reached the conclusion that ICI was still trying to do far too much. In February 1991, he announced that ICI would in future concentrate on seven sectors – pharmaceuticals, agrochemicals, specialities, explosives, paints, materials (principally acrylics, films and polyurethanes) and industrial chemicals. Other businesses would be sold or put into joint ventures with other companies.

Three months later Lord Hanson entered the scene. Announcing the purchase of a 2.8 per cent stake in ICI, he declared that ICI needed to take urgent action to increase shareholder value; Hanson's experience in improving the profitability of 'under-performing and over-managed companies' could help the ICI board achieve this objective.[44] Despite Lord Hanson's offer of co-operation, Henderson regarded the share purchase as the precursor to a take-over bid, which he resolved to resist with all guns blazing. Aided by a team of merchant bankers and public relations advisers, he laid into Hanson's management style and financial record with a ferocity which appeared to rattle Hanson and his colleagues. A phony war lasted for several months, and ICI was generally thought to have won on points.[45] No bid was made and in May 1992, Hanson sold its ICI shares at a substantial profit.

The Hanson affair gave the ICI directors a nasty fright. Size was clearly no protection against take-over, and the question which had to be addressed was whether Henderson's restructuring plan would enhance shareholder value in the timescale which investors had in mind. During the battle with Hanson, Henderson had made some play of the fact that ICI was an integrated chemical company for which unbundling was entirely inappropriate. In the internal reappraisal which followed Hanson's withdrawal this argument came under closer scrutiny. By the spring of 1992 the conclusion was reached that a division of ICI into two free-standing companies would have industrial and financial advantages.[46]

The starting-point for this decision was the recognition that the Pharmaceutical Division had outgrown ICI. It no longer needed the financial support of the parent, and, thanks in part to the growing importance of biotechnology, the technological links between pharmaceuticals and chemicals were looser than they had been twenty years earlier. Separation would provide for a dedicated management team which could concentrate entirely on pharmaceuticals without the distraction of being part of a chemical conglomerate. The other part of ICI that fitted logically with pharmaceuticals was agrochemicals, which used similar technology and similar manufacturing techniques.[47]

Outside these two sectors, ICI consisted of a somewhat heterogeneous collection of businesses. Although there were technological links between some of them, they formed a less coherent package than pharmaceuticals and agrochemicals, and posed more difficult management problems. Henderson and his colleagues believed that these problems would be more effectively tackled by a management team which was not also trying to look after the pharmaceutical business. The challenge would be to identify the potential winners in the portfolio and to put sufficient resources behind them, while at the same time withdrawing from the losers. This was a continuation of the strategy which had been in place since the mid-1980s. An important step, announced in 1992 before the demerger, was the sale of ICI's nylon interests to Du Pont, in return for the latter's acrylic materials business.

The demerger, which took effect from the start of 1993, was ICI's response to the maturing of the chemical industry. In the context of ICI's history – and its place in the British economy – it was a bold decision which upset many current and former employees. Some commentators suggested that a great British company was being sacrificed on the altar of financial short-termism: ICI was simply reacting to the threat of another take-over bid. It is certainly true that part of the purpose of the split was to increase shareholder value, but this is a case where financial, managerial and industrial arguments supported each other.

As expected, the flotation of the pharmaceutical company, Zeneca, was highly successful. It was seen by investors as a well-managed, internationally competitive business with a number of promising drugs in the pipeline. It was also well placed to participate in the restructuring of the world pharmaceutical industry which was then in progress, and which is described more fully in the next chapter. For the new ICI the aftermath of the demerger was more problematic. Although good progress was made in cutting costs – the workforce was reduced from 100,000 to 65,000 in the first two years – investors began to question whether the rationale for the company's existence, as set out at the time of the demerger, was valid. There were no obvious links between, say, paints and explosives, and the company still had a large commitment to low-margin petrochemicals. After reaching a peak of nearly £1bn in 1995, pre-tax profits fell sharply in the following year. The old problems of cyclicality and over-diversification had not gone away.

In responding to these complaints Ronnie Hampel, who took over from Henderson as chairman in 1995, and Charles Miller Smith, recruited from Unilever to be chief executive, adopted a solution which was in some respects even more radical than the demerger. They decided that ICI had to shed completely the bulk chemicals in which it no longer had a competitive advantage and to reinvent itself as a manufacturer of high-value-added speciality chemicals. To achieve this transformation it was not enough to rely on an incremental programme of acquisitions and disposals. A much larger take-over was necessary, and in 1997 Hampel and Miller Smith found the opportunity they were looking for when Unilever put its speciality chemical subsidiaries up for sale. ICI paid £4.9bn for a range of businesses, which included food additives, adhesives and surfactants; the impact on ICI's profits and revenues is shown in TABLE 12.4. The purchase was to be financed in part by the sale of a large part of ICI's industrial chemicals business to Du Pont and by the divestment of its controlling interest in ICI Australia.

TABLE 12.4 *ICI's businesses in 1998*

	Turnover (£m)	Trading profit (loss) £m
Speciality products	3,329	397
Coatings	2,167	143
Materials	1,352	114
Industrial chemicals	2,466	(41)

Source: ICI 1998 Annual Report.

The disposal programme suffered a setback in the autumn of 1998 when the US Federal Trade Commission ruled that part of the sale to Du Pont contravened the antitrust laws. The consequent sharp fall in the share price reflected concern among investors about the large amount of debt which ICI had taken on to finance the Unilever acquisition. However, in April 1999 ICI found another American company, Huntsman, which was willing to purchase most of the assets that had previously been destined for Du Pont. At the same time ICI announced that it would be selling its polyurethane and acrylics businesses; both these products were regarded as too close to commodities to fit Miller Smith's concept of ICI as a 'high value business, low in capital intensity, high in innovation and low in cyclicality'.[48] When the remaining disposals had been completed, what had once been the world's most diversified chemical manufacturer would be competing on a much narrower front, concentrating on speciality products (mostly derived from the Unilever purchase) and paints.

The reshaping of ICI in the 1980s and 1990s was driven by increasing global competition and a more demanding capital market. The same forces were at work in the rest of the industry, although the form and extent of restructuring varied from company to company – and from country to country. The process began earlier in the US than in Europe, because capital market disciplines were stronger.[49] An extreme case was that of Monsanto, which abandoned commodity chemicals during the 1980s in order to concentrate on pharmaceuticals, agrochemicals and specialities. The next step, which came in 1996, was to float off speciality chemicals as a separate company, leaving Monsanto as a pure life sciences business.

European companies, apart from ICI, were slower to abandon the conglomerate model. It was particularly hard for the German firms, which had invented the model in the nineteenth century, to break with their traditions. But they could not insulate themselves from the forces that were affecting the rest of the industry. Although, unlike ICI, they were not exposed to the threat of hostile take-over, an increasing proportion of their shares was held by foreign, mainly American investors, who looked for returns comparable with those obtainable in the US. The concept of shareholder value gained ground in Germany during the 1990s, leading some companies to do things which would have been inconceivable twenty years earlier. Of the three big German companies, Hoechst was the most radical. In 1994 its chairman, Jürgen Dormann, embarked on a strategy that would allow the company to concentrate entirely on pharmaceuticals and agrochemicals; all the other businesses were to be sold or put into joint ventures with other firms.

Rhône-Poulenc, the French chemical manufacturer, had been following a similar line, and in 1999 these two companies agreed on a merger which, if completed, would create one of the world's largest pharmaceutical groups.

The other two big German firms, BASF and Bayer, were more cautious, arguing that there were still synergies to be obtained within an integrated chemical/pharmaceutical group. But they, too, followed the general trend towards specialisation. Bayer announced in 1999 that it would sell up to 75 per cent of its AGFA film and graphic systems subsidiary. 'Our strategy,' said the chairman, Manfred Schneider, 'is to focus more strongly on our core competences, with the stress on our life sciences operations.'[50]

At the end of the 1990s the world chemical industry appeared to be rearranging itself into three groups, although the boundaries between them were not rigid and some firms straddled all three. One group consisted of commodity producers. This included the oil companies and a new breed of commodity specialists which had emerged in the US, often through the vehicle of management buy-outs. Unburdened by elaborate central services and other corporate overheads, they were better equipped to compete in cyclical, low-margin businesses than the old-established chemical groups. The second group consisted of the life sciences firms, some of which, like Zeneca, had originally been offshoots of diversified chemical manufacturers. The third, more disparate group consisted of speciality chemical manufacturers such as ICI was seeking to become.

ICI and the British Environment

Did ICI do well or badly? Unlike many of the British firms discussed in earlier chapters, ICI held its position as one of the world leaders in its field from the 1950s to the 1990s. The capabilities which it had acquired in the inter-war years were well suited to the conditions which it faced after the Second World War, and it made good use of the post-war boom. On the other hand, ICI was slow to reduce its dependence on Britain and the Commonwealth. Although the first steps towards Europeanisation were taken in the early 1960s, the follow-up was poor and ICI did not push as strongly into Continental Europe and the US as it might have done.

The consequence was to limit the options open to ICI in the 1980s and 1990s. The issue was to decide which businesses could be internationalised from a weak domestic base. By far the strongest of ICI's businesses was pharmaceuticals; the nurturing of Zeneca has been one of ICI's greatest achievements. For the rest of the portfolio the strategic choices were more difficult, and it is not yet clear whether the focus on speciality chemicals will succeed. But ICI, following the shocks of the early 1980s, cannot be faulted for lack of boldness in tackling these problems.

Like the rest of British industry, ICI suffered from the fact that Britain was not a member of the EEC until 1973. Earlier exposure to Europe-wide competition might have forced ICI to act earlier to narrow its spread of products and to concentrate on businesses where it had a long-term competitive advantage. Excessive diversity made ICI hard to manage, and almost certainly caused it to miss some opportunities for building world-leading businesses.

In other respects Britain provided a relatively favourable global platform for this industry. Of the three institutions which have been discussed throughout this book, labour relations were not an important issue in the case of chemicals. Although ICI was affected to some extent by the general deterioration in British labour relations in the 1960s and 1970s, strikes were rare. This was partly due to ICI's sophisticated approach to personnel management, but it also reflected differences in the organisation of labour between continuous-flow process industries like chemicals and assembly-type industries like cars or shipbuilding. The problem of multiple unionism and demarcations between trades was much more severe in the latter (TABLE 12.5). ICI was not immune to the British disease of over-manning – correcting this weakness was part of the adjustment that the company went through in the 1980s – but the labour relations system was not a serious competitive handicap for ICI.

TABLE 12.5 *The incidence of strikes in chemicals and other industries*

(average number of working days lost in each year per 1000 employees through industrial disputes)

	Chemicals	Motor vehicles	All industries and services
1970s	240	4183	472
1980s	127	1397	334

Source: Melanie Lansbury, 'UK Manufacturing Employment since Beveridge: The Chemical and Motor Vehicle Industries', National Institute of Economic and Social Research, Discussion Paper no. 83, August 1995, p. 26.

The training and education system has served the chemical industry well. This is an industry that relies heavily on graduate scientists and engineers, a resource with which Britain has been well endowed. Relations between the industry, the universities and the professional engineering institutions have been close and constructive, especially in the field of chemical engineering, and there have been no serious shortages of qualified personnel. While the German chemical industry derived a competitive advantage from its well-organised higher education system before 1914, and to a lesser extent in the inter-war years, this did not apply to the post-war period. In the 1980s and 1990s, according to a recent study of the chemical industry, Germany's higher education system has 'dramatically declined' in relation to the British one.[51] At the shop floor level, craft skills play a smaller role in chemical manufacture than, say, in machine tools; deficiencies in the British apprenticeship system have not impinged greatly on the chemical industry.

There is no evidence that ICI was held back, before or after 1979, by lack of access to finance.[52] As for the role of shareholders, it is arguable that one of the reasons why ICI was slow to 'de-diversify' between the 1950s and the 1970s was the failure of investors to press for higher returns.[53] But there was not much difference in this respect between Britain and the US; this was the era of managerial capitalism, in which managers rather than investors called the tune. After 1980 the stock market played a larger role in ICI's affairs. The power of institutional investors increased, and companies came under greater pressure to maximise shareholder value. A new generation of corporate predators came on the scene, and even the largest companies were not immune to the threat of take-over. On balance these developments were good for British industry, since they forced companies to allocate resources to activities which yielded the highest return. In the case of ICI, capital market pressures in the 1980s and 1990s stimulated desirable changes in strategy and organisation.

————•◦•————

THIRTEEN

Pharmaceuticals: A Winning Formula

I f Britain was a good global platform for the chemical industry, it was an even better one for pharmaceuticals. Britain is one of the leading exporters of pharmaceuticals, and a high proportion of the world's best-selling drugs have been developed in British laboratories. Some credit for this achievement is due to foreign drug manufacturers which built factories and laboratories in Britain after the Second World War, but British-owned firms have also played a prominent role. At the end of the 1990s three British or partly British companies – Glaxo Wellcome, AstraZeneca and SmithKline Beecham – ranked among the largest pharmaceutical companies in the world. Why have British firms done so well in this field, but not in other science-based industries, such as computers and semiconductors? Is pharmaceuticals a special case, or can wider lessons be drawn from it about the impact of institutions and policies on industrial performance?

The World Pharmaceutical Industry before 1939

The origins of the pharmaceutical industry can be traced to the seventeenth century when pharmacy emerged as a distinct branch of medicine. The apothecaries, members of a well-respected trade that descended from the pepperers and spicers of the early Middle Ages, made up and dispensed a variety of medicines, mostly derived from vegetable sources. Advances in chemistry during the eighteenth century made it possible to identify more precisely substances that had therapeutic value, and there was a gradual improvement in extraction and purification techniques.

In the 1820s French scientists isolated a group of biologically active compounds known as alkaloids; they included quinine, widely used as an anti-malarial medicine. Some of the apothecaries' shops, such as Allen & Hanburys in Britain and Merck in Germany, turned themselves into manufacturing chemists, supplying a range of medicines, often under their own brand name, to wholesalers and retailers.[1] The more progressive of these firms built small laboratories for testing and quality control. In Britain, for example, May & Baker, a partnership formed in 1840, won a considerable reputation for the quality of its products, winning the Prize Medal at the Great Exhibition in 1851 for its acids, metallic salts and other pharmaceutical preparations.[2]

In the US the first school of pharmacy was established in Philadelphia in 1821, and this city became, with New York, one of the two main centres of American pharmaceutical production.[3] Smith Kline & French was one of several Philadelphia-based firms that were founded in the first half of the nineteenth century and now rank among the world leaders in the field. There was also a substantial German influence on the US pharmaceutical industry, arising partly from the emigration of German doctors and pharmacists, many of whom settled in New York, and partly from the establishment of American subsidiaries by German drug manufacturers. Merck began exporting to the US in the 1850s and set up a manufacturing operation at Rahway in New Jersey in 1899.

Most of these firms were small and family-owned, and their technical capabilities were limited by the state of ignorance about the causes of illness. In the closing decades of the nineteenth century two crucial advances were made in France and Germany. First, Louis Pasteur showed how harmful micro-organisms in animals and humans could be destroyed by injecting into the body an attenuated version of the same bacteria that were causing the disease. Although this approach had been found to be effective many years earlier in the treatment of smallpox, Pasteur's work on immunology extended the use of vaccines as a cure for infectious diseases. Second, a group of German scientists, working closely with the country's leading chemical manufacturers, invented a new way of making drugs. This was based on the same technique – synthetic organic chemistry – that had been used to make dyestuffs. Work in this field began in the 1870s and led to a number of major innovations, including Bayer's Aspirin in 1899 and Hoechst's Salvarsan, an anti-syphilitic drug, in 1909. Hoechst, Bayer and other dyestuffs makers were new entrants to the pharmaceutical industry, competing against the older manufacturers such as Merck and Schering.

The German example was soon followed by the Swiss dyestuffs manufacturers – Ciba, Geigy and Sandoz – and they were later joined by Roche. In Britain and the US, where synthetic dyestuffs production had not yet been established on a significant scale, the response was slower. The pharmaceutical industry in these two countries was made up of older firms which had entered the business by the traditional apothecary/manufacturing chemist route. They were aware of the discoveries that had been made in Germany, but were content for the most part to import the new drugs rather than set up in competition with the German manufacturers. A few American firms began to recruit larger teams of medical scientists, including bacteriologists, but their skills were used primarily for quality control, not for scientific research.[4]

In Britain the company that came nearest to the German model of organised research and new product development was Burroughs Wellcome. This firm was founded in 1894 by two Americans, Henry Wellcome and Silas Burroughs, both of whom had been trained at the Philadelphia School of Pharmacy. They came to Britain as sales agents for American pharmaceutical firms, but decided to set up their own company to manufacture the vaccines and antitoxins which had been developed in Germany and France. A large, well-funded laboratory was built for this purpose. Henry Wellcome, who became a British citizen, took a personal interest in recruiting scientific staff and in directing their research programmes.[5] Most of the other British firms, including Allen & Hanburys and May & Baker, were still managed on traditional lines.

The First World War was a turning-point for the American and British pharmaceutical industries. The cut-off in supplies of drugs from Germany made governments in both countries aware of the need to build up domestic capabilities. In the US several companies increased their expenditure on research and development to produce substitutes for the drugs which had previously been imported. At first they had to find a way round the German patents, but at the end of the war the Federal government seized all German-owned properties, including the patents of the German pharmaceutical companies. The subsequent sale of these assets to American companies gave a stimulus to the domestic pharmaceutical industry. In the case of Merck, the head of the American subsidiary, George Merck, voluntarily handed over control of the company to the Alien Property Custodian. After the war the company was sold to private investors, but George Merck retained a 20 per cent stake and continued as chairman.

In the inter-war years new laboratories were built, and several American firms, working closely with academic scientists, were involved in major drug discoveries. Eli Lilly, for example, was the first to take up production of insulin, discovered by scientists at the University of Toronto in 1921. Although direct links with Germany had been broken, the German influence on the industry was still strong. Merck, one of the most research-conscious American firms, built an Institute of Therapeutic Research at Rahway in 1933, partly to accommodate Dr Hans Molitor, who had been professor of pharmacology at the University of Vienna. Another company with a German background was Pfizer, a leader in fermentation chemistry; it was active in the production of vitamins, which had been identified before the war as 'accessory food factors', essential to a healthy diet. The rise of fascism prompted a number of German scientists to emigrate to the US and join American pharmaceutical companies.[6]

Unlike their German counterparts, the big American chemical companies such as Du Pont, Monsanto and Dow played virtually no role in the development of the pharmaceutical industry. Apart from Du Pont, they were not much involved in dyestuffs and did not have the skills that would have enabled them to follow the German route into pharmaceuticals. The industry consisted almost entirely of traditional firms, whether of American origin, like Smith Kline and Eli Lilly, or German, like Merck and Pfizer. They were small companies, with no more than a few hundred employees each, and their strength lay in creating medicines out of natural substances, not in synthetic organic chemistry, which remained a German and Swiss speciality.

The British pharmaceutical industry also made progress in the 1920s and 1930s. During the First World War several firms were involved in import substitution programmes, learning how to make Salvarsan and other German drugs. From 1921, when the Safeguarding of Industries Act was passed, the British pharmaceutical industry was partially protected against German competition, and this gave the manufacturers greater confidence to spend money on development. Burroughs Wellcome and May & Baker were the most research-conscious firms (the latter formed a link with a French pharmaceutical manufacturer, Poulenc Frères, and in 1927 the French company, later part of Rhône-Poulenc, acquired majority control). Sir Henry Wellcome died in 1936, and ownership of the company, now called the Wellcome Foundation, was transferred to a charitable trust. Allen & Hanburys, the oldest of the British manufacturers, slipped back during this period. Despite some success with insulin, most of its business, which included dried milk, surgical instruments and a variety of other lines, was far removed from the new world of science-based pharmaceuticals which was beginning to dawn; old-fashioned family management was partly to blame.[7]

More surprising was the failure of Imperial Chemical Industries to make more impact in pharmaceuticals. Part of the purpose of the merger which created ICI in 1926 was to strengthen the British dyestuffs industry, and this was the logical route through which ICI might have developed a pharmaceutical business. But research in this field had a low priority for ICI's senior managers before the Second World War; they were preoccupied with problems in other parts of the group, principally the ammonia project at Billingham.[8]

Two other companies which were to play an important part in the development of the industry after 1945 took a closer interest in pharmaceuticals during this period. One was an old-established manufacturer of proprietary medicines, Beecham's Pills, founded in 1842 by Thomas Beecham, grandfather of the famous conductor. This company established a strong brand name for its products and in 1926 launched an aspirin-based cold remedy, Beechams Powders, which became one of the most successful analgesics. In the following year the family shareholdings were acquired by Philip Hill, a leading City financier, who set about enlarging the business by acquisition. One of the acquired companies was Macleans, which, in addition to its well-known brand of toothpaste, had a development laboratory run by a gifted analytical chemist, Walter McGeorge. A rising manager in Macleans was H. G. Lazell, who had joined the company as an accountant and was appointed company secretary of the Beecham group after the acquisition; he returned to Macleans as managing director in 1940. Lazell and McGeorge saw that if Beecham was to compete effectively against the big American companies in proprietary medicines, it would need to devote more resources to research. This view won the support of Philip Hill; he had become interested in scientific medicine through his friendship with Professor E. C. Dodds, a distinguished scientist who became a consultant to the company. In 1942 Hill approved Lazell's proposal for a central laboratory to serve all the companies in the group; one of the areas to be given special attention was biological and bacteriological research. Although the company's main interest at this stage was in over-the-counter medicines, Beecham was beginning to acquire the capabilities needed to compete in the pharmaceutical industry.[9]

The other new entrant was a New Zealand-based firm, Joseph Nathan. Founded in 1873 as a trader in agricultural products, this company had diversified into dried milk, sold under the Glaxo name and advertised as 'the food that builds bonnie babies'. The company was concerned about the quality of the milk powder coming from New Zealand, and in 1919 appointed Harry Jephcott, a young man with chemical and pharmaceutical qualifications, to sort the problem out. Under Jephcott's influence the company took a closer interest in the science of nutrition. In 1924 the Glaxo department of which Jephcott was general manager launched a Vitamin D product called Ostelin, and over the next decade more resources were devoted to research into vitamins and related areas. In 1935 Glaxo Laboratories was set up as a separate subsidiary, and its policy was 'to market proprietary pharmaceutical products having a reasonable claim to novelty'.[10]

By the Second World War the British pharmaceutical industry was in a better state than it had been before 1914, and more committed to research. But the strongest force in the world market continued to be Germany, and it was in the Elberfeld laboratories of Bayer that the next major advance in chemotherapy took place. During the First World War Gerhard Domagk, head of the company's Institute for Experimental Pathology and Bacteriology, had seen at first hand the disastrous effect of gangrene and other infections on wounded soldiers. After experimenting with a variety of dyes, he found that azo dyestuffs containing sulfonamide were effective against bacteria. The new drug, launched by Bayer in 1935 under the trade name Prontosil, opened up a new line of attack in the battle against infectious diseases. It was the first of the sulfa drugs, several variants of which were introduced over the subsequent twenty years. Although German companies took the lead, research was quickly taken up in other countries, including Britain. In 1937 a team of researchers at May & Baker, working with pathologists at Middlesex Hospital, synthesised over six hundred derivatives of sulfonamide before finding a compound, known as M&B 693, that was effective against pneumonia; it was also widely used during the Second World War to prevent wounds becoming gangrenous.[11]

Bayer's Prontosil was an example of well-organised scientific research applied to the solution of a clearly defined problem. The invention of penicillin, by contrast, came about by accident, and its full importance was not recognised for more than a decade after the original discovery had been made. In 1928 Alexander Fleming, Professor of Bacteriology at London University, was experimenting at St Mary's Hospital with fungus cultures. He found that the growth of bacteria called staphylococci had been stopped by a mould, later classified as *Penicillium*, or penicillin, which had settled on the culture. However, Fleming was unable to isolate penicillin or to determine its chemical structure. Little further work was done until 1939, when Howard Florey at Oxford University, assisted by Ernst Chain, Norman Heatley and others, found a way of producing penicillin in stable form and demonstrating its effectiveness in clinical experiments.

The discovery of penicillin, together with the sulfa drugs, had enormous implications for public health and for the commercial future of the pharmaceutical industry. Governments, scientists and entrepreneurs recognised that new opportunities for pharmaceutical research had been created, opening up the possibility of treating illnesses that had previously been regarded as incurable. A therapeutic revolution was under way, leading to a period of unprecedented growth and prosperity for pharmaceutical manufacturers.

1939–60: The Therapeutic Revolution

At the end of the 1930s, despite the progress that had been made since the First World War, Britain was still dependent for supplies of some essential drugs on imports from Germany. The outbreak of war prompted an urgent programme of import substitution, with the highest priority being given to medicines that were likely to be needed by the armed forces. Several companies, including ICI, May & Baker and Boots, worked on making substitutes for the anti-malarial drugs that the Germans had developed before the war.[12] ICI later introduced a superior anti-malarial of its own, Paludrine, which was widely used in the Far East towards the end of the war. To make better use of the industry's research and development facilities a co-operative organisation, the Therapeutic Research Corporation, was formed in 1941; the founder members were Wellcome, Glaxo, May & Baker, Boots and British Drug Houses.[13] One of its aims was to identify promising new drugs and to allocate development work to the firms best qualified to carry it out. An early target, following the successful clinical trials conducted by Florey and his team, was penicillin, and ICI was brought in as a collaborator on this programme.

At this stage the only way of producing penicillin was by scaling up the laboratory methods that had been used by Florey and his colleagues. Penicillin mould was grown by surface culture in vessels such as milk churns and glass bottles. This process had some similarities to the manufacture of processed cheese and dairy products, a field in which Glaxo had experience. Jephcott was eager to start penicillin production as soon as possible, and a small plant was opened in 1942, in a disused cheese factory at Aylesbury; Wellcome later came in as a partner, sharing the cost of the Aylesbury plant.[14] In the meantime strenuous efforts were under way in the US to find a way of producing penicillin on a larger scale.

American involvement in penicillin had begun in 1941 when Florey visited the US and described the new drug to the research directors of major pharmaceutical companies. In view of the urgent need to speed up production, the British government agreed that the technology should be made freely available to the Americans, and a large development programme was set in train. Co-ordinated by the Office for Scientific Research and Development, this work involved government laboratories as well as most of the leading pharmaceutical manufacturers, and the outcome was a new manufacturing process, based on deep fermentation, which was more economic than the surface culture methods used in Britain. The crucial breakthrough was made by Pfizer, whose earlier experience in fermentation chemistry was relevant to the penicillin problem. Other American firms, including Merck and Squibb, made important contributions to the penicillin programme.[15]

The American pharmaceutical industry was larger than its British counterpart, and had the resources to devote attention during the war not only to penicillin, but to the quest for other antibiotics that might have even greater therapeutic value. One promising line of research, led by Dr Selman Waksman at Rutgers University, focused on the anti-bacterial properties of micro-organisms in the soil. Merck was closely associated with this work, which led in 1943 to the discovery of the first of the broad-spectrum antibiotics, streptomycin; it was patented by Merck in 1948. In an important ruling the US Patent Office decided that chemical modifications of natural substances which had therapeutic properties could be patentable. In the case of streptomycin, Merck chose to hand over the patent to the Rutgers Research Foundation, which licensed the drug widely to other manufacturers in the US and overseas.

Over the next few years three more broad-spectrum antibiotics were introduced in the US – Aureomycin from Lederle, Chloromycetin from Parke Davis, Terramycin from Pfizer. These companies, once they had patented the drugs, decided not to license them to other manufacturers, but to retain a monopoly over their production. By keeping responsibility for manufacturing and marketing in their own hands, they could control the price at which the drugs were sold and thus maximise their profits for as long as the patent lasted.[16] By the mid-1950s the American pharmaceutical industry had acquired a structure that continued without much change until the 1980s – a group of about twenty research-based companies which had integrated the three main stages in the pharmaceutical 'value chain' – research and development, production, and marketing. Although some of these companies made over-the-counter medicines, the largest and most profitable part of their business was in prescription drugs, protected by patents and trade names. Since the decision on what drugs should be prescribed lay with doctors, the industry's marketing effort was directed not to the general public, but to the medical profession.

The success of the American companies in the new field of antibiotics shifted the balance of power in the world pharmaceutical industry away from Europe to the US. Although work on sulfa drugs was resumed in Germany and Switzerland after the war and some new discoveries were made, they were less effective than antibiotics. The American tradition of developing drugs through the chemical modification of natural substances proved to be more fruitful during this period than synthetic organic chemistry, and the US became the leading drug exporter (TABLE 13.1).

TABLE 13.1 *World exports of drugs, 1938–63:*
shares of leading countries

(per cent)

	1938	1955	1963
Germany	39	10	15
US	13	34	25
Britain	12	16	14
France	12	12	9
Switzerland	7	14	14
Others	17	14	23

Source: M. H. Cooper, *Prices and Profits in the Pharmaceutical Industry*, Pergamon 1966, p. 249.

The competitive situation of the British pharmaceutical industry had also been greatly improved as a result of penicillin and the developments which flowed from it. There was some resentment after the war about the extent to which the Americans had benefited more than the British from the pioneering work on penicillin by British scientists. But British drug manufacturers had also acquired new skills which would enable them, if not to lead the therapeutic revolution, at least to follow very closely behind the Americans. Although the Therapeutic Research Corporation was wound up after the war, the experience of working together had made member firms more aware of the importance of well-directed research and of the scope for profitable collaboration with academic scientists.

The quickest off the mark was Glaxo. Jephcott was determined to build on the company's wartime achievements in penicillin and in 1945 he obtained licences from the US for the deep fermentation process; two years later he reached agreement with Merck for the manufacture of streptomycin in Britain. At the end of the war Glaxo was still a subsidiary of Joseph Nathan, but it was now clear that the future of the company lay in pharmaceuticals and this was confirmed in the reorganisation that took place in 1947.[17] Joseph Nathan was placed in voluntary liquidation, and the name of the company was changed to Glaxo Laboratories. Jephcott's strategy was to expand from penicillin into other antibiotics, to look for new drugs which fell within Glaxo's skills and experience, and to build up the vitamins business. By the end of the 1950s Glaxo's range included cortisone products and vaccines as well as antibiotics. Most of these activities drew on research carried out by other companies, principally in the US, or by government research laboratories in Britain. Jephcott saw Glaxo primarily as a development organisation, not as an originator of novel drugs, and he was sceptical about the value of research which did not promise an early pay-off.

ICI was tentative in its approach to pharmaceuticals after the war, perhaps because so many other parts of the group, including petrochemicals and plastics, were clamouring for attention. Despite its wartime success with anti-malarial medicines, this field was regarded as too crowded to justify further investment. Antibiotics looked more promising, but ICI made the mistake of trying to develop its own manufacturing process instead of going to the US for deep fermentation technology, as Glaxo had done. As the price of penicillin fell after the war, ICI was unable to compete. Some consideration was given to acquiring an established pharmaceutical company, but none of the approaches which were made bore fruit; the pharmaceuticals business remained a somewhat neglected offshoot of the Dyestuffs Division.[18] The turning-point was the discovery in the early 1950s that fluorocarbon chemicals had anaesthetic properties. Collaboration between scientists in the General Chemicals Division, where these chemicals were made, and the Dyestuffs Division led to the synthesis of halothane, marketed by ICI as Fluothane, which became one of the most widely used anaesthetics.[19] In 1957 a separate pharmaceutical division was established and new laboratories were built at Alderley Park in Cheshire. In the following year James Black was recruited from Glasgow University to head a research programme into cardiovascular disease, and out of this work came the world's first beta-blockers, the mainstay of ICI's pharmaceutical business in the 1960s and 1970s.

Of the old-established British pharmaceutical companies, Wellcome had gone through a lean period after the death of the founder, but the business was revived in the 1950s under the chairmanship of Michael Perrin, a former ICI research chemist; he had been involved in the discovery of polythene and had played a leading part in the wartime atomic weapons programme. New products introduced by Wellcome during this period included the British version of the Salk polio vaccine. Allen & Hanburys also staged a revival after the war. Cyril Maplethorpe, a research chemist who was appointed managing director in 1944, steered what had been a technically conservative, family-controlled company into new therapeutic areas, including antibiotics and anti-depressants, and stepped up spending on research.[20]

Beecham went through a period of drift after the death of Philip Hill in 1944, but the appointment of Lazell as managing director in 1949 brought a clearer sense of direction to the group and a stronger focus on pharmaceuticals. A new research laboratory had been set up after the war at Brockham Park, near London, with Professor Dodds as chief consultant. At Dodds' suggestion, Professor Ernst Chain was brought in as a consultant to work on new variants of penicillin. Out of this research came the discovery, in 1957, of the first semi-synthetic penicillin, which greatly extended the range of penicillin therapy and helped to make Beecham one of Britain's leading pharmaceutical companies.

The market conditions in which these companies were operating were similar in most respects to those faced by their American counterparts. There was the same emphasis on patentable drugs as a source of temporary monopolies, and the same distinction between prescription and over-the-counter drugs. As the flow of innovative drugs increased, new procedures were introduced in both countries to monitor safety. But there was one important difference. In Britain, following the creation of the National Health Service in 1948, the ultimate paymaster for the bulk of the industry's sales was the government. In order to keep the cost to the taxpayer within reasonable bounds, a system had to be devised to monitor the prices which the manufacturers charged to the NHS. Piecemeal attempts to control prices in the early years of the Health Service were followed by the introduction in 1957 of the Voluntary Price Regulation Scheme (VPRS). This was a non-statutory arrangement aimed at securing 'fair and reasonable' prices. Maximum prices were determined by using one of three formulas, the most important of which related the domestic price to prevailing export prices for the same drug. There was also a three-year freedom period for new drugs so that research and development costs could be recouped.[21] Although the scheme was subsequently modified, and there were several clashes between the government and individual manufacturers during the 1960s, two of the principles underlying the VPRS – flexibility and voluntary compliance – proved durable.

'Socialised medicine', as the Americans called it, did nothing to diminish the attractiveness of Britain as a market for American drug manufacturers. The 1940s and 1950s saw a considerable inflow of overseas capital into the British pharmaceutical industry, principally from US and Swiss companies. They came to Britain partly to participate in a large, government-supported market, but also to gain access to a pool of scientific talent. The quality of British academic science in chemistry and biology was outstanding, and salary costs were low by American standards. Several US companies, including Pfizer and Smith Kline & French, used their British laboratories as an important source of innovative drugs, which were often introduced earlier in Britain than in the US. The NHS did not discriminate in its purchasing policy in favour of British-owned firms, and by the early 1960s more than half the British market was supplied by non-British companies. Of the top twenty suppliers to the NHS in 1962 only four – Glaxo, Beecham, Allen & Hanburys and Wellcome – were British-owned. Twelve of the remaining sixteen were US-owned, three Swiss-owned (Ciba, Geigy and Roche) and one French-owned (May & Baker).[22]

The foreign invasion provoked some anxiety in the industry that British firms might be squeezed out of the market by companies which had larger technical and financial resources. Glaxo carried out a study in 1957 which underlined the size of the gap in sales, profits and research expenditure with the leading American firms. Jephcott's conclusion was that 'having regard to the weight of certain US companies in men and money, it was only a matter of time before the British firms were swamped out of existence, the smaller going to the wall first'.[23] Maplethorpe at Allen & Hanburys shared this view, and the two companies were merged in 1958; two years later Jephcott added a smaller company, Evans Medical, to the Glaxo group.

Yet despite Jephcott's fears, this was not an industry where large size was necessary for success. A company's ability to produce innovative drugs depended on the quality rather than the quantity of its scientific effort. The leading American firms were bigger than their British counterparts because of the size of their home market, but that did not make their research more productive. Smaller firms could compete profitably by concentrating on one or two of the therapeutic categories into which the pharmaceutical market was divided. No single drug could cure all diseases, and a company which held a dominant position in, say, antibiotics was not necessarily better equipped to compete in heart drugs. A company might secure a temporary monopoly in one therapeutic category, but it could not do so across the market as a whole.[24]

At the end of the 1950s, when the therapeutic revolution was running strongly, the leading British firms were in no imminent danger of being 'swamped out of existence'. Indeed the presence of leading international companies in the British market proved to be a stimulus rather than a threat. British-owned firms were forced to compete against the world's best and to match their skills in development and in marketing. This openness to foreign investment was one of the factors which underpinned the continuing strength of the British pharmaceutical industry in the 1960s and 1970s.

1960–1980: Consolidation

The distinctive characteristics which the pharmaceutical industry acquired in the first fifteen years after the war continued with no fundamental change into the 1960s and 1970s. Until the appearance of genetic engineering towards the end of this period, there was no technological breakthrough which might have drastically altered the structure of the industry. The market continued to expand, but as the easier targets were picked off and the flow of wonder drugs slowed down, an increasing proportion of the industry's research effort was devoted to alleviating the symptoms of diseases for which there was no known cure. The testing of drugs for their safety and efficacy became more complex and more time-consuming, and there was greater concern about side-effects, especially after the thalidomide tragedy of the early 1960s. Thalidomide, a tranquilliser developed in Germany and marketed in Britain by the Distillers Company, had passed all the required clinical tests, but was found to cause deformities in babies born to mothers who had been prescribed the drug during their pregnancies. More onerous safety regulations lengthened the period between the discovery of a drug and its commercial launch – in Britain from an average of three years in the early 1960s to ten years or more by the 1980s.[25] In these conditions it was harder for new entrants to break into the market, but the firms which had established themselves in the early post-war years generally held their position.[26]

American companies continued to be the most prolific source of innovative drugs, with the competition coming principally from Germany, Switzerland, Britain and France. Japan was a late-comer in research-based pharmaceuticals, and, although several Japanese companies ranked among the top fifty in 1980, their activities were largely confined to their home market.[27] Italy, too, was a laggard in this field, mainly because of the absence of effective patent protection. Competitive success in pharmaceuticals depended on a domestic environment which encouraged firms to invest in costly research and development programmes and rewarded them when those programmes bore fruit. Apart from the patent laws, the two areas of most concern to governments were the monitoring of safety and – in countries such as Britain where health care was funded wholly or partly by the taxpayer – the control of prices.

The British approach to drug safety was based on co-operation between the government, the medical profession and the manufacturers.[28] Following the thalidomide tragedy the Standing Committee on Health, chaired by Lord Cohen, was asked in 1962 by the government to review the safety issue. This led to the creation of the Committee on the Safety of Drugs, staffed by academic experts and charged with the task of advising on the toxicity of new drugs, on clinical testing and efficacy, and on side-effects. The industry, through its trade association, agreed that no new drug would be introduced without the Committee's approval. This voluntary arrangement, operated in a flexible, non-bureaucratic manner, proved to be an effective means, not only of weeding out potentially unsafe drugs, but also of ensuring that new drugs which passed the tests had genuine therapeutic value. Although the Committee was later placed on a statutory basis, the essential feature of the original scheme – a joint commitment by the industry, the medical profession and academic scientists to the highest standards of safety and efficacy – was retained. It was a stringent regime which discriminated against drugs that were little more than imitations of medicines already available. The manufacturers were encouraged to focus their research on products which, because of their therapeutic novelty, were likely to win orders from overseas as well as Britain. Indirectly, therefore, the safety regulations helped to upgrade the industry's innovative capabilities and its export performance.[29]

The pricing issue was more contentious, but here, too, successive British governments preferred to rely on co-operation rather than compulsion. The Voluntary Price Regulation Scheme came under strain at the end of the 1950s as the size of the NHS drug bill increased, and in 1961 Enoch Powell, Minister of Health in the Conservative government, sent a warning shot across the industry's bows by invoking Section 49 of the Patents Act; this enabled the NHS to import cheaper, unbranded versions of some widely used drugs, principally the broad-spectrum antibiotics. But neither this episode nor the subsequent confrontation with the Swiss company Roche over the price of its Valium and Librium tranquillizers undermined the principle that the prices of innovative drugs had to be set at a level which gave an incentive to manufacturers to spend money on research. This principle was supported in 1967 by a committee of inquiry (the Sainsbury committee) which had been set up by the Labour government to investigate the industry's pricing practices.[30] One of the committee's conclusions was that 'in the absence of the prospect of "abnormal" profits, private industry would have no special inducement to undertake research to which attached an abnormal risk of failure'. Some changes were made as a result of the Sainsbury report, with a shift away from the export criterion to an assessment of the supplier's aggregate profits on its sales to the NHS. This took into account the amount of investment which the company carried out in Britain, including its investment in research.

Thus the pharmaceutical industry benefited from a generally supportive relationship with the government during the 1960s and 1970s. Perhaps because the industry's sponsor in government was the Ministry of Health rather than the Ministry of Industry, there was no attempt to create a national champion, or to protect British companies from foreign competition. The government maintained a stable but demanding regulatory framework within which the drug manufacturers could profit from an expanding domestic demand for their products and build up their export business. At a time when many other British industries were losing ground to their overseas competitors, the pharmaceutical industry increased its share of world exports. In 1980 Britain's trade surplus in pharmaceuticals was one of the largest among the leading exporting nations (TABLE 13.2).

A substantial proportion of the industry's exports, perhaps as much as half, came from foreign-owned companies operating in Britain, but the leading British-owned firms were also making good progress. Glaxo, which had built its pharmaceutical business primarily through licences acquired from other companies, began to make the transition towards an innovation-based strategy. The change came about through two unconnected events – the replacement of Jephcott by Alan Wilson as chairman of Glaxo in 1963 and the appointment of David Jack as research director at Allen & Hanburys. Wilson, a distinguished scientist who had come to Glaxo from Courtaulds, took a different view from Jephcott about the value of speculative, long-term

TABLE 13.2 *World trade in pharmaceuticals in 1980*

(figures in millions of DM)

	Exports	Imports	Balance
Germany	4,128	2,345	1,783
France	2,720	1,273	1,447
Italy	1,249	1,186	63
Japan	536	1,952	−1,416
Britain	3,150	939	2,211
US	3,699	1,459	2,240
Switzerland	2,935	747	2,188

Source: UN world trade statistics, quoted in Robert Chew et al., *Pharmaceuticals in Seven Nations*, Office of Health Economics, London, 1985.

research. Although he was not involved in the details of the research programme (his scientific background had been in physics), he gave Glaxo's
scientists their head and presided over a gradual increase in the research
budget.[31] These funds were shared between the Glaxo laboratory at Greenford
and the Allen & Hanburys laboratory at Ware, and it was the latter, under
the leadership of David Jack, which was largely responsible for lifting Glaxo
into the front rank of the world pharmaceutical industry.

After studying pharmacy and pharmacology at Glasgow University in
the 1950s, David Jack had worked briefly for Glaxo, then for Smith Kline &
French, the American company which had a substantial research operation
in Britain. When he joined Allen & Hanburys in 1961, not long after the
merger with Glaxo, he insisted that his team at Ware should be managed
independently, operating in areas which did not duplicate Greenford's work
in antibiotics, vaccines and corticosteroids. Jack believed that an original
contribution could be made by finding ways of manipulating the physiological 'mediators' (including nerve transmitters and hormones) which control
the functions of the body.[32] An early target was the respiratory system, and
in 1966 Jack's team discovered salbutamol (launched three years later as
Ventolin), a more effective treatment for bronchial asthma than any drug
then on the market. This drug, according to the company's historian,

'changed everything – the commercial standing of Allen and Hanburys, the future of drug research at Ware, and, not least, Jack's understanding of how to look for drugs'.[33] Meanwhile the Greenford laboratory was making progress in its chosen fields, launching Ceporin, an injectable antibiotic, in 1964 and Ceporex, an oral version, in 1970. Research into corticosteroids led in 1964 to the launch of Betnovate, a widely used treatment for skin disorders.

The other leading British manufacturers also moved forward during the 1960s – ICI in heart drugs, Wellcome in anti-viral medicines, Beecham in antibiotics. But there was still some concern in the industry and among outside observers about whether these companies were big enough to compete on the world stage. The development of new drugs was becoming more expensive, and these costs could only be recouped by higher sales outside Britain. Competition was increasingly international, and, compared to the world leaders, the British firms looked puny (TABLE 13.3).

TABLE 13.3 *World's leading pharmaceutical companies in 1970*

Rank	Company	Nationality	Sales ($m)
1	Roche	Switzerland	840
2	Merck	US	670
3	Hoechst	Germany	497
4	Ciba-Geigy	Switzerland	492
5	American Home Products	US	479
6	Lilly	US	421
7	Sterling	US	418
8	Pfizer	US	416
9	Warner Lambert	US	408
10	Sandoz	Switzerland	346
16	Glaxo	Britain	261
26	Wellcome	Britain	136
27	Beecham	Britain	132
37	ICI	Britain	67

Source: Monopolies Commission, A report on proposed mergers between Beecham and Glaxo, and between Boots and Glaxo, HC341, HMSO, July 1972.

This was the context in which Beecham announced an unsolicited take-over bid for Glaxo in 1971. Lazell had retired from the chairmanship of Beecham in 1968. His successor, Sir Ronald Edwards, was an economist with a special interest in industrial organisation; prior to joining Beecham he had been chairman of the Electricity Council. His appointment came about partly through the intervention of Kenneth Keith, who as chairman of Philip Hill (later Hill Samuel), was an influential member of the company's board. Lazell felt that after the company's rapid growth in the 1950s and 1960s a different style of management was needed; it would also be helpful, in Lazell's view, for the company 'to be led for a few years by a member of the Establishment'.[34]

Edwards believed that a merger between Beecham and Glaxo would facilitate a larger research programme and a stronger international marketing effort. Before Beecham's move there had been tentative discussions, in which the National Economic Development Office was involved, about the possibility of amalgamating the pharmaceutical interests of Beecham, Glaxo and ICI.[35] But Alan Wilson at Glaxo was firmly opposed to this idea, arguing that larger research organisations were unlikely to be more productive than small ones. Even within Glaxo, he pointed out, the Ware and Greenford laboratories had been kept separate, with beneficial results. He also suggested that Beecham was motivated in part by its own weakness; it was heavily dependent on a narrow range of antibiotics, some of which were nearing the end of their patent lives.

Wilson's fellow directors agreed with this view, and the Beecham proposal was vigorously resisted. But because of its consumer product businesses, Beecham was a bigger company than Glaxo and could afford to pay a generous price. Hence Wilson felt obliged to look for a more acceptable merger partner. In January 1972, an agreed merger was announced between Glaxo and Boots. This was presented as a 'true merger', since Boots' relatively small pharmaceutical interests were complementary to those of Glaxo and could easily be fitted into the Glaxo organisation, leaving the retail chemists' shops undisturbed. In view of the public controversy aroused by these manoeuvres, the government decided to refer both proposed mergers to the Monopolies Commission.

In a report which echoed many of Wilson's arguments the Commission decided that neither merger should be allowed to proceed.[36] The Commission pointed out that the number of research-based British firms was small; if that number was reduced by merger, the consequence might be to lessen the flow of ideas and thus reduce the competitiveness of the industry. What mattered, in the Commission's view, was innovative ability, not size. It was not impressed by Beecham's argument that British companies could only compete in world markets if they were as big as their American and German counterparts.

Glaxo's success in fighting off the Beecham bid enhanced the influence of Paul Girolami, the finance director, who had played an important role in organising the defence. Girolami, born in Italy but brought up in England, was a chartered accountant who had joined Glaxo as financial controller in 1965; he was promoted to finance director in 1968. In the reorganisation which followed the Beecham affair Girolami was a member of the head office team which set about integrating the group's disparate businesses and defining a clear strategy for pharmaceuticals. The strategy had two prongs, to speed up the introduction of innovative drugs, and to push more strongly into overseas markets, especially Continental Europe and the US.

Following the success of Ventolin, David Jack and his team looked for ways of applying the same research methodology to other therapeutic areas. Shortly before the Beecham bid they had begun work on anti-ulcerant drugs. Their thinking was influenced by a lecture given in 1973 by James Black, who after his success with beta-blockers at ICI was now working for Smith Kline & French.[37] In his lecture Black described how the acid secretion process which caused ulcers was linked to a physiological controller called histamine. The key to a successful treatment for ulcers lay in finding a way of inhibiting the body's reaction to histamine. Black later identified cimetidine as an effective histamine antagonist, and this was the generic name for Smith Kline & French's Tagamet, which became one of the world's best-selling drugs. Jack believed that there was room in the market for another drug which would be based on the same principle as Tagamet but use a different antagonist with fewer side-effects. A suitable compound was found, known as ranitidine, and clinical trials began in 1978; it was launched in 1981 as Zantac.[38]

While this work was going on, Glaxo was building a stronger marketing organisation in Europe, including the establishment of manufacturing plants in France and Germany. By the end of the 1970s Continental Europe had taken over from the Commonwealth as the principal outlet for the company's exports. The next target was the US, which had been regarded in the past as too big and difficult a market to attack directly. Like other British manufacturers, Glaxo had licensed its new drugs to US manufacturers, but Girolami and his colleagues recognised that without an operation of its own in the US Glaxo would remain a 'minor league' player, and vulnerable to another take-over attempt. In 1978 Glaxo bought Meyer Laboratories, a small, Florida-based pharmaceutical company. The name of the company was subsequently changed to Glaxo Inc, and a new headquarters, including laboratories for clinical testing, was established in North Carolina.

At the start of the 1980s Glaxo was the largest of a group of six British-owned pharmaceutical companies (TABLE 13.4). Of the other five, ICI had made the most progress during the 1960s and 1970s, mainly because of the success of its cardiovascular drugs. The pharmaceutical division was growing fast and beginning to command greater management attention in a company which had traditionally been dominated by heavy chemicals.

TABLE 13.4 *Leading British pharmaceutical manufacturers in 1982*

	Pharmaceutical sales ($m)	Pharmaceutical sales as per centage of total sales	World ranking
Glaxo	990	83.0	18
ICI	839	7.0	23
Wellcome	837	80.0	24
Beecham	782	31.3	25
Boots	399	16.0	42
Fisons	206	36.0	66

Source: M. L. Burstall and I. Senior, *The Community's Pharmaceutical Industry*, European Commission, 1985, p. 52.

The other British firms also had strengths in particular therapeutic areas, and if the logic of the Monopolies Commission report was correct, they were large enough to compete in the world market. The Commission's judgement appeared to be supported by the absence of merger activity in other countries. Ciba and Geigy got together in 1970, but these two Basle-based companies had been closely associated for many years, and their merger was not part of a general trend towards consolidation.

The 1980s and 1990s: The Restructuring of the Pharmaceutical Industry

In 1973 two American scientists, Herbert Boyer and Stanley Cohen, discovered recombinant DNA, whereby genes could be transferred from one organism to another in order to produce new substances with different properties. Together with a related technique for fusing and multiplying cells, which was discovered two years later, recombinant DNA opened up the possibility of genetically engineering micro-organisms, such as antibodies, that would have therapeutic value. It was a different approach to developing new drugs from the methods on which the pharmaceutical industry had relied since the 1930s – the screening of naturally occurring substances, as with penicillin, or chemical synthesis, as with the sulfa drugs.[39]

To commercialise these discoveries some American scientists set up their own companies, retaining close links with the university departments that were continuing to work on the basic science.[40] The first of the new breed was Genentech, of which Herbert Boyer was a co-founder, and in 1982 this firm launched the first genetically engineered drug, human insulin, for the treatment of diabetes. In the late 1970s and early 1980s a host of other scientist-entrepreneurs, mostly American, followed Boyer's example, and it was widely predicted that biotechnology firms would rapidly enlarge their share of the pharmaceutical market. The assumption at that time was that successful biotechnology firms would become fully fledged pharmaceutical manufacturers, responsible not just for research and development, but also for clinical testing, production and marketing. The incumbent pharmaceutical firms would be at a competitive disadvantage because they lacked the bio-engineering skills which were necessary to exploit the new technology.

However, the flow of genetically engineered drugs was slower than expected, and when a promising discovery was made the task of developing and testing the new compound to the point where it could be launched on the market was often beyond the resources of the small biotechnology firm. A division of labour began to emerge between the newcomers and the established pharmaceutical companies, with the former concentrating mainly on research and the latter taking responsibility for development, production and marketing. This was not a uniform pattern; some of the new firms, such as Amgen in the US, did turn themselves into integrated pharmaceutical manufacturers. But the typical arrangement was for the established pharmaceutical company to form relationships, sometimes involving a shareholding link, with one or more of the biotechnology firms and to use them as a source of new products.[41] At the same time the pharmaceutical companies took steps to acquire the new biotechnology skills. They did so through a combination of in-house research, close links with academic science and co-operation with the biotechnology entrepreneurs.

The rise of biotechnology coincided with a period of structural change in the world chemical industry. As described in the last chapter, this involved a reorientation of strategy on the part of several large firms from commodities towards products with higher added value and higher profit margins; the pharmaceutical industry was seen as an attractive target for new investment. In the US Dow bought Richardson-Merrell, a medium-sized American pharmaceutical firm in 1981, and four years later G. D. Searle, another drug manufacturer in the same size bracket, was acquired by Monsanto.[42] Similar forces were at work in Europe, reflecting a growing consensus that the old-style chemical conglomerate, combining pharmaceuticals with a wide range of other products, had had its day. The demerger of Zeneca from ICI in 1993 was part of this process.

While this reshuffling of assets was taking place in the chemical industry, pressures for consolidation were at work within the pharmaceutical sector itself.[43] One factor, seen most clearly in the case of Smith Kline's Tagamet, was that some companies had become over-dependent on a single, best-selling drug; unless they could develop equally successful follow-on drugs, they faced the prospect of a profits collapse when the patent expired. In the mid-1980s Tagamet accounted for 40 per cent of Smith Kline's profits, but it was coming under heavy attack from Glaxo's Zantac. Since the departure of James Black and William Duncan, the two men responsible for Tagamet's success, Smith Kline failed to recruit other scientists who might have maintained the creative momentum. At the end of the decade the pipeline of new drugs under development was looking dangerously thin, and a partnership with another company seemed the only solution.[44] In 1989 Smith Kline merged with Beecham, a company which, though never as dependent on a single drug as Smith Kline, had most of its eggs in the antibiotics basket.

Since the failed bid for Glaxo in 1972, Beecham had been diversifying without much success outside pharmaceuticals, and by the mid-1980s the company appeared to have lost its way. A boardroom upheaval in 1985 brought in an American chief executive, Robert Bauman, who concluded that Beecham should refocus on pharmaceuticals, but that the company, ranked twenty-third in the world league, was too small. Merger talks were held with ICI, which was seen as a compatible partner, but in view of the importance of the US market Bauman and his colleagues were attracted to the idea of a union of equals with an American company. The justification for the merger with Smith Kline was that neither company on its own could achieve the critical mass in research and development and in marketing that was necessary for success in an increasingly demanding industry.[45]

The Smith Kline/Beecham deal came at the start of a wave of mergers and acquisitions which transformed the structure of the world pharmaceutical industry over the subsequent decade (TABLE 13.5). While some of these transactions were prompted by the weakness of one or both of the merging partners, another factor was a tougher attitude on the part of the industry's paymasters – mainly governments and insurance companies – towards drug prices. The rising costs of health care prompted a series of moves, starting in the early 1990s, to limit the prescribing of expensive branded drugs and

TABLE 13.5 *Mergers and acquisitions in pharmaceuticals, 1989–99*

1989	Dow (US)/Marion (US)
	Bristol-Myers (US)/Squibb (US)
	SmithKline (US)/Beecham (Britain)
1990	Rhône-Poulenc (France)/Rorer (US)
	Roche (Switzerland)/Genentech (US)
1994	SmithKline Beecham (US/Britain)/Sterling Health (US)
	BASF (Germany)/Boots (Britain)
	American Home Products (US)/American Cyanamid (US)
	Elf Sanofi (France)/Sterling Drug (US)
	Roche (Switzerland)/Syntex (US)
1995	Glaxo (Britain)/Wellcome (Britain)
	Hoechst (Germany)/Marion Merrell Dow (US)
	Pharmacia (Sweden)/Upjohn (US)
	Rhône Poulenc (France)/Fisons (Britain)
1996	Ciba-Geigy (Switzerland)/Sandoz (Switzerland)
1997	Roche (Switzerland)/Boehringer Mannheim (Germany)
1999	Hoechst (Germany)/Rhône Poulenc (France)
	Astra (Sweden)/Zeneca (Britain)

to replace them wherever possible with cheaper generic alternatives. The high profit margins enjoyed by the pharmaceutical companies made them an easy target. Many pharmaceutical companies believed that mergers and acquisitions would generate savings in research, development and marketing, and enable them to live with lower prices.

Among the British-owned companies, Glaxo seemed in the 1980s to be immune to these pressures; it did not need to merge because it was doing extraordinarily well on its own. The anti-ulcerant Zantac, launched in 1981, proved to be one of the most successful drugs of all time, lifting Glaxo into second position in the world league, just behind Merck. That the drug was so successful was due as much to skilful marketing as to scientific prowess, and in this the contribution of Paul Girolami, who became chief executive in 1981, was crucial. Girolami decided, against the advice of most of his colleagues, that Zantac should be priced higher than Tagamet, and that its superior properties – it could be taken in fewer doses and had fewer side-effects – should be promoted aggressively as a major advance in the treatment of ulcers.[46] The key market was the US, and Girolami saw that more firepower was needed to support the sales organisation which had been built up after the acquisition of Meyer Laboratories; a co-marketing agreement for Zantac in the US was reached with Roche. The drug was launched in the US in 1983 and by 1987 it had taken 50 per cent of the anti-ulcerant market. Glaxo's total sales in the US, including Ventolin and other drugs, rose from $44m in 1983 to nearly $2bn at the end of the decade.

Girolami believed that Glaxo should concentrate exclusively on prescription medicines and that its growth should be based on original innovations coming out of in-house research and development. All the non-pharmaceutical businesses which had come into the group through earlier acquisitions were sold, and the profits earned from Zantac were ploughed back into research. In 1989 Zantac was the world's top-selling drug, with worldwide sales of $2.2bn, and another Glaxo drug, the anti-asthmatic Ventolin, was in the top twenty, with sales of $500m. But the pace of Zantac's growth was slowing, and it was facing competition from a new anti-ulcerant, Losec, developed by the Swedish company Astra and marketed in the US by Merck. The Zantac patents were due to run out in 1997. To avoid the trap that Smith Kline had fallen into with Tagamet, Glaxo needed top-selling drugs in other therapeutic categories.

Girolami's strong preference was to achieve this goal through in-house research. Organic growth, he said in 1990, 'avoids the enormous disruption inherent in mergers and acquisitions, which are often symptoms of structural weakness'.[47] Yet Girolami did not close his mind to mergers, and shortly before his retirement in 1994 preliminary talks were held with Pfizer in the US.[48] By this time it was clear that although there were some promising new drugs in the pipeline, none of them was likely to be in the Zantac class. The Pfizer plan was not pursued, but the merger issue was now on the agenda. In 1995 Girolami's successor, Sir Richard Sykes, announced a take-over bid for Wellcome.

This was a huge transaction, one of the largest in British corporate history; Glaxo was offering shares and cash worth a total of £9bn. Sykes argued that the combination would produce a more balanced research programme, as well as big savings in marketing and distribution. Wellcome had only recently become a public company. The Wellcome Trust had sold 25 per cent of its shares in 1985, and further disposals had taken the Trust's holding down to 45 per cent at the time of Glaxo's approach. The transition had been handled successfully, but, like Glaxo, Wellcome was uncomfortably dependent on one product, the anti-viral Zovirax, which had been launched in 1981; the patent was due to expire in 1997. The merger went through in March, 1995, and a programme of rationalisation got under way. By the end of the year the merged group had reduced its R & D staff from 11,500 to 9,500, including the closure of Wellcome's long-established laboratory at Beckenham in Kent.

Sykes had remarked in the course of the take-over battle that the world pharmaceutical industry was consolidating, 'and we had to lead the consolidation, not be carried along by it'.[49] There was no let-up in the pace of merger activity in the period following the Wellcome acquisition (see Table 13.5). One of the largest transactions was the merger between Ciba-Geigy and Sandoz in Switzerland. At the same time some of the medium-sized companies were absorbed by larger groups. In Britain Boots, which had to abandon a promising new heart drug because of side-effects found in clinical tests, sold its pharmaceutical business to BASF in 1994. In the following year Fisons, having failed to build on the success of Intal, its anti-asthmatic drug, sold its R & D operation to Astra; later in the same year the whole company was bought by Rhône-Poulenc.

The case for and against large-scale mergers in pharmaceuticals remained a matter of controversy. Some observers argued, as the Monopolies Commission had done in 1972, that there was no correlation between size and innovative ability and that mergers were as likely to disrupt research programmes as to improve them.

One man who had no doubt about the virtues of size was Jan Leschly, a Dane who took over from Bauman as chief executive of SmithKline Beecham in 1994. In 1997 he embarked on merger talks with American Home Products, which, if they had succeeded, would have created a company of about the same size as Glaxo Wellcome. When news of these talks reached Sykes, he quickly decided that a better deal would be an all-British merger between Glaxo Wellcome and SmithKline Beecham; informal discussions about such a possibility had taken place over the previous year, but no concrete proposals had emerged. Sykes contacted Leschly and a few weeks later, in January 1998, plans for a merger were announced. The stock market responded enthusiastically, and the shares of both companies rose sharply. A few weeks later the merger was abruptly called off, apparently because of disagreements about the roles and responsibilities of the men who were to form the senior executive management in the new company.

Throughout this period there had been speculation that Zeneca, demerged from ICI in 1993, would be taken over by a larger pharmaceutical company. The company insisted that, with a number of promising drugs in the pipeline, it had no need to merge with anyone. However, the pressure for consolidation appeared to be irresistible, and in 1999 Zeneca merged with Astra of Sweden to create the world's largest prescription drug manufacturers, narrowly ahead of Glaxo Wellcome. The Swedish company's success had been largely based on its anti-ulcerant drug, Losec, which was due to come off patent in 2001, and the two companies argued, as Sykes had done in the Glaxo/Wellcome case, that the merger would produce a larger and better balanced research programme, as well as savings in administration and in marketing.

How much further the merger wave would go was still uncertain in 1999. From a British point of view the critical question was not how many British companies ranked in the top ten, but whether Britain would continue to be an attractive location for research and development, both in pharmaceuticals and in biotechnology. The success of the industry since 1945 had been based on innovation. A remarkable number of the world's best-selling drugs – including Tenormin from ICI, Tagamet from Smith Kline, Augmentin from Beecham, Zantac from Glaxo and Zovirax from Wellcome, and many more – had come from British laboratories. This achievement had been made possible by outstanding scientists, good managers and a helpful regulatory environment. There had also been a promising start, by European if not by American standards, in biotechnology; more new biotechnology firms were created in Britain in the 1980s and 1990s than in the rest of Europe and, despite some well-publicised disappointments, there was a good prospect that they would constitute a cluster of R & D activity, complementary to an already strong pharmaceutical industry.

How Special a Case?

British pharmaceutical manufacturers did well because there was a good fit between the industry they were competing in and their domestic environment. The argument can be illustrated by comparing pharmaceuticals with an industry in which British firms did much less well, semiconductors. In both cases the character of competition was shaped by technical advances which took place during or shortly after the war. In pharmaceuticals the discovery and exploitation of penicillin, followed by the development of the broad-spectrum antibiotics, opened up new possibilities for using scientific research to find ways of treating illness. In semiconductors the invention of the transistor in 1947 set in train a line of research which led to the integrated circuit and the microprocessor.

In principle, the opportunities which these innovations created were exploitable by firms in any of the advanced industrial countries. But, as explained in Chapter 10, the US had particular advantages in semiconductors which European countries did not share. The demand for semiconductors grew faster in the US than in Europe in the first twenty years after the war, mainly because of space and defence programmes; government support for research and development was greater than in Europe; and the speed with which technical advances in semiconductors were transferred from university laboratories into commercial use owed a great deal to America's large and sophisticated venture capital industry.

In pharmaceuticals the size of domestic demand was less important as a source of competitive advantage. The British market was as receptive to innovative drugs as that of the US, and large enough in the 1950s and 1960s – the formative period of the industry – to support company-financed scientific research on the scale that was necessary. The leading American firms were larger than their British counterparts, but this did not make them better at developing new drugs. Small and medium-sized firms could compete successfully by focusing on one or two therapeutic categories; there was no single discovery which would enable one company to dominate the market as a whole.

Firms based in medium-sized European countries which were well endowed with high-quality academic scientists in the relevant disciplines could compete successfully with American manufacturers. Why, then, did British firms do particularly well, relative to their German and French rivals? First, the pharmaceutical industry in Britain benefited from a stable regulatory framework which put pressure on firms to develop innovative drugs and rewarded them handsomely when they did so. The controls over safety and efficacy stimulated the search for genuine innovations and weeded out drugs of little therapeutic value. The pricing regime recognised the need for high profit margins as an incentive for firms to engage in costly and speculative research, while keeping the cost to the taxpayer under control. The liberal approach to inward investment meant that British-owned firms were forced to compete against the world leaders and learn from them.

Second, the pharmaceutical industry was largely free from the negative factors which affected other British industries between the 1950s and the 1970s. There were no serious labour relations problems, mainly because the industry's manufacturing plants made small quantities of high-value materials by batch-production methods; there were no big concentrations of labour on a single site. The pharmaceutical industry did not suffer from deficiencies in the British training and education system; while there were periodic complaints about shortages of graduate scientists, this does not appear to have put a serious brake on the industry's progress. Finally, in contrast to some of the other industries discussed in this book, Britain's delayed entry into the EEC did not have an adverse impact on pharmaceuticals. Because of differing national regulations, there was no unified European market in pharmaceuticals, and British firms were no worse placed than their French and German counterparts in selling to other European countries.

Pharmaceuticals was a special case in a number of respects, but the fact that British firms did better in this industry than in others is relevant to the theme of the next four chapters, which assess the impact of national institutions and policies on industrial performance.

PART III

Institutions and Policies

FOURTEEN

————•○•————

The Financial System

T
he financial system, and the City of London in particular, has been
a favourite whipping-boy for the 'declinist' school of economic
commentators. Complaints about lack of support from banks and
other financial institutions were voiced by manufacturers before the First
World War, when Britain's industrial hegemony was under attack from
American and German competition. One of the charges made at that time,
echoed by later historians, was that the great concentration of financial
expertise in the City was geared, not to the needs of domestic manufacturers,
but to raising funds for overseas investment.[1] The separation between industry and finance was reinforced, according to this view, by class divisions in
British society. The merchants and traders of the City, educated at Eton and
other leading public schools, were 'gentlemanly capitalists', who despised
the world of the factory and had little in common with the self-made industrialists of Birmingham, Manchester and other provincial cities.[2]

Another line of attack is that the commercial banks, despite their provincial origins, did not get close enough to their industrial clients. By restricting
themselves to short-term lending, they failed to develop the mutually supportive partnership with industry which was built up in other countries,
especially Germany.[3] More recently the focus of attention has switched to a
different form of 'short-termism'. It is alleged that British capital markets
put too much pressure on firms to maximise profits in the short term.[4]
Unlike their counterparts in Germany, where investors take a longer view,
managers of publicly quoted companies in Britain face the prospect of a
hostile take-over bid if their profits are temporarily depressed; hence they
are reluctant to adopt strategies which will only pay off in the long term.

What light do the case studies presented in the last ten chapters shed on
these criticisms?

Finance and Industry before 1939

In the first phase of the British industrial revolution, up to the middle of the nineteenth century, entrepreneurs had no great difficulty in raising the funds which they needed to run their manufacturing ventures.[5] Industries such as cotton spinning called for modest amounts of start-up capital, which could usually be obtained from family, friends and associates. If external finance was required, it came from the country banks which were set up in increasing numbers after 1750. These banks provided mainly short-term credits, although their advances could turn into long-term loans as lender and borrower established a closer working relationship.[6] Most industrial firms were sole proprietorships or partnerships. Recourse to outside investors, through the medium of the joint stock company, was restricted by legislation passed in the wake of the South Sea Bubble affair in 1720: any new joint stock company had to be authorised by an Act of Parliament. The canal companies and later the railways followed this route, but few manufacturing enterprises had any need to do so.

In the second half of the nineteenth century, as industrial firms grew larger, demands on the country banks increased and they found themselves uncomfortably exposed to the risk of default. A series of bank failures, culminating in the collapse of the City of Glasgow Bank in 1878, prompted a wave of bank amalgamations. By 1920 two-thirds of the banking system in England and Wales was in the hands of five banks – Lloyds, Barclays, Midland, National Provincial and Westminster. These London-based institutions had greater financial resources than the old country banks, but chose to confine their industrial lending almost entirely to short-term loans.

The alternative to bank finance was to raise money from investors through a stock market flotation. This was made easier by the Joint Stock Companies Act of 1856 and the Companies Act of 1862, which introduced limited liability and allowed firms to incorporate without a special Act of Parliament. Over the next twenty years a growing number of industrial enterprises converted from partnerships to joint stock companies, although many of them remained private, owned by the founding family and not listed on a stock exchange. Those which went public did so for a variety of reasons – to provide members of the family with a marketable asset, to facilitate acquisitions of other firms and, in some cases, to raise new capital for expansion.[7]

Most of these flotations were handled by the provincial stock exchanges, which had hitherto dealt mainly in the shares of canal and railway companies. There were twelve of them in existence in 1885, providing a means whereby investors could buy shares in their local companies. In Lancashire, for example, there was a wave of flotations of cotton firms in the 1870s, known as the 'Oldham Limiteds'. The London stock exchange, which was by far the biggest, was largely detached from manufacturing industry. Its main business was raising funds for the British government and for overseas borrowers. In 1853 70 per cent of the securities quoted in London were British Government issues, and most of the rest were domestic railway shares. Over the next few decades the number of foreign securities greatly increased – from 10 per cent of the total in 1853 to 60 per cent in 1913 – as the City expanded its role as a supplier of capital for overseas investment.[8] The merchant banks, led by Barings and Rothschilds, were busy with their international customers, and, apart from a few large and prestigious firms such as Guinness (whose flotation in 1886 was handled by Barings), they did not take much interest in domestic industrial companies. Firms which wanted a London listing had to rely on the services of promoters, some of whom were more interested in quick profits for themselves than in the long-term health of the businesses they were promoting.[9] Numerous cases of over-optimistic or even fraudulent prospectuses gave industrial issues a bad reputation among investors, and made respectable companies reluctant to come to the market.[10]

A much-debated question is whether these flaws in the organisation of the capital markets, together with the City's focus on overseas investment, reduced the supply of long-term capital to British industry and thus contributed to Britain's alleged entrepreneurial failure between 1870 and 1914.[11] The 'failure' hypothesis relates principally to the newer industries, such as electrical engineering, where British firms fell behind their German and American competitors. But, as earlier chapters have shown, the British lag in these industries was not primarily due to a shortage of capital. In the case of synthetic dyestuffs, for example, the crucial German asset was a higher education system which provided an ample supply of well-trained chemists and engineers (Chapter 12). In electrical engineering the main obstacle in Britain was a regulatory system which discouraged investment in large-scale electricity supply undertakings (Chapter 8).

While there was room for improvement in the way industrial flotations were handled, the supply of long-term capital was generally adequate despite the City's orientation towards overseas investment.[12] From the 1880s onwards the flow of domestic industrial issues on the London stock market increased.

Of the fifty companies with the highest market capitalisation in 1904, the largest were the railways, but the list contained a number of manufacturing firms such as J and P Coats, the textile company, Vickers and Armstrong Whitworth, the armaments makers, and Brunner Mond, the chemical company which later became part of ICI.[13] Another recent arrival was Courtaulds, which went public in 1903 and used the proceeds of the flotation to acquire the patents to rayon.[14] The motor industry may have been damaged in its early years by the activities of unscrupulous promoters, but well-run firms such as Austin (which went public in 1914) were able to find finance without much difficulty.

Were these financing arrangements inferior to those which were developed in Germany? As described in Chapter 2, the rapid growth of German industry in the second half of the nineteenth century was assisted by the creation of universal banks, which, in addition to making short-term loans, looked after the long-term needs of their industrial clients and handled the flotation of their shares on the stock market; in some cases the banks acquired shares in these firms on their own account. The biggest of the universal banks were the three *Grossbanken* – Deutsche Bank, Dresdner Bank and Commerzbank – and they acted as 'house banks' for some of Germany's largest industrial companies. Under legislation passed in 1870, German joint stock companies were required to establish a two-tier board, whereby the managing board, made up of full-time executives, was monitored by a supervisory board, consisting of outsiders. The banks normally took seats on the supervisory boards of the companies which they sponsored, and this gave them an insight into the way the managers were performing, and an opportunity to influence the company's strategy.

The combination of commercial and investment banking within the same institution was a distinctively German phenomenon made necessary by the absence of well-developed capital markets.[15] It was also a reflection of the greater importance of heavy industries, especially coal, iron and steel, in the first phase of Germany's industrial revolution. These industries needed larger amounts of initial capital than, say, cotton textiles, and the universal bank was the vehicle through which the funds were assembled. The Deutsche Bank's first successful industrial flotation was that of Emil Rathenau's AEG in 1887. Three years later the same bank handled the flotation of Mannesmann, the steel company.[16] Outside heavy industry the influence of the *Grossbanken* was less strong. The financial needs of small and medium-sized firms in such industries as textiles and mechanical engineering were met by locally based savings and co-operative banks. The vast majority of these firms – which accounted for well over half of Germany's total industrial production – did not adopt the joint stock company form, and remained family-controlled.[17]

The *Grossbanken* had closer ties to their industrial clients, through supervisory board membership and in other ways, than the British commercial banks, but the difference can be overdrawn. The aversion to long-term lending on the part of British banks did not imply a lack of interest in the long-term prosperity of their customers. It was not uncommon for bankers to provide advice and support which went well beyond the provision of short-term credit. A notable example was Edward Holden, head of the Midland Bank, who worked closely with several large manufacturing companies.[18] Hugo Hirst at GEC drew on Holden's advice and support as he built up the company in the years leading up to the First World War.

If there was an entrepreneurial failure in Britain before the First World War, the financial system cannot be blamed for it. The British system was different from Germany's, but it catered adequately for the needs of manufacturing industry. It also had the great merit of stability. There were no bank collapses after 1898, and, as one historian has written, 'the English banking system may have contributed just as much to economic growth through pursuing a type of banking which did not lead to financial crisis as the German banks did by facilitating industrial capital formation and the export of manufactures'.[19]

The inter-war period presented a different challenge, arising from the depression in world trade and the financial difficulties experienced by the big exporting industries such as cotton textiles and steel. The banks have been criticised for not doing more to help these industries by promoting mergers and rationalisation.[20] The initiative for industrial reorganisation came not from the banks, but from the Bank of England, leading to the creation of Lancashire Cotton Corporation (Chapter 4) and some mergers in the steel industry (Chapter 6). But the banks had no power to impose industry-wide rationalisation schemes, and it is far from certain that more mergers would have solved the problems of these industries. What the banks did do, with some success, was to nurse individual companies through their difficulties, often insisting on management changes as a condition for further support. It was a pragmatic, case-by-case approach which did not amount to a German-style bank–industry nexus, but it was more than a hands-off relationship based on short-term lending.[21]

The inter-war years also saw a partial *rapprochement* between industry and the merchant banks. Faced with a dearth of overseas business, Barings,

Rothschilds and others began to compete more actively for domestic issues and to offer their services as financial advisers to industrial companies.[22] More opportunities were available, since the flow of industrial flotations on the London Stock Exchange was increasing. The number of domestic industrial and distribution companies quoted in London reached 1712 in 1939, compared with 569 in 1907.[23] The newer industries such as cars and electrical engineering were not held back by lack of finance in the inter-war years.

Yet many industrialists, supported by trade union leaders, continued to criticise the shortcomings of the financial system, and in 1929 the newly elected Labour government set up a high-level committee, under Lord Macmillan, a Scottish judge, to examine the relationship between finance and industry.[24] The Macmillan committee identified some gaps in the services provided by the capital markets; it recommended that special arrangements should be made for small industrial issues, between £50,000 and £200,000, for which the London stock exchange was not adequately equipped. But the banks came out of the inquiry with their reputation more or less intact; the committee did not recommend the adoption of universal banking on the German model.

In any case the performance of Germany's banks looked considerably less impressive in the inter-war period than it had done before 1914. The German banking crisis of 1931 was primarily due to an exceptionally difficult economic situation, but it was exacerbated, some observers believed, by over-lending to industry. There were suggestions at that time that the German banks should be reorganised along British lines, with a separation between deposit business and long-term industrial finance.[25] Although this idea was not pursued, there are no grounds for believing that universal banking was a competitive advantage for German industry in the inter-war years.

The Post-War Years: A Shortage of Capital?

When the Attlee government took office in 1945, reform of the financial system was not a high priority.[26] Apart from the largely symbolic take-over of the Bank of England, financial institutions were not included in the nationalisation programme. Ministers believed that they could get what they wanted out of the system through formal and informal controls; radical changes in structure were not thought to be necessary. But the old questions about relations between finance and industry had not gone away. During the 1960s and 1970s, when explanations were sought for Britain's failure to match the economic growth of the leading Continental countries, the financial system was again identified as a possible culprit. The criticisms were familiar: that capital, especially long-term capital, was not available in the right amounts and on the right terms, and that banks and other financial institutions were too detached from the needs of industrial companies.

Of these two criticisms, the first is the least convincing. British industry's loss of ground to overseas competitors in the first thirty years after the war cannot be blamed on a shortage of capital. The commercial banks expanded their services to industry during this period, especially in the field of medium-term finance.[27] Access to the stock market was easier than it had been before the war, and the merchant banks were more fully committed to domestic industrial business. A growing proportion of their profits came from advising companies on how and when to raise capital, and on mergers and acquisitions.

If there was a weakness in the early post-war years, it was that large, established companies found it too easy to raise finance, without sufficient scrutiny from banks or shareholders of how the money was to be spent. The case studies contained in the last ten chapters suggest that what was wrong with British industry in the 1950s and 1960s was not that capital was in short supply, but that too much of it was used unproductively. When Frank Kearton of Courtaulds attempted to modernise the textile industry, he had no difficulty in financing his ambitious programme of acquisitions and new factories. Where companies were reluctant to invest after the war, as in shipbuilding, this was due to the cautious view which owners and managers took about the prospects for demand, not to a lack of support from financial institutions.

It is possible that the cartel which was operated by the clearing banks until 1971 caused some distortion in lending patterns. The banks found it easier to supply a standard financial package to clients they knew well than to incur the trouble and expense of seeking out smaller and more innovative companies which did not have a proven record of profitability.[28] On the other hand, the banks did establish a new institution, the Industrial and Commercial Finance Corporation (ICFC), to supply long-term capital for small firms. The ICFC's activities were praised by the Radcliffe Committee, a body set up by the Conservative government in 1958 to review the workings of the financial system.[29] This committee was critical of some aspects of the banks' lending policies, but its overall conclusions were favourable; there were no grounds for concern about the cost of capital or about the availability of external finance. A similar judgement was reached twenty years later by another government committee, chaired by Harold Wilson, the former Prime Minister.[30]

Too Many Take-overs?

If access to capital was not a problem for British companies, were there other ways in which the financial system let British industry down? Some commentators believe that a serious weakness has been the excessive reliance on take-overs as a means of correcting managerial failure. According to this view, hostile take-overs are costly and disruptive manoeuvres which frequently fail to achieve the objectives set by their promoters, and they are often directed against the wrong targets.[31] In Germany, by contrast, hostile take-overs are extremely rare, and this has been seen as a source of strength for German industry.

At the start of the post-war period most publicly quoted companies in Britain were owned predominantly by private investors. During the 1950s, and at an accelerating rate in the 1960s and 1970s, the pattern of ownership changed as financial institutions, principally insurance companies and pension funds, increased their holdings of industrial shares.[32] This resulted from the increase in inflation, which made equities a more attractive investment than fixed-interest securities, and from the rapid growth in long-term savings, especially in the form of company-based pension schemes. In 1975 institutional investors owned 43 per cent of the ordinary shares of listed British companies and by 1990 this figure had risen to 61 per cent. Their investments were spread across a large number of companies, and it was rare for their shareholdings in any individual firm to exceed 5 per cent.

This dispersal of ownership was one of the factors which made possible an active take-over market. In the 1950s several entrepreneurs, of whom Charles Clore was the best known, saw that the share price of some publicly quoted companies was below the underlying value of their assets. They appealed above the heads of the directors to the shareholders of the target company, offering them a price (either in cash or in the shares of their own companies) which was large enough to persuade them to sell out. At first these activities were frowned on by the government and the Bank of England, but by the end of the 1950s the authorities came to regard take-overs as a useful way of promoting industrial reorganisation.[33]

No such market developed in Germany, mainly because of differences in the ownership and governance of German publicly quoted companies. In the inter-war years a pattern of cross-holdings was established, whereby large industrial firms acquired shares in other firms as a means of cementing long-term business relationships. This practice continued after the war, so that in 1960 nearly half of the shares in Germany's publicly quoted companies were held by non-financial enterprises. Although ownership of shares by private individuals tended to fall, as it did in Britain, there was not the same growth of institutional investment through pension funds and insurance companies. When German companies set up pension schemes, employer and employee contributions were retained within the firm rather than invested by professional fund managers in a portfolio of shares. The differences in the ownership structure of British, German and American companies are set out in TABLE 14.1.

TABLE 14.1 *Ownership of common stock in Britain, the US and Germany*

(per centage of outstanding shares held by each type of shareholder)

	Germany (1993)	Britain (1993)	US (1990)
Financial institutions	29.0	61.8	30.4
of which:			
Banks	14.3	0.6	0
Insurance companies	7.1	17.3	4.6
Pension funds and others	7.7	43.9	25.8
Non-financial institutions	71.0	38.2	69.6
of which:			
Non-financial enterprises	38.8	3.1	14.1
Households	16.6	17.7	50.2
Public authorities	3.4	1.3	0
Non-residents	12.2	16.3	5.4

Source: OECD Economic Surveys, Germany, 1994–95, Organisation for Economic Co-operation and Development, Paris, 1995. (Figures do not add up to 100 per cent because of rounding.)

Most German publicly quoted companies had at least one shareholder – usually another industrial firm – owning 25 per cent or more of their equity.[34] These large investors held their shares for control purposes, not as part of an actively traded portfolio. They were represented on the supervisory board and they regarded their investment as effectively permanent. For any would-be take-over bidder this solid shareholding block was a formidable obstacle. Two other factors militated against the emergence of an active take-over market. The first was the large role played by banks in the governance of public companies. Although the old 'house bank' relationship, in the sense of an exclusive link with a single bank, had faded, it was customary for a company's lead bank to be represented on its supervisory board, often occupying the post of chairman. In a few cases, as with Deutsche Bank and Daimler-Benz, the lead bank was also the principal shareholder, but direct shareholdings were less important as a source of bank influence than the proxy voting system. This was a long-standing arrangement, dating back to before the First World War, whereby small investors could deposit their shares with the banks to be voted on their behalf. The combination of proxy votes and direct shareholdings put the banks in a strong position to block or approve resolutions at the annual shareholders' meeting. The influence of the banks, through their supervisory board membership and their voting power, was particularly important in the minority of German companies whose shares were widely held. In the improbable event of a hostile take-over bid, they were likely to support the incumbent management.

The other obstacle to hostile take-overs was the presence on the supervisory board of employee and trade union representatives. Under the German co-determination system, as extended in 1976, half the board seats in publicly quoted companies employing more than 2,000 people were assigned to employees, and they, too, were unlikely to welcome the disruption and uncertainty of a hostile take-over.

Admirers of the German system believe that the concentration of ownership, together with the presence of committed 'stakeholders' on the supervisory board, ensures that the managers are monitored continuously and constructively by knowledgeable insiders. In addition, the insulation of managers from the threat of take-over allows them to concentrate on building the business for the long term, without worrying that a temporary downturn in profits will invite the attentions of a predator. This favourable assessment depends crucially on how effectively the insiders perform the monitoring function. In practice the supervisory board plays more of an advisory than a monitoring role. Its ability to control the managers of the company is limited by the infrequency of its meetings (often no more than four times a year) and by the sparseness of the information that it receives from the managing board.[35] The presence of employees can sometimes inhibit discussion of difficult issues. According to one account, 'it is only by accident if the supervisory board recognises something earlier than the management board'.[36]

It is also doubtful whether members of the supervisory board have the incentive to monitor aggressively on behalf of all shareholders. The banks, for example, may be reluctant to jeopardise a valuable business relationship by proposing radical measures, such as the sale of an unprofitable subsidiary.[37] In recent years German investors have been increasingly critical of the failure of supervisory board members, and of bankers in particular, to prevent companies from taking bad decisions. A celebrated example was the ill-judged policy of diversification adopted by Daimler-Benz in the early 1990s. This converted what had been a profitable car and truck manufacturer into a conglomerate with interests in aircraft production, electrical engineering, information technology and other businesses. The architect of the strategy was Edzard Reuter, the chief executive, who had a vision of making Daimler-Benz 'an integrated technology concern', and persuaded Deutsche Bank, the company's principal shareholder, to go along with it. The outcome, in 1995, was a loss of nearly DM6bn and a cut in the dividend for the first time for more than four decades. 'This case alone,' two German observers have written, 'is enough to destroy the notion that German banks act as efficient monitors of industrial corporations.'[38]

The German system of concentrated shareholdings and bank-dominated corporate governance does not prevent managerial empire-building. It can also be dysfunctional in situations where industrial restructuring is needed. One example was the slow pace of rationalisation in the German steel industry during the 1980s, discussed in Chapter 6; it was not the banks, but a highly unGerman device – Krupp's hostile take-over of Hoesch in 1991 – which got the process moving. Another was the prolonged effort by the banks to preserve the loss-making giant of the electrical industry, AEG. This company expanded rapidly after the war, partly in the hope of catching up with Siemens, but it failed to digest its numerous acquisitions and its financial condition deteriorated; by 1979 it was close to bankruptcy. A financial reconstruction was organised by Dresdner Bank, but the rescue did not provide a permanent solution. In 1982 AEG filed for protection under the bankruptcy laws. Once again a reconstruction was arranged, with the Federal and state governments guaranteeing some of the new loans. The company continued to limp on until it was acquired by Daimler-Benz in 1986. According to an analysis by Goldman Sachs, the American investment bank, AEG suffered from a classic German weakness – excessive diversification linked to a desire to maximise sales growth.[39] Even after the merger with Daimler-Benz, the new owners were slow to address the company's problems. The Olympia typewriter subsidiary went on making large losses until it was finally closed down in 1991.[40] In the British environment AEG would probably have been a candidate for take-over and break-up much earlier in its history.

No financial system can prevent managers from making mistakes. A system which relies on control by insiders is not obviously superior to one in which the capital market plays a larger role. The absence of hostile take-overs cannot be regarded as an unmixed blessing for German industry. But does the British system go too far in the other direction? It is undoubtedly true that take-over fever in Britain can be taken to excess, and that the tactics used by firms to ward off hostile bids can sometimes be counter-productive. But the case studies presented in earlier chapters indicate that hostile take-overs were not a significant factor in Britain's poor industrial performance in the first three decades after the war. In sectors which did badly during this period, such as shipbuilding, cars and machine tools, hostile bids, actual or threatened, were rare. Most of the mergers which took place in these and other industries during the 1960s were agreed transactions. The promoters of some of these mergers, including the government, can be criticised for exaggerating the advantages of size, but that was their misjudgement; it can hardly be blamed on the financial system. One of the few big mergers which worked well – GEC's acquisition of AEI – came about through a contested take-over.[41] The subsequent merger between GEC and English Electric was the direct result of an earlier attempt by Plessey to take over English Electric. These moves broke the logjam in an industry which needed rationalisation, and helped to create a strong, British-owned electrical engineering company (Chapter 8).

The second post-war merger wave, starting in the 1980s, involved hostile bids on a larger scale. This was the heyday of the acquisitive predators, led by Hanson and BTR, which used their highly valued shares to launch a series of ambitious take-overs. Their targets were often diversified groups, like Thomas Tilling (acquired by BTR in 1983) and Imperial Group (bought by Hanson in 1986), which benefited from a more rigorous style of management. On balance, these activities made a helpful contribution to the efficiency of British industry. A striking example was the impact on ICI of the take-over approach from Hanson in 1992. Although Hanson did not in the end make a bid, its intervention precipitated changes in ICI, including the demerger of Zeneca, which were desirable on industrial as well as financial grounds (Chapter 12).

If hostile take-overs induce a short-termist mentality on the part of industrial managers, the effects might be expected to be particularly damaging in industries which demand long-term investment in research and development. Could this explain the weak performance of British companies in electronics? Such an explanation would be more plausible if long-termist Germany had done well in this industry, but it did not. The US, on the other hand, where the take-over market is even more active than in Britain, has a strong electronics industry; so, too, does Japan, where hostile take-overs are as rare as in Germany. Another high-technology industry, pharmaceuticals, presents a different picture. Long-termist Germany and short-termist Britain and the US have been outstandingly successful in this industry, while long-termist Japan has not.

The financial system on its own does not have a decisive influence on which countries succeed in particular industries, although it may play a supporting role. The US electronics industry, for example, derives part of its strength from entrepreneurial start-up firms, backed by venture capitalists with a view to early flotation on the stock market. But, as explained in Chapter 10, the availability of venture capital was only one of several factors which underpinned American success in this industry.

Banks Versus Stock Markets

The controversy about hostile take-overs is part of the wider debate over the relative merits of bank-dominated financial systems, such as that of Germany, and systems like that of Britain and the US where the stock market plays a larger role. The distinction between the two systems is more blurred than some traditional accounts have suggested, at least as far as the raising of capital is concerned. Since 1970 German publicly quoted companies have been no more dependent on bank finance than British ones; in both countries firms generate the bulk of their funds internally, with little recourse to bond or equity markets.[42] There is, however, an important difference between Britain and Germany in the number of companies which are listed on stock exchanges (TABLE 14.2).

The small number of listed companies in Germany is sometimes

TABLE 14.2 *Number of listed companies in Britain, Germany and the US*

	Germany	Britain/Ireland	US*
No. of listed domestic companies at			
end of 1993	664	1,865	7,313
Market value of listed companies,			
DM billions, at end of 1993	800	2,056	9,006

*including stocks quoted on New York stock exchange, Amex and NASDAQ.

Source: Economic Surveys, Germany, 1994–95, OECD, Paris, 1995.

attributed to the mentality of German entrepreneurs, who are said to be reluctant to submit to public disclosure. Another factor has been the high cost of going public. But the main reason is the structure of the German banking industry. The principal suppliers of finance for German small and medium-sized companies – the *Mittelstand* – are the savings and co-operative banks, which have deep roots in their local communities. The relationship has been supported by an array of subsidies provided by the Federal and state governments; the most important instrument has been the Kreditanstalt für Wiederaufbau (KfW), set up in 1948 to administer Marshall Plan funds.[43] These arrangements have made it less necessary for *Mittelstand* firms to go to the stock market for capital; they continue to rely on bank finance even when they reach a size which, in Britain, would justify a stock market listing.[44]

Is this a strength or a weakness? The vitality of the *Mittelstand*, especially in industries such as textiles and engineering, has made an important contribution to Germany's post-war industrial success. But the decentralised banking system is only one of the elements contributing to that success. The savings and co-operative banks form part of a network of local institutions, including trade associations, chambers of commerce and training centres, which underpin the technical competence and financial stability of German companies.[45] It is the network as a whole, rather than the banking system on its own, on which the strength of the *Mittelstand* depends.

There has been much discussion in Britain about how a British equivalent to the *Mittelstand* might be created. The Small Firms Loan Guarantee

Scheme, introduced in 1981, was a modest step in the German direction, and some observers believe that more could be done, perhaps including the creation of an agency similar to the KfW in Germany.[46] The British system, however, has strengths of its own in the form of a more highly developed stock market and a bigger venture capital industry. Fast-growing firms, especially in high-technology industries, need large amounts of equity capital early in their lives, and their requirements are looked after better in Britain than in Germany.[47] This is one of the reasons why the biotechnology industry took off faster in Britain than in Germany during the 1980s.

Thus the advantages are not all on one side. Indeed, while British observers have looked enviously at the German banks, the Germans have been seeking to emulate some features of the British system. In 1997, for example, the Neuer Markt, a stock market for young, fast-growing firms loosely modelled on Britain's Alternative Investment Market, was established in Germany. It has been a big success, revealing a large unsatisfied demand for equity capital among small German firms and helping to develop an equity culture among German investors. There has also been a substantial expansion of the German venture capital industry. This is part of a growing convergence between the German and British financial systems.

The most surprising change has been the greater readiness of German companies to embrace the Anglo-American concept of shareholder value.[48] An increasing proportion of the shares of German public companies is held by foreign investors. In addition, several large German firms, including Daimler-Benz, have listed their shares on the New York stock exchange. This has had a considerable impact on the behaviour of managers. Examples have been given in earlier chapters of German companies responding to shareholder pressure in ways which would have been unthinkable in the 1960s and 1970s. The restructuring of Hoechst, the chemical company, is one such case (Chapter 12); the decision by Siemens to withdraw from semiconductors is another (Chapter 10). Even more remarkable was Krupp's hostile take-over bid for Thyssen in 1997 (Chapter 4). Although the bid was withdrawn in the face of political and trade union opposition and the two companies subsequently negotiated an agreed merger, the fact that it was made at all showed how far previously outlandish Anglo-American methods had become acceptable.

The City and Industry

A unique feature of the British economy, which has persisted for more than a hundred years, is the importance of the City of London as an international financial centre. In the world market for financial services, Britain still punches above its weight. Some industrialists contrast the strength of the financial services sector with the decline of British manufacturing, and suspect there must be some connection between the two. John Harvey-Jones, former chairman of ICI, told an interviewer in 1995 that British industry had paid 'a very high price' for the City's international success. The City, in his view, had 'performed less well in respect of industrial support than our main industrial competitors, including America'. Harvey-Jones also complained about the 'ludicrous salaries' paid by City firms. 'When I was chairman of ICI, all the advisers that we used, advisers mark you, were paid more than I was, be they the auditors, be they the merchant banks, be they the City solicitors. Now I ask you, in realistic national terms, who is likely to have the biggest impact on the fate of the bloody country?'[49]

Overpaid they may be, but the evidence presented in this book does not suggest that the denizens of the City can be blamed for the failings of British industry after the Second World War. Britain's financial system is not perfect, but the same is true of other countries; it should be struck off the list of factors contributing to British industrial decline.

Training, Education and Culture

B ritain is widely believed to have entered the post-war period with a training and education system unworthy of a leading industrial nation.[1] The failure to reform the system has been seen as an important reason for the country's poor economic performance. The main targets for criticism have been governments, for their neglect of vocational education, and employers, for their reluctance to invest in the skills of their workforce. Trade unions have also come under attack for using apprenticeship to preserve demarcations between crafts rather than to upgrade the skills of their members.

Some historians link these weaknesses to deep-seated social and cultural factors. Correlli Barnett argues that the rot set in during the second half of the nineteenth century. An anti-industrial bias within the educational establishment, reflecting the values of the ruling élite, was matched by an anti-intellectual bias on the part of entrepreneurs, who believed there was no substitute for on-the-job experience. Neither group, according to Barnett, was much interested in using schools and universities to teach practical skills.[2] Michael Sanderson thinks the English reverence for liberal education stunted the growth of technical schools for the 13–18 age group. This gap within the secondary education system, in Sanderson's view, lies 'near the heart of England's educational defects and declining economic performance in the post-war years'.[3]

Unfavourable comparisons have regularly been drawn with Germany and to a lesser extent with the US. Starting in the 1850s, a stream of reports by British visitors has praised the excellence of German scientific education and the high value placed on technical competence at all levels of the workforce. The US has been admired as the progenitor and principal developer of professional management. The idea that management was a discipline which could be taught in universities took root earlier in the US than in other countries. Harvard's graduate school of business administration was established in 1908, and by the time of the Second World War management studies were well established at most leading American universities. In Britain the first graduate business schools designed according to the US model did not open their doors until the 1960s.

In the light of the evidence contained in the earlier part of the book, this chapter looks at three areas where the British system is thought to have been deficient – shop floor skills, the supply of engineers and scientists, and the training of managers.

Shop Floor Skills

The main criticism of vocational training in Britain has been the failure to provide an adequate supply of intermediate or craft skills below the level of scientists and engineers. Apprenticeship has traditionally been the principal formal means of skill formation at this level, but since the 1960s the number of apprentices in British industry has declined, and attempts by successive governments to revive the system, or to replace it with alternative training arrangements, have not had much success. The consequence, according to the critics, has been to put British manufacturers at a disadvantage against competitors which have access to a larger pool of shop floor skills.

Persuasive evidence for this view came from a series of Anglo-German comparisons conducted in the 1980s and 1990s by the National Institute of Economic and Social Research. These studies, based on matched samples of British and German factories in selected industries, pointed to a strong link between skills and productivity. They showed, for example, that machinery breakdowns were less frequent in Germany than in Britain, because the skilled German worker was better able to maintain complex equipment in good working order.[4] Another conclusion from this research was that a poorly skilled workforce made it difficult for British firms in such industries as textiles and mechanical engineering to manufacture high-quality, technically demanding products. Trapped in a 'low-skill, low-quality equilibrium', they were forced to compete on the basis of price rather than performance, and this made them more vulnerable than their German counterparts to competition from low-wage countries.[5]

The differences between Britain and Germany in this field have their origins in the form which industrialisation took during the eighteenth and nineteenth centuries.[6] In Britain the industrial revolution made some traditional skills obsolete but created the need for new ones, especially in industries such as engineering and shipbuilding. In these industries employers found that the ancient system of apprenticeship could be adapted in a way which generated an adequate supply of craft skills at low cost.[7] Apprentices were taken on at the age of fourteen or sixteen and qualified as craftsmen after a period of training which usually lasted for five or seven years.

The responsibility for training was largely delegated to the craftsmen themselves, and it was this group of workers which formed some of the most durable trade unions.[8] Apprenticeship was the key to their bargaining power, since it was a means of limiting entry into their trade. A major preoccupation for the unions was to ensure that skilled work was reserved for men who had served their time as apprentices. The system created a pool of mobile labour with qualifications which were accepted as valid throughout the industry. At a time when most employers hired and fired their workers as demand for their products rose and fell, union membership provided the skilled craftsman with a measure of job security which was denied to semi-skilled and unskilled workers.

Although there was no serious concern about the supply of shop floor skills up to the First World War, the quality of training varied considerably from firm to firm. Some employers recognised the need to combine on-the-job training with more formal instruction, but there was no systematic link between factory-based and school-based learning, and there were no external examinations which apprentices had to pass. To tackle these problems the Engineering Employers Federation proposed in 1919 a wide-ranging reform of the industry's training arrangements. These proposals called for a systematic approach to the training of apprentices, all of whom would serve under written agreements, and a national scheme for supplementing on-the-job training with part-time attendance at school. The EEF invited the trade unions to co-operate in implementing and monitoring these reforms.[9] However, enthusiasm among EEF members for a collective programme of training reform faded as the post-war boom came to an end. The priority was to reduce costs, and arguments over wages, manning levels and working hours led to a rash of local disputes, culminating in a national lock-out in 1922, in which the union suffered a crushing defeat. This removed any possibility of a joint approach to apprenticeship reform.

With skilled craftsmen in ample supply because of high unemployment, the issue of training reform lost much of its urgency. Some progressive firms, such as Metropolitan Vickers and ICI, developed more sophisticated

personnel policies during this period, and improved their training arrangements. But there was no fundamental reform of the apprenticeship system,
and many firms used their trainees as a source of cheap labour.[10]

The government had little involvement in the regulation of the apprenticeship system. Training in industry, like other aspects of the employment
relationship, was a matter for employers and unions to work out for themselves. But there was concern around the turn of the century about the
number of young people who went into industry with little education,
received no formal training from their employers, and found themselves in
dead-end jobs. One of the reforms planned by Robert Morant, senior civil
servant at the Board of Education, was the creation of junior technical
schools, designed to fill the gap between leaving school and the start of
apprenticeship. Morant was a supporter of the 'national efficiency' movement
which had gained wide support after the turn of the century, and he was
impressed by the German system of technical education. However, only a
few technical schools were established before 1914, and hopes for a substantial
expansion after the First World War were dashed by the squeeze on public
expenditure and by the government's decision to give a higher priority to
the expansion of grammar schools.[11]

The attitudes of employers to technical schools were mixed. Some felt
that a good general education was the best preparation for work. Others,
especially in engineering, thought that boys who had gone to junior technical
schools were more likely to make a success of apprenticeship. These issues
formed part of the wartime debate on educational policy which led to the
Education Act of 1944.[12] The number of technical schools had increased
during the war, and some officials in the Board of Education recommended
further expansion in order to offset what they saw as the over-academic bias
of the grammar schools. R. A. Butler, appointed president of the Board of
Education in 1941, was persuaded that technical schools should form part of
a tripartite structure of secondary education, alongside grammar schools and
secondary modern schools. But the 1944 Act was permissive rather than
mandatory on this point, and many officials in the local education authorities
believed that technical education could be adequately provided for in the
grammar and secondary modern schools. With no push from the centre,
few new technical schools were established, and the concept of a separate
technical stream in secondary education faded in the 1960s when comprehensive schools were introduced.

The 1944 Act did not directly affect apprenticeship, and for the first
decade or so after the war this system appeared to be working rather better

than in the 1930s. Employers and trade unions seemed broadly content with the quality and quantity of apprenticeship training, which was now linked more effectively to part-time attendance at school. Towards the end of the 1950s, however, there was increasing concern about shortages of skilled labour, and the apprenticeship system became the subject of more critical scrutiny. Employers complained that apprenticeships were too narrowly based, being restricted to young males in a limited number of trades; that the system involved too much time-wasting and time-serving rather than training to standards; and that it perpetuated unnecessary demarcations between trades.[13] In 1963 the Conservative government, breaking with the hands-off policy of the past, proposed a new statutory framework under which Industrial Training Boards would be set up in each major industry. Although the government fell before the legislation was enacted, these proposals were implemented with little change by Harold Wilson's Labour government after the 1964 election.

The Training Boards were given the power to impose a levy on employers, to be reimbursed if their training programmes met approved standards. The levy-grant system turned out to be over-bureaucratic and was greatly resented by small firms. Far from reviving the apprenticeship system, the number of apprentices fell sharply, from 240,000 in 1964 to 140,000 in 1974. The decline was partly due to young people staying on longer at school, but it also reflected the waning commitment of employers to a system which had become rigid. Another factor was the narrowing of wage differentials, under trade union pressure, between apprentices and fully trained craftsmen. The unions were more concerned to prevent the exploitation of apprentices as cheap labour than with the quality of the training they received.[14]

By the early 1970s it was clear that the Industrial Training Act had failed, and a new attempt was made, through the creation of the Manpower Services Commission in 1973, to engage employers and unions in a joint attack on the training problem. But, with unemployment rising in the second half of the 1970s, the number of apprentices continued to fall, and the decline accelerated in the 1980s. In the early years of Margaret Thatcher's Conservative government, training policy was geared more to alleviating youth unemployment than to improving the quality of training. The government was also suspicious of the traditional apprenticeship, which was seen as an instrument of trade union power in the workplace, and hostile to tripartite bodies such as the Manpower Services Commision.[15] In place of the Industrial Training Boards, employer-led Training and Education Councils were set up to take responsibility for training provision. At the same time the government introduced a system of National Vocational Qualifications to establish nationally recognised standards for each level of technical competence. In 1993 the government announced plans for the Modern Apprenticeship, an attempt to recreate the virtues of the old system – the training it offered in broad, transferrable skills – while eliminating its drawbacks – the lack of externally monitored standards of competence.[16]

By the time of the 1997 election training was firmly on the political agenda, and the new Labour government took over and extended most of the initiatives started by the Tories. Although there were some dissenting voices, there was broad agreement across the political spectrum that an under-trained workforce continued to put British industry at a competitive disadvantage, especially in relation to Germany.

In Germany there has been greater continuity in training policy, based on a consensus between employers, trade unions and governments (both Federal and regional) about the importance of vocational training and how it should be organised. The starting-point, as in Britain, was the evolution of apprenticeship out of the medieval guilds, but in Germany the transition took a different form. Although the privileges of the guilds were abolished in 1807, the traditional handicraft trades, the *Handwerk*, continued to play an important role in the German economy even after industrialisation was well advanced. Towards the end of the century, when the factory workforce was expanding rapidly and trade unions were becoming more powerful, the authorities saw the *Handwerk* sector as a bulwark against socialism.[17] In 1897 the Chambers of Handicraft were given statutory control over the qualification and certification of skilled craftsmen, and all handicraft firms were obliged to become members of the chamber which governed their trade. These arrangements helped to preserve a tradition of skilled craftsmanship and a tier of small, craft-based firms which co-existed with large-scale manufacturing industry. The 1897 law set a pattern for the governance of apprenticeship training which was extended in the inter-war years to the chambers of commerce and industry, whose members included the large industrial employers.[18]

There were two other important differences between Britain and Germany. First, most German states, before and after the unification of the country in 1871, established continuation schools to provide part-time vocational training for young people after entering employment. Attendance at these schools was made compulsory, and the combination of factory-based and school-based training has remained a key element in the German system. Second, the German trade unions did not play a significant role in the development of the apprenticeship system. The initiative in training policy lay with the employers.

During the Nazi years factory-based vocational training was extended and made more systematic. The motivation was as much ideological as economic. The authorities wanted to establish the factory rather than the trade union as the nucleus of social and political organisation. But the effect was to reinforce the long-standing German commitment to a high level of workforce skills. One historian has suggested that National Socialism 'prepared the ground for the skilled industrial economy of the Federal Republic'.[19]

After 1945, the vocational training system, including the self-regulatory role of the chambers of commerce and industry, continued with little change. When the Federal Republic was established in 1949, the Christian Democratic government resisted pressure from the trade unions to take responsibility for training away from the employers. Ludwig Erhard, the Economics Minister, believed that to tamper with a system which had proved itself in the past would put economic recovery at risk.[20] The governance of training in the workplace remained a controversial issue with the trade unions during the 1950s and 1960s, and some concessions to union demands were made in the Vocational Training Act of 1969. This measure provided for employee representation on the training committees to be set up within each chamber, and for the establishment of a Federal Vocational Training Research Institute, which was given a general oversight over training policy.[21] But the main thrust of the Act was to strengthen the existing system.

The resilience of Germany's vocational training arrangements is intimately linked to German industry's long-standing orientation towards skill-intensive, technically demanding products.[22] As explained in Chapter 2, this was a distinctive feature of German industrialisation from the early days. The reconstruction of the West German economy after 1945 created more opportunities for American-style mass production – the success of Volkswagen being the most spectacular example – but in much of German industry there was still a strong emphasis on craft skills, quality and customisation.

The apprenticeship system has undoubtedly been a source of strength for Germany in the post-war period. It is less clear whether deficiencies in vocational training have been a major cause of British industrial decline. That decline, as measured by productivity growth and by shares of world markets, was most marked in the 1950s and 1960s. During those years the British apprenticeship system was in reasonable working order. Moreover, Britain was losing ground, not only to Germany, but to other European countries, notably France, whose vocational training arrangements at that time were not much superior to those of Britain.

The industry studies presented in this book do not indicate, except in one important case, that an inadequate supply of workforce skills was a central element in the industrial failures of the early post-war decades. The fact that the shipbuilders were slow to adopt flow-line production techniques, or that the attempted reorganisation of the Lancashire cotton textile industry was misconceived, or that productivity in steel-making fell behind that of Germany, cannot be blamed on flaws in the training system. Equally, the skills issue has not figured prominently in any of the numerous studies of the post-war decline of the British motor industry.

The exception is mechanical engineering. As described in Chapter 8, German firms have been pre-eminent in skill-intensive branches of engineering such as machine tools. The manufacture of complex, technically sophisticated machinery, produced in small batches, suits the skill profile of the German workforce, based on a combination of basic theoretical knowledge and in-depth practical know-how.[23] British firms have been less good in industrial processes of this kind – hence the decline in machine tools and textile machinery. But other industrial countries have fared almost as badly. The decline of the American machine tool industry in the 1970s and 1980s has been blamed in part on the same weaknesses in vocational training that have been the subject of so much criticism in Britain. French firms have also performed poorly in machine tools.

The German apprenticeship system has been less helpful in other industries where different skills are required, such as the production of consumer goods in large batches, or some branches of electronics. Indeed, there has been growing anxiety in Germany in recent years about what is seen as an over-commitment to medium-technology industries such as mechanical engineering, and an inability to shift resources into high-technology sectors. Some observers have warned that the technological conservatism of German firms, their preference for competing on the basis of product differentiation and technical perfection rather than cost efficiency, may become a competitive handicap.[24]

None of this shows that British industry would not have performed better if apprenticeship had been thoroughly reformed after the war, or if technical schools had been given a larger part in the tripartite system of secondary education, or if employers had invested more in workforce training. British firms certainly did better in industries such as chemicals and pharmaceuticals which did not depend on craft skills than in industries such as machine tools which did. But deficiencies in the training system do not appear to have been a major cause of the productivity lag behind Germany and France in the first thirty years after the Second World War, nor did they prevent the productivity catch-up which took place in the 1980s.[25]

Engineers and Scientists

Judged by the number of Nobel prizes won by British scientists, Britain's scientific prowess throughout the twentieth century compares well with that of other industrial countries. What has been missing, it has been argued, is the ability to commercialise the results of scientific research. This is often attributed to the same social and cultural factors which are said to have held back the development of technical education – a bias within the universities in favour of pure rather than applied science, and a disdain for industrially relevant subjects. Engineering has been regarded as the poor relation of science, and has attracted too small a proportion of the most talented students. It has also been undervalued as a qualification for senior management posts in industry. The usual comparison, once again, is with Germany, where the education system is said to produce engineers and scientists with the right combination of theoretical knowledge and practical skill, and engineering graduates are strongly represented in senior management.

These weaknesses are often seen as a legacy of the first industrial revolution. Between 1750 and 1850 the expansion of manufacturing industry in Britain was in sectors such as cotton textiles and iron-making that did not depend on the application of scientific knowledge. This was the age of the 'practical man', who acquired his skills on the shop floor, not in the class room or lecture theatre. The universities played almost no role either as a source of trained manpower for industry or as a provider of useful knowledge. By the middle of the nineteenth century engineering was emerging as a distinct profession, but the qualification for membership of the professional engineering institutions was a period of workshop training under the supervision of an established practitioner, not a university degree.

In Germany, by contrast, investment in scientific and technical education at the university level began earlier than in Britain and was expanded more vigorously.[26] Starting in the early decades of the nineteenth century, Prussia and other German states embarked on a thorough reform of their education systems. This involved the revival of the classical universities, which, though strictly non-vocational in purpose, were encouraged to aspire to the highest standards of teaching and research; by the second half of the century natural sciences, including medicine and chemistry, formed an important part of their curriculum. In addition, most states created technical high schools, which offered a practical education for the sons of entrepreneurs and industrial managers.

British businessmen were slow to recognise the importance of scientific education, as was the government, but from the 1870s, as international competition hotted up, attitudes began to change. A series of Royal Commissions into the state of British science led to the Technical Instruction Act of 1889, which allowed borough and county councils to support technical education with money raised from the rates. In 1878, in response to government pressure, the livery companies in the City of London set up the City and Guilds Institute for the Advancement of Technical Education; this was followed by the creation of the Finsbury Technical College for artisans and, in 1884, the more advanced Central Technical College in South Kensington. Meanwhile a challenge to the non-vocational view of university education was launched by industrialists, mainly in the Midlands and the North. The foundation of Owens College in Manchester in 1851 marked the start of a movement which spread over the next three decades to Newcastle, Leeds, Bristol, Sheffield, Nottingham and Liverpool. These civic colleges, later upgraded to universities, were designed to serve the needs of local industry, and they did so effectively.[27]

These provincial initiatives finally stirred the ancient universities out of their lethargy. The creation of the Cavendish and Clarendon laboratories in the 1870s marked the full recognition by Cambridge and Oxford of the 'progressive' sciences.[28] Cambridge appointed its first professor of engineering in 1875, and Oxford followed a few years later. In London the Royal College of Chemistry, the Royal School of Mines and the Central Technical College were merged in 1907 to form the Imperial College of Science and Technology, modelled on the technical high school in Berlin. By the time of the First World War technical education in Britain at the university level had partially recovered from the earlier lag. The output of university-trained engineers and scientists was lower than in Germany, but this was partially offset by the wide range of non-university courses which had sprung up in Britain. The First World War underlined the importance of science-based industries to Britain's security, and while the direct involvement of government was mainly confined to military technology (as, for example, in the

Royal Aircraft Establishment at Farnborough), the Department of Scientific and Industrial Research was set up to support civil research.

The cult of the practical man had not disappeared, and there was still some prejudice in parts of British industry against the university graduate. But by the 1920s the engineering institutions had come to accept that academic education was a necessary supplement to practical experience, and they worked closely with the universities to devise curricula which suited their requirements.[29] There was also an expansion of engineering education below the university level, mainly involving part-time study at technical colleges; a new sub-degree qualification, the Ordinary National and Higher National Certificate, was widely accepted by employers.

The Second World War, like the first, greatly enhanced the prestige of academic science, and gave a fillip to industries such as aircraft and electronics that were large employers of science and engineering graduates. A series of government reports in the late 1940s and early 1950s recommended an increase in the provision of university-level technical education, and new institutions – the Colleges of Advanced Technology (the former technical colleges) and later the Polytechnics – were set up for this purpose. By the mid-1950s the British higher education system was turning out more science and engineering graduates than in Germany or France.[30] A decade later, according to a report published in 1967, Britain had a larger stock of science graduates than any other West European country and employed a larger proportion of them in industry. 'Britain, far from being short of scientists, is more richly endowed with them than is any country except the USA.'[31]

Some commentators have argued that too much of the nation's scientific and engineering talent was devoted to aircraft and other defence-related industries, especially in the first thirty years after the war, and that this had a detrimental effect on such industries as motor vehicles and mechanical engineering. But the evidence contained in earlier chapters does not suggest that lack of availability of engineering and science graduates played a central part in the decline of such companies as British Motor Corporation, Alfred Herbert and Stone-Platt. In general, Britain appears to have had a comparative advantage in science-based industries – hence the success of British firms in chemicals and pharmaceuticals.[32] In the one science-based industry where British firms did badly, electronics, the failure was due to a range of factors which were not related to the supply of scientists and engineers.

The Making of Managers

The third charge against the education system relates to what many regard as the most important single cause of Britain's post-war industrial decline – the poor quality of the country's managers. The criticism comes in two parts: that Britain's schools and universities, infected by a social and intellectual bias against manufacturing industry, discouraged talented young people from taking up careers in industrial management, and that those who did go into industry and reached senior executive positions were inadequately trained for the job. Hence the average manager in Britain was less competent and less dynamic than his counterpart in countries where there was no cultural prejudice against industry and where management education was taken more seriously.

The idea that Britain has suffered from an anti-industrial culture was given powerful support in the early 1980s by an American historian, Martin Wiener. In his book, *English Culture and the Decline of the Industrial Spirit*, he argued that during the second half of the nineteenth century the British entrepreneur went through a process of gentrification.[33] The rise of the industrial bourgeoisie had left intact the cultural and social hegemony of the ruling élite, consisting of the landowning aristocracy and the bankers and merchants of the City of London. These two groups represented a form of capitalism which was *rentier* in character rather than entrepreneurial or productive, and their life-style was that of the cultivated country gentleman, who kept as far away as possible from the dirt and squalor of factories. This was the world which the successful businessman, eager for social acceptance, was determined to enter. He did so, according to Wiener, by sending his sons to public schools, where they studied classics, played team games and absorbed the anti-industrial values of the upper class. The outcome was a haemorrhage of talent out of industry as the children of entrepreneurs abandoned the factory in favour of more gentlemanly occupations.

To the extent that Wiener is seeking to explain why British entrepreneurs 'failed' between 1870 and 1914 (a proposition which is itself highly questionable, as earlier chapters have shown), the public schools cannot be given the weight he attaches to them, since a very small proportion of businessmen sent their sons to public schools during those years.[34] Moreover, most sons of businessmen who did attend public schools followed the same career as their fathers, and this continued to be the case after the turn of the century.[35] As for the education which the public schools provided, it is true that the curriculum favoured by Thomas Arnold at Rugby and the other nineteenth-century reformers was non-vocational, with a bias towards the classics. But the aim was not to prepare a leisured class for the life of a country gentleman, but to form 'an active, responsible, physically fit, self-disciplined élite of professional men and administrators for public service in church and state, the empire and the liberal professions'.[36] The qualities which the public schools sought to inculcate – leadership, self-reliance, the willingness to back one's own judgement – were as valuable in an entrepreneur or manager as in a colonial administrator.[37]

The desire for social advancement was certainly one of the reasons why businessmen sent their sons to public schools. But a public school background did not imply an amateurish approach to management. In a much-quoted article published in 1973 the economic historian, Donald Coleman, claimed that in the boardrooms of large British companies ex-public schoolboys formed a clique of 'gentlemen', separated by education, life-style and accent from lower-class 'players' who performed the humdrum tasks of production and selling.[38] Coleman used Courtaulds, the textile company, to illustrate his point. In 1938 the board consisted of seventeen directors, fourteen of whom had been at public schools. When Samuel Courtauld, a descendant of the founder, retired from the chairmanship in 1946, he chose as his successor John Hanbury-Williams, a Wellington-educated aristocrat who 'knew little or nothing about production technology, despised technical men, remained ignorant of science, and wholly indifferent to industrial relations'.

The appointment of Hanbury-Williams (who remained chairman of Courtaulds until 1962) apparently reflected Samuel Courtauld's belief that 'gentlemen' were likely to be better leaders than 'players'.[39] This distinction, Coleman suggested, had taken root in the inter-war years and was beginning to break down in the 1960s. But Hanbury-Williams was not typical of the kind of person who reached the top in British industry in the inter-war and early post-war years. It was common practice for public schoolboys, if they did not go on to university, to undergo some form of technical training after leaving school, perhaps as a premium apprentice in an industrial company. Leonard Lord, one of the outstanding figures in the inter-war motor industry, and George Nelson, chairman of English Electric from 1930 to 1962, were among many businessmen who followed this path. There was also a gradual broadening of the public schools' curriculum, with a greater emphasis on science and technology, and this trend accelerated after the Second World War.[40]

If there was an anti-industrial bias in the education system, it was to be found at Oxford and Cambridge, where some professors regarded a career in business as intellectually and morally demeaning. One Oxford student in the 1920s, later a senior government economist, was advised against industry on the grounds that he had a moral duty not to seek personal gain but to carry out public service.[41] But the fact that a small number of intellectual high-flyers at Oxford and Cambridge chose to work for the government rather than for industry hardly amounts to a haemorrhage of talent. Even if industry recruited a smaller proportion of firsts than might have been economically desirable, the flow of Oxbridge graduates into industry, which had begun before 1914, increased steadily in the inter-war years.

There remains the second charge – that British businessmen were less well trained for management than their counterparts in other countries. The neglect of management education has long been seen as a serious weakness in Britain, only partially corrected by the creation of graduate business schools in the 1960s.[42] As late as 1989 an authoritative report was complaining that management education in British industry was 'too little, too late, and for too few'.[43] The standard of comparison in most of these analyses is the US. As discussed in Chapter 2, the transition from owner-managed to professionally managed companies came earlier in the US than in Britain. The large investor-owned companies such as General Electric and United States Steel Corporation which were formed in the closing years of the nineteenth century needed teams of well-trained managers, some with specialised skills in engineering and finance, others with broader administrative capabilities. The higher education system was adapted to meet this requirement, and part of the expansion took the form of business schools, mostly attached to existing universities.[44]

In Britain the professionalisation of management came later, and took a different form. Up to the First World War most British companies were small enough not to need complex managerial hierarchies, and there were no business schools of the American type, although several universities, principally Birmingham, Manchester and the London School of Economics, introduced courses in commerce, accounting and other management-related subjects. With the trend towards mergers and acquisitions in the 1920s and 1930s, there was a greater need for professional managers, and it was met in a variety of ways. More universities offered courses in business administration, and the leading engineering institutions began to include training in management as part of the qualification for membership.[45]

Another source of management expertise was the accountancy profession.

This stemmed from the growth of joint stock companies in the second half of the nineteenth century. As the number of companies seeking a stock exchange quotation increased, investors insisted that their accounts should be independently audited. The Institute of Chartered Accountants in England and Wales, the largest of the accountancy bodies, was founded in 1880. Accounting firms acted as financial advisers to the companies whose accounts they audited, and were often involved in mergers and financial reconstructions. It was not uncommon for senior accountants to be taken on by clients as full-time managers; a well-known case was that of Francis d'Arcy Cooper, who joined Lever Brothers in 1923 and became chairman two years later. Employers saw that the rigorous training which accountants had to undergo was a good preparation for management. By 1931 about a third of all chartered accountants worked in business, and several of the country's leading industrialists, such as Allan Macdiarmid at Stewarts and Lloyds, had an accountancy background. In the absence of business schools, and with only a limited provision of management courses at universities, chartered accountancy was one of the best available routes into general management.[46]

By the time of the Second World War a partial professionalisation of British management had taken place. If the number of university graduates among senior managers was less than in the US or Germany, this was offset by the spread of professional qualifications, most of which included some element of management training. It is true that, among the graduates who reached senior positions, some could be classified as generalists, having studied classics or other non-technical subjects. A few employers favoured this background on the grounds that an arts-based education was more likely than science and engineering to instil leadership and character. But there were at least as many others who looked to the universities for highly trained technical experts. ICI, for instance, wanted chemists and engineers, some of whom could be developed into general managers.

After 1945 the issue of management training and education acquired greater prominence as part of the general drive to raise British productivity closer to US standards. The Attlee government was instrumental in setting up the British Institute of Management (BIM), and several colleges offered courses leading to the BIM's Diploma in Management Studies. A group of businessmen financed the Administrative Staff College at Henley, designed for senior managers and directors. The arrival in Britain of numerous American companies and management consultants helped to spread awareness of modern management techniques. Ford Motor Company was well-known for its graduate recruitment programme, and many ex-Ford managers went on to occupy senior positions in other British companies. The admiration of American management led to the creation, with government support, of graduate business schools at London and Manchester.[47] Once these new schools were in operation, other universities followed suit and management education expanded rapidly in the 1970s and 1980s. Even Oxford and Cambridge established graduate business schools in the 1990s.

It is possible that British industry would have performed better if the expansion of management education had taken place earlier, but the example of West Germany suggests that business schools on the US model were not a necessary condition for economic success. The American concept of professional management, unrelated to a specific technical discipline such as engineering, was regarded with some scepticism in Germany.[48] The distinctive feature of German management has been the predominance of technical qualifications, especially in engineering, among senior executives, although this has recently begun to change.

Some observers believe that what was wrong with British management was not the failure to be more like the Americans, but the under-valuation of technical competence as a qualification for senior posts. A particular cause for complaint, especially from engineers, is the over-representation of accountants on the boards of British companies; this was one of the themes of the Finniston report on the engineering profession, published in 1980.[49] Yet, as explained earlier, there are historical reasons for the special role played by accountants in British management, and there is no reason to believe that the consequences have been detrimental to British industrial performance. It is as easy to find examples of companies which have been run successfully by accountants (GKN under Trevor Holdsworth, Glaxo under Paul Girolami) as it is to find cases where companies have been mismanaged by engineers (BMC under George Harriman).

Is the quality of management, then, irrelevant as a source of Britain's post-war industrial decline? There is no doubt that some British companies were badly managed in the 1950s and 1960s and that there was a significant improvement in the 1980s and 1990s. Part of the improvement may have been due to the more meritocratic approach adopted by large industrial companies to board-level appointments.[50] The wider availability of management education may also have been helpful. But a more important factor was the increasing intensity of competition, which made it hard for badly managed companies to survive. To the extent that there were management weaknesses in Britain after the Second World War, they stemmed not so much from nepotism, or from the class system, or from the failure to invest in management training, as from soft markets. The war and the seller's market which followed bred a certain complacency in the boardrooms of some large British companies and an undemanding approach to management recruitment. There were, of course, plenty of exceptions: men like like H. G. Lazell at Beecham, Patrick Hennessy at Ford and Arnold Weinstock at GEC cannot be regarded as unprofessional or undynamic. As competition increased, more such men rose to the top of their companies – Christopher Hogg at Courtaulds, John Harvey-Jones at ICI, Roger Hurn at Smiths Industries, and many more – and they were reinforced by a sprinkling of talent imported from overseas. A modernisation of British management was taking place, in line with the internationalisation of British industry.

———•○•———

SIXTEEN

Trade Unions and Labour Relations

F or the first few years after the Second World War labour relations in
Britain seemed to be in good working order. There had been few
serious industrial disputes since the 1926 General Strike, the prestige
of trade union leaders had been enhanced by the war, and neither the Labour
government nor the Conservative opposition wished to tamper with the legal
framework within which unions and employers dealt with each other. It was
not unreasonable to believe, as did civil servants in the Ministry of Labour,
that 'here as in their unwritten constitution the British people had been able
to work out a flexible and pragmatic way of managing their affairs that was
an example to the world'.[1]

This mood of complacency faded in the course of the 1950s. By the end
of the decade it was clear that something had gone seriously wrong. The
number of strikes was increasing, and there was growing concern that union-
imposed restrictive practices were hampering the growth of productivity.
Labour relations came to be seen during the 1960s and 1970s as part of the
'British disease', and no cure was in sight. The unpopularity of the trade
unions – and the failure of the Labour government's policy of accommodation and partnership – contributed decisively to the Conservative victory in
the election of May 1979. What followed was a remarkable transformation
of the labour relations system. Margaret Thatcher's government introduced
a series of legislative changes which restricted the ability of trade unions and
their members to take industrial action against employers. The Prime Minister was also far more robust than her predecessors in resisting unions which
attempted to obstruct her policies. The defeat of the National Union of
Mineworkers in the long strike of 1984–5 was a turning-point in Britain's
labour relations history.

These events took place when the bargaining strength of organised labour
was diminishing for other reasons.[2] Unemployment was running at a high
level, averaging over 9 per cent of the workforce between 1980 and 1995,

compared with 4 per cent between 1965 and 1980; job losses were especially severe in heavily unionised industries such as steel and engineering. At the same time fiercer international competition was forcing companies to reduce their labour costs. The outcome was a shift in the balance of power from unions to employers, leading to a vigorous attack on inefficient working practices and a reduction in the number of strikes (TABLE 16.1).

TABLE 16.1 *Strikes in Britain 1950–95*

(annual averages)

	No. of stoppages	No. of workers involved (000s)	No. of working days lost per 1000 employees
1950–59	2116	663	3252
1960–69	2446	1357	3554
1970–79	2598	1616	12,870
1980–89	1116	1040	7213
1990–95	286	223	758

Source: *Employment Gazette* and Office for National Statistics.

Many observers believe that the taming of the trade unions was Margaret Thatcher's greatest achievement. Even the Labour Party came to accept that the new legal framework was here to stay, and that too close an association with the trade union movement was politically damaging. Although Tony Blair's New Labour government elected in 1997 made some concessions to trade union demands, the influence of union leaders on ministers was much less than it had been under the Labour administrations of the 1960s and 1970s.

That labour relations in Britain changed for the better in the 1980s is not in dispute. What remains a matter of controversy is the extent of the damage caused by the failure to reform the system in the pre-Thatcher period. How far can trade unions be blamed for what went wrong in British industry after the war?

The Distinctiveness of British Labour Relations

Britain entered the post-war period with a labour relations system which, like many British institutions, had evolved over a long period in an unplanned, incremental way. After the repeal of the Combination Acts in 1824, a large number of trade unions were established, some of which, like Robert Owen's Grand National Consolidated Trade Union, had ambitions to become mass working-class movements. The authorities, fearing revolution, responded harshly, and there were some flagrant acts of repression. A famous example was the prosecution in 1834 of the Tolpuddle martyrs, a group of Dorset farm labourers who were trying to organise a union. The struggle for social and political reform was taken up by the Chartists, but Chartism faded in the 1840s as standards of living improved and government policy towards working-class demands became more accommodating. The energies of the labour movement turned from political agitation to more narrowly economic objectives, in the form of the 'New Model' trade unions.

These unions were formed by the 'aristocrats of labour', skilled workers who had a stake in the existing economic order and were aware of their own importance to it. Some of them were craftsmen who had experience of self-help organisations through the journeymen's societies which had existed in pre-industrial times. In these cases the bond which united members of the same trade was apprenticeship. In engineering, for example, several skilled trades came together in 1851 to form the Amalgamated Society of Engineers (ASE). In shipbuilding the shift from wooden to iron hulls in the 1850s created a demand for skilled metal-workers, most of whom were represented by the Boilermakers Society.[3] In industries where production workers did not undergo a formal apprenticeship, such as cotton textiles, iron-making and coal-mining, the labour aristocracy consisted of the more skilled and experienced workers – the mule spinners, the senior melters, and the hewers – all of whom formed strong and durable trade unions.

Members of these unions owed their loyalty to practitioners of the same trade, not to fellow workers in the same enterprise – still less to all workers in the same industry. Part of their *raison d'être* was to maintain control over the jobs for which their members were trained, and to resist incursions from unskilled workers or from members of other unions. The various unions were prepared to work together for common political objectives – the first meeting of the Trades Union Congress (TUC), representing some 118,000 trade unionists, took place in Manchester in 1868 – but they were primarily concerned with the interests of their own trade, not with those of the working class as a whole. The sectionalism of the early trade unions left an enduring mark on the British labour movement.

Unlike the Chartists, the skilled workers' unions posed no threat to the capitalist system. Conservatives as well as Liberals formed a benign view of trade unions as a force for social peace. Both parties agreed that employers and employees should be free to regulate their affairs without the intervention of the law. The Trade Union Act of 1871 and the Conspiracy and Protection of Property Act of 1875 – the first passed by Gladstone's Liberal government, the second by the Conservatives under Disraeli – established that a union could instruct its members to go on strike without the risk of being sued for criminal conspiracy.

As the unions strengthened their position, most employers recognised that 'if there had to be unions at all, then in practice industrial relations were most orderly when the unions were solidly organised and met a no less solid organisation of employers in regular and reasonable discussion'.[4] Employers' associations were formed to negotiate with unions on a regional and later on a national basis, and these arrangements often included elaborate procedures for handling disputes.

In the closing years of the century, as economic growth slowed down and international competition increased, labour relations deteriorated. Employers sought to reduce their production costs by cutting wages or intensifying the pace of work, and the number of disputes increased. This period also saw a change in the character of trade unionism. Starting in the 1880s, general unions were formed for semi-skilled and unskilled workers. This was a more aggressive, class-conscious type of unionism, and more influenced by socialist ideas; some of the leaders of the new unions were members of the Marxist-oriented Social Democratic Federation, although Marxism was never more than a minority strand within the trade union movement.

Employers began to chafe at the legal immunities which the unions had won in the 1870s. In 1900 the Taff Vale railway company in South Wales sued the Society of Railway Servants for attempting to prevent, through picketing, the employment of non-unionised labour. The House of Lords ruled in the following year that the union's actions were illegal. There followed a great debate, the establishment of a Royal Commission and strong pressure from the unions to have the ruling reversed through legislation. After the Liberal victory in the 1906 election, the Trade Disputes Act was passed, giving the unions even more sweeping immunities than they had won in 1875. The Prime Minister, Sir Henry Campbell-Bannerman, argued that trade unions had performed a great service 'in the prevention of conflict and the promotion of harmony between capital and labour', and that the Taff Vale judgement was an unwarranted intrusion by the courts into matters which should be settled voluntarily between employers and employees.[5]

The Taff Vale episode convinced the unions that they needed stronger representation in Westminster. There were already trade unionists in Parliament – the first had been elected in 1874 – but they relied on organisational support from the Liberal Party. In 1900 the TUC, together with a group of socialist societies – the Independent Labour Party, the Social Democratic Federation and the Fabian Society – formed the Labour Representation Committee. Six years later this body was converted into the Labour Party. It won twenty-nine seats in the 1906 election. The new party was largely funded by the unions, and its policies reflected the generally reformist, non-revolutionary character of the labour movement.

Between 1906 and 1914, as the unions extended their reach into previously unorganised industries, trade union membership almost doubled, and towards the end of this period labour relations became more turbulent. Some of the most serious strikes were in coal-mining, where employers faced severe cost pressures and strenuously resisted demands for wage increases. Others were in sectors such as the London docks where unions were seeking to establish negotiating rights for the first time in the face of vigorous employer opposition. There was a trend towards more violent forms of protest, and a greater willingness to use the strike weapon as a means of putting pressure on the government.[6] Another source of tension was the increasing assertiveness of plant-based shop stewards, often acting independently of union officials. Several unions had created the post of shop steward to ensure that union rules were strictly observed in the factory; but their responsibilities went further than carrying out union instructions. In engineering, for example, where many firms had adopted the piecework method of payment, national agreements between the Engineering Employers Federation and the unions settled only basic wages, leaving piece rates to be worked out locally: piecework bargaining formed an important part of the shop steward's work.

The government's response to labour unrest was to offer its services as a conciliator through the Labour Department of the Board of Trade (converted into the Ministry of Labour during the First World War). In 1917 a committee chaired by J. H. Whitley, Speaker of the House of Commons, recommended that joint industrial councils should be set up in each industry, linked to joint works committees in factories. But these proposals met a lukewarm response. Employers feared their managerial freedom would be undermined if workers were given a statutory right to consultation, while unions were concerned that consultative committees might by-pass the estab-lished bargaining channels. A few joint works committees were formed after the war, but most of them were abandoned in the 1920s.[7]

Union membership continued to rise during and after the First World War, reaching a peak of 8.3m, about 45 per cent of the working population, in 1920 (TABLE 16.2). But the recession which began in that year led to a sharp increase in unemployment, and the unions were in a weak bargaining position for the rest of the decade. With profits under pressure, the main concern for most employers was to reduce production costs, and there was a rash of wage disputes. In 1922 the engineering employers clashed with the Amalgamated Engineering Union, and after a lengthy lock-out the union suffered a crushing defeat. These years also saw an intensification of the long-running battle between the mine-owners and the mineworkers' union. In 1926 the owners sought to impose another wage cut. The miners were determined to resist, and successfully appealed to the TUC for support. The outcome, for the first and only time in the history of the labour movement, was a general strike. The Baldwin government stood firm, and the strike collapsed after nine days.

TABLE 16.2 *Trade union membership in Britain, 1900–1939*

Year	No. of members (millions)
1900	2.0
1910	2.6
1920	8.3
1930	4.8
1939	6.3

Source: B. R. Mitchell and H. G. Jones, *Second Abstract of British Historical Statistics*, Cambridge, 1971.

This period of turmoil left the institutions of collective bargaining surprisingly unscathed. The only legislative change resulting from the General
Strike was the Trade Disputes and Trade Unions Act of 1927, banning political
strikes. Although this measure was strongly opposed by the unions, it had
little practical impact. A more important consequence of the General Strike
was the reappraisal of policy within the trade union movement. The tactics
of confrontation were replaced by a more conciliatory approach, promoted
by Walter Citrine, newly appointed general secretary of the TUC. The unions,
Citrine declared in 1927, were ready to work with employers 'in a concerted
effort to raise industry to its highest efficiency by developing the most
scientific methods of production, eliminating waste and harmful restrictions,
removing causes of friction and avoidable conflict, and promoting the largest
possible output'.[8] Citrine had a powerful ally in Ernest Bevin, head of the
Transport and General Workers Union, and these two men steered the labour
movement, not without protests from the Left, into a more constructive
relationship with the employers.

The unions' change of tack evoked a sympathetic response from a group
of industrialists led by Sir Alfred Mond, chairman of ICI, who shared
Citrine's view that labour relations should be put on a new basis after the
bitterness of the General Strike. This group contained several prominent
business leaders, including Hugo Hirst of GEC and Herbert Austin of the
Austin Motor Company. They invited Ben Turner, the textile workers' leader
who was president of the TUC, to hold discussions about labour relations
and about wider issues of industrial efficiency. Agreement was reached on
a set of proposals including the establishment of a National Industrial Council, made up of an equal number of representatives from the TUC and the
two employer bodies – the National Confederation of Employers' Organisations (NCEO) and the Federation of British Industry (FBI). The Council
was to be given a general oversight over labour relations questions.[9]

These ideas were greeted without enthusiasm by most employers: they
had no interest in new institutions which would enhance the power of
organised labour, least of all at a time when, because of high unemployment
and the failure of the General Strike, the unions were less troublesome than
they had been for a long time.[10] Employers were also doubtful whether
national agreements would have much effect on behaviour on the shop floor.
Although the NCEO agreed to discuss the Mond–Turner proposals with
the TUC, there was no meeting of minds and the talks petered out in 1931.

Some historians believe that this was a missed opportunity to reconstruct
the British labour relations system on non-adversarial lines.[11] But in the

years which followed the Mond–Turner talks the case for reform seemed less pressing. Apart from three big stoppages in textiles in 1929–31 (caused by union resistance to wage cuts), there were no major national disputes between the General Strike and the Second World War. Moreover, although unemployment remained high until the onset of rearmament in the mid-1930s, the absence of strikes was not simply a reflection of union weakness. Thanks to the intelligent leadership of Citrine and Bevin, collective bargaining was strengthened in industries where it already existed, and extended to some of those where it did not. By the time of the Second World War the trade unions were accepted by most employers, with varying degrees of reluctance, as negotiating partners. Union membership, having fallen to a low point of 4.4m in 1933, recovered to 6.3m in 1939.

Yet there were defects in the system. One was the fragmented structure of the trade union movement, reflecting its origins as a group of job-protection societies. Although the number of unions was reduced through mergers in the inter-war years, there was no trend towards industrial unions – unions which represent all workers in a given industry. Some large employers had to deal with several unions, which were often at loggerheads with each other. In shipbuilding, for example, the proliferation of craft unions was a fertile source of demarcation disputes. In steel, the Iron and Steel Trades Confederation, formed in 1917, covered most production workers, but the National Union of Blastfurnacemen stayed outside, as did the numerous craft unions with members in the industry.

Another weakness stemmed from the practice of industry-wide bargaining, which had been established in textiles and some other industries towards the end of the nineteenth century and spread more widely in the inter-war years. This system allowed employers to delegate the task of dealing with unions to their trade associations. However, in some industries national agreements left a number of issues to be settled at the workplace. These were handled informally by foremen and supervisors, without much involvement by senior managers, most of whom wanted as little as possible to do with trade unions. A few large, professionally managed companies made their own arrangements with the unions: ICI, for instance, created an elaborate structure of consultative councils to handle employment issues. In general, however, personnel management was an under-developed skill in British industry in the inter-war years.[12]

Finally, the memory of past struggles left a legacy of mutual suspicion and mistrust which the high unemployment of the 1930s did nothing to dispel. This did not apply equally to all industries. In steel, for example, there was a long history of peaceful resolution of disputes – although this did not prevent the unions from pressing for steel nationalisation during the 1930s. The general view among employers was that unions were an unpleasant but unavoidable constraint, and that their influence should be kept to a minimum.

Was British experience before 1939 a worse preparation for the post-war period than that of other European nations? Of the larger Continental countries, Germany had the most highly developed labour movement before the Second World War. German trade unions had begun to establish themselves in the 1860s, principally among skilled workers, but their growth was held back by Bismarck's repressive legislation and by the hostility of most employers. Partly for this reason, craft exclusiveness never had as strong a hold in Germany as it did in Britain. The unions saw themselves, not as job-protection societies, but as part of a working-class movement struggling to secure its rightful place in society.[13] After the repeal of Bismarck's Anti-Socialist Law in 1890, union membership increased, and the trade unions began to organise themselves more effectively.

The First World War was a turning-point for the German trade unions. By their support for the war effort they made themselves indispensable to the state, and employers were forced to accept that the labour movement had to be integrated into society. At the end of the war, with Germany facing the threat of Communist revolution, the unions were seen as a bulwark against social disorder. In November 1918 a historic agreement between prominent businessmen and union leaders – the Stinnes–Legien pact – gave the labour movement a legitimacy which was consolidated when the Weimar Republic was formed. A major advance for the unions was the Works Councils Act of 1920, providing for works councils to be established in all firms employing more than fifty workers.

Like the Republic itself, however, the reconciliation between capital and labour was built on fragile foundations. Many employers resented the growth of trade union power and sought to undermine the 1918 agreement.[14] The onset of depression at the end of the 1920s made them even more determined to roll back union gains. The lock-out of 250,000 iron and steel-workers in the Ruhr in 1928 was the start of an aggressive anti-union campaign, which continued until the unions were dissolved by the Nazis. The behaviour of German employers before and after Hitler's rise to power left a legacy of bitterness among German trade unionists which would not be easily erased.

In France the trade unions were weaker before the Second World War than in Germany and Britain. The stance of French employers in the early stages of industrialisation was authoritarian and paternalistic. A wave of strikes at the turn of the century caused concern among politicians about the alienation of industrial workers, and new conciliation machinery was set up. But there was virtually no collective bargaining on the British model, and the spread of syndicalist and Marxist ideas before the First World War stiffened the resistance of employers to unionisation. The war brought a partial truce between employers and unions. The strongest union federation, the Confédération Générale du Travail (CGT), played an active part in the war effort and achieved a substantial increase in membership. But there was no basic change in employer attitudes and high unemployment during the 1920s undermined the power of organised labour. In 1936 the election of Leon Blum's Popular Front government brought gains for the trade unions, but they were short-lived. With the defeat of the unions in the 1938 General Strike, called to protest against the abandonment of the forty-hour week, the balance of power in industry shifted back to employers.[15]

Of the three countries Britain was the only one at the time of the Second World War with a strong, politically secure trade union movement and a set of collective bargaining institutions with which employers, unions and governments seemed broadly content. Few could have predicted that the labour relations system would come to be seen as the Achilles' heel of the British economy.

The Post-war Deterioration in Labour Relations

The Second World War was a watershed in the history of the British trade union movement. Thanks to the appointment of Ernest Bevin as Minister of Labour in Winston Churchill's coalition, the interests of the trade unions were represented at the highest levels of government. Manpower planning was crucial to the war effort, and Bevin's skill in dealing with employers and union leaders helped to ensure that the redeployment of labour was handled with the minimum of friction. The unions were accepted, together with the employers and the government, as part of a tripartite system of planning and consultation, and this was to set the pattern for the early post-war years. Union membership rose during the war, reaching a total of just under 8m in 1945, and an increasing number of employers gave formal or informal recognition to shop stewards.[16]

Following Labour's landslide victory in the 1945 election, the political climate was exceptionally favourable for the unions. Many of the measures taken by the Attlee government, such as nationalisation of the coal-mines, had been on their wish-list since the 1920s. The Trade Disputes Act of 1927, which had banned political strikes, was repealed. But the Conservatives were also anxious to cultivate friendly relations with the trade unions. Their Industrial Charter, published in 1947, referred with pride to the role played by past Conservative governments in strengthening the legal position of unions. 'We desire to state quite clearly,' wrote the authors of the Charter, 'that the official policy of the Conservative Party is in favour of trade unions.'[17]

A central feature of the post-war settlement was the commitment to full employment, to be achieved by Keynesian demand management policies, and this called for the co-operation of the unions in keeping wage increases under control. The unions wanted to be free to conduct their negotiations with employers without interference, but they recognised the need, in the difficult economic circumstances of the early post-war years, to exercise restraint over wage demands. Between 1948 and 1950 the TUC agreed to a virtual freeze on wages, and for the most part union negotiators followed the TUC's lead. However, this policy caused resentment among the rank and file, and contributed to an increasing number of unofficial strikes. (Official strikes were banned until 1951 under the wartime emergency regulations, known as Order 1305.)

Despite these difficulties the spirit of tripartism was maintained when the Conservatives, led by Winston Churchill, took office in 1951. Churchill gave his Minister of Labour, Walter Monckton, a clear mandate to keep the peace, even at the cost of making concessions to union demands. In the second half of the 1950s, however, the policy of accommodation was in danger of collapse in the face of growing wage pressure and a shift to the left within the trade union leadership. Frank Cousins, who took over as General Secretary of the Transport and General Workers Union in 1956, was closer in outlook to the shop floor activists than his predecessor, Arthur Deakin, and he vigorously opposed any form of wage restraint.

The problem of unofficial strikes was also worsening, especially in the motor industry,[18] where militant shop stewards were building up powerful shop floor organisations. The role of the stewards was highlighted in the famous 'bell ringer' strike at Ford's Dagenham plant in 1957. A court of inquiry was set up to investigate the dispute and found that over a two-year period there had been 234 work stoppages, often called without discussion or warning of any sort. The inquiry report referred to the shop steward organisation as 'a private union within a union, enjoying immediate and continuous contact with the men in the shop, answerable to no superiors and in no way officially or constitutionally linked with the union hierarchy'.[19] Communist Party members were prominently represented in this organisation.

The deterioration in labour relations came at a time when the post-war seller's market was fading and international competition was increasing. Employers sought to tackle inefficient working practices which had been allowed to take root in the early post-war years. In 1960 Esso, the American-owned oil company, negotiated a pioneering agreement with its unions at the Fawley oil refinery, which bought out restrictive working practices in return for higher pay. This was the start of the productivity bargaining movement which spread to much of British industry during the 1960s. Allan Flanders, the academic who studied the Fawley agreement and became the chief propagandist for productivity bargaining, saw it as a way of shifting enployers from a reactive to an active labour relations policy.[20]

The idea was to bring shop stewards and managers into a partnership, involving detailed agreements on manning levels, flexibility between trades, and all the other sources of inefficiency which had previously been accepted by both sides as part of the status quo. Companies were urged 'to regain control by sharing it'. But in replacing informal shop floor bargaining with more formal procedures, companies often created a new set of rules which shop stewards could argue about, and the tendency was to give away more in pay increases than was recovered through greater efficiency.[21]

As public concern over labour relations increased, the issue of the unions' legal immunities came under closer scrutiny. In 1963, while the Conservatives were still in office, the House of Lords made a judgement which was to have far-reaching consequences. They ruled, in the case of Rookes v. Barnard, that a non-unionist who had been sacked by his employer because the union threatened to strike in support of a closed shop was entitled to damages from the union. This appeared to undermine the immunities which had been granted as part of the 1906 Trade Disputes Act. The TUC, fearing a repetition of Taff Vale, pressed the government to reverse the judgement through legislation. The government responded by setting up a committee of civil servants to review the implications of the Rookes judgement. The Conservatives also promised, in their manifesto for the 1964 election, to appoint a Royal Commission to examine labour relations law.[22] The same pledge was made by Labour.

Following Labour's victory the Rookes judgement was quickly reversed, and in 1965 a Royal Commission was set up under Lord Donovan. Some employers argued before the Commission that collective agreements should be made legally binding, as in the US and Germany. This was rejected by Lord Donovan and a majority of his colleagues.[23] The fundamental problem, in their view, was the gap between formal bargaining at industry level and informal bargaining within the plant. The Commission recommended that the informal arena should be made more orderly and that employers should develop company-based bargaining arrangements along the lines of the Fawley agreement.

An important consequence of the Donovan report was to bring shop stewards into the official fold; employers had to accept them as part of their negotiating procedures.[24] However, the report was a deep disappointment for those who had hoped for a thorough-going reform of the labour relations system. Even the Labour government, which had no wish to offend the trade unions, regarded it as wholly inadequate: something more was needed to curb the proliferation of unofficial strikes. In 1969 the government published proposals, under the title, 'In place of strife', whereby in certain circumstances sanctions would be imposed on workers who engaged in unconstitutional action.[25] But for Labour's allies in the trade union movement free collective bargaining, untrammelled by the law, was a principle to which they were totally committed; their fierce opposition forced the government to withdraw its proposals.

By the time of the 1970 election, reform of trade union law was firmly on the political agenda. The new Conservative government under Edward Heath entered office with a commitment to replace the 1906 Trade Disputes Act: the Industrial Relations Act of 1971 was designed to narrow the scope of trade union immunities and establish a statutory framework for the conduct of labour relations. Collective agreements between unions and employers would be legally enforceable unless a written provision to the contrary was included, and trade union leaders would be made responsible for actions taken in their name. The closed shop would be prohibited, and workers given the legal right not to belong to a trade union.

These measures were adamantly opposed by the trade unions. They regarded the Act as an assault on the hallowed principle of 'voluntarism' in labour relations, and they refused to co-operate with it. Many employers were also unhappy with the Act; they feared – correctly as it turned out – that the use of the law would create martyrs. The Act was over-complicated and over-ambitious, and introduced with inadequate consultation. It also greatly reduced the prospect of any agreement between the Heath government and the trade unions over wages. In 1972 the National Union of

Mineworkers staged a successful strike in pursuit of a wage claim which far exceeded the government's guidelines. Another dispute with the mines in the autumn of 1973, leading to the declaration of a State of Emergency and the introduction of a three-day week, precipitated an early general election in which Heath hoped to obtain a renewed mandate for a firm policy towards the unions. Instead, he was blamed by the public for provoking confrontation, and the election resulted in a narrow win for Labour.

The new government, led by Harold Wilson, promptly repealed the Industrial Relations Act and launched the Social Contract, an ambitious attempt to secure wage restraint in return for economic, industrial and social measures which were to the unions' advantage. Between 1974 and 1979 trade unions exerted more influence over government policy than at any time since the Attlee government. Jack Jones, General Secretary of the Transport and General Workers Union and one of the principal architects of the Social Contract, was widely regarded as a more important figure than most ministers. This period also saw an increase in trade union membership (from 10.5m in 1969 to 13.3m in 1979) and in the strength of shop steward organisation. Jack Jones and his counterpart in the Amalgamated Engineering Union, Hugh Scanlon, strongly favoured the delegation of authority to the shop floor. The political climate was such that employers were unable or unwilling to resist the increase in trade union power. Many of them, in line with the recommendations of the Donovan report, gave shop stewards and shop stewards' committees a larger role in negotiations, and there was a continuing drift away from industry-wide bargaining.

The partnership between unions and the Labour government eventually fell apart, not on the issue of unofficial strikes as in 1969, but over wages. For the first three phases of the Social Contract, up to the wage round of 1977–8, the unions had agreed to restrain wage increases in line with the government's guidelines. But for the next round the government laid down a limit of 5 per cent for wage increases, and this provoked widespread resistance, especially among public sector workers. A rash of strikes in the winter of 1978–9, the so-called Winter of Discontent, signalled the end of the Social Contract, and of the Labour government. Following the election of May 1979, the unsolved problem of British labour relations was handed over to Margaret Thatcher.

Comparisons with Germany and France

How did this experience compare with that of other European countries? The sharpest contrast was with West Germany, where the Nazi era and defeat in the war had left an institutional void in the labour relations field. The unions, which were in a strong moral position because they were not tainted with Nazism, pressed strongly for co-determination – an equal role for workers and employers in the governance of companies. As described in Chapter 3, the British occupation authorities agreed in 1947 that the reconstituted steel companies in the Ruhr should have supervisory boards divided equally between worker and employer representatives. How far this arrangement should be extended to other industries was the subject of intense debate after the foundation of the Federal Republic in 1949. The compromise reached in 1951 preserved what the unions had won in coal and steel and extended a more limited form of co-determination to other industries. This was followed in 1952 by the creation of company-based works councils under the Works Constitution Act.

Although these reforms drew on the experience of the Weimar Republic, the unions were determined not to repeat the mistakes made during that period. Above all, the labour movement had to be united. A single umbrella organisation, the Deutscher Gewerkschaftsbund (DGB), was established in 1949, providing a federal structure within which a small number of autonomous industrial unions bargained on behalf of all employees in their industry. In contrast with Britain, wage bargaining at the industry level was separated from the handling of labour issues within companies, which was the domain of the works council.[26] By reducing the number of unions and creating a dual channel of worker representation, through the union and through the works council, the Germans avoided two of the problems which affected the British system: inter-union rivalry and sectional shop floor bargaining. The new system was underpinned by laws which set out in detail the rights and responsibilities of each of the participants.

The old hostility between unions and employers was not instantly dissipated, but two forces were at work during the 1950s which helped to consolidate the new arrangements. In contrast to Britain, first, the anti-capitalist strand in the German labour movement, with its demands for public ownership and central planning, was marginalised. The leadership, like that of the Social Democratic Party, accepted that the interests of workers could best be promoted within the market economy. There was more common ground than in

Britain between unions and employers, and between the two largest political parties, about how industry and the economy should be organised. The second factor was the extraordinary success of the German economy; unions did not have to be especially militant to secure large material gains for their members.[27]

In France no similar reform of labour relations took place after the war. Far from achieving unity on the German pattern, the divisions in the French labour movement increased. In 1948 the moderate Force Ouvrière (FO) broke away from the Communist-dominated Confédération Générale du Travail (CGT). The separate Catholic trade union confederation, the Confédération Française des Travailleurs Chrétiens (CFTC), was also riven by internal strains; in 1964 the more militant element quit the CFTC to set up a separate organisation, the Confédération Française Démocratique du Travail (CFDT). One of the consequences of these rivalries was that union membership in France was lower than in Britain and shop floor organisation much weaker. Although France's labour relations were as adversarial as Britain's, divisions among the unions and their low level of membership gave French employers greater freedom in the management of labour.

How Much Damage was Done?

The most visible aspect of Britain's deteriorating labour relations in the 1960s and 1970s was the frequency of strikes, especially unofficial strikes. Because of the publicity attached to these events, there has been a tendency to exaggerate their importance. As TABLE 16.3 shows, Britain was not exceptionally strike-prone during this period compared to France and Italy, although Germany had a far better record. Moreover, the vast majority of workers in manufacturing industry were hardly affected by strikes; in a typical year, less than a tenth of one per cent of the available work time was lost through industrial disputes.[28]

Of the industries discussed in this book, the most strike-prone were motor vehicles and shipbuilding. Both were complex, assembly-type industries with large concentrations of labour on a single site. Both were affected to a greater extent than other industries by inter-union rivalry and sectional shop floor bargaining. In both there was a history of insecurity of employment and earnings. Even in these two cases, however, as earlier chapters have shown, strikes were only one element in the decline which took place during the 1960s and 1970s.

TABLE 16.3 *Working days lost in industrial disputes per 1000 employees (annual averages) in Britain, Germany, France and Italy, 1961–80*

	1961–5	1966–70	1971–5	1976–80
Britain	127.0	222.6	538.6	521.7
Germany	18.3	6.0	47.7	44.1
France	146.3	134.0	186.7	154.2
Italy	684.4	933.6	1063.9	940.0

Source: International Labour Organisation, *Yearbook of Labour Statistics.*

The collapse of the truck industry was not due to strokes, but to failings in engineering, design and marketing. On the car side, the under-pricing of the Mini, the mismanagement of British Leyland after the 1968 merger, the failure of the Allegro and the Marina – none of these errors can be blamed on trade unions or shop stewards. On the other hand, the persistence of unofficial stoppages – and the inability or unwillingness of union leaders to control their shop floor activists – did cause serious damage. In the case of British Leyland, the reassertion of management control over the shop floor which took place under Michael Edwardes between 1977 and 1982 was a necessary condition for the rehabilitation of the company, although, as subsequent events were to show, not a sufficient one. The strike problem was also one of the reasons why Ford and General Motors shifted more of their investment to Germany and Spain during the 1970s, and largely abandoned exporting cars from their British factories.

In shipbuilding, too, avoidable mistakes by management were at least as important in causing the decline of the industry as bad labour relations. In the early post-war years British yards were slow to abandon an approach to designing, building and marketing ships which had become obsolete. The fact that they missed out on the oil tanker boom, and failed to profit from the new market for specialised vessels such as roll-on/roll-off ferries, was not the fault of trade unions. Conversely, the case of Austin & Pickersgill, the Wearside yard, showed that labour relations were not an insuperable obstacle to commercial success.

It is certainly possible that the shipbuilding industry would have done better if labour relations had been reformed in the 1950s. The sectionalism of the industry's trade unions, leading to fragmented wage bargaining and frequent demarcation disputes, complicated the task of management, and the delivery delays resulting from strikes were partly responsible for the loss of market share. But any labour relations reform would have had to be accompanied by a realistic product and marketing policy of the sort which Austin & Pickersgill introduced in the 1960s (Chapter 5).

Outside these two industries, the incidence of strikes was low. In process industries such as chemicals, with a high degree of automatic control in factories, it was easier to avoid the friction between different work groups which bedevilled industries such as cars and shipbuilding. This was also true of paper-making, although some of the larger mills, especially those situated near the big population centres of London and Liverpool, were subject to sporadic labour disputes. More generally smaller factories employing less than 500 people were rarely troubled by strikes.[29]

In terms of damage to the economy, strikes were less important than inefficiency in the use of labour. How far this can be blamed on the trade unions is debatable. Some restrictive labour practices – for example, those arising from demarcation between trades – arose from agreements made between employers and trade unions which were entirely rational when first introduced, but were made obsolete by changing technology. The fact that they persisted for so long was due as much to the acquiescence of employers as to the obstinacy of trade unions. Other practices – for example, bad time-keeping, excessive tea breaks, late starting and early stopping – were the result of lax management rather than trade union power. The easy markets of the early post-war years allowed both types of inefficiency to become more solidly entrenched. They acquired the status of 'custom and practice', which unions were determined to defend and employers had no great incentive to attack.

When employers did try to tackle the problem, in the 1960s and 1970s, it proved difficult to win the co-operation of shop stewards and trade unions, especially in industries characterised by large sites and multiple unions.[30] In the steel industry, for example, agreements on new working practices had to be negotiated with several different unions – the Iron and Steel Trades Confederation, the National Union of Blastfurnacemen, and the numerous craft unions. The persistence of these problems contributed to the sluggish growth of productivity in steel before and after nationalisation in 1967.

The impact of overmanning varied widely from industry to industry. Many of the industries which lost ground to competitors in the 1960s and

1970s, such as motorcycles, machine tools and cotton textiles, did so for reasons which had little or nothing to do with labour relations. Nevertheless, inefficiency in the use of labour was a drag on the performance of the economy as a whole.

For employers to have imposed new working practices without union agreement was virtually impossible in the political climate of the times. Such action would almost certainly have provoked a strike, and the prospects of the employers winning it were not good. Apart from the brief period when the Conservatives under Edward Heath were trying to implement the Industrial Relations Act of 1971 the stance of successive governments was to discourage confrontation with the trade unions and to seek their co-operation in keeping wage increases under control. Keeping the trade unions sweet was regarded as a price worth paying for the sake of maintaining the post-war commitment to full employment and low inflation. Reform had to await a change in the political environment, opening up the possibility of economic and industrial policies which had previously been regarded as unthinkable.

Labour Relations in the 1980s and 1990s

The 1980s began with a deep recession in which the appreciation of sterling, due partly to the government's tight monetary policies and partly to North Sea oil, put exporters under extreme financial strain. Companies were forced to make drastic reductions in costs, often involving plant closures and redundancies. In some cases this was linked to a reappraisal of strategy which had started before Mrs Thatcher took office. But the new government's policies, including privatisation, deregulation and a firm refusal to rescue 'lame ducks', added to the pressures that were coming from the world market.

Economic necessity was the principal cause of the sustained attack on inefficient working practices which began at that time. But the confidence of management in making changes was increased by a series of Employment Acts, starting in 1980. These measures reduced the unions' legal immunities by defining more narrowly what constituted a trade dispute; exposed unions to penalties for unlawful behaviour carried out in their name; prohibited secondary action – that is, action directed against employers not party to the original dispute; and barred unions from calling strikes without conducting a secret ballot among the workers concerned. Statutory support for collective bargaining was removed; the legal position of non-unionists was strengthened and, in the 1990 Act, all forms of closed shop were outlawed. These legislative reforms were reinforced by an uncompromising government attitude towards unions in the public sector, the most spectacular example being the defeat of the miners in the 1984–5 strike.

Meanwhile high unemployment led to a sharp fall in union membership. Between 1980 and 1995 the unions lost more than 4m members (TABLE 16.4). There was also a decline in the number of workplaces with recognised unions, from 52 per cent to 40 per cent. Part of that decline was due to derecognition, but the more important change was that new workplaces were less likely to recognise unions than in the past.[31]

TABLE 16.4 *Trade union membership in Britain, 1945–95*

Year	No. of members (millions)
1945	7.9
1950	9.3
1955	9.7
1960	9.8
1965	10.3
1970	11.2
1975	12.2
1980	12.9
1985	10.8
1990	9.9
1995	8.1

Source: Chris Wrigley, *British Trade Unions 1945–1995*, Manchester, 1997, p. 30.

The decline in industry-wide bargaining continued after 1979. Engineering and cotton textiles were among several industries where national agreements collapsed or were reduced in influence. The competitive shocks of the 1980s convinced many companies that joint negotiation through their trade association was irrelevant or even harmful to the quest for higher productivity in their own plants. Meanwhile changes in the law encouraged employers to take a more aggressive line with their own unions. Instead of the 1960s idea of regaining control by sharing it, the emphasis was on regaining control and keeping it; if unions resisted, they would be confronted and defeated.

The experience of British Steel Corporation in the first half of the 1980s illustrates the crucial importance of competition as a spur to changes in working practices. Nationalised since 1967, BSC had been partially insulated from market forces: by 1980 costs per tonne were almost a third higher than those of German producers. A critical event in the turnround, as described in Chapter 6, was the thirteen-week strike in 1980. One of its central issues was the management's decision to replace the usual across-the-board pay increase with local bonuses tied to the performance of individual plants. Although the strike was settled with an improved pay offer, the unions were unable to prevent the management from virtually abandoning national bargaining on pay and other issues. New manning arrangements, including greater flexibility between production and craft workers and more use of team-working, were negotiated at plant level.

Another industry in which labour relations dramatically improved was cars. A special factor in this case was the decision by three Japanese companies, Nissan, Honda and Toyota, to build assembly plants in Britain: the Japanese model could be observed at close quarters. But 'Japanisation' also had an influence on other industries. Innovative labour agreements signed by several Japanese investors, starting with the Toshiba TV-set factory at Plymouth in 1981, were widely seen as marking the start of a new era in British industrial relations.[32] The most controversial aspect of these agreements was that they involved a single union representing all employees in the plant. Other features included abolition of the distinction between blue and white collar employees, provision for binding arbitration in the event of disputes, the creation of a broadly based company council elected by all employees, and complete flexibility in the deployment of labour.

Despite the publicity given to these agreements, the number of workplaces covered by Japanese-style single-union deals was small. Few employers tried to shift from multiple to single unionism in an established plant. But multiple unionism no longer imposed the same constraints on what management wanted to do. Thus the 1992 'New Deal' at Rover was described by a personnel manager as 'an opportunity for a traditional British workforce to demonstrate that, working together, they can do the job as well as people who don't have trade unions or people with single-union agreements'.[33]

By the end of the 1990s the number of strikes in Britain had been reduced to levels roughly comparable with Germany and France. More important, the productivity gap with the two Continental countries, which had widened alarmingly in the 1960s and 1970s, had been substantially narrowed. The labour relations system was no longer a competitive handicap for British industry.

Although Thatcherism was unique to Britain, some of the same economic pressures, including Japanese competition and a partial shift towards deregulation and privatisation, were also at work on the Continent, with important consequences for labour relations.

In Germany the dual system of industry-wide bargaining and works councils had been remarkably stable since the 1950s, but the social consensus began to fade in the second half of the 1970s. Union demands for a shorter working week led to the two biggest strikes in the history of the Federal Republic – in steel in 1978–9 and in engineering in 1984. As in Britain, high unemployment and the decline of strongly unionised heavy industries put the labour movement on the defensive. At the same time employers were objecting to the straitjacket of industry-wide wage settlements; some of them withdrew from their employers' associations in order to negotiate separately with their workers. Even when companies stayed within the national framework, the unions were unable to prevent a shift in the locus of collective bargaining to individual companies, leading to greater variation in terms and conditions of work. Some observers believed that the link between union and works council could weaken to the point where the dual system might unravel and a form of company-based unionism might emerge.[34]

However the system might evolve, it was no longer as obvious as it had been in the 1950s and 1960s that Germany's collective bargaining arrangements constituted a competitive advantage for German industry. The checks and balances built into the system made for a sluggish response to market changes. In steel, for example, the slow pace of rationalisation during the 1980s was due in part to the reluctance of unions and works councils to accept the redundancies which mergers would have involved.[35]

In France, where the unions were weaker, employers had greater freedom to rationalise and modernise their factories in response to international competition during the 1980s. There was an almost Thatcherite ruthlessness in the changes which took place at Renault; the power of the CGT was drastically reduced as this state-owned company was prepared for privatisation. In steel, too, the state-owned industry went through a rationalisation process not dissimilar to that of British Steel.

It is quite wrong to regard trade unions as the all-encompassing cause of Britain's poor industrial performance between 1945 and 1979. Nevertheless, the labour relations system, shaped as much by employers and governments as by unions, provides part of the explanation for the sluggish growth of productivity, relative to other European countries, during those years. The problem stemmed partly from defective institutions (multiple unionism, shop steward autonomy, the absence of a legal framework for collective bargaining), partly from a political and economic environment which discouraged or frustrated reform. It took a severe shock to the body politic to create the conditions in which radical change became possible.

SEVENTEEN

The Role of Government: From Consensus to Competition

T he remaining culprit in the search for explanations of British industrial decline is the government. Could post-war governments have done more to foster the international competitiveness of British industry? Did avoidable policy errors put British firms at a disadvantage *vis-à-vis* their German and French rivals? Some aspects of government policy, relating to trade unions and training, have already been discussed. This chapter focuses on three issues: the extent to which opportunities for industrial modernisation were missed between 1945 and 1960; the impact of government intervention in industry during the 1960s and 1970s; and the industrial consequences of Thatcherism.

1945–60: A Missed Opportunity?

Some commentators believe that governments could and should have done more in the first fifteen years after the war to improve the performance of manufacturing industry. Their failure to do so is often blamed on the mood of complacency induced by the outcome of the war. The obvious contrast is with France, where industrial modernisation was seen as a way of restoring the country's independence and self-respect after the humiliation of 1940. In Britain the priorities were different. The British people, having won the war, expected to be rewarded for it, and looked to the government for improvements in living standards and in social welfare provision – above all, for policies which would banish the unemployment and deprivation of the inter-war years.

Correlli Barnett has criticised the Attlee government for devoting resources to the welfare state which would have been better spent on remedying the weaknesses of British industry. According to this view, the availability of American aid under the Marshall Plan provided a unique opportunity to remake Britain as an industrial power. The squandering of that opportunity was a 'cardinal blunder', which had disastrous consequences for the British economy.[1] However, as other writers have pointed out, Britain's expenditure on social welfare was not exceptional among European countries. By the early 1950s both Germany and France were spending more on social security, as a proportion of gross domestic product, than Britain.[2] Although Britain was unusual in establishing a tax-financed National Health Service, free at the point of delivery, total expenditure on health, measured on a per capita basis, was lower during the 1950s than in all other European countries except Italy and Ireland.

Earlier chapters have shown that lack of finance, whether from public or private sources, cannot be blamed for the slow pace of modernisation in such industries as cotton textiles, shipbuilding and steel after the war.[3] Moreover, the idea that the government could have taken these industries by the scruff of the neck and imposed modernisation on them is not realistic. Whitehall was at least as likely to make mistakes as the managers of the companies concerned.

A more valid criticism of the Attlee government was its lack of interest in competition as a means of putting pressure on industry to modernise itself. Despite the creation of the Monopolies and Restrictive Practices Commission in 1948, there was no serious attempt to deal with cartels, and the government's industrial policy consisted of a vague belief in planning and controls, together with a somewhat naïve hope that the two sides of industry could be persuaded to work together more constructively. This is not to denigrate the efforts made by Stafford Cripps and other ministers to promote higher productivity and to encourage the diffusion of modern management techniques, but at a time when markets were booming and the priority for most firms was to produce more, rather than to produce more efficiently, exhortation was not enough.

The Attlee government's room for manoeuvre was severely limited by the economic legacy of the war, and it is possible to argue that any errors in industrial policy were more than outweighed by its success in maintaining full employment and price stability, and in restoring a balance of payments equilibrium. By 1951, when Labour left office, conditions had been created in which more liberal policies could have been introduced if Winston Churchill's Conservative government had wished to do so. In the event, the shift to free markets was only partial.[4]

The most important change in micro-economic policy was a tougher approach to cartels. In 1956, after a series of reports from the Monopolies Commission had revealed the extent of cartelisation in industry, a new Restrictive Trade Practices Act was passed. All price-fixing agreements were declared illegal unless the parties could demonstrate that their agreements brought benefits to the public interest. Although the effect of the Act was partially offset by an increase in the number of mergers, it was an important step towards a more competitive economy, reflecting the influence of what has been called the pre-Thatcherite wing of the Conservative Party, led by Peter Thorneycroft, President of the Board of Trade and later Chancellor of the Exchequer.[5]

In other respects, however, the commitment of the Conservatives to the market as the principal regulator of economic activity was far from whole-hearted. Of the industries which had been nationalised under Labour, only two – steel and road haulage – were returned to private ownership, and there was no question of exposing the denationalised steel industry to the rigours of price competition. The framework of regulation and protection which had been in place since the 1930s was left largely untouched. The persistent tendency to intervene in what was nominally a private-sector industry was highlighted in 1958, when the Prime Minister, Harold Macmillan, made his famous judgement of Solomon over the location of the country's fourth strip mill (Chapter 6).

In trade policy, too, there was continuity between Labour and the Conservatives, particularly in regard to Europe. Shortly after the 1951 election the Churchill government rejected a second opportunity to join the European Coal and Steel Community. Although an association agreement between Britain and the Community was signed in 1954, it was not much more than an expression of goodwill, and did nothing to expose the British steel industry to European competition.[6] Britain's position on Europe was set out by Churchill in a memorandum to the Cabinet. 'We help, we dedicate, we play a part, but we are not merged and do not forfeit our insular and Commonwealth-wide character.'[7]

It was not until the start of 1956, when the movement towards integration on the Continent was well advanced, that the British government changed its position. Ministers finally recognised that exclusion from what seemed likely to be a German-dominated trade bloc, discriminating against outsiders, would be politically and economically dangerous. The British proposal for a broader European Free Trade Area, which would encompass the six members of the Coal and Steel Community as well as Britain and other European states, was designed to appeal to politicians in Germany (including Ludwig Erhard) who were uneasy about the creation of a 'little Europe' of the Six. But the political momentum behind the creation of a six-nation customs union was unstoppable, and the Treaty of Rome, setting up the European Economic Community, was signed in 1957. The Free Trade Are British proposal was formally rejected in 1958.[8]

The clear failure of Britain's European diplomacy, coming not long after the humiliation of Suez, precipitated a fundamental reappraisal of Britain's place in the world. Harold Macmillan, who had taken over as Prime Minister from Anthony Eden after Suez, formed the view that British membership of the Common Market was essential for political and economic reasons. The first application for membership was made in 1961.

The decision to opt out of European integration was the biggest missed opportunity of the 1945–60 period, more important than any mistakes in macro-economic policy. Indeed, it is hard to argue that Britain suffered from uniquely incompetent macro-economic management during these years. Unemployment and inflation were kept low, and if productivity was rising more slowly than in France and Germany, this was at least partly due to factors outside the government's control. The Conservative governments of the 1950s and early 1960s have been criticised for 'stop-go' policies – allowing the economy to expand too fast, then slamming on the brakes when inflation threatened to get out of control and the balance of payments came under strain. Yet cyclical fluctuations were not much greater in Britain than on the Continent.[9] The difference was that the Continental economies were growing faster and the fluctuations were less painful. The stop-go phenomenon was more the result than the cause of Britain's slow productivity growth.[10]

Apart from the Restrictive Practices Act of 1956 the Conservative governments of the 1950s paid little attention to supply-side policies aimed at improving industrial efficiency. Their main concern was with the management of demand, through fiscal and monetary policy, and, in the latter part of the decade, with policies to restrain the growth of wages. But by 1960, as the disparity in economic performance between Britain and the leading Continental countries became more evident, attention shifted back to the supply side of the economy. The search began for policies which would lift Britain's growth rate closer to that of France and West Germany.

1960–79: The Failure of Industrial Policy

A new departure at the start of the 1960s was the Conservative government's conversion to French-style indicative planning. Ministers, in common with many other British observers, believed that this system had been partly responsible for the rapid growth of the French economy during the 1950s. (The fact that West Germany, the most successful of the Continental countries, had no such planning system was curiously ignored.) The value of the planning exercise, it was thought, was that it created a consensus among employers, trade unions and the government about economic objectives and how to achieve them. Businessmen would invest with greater confidence because they knew that other decision-makers, including the government and its agencies, were committed to the same growth targets. With this aim in mind, the National Economic Development Council, popularly known as Neddy, was set up in 1962. It was supported by the National Economic Development Office and later by Economic Development Committees (little Neddies), which examined the problems of individual industries.

As an attempt to raise the economy to a higher rate of growth these arrangements were wholly unsuccessful. The objective set by Neddy was for the economy to grow at an annual rate of 4 per cent up to 1966, compared to an average of 2.5 per cent in the 1950s. But the plan was upset by the same constraint which had undermined earlier dashes for growth – a deteriorating balance of payments as the economy expanded too fast. Far from promoting a more stable economic environment, the 4 per cent goal may itself have been destabilising, since it encouraged the government to stimulate demand in 1963 when a cyclical upturn was already under way.[11] The outcome was another slam on the brakes and a loss of credibility for the new Council. Other aspects of Neddy's work were more helpful, since it focused attention on obstacles to higher productivity and how they might be removed. For example, new initiatives were launched during this period in the field of training and management education.

After General de Gaulle's veto on Britain's EEC application in 1963 supply-side issues acquired even greater prominence. Edward Heath, who had been the government's chief negotiator in Brussels, suggested that Britain should reduce its tariffs unilaterally, so as to expose industry to the same competitive pressure which it would have faced if Britain had been part of the Common Market. This proposal was not pursued on the grounds that it would reduce Britain's bargaining power in the tariff negotiations which were about to begin under the General Agreement on Tariffs and Trade.[12] However, domestic competition policy was strengthened in 1965 by extending the Monopolies Commission's remit to cover mergers.[13]

A different and in some ways contradictory approach to the promotion of industrial efficiency was for the government itself to intervene directly in industry. This had begun tentatively under the Tories (help for cotton textiles in 1959 and for the shipbuilders in 1963), but was taken much further by Labour after the 1964 election – the first election since the war in which industrial modernisation was a major campaign issue.[14] The Labour government, led by Harold Wilson, believed that Britain's competitive shortcomings were too deep-seated to be corrected by market forces alone. This applied not only to older industries like steel and shipbuilding, which had failed to modernise after the war, but to newer high-technology industries such as computers, where British firms were falling behind their American rivals. Two new instruments of intervention were established. One was the Ministry of Technology, charged with 'guiding and stimulating a major national effort to bring advanced technology and new processes into British industry'.[15] This new department later absorbed the Ministry of Aviation and took over the government's responsibility for the aircraft industry. The other was the Industrial Reorganisation Corporation, with a remit to promote mergers in industries which were too fragmented to compete effectively in world markets.

During the 1960s the fashion for mergers was in full swing, and the government shared the widely held view that bigger companies were needed to exploit economies of scale and to assemble the resources which were needed to meet international competition. This was the ostensible purpose of taking over the steel industry in 1967: to bring about the rationalisation which the private owners had been unable or unwilling to undertake. It was also the central recommendation of the Geddes report on shipbuilding, which led to the creation of new regional groups in Scotland and the north-east. The computer industry was concentrated in the hands of a single company, ICL, and virtually all the British-owned car and truck manufacturers were brought together to form British Leyland Motor Corporation. But the government failed to appreciate that size was no guarantee of efficiency, especially where one or more of the merging companies suffered from deep-rooted managerial weaknesses.

Moreover, where reorganisation was accompanied by an injection of government money, as in steel, shipbuilding, cars and to some extent in computers, the effect was to lessen the financial pressures on the companies concerned and to allow them to pursue strategies which could not have been justified on commercial grounds.

The results of Labour's interventionist policies between 1964 and 1970 were disappointing and in some cases, like that of British Leyland, disastrous. When the Conservatives returned to office under Edward Heath, they were determined to change course. Since their defeat in 1964, the party's thinking had moved away from planning towards a greater emphasis on competition. The policy of 'disengagement' to which the new government was committed was partially implemented during its first year. The Industrial Reorganisation Corporation was disbanded, as was the Shipbuilding Industry Board, and the Ministry of Technology was merged with the Board of Trade to form the Department of Trade and Industry. But events began to weaken the government's resolve.

The take-over of Rolls-Royce, following its bankruptcy in 1971, could be defended on the grounds that the aero-engine maker was crucial to the nation's defence. But the rescue of Upper Clyde Shipbuilders a few months later was a different matter. Unemployment was rising, and the political pressure on the government to relax its hard line on 'lame ducks' had become irresistible. The Industry Act of 1972 gave the government sweeping powers to intervene in industry, and for the next two years the Department of Trade and Industry pursued an industrial policy which was entirely contrary to the spirit of 'disengagement'.

The one clear success for the Heath administration was Britain's entry, at the third time of asking, to the EEC. (A second application had been made by Labour in 1967, and promptly vetoed by de Gaulle.) Terms were agreed in 1971, and Britain became a member in January 1973. This was a personal triumph for the Prime Minister, but it came fifteen years too late. The long post-war boom was nearing its end and the trade-creating impetus coming from European integration was losing its force.

The Heath government fell from office in 1974 in the midst of a confrontation over wages with the National Union of Mineworkers. The new Labour administration, led once again by Harold Wilson, was even more convinced that the ills of the British economy could only be solved by an extension of government ownership and control. Left-wingers in the Party (including Tony Benn, who was to become Secretary of State for Trade and Industry) prepared a programme which was far more interventionist than the policies pursued by the previous Labour government.[16]

The spearhead of modernisation was to be the National Enterprise Board, which would take a controlling stake in many of the country's leading companies. The NEB's activities would be complemented by a system of planning agreements, whereby companies would commit themselves to expansion in return for government financial assistance. Two of the industries which had already received large sums of public money – aircraft and shipbuilding – would be nationalised.

These proposals were too extreme for the moderate wing of the party, including the Prime Minister, and many of them were watered down by the time the Industrial Expansion Act of 1975 was passed. Planning agreements were made voluntary (only two were signed) and the NEB's powers to take over companies were restrained.[17] Although the shipbuilding and aircraft industries were nationalised, most of the other interventions were *ad hoc* responses to crises in individual companies such as British Leyland, Ferranti and Alfred Herbert. The NEB made some attempts to promote high-technology industries (Inmos, the semiconductor firm discussed in Chapter 10, being a notable example), but most of its energies were devoted to looking after 'lame ducks'.

Intervention in industry between 1964 and 1979 must be regarded as a failure.[18] Was this because governments were bad at intervening or because intervention itself was a bad policy? Comparisons are often drawn with France, which is said to have benefited from a closer rapport between government officials and industrialists, especially in big companies.[19] This has led, according to admirers of the French system, to intelligent and well-executed intervention, and has given French industry a competitive advantage. Earlier chapters, however, have shown that the record of French industrial policy was patchy at best, and it included some costly mistakes, of which steel and computers are examples. The promotion of national champions was not much more successful than in Britain, with the notable exception of telecommunications equipment and perhaps aircraft. Indeed, a plausible argument can be made that the success of the French economy was achieved in spite of industrial policy rather than because of it.[20] The decisive factor was the opening-up of the French economy to competition through the Common Market.[21] It was this competitive pressure, rather than industrial policy, which enabled the French car manufacturers to make spectacular gains in productivity in the 1960s.

The most successful of the large European countries in the 1960s and 1970s was the one in which there was the smallest amount of selective intervention in industry. One of the principles of the German social market economy was that the government should confine itself to the preservation of price stability and the maintenance of competition. Although this did not preclude some *ad hoc* intervention in response to social and political pressures, there was no industrial policy along the lines practised in Britain and France.[22] For the most part, industrial adjustment was left to firms and their workers to handle on their own. Even in the Volkswagen crisis of 1974–5, where the Federal government was directly involved as a shareholder in the company and the Social Democratic Party was in power, a private-sector solution was always the preferred outcome. The Chancellor, Helmut Schmidt, used his influence to bring this about (Chapter 9).

Germany was infected to some degree by the techno-nationalism which prompted France and Britain to subsidise high-technology industries such as computers, aircraft and nuclear power – most of the Federal government's efforts in these fields were unsuccessful.[23] But the main thrust of policy was towards general measures to encourage the diffusion of technology, rather than the promotion of mergers and support for national champions.[24]

In Britain, selective intervention was a costly distraction which slowed down the adaptation of industry to international competition. It was based on the misguided belief, largely shared by both major political parties, that governments had the power to identify and correct competitive weaknesses in particular industries and companies. By 1979, when Margaret Thatcher entered Downing Street, these illusions had been dispelled, and the stage was set for a very different kind of industrial policy.

The Industrial Consequences of Margaret Thatcher

The Thatcher government rejected most of the assumptions which had guided post-war economic management.[25] First, macro-economic policy was geared to the conquest of inflation rather than the maintenance of full employment. This called for strict limits on government spending, tight control of the money supply and the rejection of incomes policies. Second, micro-economic policy was directed towards the promotion of competition and the withdrawal of government from direct intervention in industry. Third, tripartism was abandoned. The trade union movement was regarded, not as a partner in government, but as an over-powerful interest group which had been allowed to wield too great an influence over economic policy.

The starting-point for these changes was the exceptionally severe recession in the two years following the 1979 election. For many companies this was a traumatic experience which stimulated an urgent drive for lower costs and greater efficiency, often accompanied by a fundamental reappraisal of strategy.

Despite widespread complaints that Mrs Thatcher's policies were destroying the country's industrial base, the resulting spurt in productivity might not have occurred if the government's original plans for a more gradual reduction of inflation had been fulfilled. With hindsight, the overvaluation of sterling could be regarded as a fortunate accident which contributed to the subsequent success of the Thatcher government's supply-side policies.

An early decision was to abolish exchange control. Taken together with the increasing integration of the world's financial markets, this made it impossible for firms to survive with a rate of return below the international average.[26] On the domestic front, the most eye-catching part of the programme, which began slowly but gathered pace during the 1980s, was privatisation. This programme included not only the industries and companies which had been taken over in the 1960s and 1970s – British Steel, British Shipbuilders, British Aerospace and Rolls-Royce – but most of the government-owned monopolies which had been created under the Attlee administration after the war. The consequence, seen most clearly in the case of British Steel, was a sharp improvement in competitiveness.

Subsidies to industry were cut back and the old policy of supporting national champions was abandoned. With the partial exception of defence and aerospace, high-technology industries could no longer expect privileged treatment from the state. The one aspect of industrial policy in which the Thatcher government did take a direct interest was the promotion of inward investment. Strenuous efforts were made to persuade Japanese car and electronics companies to build factories in Britain, and government grants were made available for this purpose. In addition, the government took a more relaxed view about foreign ownership of what had once been regarded as flagship companies. However nationalistic the Prime Minister may have been on other issues, she had no inhibitions about making the British economy more dependent on foreign companies. Some commentators deplored the loss of domestic control over strategic technologies such as computers and semiconductors.[27] But, as Chapter 10 showed, greater reliance on inward investment in these and other high-technology sectors was not obviously a disadvantage for the British economy. In a world in which capital and technology flowed easily across national borders, the case for propping up national champions was even weaker than it had been in the 1960s.

The effect of the Thatcher government's industrial policies, taken together with the reforms of trade union law discussed in the last chapter, was to accelerate British industry's adjustment to international competition and to remove obstacles which stood in the way.

Were Governments to Blame?

It is arguable that if Thatcherite policies had been introduced in the 1950s rather than the 1980s, British industry would have been more successful.[28] Whether such policies would have been politically feasible at that time is another matter. The reforming zeal of a Margaret Thatcher would have had little appeal for a population basking in the after-glow of victory. A consensual approach to economic management, with the emphasis on full employment, was to some extent the inevitable result of the war. The fact that these policies worked rather well in the 1950s and 1960s, at least by comparison with Britain's pre-war performance, reduced the incentive for change.

It was not helpful, to say the least, that one of the two major political parties – until the arrival of Tony Blair's New Labour in the 1990s – was deeply suspicious of the free market and ideologically inclined to enlarge the role of government. This contributed to unnecessary conflicts over nationalisation, which were especially damaging in the case of steel. But for much of the period up to the end of the 1970s the Conservatives were almost as interventionist as Labour. Their record on competition and trade policy did not live up to their rhetorical commitment to liberalism.

It was also unfortunate that when the reappraisal of policy began at the end of the 1950s, the wrong lessons were drawn from French and German experience: successive governments embarked on a futile exercise in industrial intervention. Things had to get much worse – the failure of industrial policy and the breakdown of the post-war consensus – before the conditions were ripe for the Thatcher revolution.

EIGHTEEN

Conclusion

T he purpose of this book has been to describe how British firms in the country's major industries responded to international com- petition after the Second World War and to assess the validity of some widely canvassed explanations of British industrial decline.

The overall picture which emerges from the case studies does not justify the gloomy judgements commonly made about Britain's post-war industrial performance. There were successes as well as failures, with chemicals at one end and the motor industry – until the partial revival of the 1980s – at the other. Much depended on the economics of the industry concerned, the severity of international competition and the behaviour of individual man- agers and entrepreneurs. Some of the failures, as in electronics and shipbuild- ing, were shared with other European countries.

Companies succeed or fail for many different reasons, with chance play- ing a large role, and it is impossible to assign precise weights to each of the factors involved. Some broad conclusions, however, can be drawn from the evidence set out in this book.

First, what happened to British industry after 1945 was not a continuation of a decline which had started in the closing decades of the nineteenth century. The fact that Britain lost ground to the US and Germany between 1870 and 1914 was mainly due to the timing and character of industrialisation in the two follower countries, not to deep-rooted and persistent institutional or managerial deficiencies. The lag was partially made up in the inter-war years, and there was no lack of entrepreneurial vitality in the newer industries.

Second, although coming first in the industrial revolution was not a long-term competitive handicap for British industry, it left two legacies which are relevant to an understanding of what happened after 1945. One was a large commitment to older industries – cotton textiles and shipbuilding being the two outstanding examples – in which British entrepreneurs had achieved a dominant market position before the First World War. The other was a bias towards the Empire and other non-European markets as the principal destination for British exports. This bias was compounded by the general retreat into protection and cartelisation in the inter-war years.

Third, the superior industrial performance of West Germany and France in the first thirty years after the Second World War was partly due to forces over which neither British governments nor British managers had any control. The two Continental countries were starting from a lower base than Britain; their economies had been less highly industrialised before the war; and, unlike Britain, they had a pool of surplus agricultural labour which could be transferred into industry.

Fourth, these initial advantages were reinforced, especially in Germany, and to a lesser extent in France, by policy changes and institutional reforms which were inspired by a national determination to make a fresh start after the disasters of the preceding decade. The reforms removed some of the obstacles which had impeded economic growth in those two countries in the 1920s and 1930s. In Britain there was no such stimulus for national renewal, and no fundamental questioning of institutions which had proved their worth during the war. The priority in economic policy was to prevent a return to the high unemployment and social distress of the 1920s and 1930s. The instruments used to achieve this objective depended on a partnership between employers, trade unions and the government. Reforms which might have jeopardised this co-operation – for example in the field of labour relations – were not on the political agenda.

Fifth, German and French industry benefited from the early commitment of their governments to European economic integration. Easy access to a fast-growing, homogeneous, tariff-free market was an important advantage for German and French manufacturers *vis-à-vis* their British counterparts, especially in industries such as cars in which economies of scale are critical. Britain saw itself as an imperial rather than a European power and stayed aloof from Europe. The delay in Britain's accession to the EEC meant that British industry largely missed out on the expansion of intra-European trade which took place in the 1960s and early 1970s.

Sixth, the evidence in this book runs counter to some popular 'institutional' explanations of British industrial decline. The financial system did not let British industry down. The training and education system was flawed in some respects, and these flaws affected the performance of British firms in certain industries, principally those which relied heavily on craft skills. But it was not a central source of weakness in manufacturing as a whole.

Seventh, the labour relations system was a specifically British problem, and a serious drag on productivity, as well as damaging the image of British industry in the world. However, it was by no means the sole cause of Britain's poor industrial performance in the 1960s and 1970s. The decline of industries such as machine tools and semiconductors cannot be blamed on strikes, demarcation disputes or overmanning. Even in cars and shipbuilding – both badly affected by strikes – labour relations were only one element in the collapse of these industries, and probably not the most important.

If these explanations of industrial decline are ruled out, or given less weight than in most accounts of Britain's post-war industrial history, the finger points at governments. British industrial performance between 1945 and 1979 might have been better if governments had pursued different policies. The biggest single mistake was to opt out of European integration in the 1950s. A second error was to give insufficient priority to competition as the main driver of higher productivity.

This is not to say that British industrial performance would have been transformed if there had been a full-blooded attack on cartels after 1945, or if Britain had joined the Common Market in 1958 rather than 1973, or if industrial policy in the 1960s and 1970s had been geared to the promotion of competition rather than the creation of national champions and the preservation of jobs. But a more consistently pro-competitive and pro-European stance on the part of successive governments might have brought forward some of the changes in industry which took place in the 1980s.

Yet criticism of governments needs to be kept in proportion. There was no miraculous remedy available which politicians were too stupid or short-sighted to apply. The most that can be said is that, through avoidable errors, they made British industry's adjustment to the post-war world more difficult than it otherwise might have been.

In industry, as in other aspects of British society, the transition from imperial power to 'just another European country' was bound to be a slow and painful process. Because of history, because of what had happened in the 1930s, and because of the victorious outcome of the war, the obstacles to change were greater in Britain than in Germany or France – and the incentive to remove them was weaker. Moreover, for the first thirty years after the war, the political climate militated against the single-minded pursuit of industrial efficiency and international competitiveness. The tide turned in the 1980s, when two powerful forces came together and reinforced each other: external economic pressure and domestic policy reform. By the end of the 1990s Britain had found a role for itself as a medium-sized industrial nation, well integrated into the world market.

Notes

CHAPTER 1

1 The EFTA agreement came into effect in 1960. Finland became an associate member in 1961.
2 Sir Trevor Holdsworth, speech to Institute of Chartered Accountants of Scotland, 6 September 1990.
3 Michael Porter, 'Changing patterns of international competition', in David J. Teece (ed.), *The competitive challenge*, Harper & Row, 1987. See also Michael Porter, *The competitive advantage of nations*, Macmillan, 1990.

CHAPTER 2

1 Alfred D. Chandler, *Scale and Scope: The Dynamics of Industrial Capitalism*, Harvard, 1990, ch. 7.
2 Joel Mokyr, *The Lever of Riches*, Oxford, 1990, p. 93.
3 Sidney Pollard, *Peaceful Conquest: The Industrialisation of Europe 1760–1970*, Oxford, 1981, ch. 1.
4 Joel Mokyr, 'Technological Change 1700–1830', in Roderick Floud and Donald McCloskey (eds.), *The Economic History of Britain since 1700*, 2nd edn, vol. 1: 1700–1860, Cambridge, 1994, p. 36.
5 William Lazonick, *Competitive Advantage on the Shop Floor*, Harvard, 1990, ch. 3.
6 Douglass C. North and Barry R. Weingast, 'Constitutions and Commitment: The Evolution of Institutions Governing Public Choice in Seventeenth-century England', *Journal of Economic History*, vol. 49, no. 4, December 1989.
7 Christopher Hill, *The Century of Revolution, 1603–1714*, Nelson, 1961, p. 213.
8 Harold Perkin, *Origins of Modern English Society*, Routledge, 1969, p. 315.
9 Robert Blake, *Disraeli*, Eyre & Spottiswoode, 1966, p. 293.
10 Perkin, *Origins of Modern English Society*, ch. 9.
11 Anthony Howe, *Free Trade and Liberal England 1846–1946*, Oxford, 1998. pp. 73–81.
12 Gavin Wright, 'The Origins of American Industrial Success 1879–1940', *American Economic Review*, no. 80, September 1990. See also Paul David and Gavin Wright, 'Increasing Returns and American Resource Abundance', *Industrial and Corporate Change*, vol. 6, no. 2, March 1997.
13 Alfred D. Chandler, *The Visible Hand: the Managerial Revolution in American Business*, Harvard, 1977, p. 249.
14 David A. Hounshell, *From the American System to Mass Production 1800–1932*, Johns Hopkins University Press, 1984.
15 Bernard Elbaum, 'The persistence of Apprenticeship in Britain and Its Decline in the United States', in Howard F. Gospel (ed.), *Industrial Training and Technological Change*, Routledge, 1991.
16 Lazonick, *Competitive Advantage on the Shop Floor*, p. 216.
17 William Lazonick, 'Social Organisation and Technological Leadership', in William J. Baumol, Richard R. Nelson and Edward N. Wolff (eds.), *Convergence of Productivity*, Oxford, 1994. See also William Lazonick, 'Strategy, Structure and Management Development in the US and Britain', in Kesaji Kobayashi and Hidemasa Morikawa (eds.), *Development of Managerial Enterprise*, University of Tokyo Press, 1986.
18 Richard R. Nelson and Gavin Wright, 'The Erosion of US Technological Leadership as a Factor in Post-war

Economic Convergence', in Baumol, Nelson and Wolff, *Convergence of Productivity*, p. 138.

19 David Blackbourn, *The Fontana History of Germany 1780–1918*, Fontana, 1997, p. 178.

20 John C. Brown, 'Imperfect Competition and Anglo-German Trade Rivalry: Markets for Cotton Textiles before 1914', *Journal of Economic History*, vol. 55, no. 3, September 1995.

21 Gary B. Herrigel, 'Industrial Order and the Politics of Industrial Change: Mechanical engineering', in Peter J. Katzenstein (ed.), *Industry and Politics in Germany: Towards the Third Republic*, Cornell, 1989.

22 Wilfried Feldenkirchen, 'Banking and Economic Growth: Banks and Industry in Germany in the Nineteenth Century and Their Changing Relationships during Industrialisation', in W. R. Lee (ed.), *German Industry and German Industrialisation*, Routledge, 1991.

23 Gary Herrigel, *Industrial Constructions: the Sources of German Industrial Power*, Cambridge, 1996. ch. 2.

24 Richard E. Deeg, 'Banks and the State in Germany: the Critical Role of Subnational Institutions in Economic Governance', Ph.D. dissertation, Department of Political Science, MIT, 1992.

25 Robert Currie, *Industrial Politics*, Oxford, 1979, p. 15.

26 Jürgen Kocka, 'The Rise of the Modern Industrial Enterprise in Germany', in Alfred D. Chandler and Herman Daems, *Managerial hierarchies: Comparative Perspectives on the Rise of the Modern Industrial Enterprise*, Harvard, 1980.

27 V. R. Berghahn, *Germany and the Approach of War in 1914*, Macmillan, 1973, p. 10.

28 Peter Temin, 'The Relative Decline of the British Steel Industry 1880–1913', in Henry Rosovsky (ed.), *Industrialisation in Two Systems*, Wiley, 1966.

29 William P. Kennedy, *Industrial Structure, Capital Markets and the Origins of British Industrial Decline*, Cambridge, 1987, pp. 134–8.

30 Chandler, *Scale and Scope*, p. 276.

31 Ranald Michie, 'The Finance of Innovation in Late Victorian and Edwardian Britain: Possibilities and Constraints', *Journal of European Economic History*, vol. 17, no. 3, Winter 1988.

32 D. C. Coleman, *Courtaulds: an economic and social history*, vol. 2, Oxford, 1969, chs. 2 and 8.

33 Sidney Pollard, 'Entrepreneurship 1870–1914', in Floud and McCloskey, *The Economic History of Britain since 1700*, vol. 2.

34 Sidney Pollard, *Britain's Prime and Britain's Decline*, Edward Arnold, 1969, p. 161.

35 Kennedy, *Industrial Structure*, pp. 117–19.

36 Michael Edelstein, 'Foreign investment and accumulation 1860–1914', in Floud and McCloskey, *The Economic History of Britain since 1700*, vol. 2.

37 Lazonick, *Competitive Advantage on the Shop Floor*, ch. 6.

38 C. Knick Harley, 'Substitutions for Prerequisites, Endogenous Institutions and Comparative Economic History', in Richard Sylla and Gianni Toniolo (eds.), *Patterns of European Industrialisation*, Routledge, 1991.

39 Jürgen Kocka, 'The Rise of the Modern Industrial Enterprise in Germany', in Alfred D. Chandler and Herman Daems, *Managerial Hierarchies*; Jeffrey R. Fear, 'Constructing Big Business: The Cultural Concept of the Firm', in Alfred D. Chandler, Franco Amatori and Takashi Hikino (eds.), *Big Business and the Wealth of Nations*, Cambridge, 1997.

40 D. A. Hounshell and J. K. Smith, *Science and Corporate Strategy: Du Pont R and D, 1902–1980*, Cambridge, 1988.

41 Leonard S. Reich, *The Making of American Industrial Research: Science and Business at GE and Bell 1876–1926*, Cambridge, 1985.

42 See, for example, Mary Nolan, *Visions of Modernity, American Business and the Modernisation of Germany*, Oxford, 1994.

43 R. J. Overy, *The Nazi Economic Recovery, 1932–1938*, Macmillan, 1982, p. 13.

44 John Gillingham, *Coal, Steel and the Rebirth of Europe, 1945–1955*, Cambridge, 1991, p. 197.

45 Harold James, *The German Slump*, Oxford, 1986, p. 149.

46 Bernd Dornseifer, 'Strategy, Technological Capability and Innovation: German Enterprises in Comparative Perspective', in François Caron, Paul Erker and Wolfram Fischer (eds.), *Innovations in the European Economy Between the Wars*, de Gruyter, 1995.

47 Leslie Hannah, *The Rise of the Corporate Economy*, Methuen, 1976, p. 141. Leslie Hannah, 'Managerial Innovation and the Rise of the Large-Scale Company in Inter-war Britain', *Economic History Review*, vol. 27, no. 2, May 1974.

48 Derek Matthews, Malcolm Anderson and John Richard Edwards, 'The Rise of the Professional Accountant in British Management', *Economic History Review*, vol. 50, no. 3, August 1997.

49 S. N. Broadberry and R. Fremdling, 'Comparative Productivity in British Industry 1907–37', *Oxford Bulletin of Economics and Statistics*, vol. 52, no. 4, 1990.

CHAPTER 3

1 The remark, 'You've never had it so good', is reported to have been made in response to a heckler at a political meeting in Bedford; Kenneth O. Morgan, *The People's Peace: British History 1945–1989*, Oxford, 1990, p. 176.

2 Michael Shanks, *The Stagnant Society*, Penguin, 1961, p. 207.

3 Charles Feinstein, 'Success and Failure: British Economic Growth since 1948', in Roderick Floud and Donald McCloskey (eds.), *The Economic History of Britain since 1700*, vol. 3: *1939–1992*, Cambridge, 1994.

4 Holger Wolf, 'Post-war Germany in the European Context', in Barry Eichengreen (ed.), *Europe's Post-war Recovery*, Cambridge, 1995.

5 Rolf H. Dumke, 'Reassessing the Wirtschaftswunder: Reconstruction and Post-war Growth in West Germany in an International Context', *Oxford Bulletin of Economics and Statistics*, vol. 52, no. 4, 1990.

6 Michael J. Hogan, *The Marshall Plan*, Cambridge, 1987, pp. 427–45.

7 A. J. Nicholls, *Freedom with Responsibility: the Social Market in Germany 1918–1963*, Oxford, 1994, p. 131.

8 Geoffrey Denton, Murray Forsyth and Malcolm Maclennan, *Economic Planning and Policies in Britain, France and Germany*, Allen & Unwin, 1968, p. 49.

9 Nicholls, *Freedom with Responsibility*, pp. 73–6.

10 Herbert Giersch, Karl-Heinz Paqué, Holger Schmieding, *The Fading Miracle: Four Decades of Market Economy in Germany*, Cambridge, 1992, p. 39.

11 The new central bank, Bank deutscher Lander, forerunner of the Bundesbank, was established by the Allies in March 1948.

12 Nicholls, *Freedom with Responsibility*, p. 241.

13 Volker Berghahn, *The Americanisation of West German Industry 1945–1973*, Berg, 1986, p. 95.

14 Giersch et al., *The Fading Miracle*, p. 85.

15 Alan S. Milward, *The European Rescue of the Nation-state*, Routledge, 1992, p. 166.

16 Nicholls, *Freedom with Responsibility*, pp. 340–41.

17 Ludger Lindlar and Carl-Ludwig Holtfrerich, 'Four Decades of German Export Expansion: An Enduring Success Story?', Discussion Paper, no. 10, German Institute for Economic Research, Berlin, January 1996.

18 Berghahn, *The Americanisation of West German Industry*, p. 217.

19 Karl-Heinz Paqué, 'The Causes of Postwar Slumps and Miracles: An Evaluation of Olsonian Views on German Economic Performance in the 1920s and 1950s', Discussion Paper, no. 981, Centre for Economic Policy Research, July 1984. See also Wendy Carlin, 'West German Growth and Institutions, 1945–90', in Nicholas Crafts and Gianni Toniolo (eds.), *Economic Growth in Europe since 1945*, Cambridge, 1996.

20 Helge Berger and Albrecht Ritschl, 'Germany and the Political Economy of the Marshall Plan, 1947–52: A Re-revisionist View', in Eichengreen, *Europe's Post-war Recovery*.

21 Richard F. Kuisel, *Capitalism and the State in Modern France*, Cambridge, 1981, p. 128.

22 Pierre Sicsic and Charles Wyploz, 'France 1945–92', in Nicholas Crafts and Gianni Toniolo (eds.), *Economic Growth in Europe since 1945*, Cambridge, 1996.

23 J-J. Carre, P. Dubois and E. Malinvaud, *French Economic Growth*, Oxford, 1975, p. 499.

24 Kuisel, *Capitalism and the State in Modern France*, p. 128. See also E. N. Suleiman, *Politics, Power and Bureaucracy in France*, Princeton, 1974.

25 Jean-Louis Loubet, *Citroën, Peugeot, Renault et les autres: soixante ans de stratégies*, Le Monde Editions, 1995; John Sheahan, *Promotion and Control of Industry in Post-war France*, Harvard, 1963.

26 See Frances M. B. Lynch, 'Resolving the Paradoxes of the Monnet Plan: National and International Planning in French reconstruction', *Economic History Review*, vol. 37, no. 2, May 1984.

27 Hogan, *The Marshall Plan*, p. 367.

28 Milward, *The European Rescue of the Nation-state*, p. 302.

29 Ibid., p. 207.

30 Andrew Sherman, *Rethinking France*, Oxford, 1989, p. 201.

31 François Duchêne, *Jean Monnet: The First Statesman of Interdependence*, Norton, 1994, p. 179.

32 Alan S. Milward, *The Reconstruction of Western Europe 1945–51*, Methuen, 1984, p. 141.

33 Eric Roll, *Where Did We Go Wrong?*, Faber, 1995, p. 14.

34 Michael Foot, *Aneurin Bevan: A Biography*, vol. 1: *1897–1945*, Atheneum, 1963, p. 506.

35 Paul Addison, *The Road to 1945*, Cape, 1975, p. 261.

36 Alec Cairncross, *Years of Recovery: British Economic Policy, 1945–51*, Methuen, 1985.

37 Correlli Barnett, *The Lost Victory: British Dreams, British Realities 1945–1950*, Macmillan, 1995.

38 Jim Tomlinson, *Government and the Enterprise Since 1900*, Oxford, 1994, p. 175.

39 Michael Foot, *Aneurin Bevan: A Biography*, Vol. 2: *1945–60*, Davis-Poynter, 1973, p. 260.

40 Robert Millward and John Singleton, 'The Ownership of British Industry in the Post-war Era: An Explanation', in Robert Millward and John Singleton (eds.), *The Political Economy of Nationalisation in Britain 1920–1950*, Cambridge, 1995.

41 Nick Tiratsoo and Jim Tomlinson, *Industrial efficiency and state intervention: Labour 1939–51*, Routledge, 1993, p. 145.

42 Ibid., pp. 95–6.

43 Alan Booth, Joseph Melling and Christoph Dartmann, 'Institutions and Economic Growth: The Politics of Productivity in West Germany, Sweden and the United Kingdom, 1945–1955', *Economic History Review*, vol. 57, no. 2, June 1997. Alan Booth, 'Corporate Politics and the Quest for Productivity: The British TUC and the Politics of Industrial Productivity, 1947–1960', in Joseph Melling and Alan McKinlay (eds.), *Management, Labour and Industrial Politics in Modern Europe*, Elgar, 1996.

44 Helen Mercer, *Constructing a Competitive Order*, Cambridge, 1995, p. 13.

45 A statement made at a meeting with US officials in 1947, quoted in Milward, *The European Rescue of the Nation-State*, p. 354.

46 Edmund Dell, *The Schuman Plan and the British Abdication of Leadership in Europe*, Oxford, 1995.

47 Michael Foot, *Aneurin Bevan*, vol. 2, p. 234.

48 Hogan, *The Marshall Plan*, p. 440.

49 Milward, *The European Rescue of the Nation-state*, p. 406.

50 Ibid., p. 425.

51 Keith Middlemas, *Power, Competition and the State*, vol. 1: *Britain in Search of Balance*, Macmillan, 1986, p. 235.

CHAPTER 4

1 Geoffrey Timmins, 'Technological Change', in Mary B. Rose (ed.), *The Lancashire Cotton Industry: A History*

since 1700, Lancashire County Books, 1996.

2 Mary B. Rose, 'The Rise of the Cotton Industry in Lancashire to 1830', in Rose, *The Lancashire Cotton Industry*.

3 D. A. Farnie, 'The Textile Machine-making Industry and the World Market, 1870–1960', *Business History*, vol. 32, no. 4, October 1990.

4 William Lazonick, *Competitive Advantage on the Shop Floor*, Harvard, 1990, ch. 3.

5 Michael Winstanley, 'The Factory Workforce', in Rose, *The Lancashire Cotton Industry*.

6 John C. Brown, 'Imperfect Competition and Anglo-German Trade Rivalry: Markets for Cotton Textiles before 1914', *Journal of Economic History*, vol. 55, no. 3, September 1995.

7 R. E. Tyson, 'The Cotton Industry', in D. H. Aldcroft (ed.), *The Development of British Industry and Foreign Competition 1875–1914*, Allen & Unwin, 1968.

8 Marguerite Dupree, 'Foreign Competition and the Inter-war Period', in Rose, *The Lancashire Cotton Industry*.

9 William Mass and William Lazonick, 'The British Cotton Industry and International Competitive Advantage: The State of the Debates', *Business History*, vol. 32, no. 4, October 1990.

10 W. R. Garside and J. I. Greaves, 'The Bank of England and Industrial Intervention in Inter-war Britain', *Financial History Review*, vol. 3, part 1, April 1996.

11 Leslie Hannah, *The Rise of the Corporate Economy*, Methuen, 1976, p. 84.

12 Alex J. Robertson, 'Lancashire and the Rise of Japan, 1910–1937', *Business History*, vol. 32, no. 4, October 1990.

13 Marguerite Dupree, 'Foreign Competition and the Inter-war Period', in Rose, *The Lancashire Cotton Industry*.

14 William Lazonick, 'The Cotton Industry', in Bernard Elbaum and William Lazonick (eds.), *The Decline of the British Economy*, Oxford, 1986.

15 For a sceptical view, see Andrew Marrison, 'Indian Summer 1870–1914', in Rose, *The Lancashire Cotton Industry*.

16 Political and Economic Planning, *Report on the British Cotton Industry*, 1934, quoted in Steven H. Cobrin, 'Two Paths of Industrial Adjustment to Shifting Patterns of International Competition: The Political Economy of Specialisation and Mass Production in British Textiles', Ph.D. thesis, Harvard, 1990, pp. 211–17.

17 Marguerite Dupree, 'The Cotton Industry: A Middle Way between Nationalisation and Self-government?', in Helen Mercer, Neil Rollings and Jim Tomlinson (eds.), *Labour Governments and Private Industry*, Edinburgh, 1992.

18 *Report of the Cotton Textile Mission to the US, March–April 1944*, HMSO, 1944.

19 *Board of Trade Working Party Report: Cotton*, HMSO, 1946, p. 164, quoted in Cobrin, 'Two Paths of Industrial Adjustment', pp. 234–41.

20 *Board of Trade Working Party Report: Cotton*, p. 234.

21 Martin Chick, *Industrial Policy in Britain 1945–1951*, Cambridge, 1998, ch. 7.

22 John Singleton, 'Showing the White Flag: The Lancashire Cotton Industry 1945–1965', *Business History*, vol. 32, no. 4, October 1990; John Singleton, *Lancashire on the Scrapheap: The Cotton Industry 1945–70*, Oxford, 1991.

23 Cotton Board Trade Letter, November 1952.

24 Caroline Miles, *Lancashire Textiles: A Case Study of Industrial Change*, Cambridge, 1967, p. 75.

25 Benyamin Bardan, 'The Cotton Textile Agreement 1962–1972', *Journal of World Trade Law*, vol. 7, no. 1, January–February, 1973.

26 D. M. Higgins, 'Re-equipment as a Strategy for Survival in the Lancashire Spinning Industry, c. 1945–c. 1960', *Textile History*, vol. 24, no. 2, Autumn 1993.

27 For a full account of these debates, see Cobrin, 'Two Paths of Industrial Adjustment'.

28 John Blackburn, 'The British Cotton Textile Industry since World War II: The Search for a Strategy', *Textile History*, vol. 24, no. 2, Autumn 1993.

29 D. C. Coleman, *Courtaulds: An Economic and Social History*, vol. 2, Oxford, 1969, p. 500.

30 In 1928 Courtaulds and ICI had signed a non-aggression pact whereby they agreed to keep out of each other's territory. Courtaulds was a large buyer of chemicals from ICI, and ICI had a policy of not competing with its customers. Courtaulds also had skills in fibre production which ICI lacked; this was one of the reasons for the formation of the joint company, British Nylon Spinners.

31 D. C. Coleman, *Courtaulds: An Economic and Social History*, vol. 3, Oxford, 1980, p. 226.

32 Arthur Knight, *Private Enterprise and Public Intervention*, Allen & Unwin, 1974, p. 37.

33 See, for example, the article by A. M. Alfred, chief economist of Courtaulds, 'UK Textiles – A Growth Industry', in *Transactions of Manchester Statistical Society 1965–66*.

34 Coleman, *Courtaulds*, vol. 3, p. 273.

35 Z. A. Silberston, *The Multi-Fibre Arrangement and the UK Economy*, HMSO, 1984.

36 Arthur Knight, *Private Enterprise and Public Intervention*, p. 170.

37 F. A. Wells, *Hollins and Viyella: A study in business history*, David & Charles, Newton Abbott, 1968.

38 John A. Blackburn, 'The British Cotton Textile Industry since World War II: The Search for a Strategy', *Textile History*, vol. 24, no. 2, Autumn 1993.

39 Ibid.

40 Monopolies Commission, *Report on the Supply of Man-made Cellulosic Fibres*, HMSO, 1968.

41 Edmund Dell, *Political Responsibility and Industry*, Allen & Unwin, 1973, p. 91.

42 Coats Patons was the product of a 1960 merger between J. and P. Coats, the Scottish thread producer, and Patons and Baldwins, a wool textile company based in Yorkshire. Coats had been since the late nineteenth century the world's largest sewing-thread manufacturer, with a network of factories around the world; it is often regarded as Britain's first multinational. Its acquisitions during the 1960s were partly driven by tax considerations; it needed a larger source of profits in the UK to offset the tax payable on its overseas earnings. Coats was also looking for new avenues of growth in the face of a likely decline in its international thread business. Most of its acquisitions were of knitwear companies in the East Midlands.

43 *Cotton and Allied Textiles: a report on Present Performance and Future Prospects*, The Textile Council, Manchester, 1969.

44 Knight, *Private Enterprise and Public Intervention*, p. 114.

45 Stanley Chapman, 'Mergers and Take-overs in the Post-war Textile Industry: The Experience of Hosiery and Knitwear', *Business History*, vol. 30, no. 2, April 1988.

46 Quoted in the *Financial Times*, 2 July 1981.

47 Interview with author, 13 October 1992.

48 Michael Cannell, 'The rise of Shiloh: Bucking the Trend in the UK Spinning Industry', *Textile Outlook International*, May 1997.

49 'Profile of Courtaulds Textiles', *Textile Outlook International*, January 1999.

50 John A. Blackburn, 'The British Cotton Textile Industry since World War II: The Search for a Strategy', *Textile History*, vol. 24, no. 2, Autumn 1993.

51 Martin Taylor, 'Large Textile Companies: Utility or Futility?', The Mather Lecture, delivered to the Textile Institute Annual World Conference, Nottingham, 18 October 1989.

52 *The Times*, 11 March 1999.

53 Cobrin, 'Two Paths of Industrial Adjustment', pp. 134–44.

54 Geoffrey Shepherd, 'Textile-Industry Adjustment in Developed Countries', Trade Policy Research Centre, London, 1981.

55 Stephan H. Lindner, 'Facing Global Competition: The Social Impact of the West German Textile Industry's Adjustment Strategies, in René Leboutte and Jean-Paul Lehners (eds.), *Formation et mutations des bassins industriels en Europe: impacts sociaux et environnementaux*, Luxembourg: Centre Universitaire de Luxembourg, 1997.

56 U. Hartmann, 'Experiences in Restructuring the Textile Industry in

West Germany and Some Other Industrialised Countries', in *World Textiles: Investment, Innovation, Invention*, Textile Institute, Manchester, 1985.

57 B. Toyne, J. S. Arpan, D. A. Ricks, T. A. Shimp and A. Barnett, *The Global Textile Industry*, Allen & Unwin, 1984, p. 150.

58 Patrick Kenis, *The social construction of an industry: A World of Chemical Fibres*, Campus Verlag, Frankfurt, 1992, p. 62.

59 Michael Scheffer, 'The Changing Map of European Textiles, Production and Sourcing Strategies of Textile and Clothing Firms', *L'Observatoire Européen du Textile and de l'Habillement*, Brussels, 1994.

60 Toyne et al., *The Global Textile Industry*, pp. 151-3.

61 Stephan H. Lindner, 'The French Textile Industry in the Depressions of the 1970s and 1980s', in Pierre Lanthier and Hubert Watelet (eds.), *Private Enterprise during Economic Crises, Tactics and Strategies*, International Economic History Congress, Milan, 1994.

62 John A Blackburn, 'The Vanishing UK Cotton Industry', *National Westminster Quarterly Review*, November 1982.

63 Stanley Chapman, 'Mergers and Take-overs in the Post-war Textile Industry', *Business History*, vol. 30, no. 2, April 1988.

64 Anna Bull, Martyn Pitt and Joseph Szarka, *Entrepreneurial Textile Communities*, Chapman & Hall, 1993, p. 151.

65 'Textile and Clothing Industries: Structural Problems and Policies in OECD Countries', OECD, Paris, 1983.

CHAPTER 5

1 Sidney Pollard and Paul Robertson, *The British Shipbuilding Industry 1870–1914*, Harvard, 1979, p. 11.

2 Leslie Jones, *Shipbuilding in Britain*, Cardiff, 1957, ch. 1.

3 Michael Davies, *Belief in the Sea*, Lloyd's of London Press, 1992, ch. 2.

4 Pollard and Robertson, *The British Shipbuilding Industry*, ch. 10.

5 Keith McClelland and Alastair Reid, 'Wood, Iron and Steel: Technology, Labour and Trade Union Organisation in the Shipbuilding Industry, 1840–1914', in Royden Harrison and Jonathan Zeitlin (eds.), *Divisions of Labour: Skilled Workers and Technological Change in 19th Century England*, Harvester Press, Sussex, 1985.

6 E. H. Lorenz, *Economic Decline in Britain: The Shipbuilding Industry 1890–1970*, Oxford, 1991, ch. 3.

7 John Lovell, 'Employers and Craft Unionism: A Programme of Action for British Shipbuilding, 1902–5', *Business History*, vol. 34, no. 4, October 1992.

8 Alastair Reid, 'Employers' Strategies and Craft Production: The British Shipbuilding Industry 1870–1950', in Steven Tolliday and Jonathan Zeitlin (eds.), *The Power to Manage? Employers and Industrial Relations in Comparative Historical Perspective*, Routledge, 1991.

9 Quoted in Lovell, 'Employers and Craft Unionism'.

10 Lorenz, *Economic Decline in Britain*, p. 59.

11 Alastair Reid, 'Employers' Strategies and Craft Production', in Tolliday and Zeitlin, *The Power to Manage?*.

12 Pollard and Robertson, *The British Shipbuilding Industry 1870–1914*, p. 169.

13 Sidney Pollard, 'British and World Shipbuilding 1890–1914: A Study in Comparative Costs', *Journal of Economic History*, vol. 17, no. 3, September 1957.

14 S. G. Sturmey, *British Shipping and World Competition*, London, 1962, p. 81.

15 A. Slaven, 'British Shipbuilders: Market Trends and Order Book Patterns Between the Wars', *Journal of Transport History*, vol. 3, no. 2, September 1982.

16 A. Slaven, 'Self-liquidation: The National Shipbuilders Security Ltd and British Shipbuilding in the 1930s', in Sarah Palmer and Glyndwr Williams (eds.), *Charted and Uncharted Waters*, National Maritime Museum, 1981.

17 Lorenz, *Economic Decline in Britain*, p. 111.

18 J. R. Parkinson, 'Shipbuilding', in N. K. Buxton and D. H. Aldcroft (eds.), *British Industry between the Wars*, Scolar Press, 1979.

19 Ibid.

20 Sturmey, *British Shipping and World Competition*, ch. 7.

21 Peter Hilditch, 'Management Strategy in the British Shipbuilding Industry', Ph.D. thesis, University of Kent, 1986.

22 Tomohei Chida and Peter N. Davies, *The Japanese Shipping and Shipbuilding Industries*, Athlone Press, 1990.

23 Ibid., pp. 111–14

24 A. Slaven, 'From Rationalisation to Nationalisation: The Capacity Problem and Strategies for Survival in British Shipbuilding 1920–1977', in Wilfred Feldenkirchen et al. (eds.), *Hans Pöhl Liber Amicorum: Wirtschaft Gesellschaft Unternehmen*, Stuttgart, 1995, pp. 1128–55.

25 Department of Scientific and Industrial Research, *Research and Development Requirements of the Shipbuilding and Marine Engineering Industries*, HMSO, 1960.

26 British Productivity Council, *Shipbuilding in Sweden*, October 1959.

27 *Productivity and Research in Shipbuilding*, report of the main committee under the chairmanship of Mr James Patton to the Joint Industry Committee, 1962.

28 Sydney Paulden and Bill Hawkins, *Whatever Happened at Fairfields?*, Gower, 1969.

29 Brian Hogwood, *Government and Shipbuilding: The Politics of Industrial Change*, Saxon House, 1979, ch. 4.

30 *Shipbuilding Inquiry Committee, 1965–6*, Cmd 2937, HMSO, 1966.

31 R. M. Stopford and J. R. Barton, 'Economic Problems of Shipbuilding and the State', *Maritime Policy Management*, vol. 13, no. 1, 1986.

32 Michael Moss and John R. Hume, *Shipbuilders to the World: 125 Years of Harland & Wolff*, Belfast, 1986.

33 J. McGoldrick, 'Industrial Relations and the Division of Labour in the Shipbuilding Industry since the War',

British Journal of Industrial Relations, vol. 21, no. 2, July 1983.

34 Commission on Industrial Relations, *Shipbuilding and Shiprepairing*, Report no. 22, Cmd 4756, HMSO, August 1971.

35 Peter Hilditch, 'Management Strategy in the British Shipbuilding Industry 1945–1986', Ph.D. thesis, University of Kent, 1986, ch. 10.

36 Ibid.

37 Hogwood, *Government and Shipbuilding*, p. 206.

38 Ian Roberts, *Craft, Class and Control*, Edinburgh, 1993, p. 201.

39 *Financial Times*, 9 November 1993, quoted in John Stirling and Jeff Bridgford, 'British and French Shipbuilding: The Industrial Relations of Decline', *Industrial Relations Journal*, vol. 16, no. 4, Winter 1985.

40 Robert Gordon, 'Manpower Utilisation and Flexibility in Shipbuilding: A Case Study on Organisational Change', Ph.D. thesis, University of Glasgow, June 1993.

41 Bo Stråth, *The Politics of De-industrialisation: The Contraction of the West European Shipbuilding Industry*, Croom Helm, 1987.

CHAPTER 6

1 Mary O'Mahony and Karin Wagner, 'Changing Fortunes: An Industry Study of British and German Productivity Growth over Three Decades', Report Series no. 7, National Institute of Economic and Social Research, 1994.

2 Bernard Elbaum, 'The Steel Industry before World War I', in Bernard Elbaum and William Lazonick (eds.), *The Decline of the British Economy*, Oxford, 1986.

3 Norman J. G. Pounds and William N. Parker, *Coal and Steel in Western Europe*, Faber & Faber, 1957.

4 Steven B. Webb, 'Tariffs, Cartels, Technology and Growth in the German Steel Industry, 1879–1914', *Journal of Economic History*, vol. 40, June 1980. See also R. Fremdling, 'The German Iron and Steel industry in the 19th Century', in Etsuo Abe and Yoshitaka Suzuki (eds.), *Changing Patterns of International*

Rivalry: Some Lessons from the Steel Industry, University of Tokyo Press, 1991.

5 Peter Temin, 'The Relative Decline of the British Steel Industry 1880–1913', in Henry Rosovsky (ed.), *Industrialisation in Two Systems*, Wiley, 1966. See also P. L. Payne, 'Iron and Steel Manufactures', in D. H. Aldcroft (ed.), *The Development of British Industry and Foreign Competition 1875–1914*, Allen & Unwin, 1968.

6 Duncan Burn, *The Economic History of Steelmaking, 1967–1939*, Cambridge, 1940, ch. 9.

7 Ulrich Wengenroth, *Enterprise and Technology*, Cambridge, 1994; Steven Tolliday, 'Competition and Maturity in the British Steel Industry 1870–1914', in Etsuo Abe and Yoshitaka Suzuki (eds.), *Changing patterns of International Rivalry*.

8 Wengenroth, *Enterprise and Technology*, pp. 265–6.

9 Geoffrey Tweedale, *Steel City, Entrepreneurship, Strategy and Technology in Sheffield 1743–1993*, Oxford, 1995, pp. 95–8.

10 Ibid., p. 112; M. Sanderson, 'The Professor as Industrial Consultant: Oliver Arnold and the British Steel Industry 1900–1914', *Economic History Review*, vol. 31, November 1978.

11 Frank Wilkinson, 'Collective Bargaining in the Steel Industry in the 1920s', in Asa Briggs and John Saville (eds.), *Essays in Labour History 1918–1939*, Croom Helm, 1977.

12 P. Bowen, *Social Control in Industrial Organisations*, Routledge, 1976.

13 Frank Wilkinson, 'Industrial Organisation, Collective Bargaining and Economic Efficiency', *International Contributions to Labour Studies*, vol. 1, 1991.

14 W. H. Scott, A. H. Halsey, J. A. Banks and T. Lupton, *Technical Change and Industrial Relations*, Liverpool University Press, 1956, p. 131.

15 Wengenroth, *Enterprise and Technology*, p. 268.

16 Steven Tolliday, *Business, Banking and Politics: The Case of British Steel, 1918–1935*, Harvard, 1987.

17 Burn, *The Economic History of Steelmaking*, pp. 436–40.

18 Tolliday, *Business, Banking and Politics*, ch. 4.

19 Ibid. p. 348.

20 Ibid. pp. 149–55.

21 Jonathan S. Boswell, *Business Policies in the Making: Three Steel Companies Compared*, Allen & Unwin, 1983.

22 Derek Matthews, 'The Business Doctors: Accountants in British Management from the Nineteenth Century to the Present Day', *Business History*, vol. 40, no. 3, July 1998.

23 Wilfried Feldenkirchen, 'Concentration in German Industry 1870–1939', in Hans Pohl (ed.), *The Concentration Process in the Entrepreneurial Economy since the Late 19th Century*, German Society for Business History, Frank Steiner Verlag, Stuttgart, 1988; Wilfried Feldenkirchen, 'Big Business in Inter-war Germany: Organisational Innovation at Vereinigte Stahlwerke, IG Farben and Siemens', *Business History Review*, vol. 61, no. 3, Autumn 1987; Alfred Chandler, *Scale and Scope*, Harvard, 1990, pp. 551–61.

24 Ingvar Svennilson, *Growth and Stagnation in the European Economy*, UN Economic Commission for Europe, Geneva, 1952.

25 S. N. Broadberry, *The Productivity Race*, Cambridge, 1997, p. 227.

26 Ruggero Ranieri, 'Partners and Enemies: the Government's Decision to Nationalise Steel 1944–8', in Robert Millward and John Singleton (eds.), *The Political Economy of Nationalisation in Britain 1920–50*, Cambridge, 1995.

27 Duncan Burn, *The Steel Industry 1939–1959*, Cambridge, 1961, ch. 4.

28 Richard Thomas merged with Baldwins, another South Wales tinplate firm, in 1944.

29 Martin Chick, *Industrial Policy in Britain 1945–1951*, Cambridge, 1998, ch. 7.

30 Ranieri, 'Partners and enemies', in Millward and Singleton, *The Political Economy of Nationalisation*, p. 281.

31 Burn, *The Steel Industry 1939–1959*, p. 318.

32 Edmund Dell, *The Schuman Plan and*

the British Abdication of Leadership in Europe, Oxford, 1995.

33 Ruggero Ranieri, 'Inside or outside the Magic Circle: The Italian and British Steel Industries Face to Face with the Schuman Plan and the European Coal and Steel Community', in A. S. Milward, Frances Lynch, Ruggero Ranieri, Federico Romero and Vibeke Sorensen, *The Frontier of National Sovereignty*, Routledge, 1993.

34 Kathleen Burk, *The First Privatisation*, The Historians' Press, London, 1988.

35 Anglo-American Council on Productivity, *Report on Iron and Steel*, June 1952.

36 Private communication.

37 E. Owen Smith, *Productivity bargaining: A Case Study of the Steel Industry*, Pan, 1971.

38 As part of the government's plan to create new jobs in Scotland, Rootes built a plant at Linwood to manufacture a new small car, while British Motor Corporation built a truck plant at Bathgate.

39 Burn, *The Steel Industry 1939–1959*, p. 656. See also Duncan Burn, *The Future of Steel*, Institute of Economic Affairs, 1965.

40 Burn, *The Steel Industry 1939–59*, pp. 556–7.

41 Frances Lynch, *France and the International Economy: From Vichy to the Treaty of Rome*, Routledge, 1997, pp. 59–66.

42 Matthias Kipping, 'Competing for Dollars and Technology: The United States and the Modernisation of the French and German Steel Industries after World War II', *Business and Economic History*, vol. 23, no. 1, Fall 1994.

43 Alastair Forsyth, *Steel Pricing Policies*, Political and Economic Planning, December 1964.

44 Michel Freyssenet, *La Sidérurgie Française 1945–1979*, Savelli, Paris, 1979.

45 Volker Berghahn, *The Americanisation of West German Industry, 1945–1973*, Berg, 1986, pp. 84–110.

46 Isabel Warner, *Steel and Sovereignty: The Deconcentration of the West German steel industry 1949–1954*, Verlag Philipp von Zabern, Mainz, 1996.

47 Gary Herrigel, *Industrial Constructions: The Sources of German Industrial Power*, Cambridge, 1996, pp. 216–19.

48 Kipping, 'Competing for Dollars and Technology'.

49 Seiichiro Yonekura, 'The Post-war Japanese Iron and Steel Industry: Continuity and Discontinuity', in Abe and Suzuki, *Changing Patterns of International Rivalry*.

50 *The Steel Industry*, the stage 1 report of the development co-ordinating committee of the British Iron and Steel Federation (the Benson report), July 1966.

51 Owen Smith, *Productivity Bargaining*.

52 Keith Ovenden, *The Politics of Steel*, Macmillan, 1978, p. 17.

53 Ibid., p. 81.

54 The Benson report.

55 Ovenden, *The Politics of Steel*, pp. 173ff.

56 *British Steel Corporation: Ten Year Development Strategy*, February 1973, Cmd 5226, HMSO.

57 Quoted in Bowen, *Social Control in Industrial Organisations*, p. 158.

58 G. F. Dudley and J. J. Richardson, *Politics and Steel in Britain, 1967–1988*, Dartmouth, 1990, p. 82.

59 Charles Villiers, *Beyond the Sunset*, Thomas Harmsworth, 1992, p. 166.

60 *British Steel Corporation: The Road to Viability*, March 1978, Cmd 7149, HMSO.

61 Bowen, *Social Control in Industrial Organisations*, p. 148.

62 James Kelly, 'Management Strategy and the Reform of Collective Bargaining: Cases from the British Steel Corporation', *British Journal of Industrial Relations*, July 1984.

63 Martin Upham, 'British Steel: Retrospect and Prospect', *Industrial Relations Journal*, vol. 11, no. 3, July–August 1980.

64 Martin Upham, *Tempered not Quenched: The History of the ISTC, 1951–1997*, Lawrence & Wishart, 1997, p. 118.

65 Villiers, *Beyond the Sunset*, p. 162.

66 Jack Hayward, 'The Nemesis of Industrial Patriotism: The French Response to the Steel Crisis', in Yves

Mény and Vincent Wright (eds.), *The Politics of Steel: Western Europe and the Steel Industry in the Crisis Years (1974–1984)*, de Gruyter, Berlin, 1987.

67 Philippe Mioche, *Jacques Ferry et la Sidérurgie Française depuis la seconde guerre mondiale*, Publications de l'Université de Provence, 1993.

68 James Bell, 'The Fall of the House of Krupp', *Fortune*, August 1967.

69 Martin F. Parnell, *The German Tradition of Organised Capitalism: Self-government in the Coal Industry*, Oxford, 1994.

70 Josef Esser and Werner Vath, 'Overcoming the Steel Crisis in the Federal Republic of Germany', in Mény and Wright, *The Politics of Steel*.

71 Lutz Schröter, ' "Steelworks Now!" The Conflicting Character of Modernisation: A Case Study of Hoesch in Dortmund', in Walter H. Goldberg (ed.), *Ailing Steel: the Transatlantic Quarrel*, Gower, 1986.

72 Upham, *Tempered Not Quenched*.

73 Margaret Thatcher, *The Downing Street Years*, HarperCollins, 1993, pp. 108–114.

74 Ian MacGregor, *The Enemies Within: the Story of the Miners' Strike 1984–5*, Collins, 1986.

75 Christopher Beauman, 'British Steel: A Turnround under Public Ownership', *Business Strategy Review*, vol. 7, no. 3, Autumn 1996. Published by London Business School.

76 Jonathan Aylen, 'Privatisation of British Steel', in Matthew Bishop, John Kay and Colin Mayer (eds.), *Privatisation and Economic Performance*, Oxford, 1994.

77 Paul Blyton, 'Steel', in Andrew Pendleton and Jonathan Winterton (eds.), *Public Enterprise in Transition: Industrial Relations in State and Privatised Corporations*, Routledge, 1993. See also Jonathan Morris, Paul Blyton, Nick Bacon and Hans-Werner Franz, 'Beyond Survival: The Implementation of New Forms of Work Organisation in the UK and German Steel Industries', *International Journal of Human Resource Management*, vol. 3, no. 2, September 1992.

78 Peter F. Marcus and Karlis M. Kirsis, *World Steel Dynamics*, no. 14, 10 December 1987.

79 Raymond Levy, 'Industrial Policy and the Steel Industry', in William J. Adams and Christian Stoffaes (eds.), *French Industrial Policy*, Brookings, 1986.

80 Schröter, 'Steelworks Now!', in Goldberg, *Ailing Steel*.

81 Aylen, 'Privatisation of British Steel', in Bishop, Kay and Mayer, *Privatisation and Economic Performance*.

82 Anthony Cockerill, 'Steel', in Peter Johnson (ed.), *The Structure of British Industry*, Unwin Hyman, 1988.

83 Hayward, 'The Nemesis of Industrial Patriotism', in Mény and Wright, *The Politics of Steel*.

CHAPTER 7

1 C. D. M. Ketelbey, *Tullis Russell: The history of R. Tullis & Company and Tullis Russell & Co. Ltd. 1809–1959*, Tullis Russell, 1959.

2 Joan Evans, *The Endless Web: John Dickinson & Co Ltd 1804–1954*, Cape, 1955.

3 Ketelbey, *Tullis Russell*, p. 4.

4 D. C. Coleman, *The British Paper Industry, 1495–1860*, Oxford, 1958.

5 Gary Bryan Magee, *Productivity and Performance in the Paper Industry*, Cambridge, 1987, ch. 7.

6 W. J. Reader, *Bowater: A history*, Cambridge, 1981, p. 28.

7 Ibid., p. 100.

8 Ibid., p. 59.

9 Ibid., p. 142.

10 1937 Annual report of British Paper and Board Makers Association, quoted in Margaret Wray, *The British Paper Industry: A Study in Structural and Technological Change*, British Paper and Board Industry Federation, 1979, p. 44.

11 Representations to HM Government on post-war policy, submitted by the Paper Makers Association of Great Britain and Ireland, 1944. Quoted in Wray, *The British Paper Industry*, p. 57.

12 Alan S. Milward and George Brennan, *Britain's Place in the World: A Historical Enquiry into Import Controls 1945–60*, Routledge, 1996, p. 284.

13 Richard L. Hills, *Paper-making in Britain*, Athlone, 1988, p. 205.

14 Ibid., p. 197.
15 Ketelbey, *Tullis Russell*.
16 Reader, *Bowater*, p. 295.
17 K. J. Funnell, *Snodland Paper Mill, C. Townsend Hook and Company from 1854*, Townsend Hook, 1979.
18 In 1998 BPB Industries announced its intention to close the Radcliffe mill in Manchester, while retaining the Davidson mill in Aberdeen and the Purfleet mill in Essex.
19 Oscar Haus, Verband Deutscher Papierfabriken, letter to the author, 17 August 1993.
20 Reader, *Bowater*, p. 296.
21 P. B. Beaumont and L. C. Hunter, 'Continuous Process Technology, Annualised Hours and National Bargaining', *New Technology, Work and Employment*, vol. 11, no. 2, September 1996, pp. 118–24.

CHAPTER 8

1 Ann Daly and Daniel Jones, 'The Machine Tool Industry in Britain, Germany and the US', *National Institute Review*, no. 92, May 1980.
2 D. A. Hounshell, *From the American system to mass production 1800–1932*, Johns Hopkins University Press, 1984.
3 Jonathan Zeitlin, 'Between Flexibility and Mass Production: Strategic Ambiguity and Selective Adaptation in the British Engineering Industry, 1830–1914', in Charles F. Sabel and Jonathan Zeitlin (eds.), *World of Possibilities, Flexibility and Mass Production in Western Industrialisation*, Cambridge, 1997.
4 A. E. Harrison, 'The Competitiveness of the British Cycle Industry 1890–1914', *Economic History Review*, vol. 22, no. 2, August 1969, pp. 287–303.
5 Paul Rosen, 'Modernity, Post-modernity and Socio-technical Change in the British Cycle Industry', Ph.D. thesis, University of Lancaster, 1995.
6 S. B. Saul, 'The Machine Tool Industry in Britain to 1914', in R. P. T. Davenport-Hines (ed.), *Capital, Entrepreneurs and Profits*, Cass, 1990.
7 Jonathan Zeitlin, 'The Labour Strategies of British Engineering Employers, 1890–1922', in H. Gospel and C. R. Littler (eds.), *Managerial Strategies and Industrial Relations: an Historical and Comparative Study*, Heinemann, 1983.
8 Alex McKinlay and Jonathan Zeitlin, 'The Meanings of Managerial Prerogative: Industrial Relations and the Organisation of Work in British Engineering, 1880–1939', *Business History*, vol. 31, no. 2, April 1989.
9 Klaus Harney, 'The Emergence of the Technical School System in Prussia', in Ian Inkster (ed.), *The Steam Intellect Societies*, Nottingham Studies in the History of Education, Nottingham University, 1985.
10 B. Dornseifer and J. Kocka, 'The Impact of the Pre-industrial Heritage: Reconsiderations of the German Pattern of Industrial Development in the Late 19th and Early 20th Centuries', *Industrial and Corporate Change*, vol. 2, no. 2, 1993.
11 Gary Herrigel, *Industrial Constructions: The Sources of German Industrial Power*, Cambridge 1996, ch. 2. See also Gary Herrigel, 'Industrial Order and the Politics of Industrial Change: Mechanical Engineering', in Peter J. Katzenstein (ed.), *Industry and Politics in West Germany*, Cornell, 1989.
12 Zeitlin, 'Between Flexibility and Mass Production', in Sabel and Zeitlin, *World of Possibilities*. See also S. B. Saul, 'The American Impact upon British Industry 1895–1914', in Davenport-Hines, *Capital, Entrepreneurs and Profits*.
13 I. C. R. Byatt, *The British Electrical Industry*, Oxford, 1979.
14 T. P. Hughes, *Networks of Power: Electrification in Western Society 1880–1930*, Johns Hopkins, 1983.
15 Wilfried Feldenkirchen, *Werner von Siemens*, Ohio State University Press, 1994.
16 J. F. Wilson, *Ferranti and the British Electrical Industry 1864–1930*, Manchester University Press, 1988.
17 Alfred D. Chandler, *Scale and Scope: The Dynamics of Industrial Capitalism*, Harvard, 1990, p. 276.
18 William P. Kennedy, *Industrial Structure,*

Capital Markets and the Origins of British Economic Decline, Cambridge, 1987.

19 Ranald Michie, 'The Finance of Innovation in Late Victorian and Edwardian Britain: Possibilities and Constraints', *Journal of European Economic History*, vol. 17, no. 3, Winter 1988.

20 Michie, 'The Finance of Innovation', p. 513. See also T. P. Hughes, 'The British Electrical Industry Lag, 1882–1888', *Technology and Culture*, vol. 3, no. 1, Winter 1962.

21 R. P. T. Davenport-Hines (ed.), *Speculators and Patriots: Essays in Business Biography*, Cass, 1986, p. 127.

22 The name Osram was a contraction of osmium and wolfram, the ores from which tungsten is made.

23 John Wilson, 'A Strategy of Expansion and Combination; Dick Kerr & Co, 1897–1914', *Business History*, vol. 27, no. 1, March 1985.

24 D. A. Farnie, 'The Textile Machine-making Industry and the World Market, 1870–1960', *Business History*, vol. 32, no. 4, October 1990.

25 Jonathan Zeitlin, *Between Flexibility and Mass Production: Strategic Debate and Industrial Reorganisation in British Engineering*, Oxford (forthcoming), ch. 3.

26 Leslie Hannah, 'A pioneer of public enterprise: The Central Electricity Board and the National Grid, 1927–1940', in Barry Supple (ed.), *Essays in British Business History*, Oxford, 1977.

27 The inter-war mergers in the British electrical industry are described in Robert Jones and Oliver Marriott, *Anatomy of a merger: A history of GEC, AEI and English Electric*, Cape, 1976.

28 R. P. T. Davenport-Hines, *Dudley Docker: The Life and Times of a Trade Warrior*, Cambridge, 1984, pp. 155–9.

29 T. A. B. Corley, *Domestic Electrical Appliances*, Cape, 1966, p. 35.

30 A. S. Milward, *The European Rescue of the Nation-state*, Routledge, 1992, ch. 7.

31 Alan Kramer, *The West German economy 1945–1955*, Berg, 1991, p. 189.

32 Milward, *The European rescue of the Nation-state*, p. 154.

33 The first was an unpublished report by the Department of Scientific and Industrial Research. The second was commissioned by the Board of Trade and published as *The Machine Tool Industry: A Report by the sub-committee of the Machine Tool Advisory Committee*, HMSO, 1960.

34 The Marconi Company had been merged in 1929 with Associated Cables Company to form Cable and Wireless. The Labour Government nationalised this company in 1946, mainly in order to safeguard the provision of telecommunications services between Britain and the Commonwealth. The Marconi side of the business, engaged in the design and manufacture of electronic equipment, was then put up for sale. These events are described in Chapter 10.

35 Since the end of the First World War Siemens Brothers had been a quoted British company, but it had re-established its links with Siemens in Germany, and at the time of the Second World War 15 per cent of the shares were held by its former parent. This block of shares was taken over by the Custodian of Enemy Properties during the war, and sold in 1951 to AEI. Three years later AEI made a full bid for the company. See Jones and Marriott, *Anatomy of a Merger*, ch. 10.

36 Jones and Marriott, *Anatomy of a Merger*, pp. 204–7.

37 S. A. Pandit, *From Making to Music: The History of Thorn EMI*, Hodder & Stoughton, 1996, p. 11.

38 Jones and Marriott, *Anatomy of a Merger*, p. 310.

39 Patrizio Bianchi and Luigi Forlai, 'The Domestic Appliance Industry 1945–1991', in H. W. de Jong (ed.), *The Structure of European Industry*, 3rd rev. edn, Kluwer, 1993. See also Nicholas Owen, *Economies of scale, Competitiveness and Trade Patterns within the European Community*, Oxford, 1983, ch. 6.

40 Quoted in S. Koerner, 'The British Motor Cycle Industry 1935–1975', Ph.D. thesis, Warwick University, 1995.

41 Ibid. See also *Strategy alternatives for the British motorcycle industry: A Report by*

the Boston Consulting Group, HMSO, 1975.

42 Davenport-Hines, *Dudley Docker*, p. 231.

43 Staffan Jacobsson, *Electronics and Industrial Policy: The Case of Computer Controlled Lathes*, Allen & Unwin, 1986.

44 D. J. Collis, 'Bearings: The Visible Hand of Global Firms', in David B. Yoffie (ed.), *Beyond Free Trade: Firms, Governments and Global Competition*, Harvard, 1993. For the IRC's involvement in ball bearings see Douglas Hague and Geoffrey Wilkinson, *The IRC: An Experiment in Industrial Intervention*, Allen & Unwin, 1983, ch. 6.

45 Andrew Lorenz, *A Fighting Chance*, Hutchinson, 1989, pp. 90–97.

46 Sir Trevor Holdsworth, speech given at Institute of Chartered Accountants of Scotland, September 1990.

47 Massey-Ferguson, the Canadian farm equipment company, changed its name to Varity in 1986 and moved its headquarters to the US. In 1989 Varity bought Kelsey-Hayes, an American brake manufacturer. In 1994 the Massey-Ferguson tractor business, based in Coventry, was sold to Agco of the US. In 1997, after the merger with Lucas, Varity's other main British subsidiary, Perkins Engines, was sold to Caterpillar of the US.

48 Interview with author, 28 June 1993.

49 Speech by Sir Ronald Garrick, chief executive, Weir Group, to Fellowship of Engineering, May 1992.

50 *Financial Times*, 3 January 1995.

51 Andrew Lorenz, *A Fighting Chance*, ch. 2.

52 Steve Thomas and Francis McGowan, 'The World Market for Heavy Electrical Equipment', *Nuclear Engineering International*, 1990.

53 In 1987 GEC sold 50 per cent of the Hotpoint subsidiary to General Electric of the US, but this did not lead to any change in marketing policy.

54 S. A. Pandit, *From Making to Music*, ch. 14. Thorn-EMI retained the profitable light-fittings and fixtures business, but this, too, was sold in 1994.

CHAPTER 9

1 James Laux, *The European Automobile Industry*, Twayne, 1992, ch. 2.

2 Roy Church, *Herbert Austin: The British Motor Car Industry to 1941*, Europa, 1979, p. 16.

3 S. B. Saul, 'The Motor Industry in Britain to 1914', *Business History*, vol. 5, no. 1, December 1962.

4 R. J. Overy, *William Morris, Viscount Nuffield*, Europa, 1976; Martin Adeney, *Nuffield: A biography*, Robert Hale, 1993.

5 G. Maxcy and A. Silberston, *The Motor Industry*, Allen & Unwin, 1959, p. 13.

6 Roy Church and Michael Miller, 'The Big Three: Competition, Management and Marketing in the British Motor Industry, 1922–1939', in Barry Supple (ed.), *Essays in British Business History*, Oxford, 1977.

7 Allan Nevins and Frank Ernest Hill, *Ford: expansion and challenge, 1915–1933*, Scribner, New York, 1957, ch. 21.

8 Church and Miller, 'The Big Three', Supple, *Essays in British Business History*.

9 Richard Whipp and Peter Clark, *Innovation and the Auto Industry*, Pinter, 1986, pp. 67–9.

10 Laux, *The European Automobile Industry*, 1992, pp. 123–4.

11 Lothar Gall et al., *The Deutsche Bank, 1870–1995*, Weidenfeld & Nicolson, 1995, pp. 217–18.

12 R. J. Overy, *War and Economy in the Third Reich*, Oxford, 1994, ch. 2.

13 Karel Williams, Colin Haslam, Sukhdev Johal and John Williams, *Cars: Analysis, History, Cases*, Berghahn, 1994, p. 138.

14 Jonathan Wood, *Wheels of Misfortune: The Rise and Fall of the British Motor Industry*, Sidgwick & Jackson, 1988, p. 60.

15 In Germany the licensee was the Dixi Motor Works in Eisenach, later taken over by BMW. Horst Mönnich, *The BMW Story*, Sidgwick & Jackson, 1991.

16 Roy Church, 'Deconstructing Nuffield: The Evolution of Managerial Culture in the British Motor Industry', *Economic History Review*, vol. 49, no. 3, 1996.

17 Wayne Lewchuk, *American Technology*

and the British Vehicle Industry, Cambridge, 1987, ch. 8.

18 Steven Tolliday, 'Management and Labour in Britain 1896–1939', in Steven Tolliday and Jonathan Zeitlin (eds.), *Between Fordism and Flexibility: The Automobile Industry and Its Workers*, Berg, 1992. See also Steven Tolliday, 'The Diffusion and Transformation of Fordism: Britain and Japan Compared', in Robert Boyer, Else Charron, Ulrich Jürgens and Steven Tolliday (eds.), *Between imitation and innovation: the Transfer and Hybridization of Productive Models in the International Automobile Industry*, Oxford, 1998. The debate is summarised in Roy Church, *The Rise and Decline of the British Motor Industry*, Macmillan, 1994, ch. 1.

19 Tim Claydon, 'Trade Unions, Employers and Industrial Relations', in 'The British Motor Industry c.1919–45', *Business History*, vol. 29, no. 3, July 1987.

20 Howard F. Gospel, *Markets, Firms, and the Management of Labour in Modern Britain*, Cambridge, 1992, p. 128.

21 D. G. Rhys, *The Motor Industry: An Economic Survey*, Butterworths, 1972, p. 379.

22 Jonathan Zeitlin, 'Reconciling Automation and Flexibility? Technology and Production Organisation in the Postwar British Motor Vehicle Industry', in *Enterprise and Society: An International Journal of Business History*, Oxford, vol. 1, 2000.

23 Williams, Haslam, Johal and Williams, *Cars*, p. 143.

24 Wood, *Wheels of Misfortune*, p. 133.

25 In 1953 Ford acquired its body supplier, Briggs Bodies, where a strong shop steward organisation already existed. The integration of the two businesses exacerbated Ford's labour relations problems. See Steven Tolliday, 'Ford and Fordism in Post-war Britain', in Steven Tolliday and Jonathan Zeitlin (eds.), *The Power to Manage? Employers and Industrial Relations in Comparative Historical Perspective*, Routledge, 1991, p. 88.

26 H. A. Turner, Garfield Clack and Geoffrey Roberts, *Labour Relations in the Motor Industry*, Allen & Unwin, 1967, p. 187.

27 Steven Tolliday, 'Competition and the Workplace in the British Automobile Industry, 1945–1988', *Business and Economic History*, vol. 17, 1988.

28 Alan Milward, *The European Rescue of the Nation-state*, Routledge, 1992, p. 418.

29 Steven Tolliday, 'Enterprise and State in the West German Wirtschaftswunder: Volkswagen and the Automobile Industry, 1939–1962', *Business History Review*, no. 69, Autumn 1995.

30 Jean-Louis Loubet, *Citroën, Peugeot, Renault et les autres: soixante ans de stratégies*, Le Monde Editions, 1995.

31 G. Maxcy and A. Silberston, *The Motor Industry*, Allen & Unwin, 1959, p. 187.

32 Triumph was a manufacturer of motorcycles and cars which went into receivership in 1939. The motorcycle enterprise was sold as a separate business, and the car side was acquired by Standard in 1944.

33 Wood, *Wheels of Misfortune*, p. 154.

34 Graham Robson, *The Rover Story*, Patrick Stevens, 1977.

35 *Economist*, 11 August 1962.

36 Timothy R. Whisler, 'The Outstanding Potential Market: The British Motor Industry and Europe 1945–75', *Journal of Transport History*, vol. 15, no. 1, March 1994.

37 Williams, Haslam, Johal and Williams, *Cars*, p. 146.

38 K. Williams, J. Williams and D. Thomas, *Why are the British Bad at Manufacturing?*, Routledge, 1983, p. 220.

39 Sue Bowden and Josephine Maltby, 'Under-performance, Short-termism and Corporate Governance: The City and British Motor Corporation, 1952–67', *Financial History Review*, vol. 5, part 2, October 1998.

40 The merger negotiations are described in Graham Turner, *The Leyland Papers*, Eyre & Spottiswood, 1963. For the IRC's role, see Douglas Hague and Geoffrey Wilkinson, *The IRC: An Experiment in Industrial Intervention*, Allen & Unwin, 1983.

41 Karel Williams, John Williams, D. Thomas, *Why are the British Bad at*

Manufacturing?, Routledge, 1983, p. 233.

42 Jonathan Wood, *Wheels of Misfortune*, p. 176.

43 Richard Whipp and Peter Clark, *Innovation and the Auto Industry*, p. 109.

44 *Turner, The Leyland Papers*, p. 211.

45 Steven Tolliday, 'High Tide and After: Coventry's Engineering Workers and Shop Floor Bargaining 1945–80', in Bill Lancaster and Tony Mason (eds.), *Life and Labour in a Twentieth Century City: The Experience of Coventry*, Cryfield Press, 1986.

46 Tolliday, 'Ford and Fordism in Post-war Britain', in Tolliday and Zeitlin, *The Power to Manage*, p. 95.

47 Lewis Whyte, *One increasing purpose: The Annals of an Investor*, Hutchinson, 1984.

48 *British Leyland: The Next Decade*, HMSO, April 1975.

49 *The Motor Vehicle Industry*, a report by the House of Commons Expenditure Committee, August 1975.

50 A. Manwaring, D. Marsden and S. Wood, 'Developments in Industrial Relations in the Post-war British Motor Industry', in Wolfgang Streeck and Andreas Hoff (eds.), *Industrial relations in the world motor industry: the experiences of the 1970s*, International Institute of Management, Berlin, 1982, p. 147.

51 David Marsden, Timothy Morris, Paul Willman and Stephen Wood, *The Car Industry: Labour Relations and Industrial Adjustment*, Tavistock, 1985, p. 131.

52 Central Policy Review Staff, *The Future of the British Car Industry*, HMSO, 1975. See also in Stephen Wilks, *Industrial Policy and the Motor Industry*, Manchester, 1984; S. Young and N. Hood, *Chrysler UK, a Corporation in Transition*, Praeger, 1977.

53 Edmund Dell, 'The Chrysler UK Rescue', *Contemporary Record*, vol. 6, no. 1, Summer 1992.

54 Jean-Louis Loubet, *Automobiles Peugeot*, Economica, 1990, ch. 7.

55 Wolfgang Streeck, *Industrial Relations in West Germany: A Case Study of the Car Industry*, Heinemann, 1984.

56 Michael Cusumano, *The Japanese Automobile Industry*, Harvard, 1991; James P. Womack, Daniel T. Jones and Daniel Roos, *The Machine that Changed the World*, Rawson, New York, 1990.

57 Margaret Thatcher, *The Downing Street Years*, HarperCollins, 1993, pp. 496–7.

58 Michael Edwardes, *Back from the Brink*, Pan, 1984, p. 35.

59 Ibid., p. 135.

60 Ray Horrocks, managing director (cars), interviewed in *Motor*, 25 August 1979.

61 Frank Mueller and Michael Roper, 'Technological Innovation and Commercial Success: The Development of the K-series Engine at Rover', Technology Project Papers, no. 15, London Business School, November 1991.

62 Margaret Thatcher, *The Downing Street Years*, p. 118.

63 Sir Graham Day, Price Waterhouse lecture to the Cardiff Business School, 16 May 1990.

64 Andrew Mair, *Honda's Global Local Corporation*, Macmillan, 1994, p. 278.

65 Lord Young, *The Enterprise Years*, Headline, 1990, p. 288.

66 Ibid., p. 292.

67 *Financial Times*, 13 September 1995.

68 Nick Oliver and Barry Wilkinson, *The Japanisation of British Industry*, Blackwell, 1988, p. 221.

69 Interview with author, 31 March 1992.

70 Ken Starkey and Alan McKinlay, *Strategy and the Human Resource: Ford and the Search for Competitive Advantage*, Blackwell, 1993.

71 Steven Tolliday, 'Ford and Fordism in Post-war Britain', in Tolliday and Zeitlin, *The Power to Manage*, p. 103.

72 *Financial Times*, 22 April 1999.

73 Ibid., 16 September 1996.

74 Daniel T. Jones, 'Maturity and Crisis in the European Car Industry: Structural Change and Public Policy', Sussex European Papers, no. 8, Sussex University, 1981.

75 Patrick Messerlin, 'France', in François Duchène and Geoffrey Shepherd (eds.), *Managing Industrial Change in Western Europe*, Pinter, 1987.

CHAPTER 10

1 W. J. Baker, *A History of the Marconi Company*, Methuen, 1970, ch. 6.

2 Sigfrid von Weiher and Herbert Goetzeler, *The Siemens Company: Its Historical Role in the Progress of Electrical Engineering, 1847–1980*, Siemens, 1977, p. 64.

3 Leonard S. Reich, *The making of American industrial research: Science and Business at GE and Bell, 1876–1926*, Cambridge, 1985, ch. 9.

4 Baker, *A History of the Marconi Company*, p. 181; Alfred Chandler, *Scale and Scope: The Dynamics of Industrial Capitalism*, Harvard, 1990, p. 219.

5 Peter Young, *Power of speech, a history of Standard Telephones 1883–1983*, Allen & Unwin, 1983.

6 J. F. Wilson, *Ferranti and the British Electrical Industry, 1864–1930*, Manchester, 1988, p. 135.

7 S. G. Sturmey, *The Economic Development of Radio*, Wyman, 1958.

8 Keith Geddes and Gordon Bussey, *The Setmakers*, British Radio and Electronic Equipment Manufacturers Association, 1991, p. 31.

9 Baker, *A History of the Marconi Company*, p. 231.

10 Geoffrey Jones, 'The Gramophone Company: An Anglo-American Multinational 1898–1931', *Business History Review*, vol. 59, no. 1, Spring 1985.

11 S. A. Pandit, *From Making to Music: The History of Thorn EMI*, Hodder & Stoughton, 1996, p. 62.

12 Thomas Wilson, 'The Electronics Industry', in Duncan Burn (ed.), *The Structure of British Industry*, vol. 2, Cambridge, 1958.

13 Paul Erker, 'The Choice between Competition and Co-operation: Research and Development in the Electrical Industry in Germany and the Netherlands', in François Caron, Paul Erker and Wolfram Fischer (eds.), *Innovations in the European Economy between the Wars*, de Gruyter, 1995.

14 Ibid.

15 Thomas Wilson, 'The Electronics Industry', in Duncan Burn (ed.), *The Structure of British Industry*, vol. 2.

16 Richard R. Nelson, 'The Link between Science and Invention: The Case of the Transistor', in *The Rate and Direction of Inventive Activity: Economic and Social Factors*, National Bureau of Economic and Social Research, Princeton, 1962.

17 J. E. Tilton, *International Diffusion of Technology: The Case of Semiconductors*, Brookings, 1971, p. 76.

18 The launch of the Fairchild semiconductor business was financed by Fairchild Camera and Instrument, which later acquired full control of the operation. It was partly because of the constraints of operating within a large corporation that Noyce and Moore struck out on their own to form Intel.

19 Franco Malerba, *The Semiconductor Business*, Pinter, 1985, p. 97.

20 Tilton, *The International Diffusion of Technology*, pp. 89–92.

21 Kenneth Flamm, *Creating the Computer*, Brookings, 1988, p. 51.

22 In 1955 Remington Rand merged with Sperry Corporation to form Sperry Rand.

23 Flamm, *Creating the Computer*, ch. 4.

24 Martin Fransman, *Japan's Computer and Communications Industry*, Oxford, 1995.

25 John Hendry, *Innovating for Failure: Government Policy and the Early British Computer Industry*, MIT Press, 1989, p. 33.

26 David Caminer, John Aris, Peter Hermon and Frank Land, *User-driven innovation: The World's First Business Computer*, McGraw Hill, 1996; John Hendry, 'The Teashop Computer Manufacturer: J. Lyons, LEO and the potential limits of high-tech diversification', *Business History*, vol. 29, January 1987.

27 John Hendry, *Innovating for Failure*, p. 11.

28 Martin Campbell-Kelly, *ICL: A Business and Technical History*, Oxford, 1989, p. 143.

29 Hendry, *Innovating for Failure*, p. 161.

30 Ibid., p. 154.

31 Harold Wilson, *The Labour Government*

1964–70: A Personal Record, Penguin, 1974, p. 31.

32 Campbell-Kelly, *ICL*, p. 260.

33 General Electric sold its computer interests to Honeywell, RCA to Sperry Rand.

34 Campbell-Kelly, *ICL*, p. 331.

35 Interview in Robert Heller, *The state of British industry: Can Britain Make It?*, BBC Books, 1987, p. 152.

36 A full and critical account of French computer policy is Jean-Pierre Brule, *L'informatique malade de l'Etat, du Plan Calcul à Bull nationalisé: un fiasco de 40 milliards*, Les Belles Lettres, Paris, 1993. For an earlier overview of French policy in electronics, see John Zysman, *Political strategies for industrial order: State, market and industry in France*, University of California Press, 1977.

37 Pierre-E. Mounier-Kuhn, 'Product Policies in Two French Computer Firms: SEA and Bull (1948–64)', in Lisa Bud-Frierman (ed.), *Information Acumen: The Understanding and Use of Knowledge in Modern Business*, Routledge, 1994.

38 Pascal Griset (ed.), *Informatique, politique industrielle, Europe: entre Plan Calcul et Unidata*, Institut d'Histoire de l'Industrie, Editions Rive Droite, Paris, 1998.

39 *Financial Times*, 17 June 1999.

40 Flamm, *Creating the Computer*, p. 170.

41 John Zysman and Michael Borrus, *From Failure to Fortune? European Electronics in a Changing World Economy*, Annals of the American Academy of Political and Social Science, vol. 531, January 1994.

42 Malerba, *The Semiconductor Business*, ch. 4.

43 W. B. Willott, 'The NEB Involvement in Electronics and Information Technology', in Charles Carter (ed.), *Industrial Policy and Innovation*, Heinemann, 1981.

44 T. Rowland and M. McLean, *The Inmos Saga*, Pinter, 1985; Romano Dyerson, 'Inmos: a case of unsuitable corporate governance?', *Business Strategy Review*, vol. 3, no. 1, Spring 1992.

45 Stephen Aris, *Arnold Weinstock and the Making of GEC*, Aurum, 1998, ch. 7.

46 Interview with *Financial Times*, 4 November 1988.

47 For a criticial view of this take-over, and its implications for semiconductors, see Kevin Morgan et al., 'The GEC-Siemens Bid for Plessey: The Wider European Issues', Working Paper no. 2, January 1989, Centre for Information and Communications Technologies, Science Policy Research Unit, University of Sussex.

48 This plan was outlined to the Monopolies Commission, which investigated and cleared the GEC/Siemens take-over of Plessey. *The General Electric Company plc, Siemens AG and the Plessey Company plc: A Report on the Proposed Mergers*, Monopolies and Mergers Commission, April 1989.

49 Quoted in *Financial Times*, 14/15 February 1998.

50 William Walker, 'National Innovation Systems: Britain', in Richard R. Nelson (ed.), *National Innovation Systems: A Comparative Analysis*, Oxford, 1993.

51 J. Nicholas Ziegler, *Governing Ideas: Strategies for Innovation in France and Germany*, Cornell, 1997, p. 195.

52 Study of Siemens by S. G. Warburg Securities, May 1991.

53 *Financial Times*, 1/2 August 1998.

54 *Financial Times*, 5 November 1998.

55 Alan Cawson, Kevin Morgan, Douglas Webber, Peter Holmes, and Anne Stevens, *Hostile Brothers: Competition and Closure in the European electronics industry*, Oxford, 1990, p. 224.

56 In 1969 EMI had made a spectacular breakthrough in electronic body scanners. But EMI had no previous experience of the medical field, and it made the mistake of trying to market the scanner in the US on its own. Losses in this business, together with a down turn on the music side, contributed to a financial crisis at the end of the 1970s, leading to the takeover by Thorn in 1979.

57 Interview with Sir Richard Cave, chairman of Thorn, *Financial Times*, 10 November 1979.

58 *Financial Times*, 19 June 1987.

59 Pandit, *From Making to Music*, p. 174.
60 *Financial Times*, 14 April 1997.
61 These events are described in Alan Cawson, Kevin Morgan, Douglas Webber, Peter Holmes and Anne Stevens, *Hostile Brothers: Competition and Closure in the European electronics industry*, Oxford, 1990, ch. 11.
62 *Le Monde*, 28 November 1997.
63 Robert J. Chapuis and Amos E. Joel, *Electronics, Computers and Telephone Switching*, Amsterdam, 1990, p. 60.
64 Alfonso H. Molina, 'The Development of Public Switching Systems in the UK and Sweden: The Weight of History', Edinburgh PICT Working Paper, no. 19, University of Edinburgh, 1990. See also Peter C. Grindley, 'System X: The Failure of Procurement', Working Paper Series, no. 29, London Business School, August 1987.
65 Cawson et al., *Hostile Brothers*, p. 111.
66 Henry Ergas, 'France Telecom: Has the Model Worked?', paper for a seminar organised by the Royal Norwegian Council for Scientific and Industrial Research, Oslo, 29 January 1992.
67 Elie Cohen, *Le Colbertisme 'high tech': Economie des Télécom et du Grand Projet*, Hachette, 1992.
68 Razeen Sally, 'Alcatel's Relations with the French State: The Political Economy of a Multinational Enterprise', *Communications and Strategies*, no. 9, 1st quarter, 1993.
69 Cawson et al., *Hostile Brothers*, p. 161.
70 Ziegler, *Governing Ideas*, p. 84.
71 *Financial Times*, 25 June 1998.
72 *Financial Times*, 5 March 1999.
73 See note 56 above.
74 According to a study published in *Management Today* (March 1997), Racal was the second highest performer in terms of total shareholder return between 1966 and 1995, slightly behind Hanson.
75 Criticisms along these lines are contained in Karel Williams, John Williams and Dennis Thomas, *Why are the British Bad at Manufacturing?*, Routledge, 1983; Alex Brummer and Roger Cowe, *Weinstock: the Life and Times of Britain's Premier Industrialist*, HarperCollins, 1998; and Aris, *Arnold Weinstock and the Making of GEC*.
76 *GEC in Ascension*, Smith New Court, April 1993.
77 Interview in *Financial Times*, 9 July 1992.
78 National Economic Development Council, 'Strengthening the Competitiveness of the UK Electronics Industry', a report by McKinsey and Company to the electronics industry Economic Development Committee, June 1988.
79 *The General Electric Company Limited and Averys Limited*, Monopolies and Mergers Commission, HMSO, September 1979.
80 Williams, Williams and Thomas, *Why are the British Bad at Manufacturing?* p. 175.

CHAPTER 11

1 Ronald Miller and David Sawers, *The Technical Development of Modern Aviation*, Routledge, 1968, p. 9.
2 David Edgerton, *England and the Aeroplane*, Macmillan, 1991, p. 4.
3 P. Fearon, 'The Formative Years of the British Aircraft Industry, 1913–1924', *Business History Review*, vol. 43, 1969, pp. 476–9.
4 J. D. (later Sir John) Siddeley was one of the earliest British car manufacturers. In 1905 he took over from Herbert Austin as general manager of Wolseley (then owned by Vickers), and four years later he left to join with Captain H. H. P. Deasy to build Siddeley-Deasy cars. Jonathan Wood, *Wheels of Misfortune*, Sidgwick & Jackson, 1988, p. 6.
5 Robert Schlaifer and S. D. Heron, *Development of Aircraft Engines and Aviation Fuels*, Harvard, 1950.
6 E. W. Constant, *The Origins of the Turbojet Revolution*, Johns Hopkins University Press, 1980, ch. 4.
7 Miller and Sawers, *The Technical Development of Modern Aviation*, p. 54.
8 Sir Roy Dobson, 'Development and Organisation of the Hawker Siddeley Group', in R. S. Edwards and H. Townsend, *Business Growth*, Macmillan, 1966.

9 Peter J. Lyth, 'The Changing Role of Government in British Air Transport', in Robert Millward and John Singleton (eds.), *The Political Economy of Nationalisation in Britain 1920–50*, Cambridge, 1995.

10 Miller and Sawers, *The Technical Development of Modern Aviation*, ch. 4. See also John Sutton, *Technology and Market Structure*, MIT Press, 1998, pp. 419–28.

11 Lyth, 'The Changing Role of Government in British Air Transport', p. 77.

12 Sebastian Ritchie, *Industry and Air Power: The Expansion of British Aircraft Production, 1935–1941*, Cass, 1997, p. 197.

13 Ibid., p. 157.

14 Miller and Sawers, *The Technical Development of Modern Aviation*, p. 71.

15 Correlli Barnett, *The Audit of War*, Macmillan, 1986, ch. 7.

16 Jonathan Zeitlin, 'Flexibility and Mass Production at War: Aircraft Manufacture in Britain, the United States and Germany, 1939–45', *Technology and Culture*, vol. 36 January 1995. See also Edgerton, *England and the Aeroplane*, pp. 79–82, and R. J. Overy, *The Air War, 1939–1945*, London, 1980.

17 Cripps was unusual among politicians in having had industrial experience; he had managed a munitions factory during the First World War.

18 Ritchie, *Industry and Air Power*, p. 264.

19 Andrew Nahum, 'Two-stroke or Turbine? The Aeronautical Research Committee and British Aero-engine Development in World War II', *Technology and Culture*, vol. 38, no. 2, April 1997.

20 Miller and Sawers, *The Technical Development of Modern Aviation*, p. 173.

21 Alec Cairncross, *Planning in Wartime*, Macmillan, 1991, pp. 140–44.

22 Miller and Sawers, *The Technical Development of Modern Aviation*, p. 161.

23 Keith Hayward, *The British Aircraft Industry*, Manchester, 1989, p. 40.

24 Andrew Nahum, Ph.D. thesis in preparation, London School of Economics.

25 David Edgerton, 'Public Ownership and the British Arms Industry 1920–1950', in Robert Millward and John Singleton (eds.), *The Political Economy of Nationalisation in Britain, 1920–1950*, Cambridge, 1995.

26 Edgerton, *England and the Aeroplane*, p. 89.

27 Hayward, *The British Aircraft Industry*, p. 63.

28 P. D. Henderson, 'Government and Industry', in G. D. N. Worswick and P. H. Ady (eds.), *The British Economy in the 1950s*, Oxford, 1962.

29 Hayward, *The British Aircraft Industry*, p. 79.

30 A. F. C. Hunter (ed.), *TSR-2 with Hindsight*, RAF Historical Society, 1998.

31 John Costello and Terry Hughes, *The Battle for Concorde*, Compton Press, 1971.

32 Sutton, *Technology and Market Structure*, p. 440.

33 Ely Devons, 'The Aircraft Industry', in Duncan Burn (ed.), *The Structure of British Industry*, vol. 2, Cambridge, 1958.

34 D. J. Hickie, 'The Government and Civil Aircraft Production 1942–1951', Ph.D. thesis, Birkbeck College, London University, 1988, ch. 11.

35 Chris Harley, *Innovation and Productivity under Nationalisation*, Allen & Unwin, 1977, p. 49.

36 This was also the view of a team of economists from the Brookings Institution in the US which studied the British economy in 1967. See Merton J. Peck, 'Science and Technology', in Richard E. Caves and Associates, *Britain's Economic Prospects*, Allen & Unwin, 1968.

37 Jock Bruce-Gardyne and Nigel Lawson, *The Power Game*, Macmillan, 1976, pp. 29–34.

38 *Report of the Committee of Inquiry into the Aircraft Industry*, Cmd 2853, HMSO, December 1965, p. 37.

39 Ivan Yates, *Evolution of the new European Fighter: A British Industrial Perspective*, British Aerospace, 1988.

40 VFW had been formed two years earlier to bring together Weser, Focke-Wulf and Heinkel.

41 Hayward, *The British Aircraft Industry*, p. 123.

42 Edmund Dell, *Political Responsibility and Industry*, Allen & Unwin, 1973, p. 162.

43 John Newhouse, *The Sporty Game*, Knopf, 1982, p. 192.

44 Keith Hartley, 'The European Defence Market and Industry', in Pauline Creasey and Simon May (eds.), *The European Armaments Market and Procurement Co-operation*, Macmillan, 1998.

45 *Productivity of the National Aircraft Effort*, HMSO, 1969.

46 Emmanuel Chadeau (ed.), *Airbus: un succès industriel Européen*, Institut d'histoire de l'industrie et Editions Rive Droite, Paris, 1995, p. 67.

47 Douglas Hague and Geoffrey Wilkinson, *The IRC: An Experiment in Industrial Intervention*, Allen & Unwin, 1983, p. 189.

48 Rupert Nicholson, *Rolls-Royce Limited: Recollections of the Receiver and Manager*, KPMG Peat Marwick, 1993.

49 Andrew Nahum, obituary of Sir David Huddie, *Independent*, 16 June 1998.

50 Rolls-Royce Motors was acquired in 1980 by Vickers, which sold the business in 1998 to Volkswagen (see Chapter 9).

51 N. K. A. Gardiner, 'The Economics of Launching Aid', in Alan Whiting (ed.), *The Economics of Industrial Subsidies*, HMSO, 1976.

52 Hayward, *The British Aircraft Industry*, p. 143.

53 Keith Hayward, *Government and Civil Aerospace*, Manchester University Press, 1983, p. 157.

54 The Fokker company of the Netherlands had had close connections with the German aircraft industry since its foundation by Anthony Fokker in 1912. In 1969 Fokker merged with VFW in order to rationalise the two companies' activities in short-range airliners. The merger was abandoned in 1980.

55 Hayward, *The British Aircraft Industry*, p. 147.

56 Newhouse, *The Sporty Game*, p. 201.

57 Yates, *Evolution of the New European Fighter*.

58 In 1998 the limit was increased to 49.9 per cent, but no individual foreign shareholder was allowed to hold more than 15 per cent.

59 Kim Kaivanto, 'UK Launch Aid Experience', Warwick Business School Research Bureau, Research Paper, no. 26. June 1997.

60 Laura Tyson, *Who's Bashing Whom? Trade Conflict in High-Technology Industries*, Institute for International Economics, Washington, 1992, ch. 5.

61 Mrs Thatcher's view, that the board of Westland should be free to make its own decisions, is set out in her autobiography, *The Downing Street Years*, HarperCollins, 1993, pp. 423–37.

62 These events are described in Pauline Creasey and Simon May (eds.), The *European Armaments Market and Procurement Co-operation*, Macmillan, 1988, ch. 4. In 1993 Sikorsky's American parent company, United Technologies, decided to withdraw from its shareholding in Westland, and its shares were acquired by GKN, the British engineering company. GKN subsequently acquired full control. In 1999 GKN put Westland into a 50/50 joint venture with Agusta of Italy.

63 Philip Gummett, 'Civil and Military Aircraft in the UK' *History and Technology*, vol. 9, 1992, pp. 203–222.

64 Bernard Gray, 'How BAe Pulled Back from the Brink', *Financial Times*, 18/19 December 1995.

65 *Business Week*, 21 December 1998.

66 Richard Lambert and John Makinson, 'Rolls Faces Up to Reality', *Financial Times*, 4 February 1984.

67 P. D. Henderson, 'Two British Errors: Their Probable Size and Some Possible Lessons', *Oxford Economic Papers*, vol. 29, no. 2, July 1977.

68 E. Kolodziej, *Making and Marketing Arms*, Princeton, 1987.

69 François Chesnais, 'The French National System of Innovation', in Richard R. Nelson (ed.), *National Innovation Systems*, Oxford, 1993.

70 Keith Hartley, *A Market for Aircraft*, Institute of Economic Affairs, 1974.

CHAPTER 12

1 In 1997 the chemical industry recorded a trade surplus of £4.2bn, of which pharmaceuticals accounted for just under £2bn.

2 H. W. Richardson, 'Chemicals', in D. H. Aldcroft (ed.), The Development of British Industry and Foreign Competition, 1875–1914, Allen & Unwin, 1968.

3 Fred Aftalion, A History of the International Chemical Industry, University of Pennsylvania Press, 1991, p. 39.

4 J. J. Beer, The Emergence of the German Dye Industry, University of Illinois Press, 1979.

5 The College was privately financed by a group of landowners who were interested in Liebig's work on fertilisers. They secured the backing of Prince Albert – hence the royal title.

6 Fred Aftalion, A History of the International Chemical Industry, p. 48.

7 Johann Peter Murmann and Ralph Landau, 'On the Making of Comparative Advantage: The Development of the Chemical Industries of Britain and Germany since 1850', in Ashish Arora, Ralph Landau and Nathan Rosenberg (eds.), Chemicals and Long-term Economic Growth, Wiley, 1998.

8 David A. Hounshell and John Kenly Smith, Science and Corporate Strategy: Du Pont R & D 1902–1980, Cambridge, 1988, p. 4.

9 Richardson, 'Chemicals', in Aldcroft, The Development of British Industry, p. 294.

10 D. W. F. Hardie and J. Davidson Pratt, A History of the Modern British Chemical Industry, Pergamon, 1966, p. 44.

11 J. M. Cohen, The Life of Ludwig Mond, Methuen, 1956, chs. 1–2.

12 W. J. Reader, Imperial Chemical Industries: A History, vol. 1: The forerunners, 1870–1926, Oxford, 1970, p. 93.

13 Ibid., p. 266.

14 Ibid., p. 425.

15 Ibid., p. 367.

16 Ibid., p. 385. Du Pont welcomed Nobel Industries as a shareholder in General Motors, hoping that the British company might help to promote the sale of GM vehicles in the Empire.

17 Ibid., p. 452.

18 One of the participants in this merger was Solvay Process Company, in which Brunner Mond and Solvay were large investors. Thus the two European firms became minority shareholders in Allied Chemical.

19 Reader, Imperial Chemical Industries, vol. 1, ch. 19.

20 Hounshell and Smith, Science and Corporate Strategy, ch. 3.

21 D. C. Coleman, Courtaulds: An Economic and Social History, Oxford, 1969, vol. 2, p. 265.

22 A. B. Thompson, 'Early Days of Terylene at ICI', in David Brunnschweiler and John Hearle (eds.), Polyester: Fifty Years of Achievement, Textile Institute, 1993.

23 Coleman, Courtaulds, vol. 3, p. 74.

24 Hounshell and Smith, Science and Corporate Strategy, p. 204.

25 Alfred Chandler, Strategy and Structure, MIT Press, 1962, ch. 2.

26 Leslie Hannah, The Rise of the Corporate Economy, Methuen, 1979, ch. 6.

27 A. Arora and A. Gambardella, 'Evolution of Industry Structure in the Chemical Industry', Rosenberg, Chemicals and Long-term Economic Growth.

28 Takashi Hikino, Tsutoma Harada, Yoshio Tokuhisa and James Yoshida, 'The Japanese Puzzle', in Arora, Landau and Rosenberg, Chemicals and Long-term Economic Growth.

29 Reader, Imperial Chemical Industries, vol. 2: The First Quarter Century, 1926–1952, p. 437.

30 Raymond Stokes, Divide and prosper: the heirs of IG Farben under Allied authority, 1945–1951, University of Calfornia Press, 1988, p. 202.

31 Reader, Imperial Chemical Industries, vol. 2, pp. 395–407.

32 Quoted in ibid., p. 467.

33 Graham Turner, Business in Britain, Eyre & Spottiswood, 1969, p. 146.

34 Ibid., p. 143.

35 Carol Kennedy, ICI: The company that

changed our lives, 2nd edn, Paul
Chapman, 1993, ch. 8.

36 Michael Shanks, 'ICI: the Quiet
Revolution', *Sunday Times*, 27 September
1964.

37 Turner, *Business in Britain*, p. 147.

38 Joe Roeber, *Social Change at Work: the
ICI Weekly Staff Agreement*, Duckworth,
1975. Andrew Pettigrew, *The Awakening
Giant: Continuity and Change in ICI*,
Blackwell, 1985, ch. 4.

39 Pettigrew, *The Awakening Giant*, p. 392.

40 Keith Chapman, *The International
Petrochemical Industry*, Blackwell, 1991.

41 Peter H. Spitz, *Petrochemicals: The Rise
of an Industry*, Wiley, 1988.

42 Arora and Gambardella, 'Evolution of
Industry Structure In the Chemical
Industry', in Arora, Landau and
Rosenberg, *Chemicals and Long-term
Economic Growth*.

43 Pettigrew, *The Awakening Giant*,
pp. 423–4.

44 Hanson plc press release, 26 July 1991.

45 *Financial Times*, 1/2 February 1992.

46 Geoffrey Owen and Trevor Harrison,
'Why ICI Chose to Demerge', *Harvard
Business Review*, March–April 1995.

47 Another business which had technical
links to pharmaceuticals was dyestuffs,
and this formed part of the hived-off
company, Zeneca; the dyestuffs business,
however, was relatively small by
international standards, and in 1996 it
was sold to BASF of Germany.

48 Quoted in *European Chemical News*, ICI
supplement, Spring 1999.

49 Sarah J. Lane, 'Corporate Restructuring
in the Chemical Industry', in Margaret
M. Blair (ed.), *The Deal Decade*,
Brookings, 1997.

50 *Financial Times*, 18 September 1998.

51 Murmann and Landau, 'On the Making
of Comparative Advantage', in Arora,
Landau and Rosenberg, *Chemicals and
Long-term Economic Growth*.

52 Wyn Grant, William Paterson and Colin
Whitston, *Government and the Chemical
Industry*, Oxford, 1988, ch. 5.

53 Marco Da Rin, 'Finance and the
Chemical Industry', in Arora, Landau
and Rosenberg, *Chemicals and Long-term
Economic Growth*, p. 325.

CHAPTER 13

1 Geoffrey Tweedale, *At the Sign of the
Plough: Allen & Hanburys and the British
Pharmaceutical Industry, 1715–1990*,
Murray, 1990, ch. 3.

2 Judy Slinn, *A History of May & Baker,
1834–1984*, Hobsons, 1984, p. 22.

3 M. Feldman and Y. Schreuder, 'Initial
Advantage: The Origins of the
Geographical Concentration of the
Pharmaceutical Industry in the Mid-
Atlantic Region', *Industrial and
Corporate Change*, vol. 5, no. 3, 1996.

4 Jonathan Liebenau, 'Industrial R & D in
Pharmaceutical Firms in the Early
Twentieth Century', *Business History*,
vol. 26, no. 3, November 1984.

5 Ibid.

6 Feldman and Schreuder, 'Initial
Advantage', *Industrial and Corporate
Change*, vol. 5, no. 3.

7 Tweedale, *At the Sign of the Plough*,
p. 174.

8 W. J. Reader, *Imperial Chemical
Industries: A History*, Oxford, 1973, vol.
2, p. 458.

9 H. G. Lazell, *From Pills to Penicillin: The
Beecham Story*, Heinemann, 1975;
T. A. B. Corley, 'The Beecham Group in
the World's Pharmaceutical Industry,
1914 to 1970', *German Society for Business
History*, vol. 39, no. 1, 1994.

10 R. P. T. Davenport-Hines and Judy
Slinn, *Glaxo: A History to 1962*,
Cambridge, 1992, p. 86.

11 Slinn, *A History of May & Baker*, p. 124.

12 Ibid., p. 138.

13 Jonathan Liebenau, 'The British success
with Penicillin', *Social Studies of Science*,
vol. 17, 1987, pp. 69–86.

14 Davenport-Hines and Slinn, *Glaxo*,
p. 144.

15 Basil Achilladelis, 'The Dynamics of
Technological Innovation: The Sector of
Antibacterial Medicines', *Research Policy*,
vol. 22, 1993, pp. 279–308.

16 Peter Temin, 'Technology, Regulation
and Market Structure in the Modern
Pharmaceutical Industry', *Bell Journal of
Economics*, vol. 10, 1979, pp. 429–46.

17 Edgar Jones, *A History of Glaxo from Its
Origins until 1985*, Profile, forthcoming.

18 Reader, *Imperial Chemical Industries*. vol. 2, pp. 489–460.

19 Carol Kennedy, *ICI: The Company that Changed Our Lives*, Hutchinson, 1986, p. 130.

20 Tweedale, *At the Sign of the Plough*, ch. 6.

21 Leigh Hancher, *Regulating for Competition: Government, Law and the Pharmaceutical Industry in the United Kingdom and France*, Oxford, 1990, ch. 3.

22 William Breckon, *The Drug Makers*, Methuen, 1972, p. 29.

23 Davenport-Hines and Slinn, *Glaxo*, p. 171.

24 Temin, 'Technology, Regulation and Market Structure', *Bell Journal of Economics*, vol. 10, 1979, pp. 429–46.

25 Robert Chew, George Teeling Smith and Nicholas Wells, *Pharmaceuticals in Seven Nations*, Office of Health Economics, London, 1985, p. 27.

26 M. L. Burstall and I. Senior, *The Community's Pharmaceutical Industry: Evolution of Concentration, Competition and Competitivity*, European Commission, January 1985, p. 57.

27 Michael Reich, 'Why the Japanese Don't Export More Pharmaceuticals: Health Policy as Industrial Policy', *California Management Review*, Winter 1990.

28 Hancher, *Regulating for Competition*. See also L. G. Thomas, 'Implicit Industrial Policy: The Triumph of Britain and the Failure of France in Global Pharmaceuticals', *Industrial and Corporate Change*, vol. 3, no. 2, 1994.

29 Thomas, 'Implicit Industrial Policy', *Industrial and Corporate Change*, vol. 3, no. 2, 1994.

30 *Report of the Committee of Enquiry into the Relationship of the Pharmaceutical Industry with the National Health Service* (Sainsbury Report), Cmd 3410, HMSO, 1967.

31 Matthew Lynn, *Merck v Glaxo: The Million-Dollar Battle*, Heinemann, 1991, p. 179.

32 Tweedale, *At the Sign of the Plough*, p. 209.

33 Ibid., p. 210.

34 Lazell, *From Pills to Penicillin*, p. 190.

35 Jones, *A History of Glaxo*.

36 Monopolies Commission, *A Report on Proposed Mergers between Beecham and Glaxo, and between Boots and Glaxo*, HC341, HMSO, July 1972.

37 Lynn, *Merck v Glaxo*, p. 191.

38 Jones, *A History of Glaxo*.

39 L. Orsenigo, *The Emergence of Biotechnology*, Pinter, 1989.

40 F. Malerba and L. Orsenigo, 'The Dynamics and Evolution of Industries', *Industrial and Commercial Change*, vol. 5, no. 1, 1996.

41 C. Kurdas, 'Dynamic Economies of Scope in the Pharmaceutical Industry', *Industrial and Corporate Change*, vol. 7, no. 3, September 1988.

42 Sarah J. Lane, 'Corporate Restructuring in the Chemicals Industry', in Margaret M. Blair (ed.), *The Deal Decade*, Brookings, 1993.

43 H. Grabowski and J. Vernon, 'Innovation and Structural Change in Pharmaceuticals and Biotechnology', *Industrial and Corporate Change*, vol. 3, no. 2, 1994.

44 A. Gambardella, *Science and Innovation: The US pharmaceutical industry during the 1980s*, Cambridge, 1995, p. 98.

45 Robert P. Bauman, Peter Jackson and Joanne T. Lawrence, *From Promise to Performance: A Journey of Transformation at SmithKline Beecham*, Harvard Business School Press, 1997, p. 64.

46 John Sutton, *Technology and Market Structure*, MIT Press, 1998, ch. 8.

47 Speech on 'Strategic Vision and Implementation at Glaxo', delivered to the Sloan School of Management, Massachusetts Institute of Technology, 20 March 1990.

48 Neil Bennett, 'Flawed Formula', *Sunday Telegraph*, 1 March 1998.

49 Matthew Lynn, 'Most Unwellcome', *Sunday Times*, 29 January 1995.

CHAPTER 14

1 See, for example, the speech made in 1907 by Dudley Docker, the Birmingham industrialist, quoted in David Kynaston, *The City of London*, vol. 2: *1890–1914*, Chatto & Windus, 1995, p. 451. The gap

between the City and industry is the main theme of Geoffrey Ingham, *Capitalism Divided: the City and Industry in British Social Development*, Macmillan, 1984. For a review of the controversy, see Y. Cassis, 'British Finance: Success and Controversy', in J. J. Van Helten and Y. Cassis (eds.), *Capitalism in a Mature Economy: Financial Institutions, Capital Exports and British Industry, 1870–1939*, Elgar, 1990.

2 P. J. Cain and A. G. Hopkins, *British imperialism: Innovation and Expansion 1688–1914*, Longman, 1993, ch. 3.

3 M. H. Best and Jane Humphries, 'The City and Industrial Decline', in Bernard Elbaum and William Lazonick, *The Decline of the British Economy*, Oxford, 1986.

4 Will Hutton, *The State We're In*, Cape, 1995.

5 Peter Mathias, *The First Industrial Revolution*, Methuen, 1969, ch. 5.

6 Duncan M. Ross, 'The Clearing Banks and Industry: New Perspectives on the Inter-war Years', in Van Helten and Cassis, *Capitalism in a Mature Economy*.

7 R. C. Michie, 'The Stock Exchange and the British Economy, 1970–1939', in Van Helten and Cassis, *Capitalism in a Mature Economy*.

8 Ibid.

9 John Armstrong, 'The Rise and Fall of the Company Promoter and the Financing of British Industry', in Van Helten and Cassis, *Capitalism in a Mature Economy*.

10 Kynaston, *The City of London*, vol. 2, pp. 449–72.

11 William P. Kennedy, *Industrial Structure, Capital Markets and the Origins of British Economic Decline*, Cambridge, 1987.

12 Michael Edelstein, 'Foreign Investment and Accumulation, 1860–1914', in Roderick Floud and Donald McCloskey (eds.), *The Economic History of Britain since 1700*, 2nd edn, vol. 2: *1860–1939*, Cambridge, 1994.

13 Peter Wardley, 'The Anatomy of Big Business: Aspects of Corporate Development in the Twentieth Century', *Business History*, vol. 23, no. 2, April 1991.

14 Donald Coleman, *Courtaulds: An Economic and Social History*, vol. 2, ch. 2, Oxford, 1969.

15 C. Knick Harley, 'Substitutes for Prerequisites: Endogenous Institutions and Comparative Economic history', in Richard Sylla and Gianni Toniolo (eds.), *Patterns of European Industrialisation*, Routledge, 1991.

16 Lothar Gall et al., *The Deutsche Bank, 1870–1995*, Weidenfeld & Nicolson, 1995, pp. 32–41.

17 Richard Edward Deeg, 'Banks and the State in Germany: the Critical Role of Subnational Institutions in Economic Governance', unpublished Ph.D. thesis, Massachusetts Institute of Technology, May 1992.

18 R. P. T. Davenport-Hines, *Dudley Docker: The Life and Times of a Trade Warrior*, Cambridge, 1984, p. 33. See also Kynaston, *The City of London*, vol. 2, pp. 188–94.

19 P. L. Cottrell, *Industrial Finance, 1830–1914*, Methuen, 1980, p. 244.

20 See, for example, Steven Tolliday, *Business, Banking and Politics*, Harvard, 1987. For an overview of the Bank of England's role, see W. R. Garside and J. I. Greaves, 'The Bank of England and Industrial Intervention in Inter-war Britain', *Financial History Review*, vol. 3, part 1, April 1996.

21 Duncan M. Ross, 'The Clearing Banks and Industry', in Van Helten and Cassis, *Capitalism in a Mature Economy*.

22 Stephanie Diaper, 'Merchant Banking in the Inter-war Period: The Case of Kleinwort, Sons & Co', *Business History*, vol. 28, no. 4, October 1986.

23 Leslie Hannah, *The Rise of the Corporate Economy*, Methuen, paperback edn, 1979, p. 69.

24 *Report of the Committee on Finance and Industry* (Macmillan Report), Cmd 3897, HMSO, 1931.

25 Lothar Gall et al., *The Deutsche Bank*, p. 270.

26 Jim Tomlinson, *Government and the Enterprise since 1900*, Oxford, 1994, p. 175. See also John Zysman, *Governments, Markets and Growth: Financial Systems and the Politics of*

Industrial Change, Cornell, 1983, ch. 4.

27 Forrest Capie and Michael Collins, *Have the Banks Failed British Industry?*, Institute of Economic Affairs, 1992, ch. 7.

28 Francesca Carnevali and Leslie Hannah, 'The Effects of Banking Cartels and Credit Rationing on UK Industrial Structure and Economic Performance since World War Two', in Richard Sylla and Michael Bordo (eds.), *Anglo-Saxon Finance*, Irwin, 1995.

29 *Committee on the Working of the Monetary System* (Radcliffe Committee), Cmd 827, HMSO, 1959.

30 *Committee to Review the Functioning of Financial Institutions* (Wilson Committee), Cmd 7937, HMSO, 1980.

31 Tim Jenkinson and Colin Mayer, *Hostile Take-overs: Defence, Attack and corporate Governance*, McGraw Hill, 1994.

32 Paul L. Davies, 'Institutional Investors in the United Kingdom', in D. D. Prentice and P. R. J. Holland (eds.), *Contemporary Issues in Corporate Governance*, Oxford, 1993.

33 Richard Roberts, 'Regulatory Responses to the Market for Corporate Control in Britain in the 1950s', *Business History*, vol. 34, no. 1, January 1992.

34 Colin Mayer and Julian Franks, 'Ownership and Control in Europe', in Peter Newman (ed), *The New Palgrave Dictionary of Economics and the Law*, Macmillan, 1998.

35 Jeremy Edwards and Klaus Fischer, *Banks, Finance and Investment in Germany*, Cambridge, 1994.

36 Ada Demb and F.-Friedrich Neubauer, *The Corporate Board: Confronting the Paradoxes*, Oxford, 1992, p. 96.

37 Theodor Baums, 'The German Banking System and Its Impact on Corporate Finance and Governance', in Masahiko Aoki and Hugh Patrick (eds.), *The Japanese Main Bank System*, Oxford, 1994.

38 E. Wenger and C. Kaserer, 'The German System of Corporate Governance: A Model Which Should not be Imitated', in S. W. Black and M. Moersch (eds.), *Competition and Convergence in Financial Markets*, North Holland Elsevier Science, Amsterdam, 1998.

39 *Daimler-Benz*, Goldman Sachs Investment Research, September 1993.

40 Ibid.

41 Keith Cowling, Paul Stoneman, John Cubbin, John Cable, Graham Hall, Simon Domberger and Patricia Dutton, *Mergers and Economic Performance*, Cambridge, 1980, ch. 6.

42 Jenny Corbett and Tim Jenkinson, 'The Financing of Industry, 1970–1989: An International Comparison', Discussion Paper, no. 948, Centre for Economic Policy Research, May 1994.

43 Christian Harm, 'The Financing of Small Firms in Germany', *World Bank Working Paper*, May 1992. See also Deeg, 'Banks and the State in Germany'.

44 E. P. Davis, 'Whither Corporate-Banking Relations?', in Kirsty Hughes (ed.), *The Future of UK Competitiveness and the Role of Industrial Policy*, Policy Studies Institute, 1993.

45 David Soskice, *Innovation Strategies of Companies: A Comparative Institutional Explanation of Cross-Country Differences*, WZB Berlin, mimeo, 1993.

46 Andy Mullineux, 'Do They Really Do Things Better in Germany?' in Simon Milner (ed.), *Could Finance Do More for British Business?*, Institute for Public Policy Research, 1996. See also *The Mittelstand: The German Model and the UK*, Midland Bank, September 1994.

47 Colin Mayer, 'The Financing of Innovation', in Alex Bowen and Martin Ricketts (eds.), *Stimulating Innovation in Industry*, Kogan Page, 1992; *The Financing of Technology-Based Small Firms*, Bank of England, October 1996.

48 Ulrich Schröder and Alexander Schrader, 'The Changing Role of Banks and Corporate Governance in Germany: Evolution Towards the Market?' in Black and Moersch, *Competition and Convergence in Financial Markets*.

49 Interviewed by Will Hutton on a BBC Radio programme on the City, 5 January 1995.

CHAPTER 15

1 See Peter J. Senker, *Industrial Training in a Cold Climate*, Avebury, 1992, p. 15.

2 Correlli Barnett, *The Audit of War: the Illusion and Reality of Britain as a Great Nation*, Macmillan, 1986, ch. 11.

3 Michael Sanderson, *The Missing Stratum: Technical School Education in England 1900–1990s*, Athlone, 1994, p. 153. See also Michael Sanderson, 'Technical Education and Economic Decline', in *Oxford Review of Economic Policy*, vol. 4, no. 1, Spring 1988.

4 S. J. Prais, *Productivity, Education and Training: An International Perspective*, Cambridge, 1995, ch. 3.

5 David Finegold and David Soskice, 'The Failure of Training in Britain: Analysis and Prescription', *Oxford Review of Economic Policy*, vol. 4, no. 3, Autumn 1988.

6 Howard F. Gospel, *Markets, Firms and the Management of Labour in Modern Britain*, Cambridge, 1992, ch. 2.

7 Charles More, *Skill and the English Working Class, 1870–1914*, Croom Helm, 1980.

8 Keith McClelland, 'The Transmission of Collective Knowledge: Apprenticeship in Engineering and Shipbuilding', in Penny Summerfield and Eric J. Evans (eds.), *Technical Education and the State since 1850*, Manchester University Press, 1990.

9 Jonathan Zeitlin, 'Re-forming Skills in British metalworking, 1900–1940: A Contingent Failure', paper prepared for the Panel on 'Skill Formation in Comparative Historical Perspective', 21st meeting of the Social Science History Association, New Orleans, October 10–13, 1996.

10 Alan McKinlay, '"A certain short-sightedness": Metalworking, Innovation, and Apprenticeship, 1897–1939', in Howard F. Gospel (ed.), *Industrial Training and Technological Innovation*, Routledge, 1991.

11 Michael Sanderson, *The Missing Stratum*.

12 Keith Burgess, 'British Employers and Education Policy 1935–45: A Decade of "Missed Opportunities"?', *Business History*, vol. 36, no. 3, July 1994.

13 Howard F. Gospel, 'Whatever Happened to Apprenticeship Training in Britain?', *Studies in economics*, no. 93/14, University of Kent, September 1993.

14 Paul Ryan, 'Training Quality and Trainee Exploitation', in R. Layard, K. Mayhew and G. Owen (eds.), *Britain's Training Deficit*, Avebury, 1994; Paul Ryan, 'Pay Structures, Collective Bargaining and Apprenticeship Training in Post-war British and German Metalworking Industry', paper presented for CEPR workshop on Human Capital and Post-war European Economic Growth, Dublin, March 1993.

15 Desmond S. King, 'The Conservatives and Training Policy 1979–1992: From a Tripartite to a Neo-Liberal Regime', *Political Studies*, vol. 41, no. 2, June 1973.

16 Hilary Steedman, Howard Gospel and Paul Ryan, 'Apprenticeship: A Strategy for Growth', Centre for Economic Performance, London School of Economics, October 1998.

17 Gary Herrigel, *Industrial Constructions: the Sources of German Industrial Power*, Cambridge, 1996, p. 52; Arndt Sorge and Malcolm Warner, *Comparative Factory Organisation*, Gower, 1986, ch. 13.

18 Klaus Harney, 'The Emergence of the Technical School System in Prussia', in Ian Inkster (ed.), *The Steam Intellect Societies*, Nottingham Studies in the History of Adult Education, Nottingham University, 1985.

19 John Gillingham, 'The "Deproletarianisation" of German Society: Vocational Training in the Third Reich', *Journal of Social History*, Spring 1986.

20 M. E. Taylor, *Education and Work in the Federal Republic of Germany*, Anglo-German Foundation for the Study of Industrial Society, London, 1981.

21 Peter Berg, 'The German Training System', in Layard, Mayhew and Owen, *Britain's Training Deficit*.

22 David Soskice, 'Reconciling Markets and Institutions: The German Apprenticeship System', in L. M. Lynch (ed.), *Training and the Private Sector: International Comparisons*, Chicago, 1993; Arndt Sorge and Wolfgang Streeck, 'Industrial

Relations and Technical Change: The Case for an Extended Perspective', in Richard Hyman and Wolfgang Streeck (eds.), *New Technology and Industrial Relations*, Blackwell, 1988.

23 Christoph F. Buechtemann and Kurt Vogler-Ludwig, *The 'German Model' under Pressure: Human Capital Investment and Economic Performance in Germany*, Centre for Research and Society, Santa Barbara, Report E96–05, 1996.

24 Ibid.

25 P. Robinson, 'The British Disease Overcome? Living Standards, Productivity and Education Attainment, 1979–94', Discussion Paper, no. 260, Centre for Economic Performance, London School of Economics, August 1995.

26 Robert R. Locke, *The End of the Practical Man: Entrepreneurship and Higher Education in Germany, France and Great Britain 1880–1940*, JAI Press, 1984; Göran Ahlström, *Engineers and economic growth: Higher Technical Education and the Engineering Profession During the 19th and Early 20th Centuries: France, Germany, Sweden and England*, Croom Helm, 1982.

27 Michael Sanderson, *The Universities and British Industry, 1850–1970*, Routledge, 1972. Peter Lundgren, 'Engineering Education in Europe and the USA 1750–1930: The Rise to Dominance of the School Culture and the Engineering Profession', *Annals of Science*, no. 57, 1990, pp. 33–75.

28 D. S. L. Cardwell, *The Organisation of Science in England*, Heinemann, 1958, p. 138.

29 Colin Divall, 'A Measure of Agreement: Employers and Engineering Studies in the Universities of England and Wales, 1897–1939', *Social Studies of Science*, vol. 20, 1990, pp. 65–112.

30 David Edgerton, *Science, Technology and the British Industrial 'Decline'*, Cambridge, 1996, p. 54.

31 M. C. Burstall, 'The Education of Industrial Scientists', in G. Walters and S. Cotgrove (eds.), *Scientists in British Industry*, Bath, 1967, quoted in Edgerton,

Science, Technology and the British Industrial 'Decline'.

32 William Walker, 'National Innovation Systems: Britain', in Richard R. Nelson, *National Innovation Systems*, Oxford, 1993.

33 Martin J. Wiener, *English Culture and the Decline of the Industrial Spirit 1850–1980*, Cambridge, 1981. For critiques of Wiener's thesis see Bruce Collins and Keith Robbins (eds.), *British Culture and Economic Decline*, St Martin's Press, 1990; W. D. Rubinstein, *Capitalism, Culture and Decline in Britain, 1750–1990*, Routledge, 1993; M. J. Daunton, ' "Gentlemanly capitalism" and British Industry', *Past and Present*, no. 122, February 1989.

34 H. Berghoff, 'Public Schools and the Decline of the British Economy, 1870–1914', *Past and Present*, no. 129, November 1990; H. Berghoff and R. Moller, 'Tired Pioneers and Dynamic Newcomers? A Comparative Essay in English and German Entrepreneurial History', *Economic History Review*, vol. 47, no. 2, 1994.

35 Rubinstein, *Capitalism, Culture and Decline in Britain 1750–1990*, ch. 3.

36 Harold Perkin, *The Rise of Professional Society*, Routledge, 1989, p. 368.

37 Sidney Pollard, *Britain's Prime and Britain's Decline*, Edward Arnold, 1989, p. 212.

38 D. C. Coleman, 'Gentlemen and Players', *Economic History Review*, vol. 26, no. 1, February 1973.

39 D. C. Coleman, *Courtaulds: An Economic and Social History*, Oxford, 1980, vol. 3, pp. 23–5.

40 Michael Sanderson, 'Education and Social Mobility', in Paul Johnson (ed.), *20th Century Britain*, Longman, 1994.

41 Michael Sanderson, *The Universities and British Industry 1850–1970*, Routledge, 1972, p. 283.

42 S. P. Keeble, *The Ability to Manage: A study of British Management 1890–1990*, Manchester University Press, 1992.

43 Charles Handy, Ian Gow, Colin Gordon, Colin Randlesome, Michael Moloney, *The Making of Managers*, a report prepared for the Manpower Services

Commission, the National Economic Development Council and the British Institute of Management, National Economic Development Office, 1987.

44 William Lazonick, 'Organisational Capabilities in American Industry: The Rise and Decline of Managerial Capitalism', in Howard F. Gospel (ed.), *Industrial Training and Technological Innovation*, Routledge, 1991.

45 Colin Divall, 'Professional Organisation: Employers and the Education of Engineers for Management: A Comparison of Mechanical, Electrical and Chemical Engineers in Britain, 1897–1977', *Minerva*, vol. 32, no. 3, 1994.

46 Derek Matthews, 'The Business Doctors: Accountants in British Management from the Nineteenth Century to the Present Day', *Business History*, vol. 40, no. 3, July 1998. Derek Matthews, Malcolm Anderson and John Richard Edwards, 'The Rise of the Professional Accountant in British Management', *Economic History Review*, vol. 1, no. 3, August 1997.

47 John F. Wilson, *The Manchester Experiment: A History of the Manchester Business School 1965–90*, Paul Chapman, 1992; William Barnes, *Managerial Catalyst: The Story of the London Business School, 1964–1989*, Paul Chapman, 1989.

48 Peter Lawrence, *Managers and Management in West Germany*, Croom Helm, 1980. Arndt Sorge, 'The Management Tradition: A Continental View', in Michael Fores and Ian Glover (eds.), *Manufacturing and Management*, HMSO, 1978.

49 *Engineering our Future*, report of the committee of inquiry into the engineering profession (The Finniston Report), Cmd 7794, HMSO, 1980. See also Arndt Sorge, 'Engineers in Management: A Study of British, German and French Traditions', *Journal of General Management*, vol. 5, no. 1, 1979.

50 Leslie Hannah, 'Cultural Determinants of Economic Performance: An Experiment on Measuring Human Capital Flows', in Graeme Donald

Snooks (ed.), *Historical Analysis in Economics*, Routledge, 1993.

CHAPTER 16

1 Henry Phelps Brown, *The Origins of Trade Union Power*, Oxford, 1983, ch. 10.

2 William Brown, Simon Deakin and Paul Ryan, 'The Effects of British Industrial Relations Legislation 1979–97', *National Institute Economic Review*, April 1997.

3 Keith McClelland and Alastair Reid, 'Wood, Iron and Steel: Technology, Labour and Trade Union Organisation in the Shipbuilding Industry, 1840–1914', in Royden Harrison and Jonathan Zeitlin (eds.), *Divisions of labour: Skilled Workers and Technological Change in 19th Century England*, Harvester Press, Sussex, 1985.

4 E. H. Phelps Brown, *The Growth of British Industrial Relations*, Macmillan, 1959, p. 270.

5 *Parliamentary Debates*, 1906, vol. 154, 52, quoted in E. H. Phelps Brown, *The Origins of Trade Union Power*, p. 45.

6 George Dangerfield, *The Strange Death of Liberal England*, Constable, 1936.

7 Phelps Brown, *The Origins of Trade Union Power*, p. 144.

8 H. A. Clegg, *A History of British Trade Unions since 1889*, vol. 2: *1911–1933*, Oxford, 1985, p. 463.

9 Howard Gospel, 'Employers' Labour Policy: A Study of the Mond–Turner Talks 1927–1933', in R. P. T. Davenport-Hines (ed.), *Business in the Age of Depression and War*, Cass, 1990.

10 Clegg, *A History of British Trade Unions*, vol. 2, p. 409.

11 H. A. Clegg, *The system of Industrial Relations in Great Britain*, Oxford, 1970, p. 133.

12 Gospel, *Markets, Firms and the Management of Labour in Modern Britain*, Cambridge, 1992, p. 99.

13 John A. Moses, *Trade Unionism in Germany from Bismarck to Hitler*, George Prior, 1982.

14 Volker R. Berghahn and Detlev Karsten, *Industrial relations in West Germany*, Berg, 1987, ch. 5.

15 Roger Magraw, 'Management, Labour

and the State in France 1871–1939: Industrial Relations in the Third Republic', in Peter Mathias and John A. Davis (eds.), *Enterprise and Labour from the Eighteenth Century to the Present*, Blackwell, 1996.

16 Gospel, *Markets, Firms and the Management of Labour*, p. 129.

17 Conservative Political Centre, 'The Industrial Charter, 1947', quoted in Chris Wrigley, *British trade unions 1945–1995*, documents in contemporary history, Manchester University Press 1997.

18 H. A. Turner, Garfield Clack and Geoffrey Roberts, *Labour relations in the motor industry: A Study of Industrial Unrest and an International Comparison*, Allen & Unwin, 1967, p. 23.

19 Quoted in Steven Tolliday, 'Ford and Fordism in Post-war Britain', in Steven Tolliday and Jonathan Zeitlin (eds.), *The Power to Manage? Employers and Industrial Relations in Comparative Historical Perspective*, Routledge, 1991, p. 88.

20 A. Flanders, *The Fawley Productivity Agreements*, Faber & Faber, 1964.

21 Bruce W. Ahlstrand, *The Quest for Productivity: A Case Study of Fawley after Flanders*, Cambridge, 1990.

22 Denis Barnes and Eileen Reid, *Governments and trade unions: The British Experience 1964–1979*, Heinemann, 1980, pp. 42–3.

23 *Report of the Royal Commission on Trade Unions and Employers' Associations* (The Donovan Report), Cmd 3623, HMSO, 1968.

24 Sid Kessler and Fred Bayliss, *Contemporary British Industrial Relations*, Macmillan, 1992, p. 16. See also Stephen Dunn, 'From Donovan to . . . Wherever', *British Journal of Industrial Relations*, vol. 31, no. 2, June 1993.

25 *In place of strife*, Cmd 3888, HMSO, 1969.

26 Eric Jacobs, Stanley Orwell, Peter Paterson, Friedrich Weltz, *The Approach to Industrial Change in Britain and Germany*, Anglo-German Foundation, 1978.

27 Herbert Giersch, Karl-Heinz Paqué,

Holger Schmieding, *The Fading Miracle: Four Decades of Market Economy in Germany*, Cambridge, 1992, p. 76.

28 Ray Richardson, 'Trade Unions and Industrial Relations', in N. F. R. Crafts and Nicholas Woodward (eds.), *The British Economy since 1945*, Oxford, 1991.

29 S. J. Prais, *Productivity and Industrial Structure*, Cambridge, 1981, ch. 7.

30 Nicholas Oulton, 'Supply Side Reform and UK Economic Growth: What Happened to the Miracle?', *National Institute Economic Review*, November 1995.

31 David Metcalf, 'Transformation of British Industrial Relations? Institutions, Conduct and Outcomes, 1980–1990', in Ray Barrell (ed.), *The UK Labour Market*, Cambridge, 1994.

31 Philip Bassett, *Strike Free: New Industrial Relations in Britain*, Macmillan, 1986; Nick Oliver and Barry Wilkinson, *The Japanisation of British Industry*, Blackwell, 1988.

32 *Sunday Times*, 5 April 1992.

33 Martin Baethge and Harald Wolf, 'Continuity and Change in the "German model" of Industrial Relations', in Richard Locke, Thomas Kochan and Michael Piore, *Employment Relations in a Changing World Economy*, MIT Press, 1995.

34 Susan N. Houseman, *Industrial Restructuring and Job Security: The Case of European steel*, Harvard, 1991.

CHAPTER 17

1 Correlli Barnett, *The Lost Victory: British Dreams, British Realities, 1945–1950*, Macmillan, 1995, p. 379.

2 Jose Harris, 'Enterprise and Welfare States: A Comparative Perspective', *Transactions of the Royal Historical Society*, no. 40, 1990, pp. 175–95.

3 Martin Chick, *Industrial policy in Britain 1945–1951*, Cambridge, 1998, p. 212.

4 Nigel Harris, *Competition and the Corporate Society: British Conservatives: The State and Industry 1945–1964*, Methuen, 1972.

5 Keith Middlemas, *Power, Competition and the State*, vol. 1, Macmillan, 1986,

pp. 249–256; J. D. Gribbin, 'The Post-war Revival of Competition as Industrial Policy', Government Economic Service Working Paper, no. 19, 1978.

6 Edmund Dell, *The Schuman Plan and the British Abdication of Leadership in Europe*, Oxford, 1995, ch. 13.

7 Quoted in Edmund Dell, *The Schuman Plan*, p. 231.

8 Alan Milward, *The European Rescue of the Nation-state*, Routledge, 1992, pp. 428–431.

9 A. Whiting, 'An International Comparison of the Instability of Economic Growth', *Three Banks Review*, no. 109, March 1976.

10 Charles Feinstein, 'Success and Failure: British Economic Growth Since 1948', in Roderick Floud and Donald McCloskey (eds.), *The Economic History of Britain since 1700*, 2nd edn, vol. 3, *1939–1992*, Cambridge, 1994.

11 M. W. Kirby, 'Supply-side Management', in N. F. R. Crafts and Nicholas Woodward (eds.), *The British Economy since 1945*, Oxford, 1991.

12 Nick Tiratsoo and Jim Tomlinson, *The Conservatives and Industrial Efficiency, 1951–64*, Routledge, 1998, p. 17.

13 This merger legislation was prepared by the Conservatives shortly before the 1964 election, and enacted by Labour in 1965.

14 Jim Tomlinson, 'Inventing "Decline": The Falling-Behind of the British Economy in the Post-war Years', *Economic History Review*, vol. 49, no. 4, November 1966.

15 Hansard, 26 November 1964, Cols. 214–15, HMSO.

16 Stuart Holland, *The Socialist Challenge*, Quartet, 1975; Noel Thompson, *Political Economy and the Labour Party*, UCL Press, 1996.

17 Jim Tomlinson, *Government and the Enterprise since 1900*, Oxford, 1994, pp. 301–5.

18 N. F. R. Crafts, 'Can De-industrialisation Seriously Damage Your Wealth?', Hobart Papers, no. 120, Institute of Economic Affairs, 1993. See also P. D. Henderson, 'Comment on Chapter 7', in Charles Carter (ed.), *Industrial Policy and Innovation*, Heinemann, 1981.

19 Peter Hall, *Governing the Economy: The Politics of State Intervention in Britain and France*, Polity Press, 1986.

20 Patrick Messerlin, 'France: The Ambitious State', in François Duchêne and Geoffrey Shepherd (eds.), *Managing Industrial Change in Western Europe*, Pinter, 1978.

21 Pierre Sicsic and Charles Wyplosz, 'France 1945–92', in Nicholas Crafts and Gianni Toniolo (eds.), *Economic Growth in Europe since 1945*, Cambridge, 1996.

22 Heidrun Abromeit, 'Government–Industry Relations in West Germany', in Martin Chick (ed.), *Governments, Industries and Markets*, Elgar, 1990.

23 Otto Keck, 'The National System for Technical Innovation in Germany', in Richard R. Nelson (ed.), *National Innovation Systems*, Oxford, 1993.

24 Henry Ergas, 'The Importance of Technology Policy', in Partha Dasgupta and Paul Stoneman (eds.), *Economic Policy and Technological Performance*, Cambridge, 1987.

25 N. F. R. Crafts, 'The Conservative Government's Economic Record: An End of Term Report', The 1997 Wincott lecture, Institute of Economic Affairs, 1998.

26 Nigel Lawson, *The View from No. 11*, Bantam, 1992, ch. 78.

27 William Walker, 'National Innovation Systems: Britain', in Richard R. Nelson (ed.), *National Innovation Systems: A Comparative Analysis*, Oxford, 1993.

28 Charles Bean and Nicholas Crafts, 'British Economic Growth since 1945: Relative Economic Decline . . . and Renaissance?' in Crafts and Toniolo, *Economic Growth in Europe since 1945*, Cambridge, 1996. See also N. F. R. Crafts, 'Adjusting from War to Peace in 1940s Britain', *The Economic and Social Review*, vol. 25, no. 1, October 1993.

Select Bibliography

Adams W. J., *Restructuring the French Economy: Government and the Rise of Competition since World War II*, Brookings, 1989.

Adams W. J., and C. Stoffaes (eds.), *French Industrial Policy*, Brookings, 1986.

Aris, Stephen, *Arnold Weinstock and the Making of GEC*, Aurum, 1998.

Arora, Ashish, Ralph Landau and Nathan Rosenberg (eds.), *Chemicals and Long-term Economic Growth*, Wiley, 1998.

Barnes, Denis, and Eileen Reid, *Governments and Trade Unions: The British Experience 1964–1979*, Heinemann, 1980.

Barnett, Correlli, *The Audit of War: the Illusion and Reality of Britain as a Great Nation*, Macmillan 1986.

The Lost Victory: British Dreams, British Realities 1945–1950, Macmillan, 1995.

Barrell, Ray (ed.), *The UK Labour Market*, Cambridge, 1994.

Berghahn, Volker, *The Americanisation of West German Industry 1945–1973*, Berg, 1986.

Berghahn, Volker, and Detlev Karsten, *Industrial Relations in West Germany*, Berg, 1987.

Bishop, Matthew, John Kay and Colin Mayer (eds.), *Privatisation and Economic Performance*, Oxford, 1994.

Broadberry, S. N., *The Productivity Race*, Cambridge, 1997.

Brummer, Alex, and Roger Cowe, *Weinstock: The Life and Times of Britain's Premier Industrialist*, HarperCollins, 1998.

Burn, Duncan, *The Steel Industry 1939–1959*, Cambridge, 1961.

Burn, Duncan (ed.), *The Structure of British Industry*, 2 vols., Cambridge, 1958.

Cain, P. J. and Hopkins, A. G., *British Imperialism, Innovation and Expansion, 1688–1914*, Longman, 1993.

British Imperialism, Crisis and Deconstruction, 1914–1990, Longman, 1993.

Cairncross, Alec, *Years of Recovery: British Economic Policy 1945–51*, Methuen, 1985.

Campbell-Kelly, Martin, *ICL: A Business and Technical History*, Oxford, 1989.

Capie, Forrest, and Michael Collins, *Have the Banks Failed British Industry?*, Institute of Economic Affairs, 1992.

Carter, Charles (ed.), *Industrial policy and innovation*, Heinemann, 1981.

Cawson, Alan, Kevin Morgan, Douglas Webber, Peter Holmes and Anne Stevens, *Hostile Brothers: Competition and Closure in the European Electronics Industry*, Oxford, 1990.

Central Policy Review Staff, *The Future of the British Car Industry*, HMSO, London, 1975.

Chandler, Alfred D., *The Visible Hand: The Managerial Revolution in American business*, Harvard, 1977.

Scale and Scope: The Dynamics of Industrial Capitalism, Harvard, 1990.

Chick, Martin, *Industrial Policy in Britain, 1945–1951*, Cambridge, 1998.

Chick, Martin (ed.), *Governments: Industries and Markets*, Elgar, 1990.

Church, Roy, *The Rise and Decline of the British Motor Industry*, Macmillan, 1994.

Coleman, D. C., *Courtaulds: An Economic and Social History*, vol 3, Oxford, 1980.

Collins, Bruce, and Keith Robbins (eds.), *British Culture and Economic Decline*, St Martin's Press, 1990.

Crafts, Nicholas, *Can De-industrialisation Seriously Damage Your Wealth?*, Institute of Economic Affairs, 1993.

Crafts, Nicholas, and Gianni Toniolo (eds.), *Economic Growth in Europe since 1945*, Cambridge, 1996.

Crafts, Nicholas, and Nicholas Woodward (eds.), *The British Economy since 1945*, Oxford, 1991.

Davenport-Hines, R. P. T., and Judy Slinn, *Glaxo: A History to 1962*, Cambridge, 1992.

Dell, Edmund, *Political Responsibility and Industry*, Allen & Unwin, 1973.
The Schuman Plan and the British Abdication of Leadership in Europe, Oxford, 1996.

Duchêne, François, *Jean Monnet, the First Statesman of Inter-dependence*, Norton, 1994.

Dudley, G. F., and J. J. Richardson, *Politics and Steel in Britain, 1967–1988*, Dartmouth, 1990.

Edgerton, David, *England and the Aeroplane*, Macmillan, 1991.
Science, Technology and the British Industrial 'Decline', Cambridge, 1996.

Edwards, Jeremy, and Klaus Fischer, *Banks, Finance and Investment in Germany*, Cambridge, 1994.

Eichengreen, Barry (ed.), *Europe's Post-war Recovery*, Cambridge, 1995.

Elbaum, Bernard, and William Lazonick (eds.), *The Decline of the British Economy*, Oxford, 1986.

Edwardes, Michael, *Back from the Brink*, Pan, 1984.

Flamm, Kenneth, *Creating the Computer*, Brookings, 1988.

Floud, Roderick, and Donald McCloskey (eds.), *The Economic History of Britain Since 1700*, 2nd edn, 3 vols., Cambridge, 1994.

Foreman-Peck, James, Sue Bowden and Alan McKinlay, *The British Motor Industry*, Manchester, 1995.

Giersch, Herbert, Karl-Heinz Paqué and Holger Schmieding, *The Fading Miracle: Four Decades of Market Economy in Germany*, Cambridge, 1992.

Gillingham, John, *Coal, Steel and the Rebirth of Europe 1945–1955*, Cambridge, 1991.

Gospel, Howard, *Markets, Firms, and the Management of Labour in Modern Britain*, Cambridge, 1992.

Hague, Douglas, and Geoffrey Wilkinson, *The IRC: An Experiment in Industrial Intervention*, Allen & Unwin, 1983.

Hall, Peter, *Governing the Economy: The Politics of State Intervention in Britain and France*, Polity Press, 1986.

Hannah, Leslie, *The Rise of the Corporate Economy*, Methuen, 1976.

Harris, Nigel, *Competition and the Corporate Society: British Conservatives, the State and Industry 1945–1964*, Methuen, 1972.

Hayward, Keith, *The British Aircraft Industry*, Manchester, 1989.

Hendry, John, *Innovating for Failure: Government Policy and the Early British Computer Industry*, MIT Press, 1989.

Herrigel, Gary, *Industrial Constructions: The Sources of German Industrial Power*, Cambridge, 1996.

Hogan, Michael J., *The Marshall Plan*, Cambridge, 1997.

Hogwood, Brian, *Government and Shipbuilding: The Politics of Industrial Change*, Saxon House, 1979.

Hutton, Will, *The State We're In*, Cape, 1995.

Johnson, Peter (ed.), *The Structure of British industry*, Unwin Hyman, 1988.

Jones, Edgar, *A History of Glaxo From its Origins until 1985*, Profile Books, forthcoming.

Jones, Robert, and Oliver Marriott, *Anatomy of a Merger: A History of GEC, AEI and English Electric*, Cape, 1976.

Keeble, S. P., *The Ability to Manage: A Study of British Management 1890–1990*, Manchester, 1992.

Kessler, Sid, and Fred Bayliss, *Contemporary British Industrial Relations*, Macmillan, 1992.

Kennedy, Carol, *ICI, The Company that Changed Our Lives*, Paul Chapman, 1993.

Kennedy, William P., *Industrial Structure, Capital Markets and the Origins of British Industrial Decline*, Cambridge, 1997.

Knight, Arthur, *Private Enterprise and Public Intervention*, Allen & Unwin, 1974.

Kuisel, Richard F., *Capitalism and the State in Modern France*, Cambridge, 1981.

Layard, R., K. Mayhew and G. Owen, *Britain's Training Deficit*, Avebury, 1994.

Lazonick, William, *Competitive Advantage on the Shop Floor*, Harvard, 1990.

Lewchuk, Wayne, *American Technology and the British Vehicle Industry*, Cambridge, 1987.

Lorenz, E. H., *Economic decline in Britain: The Shipbuilding Industry 1890–1970*, Oxford, 1991.

Lynch, Frances, *France and the International Economy: From Vichy to the Treaty of Rome*, Routledge, 1997.

Malerba, Franco, *The Semiconductor Business*, Pinter, 1985.

Marsden, David, Timothy Morris, Paul Willman and Stephen Wood, *The Car Industry, Labour Relations and Industrial Adjustment*, Tavistock, 1985.

Maxcy, G., and A. Silberston, *The motor industry*, Allen & Unwin, 1959.

Mény Yves, and Vincent Wright (eds.) *The Politics of Steel: Western Europe and the Steel Industry in the Crisis Years (1974–1984)*, de Gruyter, Berlin, 1987.

Mercer, Helen, *Constructing a Competitive Order*, Cambridge, 1995.

Mercer, Helen, Neil Rollings and Jim Tomlinson (eds.), *Labour Governments and Private Industry*, Edinburgh, 1992.

Middlemas, Keith, *Power, competition and the state*, 3 vols., Macmillan, 1986–1991.

Miles, Caroline, *Lancashire Textiles: A Case Study of Technical Change*, Cambridge, 1967.

Miller, Ronald, and David Sawers, *The Technical Development of Modern Aviation*, Routledge, 1968.

Millward, Robert, and John Singleton (eds.), *The Political Economy of Nationalisation in Britain 1920–1950*, Cambridge, 1995.

Milward, A. S., *The European Rescue of the Nation-state*, Routledge, 1992.

Nicholls, A. J., *Freedom with Responsibility: The Social Market in Germany 1918–1963*, Oxford, 1994.

Nelson, Richard R. (ed.), *National Innovation Systems: A Comparative Analysis*, Oxford, 1993.

Oliver, Nick, and Barry Wilkinson, *The Japanisation of British Industry*, Blackwell, 1993.

Olson, Mancur, *The Rise and Decline of Nations*, Yale, 1982.

Orsenigo, L., *The Emergence of Biotechnology*, Pinter, 1989.

Owen, Nicholas, *Economies of scale, Competitiveness, and Trade Patterns within the European Community*, Oxford, 1993.

Pandit, S. A., *From Making to Music: The History of Thorn-EMI*, Hodder & Stoughton, 1996.

Perkin, Harold, *The Origins of Modern English Society, 1780–1880*, Routledge, 1969.
The Rise of Professional Society: England since 1880, Routledge, 1989.

Pettigrew, Andrew, *The Awakening Giant: Continuity and Change in ICI*, Blackwell, 1985.

Phelps Brown, Henry, *The Origins of Trade Union Power*, Oxford, 1983.
The Growth of British Industrial Relations, Macmillan, 1959.

Pollard, Sidney, *Britain's Prime and Britain's Decline*, Edward Arnold, 1969.

Porter, Michael, *The Competitive Advantage of Nations*, Macmillan, 1990.

Prais, S. J., *Productivity and industrial structure*, Cambridge, 1981.
Productivity, education and training, an international perspective, Cambridge, 1995.

Reader, W. J., *Bowater: A History*, Cambridge, 1981.
Imperial Chemical Industries: A History, 2 vols., Oxford, 1970.

Rhys, D. G., *The Motor Industry: An Economic Survey*, Butterworth, 1972.

Ritchie, Sebastian, *Industry and Air Power: The Expansion of British Aircraft Production 1935–1941*, Cass, 1997.

Rose, Mary B. (ed.), *The Lancashire Cotton Industry: A history since 1700*, Lancashire County Books, 1996.

Rubinstein, W. D., *Capitalism, Culture and Decline in Britain*, Routledge, 1993.

Sanderson, Michael, *The Universities and British Industry 1850–1970*, Routledge, 1972.
The Missing Stratum: Technical School Education in England 1900–1990s, Athlone, 1994.

Singleton, John, *Lancashire on the Scrapheap: The Cotton Industry, 1945–1970*, Oxford, 1991.

Starkey, Ken, and Alan McKinlay, *Strategy and the Human Resource: Ford and the Search for Competitive Advantage*, Blackwell, 1993.

Stråth, Bo, *The Politics of De-industrialisation: The Contraction of the West European Shipbuilding Industry*, Croom Helm, 1987.

Streeck, Wolfgang, *Industrial Relations in West Germany: A Case Study of the Car Industry*, Heinemann, 1984.

Sutton, John, *Technology and Market Structure*, MIT Press, 1998.

Thatcher, Margaret, *The Downing Street Years*, HarperCollins, 1993.

Tilton, J. E., *International Diffusion of Technology: The Case of Semiconductors*, Brookings, 1971.

Tiratsoo, Nick, and Jim Tomlinson, *Industrial Efficiency and State Intervention: Labour 1939–51*, Routledge, 1993.

The Conservatives and Industrial Efficiency 1951–64, Routledge, 1998.

Tolliday, Steven, *Business, Banking and Politics: The Case of British Steel, 1918–1935*, Harvard, 1987.

Tolliday, Steven, and Jonathan Zeitlin (eds.), *Between Fordism and flexibility*, Berg, 1982.

Shop Floor Bargaining and the State, Cambridge, 1985.

The Power to Manage? Employers and Industrial Relations in Comparative-Historical Perspective, Routledge, 1991.

Tomlinson, Jim, *Government and the Enterprise since 1900*, Oxford, 1994.

Toyne, B. J. S. Arpan, D. A. Ricks, T. A. Shimp and A. Barnett, *The Global Textile Industry*, Allen & Unwin, 1984.

Turner, Graham, *The Leyland Papers*, Eyre & Spottiswood, 1963.

Business in Britain, Eyre & Spottiswood, 1969.

Turner, H. A., Garfield Clack and Geoffrey Roberts, *Labour Relations in the Motor Industry*, Allen & Unwin, 1959.

Tweedale, Geoffrey, *Steel City: Entrepreneurship, Strategy and Technology in Sheffield, 1743–1993*, Oxford, 1995.

Whipp, Richard, and Peter Clark, *Innovation and the Auto Industry*, Pinter, 1986.

Wiener, Martin J., *English Culture and the Decline of the Industrial Spirit 1850–1980*, Cambridge, 1981.

Wilks, Stephen, *Industrial Policy and the Motor Industry*, Manchester, 1984.

Williams, K., J. Williams and D. Thomas, *Why are the British Bad at Manufacturing?* Routledge, 1983.

Williams, Karel, John Williams and Colin Haslam, *The Breakdown of Austin Rover*, Berg, 1987.

Williams, Karel, Colin Haslam, Sukhdev Johal and John Williams, *Cars: Analysis, History, Cases*, Berghahn, 1994.

Wood, Jonathan, *Wheels of Misfortune: The Rise and Fall of the British Motor Industry*, Sidgwick & Jackson, 1988.

Zysman, John, *Governments, Markets and Growth, Financial Systems and the Politics of Industrial Change*, Cornell, 1983.

Index